NEWNES
PICTORIAL KNOWLEDGE
ATLAS

United Kingdom
GEORGE NEWNES LTD.
LONDON: 15–17, LONG ACRE, LONDON, W.C.2

Australia
GEORGE NEWNES (AUSTRALIA) PTY., LTD.

ADELAIDE: S.A.A.C.C. HOUSE, 32, HINDMARSH SQUARE
BRISBANE: REX BUILDING, 186, WICKHAM STREET, THE VALLEY
MELBOURNE: CAPITOL HOUSE, 109, SWANSTON STREET
SYDNEY: NEWNES HOUSE, 20–22, MARGARET STREET

NEWNES
PICTORIAL KNOWLEDGE
ATLAS

Foreword by

Sir JOHN HUNT, C.B.E., D.S.O., D.C.L., LL.D.

Editor-in-Chief:

PETER FINCH, M.A., F.R.G.S.

Associate Editors:

CEDRIC DOVER, M.I.Biol., F.R.A.I.

FREDERIC EVANS, M.B.E., M.A.
(Former Scholar of St. Catharine's College, Cambridge)

ERIC BURGESS, F.R.A.S.
(Past President of the British Interplanetary Society)

Cartographic Editor:

H. FULLARD, M.Sc., F.R.G.S., F.R.A.I.

GEORGE NEWNES LIMITED

15–17 LONG ACRE

LONDON, W.C.2

PRINTED IN GREAT BRITAIN
BY THE WHITEFRIARS PRESS LTD., LONDON AND TONBRIDGE,
AND BOUND BY DORSTEL PRESS LTD., HARLOW ESSEX
N.P.K. AT. 340259. W.P. 9942

FOREWORD

by

Sir John Hunt

C.B.E., D.S.O., D.C.L., LL.D.

Leader of the British Expedition to Mount Everest
1952–53

ONE of the greatest needs of to-day is to widen our knowledge of the world and increase our understanding of its peoples and problems; we need to do so in order to keep pace with the rate at which this same world is shrinking.

I do not mean that the globe is literally getting smaller, but the rapid exploitation of its resources, the development of its remoter regions, the linking of populations by the many swift means of communication, are in fact having the effect of bringing us all closer together. The interests and needs of people in China, Africa and Asia are steadily becoming similar to our own; and we must move forward towards a common meeting-point in understanding, if the affairs of our world are to be conducted smoothly and peaceably. In fact, all of us, and particularly boys and girls now growing up, must begin to think, not only as citizens of our own country—although this must still claim their first loyalty—but also as citizens of the world.

There is a common saying: " It's a small world." And to-morrow we shall be saying it more often, because it will be a smaller world still.

Curiously enough, as the need to widen our mental horizon grows, it becomes more difficult to fulfil this need. For in the complicated pattern of civilisation most of us are forced to specialise in some particular branch of knowledge—indeed, to focus our minds on one offshoot of that branch—in order to play our separate parts, whether in some department, or serving some piece of machinery, in the vast complex of the modern State.

This narrow beaming of our thinking powers, necessary though it is, represents one of the most serious human problems of to-day and to-morrow, for two main reasons. First, because it limits our understanding of the world outside our own particular job; second, because it threatens to submerge and subdue the spirit that is in us. And there is small prospect of a peaceful world of plenty in the future unless we can, despite the demands of our economic system, open wider the doors of our human understanding and give wings to our adventurous spirit.

In this lies the importance of a book which can illustrate, clearly and concisely, in a colourful and impressive way, much of the information about our world on which this understanding must be based; in a way which can also awake our innate love of adventure.

In this Atlas we can gain an insight, almost at a glance, into the power and the resources of Nature, man's immense achievement in coming to terms with many aspects of that power and the use he has learned to make of many of its resources. We can glean some inkling, too, of many problems which remain to be solved, the obstacles of climate and geography in the path of their solution, and much else besides.

So much for helping our understanding. What about adventure? Well, the story of the earth's formation and development, the history of its exploration and exploitation by man, are in themselves a great epic of adventure. And it can be a challenge to each one of us to push our own exploration a little further afield—to lose no opportunity to travel, seeing other lands and meeting other people. That is what the study of a map does to me, and I hope it will do the same to you, too.

There is one more reason why I find this Atlas useful. It sets our globe, its peoples, its resources, the past achievements and the problems which lie ahead, in the bigger perspective of the timeless universe. It thus reminds us that the power of men, machines and even the natural forces on the earth are but a microscopic part of an immensely greater pattern, fashioned by a hand of infinite skill and wisdom. This, and the fact that the greatest truth on earth is the love for each one of us, of this same Creator, is at once a humbling and a comforting thought.

I believe that this book can be a helpful contribution in the task of enabling to-morrow's citizens to widen their vision, catch the spirit by which past great deeds have been achieved, and emulate those deeds in the future.

John Hunt.

Aston,
Henley-on-Thames.

CONTENTS

THE MAPS

THE MAPS: ECONOMIC SECTION

SPECIAL SUPPLEMENTS

" Journey over all the universe in a map, without expense and fatigue, without suffering inconvenience."

—*Miguel de Cervantes*

Acknowledgements

Thanks are due to Dr. Joseph Needham, F.R.S., for providing pictures and information on early Chinese geography; and to the Syndics of the Cambridge University Press for permission to reproduce two early Chinese maps and the photograph of a Korean rain gauge from the third volume of Dr. Needham's *Science and Civilization in China*. The photographs from the Geological Survey and Museum are reproduced by permission of H.M. Stationery Office.

THE GEOGRAPHY OF SPACE

WHEN we look into a cloudless sky we obtain the impression of a vast hemisphere rising high above our heads like the roof of a great hall and on which the Sun, the Moon and the stars appear to be fixed. If we continue looking we shall see that these heavenly bodies seem to move across the concave surface of the sky, rising in the east and setting in the west. However, towards the north we find that there are a number of stars which neither rise nor set, but are always visible in the cloudless night sky. They appear to revolve in the course of a day around the bright star Polaris which is the Pole Star (Fig. 1).

In addition, if we look at the stars night after night we shall see that although they move across the sky, they preserve their constant positions relative to one another; they can be grouped into squares, triangles, rectangles and lines; these groups are called constellations. Yet at times in certain parts of the star sphere bright star-like objects will be visible which do change their positions—generally moving from west to east as the weeks pass—relative to the other stars. They were called by the Greeks wandering stars—planets.

The Planets

The Earth on which we live is one of nine worlds or planets which together with the Sun and other much smaller bodies make up the Solar System. Although at first sight we might decide that the Earth must be the centre of everything with the Sun, Moon, planets and stars revolving round it, careful observation of the motions of the heavenly bodies leads to the right conclusion that the planets are indeed revolving round the Sun all in the same direction. These worlds are Mercury, Venus, Earth, Mars, Jupiter, Saturn,

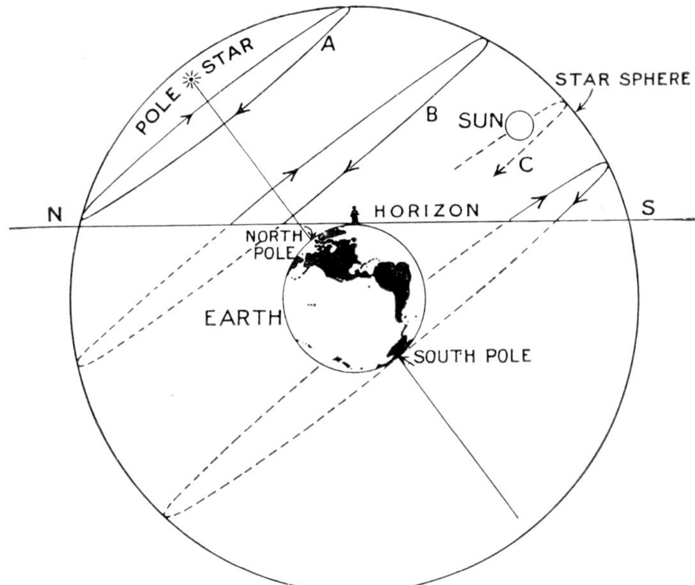

Fig. 1. THE EARTH AND THE STARS

Because the Earth rotates on its axis it appears to an observer on its surface that the planet is still while the star sphere rotates about the Pole Star. This diagram shows how some stars (position A) circle the Pole Star and never set, others (B) rise and set each day, the dotted lines indicating when they are below the horizon, while yet others (C) only rise above the horizon for a very short time. The position of the Sun as it is in spring and autumn is shown. If the observer moves towards the south pole of the Earth his horizon shifts with him and he is then able more easily to see the stars at position C and even further south in the star sphere.

Uranus, Neptune and Pluto and they are held in their almost circular paths by the attraction of the Sun's gravity. Mercury revolves at an average distance of 36 million miles, being the closest planet to the Sun, while Pluto, the most distant, is one hundred times as far away. The nearer a planet is to the Sun the faster it moves in its orbit; Mercury takes eighty-eight days for a complete revolution, while Pluto takes nearly 250 years.

Not only is the Earth circling around the Sun, but in addition the Sun itself is moving through space together with many other stars circling round the centre of a vast bun-shaped mass of stars known as the Galaxy.

The apparent daily motion of the celestial bodies in the sky is a result of the rotation of the Earth upon its own axis which passes through the north and south poles and points towards the star Polaris. That is why all the heavenly bodies appear to revolve around a point in the sky close to Polaris. Due to the revolution of the Earth around the Sun there is also an annual revolution of the heavens as seen from our planet. This makes the Sun appear to move through the star sphere from west to east through what are known as the Constellations of the Zodiac. In addition all the stars which rise and set do so a little earlier each day so that in the course of a year only certain stars are seen at the different seasons. Those stars in the part of the heavens close to the Sun at the various times of the year are, of course, not visible because they rise and set with the Sun itself.

The Sun

The most brilliant object in our heavens is the Sun, which is the nearest star to the Earth. But it is only one of millions of stars, each of which pours forth energy in the form of light, heat and other invisible radiations. This energy is generated deep in the star's interior where the core reaches high enough temperatures and pressures for thermo-nuclear reactions to take place.

The principal reaction is similar to that which occurs when a hydrogen bomb goes off, only it is continuous. The Sun is so vast that it converts 250 million tons of hydrogen into light, heat and other radiation every minute, the hydrogen being converted into helium. Though its hydrogen is thus being used up, the Sun is not getting colder like a dying fire. The physical changes which take place are actually causing it to get brighter and hotter. This process will go on for many thousands of millions of years, for there is so much hydrogen in the Sun that only 3 or 4 per cent. of the original store has been used up during the 5,000 million years of the Sun's existence.

The Sun is 866,000 miles in diameter and 93,000,000 miles from the Earth. It is more than a million times the volume of the earth. The next star is so far away, however, that it takes light, travelling at 186,000 miles per second, four and a half years to journey the 27,000,000,000,000 miles from it to the Earth.

The Multitude of Stars

And all the myriads of stars which can be seen with the aid of a powerful telescope are separated by similar distances.

With the unaided eye it is possible—though not all at one time—to see 6,000 different stars, but a large telescope reveals many millions. It is estimated that in our Galaxy there are over 100,000 million stars and if we look along the thickest part of its bun-shaped structure their combined light blends together to produce a pearly band which can best be seen stretching across our summer skies as the Milky Way. Even the Galaxy, therefore, is mostly " empty " space, though between the stars themselves there is a certain amount of very tenuous gas and dust.

Beyond the system of the Milky Way there are similar systems each containing hundreds of millions of stars. The nearest can be seen with the unaided eye as a hazy star in the constellation of Andromeda. It is at a distance of over 1,000,000 light years. It is estimated that there are at least as many of these " island universes " as there are stars in our own galaxy, and from the most distant which can be photographed the light has taken 1,000 million years to reach the Earth.

We live on a world which is thus a member of the Sun's group of planets; the Sun is one of the much larger group of stars making up the Galaxy; while the Galaxy itself is only one of a great system of island universes which stretch as far as our telescopes can penetrate into space. There are no doubt millions of other galaxies far beyond telescopic range.

Sunspots

All life on Earth depends upon the Sun. The brilliant outer layers from which the heat and light are radiated to us is called the photosphere and this is the bright disc which we can see. A telescope shows that it has a granular agitated surface in which dark cavities sometimes appear. These are sunspots which at times can be so large in area that they can be seen without a telescope if the Sun is examined through very dark glasses.

By watching these spots cross the solar disc we can find out that the Sun turns on its axis, like the Earth does, but in a period of twenty-six days. It is also found by observation that spots close to the solar equator move round more quickly than do those close to the polar regions. This informs us that the Sun does not have a solid surface; it is a great globe of intensely hot gases. Though the surface temperature is only about 6,000 degrees, the temperature at the centre of the Sun may be 20,000,000 degrees!

Solar Eclipses

Surrounding the photosphere is a region which shines with a brilliant red light which we know comes from the gas hydrogen. This region is known as the chromosphere and it is prominent when, at times of total solar eclipse, the disc of the Moon temporarily hides the brilliance of the photosphere from our view. Then the eclipsed Sun presents a really wonderful sight. The black mass of the Moon is surrounded by the vivid red chromosphere from which crimson prominences of fantastic shapes can be seen to rise like monstrous flames.

These prominences change rapidly and sometimes leap tens of thousands of miles into space. They are thought to be caused by matter plunging into the Sun from the surrounding space so that their outward motion is merely an illusion. Surrounding the whole is the pearly outer atmosphere of the Sun which is called the corona and which extends for millions of miles into space.

Total solar eclipses, when the Sun, Earth and Moon are in the same straight line with the Moon in the middle, although they occur fairly frequently, can each only be seen from a small track on the Earth's surface. The last seen in England was in 1927 and the next will not be until August 11th, 1999.

An eclipse of the Moon is more common. This is caused by the Earth coming between the Moon and the Sun so that the shadow of our planet falls on the Moon. Total lunar eclipses will be seen from England on August 25th, 1961, June 24th and December 18th, 1964.

The Moon

Although the Sun and the Moon appear to be about the same size from the Earth, the Moon is really quite a tiny globe, being only 2,160 miles in diameter. But, as the satellite of the Earth, it is relatively close—238,000 miles, or about nine times the distance round the Earth's equator. In fact, if the Earth were placed at the centre of the Sun there would be plenty of room inside the Sun for the Moon to revolve around us as it normally does.

Yet despite its small size, the Moon is of special interest because it is the nearest heavenly body to our Earth and because we can see its surface quite clearly. Modern telescopes are sufficiently powerful to reveal anything the size of a small town on the Moon.

The Moon and the Earth, held together by their mutual gravities, revolve around the Sun, but the effect of the motion to an observer on Earth is that the Moon moves around the Earth in a period of about

ROUND THE YEAR—

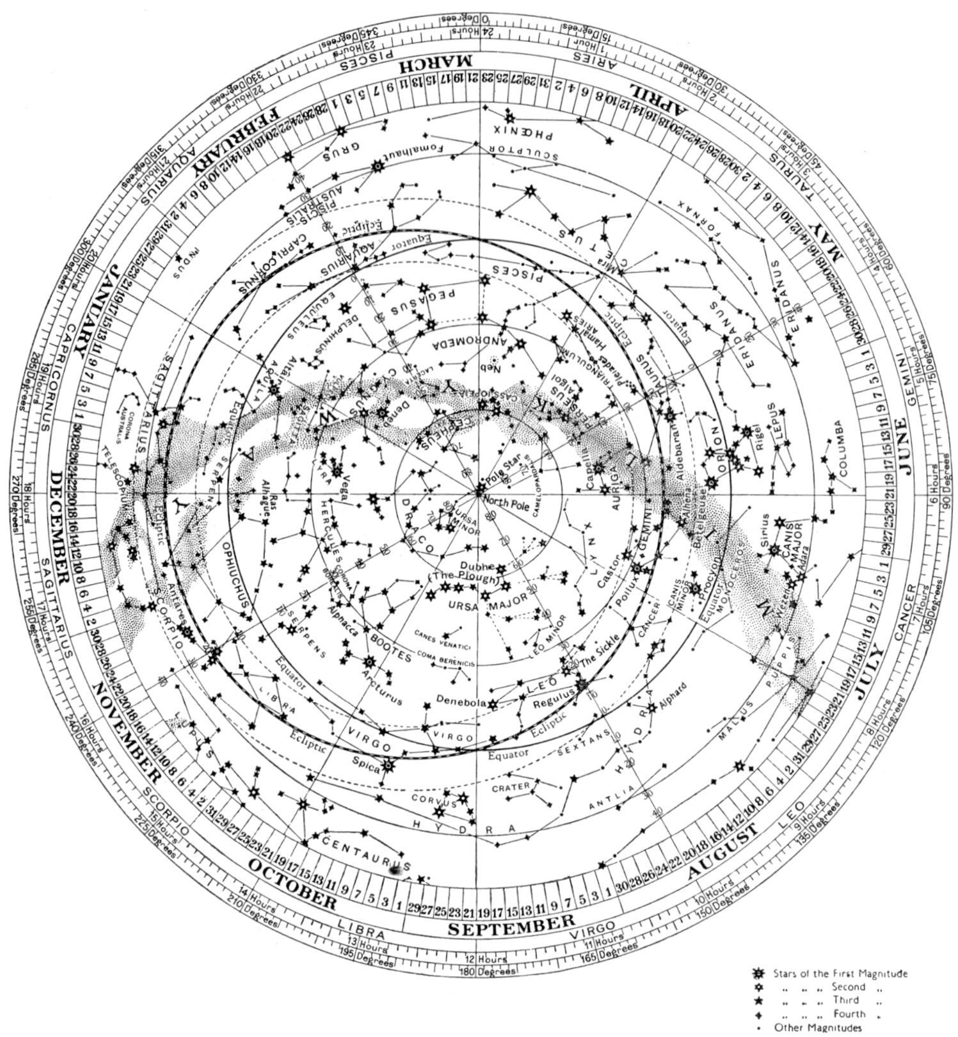

1. NORTHERN HEMISPHERE

This map shows all the principal stars visible in the Northern Hemisphere throughout the year, and it thus includes many stars which are in the Southern Hemisphere of the sky. If you hold it nearly over your head, so that its centre is in the direction of the Pole Star, and then rotate it until the day of the month is at the bottom, it shows the positions of the stars at midnight. To find their positions earlier in the evening, rotate the map in a clockwise direction for the required number of hours before midnight. The hours are marked round the edge, but you must count off the number you require—not read off the time.

Many of the stars in the foreground will be below your horizon, and to find where this comes you subtract the latitude of your place from 90 degrees and read off the answer on the nearest radius shown on the map (every third one is numbered). You will find two such numbers on the radius, and you need the one nearest the North Pole. Thus, in the position of the map on the page (showing the stars at midnight on 21st September) a person at latitude 50° N. would see the Great Bear (Ursa Major) low down on the northern horizon, for 50 from 90 leaves 40, and the 40th degree mark nearest the North Pole falls a little below the Great Bear.

To find the stars visible when you look to the south, turn the diagram exactly upside-down and face south. Now once more look for the number 40 on the nearest radius running directly down the page, only this time read inwards from the outer edge of the map. This will mark the edge of your southern horizon.

—IN THE HEAVENS

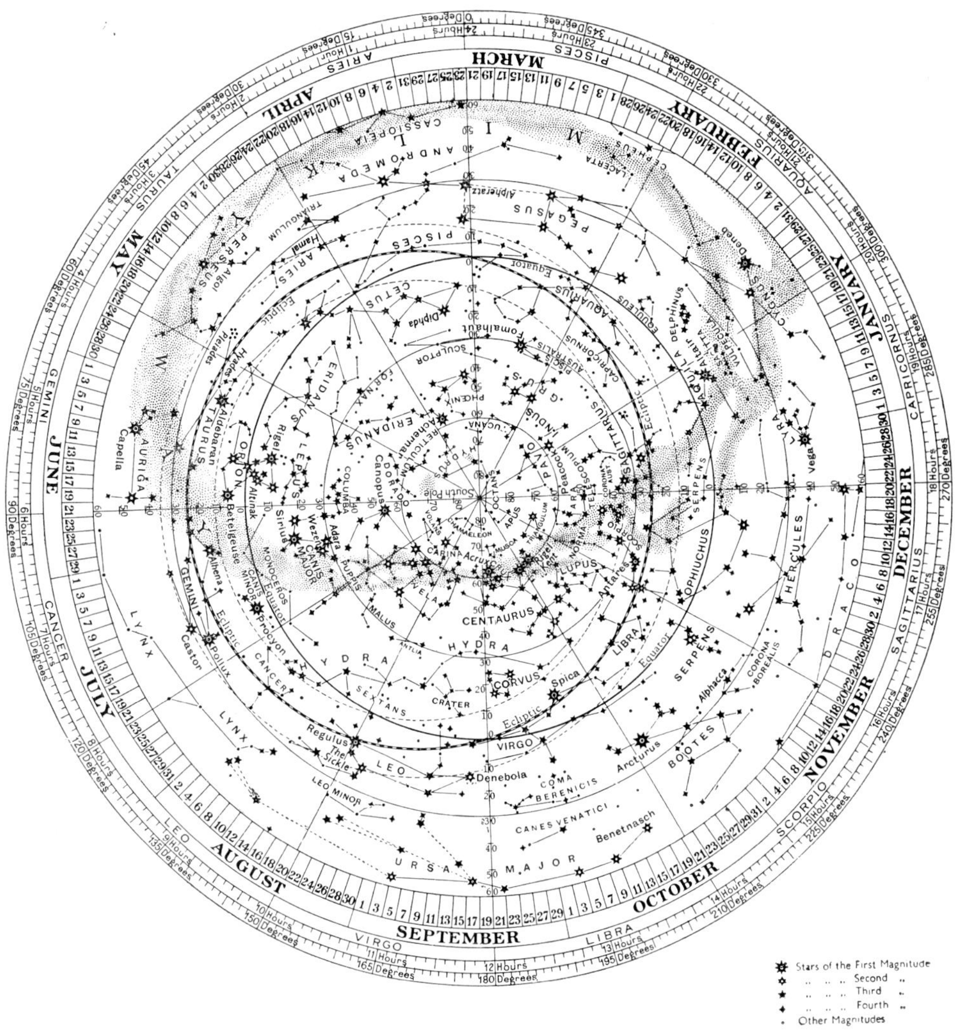

2. SOUTHERN HEMISPHERE

This map shows the stars for people living in the Southern Hemisphere. Here, the first thing is to face the South Pole, so you set up your map with the date at the bottom, as before, and turn so that the Southern Cross corresponds with the position of Crux on the map. To observe at a time earlier than midnight, proceed as in the Northern Hemisphere only rotate the map in a *counter*-clockwise direction. You then find your southern horizon on the map by subtracting your latitude from 90 and reading off the result on the radius from the Pole (taking the figure nearest the Pole).

To find your northern horizon, turn the map exactly round and face north. Now read off the same number upwards from the bottom edge. Suppose you are at latitude 34° S., this number will be 90 *minus* 34, which is 56. You have thus found two points on your map, one for the northern horizon and one for the southern. A circle passing through both of them will give you your entire horizon, but it will not be any of the circles already drawn on your map, which are all centred on the South Pole. These are all parallel with the equator (which you will find marked as a thin black line), whereas one of your points lies inside the equator and the other the same distance outside. The centre of *your* circle will correspond with the point in the sky exactly overhead.

The dark circle marked on the map as the 'ecliptic' shows the path through the stars followed by the sun all round the year. On it you will find the twelve Signs of the Zodiac, and when planets or the moon are visible they are never very far from it.

Copyright.

Fig. 2. LIGHTED BY EARTHSHINE

The Moon and the planets shine only by reflected light. The bright part of the Moon is illuminated by light from the Sun. But the sunshine also falls on the Earth from which it is reflected to the Moon. When the Moon is a fine crescent we can sometimes see the dark part lighted by the Earthshine as shown in this photograph.

twenty-seven and a half days. Because our satellite also rotates on its axis in the same period of time, it presents only one hemisphere to Earth, the other being hidden from us. In point of fact the Moon's path relative to the Earth is not a perfect circle and the speed of rotation does not always coincide with that of revolution so we are able to see four-sevenths of its surface.

The Moon, like the planets, does not shine of its own accord but by reflected sunlight. The amount of its surface which appears illuminated depends on the relative position of the Moon and the Sun as seen from the Earth. When between the Earth and the Sun the dark hemisphere is towards us and the Moon is said to be "new." When opposite to the Sun in the sky the full face of the Moon is illuminated and it is said to be "full." Sometimes when the Moon is just a thin crescent we can see the dark portion lighted up by sunlight which has been reflected from the Earth on to the night side of the Moon. This is popularly known as the "old Moon in the young Moon's arms" (Fig. 2).

Our satellite is a barren world with neither air nor water. A telescope shows great mountain ranges, extensive grey plains and circular mountain rings known as craters (Fig. 3). Some of these circular mountains are large enough to hold Wales, but scientists are not sure exactly how they were formed. They may have arisen from volcanoes which, because of the reduced lunar gravity (one-sixth that

Copyright.

Fig. 3. THE SURFACE OF THE MOON

The surface of the Moon is very inhospitable and covered with great circular mountains called craters. This photograph shows some of the lunar craters just as the Sun is rising on that part of the Moon. It was taken with the 18-inch telescope at Jodrell Bank, in Cheshire.

of the Earth), were able to throw their lava and debris for long distances across the lunar surface. Alternatively the craters might have been formed by the impact of great masses of rock which originated when the solar system was formed and were later swept up by the planets and their satellites. The Earth was still molten at the time so that the falling bodies were absorbed without trace. The Moon, because of its smaller size, cooled more quickly than the Earth and a crust formed rapidly. The crashing bodies tore and rent this surface to produce the great craters which we now see. There has, moreover, been no weather on the Moon to wear down the surface rocks and they remain just as they were formed.

Copyright.

Fig. 4. A RECORD BREAKING ROCKET

Some day men may land on the Moon by means of spaceships driven by rocket motors. This large rocket is starting off to travel at 4,000 miles an hour into the upper atmosphere of the Earth. It is a VIKING rocket which set up a height record of 156 miles. The Glenn L. Martin Company which made it later took part in the United States earth satellite programme, in the course of which the Viking's altitude has been many times exceeded.

One of the many unexplained features of the lunar surface is the series of light streaks which diverge from several of the craters and pass for hundreds of miles across both mountains and plains. They are especially prominent at Full Moon, when they make the small globe look like a peeled orange. They are neither cracks nor ridges but look as though they might have been caused by tremendous explosions blowing material from the craters out across the surface.

Although the Moon is a " dead " world, it will be the first on which we shall land when rockets can be built large enough to carry us on interplanetary journeys.

Space Travel

In order to go to the Moon a rocket spaceship would have to reach 25,000 miles an hour just outside the Earth's dense atmosphere, that is, about 100 miles above sea level. The ship would then coast through space and four or five days later would start to fall to the Moon. If nothing were done, it would crash on to the lunar surface at a speed of 5,000 miles per hour; but the spaceship would have to be designed so that it could fall towards the Moon tail first. At the right time the rocket motors would again be fired to break the fall and the ship would be cushioned on its jets to a safe landing.

Any exploration of the Moon would require the use of special suits to protect the explorers from the inhospitable conditions. During the long lunar day the Sun's rays fall on to the rocks and make them hotter than boiling water. During the lunar night, on the other hand, there is no air to prevent the heat leaking off into the vacuum of space and conditions become so cold that air, if it were present, would freeze solid. A lunar space suit has to protect its wearer from these extremes of temperature and it must also supply air for the explorer to breathe. Similar types of suits are now being designed to protect the pilots of high-flying aircraft who may have to bale out at heights where they would otherwise die before they could fall into the breathable atmosphere closer to the ground.

A Silent World

The lack of air on the Moon also produces another unusual effect. Sound waves are carried by air, so on the Moon silence will reign. A man in a space suit

Copyright.

Fig. 5. HERMES—A GUIDED MISSILE

But travelling through space requires accurate navigation which must be done by complex instruments. To-day scientists are evolving electronic brains which can guide missiles like this General Electric Company HERMES to distant targets. In the future these electronic devices may guide spaceships to other worlds.

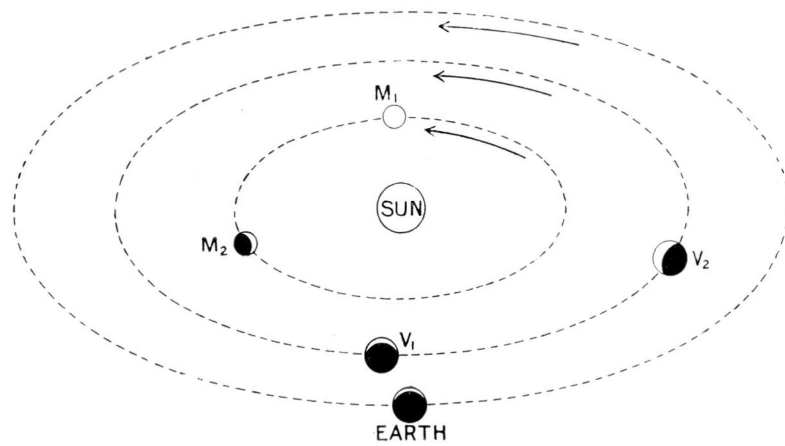

Copyright.

Fig. 6. THE ORBITS OF MERCURY AND VENUS

The orbits of the inner planets, Mercury and Venus, compared with the Earth. Mercury is shown (M1) when it is most distant from the Earth at superior conjunction and also (M2) when it appears at its greatest distance from the Sun in the sky. Venus is shown nearly at its closest approach to the Earth (V1) at inferior conjunction, and also (V2) when it is farthest from the Sun in the sky. Mercury at M2 is at eastern elongation and is an evening star; Venus at V2 is at western elongation and is a morning star.

could not hear a gun fired a few feet away. To talk to each other lunar explorers would have to use radio waves with " walkie-talkie " sets built into their space suits.

Our sky on Earth is blue because the air disperses some of the light from the Sun. On the Moon the sky would be jet black. If the explorers could shield their eyes from the glare reflected from the lunar rocks they would be able to see the stars shining in the sky even during the daytime. But most awe-inspiring would be a great globe shining brilliantly and twelve times as big as the Moon appears in Earth's skies. Fixed in the lunar sky, never rising nor setting, it would be our own planet Earth.

Although men must wear space suits to move about on the Moon they would not be unduly hindered by the weight of these suits. The reduced lunar gravity would make it possible for the explorers to take fantastic leaps, six times as high as they could on Earth.

How soon can we expect to walk on the Moon? A few scientists think that it will be possible by the end of this century, but this is probably much too optimistic. The beginning of space flight may be dated from the launching of Earth-satellites into space (Fig. 4). These are metal balls, or cylinders, which are able to circle the Earth at about 17,000 miles per hour at a height of over 200 miles. Within them are instruments to measure the light, heat, X-rays and radio waves coming from the Sun, and others to detect cosmic particles coming from distant parts of the universe. Such satellites are helping us to find out more about our own Earth by looking at it from space.

The Frontier of Space

Later, bigger Earth-satellites will be put up while other rocket vehicles, developments of to-day's guided missiles (Fig. 5), will be sent into space to journey to other worlds. Manned rocket planes are even now shooting into the upper atmosphere at speeds several times faster than that of a rifle bullet; they are carrying us to the frontier of interplanetary space. The day is fast approaching when we shall see unmanned rockets capable of landing on the Moon. These will pave the way for spaceship journeys to other worlds in the distant future.

These worlds can be conveniently divided into inner and outer planets.

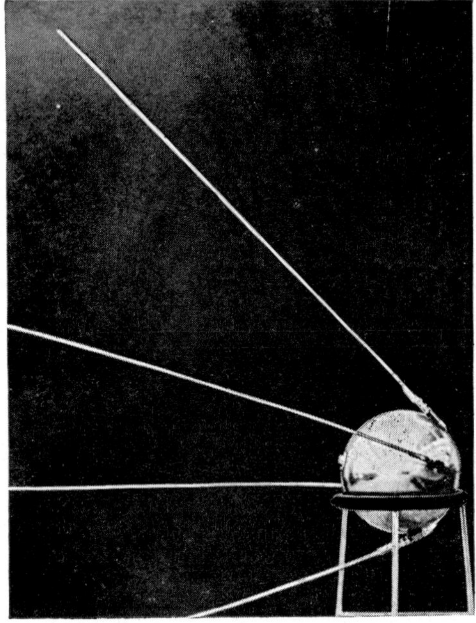

Planet News.

On October 4th, 1957, Russia startled the world by successfully launching the first earth satellite, which she called *sputnik*. This official photograph shows the satellite resting on a stand before being launched. Its weight was given as 184 lb.

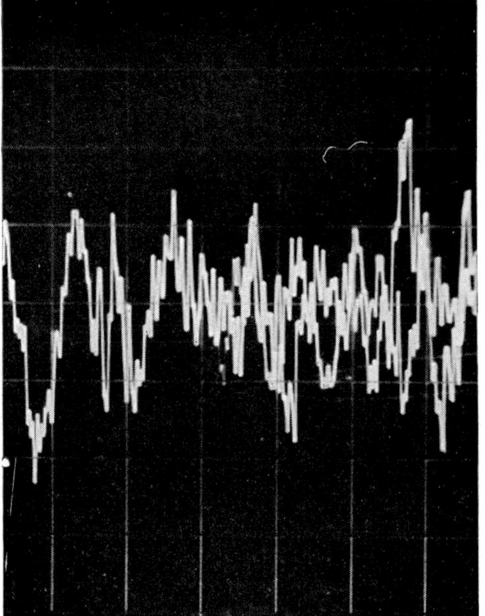

Keystone.

Circling the earth at a speed of probably more than 17,000 m.p.h. and at a height of 560 miles, the *sputnik* transmitted radio signals. This was the pattern of the signals as recorded at the B.B.C.'s receiving station at Tatsfield, Surrey.

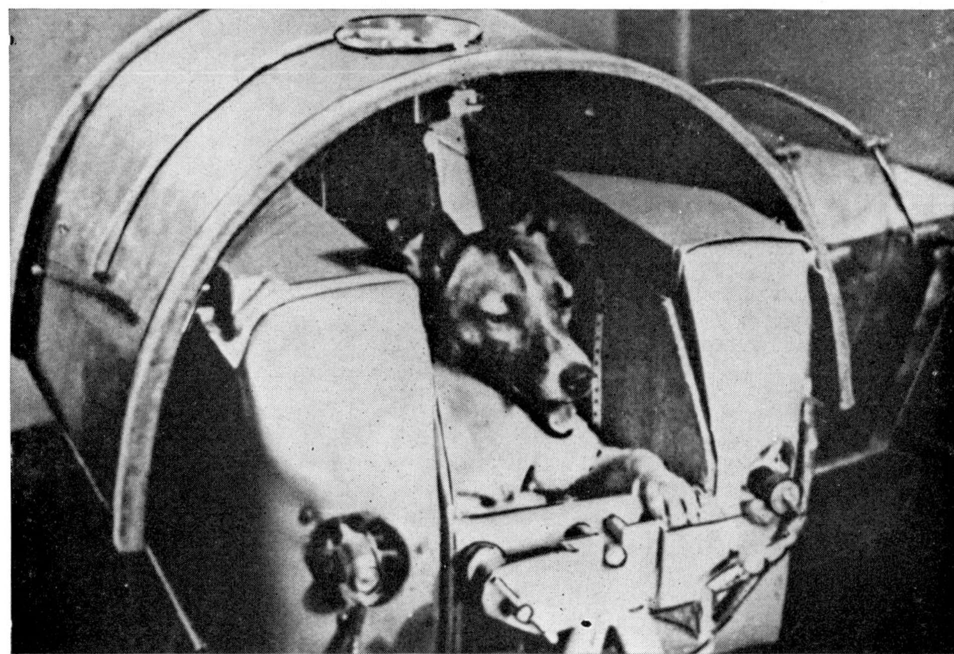

Planet News.

A second and larger satellite was launched by Russia on November 3rd, 1957. Weighing about half a ton, it carried a dog in a pressurised container (seen here before it was put in the satellite). The dog, a " husky " of the Samoyede type, was called " Laika," and had previously made rocket flights and had undergone other special training. Instruments in the satellite sent information about the dog's bodily reactions back to earth.

—RUSSIAN AND AMERICAN

Associated Press.

The first American attempt to launch a satellite was a failure, but on January 31st, 1958, the satellite called *Explorer* or *Alpha* 1958 was successfully launched by a special *Jupiter-C* rocket at Cape Canaveral, Florida. This picture shows the nose section of the rocket being joined to the main stage booster.

Keystone.

Testing the final assembly of the satellite on a " balancing tub " in the spin test rig. About 80 inches long, 6 inches wide, and weighing 30·8 lb., the satellite (containing two radio transmitters) orbited the earth once every 118 minutes.

Keystone.

Ready for firing on the launching pad at Cape Canaveral. Another satellite, *Beta* 1958, was successfully launched on March 17th, 1958, but the first attempts to send a satellite to the moon (August and October 1958) failed.

The former (Fig. 6) revolve in orbits inside that of the Earth and consequently they show phases like the Moon does. They cannot move far away from the Sun in the sky and they appear as morning and evening stars. Mercury is a small world—one-sixteenth the size of the Earth—without any atmosphere, and extremely hot due to its nearness to the Sun. It is probably very much like our Moon.

Bright Venus

Venus is almost as big as the Earth, but a thick cloud envelope hides its surface and at the same time reflects so much sunlight that, after the Moon, Venus is the brightest object in our heavens, sometimes being visible in the daytime. There may be life on Venus; we do not know, because we are not sure which gases are present in its atmosphere and we cannot see what is on the surface of the planet beneath the clouds.

The Planet Mars

The outer planets (Fig. 7) are all revolving beyond the orbit of the Earth and they are best seen shining bright and full at opposition in the midnight sky. In favourable circumstances Mars can approach to within 35,000,000 miles of the Earth. At such times astronomers looking at the bright red star-like object through their telescopes see a world with an atmosphere in which there are clouds and dust storms. They see white polar caps which may consist of snow, and red deserts and green areas near to the Martian equator.

Its "Canals"

Some observers claim to have seen long straight lines on the surface of the planet, and these have been imprudently called "canals." If they exist, which seems doubtful, they are almost certainly not canals. They may be only optical illusions.

The planet is about half the diameter of the Earth, but it is of great interest because seasonal changes take place in the green areas which may be caused by vegetation. It has been recently shown that plant life could live in an atmosphere similar to that on Mars, even though the temperature is often below freezing point. If there are Martian plants, there may also be other types of life to preserve the balance of nature, as on Earth. But sending a spaceship to Mars is much more difficult than journeying to the Moon. Before we can do

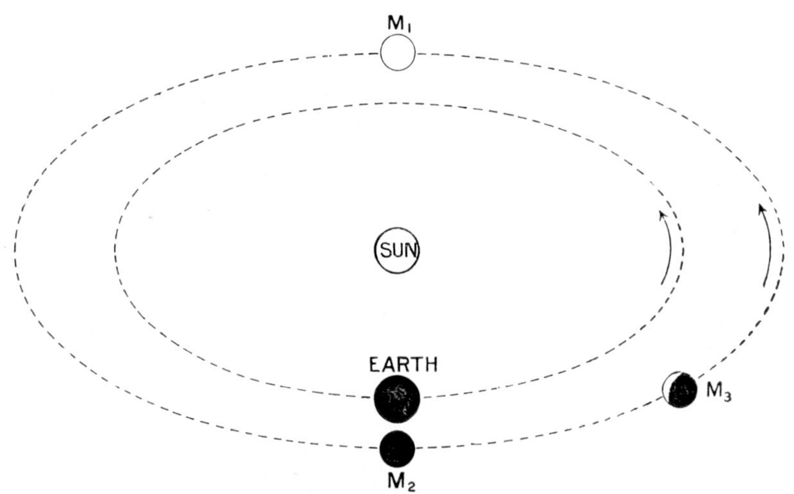

Fig. 7. THE ORBITS OF THE EARTH AND MARS

Orbits of the Earth and Mars, which is an outer planet. Mars is shown at M1 when most distant from the Earth (conjunction) and at M2 when closest to the Earth (opposition). M3 is known as the position of quadrature.

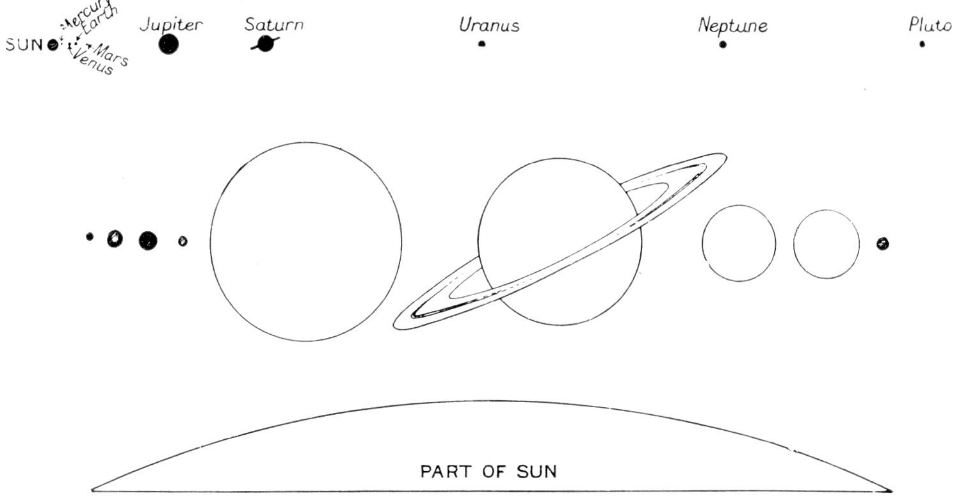

Copyright.

Fig. 8. THE PLANETS IN RELATION TO THE SUN

The planets of the Solar System are shown at their relative distances from the Sun at the top of this drawing. Below they are shown in the same order but in relative sizes together with a part of the Sun drawn to the same scale. It is important to note how small the Earth is compared with the Sun and the larger planets, and also how close it is to the Sun on the scale of the Solar System.

so it will be necessary for our scientists to develop new types of atomic or solar engines to power spaceships through the interplanetary void.

The Asteroids

Beyond Mars is a great gap in the Solar System in which there is not one world revolving round the Sun, but countless tiny bodies known as the asteroids. Some theories say that they are the remnants of a planet which disintegrated. They are of great interest to astronomers because a few of these bodies move in elongated orbits which carry them very close to the Earth, nearer than any other body except the Moon. They can then be used to measure accurately the distance of the Earth from the Sun.

Jupiter the Giant

Outside the asteroid zone revolves the largest planet of the Solar System, the giant Jupiter with its family of twelve satellites, four of which can be seen with a pair of field glasses. After Venus it is the brightest object in the sky and at present shines brilliantly in the spring. In a few years' time it will have moved farther along its twelve-year orbit around the Sun and will be best seen during the summer months.

Jupiter is mainly a ball of gas consisting of hydrogen, methane and ammonia. It probably has no solid surface and we can see that the outer atmosphere is convulsed with great storms. Its diameter is eleven times that of the Earth and it has more than twice the combined weight of all the other planets (Fig. 8).

Ringed Saturn

At a distance of 890 million miles from the Sun is the unique ringed planet Saturn, which is light enough to float on water.

The rings consist of myriads of tiny moonlets and have a diameter of 170,000 miles but are only 100 miles thick. Saturn is a gaseous world like Jupiter and has also a large family of satellites.

Far out towards the boundaries of the Solar System we find the two large cold planets, Uranus and Neptune, and then the tiny Pluto which was discovered photographically as late as 1930. These are all distant uninhabitable worlds from which the Sun itself would appear only as a very bright star.

THE NATURE OF THE EARTH

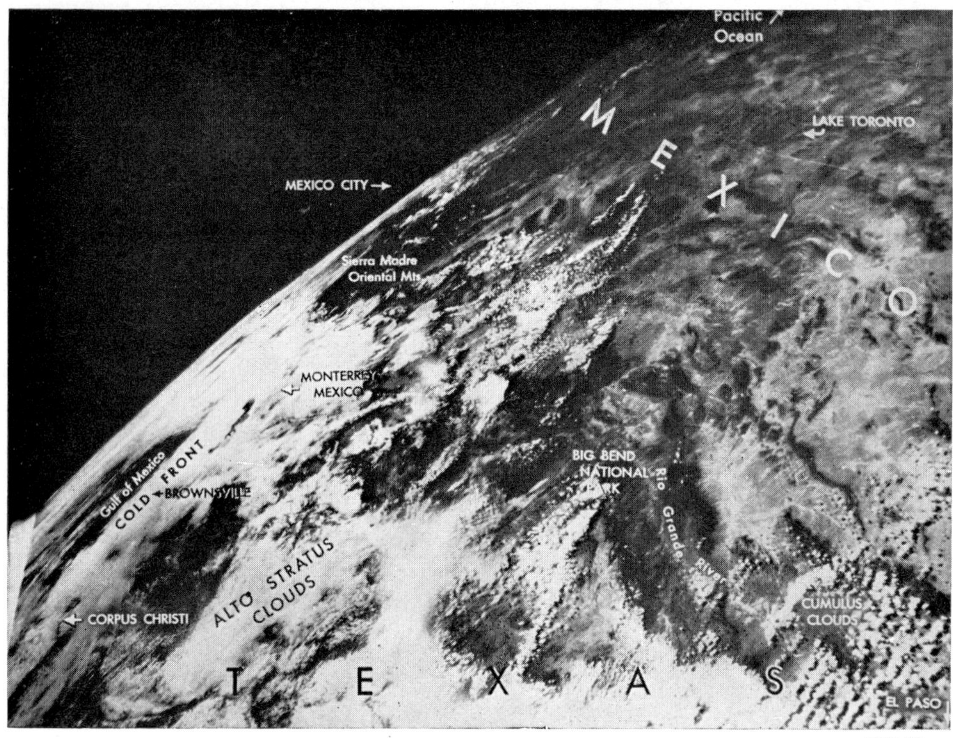

U.S. Navy.

THE WORLD *IS* ROUND

Do you remember the proofs which helped us to understand that the world is a globe? In future everyone will be able to *see*, as we do here, that it is round; for photographs taken by rocket-borne automatic cameras clearly reveal its curvature. Our dramatic " highest ever " picture shows how a great sweep of Mexico and Texas, covering about 600,000 square miles, looks to the eye of a camera 155 miles above sea level.

It is sometimes said that the Earth is a second-rate planet caught in the orbit of a third-rate star, but it will always be the most important planet to us. It is true, of course, that it has only one satellite and is much smaller than Jupiter with eleven satellites, Saturn (nine satellites), Uranus (five satellites) and Neptune (two satellites); but it is nearer (93,003,000 miles) to the life-giving Sun than these giants and its speed of 66,000 miles an hour, which takes it round the Sun in 365¼ days, is a great deal more: it takes Neptune, travelling at 12,000 miles an hour, 1,648 years to make a complete journey round the Sun.

Moreover, the Earth's measurements remain tremendously impressive. Its polar and equatorial circumferences are 24,860 and 24,902 miles respectively; its polar and equatorial diameters are 7,900 and 7,926½ miles; and its total area is 197 million square miles. Its calculated weight is 5,876 million million million tons!

How the Earth Began

All peoples have speculated about the origin of the Earth, but the first scientific attempts began with Georges Leclerc, Comte de Buffon (1707–88). He suggested that the planetary system resulted from a collision between the Sun and a passing star. Enormous bits of matter were thus sent spinning into space, where many of them were trapped, by gravitational attraction, into an eternity of orderly movement around the Sun.

Six years later (1755), Immanuel Kant (1724–1804) outlined a different view of the

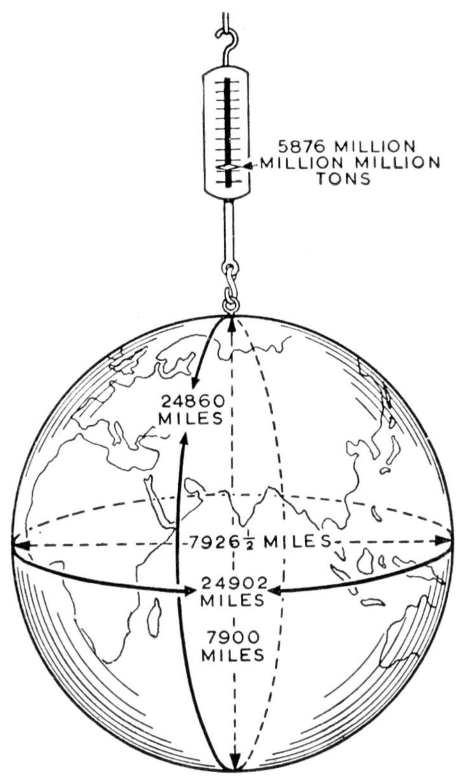

Specially drawn for this work.

"OUR GLOBE"

The measurements which should agree differ because "our globe" is not really a globe. It is flattened at the poles and bulges at the Equator—the imaginary line that equates the northern and southern hemispheres.

origin of the planets, which was elaborated in 1796 by Pierre Simon, Marquis de Laplace (1749–1827). He proposed that the Solar System began as a vast ball of gas, hot and spinning, caused by an explosion inside the Sun. As it cooled and contracted, its rotation increased and threw off bits of gaseous matter. These were held and shaped by gravitational attraction into a surrounding ring, which cooled and contracted into a globe revolving around its parent.

And so the first planet was formed. Meanwhile, a second ring was forming which developed into the next planet, the process being repeated until all the planets had appeared. Their satellites were produced in much the same way.

The Collision Theory of Buffon led to modifications in which a passing star caused an upheaval by coming too near the Sun, or by rubbing against it without actually colliding. According to the Planetesimal Theory of T. C. Chamberlin (1843–1928) and F. R. Moulton (1872–), the gravitational force of a gigantic star, which came too close to the Sun, had a breaking-up effect that also drew to itself the particles ejected by the Sun. These particles came together and formed solid bodies, called planetesimals. They grew into larger planetesimals, and eventually into planets, by attracting smaller bodies to themselves.

The Tidal Hypothesis, made popular by Sir James Jeans (1877–1946), assumed that the Sun was still in a gaseous state when it was affected by the passing star. In that event immense tidal waves would have

Royal Geographical Society.

THE FIRST PHYSICAL GLOBE

The first physical geography globe, now in the Royal Geographical Society, was made by Dr. Alexander Keith Johnston (1804–71) for the Great Exhibition, London, 1851. It is about five feet high and beautifully carved; the figures on the base represent the four continents.

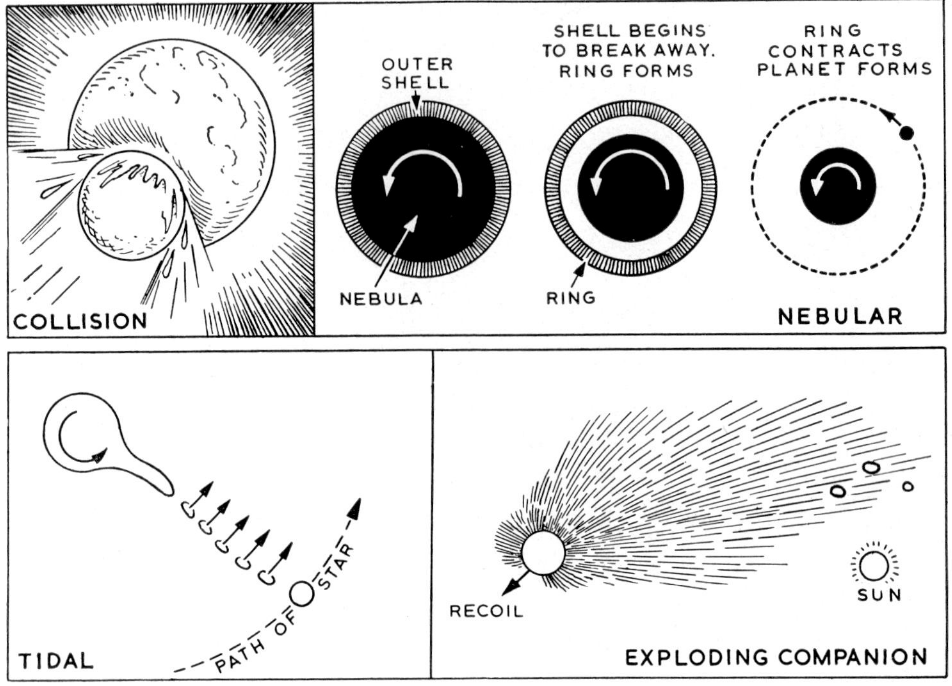

Specially drawn for this work.

THEORIES OF THE EARTH'S ORIGIN

Here we try to illustrate four of the theories of the Earth's origin described in the text: Buffon's Collision Theory, Laplace's Nebular Hypothesis, Jeans' Tidal Hypothesis and Hoyle's Exploding Companion Theory.

been set up in the Sun, distorting its shape into a gaseous " tail " drawn towards the star. This tail would have eventually broken into pieces that condensed and formed planets travelling round the Sun.

Laplace's Nebular Hypothesis lost ground against these theories, but in 1944 Carl von Weizsäcker revived it by showing that the Sun could have moved into a dense nebula of gas and dust particles which would then, through gravitational attraction, form a growing envelope around the Sun. Eventually this envelope would tighten into a vast surrounding ring from which the planets would be formed by condensation.

Weizsäcker's work had scarcely become known when Fred Hoyle advanced a theory based on the assumption that the Sun once had a companion which moved with it at a great distance. This companion was a type of star that explodes violently through nuclear reactions in its interior. Such an explosion in the Sun's companion would have had three main effects. A blazing cloud of material would have been shot out at something like three million miles an hour; as its speed decreased some of this material would have been captured, later to cool into planets, by the Sun; and the recoil would have driven the star for ever out of the path of companionship with the Sun.

These are some of the major theories of the Earth's origin. They challenge new scientific resources; and it may be that international effort can give us an agreed answer to man's oldest question: how did the world begin?

How Old is the Earth ?

The age of the Earth has also prompted speculation from very early times. Hindu thought gave us a calendar which puts the beginning of the world at 1,972,949,058 years ago (from 1957); Archbishop James

EXACTLY 4,004 B.C.

ABOUT 10 MILLION YEARS

AT MOST 100 MILLION YEARS

OVER 700 MILLION YEARS

ABOUT 4,500 MILLION YEARS

THREE CENTURIES OF GEOCHRONOLOGY

Archbishop Usher's calculation in 1650 was not seriously contested until the mid-nineteenth century. Estimates since then have advanced the age of the Earth (*geochronology*) from 10 million years to 4·55 billion years. It is thought that this is not likely to be greatly changed in the future.

Usher (1581–1656) defined the Hebrew-Christian view by announcing (1650) that the " beginning of time fell upon the night before the twenty-third day of October in the year of the Julian Calendar 710 (4004 B.C.)."

This calculation was accepted for the King James Version of the Bible, but it soon became apparent that the evolution of the Earth must have taken much more than the authorised span. Herman von Helmholtz (1821–94), urged by this changing attitude, estimated that the Sun and the Earth were both about 10 million years old.

The geologists took the record to 400 or 500 million years; but Lord Kelvin (1824–1907) argued that, as the Earth was receiving its heat from the shrinking Sun, its temperatures from the crust to the molten interior should be lower than they were if the crust had formed more than 400 million years ago. On the other hand, they would be much higher than they were if the crust had formed less than 20 million years ago. Along these lines, he concluded (1897) that the Earth was at most 100 million years old.

Meanwhile, there began the series of discoveries on the energy-releasing properties of the Earth's materials which are associated with the names of Antoine Becquerel (1852–1908), Pierre Curie (1859–1906), Marie Curie (1867–1934), Lord Rayleigh (1875–1947) and Lord Rutherford (1871–1937). They showed that the Earth made its own heat; for its materials contained elements that were slowly but

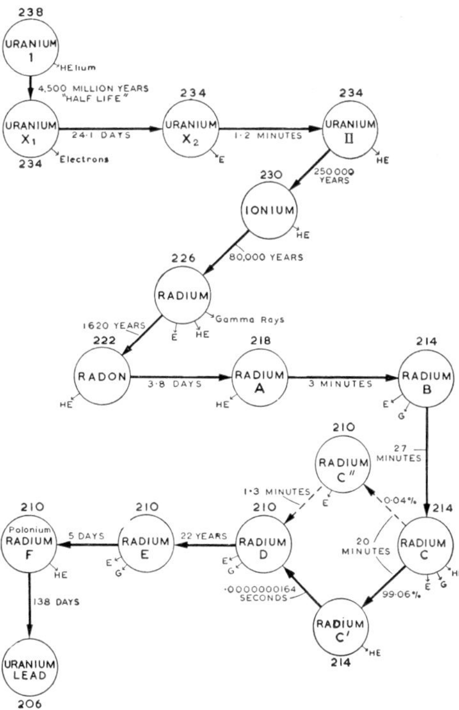

RADIOACTIVITY DATES THE PAST

Uranium, thorium, and actinium are the parent metals of a continuous cycle of changes accompanied by radioactivity, *alpha* particles or helium (HE), *beta* particles or electrons (E) and *gamma* rays (G) being discharged. The release of helium (atomic weight 4·003) decreases the atomic weight of the next substance formed by four. The time taken for each transformation is reckoned in terms of the " half life " and its regularity enables radioactive rocks to be dated with reasonable certainty.

continuously undergoing nuclear changes that released energy (which Marie Curie called *radioactivity*) and deposited lead at regular rates. Thus it became possible to devise methods for calculating the actual age of radioactive rocks that were not mixed up with rocks of other ages.

Lord Rutherford led the way by dating pitchblende (oxide of uranium) in his possession at 700 million years, but later samples reached 1,850 million years; and it became customary to say that the Earth was about 2,000 million years old. Further work revealed rocks that had begun depositing lead 2,500 million years ago, while calculations on the period since the crust was formed gave the Earth an age between 3,000 and 5,000 million years.

The most recent research has made possible a precise-looking estimate: 4·55 billion years—using billion in the American sense of 1,000 million years. Future work, it is thought, may raise this figure by half a billion or so years, but is unlikely to reduce it.

The Earth in its Infancy

The primary ingredients of the air, land and sea, and the organisms in them, are the elements which cannot be broken down into simpler ingredients: apart from 9 recently made in laboratories, 92 are now known. Only two of these, oxygen (50 per cent.) and silicon (26 per cent.), account for three-quarters of the weight of the whole Earth, the balance being mostly the contribution, as the diagram shows, of the six chief metals: aluminium, iron, calcium, sodium, potassium and manganese.

The most remarkable is oxygen. As a colourless, tasteless, odourless gas it makes up a fifth of the air we breathe; and in combination with various elements it gives us the oxides that dominate the compound materials of the Earth's crust: water is an oxide (hydrogen oxide) which gets eight-ninths of its weight from oxygen. Moreover, oxidation is a burning-process which releases energy no matter how different the burning might appear to be. The rusting of a nail, the combustion of oil in an engine, and the utilisation of food, are all examples of oxidation.

So the abundance of oxides ensures the storage of vast quantities of oxygen in the Earth, which we have learned to release and use: more than a million pounds worth of pure oxygen is manufactured in Britain every year. But the extent of oxidation renders animal life dependent on the activity of plants in restoring oxygen to the air; and it seems that plants appeared "just in time" to save the world from the disappearance of free oxygen.

How is it that we have any oxygen at all, considering that the atmosphere of the molten Earth was a great deal hotter than the 400° C. at which hydrogen is dispersed? Some authorities believe that most of the atmosphere was actually dispersed in those days, the atmosphere we know being produced by volcanic action. Others have calculated that the escaping

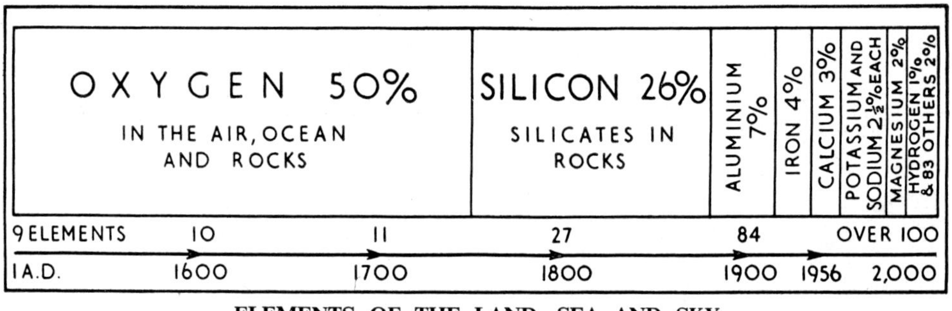

OXYGEN 50%
IN THE AIR, OCEAN AND ROCKS

SILICON 26%
SILICATES IN ROCKS

ALUMINIUM 7%
IRON 4%
CALCIUM 3%
POTASSIUM AND SODIUM 2½% EACH
MAGNESIUM 2%
HYDROGEN 1% & 83 OTHERS 2%

9 ELEMENTS	10	11	27	84		OVER 100
1 A.D.	1600	1700	1800	1900	1956	2,000

ELEMENTS OF THE LAND, SEA AND SKY

Oxygen and silicon account for 76 per cent. of the composition of the Earth; aluminium, iron and calcium for 14 per cent.; potassium, sodium and magnesium for 7 per cent. Below you see how the number of known elements has grown, especially during the Expansion of Europe, since the nine known to the ancient world. In recent years nine artificial elements have been added to the 92 natural elements.

PRECIOUS METALS

Within living memory men faced great hardships and fought each other for gold. To-day, uranium takes pride of place as " the precious metal," for uranium provides energy—the source of all wealth. Some of the richest uranium mines are in the famous copper centre at Katanga in the Belgian Congo. Slag, sliced hillsides and scrub dominate the scene.

Photos : Camera Press.

We cannot live without salt. In some countries it is still extracted as in ancient times: seawater is directed into concentrating tanks to evaporate, the dried out salt being raked on to the banks, piled up in pyramids, and then carried away. Iviza, one of the Balearic Islands, supplied salt made in this way to the first civilisations of the Mediterranean. To-day much of it goes to Norway for curing fish.

speed of oxygen, though increased by heat, was low enough to keep it earth-bound even if the influencing temperature had reached 5,000° C.

Therefore, as the gaseous Earth condensed into a seething molten mass, surrounded by acrid fumes, it is probable that the oxygen remained to assist the cooling process. In this condition, the heavier materials sank to the centre, while the lighter rose to the surface, where they hardened into a crust of *igneous* ("fire-born") rocks from which heat was rapidly lost by radiation.

It was still too hot for water to remain on the crust, but eventually it became cool enough for clouds to form here and there. And, as cooling continued, they collected in great masses which gradually covered the Earth with a thick sheet of vapour through which the Sun's rays could not pass.

The dark and waterless world, lifeless and flat, waited for rain. Then, after

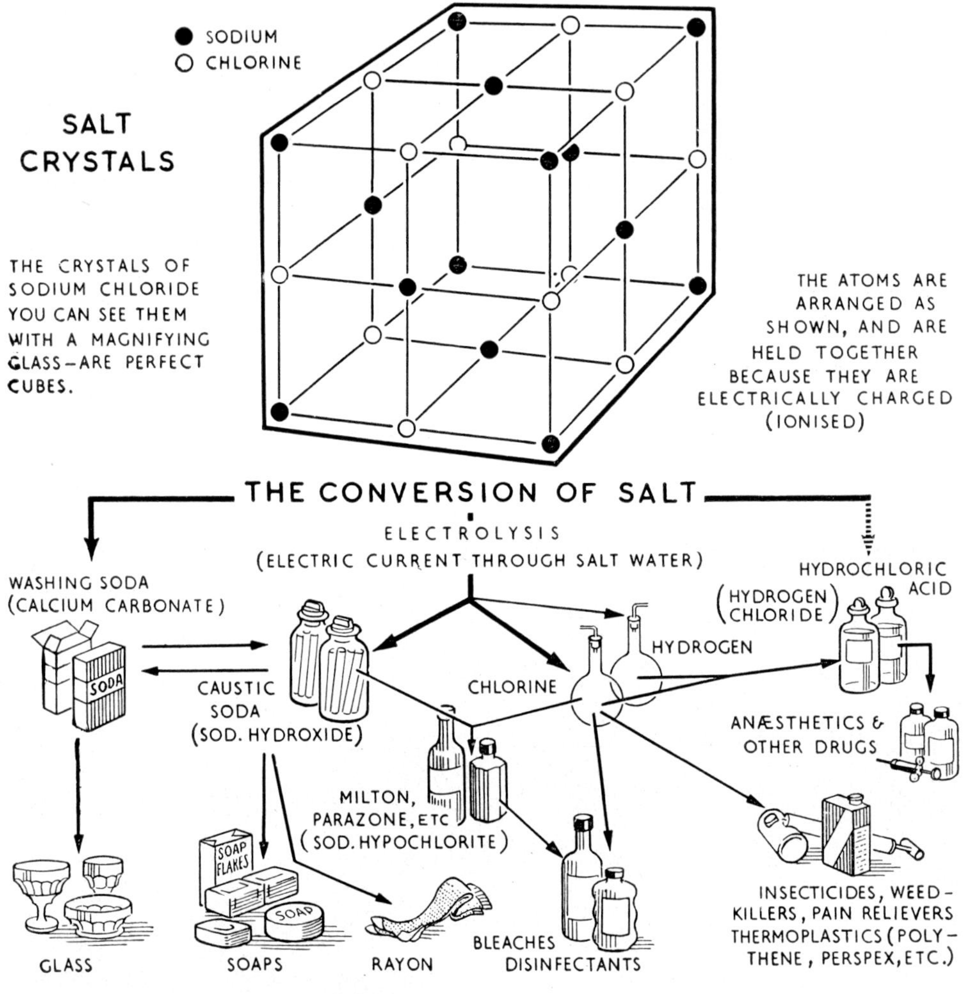

SALT AND ITS PRODUCTS

If you look at a few grains of salt with a magnifying glass, you will see that they are cube-shaped crystals. That is because their electrically charged atoms (ions) are held together at the corners of the cubical network—not just a few as shown in the greatly enlarged diagram but many millions. It is fortunate that salt is found in great abundance, for it is essential to us and many valuable products are made from it.

“FIRE-BORN” ROCKS

Coarsely crystalline granites, consisting chiefly of silica, make up the topmost layer of the igneous (“fire-born”) rocks of the Earth’s crust. This picture of rugged granitic scenery was taken in Devonshire at Bowermans Nose, Heyne Down, near Manaton, East Dartmoor.

Photos: H.M. Geological Survey.

Finely crystalline basalts, darker and heavier than granites, form the next layer of the Earth’s crust, but basaltic lava is often formed in columns at the surface, as this picture shows. It was taken on Staffa, one of the small islands of the Inner Hebrides, Scotland.

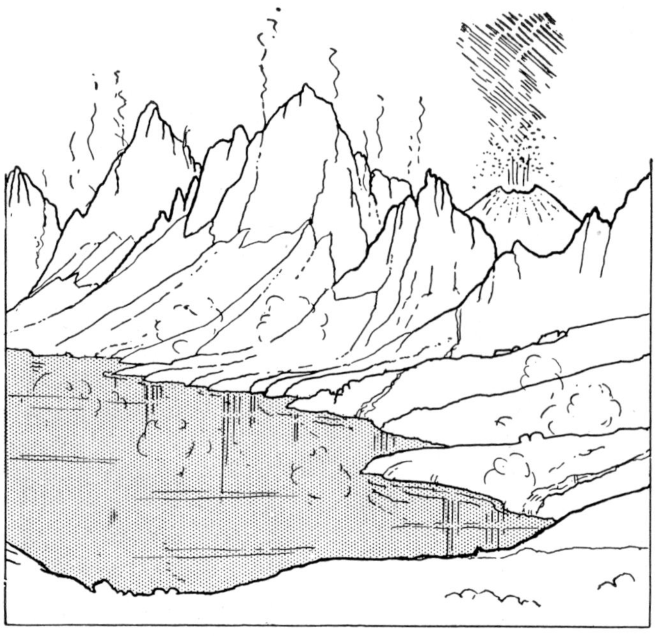

Specially drawn for this work.

AFTER THE FIRST RAINS

The long rains of the infant world filled the empty ocean basins, helped the shrinking, wrinkling and folding of the crust, and cut their own patterns on the way to the sea. And, as the perpetual night lifted, the sun shone on sharp-peaked mountains and belching volcanoes towering above the warm seas. But life was yet to come.

countless years, it came—first in great drops that were quickly returned to the clouds, later in an unceasing centuries-long deluge, accompanied by the booming and flashing of energy-releasing thunder and lightning. The water ran over the hot rocks and bubbling lava fields, cooling, scouring and dissolving salts as it went.

Vaporisation took a considerable proportion of these salts into the atmosphere, where they were electrically charged (ionised) by the abundant atmospheric energy and then returned to the Earth. Common salt (sodium chloride), which consists of electrically held atoms (ions) of sodium and chlorine, is an example of the building up of compounds by ionisation.

Thus, as the flowing waters ran into the lesser hollows to form lakes and ponds, and channelled the mighty drainage systems that fed the first seas, they carried along with them, and deposited where their speed decreased, the rock materials they had worn away or dissolved, as well as the vitalising ions returned to them from the atmosphere. In this way, new and more complex rocks were built up; water-cut ways and patterns were added to the wrinkling and folding of the cooling crust; and in the warm shoreline waters of the brimming basins there began the primeval conditions for life and future abundance.

The Beginnings of Earth Anatomy

Since the historic voyage round the world (1519–22), inspired by Ferdinand Magellan (1480–1521), many proofs have been devised to show that the Earth is a globe. Curvature photographs, taken by rocket-borne equipment, are the latest and most impressive.

Its shape is the only one which allows all its particles to be gravitationally attracted towards the centre, without causing distortions that would continue until every part of the surface was the same distance from the centre. Why, then, is it flattened at the poles and pulled out at the equator? The answer lies in the outwards-drawing or centrifugal force set up by the Earth's daily rotation. It is strongest at the equator and weakest at the poles.

Consequently, the Earth is more of a spheroid than a sphere or globe; but, as there are bulges and depressions on its surface, it is not exactly a spheroid. The bulges are the continents and mountains; the depressions are the ocean basins formed from heavier rocks. These ups and downs, so to speak, disappear when reduced proportionately in ordinary maps and globes. We must accordingly be content with seeing the Earth as a sphere in most representations "in the round," while imagining it as a *geoid* (earth-shaped mass).

LIFE IN THE PAST

A trilobite from the Cambrian Period.

A Silurian sea lily (animal) and honeycomb coral.

A fern from the Devonian Period.

Preserved stumps of Carboniferous scale trees in "The Fossil Grove," Victoria Park, Glasgow.

Photos: H.M. Geological Survey.

In early Cretaceous England, scale trees, cycads, conifers and tree ferns flourished in the sub-tropical climate. Giant reptiles ruled the land, water and skies.

ERAS	PERIODS	EARTH MOVEMENTS (MOUNTAINS, VOLCANOS)	WATER MOVEMENTS (GLACIERS, SEAS)	THE PROCESSION OF LIFE
CENOZOIC ("RECENT LIFE")	HOLOCENE ("WHOLLY RECENT")	S. America, Oceania	Postglacial. High seas	
	PLEISTOCENE ("MOST RECENT") 1 Million Years Ago	Coast ranges Western North America	Changing levels	Mammoth; Early Man; Sabre-toothed cat
	TERTIARY ("THIRD" PERIOD) 60 Millions	Great volcanism in Med., Ind. Ocean & Pacific. Vesuvius, Etna, "Fire Ring" of Pacific. Columbia Plateau, western North America, formed by 200,000 square miles of lava Pyrenees, Apennines, Alps, Carpathians, Caucasus, Himalayas	Desert conditions Seas cover many lands, including S. Europe, S.W. & Central Asia. Gondwanaland divided roughly into Africa & S. America. Britain raised, submerged, exposed again	Giant Rhinocerus; Old World Monkey; Giant ape; Flightless bird; First horse; Lemur
MESOZOIC ("MIDDLE LIFE")	CRETACEOUS ("CHALKY") 130 Millions	Lava forms vast plateaux in India (Deccan) and Siberia Rockies, Andes. Swampy estuaries raised to plateaux. Rising of Isthmus of Panama helps to form Gulf Stream by blocking N. Equatorial Current	Warm climate Much of Europe & N. America submerged but lands rising. English chalk cliffs formed	Flowering plants increase insects; Young born at advanced stage; Tiny young reared in pouch; Flesh eating Dinosaur
	JURASSIC (NAMED AFTER JURA MOUNTAINS) 155 Millions	Sierra Nevadas	Generally warm Australia Seas again invade western N. America. Most of Eurasia is dry land	Great variety of Dinosaurs; Temp. of body controlled. Warm blood; First Birds; Egg-laying mammal
	TRIASSIC (FROM "TRIAS" MEANING "THREE") 185 Millions	North America	Warm Desert conditions Seas retreat from Britain	Mammal-like reptiles; Marine Reptiles; Flying reptiles
	PERMIAN (PERM: FORMER	Urals, Southern Appalachians Guadalupe Range	Equatorial regions Invade western North America	

Side labels in The Procession of Life column: PLANTS; FLOWERING PLANTS; SEED PLANTS; MAN; MAMMALS; REPTILES

Era	Period	Mountain building	Seas	Life
PALEOZOIC ("ANCIENT LIFE")	("COAL PRODUCING") 260 Millions		Swampy plains in many areas. World's coal beds formed. Desert conditions	Insects. Some coal-making trees. Shelled egg allows Vertebrates to conquer the land
	DEVONIAN (FIRST FOSSILS FOUND IN DEVONSHIRE) 320 Millions	Great Britain; Northern Appalachians	Desert conditions; South Africa; Equable climate	Vertebrates move to the land: Amphibia. Ancestral land plant. Bony fishes. Wingless Insects
	SILURIAN (SILURES, A WELSH TRIBE) 360 Millions	Caledonian Mts. (Britian to Scandinavia); Eastern North America	Equable climate. Invade and retreat. Salt beds formed in eastern N. America. Desert conditions in many areas	Jaws develop: first sharks. LIFE APPEARS ON THE LAND
	ORDOVICIAN (ANCIENT WELSH TRIBE, THE ORDOVICES) 440 Millions	Great Britain	Advance again. More than half of North America covered	FIRST FISHES. Armoured jawless fish. Jointed backbone develops
	CAMBRIAN (OLD ROMAN WORD FOR WALES) 520 Millions		Advance covering most of Eurasia and North America	BEGINNINGS OF A BACKBONE. External skeleton & jointed legs. Ringed bodies. Soft bodies protected by a shell
PROTEROZOIC ("PRIMARY LIFE") 2,000 Millions		Killarney Mts. (Manitoba – Minnesota – Wisconsin). Worn to roots	Advancing	Simple Bodies. Cells specialise and cluster
ARCHEOZOIC ("PRIMORDIAL LIFE") 3,000 Millions		Laurentian Mts., Canada: Traces remain. Earliest dated rocks		Cells with nucleus. Cells without nucleus. BEGINNINGS OF LIFE
AZOIC ("LIFELESS") 5,000 Millions				

Side labels in Life column: FERNS, ALGAE, FISH, INVERTEBRATES

A CHRONICLE OF EARTH HISTORY

The Earth's long history is written in its rocks. They tell us, when we learn how to probe their secrets, about the upthrust and wearing away of mountains, the making and melting of vast ice sheets, the advance and retreat of the seas, and the fantastic variety and abundance of plants and animals that have had their day. Man himself has been embedded in the rocks for men to study, but on man the record fades after half a million years and on all living things after the Cambrian Period, for the simpler types of life cannot be preserved in stone. Otherwise, the story of the rocks covers five of the six great Eras of the Earth's evolution—and we have tried here to indicate their main events. The Pleistocene Period is further treated in the table on page 47.

The general pattern of the Earth's anatomy has, of course, been determined by its shape and original condition; for the confinement of gases and molten metals of different weights within a geoid must result in the formation of layers (concentric rings) around the common centre of gravity. Thus, the Earth is not a rigid, uniform mass, but a unity of variable concentric masses, with the heaviest materials forming the central core. This flexible structure gives it more than the strength of steel.

In such circumstances, the pressure towards the centre is tremendous: about 4,800 tons per square inch at 1,000 miles below the surface, and 22,000 tons at the centre. The temperature also increases with depth by roughly 1° C. for every 100 feet to boiling point at 7,200 feet. Variations in this rate of increase allow miners in South Africa, for example, to work at twice the depth possible in Britain.

The pressure on the core, which extends surfacewards for about 2,400 miles, bears down so heavily on the iron and nickel-iron comprising it that its density is twelve times that of water, though the pure iron we know is 7·8 times as heavy as water. Therefore, the core-iron cannot be in a liquid condition, unless the temperature is a great deal more than the 1,500° C. at which pure iron can be melted on the Earth's surface. It is probably high enough for a liquid core since volcanic lava, which comes from about thirty miles below the surface, usually has a tempera-

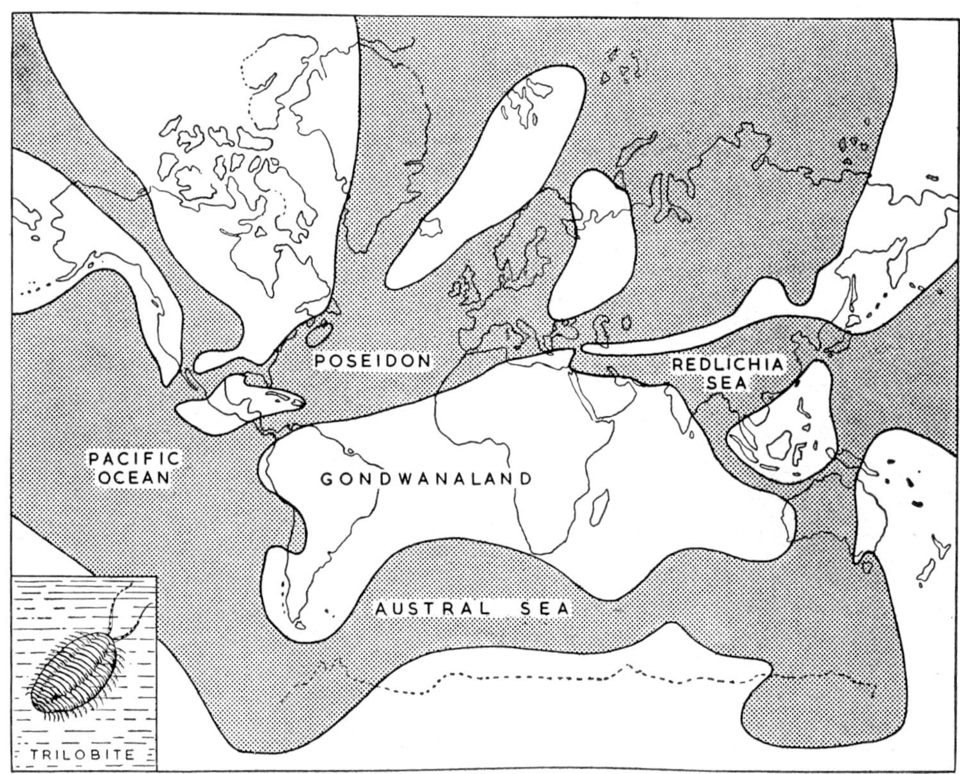

Specially drawn for this work.

FIVE HUNDRED MILLION YEARS AGO

Five hundred million years ago the face of the Earth was very different to what it is now, as you can see from the modern outline map superimposed on the map of the lands and seas at that time. Most of Eurasia had not appeared, but America, the so-called " New World," was mostly land even in those days. Africa, except for the Mediterranean strip, was part of Gondwanaland. There was no vegetation and, of course, no land animals; and in the seas the most advanced creatures were the trilobites.

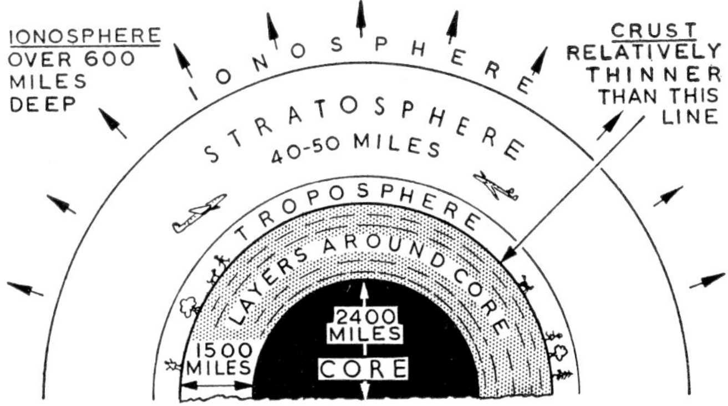

Specially drawn for this work.

THE LAYERED EARTH

The cooling of the Earth separated its materials into a series of layers. The molten core itself seems to have a lighter outer layer, around which are the four or five layers of the semi-molten plastic mantle. To enable the inclusion of the three " shells " of the atmosphere their scale is about 60 times that to which the " solid earth " is drawn, and only a part of the ionosphere is shown.

ture of 1,200° C. We also know that earthquake waves passing through the core behave as if they were passing through a liquid.

Surrounding the core to a depth of about 1,500 miles is a series of layers formed from molten or semi-molten rocks; and around these " shells," thirty to forty miles in depth, is the layered crust or *lithosphere.* It is enveloped by a globe, within two more globes, collectively called the *atmosphere*.

Properties of the Atmosphere

The gases of this globe of air are mostly nitrogen (78·03 per cent.) and oxygen (20·94 per cent.) in the rough proportion of 4 to 1. Some of the oxygen occurs several miles above sea level in the form of ozone, but air movements over the sea bring traces down to add to the tangy, bracing quality of sea breezes. Its greater value, however, is that it forms an upper layer which filters the ultra-violet rays of the Sun down to the small amounts that we can tolerate.

The other constituents of the air are about 1 per cent. of argon, neon, helium, krypton and xenon; ·03 per cent. of carbon dioxide; and variable quantities of water vapour, dust and plant spores. In polluted air there is more carbon dioxide, dust, soot, ash and additional poisonous impurities, such as sulphur dioxide from coal fires, hydrogen fluoride from chemical works, and carbon monoxide from the exhausts of cars.

The typical ingredients of the air are nowhere completely absent from the atmosphere, though three-fourths of all the air occurs in the innermost globe, of which two-thirds is found below a height of three and a half miles above sea level. That is because the air is pulled down increasingly by gravitation, the pressure at sea level reaching 15 pounds per square

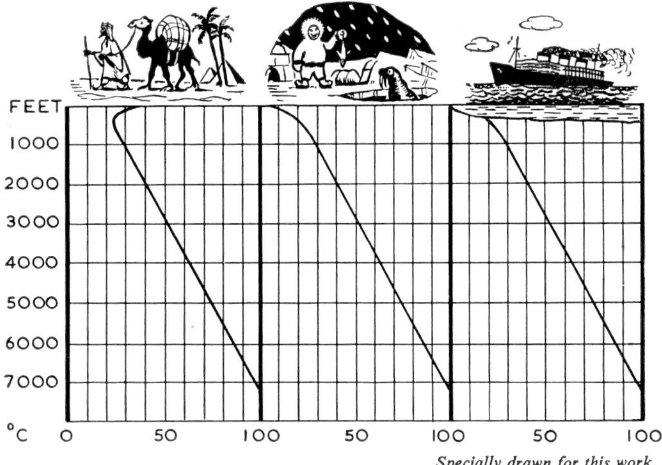

Specially drawn for this work.

TEMPERATURES OF THE CRUST

Regardless of temperatures at the surface the mean increase of temperatures in the depths is one degree Centigrade for every 100 feet, boiling point being reached at 7,200 feet. Volcanic lava from a depth of about 30 miles usually has a temperature of 1,200 degrees Centigrade, having cooled somewhat on the way up.

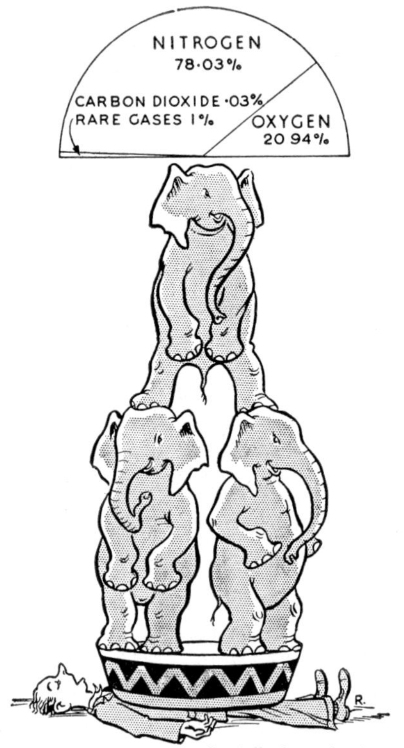

Specially drawn for this work.

ATMOSPHERIC PRESSURE

The pressure of the atmosphere, which consists mostly of nitrogen and oxygen, is 15 pounds per square inch at sea level. This is equal to the weight of three large elephants—enough to squash a man if it were not equalised. We do, however, feel rapid differences in pressure, as when we ascend a mountain by funicular railway or go up in a glider.

inch. It is equal to a weight of 13 tons on the body of a man—enough to " flatten him out " if it were not for the fact that air presses equally in all directions.

It is a characteristic of air that, unlike water, it is compressible, as everyone knows who has fired a popgun. Air can be expanded too: that is, its particles can be set in increasing motion by increases in temperature. In an air engine the alternation of the stroke is accordingly effected by heating and cooling—expanding and contracting—an enclosed body of air. Somewhat similarly, weather-making movements are created by differences in temperature and pressure.

Air temperatures cover a wider range than those of seawater. Sometimes they seem " boiling hot," though they are never high enough to make water unbearably hot; at the other extreme they are really " freezing cold," but never cold enough (minus 190° C.) to freeze air itself into a liquid—a liquid so cold that you can boil it on the comparative heat of a block of ice. We make it for various purposes, including food preservation.

The " Shells " of the Atmosphere

The innermost globe or " shell " of the atmosphere is known as the *troposphere*; and its curved ceiling, which can be " touched " at heights varying between four miles over the poles and eleven miles over the equator, as the *tropopause*. Currents of warm air rise in it and are cooled as they rise, for there is an upwards mean decrease in temperature of about 1° F. for every 300 feet, and currents of cold air descend to be warmed. So water vapour is taken up, condensed and returned as rain, snow or hail.

On a grander scale air movements between areas of high and low pressure cause the great Trade Winds; and when we also consider the effects of rotation, tides, currents, topographical features and pollution we begin to arrive at an understanding of the daily atmospheric phenomena we call weather. Climate is something more: it is regional weather over periods of time recognised as seasons.

Above the tropopause, in the rarified atmosphere of the second " shell " or *stratosphere*, there is little activity other than electrical displays and the frequent darting of the burning bits of cosmic matter familiar to us as " shooting stars " or meteors. Pressures and temperatures vary according to height, but are always low. There seems to be no upwards decrease in temperature, and there is no vertical circulation, though there are gentle winds, mostly from east to west.

Consequently there is no pollution, apart from some spores, bacteria and volcanic dust; no water vapour and therefore no clouds, except for a few straying cirrus clouds containing frost crystals; and relatively much less carbon dioxide than there is in the troposphere. Friction is, of course, greatly reduced, so that aeroplanes can reach high speeds " above the clouds."

Towards the vague ceiling or *stratopause*, forty or fifty miles up, very little atmosphere is left; and in the third " shell " or *ionosphere* there is probably less than 1 per cent. of the total atmosphere. It is free from contamination from the Earth, but we know that it contains cosmic dust since disintegrating meteors pass through it.

How far the atmospheric gases extend in the ionosphere is unknown. It has been calculated that the ionosphere could be about 21,000 miles deep, as gases can still be earth-bound at that height; but there can be so little atmosphere left at 600 miles or so that the condition of " empty space " would then be more or less reached.

The ionosphere (ionised sphere), as its name indicates, is a heavily charged region, strongly influenced

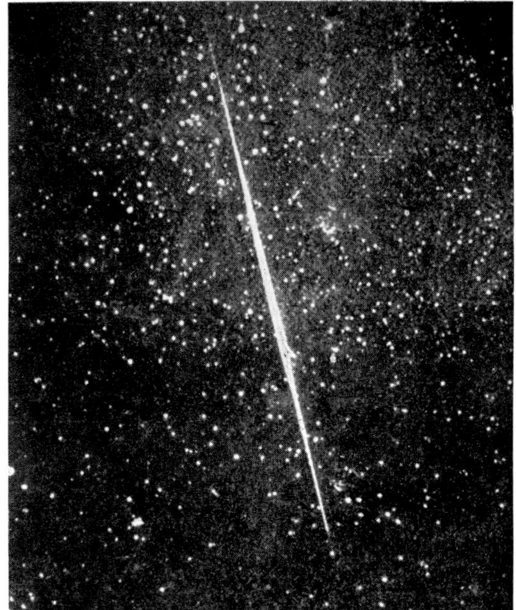

A SHOOTING STAR

Two or more observations on the flight of a meteor, as it flashes through the sky at 20–40 miles per second, allows a calculation on the height at which it became luminous; and such calculations improve estimates of the depths of the atmospheric layers. Meteors are at most pebble-sized and are vaporised before they reach the surface of the Earth's crust.

Paul Popper.

A COSMIC BOMB CRATER

Meteorites are planetary fragments large enough to reach the Earth. Over a thousand have been collected, the largest in Greenland (36½ tons) and South Africa (60 tons); but much larger meteors have " bombed " their way below the surface. The most famous of these fell in the northern part of the desert near Winslow, Arizona, over 700 years ago, perhaps several thousand years ago, leaving a crater 3,600 feet in diameter and 600 feet in depth. Below its floor is the giant meteorite weighing about 500,000 tons. The study of meteorites has helped to reveal the nature and unity of the universe.

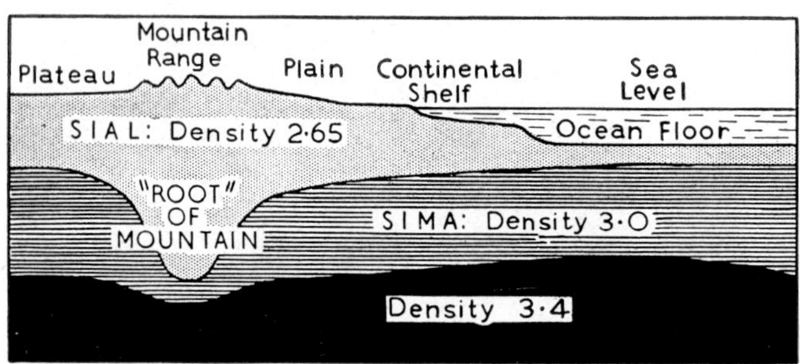

Re-Drawn after A. Holmes.

THE EARTH'S CRUST

The surface of the Earth's crust, and its relief, is composed of granitic rocks (*sial*), which is thinnest, as we see in this diagram, in the floor of the ocean. Below the sial is a relatively broad layer of heavy basaltic rocks (*sima*), and beyond it is the semi-molten plastic mantle.

by variations in solar radiation, which profoundly affect electrical phenomena on the Earth's surface. Long and medium waves are reflected by a belt of the ionosphere, known after its discoverer, Dr. Oliver Heaviside (1850–1925), as the *Heaviside Layer*, which extends to 80–120 miles from the stratopause; and short waves are reflected by a succeeding belt, some 200 miles deep, named the *Appleton Layer* in honour of Sir Edward Appleton (born 1892).

Radio communications are affected when these layers absorb radio waves instead of reflecting them. Thus, when there is a great release of ultra-violet radiation, as there is during a sunspot or flaring up of the Sun, short waves are absorbed; and there is a " fade-out " of short-wave communications wherever the Sun is shining over the Earth. Even in normal conditions reception is better at night.

The Nature of the Crust

The solidification of the Earth's surface began early, but did not continue inwards for more than a few miles. The temperature at a depth of twenty miles has only been reduced by about 800° C., while at 250 miles and beyond it has remained unchanged since the world began. In other words, the cooling of the Earth was confined to the formation of a thin crust which prevented further cooling of the interior.

In this crust the topmost layer, some ten miles thick, consists mostly of coarsely crystalline granites, such as we see in the mountain scenery of Britain. They have a density 2·65 times that of water and are made up chiefly of oxide of silicon or *si*lica (70 per cent.), with *al*uminium first among the lesser constituents. The mnemonic (memory-aiding) term *sial* is often applied to the whole granite layer.

The rocks of the next layer, twenty-five to thirty miles thick, are dark, finely crystalline or glassy basalts, with an average density of 2·85. Silica is again their main constituent, but in smaller proportions (40–50 per cent.); and *mag*nesium replaces aluminium in abundance. Hence the term *sima* for the basaltic layer.

British Aluminium Co.

A VALUABLE DEPOSIT

Deposits that remain where weathering placed them serve many useful purposes: bauxite, for instance, yields aluminium. This picture shows the mining of a bauxite deposit at Brignoles in the south of France.

It merges into a more or less molten plastic *mantle* or *substratum*.

The ages of the original rocks in both these layers can be determined by radioactivity tests, but sedimentary deposits cannot be safely dated by the same methods, for they are new rocks built from the weathering of the old.

Most sedimentary deposits have been transported, but some (*residual deposits*) remain where weathering extracted them. The reddish clay or laterite, commonly used in India and other monsoon countries for making bricks (*later* means " brick " in Latin) and surfacing roads, is a residual deposit. It is rich in the oxides of iron that remain after silicate rocks of all kinds have been weathered in countries where plentiful rain carries abundant oxygen for oxidation. Bauxite, the commercial source of aluminium, is produced in the same way.

In dry countries, winds dominate the making and moving of deposits. Loess in China, for instance, is a yellowish " rock flour " milled in the Gobi Desert by wind-action and blown southwards, where it is held by the low vegetation and compacted into vast deposits. The so-called " loess plateau," which extends eastwards from Kansu, is an example.

Water continues the spreading process—cutting the plateau into a fantastic pattern of gullies, canyons and escarpments, and covering the alluvial (flood-soil) plain of China with loess-silt. The Hwang-ho or Yellow River collects the yellow loess in such enormous quantities, as it flows through the plateau, that much of it is deposited during the long journey to the lower reaches. So, during its known history of some 4,000 years, " China's Sorrow " has changed its course frequently and earned the worst name in the chronicle of flood disasters. To-day, as it bends south and east to the Gulf of Pohai, it flows *above* the surrounding countryside on a raised bed held in by natural and man-made dykes; and it is being further " tamed " to provide controlled irrigation and hydro-electric power.

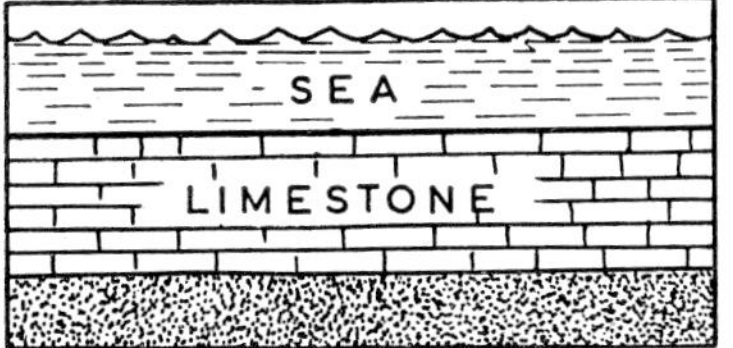

Limestone is deposited under the sea.

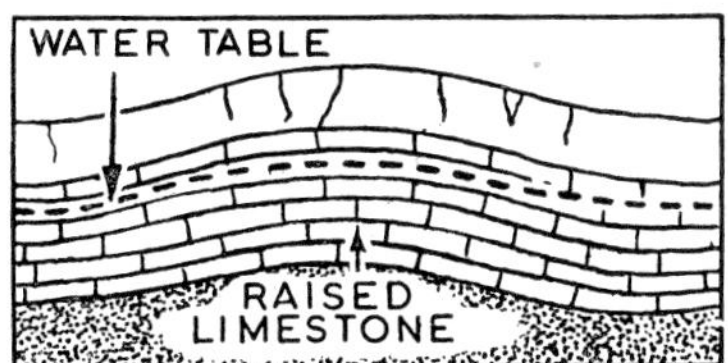

Earth movements push up the limestone.

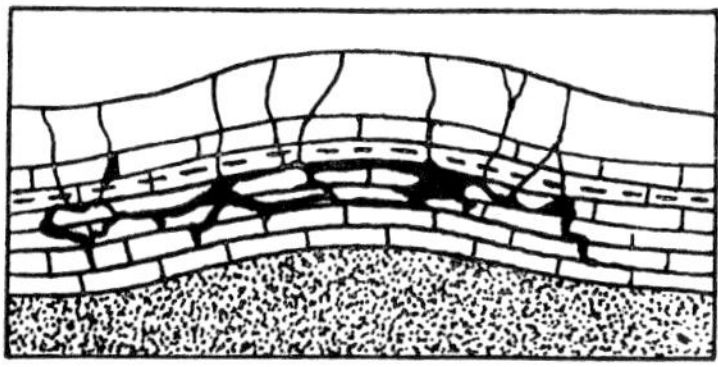

Seeping water dissolves the rock.

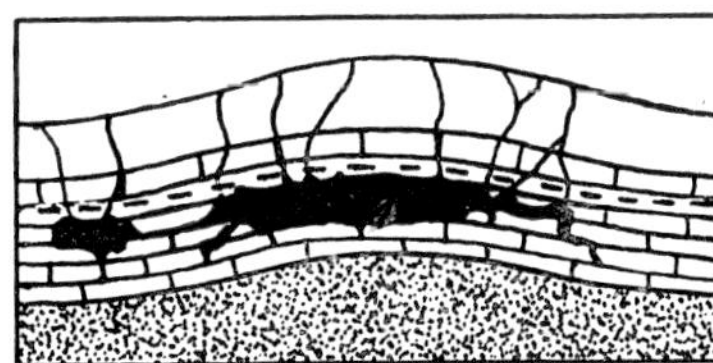

Thus water-filled caverns are formed.

Eventually the water-table falls—and that is

HOW A CAVE IS MADE
By the action of water on limestone.

THE YELLOW RIVER

RAISED BANKS (LEVEE)
RIVER
SILT
OLD BED

Chinese Embassy, London.

The Yellow River, just over 3,000 miles long, affects 40 per cent. of China's cultivated land. Here we see it flowing placidly on the raised bed (diagram above) of its lower reaches, but it has flooded 1,500 times, and changed its course 26 times, during the last 3,000 years.

Camera Press.

This is the Yellow River on its way through the Liukia Gorge in the loess plateau of Kansu. A great dam here will be the starting point of a vast scheme to prevent floods and use the river for irrigation, hydro-electric power and navigation; and by 1970 the waters of " China's Sorrow " will flow clear and always beneficially.

PINNACLES AND TERRACES

H.M. Geological Survey.

Limestones are quickly shaped by the acid action of water-erosion. Many unusual patterns result, such as these pinnacles on the foreshore below Torrs Walk, west of Ilfracombe, North Devon.

H. Armstrong Roberts.

In the Arizona desert the tops of the pre-Cambrian rocks have been worn down to flat terraces and crevices and canyons have also been cut. The Grand Canyon, shown here, is a mile-deep gorge carved by the Colorado River. It carries away 500,000 tons of silt daily.

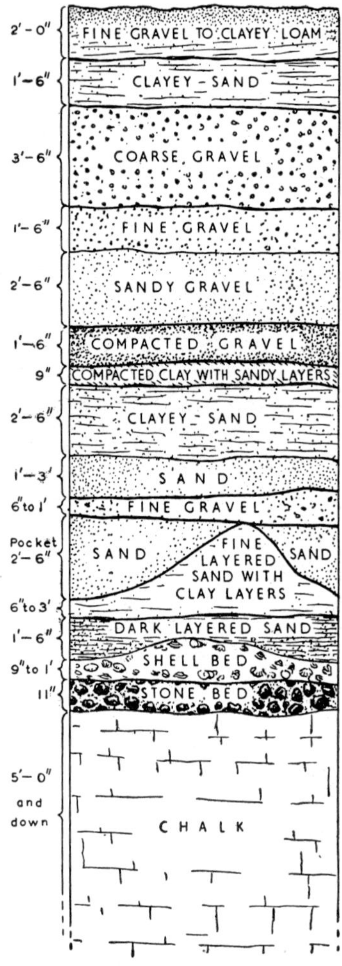

SEDIMENTATION

This "soil profile," based on the work of J. F. Sainty at Thorpe, near Norwich, Norfolk, is a simple illustration of how sedimentation takes place.

New Rocks from Old

From this example we can imagine the vast amount of rock-scourings collected, spread over the land, and deposited in the estuaries and along the shore-lines by the rivers of the world: the Mississippi alone, after enriching its fertile delta, annually pours 800 million tons of silt into the Gulf of Mexico. In this way all the continents lose a fraction, amounting perhaps to an inch in a century, of their topmost layers every year.

But, in the long run, most of this material is not lost to the land. It is deposited, after sifting by gravity and other forces, as alluvial soil and as overlying beds under the edges of the seas. These beds, and those formed from the remains of animals and plants, are compacted into layers, sand becoming sandstone, mud being squeezed to clay, and clay hardening into flaky shale. A fairly regular sequence of sedimentary rocks is accordingly laid down, and eventually pushed up by earth movements, which can be dated by the rate of sedimentation, the organic remains found in the various layers, and other methods.

Extreme pressure, which is usually accompanied by great heat, changes sedimentary (and sometimes igneous) rocks so completely that sandstones become quartzites, limestone becomes marble, shales become slates, granites become gneiss, and so on. The making of these *metamorphic* rocks (Greek *meta*, change, and *morphē*, form) is a complex business, but we can sense the process if we consider what happens when a column of molten rock begins to rise, spreading fanways as well, in the crust.

It may burst from the surface as lava from a volcano and cover the surrounding countryside repeatedly, penetrating the rocks and changing their character, and adding layers of heavy basalt mixed with dust, mud and ash. The "water-volcanoes" we call geysers are common in volcanic regions because pockets of underground water, boiled by the rising lava, come together and form a pressure jet to the surface.

Alternatively, lava may collect below the surface and push in tongues into the surrounding rocks, "cooking" them at 1,200° C. or so and setting up active chemical reactions which produce new mineral deposits in their neighbourhood and alter the nature of the rocks further away—limestone would be converted into mineral deposits nearby, and marble at some distance.

Sometimes, usually under conditions of extremely high pressures, stresses and temperatures associated with mountain-building, new rocks are made on such a scale that extensive areas are said to have

THE RESULTS OF PRESSURE

H.M. Geological Survey.

This picture, taken on the island of Kerrera, off Oban, Argyllshire, gives us an idea of the manner in which the rocks of a mountain are pushed up, folded and puckered by the Earth's pressures.

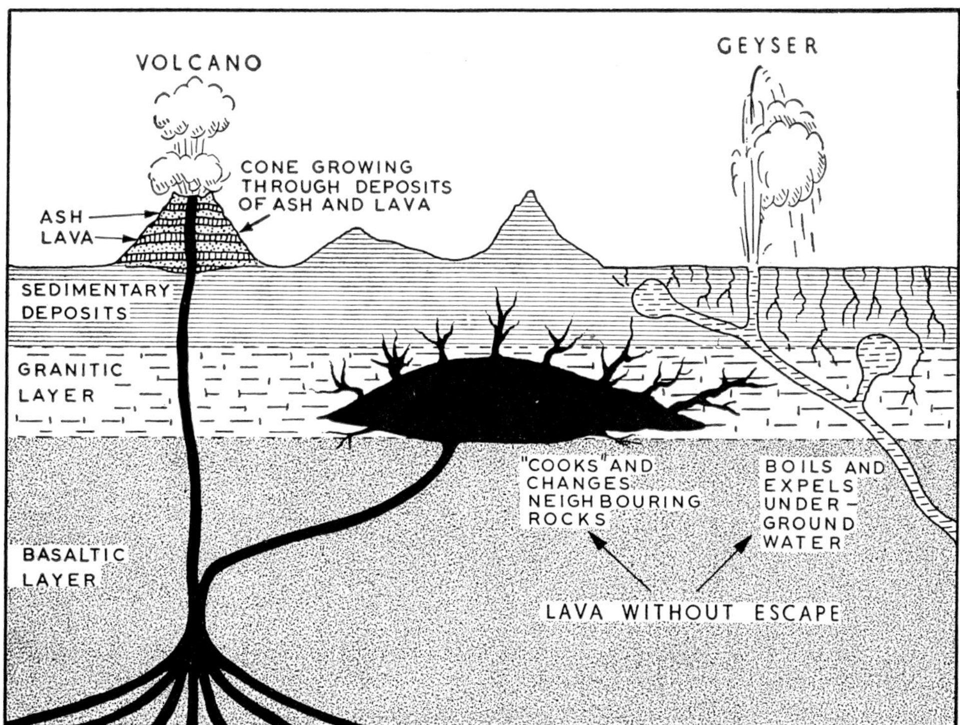

A column of molten rock, rising from below the sima, can burst from the surface (volcanic action); collect and spread below the surface, " cooking " and changing the nearby rocks (intrusive action); and heat pockets and " pipes " of water to the point of forming hot water springs and, if the pressure is sufficient, " water volcanoes " or geysers. All these effects often occur in volcanic regions.

THE FLOATING CONTINENTS

The continents, as we have tried to show in this picture, are giant granitic rafts floating high above the ocean floors on the heavier and upwards pushing sima.

undergone *regional metamorphism.* In them, as in the Grampian Highlands of Scotland, one can see remnants of the old clays and granites, followed by flaky schists (such as mica) and gneisses, in which garnet and other dense minerals are embedded.

The Form of the Land

The visible land, or continental surfaces, of the Earth equals 29·22 per cent. (57½ million square miles) of its total area. It is massed in the Northern Hemisphere, with the tails of Afro-Eurasia and the Americas pointing southwards, presumably because radial forces push away from and towards the centre of the Earth.

Why are these surfaces not covered with water? The somewhat astonishing answer is that the continents themselves are giant rafts of sial floating high above the ocean floors on the heavier and upwards-pushing sima. Shrinkage and radial forces threw up enough rock to form them; convection currents and cracking separated them into drifting masses; the filling of the oceans pressed down the bottoms of their basins and pushed the continents further up; tangential forces (which run along straight lines to points on a curve which they touch but do not cut when extended) squeezed, drew out and fractured the parts on which they acted, thus forming the first mountains and valleys.

Later earth movements, and all the other factors of breaking down (such as erosion) and building up (such as sedimentation), enlarged and repeatedly changed the relief and complicated the *topography* (the physical features) of the

THE SEA FLOOR

This diagram, based on " echo " soundings, shows the nature of a long stretch of the floor of the Southern Ocean between Bouvet Island and the South Shetland Islands.

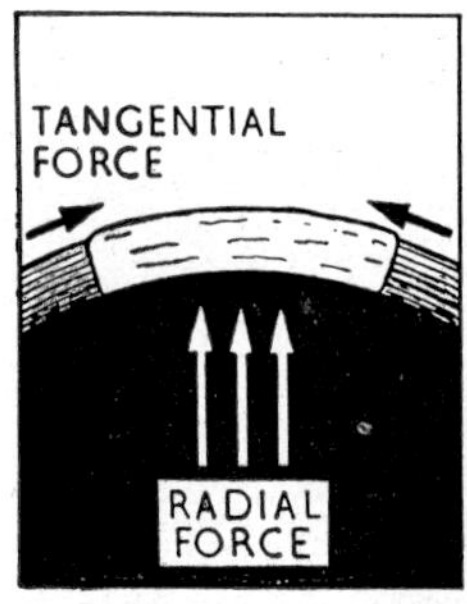

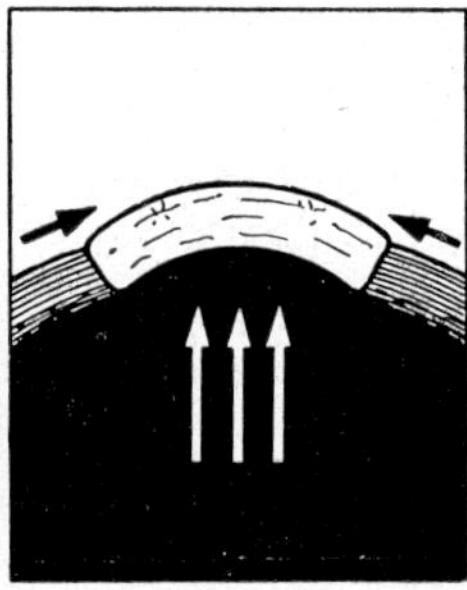

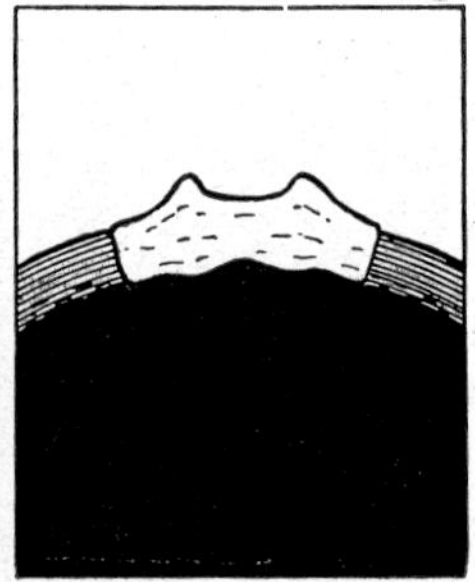

Specially drawn for this work.

HOW THE FIRST MOUNTAINS WERE MADE

The cooling and shrinking of the Earth's crust brought about compression, the lighter sial being more easily distorted by the pressure of radial and tangential forces than the heavier sima. So the first mountains were pushed up from the once unbroken surface.

VOLCANO AND GEYSER

Italian State Tourist Office.

This is Vesuvius, the volcano that has brought disaster on more than one occasion to the people living around the Bay of Naples. In A.D. 79 it destroyed the Roman city of Pompeii, leaving " basaltic statues " of the men, animals and plants that were caught by the molten lava. Vesuvius is noteworthy for the uniformity of its slopes and for the clearly discernible rhythm of its eruptions.

Iceland Tourist Information Bureau.

Geysers are " water-volcanoes " that often occur in volcanic regions. Their columns of scalding water sometimes rise terrifyingly into the sky, but men have used them beneficially from very early times. The name comes from the famous Great Geysir of Iceland, shown here. This geyser is one of a group in Haukadal, about fifty miles from Reykjavik.

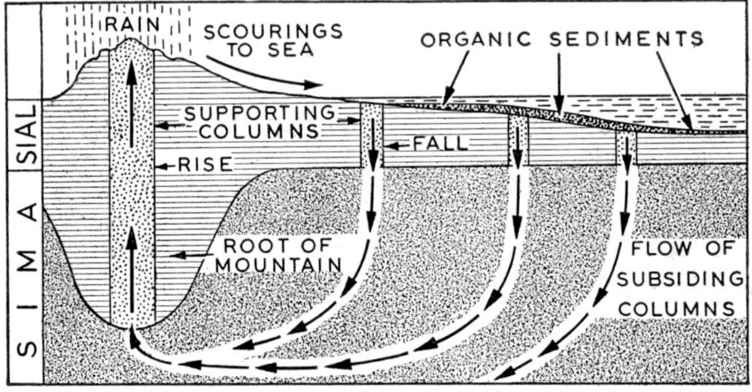

THE GROWING MOUNTAINS

Mountain ranges are washed away, but they *grow*. The weight they lose reduces the load on the supporting column of the crust; and this weight is transferred to the column supporting the already piled up sea floor. The differences in pressure set up a slow flow of rock material from the overloaded columns; and the pressure of the rising column tends to push the range upwards.

land. Living things added to the modelling.

In these ways mountains crumbled and rose again, sometimes from the thrusting up of sedimentary deposits from the sea. Seas became lands rich in the products of the ocean and lands became seas. To-day 12 million square miles of continental platform are below water—and the ceaseless gnawing away of coastal lands has become a problem for many peoples.

But the *relief*—the mountains, plateaux and plains—of all the continents has one feature in common: it slopes down from the heights to under the sea. First there is the *continental platform*, with a mean elevation of 2,707 feet and tall mountains aspiring to the height of Chomolungma or Mount Everest (29,028 feet). Then, at sea level, the *continental shelf* begins.

The shelves are covered by the sea to an average depth of 72 fathoms (432 feet), but they belong to the land. Maritime nations accordingly extend their jurisdiction to the "three-mile limit," though there is no average limit: the Pacific shelf of America reaches twenty miles, that covered by the Barents Sea is 750 miles.

The exploration of the shelf offers completely new prospects of discovery and adventure. We have begun to draw its oil and it is not beyond our capacity to probe it for other products, for new facts about the Earth's history, for hidden information about the plants, animals and men that once lived on lands now covered by the sea. And we can move on to closer

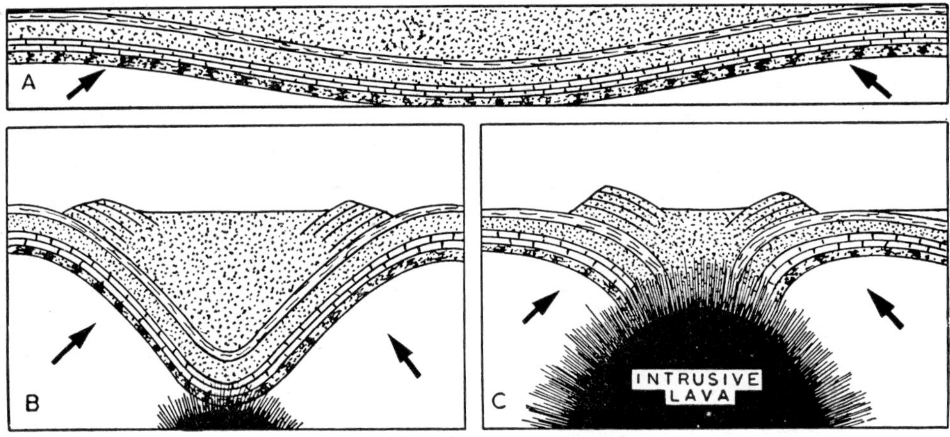

MOUNTAINS FROM THE SEA

Scourings and the remains of living things pile up on the sea floors and are pressed into layers of rock (A). They eventually reach the surface and are pushed above it by earth movements (B). In narrow seas across the land masses, sagging of the floors, radial and tangential forces, and rising lava bring about profound changes in the nature of the rocks and push up long mountain ranges (C).

THE ENCROACHING SEA

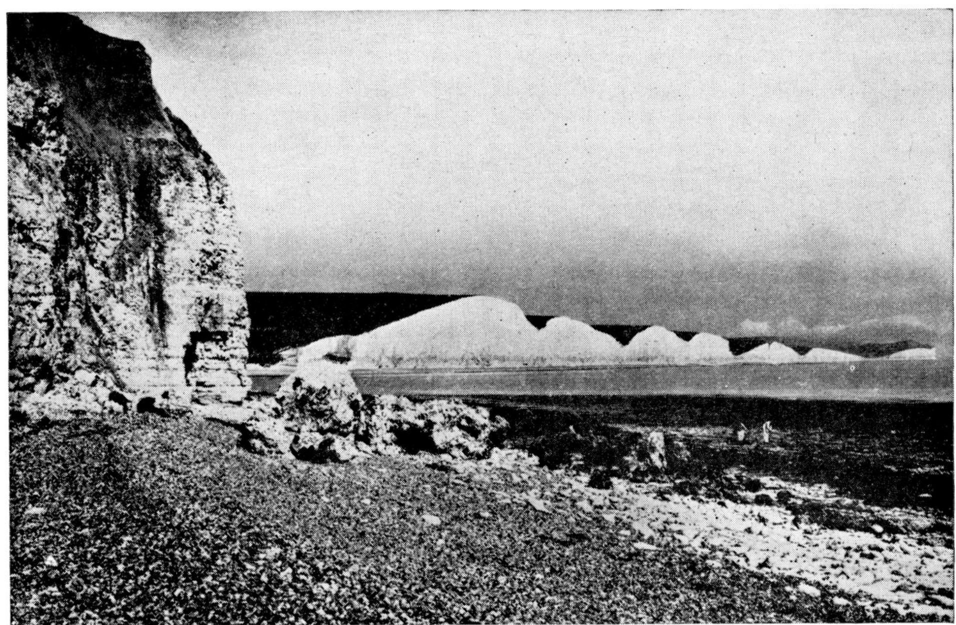

The chalk hills raised by the sea are easily carved by its eroding action. The " Seven Sisters " of the Sussex coast, near Eastbourne, are an illustration of its power. This famous series of chalk cliffs, part of the " White Walls of Old England," extends towards Beachy Head.

Photos: H.M. Geological Survey.

Many coastal areas in England which were occupied fifteen hundred years ago are now washed by the tides. This ceaseless attack on the land is an increasingly serious problem, as we see from this picture showing the damage done by a very high tide at Pakefield, near Lowestoft.

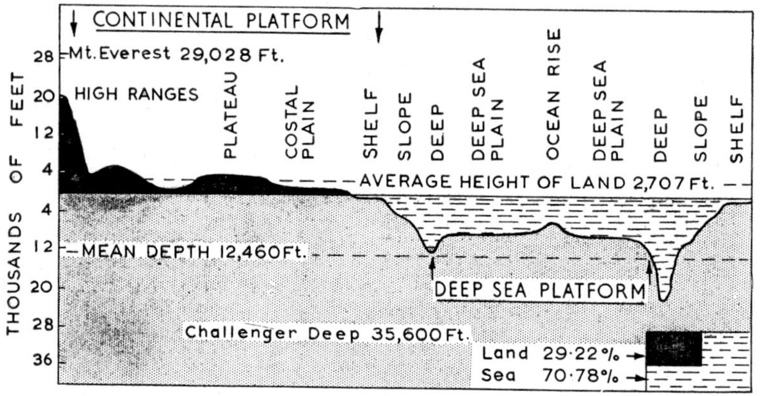

Specially drawn for this work.

FROM MOUNTAINS TO DEPTHS

This " profile " of the Earth's crust shows the succession from the heights of the *continental platform* to the flat *continental shelf* and down the *continental slope* to the depths of the *deep sea platform.*

study of the *continental slopes* which plunge from the shelves into the deeps. They are the towering continental ramparts of the seas.

The Boundless Ocean

Mankind has always been impressed by the awesome, yet challenging, immensity of the sea. Its area is 139·4 million square miles, or 70·78 per cent. of the Earth's surface: even in the Northern Hemisphere, where the continents are massed, 61 per cent. is sea.

This vast area is matched by depth and mass. The mean depth is 12,460 feet, but the deeps vary between 24,000 feet and the record of 35,600 feet reached by the Challenger Deep off Guam. The total mass is 330 million cubic miles. And we should not forget, in a world that seems to be warming up, the two or three million cubic miles of seawater in the leaking ice sheets.

The floor is unique: unlike the rest of the Earth's crust, its layer of sial is thin, broken and entirely absent from a third of its area—at least no granite has been found in any of the islands of the Pacific.

The missing sial may be in the Moon, if our satellite was torn away after the Earth's crust had formed. Or it may be in the continents, if convection currents helped to separate them and sweep away the floating sial from the areas that were to become the ocean basins.

Yet the heavy sea floor rises and falls in contours more varied than we know on land. There are majestic mountains,

Swedish Travel Bureau.

THE MELTING ICE

A tiny fraction of their three million cubic miles of water is released from the ice fields every year. If all of them were to melt suddenly the oceans would rise by some 200 feet—and most of the world's great cities would be under the sea. It is a problem to think about.

active and extinct volcanoes, sheer and long ridges, gently sloping banks, raised " islands " with a relief of their own; and between the heights are deeps, canyons, valleys, trenches and basins.

In these eerie surroundings, under pressures reaching 5 or 6 tons per square inch, two-thirds of the known kinds of non-insect life abound. All of them, from the brightly coloured and oddly shaped creatures we see in aquaria to blue whales 100 feet long and 150 tons in weight, are directly or indirectly kept alive by the plants. But the plants themselves are confined to a top layer one-fortieth of the average depth of the sea, for radiation penetrates no more than 300 feet. Beyond it, to a limit of 2,000 feet in the clearest seas, there are the familiar green and blue tints of the ocean: then there is absolute darkness, briefly pierced now and then by the natural lights that many marine animals carry.

Warmth goes deeper, for water can absorb and retain more heat than any other substance. Therefore, warm and cold currents, kept separate by weight, can travel thousands of miles without losing or gaining much temperature, while enclosed seas are nearly as warm in the depths as they are a few hundred feet below the surface. The temperature of the Red Sea, for example, drops from 26·7° C. (80° F.) at the surface to 21·1° C. (70° F.) at 1,200 feet, but below that there is little further change.

The open Indian Ocean is almost as warm at the surface, but the temperature drops from 25° C. (77° F.) to 20° at 600 feet, 10° at 1,800 feet, 5° at 3,000 feet, and slowly to 1° or 2°. It cannot go much lower, as seawater freezes at − 1·5° to − 1·9° C.

The cooling of the surface waters warms the air on a tremendous scale, for increasing the temperature of a volume of air by 1° C. only requires one-three-thousandth of the heat required to warm a comparable volume of water to the same extent. In theory this means that the heat lost when a 3-foot layer of seawater cools by ·1° can raise the temperature of the air to 100 feet above it by 10°.

But the sea is more than a convector oven for the air. It is a water and heat reservoir, wind distributor and temperature regulator as well. It increases evaporation and provides the water, eventually getting it back enriched by washings from the land; it promotes air currents and wind movements from cold high-pressure areas to warmed-up low-pressure areas; its currents, driven by the winds it has helped to produce, take warm waters to the poles and bring cold water to the equator. Ceaselessly active, it gives, takes away, and gives again.

The Treasury of the Sea

The sea is also a global treasury of mineral wealth, and acre for acre it is more productive than agricultural land. We have begun to extract the minerals, we have fished and overfished here and there, and we have hunted the great whales to the verge of extinction; but the scientific cultivation of the sea remains an occasional vision of plenty.

The minerals are not, of course, so numerous or so concentrated as they are on land: only six major constituents, nine minor constituents, and traces of thirty-five other elements have so far been found in the sea. They are arranged in the diagram on the next page.

The salts made from these elements (see diagram) vary according to place and season, warm water being saltier than cold. Thus, there are differences in weight and capacity for nourishment which help to explain the movement of layered waters, the migrations and numbers of marine organisms, and other oceanic phenomena.

But there is a *normal salinity*: 3·5 per cent., or 35 parts of salts in 1,000 parts of water (35‰). In a glass of water this percentage represents a heaped teaspoon of salt; in the ocean it accounts for more than 5,500 million tons of salt—enough to cover all the seas with adjoining " salt-bergs," each 200 feet square.

Common salt (sodium chloride) would fill seventeen-twentieths of these blocks, the remainder being substances our bodies also need. So millions still use the total

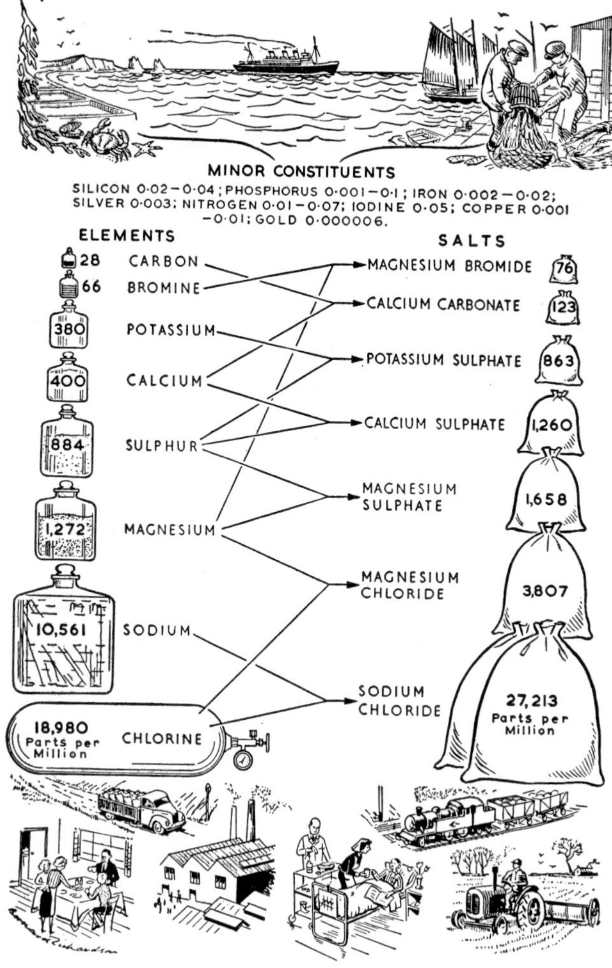

Specially drawn for this work.

THE GIFTS OF THE SEA

The sea invades and destroys, but it also provides warmth, food, health, essential chemicals and ocean highways. Its chemical constituents are important in all our basic activities.

salts obtained by " panning "; but a huge chemical industry, based on mining the deposits laid down by past seas, has given us the convenience of manufactured salts for table and kitchen.

Among the elements extracted from the sea, magnesium is indispensable to industries as separate as printing, pharmaceuticals and light metal alloys, very large quantities being used in aircraft production. Magnesium ore was the only source before the Second World War, but seawater now provides as much magnesium as the world will ever want. There are four million tons in every cubic mile.

Vanadium is another element that goes to the making of light and strong metals. Henry Ford added to his fortune by using it to lighten the weight of his cars. It occurs in deposits, but is so rare in seawater that it cannot be analysed. We know of its presence because it is highly concentrated in sea squirts and sea cucumbers.

In fact, we owe many of the lesser constituents of the sea to their concentration by marine animals and plants. Calcium, which is extracted by various organisms for making their shells, is deposited on a scale we can imagine from the limestone and chalk exposed by ancient seas. Potassium, now extracted directly, has always been obtained in quantity from seaweeds. The trace of iodine in seawater (1 part in 20 million) is also stored by seaweeds (0·5 per cent.) and is particularly abundant in lobsters. Lobsters, oysters and other " shellfish " store copper too.

The concentration of bromine by the Purple Snail (*Murex*) gave antiquity the famous purple of Tyre. Until recently it was obtained from sea plants, or as a by-product of salt manufacture, for making dyestuffs and pharmaceuticals. It is now used in making high-compression fuels and is extracted directly from seawater, which contains 250,000 tons per cubic mile—100 times more in the Dead Sea.

Petroleum itself is the gift of the sea. For mineral oil is organic oil squeezed out of plant, and some animal, remains by

PRODUCTS FOR PLENTY

I.C.I.

Ammonium sulphate, a cheap synthetic fertiliser, is extracted in large quantities from the air. Here we see it pouring into the giant silo, capable of holding 100,000 tons, at the works of Imperial Chemical Industries Ltd., in Billingham, Durham.

Chilean Nitrate Corp.

Chilean nitrate is a natural fertiliser consisting of nitrate of soda, with other essential substances. It comes from a strip of desert in northern Chile proudly called " the desert that feeds the world." Two million tons of nitrate leave it annually.

Society for Cultural Relations with U.S.S.R.

Mineral fertilisers look alike even when they are very different. This is superphosphate in a processing plant at Riga, the capital of the Latvian Republic of the Soviet Union. It is made by treating rock phosphate (calcium phosphate) with sulphuric acid. The result is an easily dissolved acid salt readily used by plants.

sedimentation and earth movements; or it is the oil remaining when certain bacteria remove the oxygen from dead organisms.

There is more oil to come—but not much. Half the oil ever used was used between 1945–55 and, allowing for new discoveries, it seems that there will be little or no oil left by A.D. 2000. But by then the sea may provide enough heavy hydrogen to solve the world's future energy problems, if we can learn how to use the principle of the hydrogen bomb for constructive purposes.

Perhaps we shall even learn to grow rich on the sea's gold and silver. Meanwhile, we should concentrate on making the best use of the sea's healing waters and its vast, cultivable, international wealth of food. These are its greatest gifts.

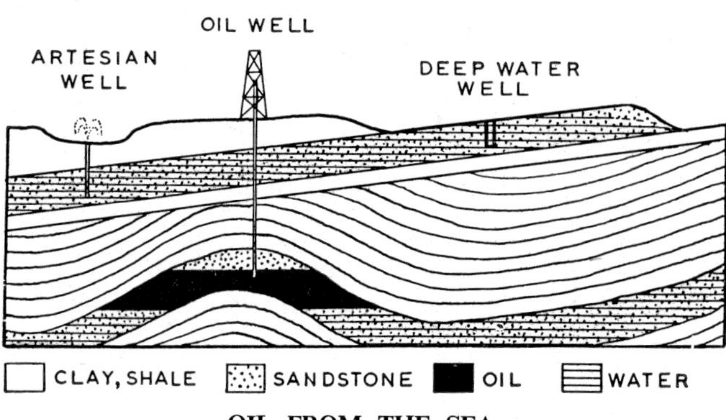

OIL FROM THE SEA

The minute plants of ancient seas were sometimes sealed up within sandy and clayey deposits. There they underwent chemical changes which produced oil. It seeped into porous rocks and separated from the water with which it was mixed, a layer of gas usually being formed above it. Therefore, oil, natural gas and water are generally stored together in areas once covered by the sea.

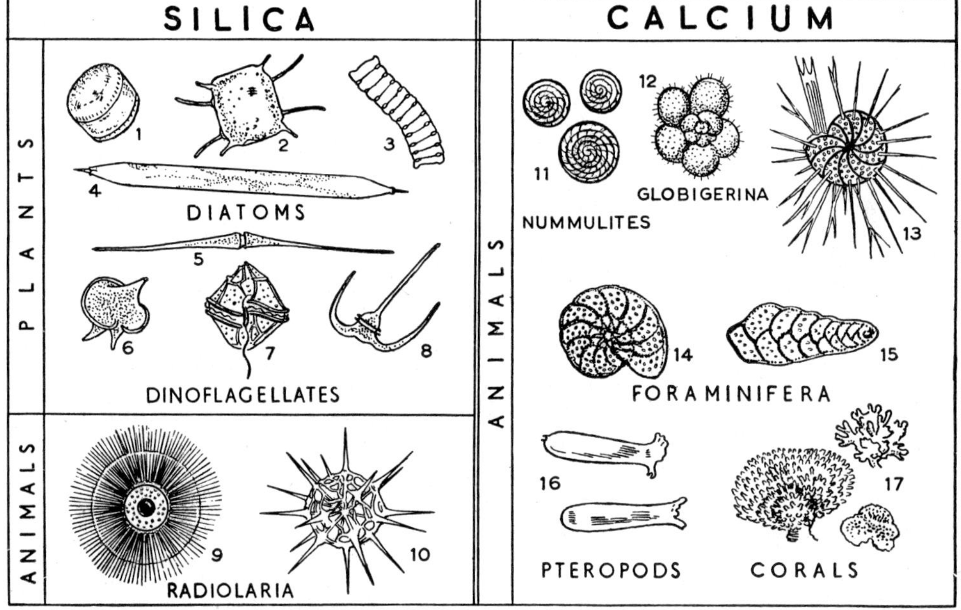

Specially drawn for this work.

ROCK-MAKING ANIMALS AND PLANTS

Diatoms (1–4) and dinoflagellates (5–8) are microscopic plants enclosed in boxes of silica. Dinoflagellates swim, diatoms drift in great abundance in the cooler seas and deposit *Diatom ooze*. *Radiolaria* (9–10) form deep beds of *Radiolarian ooze* in tropical waters. *Foraminiferan ooze* (11–15) is the most widespread deposit. It is often called *Globigerina ooze*, because the shells of this tiny animal are conspicuous in it. *Pteropod ooze* (16) is laid down in warmer and shallower waters. Corals (17) flourish on the sea floor and some grow into coral islands. Their remains are common in limestone rocks. No attempt to show relative sizes is made in these diagrammatic drawings.

MANKIND

E.N.A.

ARE THEY OUR SURVIVING ANCESTORS ?

What did our ancestors of 15,000 to 20,000 years ago look like? This picture of an Ainu family may offer a clue, for the Ainu are thought to be the survivors of an ancient white group which thrust eastwards towards Sakhalin, the Kuriles and Japan. The Ainu have been much " Mongolised," but they remain essentially white; they have no trace of yellow in their skins, seldom have " slant " eyes, and are very hairy. The older men have luxuriant beards, and the women shadow moustaches.

THERE have been people in the world for the better part of a million years, but man was in the making for sixty million years before our first human ancestors appeared. That takes us back to the end of the Cretaceous or Chalk Period, when the forerunners of men, apes and monkeys were the rat-sized tarsiers. They were the most intelligent creatures then living and their large eyes, surrounded by bony rings, gave them an almost professorial look of spectacled wisdom. Unlike other animals, they relied more on hearing and sight than on smell; they were unique, too, in being able to sit upright, which allowed them to use their forepaws almost like hands, especially as they could also oppose their thumbs to their fingers.

Improved sight, and the ability to handle things, meant that the tarsiers were more capable of discrimination—the basis of learning—than their larger contemporaries; and this gave them an advantage which brought about evolution along four different, yet somewhat similar, lines leading to the Old World monkeys, the New World monkeys, the apes, and the precursors of man. The monkeys were so superior in intelligence to the tarsiers, with whom they lived in competition, that the tarsier populations dwindled and died out. To-day only one species survives. It is a " living fossil " found in the jungles of Indonesia.

How Man Evolved

Increased size was a feature of all four lines of development. The apes and pre-human types grew so large that it became convenient for them to spend more of their time on the ground than among the trees, but the apes failed to achieve the fully erect posture typical of man. They can walk and run, " ape-fashion," on their feet, but they soon tire and have to support themselves with their long arms. The secret of our success in being able to stay on our feet is quite simple: we have larger heels and our big toes are fairly rigid.

Erect posture marked the final transition from the pre-human to the human condition. The brain grew larger, more complicated, and more concerned with speech and understanding than with hearing, sight and smell. The arms were freed from the mechanics of moving about and the hands, with their advantages of flexible wrists and opposable thumbs, could be used for making and doing things.

The chief disadvantages were that, by standing erect and living on the ground, man became less muscular, less alert, and more defenceless than other large animals; but they were turned to good account. Brains and hands were used to solve the problems of finding food, shelter, clothing and protection. Co-operation, and with it the beginnings of domestic habits and better means of communication, became necessary. Sound signals, such as animals have, were no longer adequate: they grew into language.

And so, by the middle of the Pleistocene Period, man became a thinking, planning, toolmaking, and more or less domesticated animal whose successors gradually moved forward—it took half a million years!—towards building cultures and civilisations. We know these early men only from a few remains, but we do know that they walked upright and were recognisably human; that there were several different groups of them in various parts of Eurasia and Africa; that all of them had simple cutting tools and knew the use of fire; and that they lived together in ways that are uniquely human. They were men, not wild animals with human aspects, and it is clear that they had been men for a long time.

Neanderthal Man

We know more about mankind after the third Ice Age. The Far Eastern type, represented by Java Man and Peking Man, was then extinct, but Neanderthal Man was flourishing. Several skeletons and many oddments have been found since the first discoveries in Gibraltar (1848) and a cave, which gives the type its name, in the Neanderthal ravine (1856) near Düsseldorf, Germany.

There is a popular idea, created by fanciful artists and the cave-digging habits of archæologists, that the Neanderthals

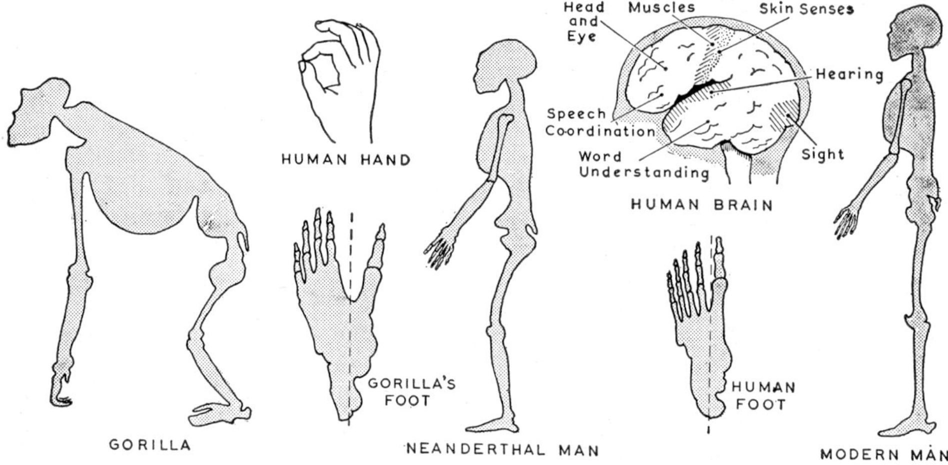

Specially drawn for this work.

THE UNIQUENESS OF MAN

Man evolved from man-like animals when his large heels and closely-set big toes enabled him to stand erect. Then his complicated brain developed and he could better employ his earlier advantage of flexible wrists and opposable thumbs and fingers. He could think, speak, and make tools. Note that, because their big toes are not rigid, gorillas soon tire when walking and have to help themselves along with their arms. Neanderthal Man inclined towards the gorilla's posture.

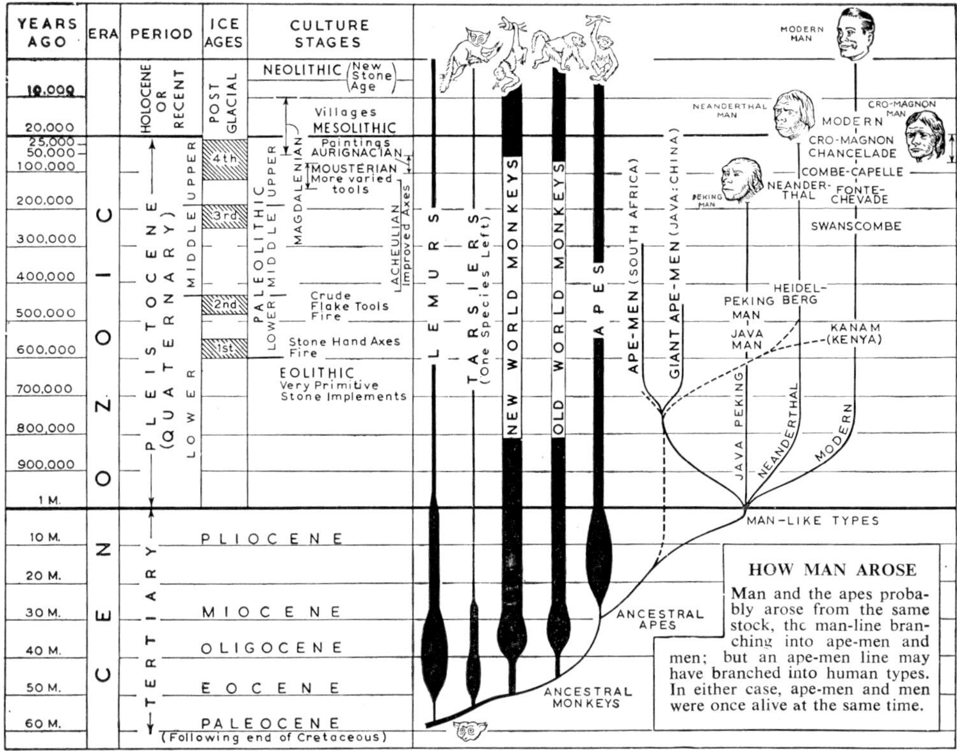

Specially drawn for this work.

THE AGE OF MAN

It used to be thought that Modern Man evolved from the Neanderthals a few thousand years ago, but it now seems certain that the whole Pleistocene Period is The Age of Man. In that million years of natural history Ice Ages came and went, the evolutionary bursts of the Tertiary Period petered out, animals and cultures disappeared. Man alone repeatedly adapted, moved, mingled and grew.

were ape-like cavemen who belaboured each other with enormous clubs. Actually they were much shorter, and had larger brains, than ourselves; and, though they lodged in caves when convenient, they lived as families in shelters built on their hunting and food-collecting grounds. But it is true that the later Neanderthals, who were heavy-browed, chinless and rather ape-like in their walk, seemed to be evolving in the direction of the apes. This is surprising, for the early Neanderthals, and the still earlier men of Java and Peking, walked as upright as we do and had skeletons like our own.

Nevertheless, the later Neanderthals were sufficiently human to live on intimate terms with the forerunners of Modern Man with whom they came in contact. Burial remains prove that they intermarried and there are striking survivals of Neanderthal characteristics in our own time—so much so that some of us can remember having seen a " Neanderthal " man.

The First Modern Men

When did Modern Man, *Homo sapiens*, appear? The older view is that our species evolved from Neanderthal Man towards the end of the last Ice Age some 25,000 years ago. But fossil bones of *sapiens* type date to the period of Peking Man; and anthropologists (students of mankind) are inclining to the opinion that Modern Man is as old as the Pleistocene.

Such a history would be in keeping with what we know about the evolution of other large animals, for no new species has appeared during the last million years, though many have become extinct. Moreover, the emergence of a new kind of animal is marked by a great burst, so to speak, of evolutionary vigour: many allied forms are produced to ensure that the fittest survive.

Human evolution conforms to this pattern. Several different species emerged, at much the same time, from pre-human ancestors, of which only two, the Neanderthals and Moderns, survived into the Upper Pleistocene. They may have been diverging stems of the same species for, as we have said, the early Neanderthals were more like Moderns than the later ones.

The last Ice Age put an end to the long history of the Neanderthals, but the Moderns began another phase as they entered the postglacial period in which we live. The men of this time benefited from the vastly increased food-lands left and watered by the retreating ice, and they responded by improving their hunting, fishing and food-gathering techniques, as well as the arts urged by their way of life.

Their populations grew and flourished accordingly; and, as they grew, they divided up again and again into groups of more manageable size which established themselves widely in Eurasia and Africa. The inter-continental land connections which still existed then helped their travels and they had the great human asset of adaptability. They adapted themselves to, and were physically modified by, variations in climate and environment; they became still more plastic and variable by intermarriage; and, in making the best of their various situations, they built up an ever-increasing variety of cultures.

Cro-Magnon Man

We began to know their story in 1868, when the bones of the Old Man of Cro-Magnon were dug out of the cave of Cro-Magnon—one of the caves, world-famous for their prehistoric art and human remains, near the little southern French town of Les Eyzies in the valley of the Dordogne. Since then many other Cro-Magnon-like remains have been found in Eurasia (chiefly Europe) and Africa, from which we know that they continued into the Recent period from about 75,000 years ago and were the first of the truly modern men. They looked much like well-fed, broad-faced western Europeans to-day and their culture was considerable: their paintings are both superb and revealing.

Their geographical range, and that of the earlier Combe Capelle type, was so wide that their remains have been found at Choukoutien near Peking, where the best known of our ancient allied species, Peking Man, lived some 500,000 years ago. These Chinese contemporaries of the Cro-Magnons are specially interesting for two reasons: they are recognisably Cro-Magnon in type, but have Mongoloid affinities; and they suggest, since they were found above the remains of Peking Man, that some areas have been inhabited by human and human-like beings for vast stretches of time.

The " Whites " Emerge

The chief centres of human habitation and dispersal in Cro-Magnon times were in Asia, where great mountain ranges affected their future growth. The Himalayas, extending westwards across northern Iran to the Caucasus, tended to isolate the south from the north. Above the Himalayas, the populations of eastern Asia suffered from enclosing rings of mountains and were largely cut off from the west by the high ranges extending from the Pamirs and the Tien Shan to beyond Lake Baikal. Further west, the Urals formed an effective barrier, while in the far south the Indian peninsula was largely separated from the plains of north India by the Vindhya Mountains. In these circumstances, the three major groupings of modern mankind were formed: the Caucasoids or " white " peoples, the Mongoloids or " yellow " peoples, and the Negroids or " black " peoples.

At one time the ancestral Caucasoids may have stretched right across northern Asia, for they seem to have left a remnant in the hairy Ainu of northern Japan ; but their chief centres were in the western steppes. From these centres they thrust westwards into Europe, south-eastwards

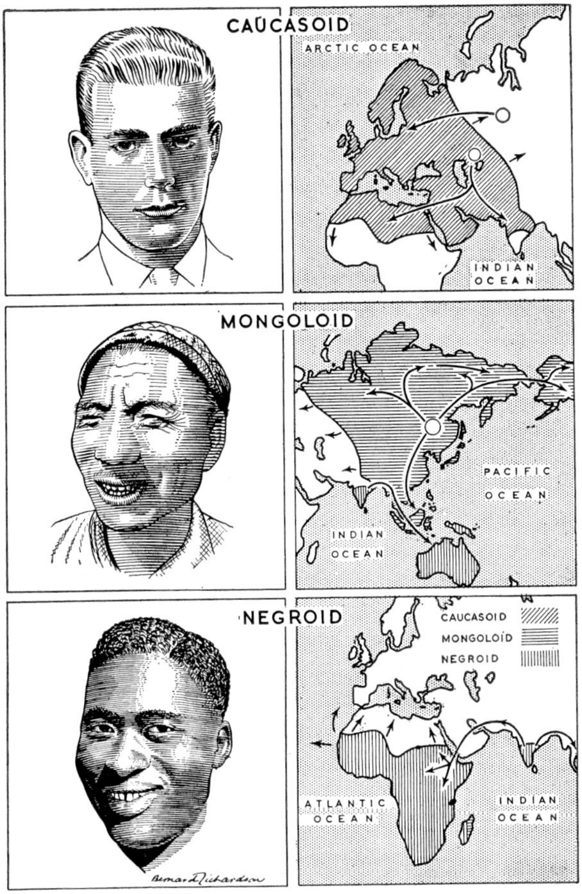

CHARACTERISTICS

Medium to tall, thickset to slender, people of pinkish to olive-brown colour. Narrow to fairly broad faces. Blue, grey, light to dark-brown eyes. Narrow to broadish, high-bridged noses. Fine, usually wavy, yellowish to dark-brown hair.

Short to fairly tall, often thickset people of pinkish to yellow-brown, or reddish-brown (Amerasians) colour. Medium to very broad, flattened faces. Light to dark-brown, typically heavy-lidded and " slanted " eyes. Rather broad, low-bridged noses. Coarse and straight, brown to black hair.

Very short (pygmies) to very tall (Nilotics), thickset to very slender people of brownish to ebony black colour (Bushmen yellow-brown). Narrow to medium broad faces. Brown to black eyes, somewhat slanted in Bushmen. Medium to very broad, low-bridged noses. Coarse and woolly to peppercorn, black hair.

Specially drawn for this work.

THE MAIN HUMAN STOCKS

Mankind is usually divided into three main stocks: the Caucasoid or white, the Mongoloid or yellow, and the Negroid or black. Above are shown the characteristics and area covered by each. The maps also indicate the directions of their earliest migrations (long lines) and continuing infiltrations (arrows). European colonisation is not shown.

towards Iran and India, south-westwards into north-eastern Africa, and then downwards into East Africa, where many early Caucasoid remains have been found.

They lost their identity in East Africa, but maintained themselves vigorously around the Mediterranean, in south-western Asia, and in north-western Europe. Wandering, invading, settling down and mingling, they covered Europe, discovered how to grow their food instead of collecting it, and built the classical cultures and civilisations of the West.

Thus they became essentially a people of temperate Eurasia and North Africa. They formed fairly distinctive groups in various regions, but never ventured far enough into extremes of climate, though they pushed up to Scandinavia, for any of these groups to become markedly different from the ancestral types. Even now, with all the technical resources that have been developed since the Industrial Revolution, the Caucasoids have only been able, with the help of native or imported labour, to colonise the more favourable areas of the territories they have acquired since the sixteenth century.

Mongoloid Adaptations to Cold

The precursors of the Mongoloid peoples lived in north-eastern Asia. It was a region in which only those could survive who were best adapted to the bitter cold—and these adaptations produced the well-known Mongoloid traits. The stocky, fat-warmed body reduces heat-loss from the skin to a minimum (see picture on p. 57). The flattened face decreases the chances of freezing: long noses are easily frostbitten. The slanted, heavy-lidded eyes can cope with exposure to cold as well as glare. They are also dark, for pigment helps the eyes to regulate the effects of light. This is specially important to hunting peoples, as it enables them to distinguish game at great distances.

But why do Mongoloid men have coarse, sparse and slow-growing beards instead of bushy, warming ones? The reason is that a frozen beard can be so dangerous to the face beneath that shaving, or plucking out the hairs, is a painful necessity in below-zero climates. In such circumstances the Mongoloid beard is the next best thing to having no beard at all.

There remains another question: why does the typical Mongoloid skin have a yellowish tinge? We know that the large amount of black pigment, melanin, in the Negroid skin is a protection against over-exposure to the sun's normally beneficial ultra-violet rays, but we have no clue to the advantage, if any, of yellow skins.

Apart from the mystery of their skins, the Mongoloid adaptations include everything but a furry coat; and that they could make for themselves from very early times. Great tailoring skill also went into building their circular skin-tents or *yurta*—the most effective portable and weather-proof homes yet designed.

The Mongoloid Migrations

Yet they were often bitterly cold. They had to eat a large amount of heat-giving foods and they wandered in search of abundant supplies. Indeed, their wanderings are the most dramatic in all human history.

The first great movements of the ancestral Mongoloids took them from their centres in north-eastern Asia into Siberia, some groups going gradually in north-westerly, and some in north-easterly, directions. They mingled with the pre-Caucasoids in North-west Siberia; in the extreme north-east they reached the Bering Strait about 20,000 years ago and crossed over into Alaska to become the first human inhabitants of the New World.

The migrations across the Bering Strait occurred at intervals for thousands of years, some following the coast, while others wandered east of the Rocky Mountains into the Great Plains of North America. Eventually they covered the Americas from Alaska to Tierra del Fuego, from the Plains to the Atlantic coast, and across Central and South America, leaving only the inhospitable regions below and just above the Equator relatively unoccupied.

The last to come were the Eskimo. They arrived about 1000 B.C. as a fully Mongoloid people so well equipped—they even had felt snow-goggles—for living in an intensely cold climate that they settled in Arctic North America. The early migrants, on the other hand, were still intermediate types, as we know from the mixture of Caucasoid and Mongoloid features in the American Indians.

In Asia itself southwards migrations took the Mongoloids to the Plateau of Mongolia, whence they thrust westwards through the mountain passes, eastwards to the coast and through the Korean Peninsula to Japan, and southwards in two prongs which took them to the shores of the China Sea and into the peninsula of Indo-China. Collecting in the fertile south, they ended their long phase of peaceful migration by moving into the Philippines, the Malay Peninsula, the large islands of Indonesia, and then across the Indian Ocean to Madagascar. Eventually they reached Micronesia and Polynesia.

Thus, as the Christian era approached, the Mongoloids had covered most of the world; but they were late in building civilisations and making a career of conquest. In the New World the great Amerasian empires of the Middle Ages were far behind the classical civilisations

FRENCH

SPANISH

ALGERIAN

N. INDIAN

THE MEDITERRANEAN TYPE

People of the Mediterranean type dominate Southern Europe, North Africa and South-west Asia. Variations of the type include the Indo-Afghan sub-type of northern India, Afghanistan and adjacent areas. (*Photos: E.N.A.*)

of South-west Asia and the Mediterranean, some of which were older by about 5,000 years. Even in China the beginnings of civilisation can at most be dated to the foundation of the Shang Dynasty about 1520 B.C.

The Shang emperors themselves were Mongoloids in a roundabout way. For they arose from partly Mongoloid peoples who had been migrating eastwards from the south-western steppes since about 3000 B.C. Their route was through a gap, known as the Dzungaria Gates, in the Tien Shan-Altai barrier east of Lake Balkhash; then south of the Great Altai range into the province of Kansu and upwards into northern China. They brought with them the methods of agriculture, animal husbandry and metalwork of the Bronze Age on which the Shang emperors based their power.

Horsepower Comes to Mongolia

Along the same route there came one of the most momentous discoveries in the history of mankind—the use of horse-drawn chariots. It can be called a world-shaking discovery, for the addition of horsepower to manpower made possible the conquest and maintenance of the extensive empires that started around 1700 B.C. But, so slowly do men learn, that the full use of horsepower did not come until the seventh century B.C., when the Medes of western Iran first bred horses for their famous Nisean cavalry.

The Chinese were quick to take advantage of all the new facilities from the West, but the nomadic herdsmen of Mongolia became enthusiastic only about the riding-horse. They had already domesticated the sturdy wild ponies, known to western science as Prjevalski's Horse (*Equus prejevalski*); and, with their long experience

NORDIC

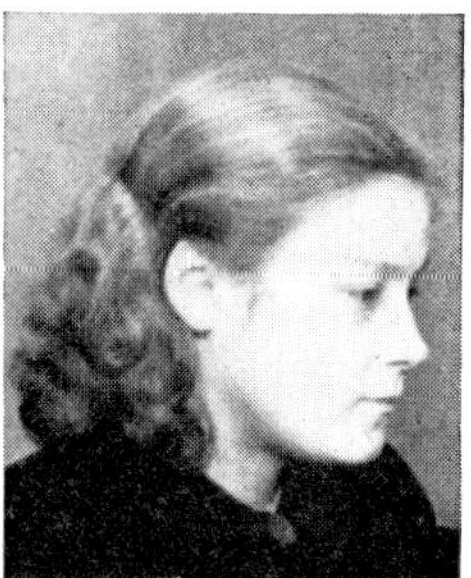
BALTIC

ALPINE

DINARIC

BLONDS AND ROUNDHEADS

The blond, longheaded Nordic type is found in pockets of Northern Europe. The roundheaded blonds found east of the Baltic belong to the Baltic or East European type. The stocky, roundheaded people of mountainous Europe are classified as the Alpine and rather similar Dinaric types. (*Photos: Swedish Embassy, S.C.R. and E.N.A.*)

TUNGUS

N. CHINESE

KOREAN

CROW INDIAN

THE MONGOLOID GROUP

The Mongoloids cover most of the world and vary greatly from place to place, but they remain recognisable as Mongoloids. The Tungus of the Amur River region are among the " classic Mongoloids." (*Photos: E.N.A.*)

of work in leather, they soon improved upon riding bareback by producing the padded tree-saddle—the most comfortable saddle known for horse and rider. Later they invented stirrups.

To-day the visitor to Outer Mongolia is astonished, in spite of all its modernising, by the many-coloured horses he sees roaming the grasslands or clustered near the *yurta*. And everybody rides, for everybody grows up in the saddle. They eat from their horses, shoot from their horses, play on their horses, line the race-track, the games, and the open-air theatre on their horses, and sing on horseback to the accompaniment of an age-old stringed instrument with the end of the fingerboard shaped like a horse's head.

Long ago they ate their horses, too, and drank their blood, but now they are content with fermented mare's milk. *Aireg*, as they call it (and not by the Russian name *Kumiss*), is the national everyday and ceremonial drink. In sickness it is more highly prized than asses' milk is in some countries: for tuberculosis patients it is invaluable.

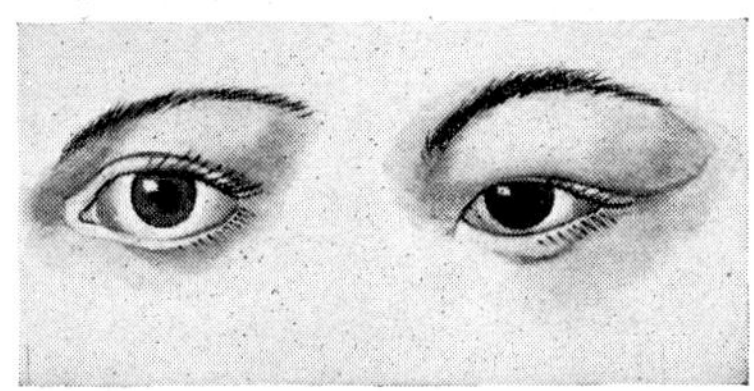

" OPEN " EYES AND " SLANT " EYES

The Mongoloid eye (right) has fat-padded lids which come closer together and fold over at the corners. This produces the well-known " slant-eyed " effect. On the left is shown the Caucasoid eye.

The Mongol Horsemen

The horse also put the word " Mongol " in the history books—a word so feared that the notion of invasion by a " Yellow Peril " still clings to it. They harried the Chinese, who found temporary security only by building the Great Wall: as Scythians and Massagetæ they fought the Greeks and the Persians and celebrated the death of Cyrus, so Herodotus tells us, by drinking from his skull; as Huns they continued to frighten the Chinese, advanced to South-west Asia and Middle and Southern Europe, and gave history and Hollywood the exploits of Attila, the " Scourge of God."

Thereafter, they were relatively quiet for several centuries. Then, in the Middle Ages, came the Mongol Conquest. Beginning with the capture of Peking in 1211 by Ghenghis Khan, and ending with the subjugation of China in 1260 by his grandson Kublai Khan, the patron of Marco Polo, it covered most of Eurasia from the Pacific to the Rhine and down to the Adriatic—and on the other side of the Mediterranean to Egypt and North Africa.

All this in fifty years, but collapse did not take much more than another century. In 1368 the Mongol (Yuan) Dynasty in China gave way to the first Ming Emperor, and a few years later Mongolia itself was invaded, the capital, Karakoram, being razed to the ground. It was the beginning of an end hastened by the revolt of the Russian princes against their Mongolian overlords.

Nevertheless, some groups survived. In Hungary, for instance, the Mongolian Magyars, form more than 90 per cent. of the population. In India Moghul rule continued into the nineteenth century and Mongoloid traits remain firmly stamped elsewhere in South-west Asia and Eastern Europe. Even in Western Europe, particularly in Germany, Mongoloid faces are common. Bismarck, the French were fond of saying, looked like Li Hung Chang's twin.

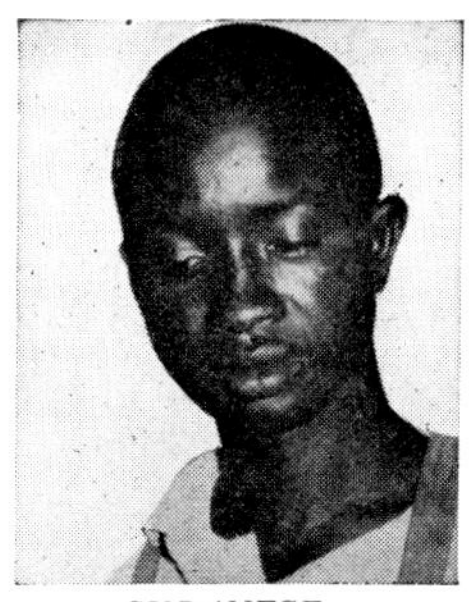

SUDANESE
(*Oloff*)

GUINEAN
(*Yoruba*)

ETHIOPIAN
(*Galla*)

NILOTIC
(*Nuer*)

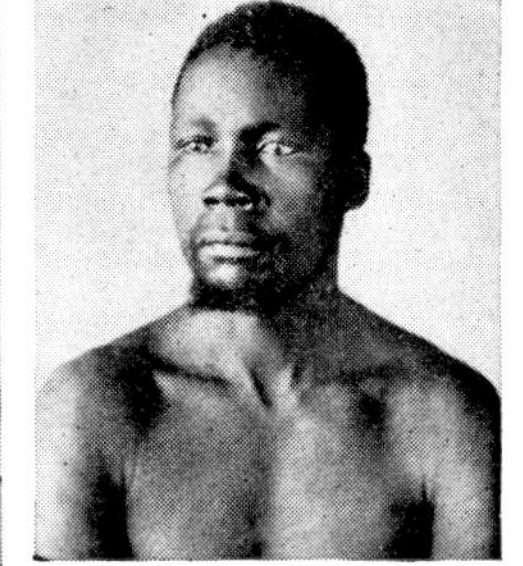

S. AFRICAN
(*Kaffir*)

S. AFRICAN
(*Masai*)

NEGROID TYPES

The Negroid group includes types ranging from the Sudanese and lanky Nilotic to the Ethiopian—the Negroid tail-end of early white migrations. The distended ear-lobes of the Masai are a good example of tribal ornamentation. (*Photos: French Embassy, C.O.I. and E.N.A.*)

The Negroid Peoples

We must turn now to the Negroid peoples. Their typical region is Africa south of the Sahara, but there are woolly-haired Negroids in Melanesia and pre-Negroid or near-Negroid types in peninsular India, Ceylon, Indonesia and Australia. Moreover, during the last four centuries, they have grown into important populations in the New World and there are pockets of them everywhere.

It is usual to regard their characteristics as adaptations, but they are not so clearly defined as the Mongoloid adaptations. Are pygmies small because they live in tropical forests? It seems so, but we do not know why. It cannot be due entirely to mineral deficiency, for the animals of pygmy lands are of normal size. At the same time we know for certain that diet influences stature. Shetland ponies bred in the United States develop into horses; and the children of immigrants there invariably grow taller than their parents.

Apart from diet, there is no doubt that " pygminess " is an advantage in moving about and hiding in tangled growth. It is true, of course, that taller peoples live in similar conditions, but they are later arrivals with more techniques for controlling forest conditions. Besides, the relatively tall Negroes who live alongside the pygmies of the Congo are a good deal shorter than Negroes who live in the grasslands.

Tall, slender stature, though definitely associated with diet, increases the surface area for evaporation from the skin (see picture on p. 55); and it is interesting that various Negro and other groups living in hot dry lands are tall. Some, such as

MORE SURVIVING ANCESTORS

E.N.A.

This is a Papuan medicine man. The Papuans are unique, both in appearance and language, among the Negroid people of Melanesia; they may be a pygmy, Australoid and Melanesian mixture.

Royal Anthropological Institute.

This aboriginal Australian group of long ago shows a chief with his wife and mother. The scarring on the chief's body is a form of tribal marking common amongst Negroid peoples.

Royal Anthropological Institute.

The Veddas are the survivors, now scattered in eastern Ceylon, of a very ancient people who may have once flourished around the Indian Ocean. They resemble various " remnant-groups " of India so closely that all of them are often spoken of collectively as Veddoids; sometimes as Indo-Australoids, for they also have traits in common with the Australian aborigines.

YURT AND IGLOO

Paul Popper.

Round houses are so well adapted to extremes of climate that they may be seen from the Equator to the Arctic. The felt *yurt* is a warm and comfortable home—not just a tent—for the seasonal nomads of Asia. They take their homes with them when they drive their flocks to summer pastures high up the mountain sides, as do the Kirghiz of the Tien Shan region.

Polar Photos.

Eskimos travel long distances when hunting and trading furs. They keep snug by building " snow-yurts " or igloos. Sleds, highly-trained huskies, double clothing, snow-goggles, blubber lamps for heating, efficient weapons and cunning traps also helped them to colonise the Arctic when man first began to make the world his own.

the Negroes of the Sudan and the Nile, the Caucasoid Somalis of the arid belts around the Horn of Africa, and other inhabitants of deserts, are exceptionally tall ; and we know that some people have grown taller in the desert within fairly recent times. Thus, the Berbers, who dominate northern Africa from Libya to the Canaries, are an agricultural Caucasoid people of average European size who acquired camels from the Persians in the fifth century. Some Berbers then moved into the Sahara on their " ships of the desert " and developed, within a few centuries, into the nomadic Tuareg. They still look like Berbers, but they are remarkably tall and skinny.

On the other hand, shorter people live comfortably in deserts and the Bushmen of the Kalahari are almost pygmies; and very tall people live in temperate climates —the lowland Scots are among the tallest people in the world. But, allowing for these exceptions, especially if we note that the Kalahari is a more genial desert than the Sahara and that the lowland Scots are heavier than the Tuareg, there does seem to be a trend in the direction of tallness in arid climates.

Black Skins and Woolly Hair

Skin colour shows a trend towards blondness in temperate climates and blackness in hot sunny regions; and we associate it largely with the importance of melanin in filtering the ultra-violet rays of the sun. Fair people have very little melanin because, it is sometimes said, they need all the ultra-violet rays they can get in their typical areas. In fact, they have so little melanin that they become red and uncomfortable during their summer holidays and suffer severe burns when they are exposed to really strong sunlight.

This argument loses strength when we consider that large numbers of brunet peoples, who tan happily in the summer and get a little paler in the winter, live quite successfully in northern Europe. But, unlike the brunets, all the blue-eyed fair peoples of the last few thousand years have lived in regions of weak sunlight covered by ice during the previous Ice Age.

Black-skinned peoples are evidently suited to tropical living, for their deep pigmentation prevents damage by the strong ultra-violet rays, while allowing enough to get through for making vitamin D—the " sunshine vitamin." This advantage would be a disadvantage in colder and less sunny lands; and it is certainly true that, until quite recently, Negroids have made no noticeable effort to move away from the climates to which they are so well suited. Consequently, we say that "black" skins (they are generally more brown than black) are an "adaptive characteristic" of the Negroid peoples.

Yet it cannot be said that survival in the tropics depends on being almost black —light brunets have

Royal Anthropological Institute.

THE LAST TASMANIANS

Charles A. Woolley, a photographer of Hobart, Tasmania, gave history these pictorial records of the last Tasmanian man and woman : William Lanne or King Billy of the Coal River Tribe who died at the age of 29 or so in 1869; and Truganini, also named Lalla Rookh after the heroine of the famous poem by Thomas Moore (1779–1852), of the Bruni Island tribe. She died in 1879, when she was nearing eighty years of age.

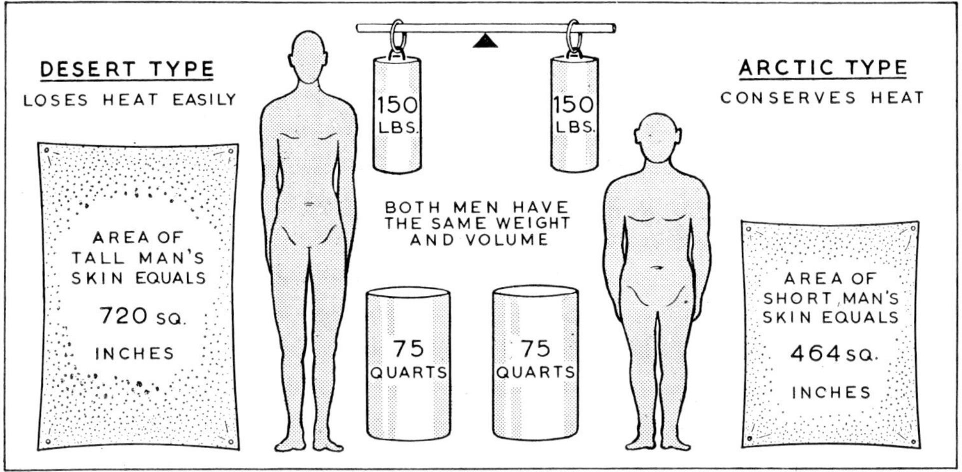

Re-drawn after C. S. Coon.

SURFACE AREA AND HEAT LOSS

The skin of the taller of the two men of the same weight and volume has more surface area from which heat can be lost. This is why people living in deserts are usually tall and thin, while those living in cold lands (who have to conserve heat) are short and bulky.

done well in Africa from early times. Why, then, did black skins arise? The obvious answer is that they arose when conditions in the tropics favoured those who were developing more pigment in their skins.

This answer is not denied by the yellowish-brown colour of the Bushmen-Hottentot or Khoisan (*khoi* is Hottentot for " men " and *san* is Bushman for " bush "). These cattle-keeping people probably inherited their Mongoloid colour, together with slant eyes and the same blood-group (B) as the majority of Asians, from ancestors who migrated from South-west Asia to north-eastern Africa. They lived in that part of Africa for a long time before moving south. Later they dominated Africa below the Sahara, but by the sixteenth century the aggressive Bantu had confined them to the inhospitable south-west.

Woolly hair is as ancient as black skins. It provides Negroids with an air-chambered protective hat. In those with peppercorn hair the curls are so tight that tiny islands of scalp are exposed so that sweat can evaporate quickly—an advantage, anthropologists say, when it is hot and humid. But the " hair-hatted " Negroids are often uncomfortable, the peppercorn heads expose numerous bits of scalp to the sun, straight and wavy haired peoples live in the tropics, some Negroids are bald and many shave their heads. In short, people anywhere can get along with any kind of hair or no hair at all; but, when all this is said, we must remember that the apparently useless characteristics of human groups to-day may once have served them well.

Negroid Origins

The early history of the Negroids is little known. The fossil records show, surprisingly, that Negroes are comparative newcomers in Africa—usually in the New Stone Age in East Africa. The earliest Africans of our own species are pre-Caucasoids, followed by ancestral Bushmen; and the native peoples of East Africa are still dominantly Caucasoid though extensively mixed with Negroids.

How, then, can we account for the origin of the African Negroes? It can be explained by crossings above the Congo between pre-Caucasoids, pre-Negroids from India, pygmies and Bushmen. By this theory the Negroes are, so to speak, enlarged pygmies who moved westwards to the coast and eastwards to the Nile, eventually populating the whole Negroid area of the Sudan. It is only a theory, but it gains respect from the two earliest Negroid skulls (10000 B.C. at most) that have been found in Africa; for one comes from Asselar in the west, some 200 miles above Timbuktu, and the other from Khartoum on the Lower Nile.

It also fits in very well with the most likely theory about the origin of the Negroids in general. According to this view the pre-Negroids, represented to-day by the forest-dwelling Veddas (see picture on p. 54), originated in the Indian peninsula, whence they migrated up the coasts.

The western branch moved into Iran, crossed Arabia into East Africa, penetrated the Sudan and wandered along the Nile to Egypt in the north and the Great Lakes in the south. The same routes were followed again and again into modern times, leaving pronounced Asian influences in various parts of Africa. The Egyptian language, for instance, contains a large number of Dravidian words.

The eastern branch reached Australia and Tasmania by way of the Malay Peninsula, Indonesia and New Guinea, from where the other Melanesian islands were also populated. Except for the Tasmanians, who could not survive the colonisation of their small island, the remnants of this wave of migration still inhabit Malaysia and Oceania.

Some of these survivals support the theory of pre-Negroid migration from peninsular India; the forest Sakai of Malaya, though dwarfs, and the Australian aborigines, though tall, both resemble the Veddas. But the Negritos, the black, woolly-haired, broad-nosed pygmies of the Andamans, Malaya, the Philippines and Melanesia, are a problem. The Negroid Melanesians may have resulted from crossing with the immigrant Veddoids, in much the same way as the African Negroes may have arisen from crossings with pygmies and Bushmen; and it is worth noting that in India itself, where the supposed presence of Negritos has been denied, the pre-Negroids never developed into woolly-haired Negroids.

Can we suppose, then, that the pygmies were already an ancient people when the first group-forming migrations of man were taking place? It seems so. At least it is certain that when we discover the origins and hidden history of these tremendously important little people we shall have closed many of the gaps in our knowledge of the making of mankind.

Movement and Variety

Movement and change, as we have seen, are the grand themes of the whole story of mankind. Men made the habitable world their own by moving into its furthest corners; and in doing so they changed themselves as well as the face of the earth. They wandered, adapted, mingled, destroyed and built, and formed distinctive populations far from their original homes. In these ways they changed into a variety of types, each containing a particular series of populations, that were very different from the original types from which they sprang.

But they continued to move and change, and to mingle with others who were moving and changing; and so their distinctiveness broke down again. To-day we are in an advanced stage of this process when no pure populations remain—even the Ainu have been Mongolised by the Japanese, the forest dwellers of Malaya are being absorbed by the Malays, and the Congo pygmies are providing wives for Negroes. In fact, all populations are mixed populations, all the so-called " races " are mongrelised races, and all peoples are compounds of peoples.

Languages reflect these movements, for they grow and change as men wander and settle and wander again. We can see how this happens by considering English speech during the five centuries after the Norman Conquest. By Chaucer's time it was another language, which grew so rapidly that we cannot read *The Canterbury Tales* as easily as we can read Hamlet; and we can only read Shakespeare because printing and increasing education had

THE PUEBLO INDIANS

Cedric Dover.

The Pueblo Indians of the south-western United States are so-called because they live in cliff dwellings and community houses of stone and adobe which are really villages (*pueblo* in Spanish). They passed their great days six centuries ago, but the famous pueblo at Taos, New Mexico, shown in this picture, gives an idea of the magnificent pueblos of old.

E.N.A.

D. H. Lawrence lived in Taos and was much attracted by the Pueblo Indians and their arts. The Pueblo men developed particular skill in weaving; the women in making and decorating pottery. The tradition continues, as can be seen from this picture of Pueblo women offering their wares for sale at a simple street stall in Santa Fé.

PIRATES AND PYGMIES

E.N.A.

These young Sea Dyaks, entertaining themselves in a clearing in the coastal Borneo forest, are the descendants of headhunters and pirates—and they are not always as peaceful as they look in this picture. Their seafaring traditions go back to the days when their Mongolian ancestors, venturing far across the Indian Ocean to Madagascar, established their island outposts. You will see that they remain dominantly Mongoloid.

Royal Geographical Society.

The pygmies of the Belgian Congo live in the heart of the equatorial forest, but they are a courageous and inventive people. They hunt elephants, trap small game, collect wild honey, and build simple cantilever bridges; and their skill and endurance have been exploited since the days of the ancient Egyptians. The inset (left) provides a height comparison with a typical European.

ORNAMENTATION

The women of the Sara-Caba tribes, south of Lake Chad, distort their lips to incredible proportions. The lip-stretching, slitting and inserting of increasingly large discs begins in childhood.

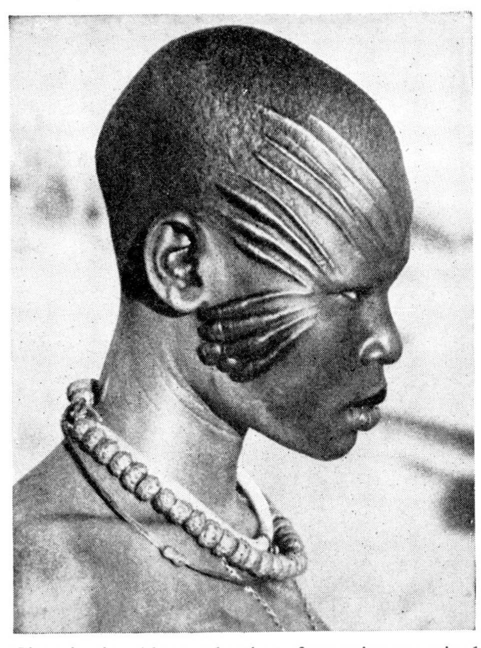

Cicatrisation (the production of conspicuous raised scars) is common among many Negroid peoples. The scars on this young Latuka woman of the Sudan show how carefully the art is practised.

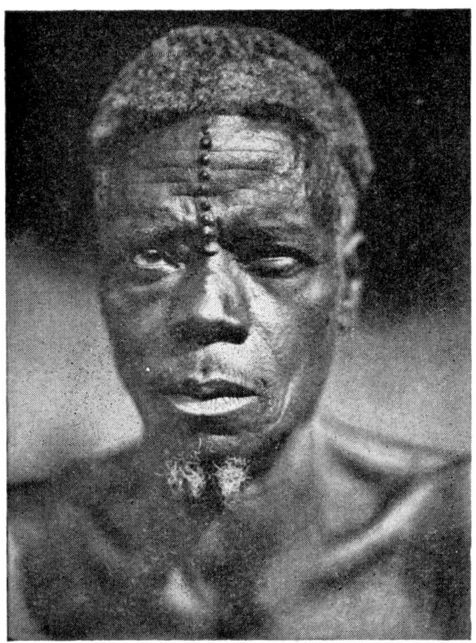

Among the M'Bouka (Congolese type) of the Belgian Congo, a characteristic row of beads down the forehead to the nose is produced by cicatrisation. Such markings have tribal significance.

Photos: E. N.A.

All tribal peoples have tribal markings, tattooing being specially common in Asia, Oceania and the New World. This picture shows tribal tattooing on a girl from the Chen Hills in Burma.

standardising effects on spelling and pronunciation. But "exported English" quickly grew into forms that Englishmen cannot understand, while domestic English absorbed large numbers of new words, often from far afield. Two of the commonest, cocoa and tomato, came from the Aztec language still spoken by more than a million Mexicans.

These two words alone show how our language grew as contacts expanded and the English way of life changed, yet Englishmen look much the same to-day as when Chaucer was alive. This is also true elsewhere. For languages evolve faster than men and many languages are spoken by one type of mankind, but word-likenesses are preserved which allow a Babel of tongues to be grouped into a few language stocks.

This diversity within large unities is illustrated in the map on p. 71. Apart from the tiny pockets of "problem stocks," such as Basque and Mon-Khmer, there are islands of languages surrounded by languages of different stock; for example, the Finno-Ugrian islands, surrounded by Slavonic languages, that extend from the Urals to Hungary. These linguistic islands are occupied by surrounded Mongoloids, whose languages retain enough of their original character for them to be included in the Finno-Ugrian branch of the Ural-Altaic stock.

In the New World the connection between migration and language-making is more conspicuous. There a few original languages were multiplied in North America within eight stocks, but as soon as the migrating peoples passed Mexico into the isolating mountains and jungles of South America a great patchwork of languages and stocks, often cutting across each other, was formed.

But the unities, even in the Americas, are still more striking; and they add to the picture we have outlined of the movements of the major human stocks. Most of Eurasia, for instance, is covered by the Indo-European languages of the Caucasoids and the Ural-Altaic and Sinitic languages of the Mongoloids.

The Caucasoid Types

The other map (p. 69), which shows the distribution of human types, gives a similar impression of diversity within unity. The types no longer distinguish whole populations, but occur in connecting geographical belts running across or enclosing various populations in which other types are also represented. And all can be grouped according to the primary stocks from which they stem.

In south-western Eurasia the Mediterranean type is dominant. The Neolithic ancestors of these long-headed, small-faced, sharp-nosed brunets of medium height were the first eastern arrivals in Europe. They came from the somewhat taller, round-headed, big-nosed mountain people of Anatolia and first established themselves in the Balkan peninsula. Moving on, some clustered, as Plato observed, like frogs around the genial Mediterranean "pond," where they discovered agriculture (to settle they had to grow food instead of gathering it) and built the first great civilisations.

But others moved on. They settled in the Iberian peninsula, occupied France and the Low Countries, crossed the still existing land bridge into England (where their famous Long Barrows still survive), and followed the Atlantic coast to Scandinavia. From Spain they reached North Africa and travelled along the fertile coastal zone towards the Asian limits of the type in north-eastern India. Now they were back in areas of previous migrations and much mingling obviously took place. This is specially evident in the Semitic branch in Arabia to which the big-nosed Anatolian element contributed; and again in Afghanistan and north-eastern India, where a tall Indo-Afghan type can be recognised.

While the first stages of these movements were taking place, the Anatolian settlers in the Balkan peninsula, who had changed slightly into a taller, long-faced Dinaric type or sub-type, moved up into Central Europe, where they seem to have been submerged by the Alpine type. This type includes all the stocky, round-headed,

E.N.A.

The head-dress of this Magyar girl denotes that she is a Calvinist. Her remote Mongoloid origins still show slightly in her broad face and faintly Mongoloid eyes.

E.N.A.

This woman of the " Reindeer People," a Norwegian Lapp of strongly Mongoloid appearance, keeps her baby snug in a type of cradle commonly used in Arctic lands. Light, warm and well-protected, it is ideally suited to nomadic family life in the Arctic cold.

E.N.A.

These members of the Hawaiian National Ballet remain seated while they dance, but they convey a tremendous feeling of rippling rhythmic movement. You will gather from their faces that there has been much mingling in Hawaii, the " melting-pot " of the Pacific.

Cedric Dover

These musicians are Miao from south-western China; the bamboo instrument is a *sheng*. Pipe music begins early in human history because Nature provides so many means of producing it.

WHEN PEOPLES MEET

E.N.A

Peoples of very different types have been meeting and mingling for a long time—and they still do so. This picture shows a slightly " mixed " aboriginal Australian boy.

E.N.A.

Strange resemblances crop up when peoples meet. This girl from Ecuador could pass for the aboriginal boy's sister; but her origins are South American Indian with " a touch of white."

Copyright.

It could be thought that this girl is related to the two young people above. But she is an Anglo-Indian—the result of generations of intermarriage within a community starting from European and Indian mixtures.

E.N.A.

This young Brazilian (he is sipping *maté* tea from a *chimarrão* through a silver tube or *bombilla*) resembles many other young Latin Americans. His ancestry is Mediterranean (Portuguese) and South American Indian.

THEY MINGLE — BUT NOT ALWAYS

E.N.A.

This woman of the San Blas Archipelago, Panama, belongs to one of the earliest of the many part-white groups fathered by buccaneers and mutineers. Her people speak a localised form of Elizabethan English and are often fair-haired.

E.N.A.

The pygmy Sakai of Malaya live by collecting plants and hunting with blowguns. This Sakai boy shows the effects of Malay mixture and better food.

Copyright.

People of Negroid-Caucasoid origin account for more than 10 per cent. of the population of the United States. They vary greatly, as this photograph of two Negro professors shows.

Hulton Picture Library.

Very few people have met without mingling. But, in spite of Romany Romances, the gypsies remain relatively " pure," though they have been in Western Europe since the early fifteenth century and roamed the Old World for unknown centuries before that.

broad-faced brunets of the mountain chain from the Black Sea to the western edges of the Central Massif of France, as well as the descendants of the Beaker Folk who arrived in England about 2000 B.C.

Two types of partly Mongoloid descent probably contributed to the origins of the Alpine type: the tall, brunet, round-headed but long-faced Turkic type, which ranges widely across the steppes from Lake Balkhash to beyond the Caspian Sea; and the Baltic or East European type, which extends in a northerly direction from east of the Baltic to the Ural Mountains. The Baltics are tall, fair, blue-eyed roundheads, with flat-tipped noses, whose ancestors must have been the pre-Caucasoids who migrated westwards, as we have already mentioned, from North Central Asia.

The only other blue-eyed blonds are the very tall, long-faced longheads of the Nordic type. It has been said that they are " bleached Mediterraneans," but their northern range suggests that they are of Baltic and later Mediterranean stock; for it may be that the East European migration continued, mingling with Mediterraneans on the way, from Poland to Northern Germany, Holland, France and Britain, while a branch followed the eastern shores of the Baltic into Scandinavia. Much that is fanciful has been written about " Nordic superiority " in recent years, for Nordic peoples have spread far and conquered widely. The Vikings, for example, reached America centuries before Columbus and began their conquest of England long before 1066; but the romantic exploits of particular types should never be allowed to become excuses for fairy-tale living.

The Fairer Mongoloids

Among the Mongoloids, the characteristics we have already discussed are found in the peoples of medium height who form the North Mongol type. They occupy a broad belt of plateaux and steppes from north-eastern Siberia to the Caspian Sea and include the Arctic Yakuts, the Tungus of the Amur River region, the Buriats of Lake Baikal, and the Kalmuks of Astrakhan. A branch, which includes the Samoyed, takes the type from the neighbourhood of Lake Baikal to the White Sea.

This branch crosses the Siberian type, often called the Paleoasiatic type because of its early origins, resulting originally from the mixture of pre-Caucasoids and pre-Mongoloids. The peoples of this type are usually shorter than the other Mongol types and many show Caucasoid affinities, but all are essentially Mongoloids. In fact, the whole Arctic and sub-Arctic area from Lapland and Finland to the Chukchee Peninsula, and the Eskimo territory of Alaska, is a North Mongol-Siberian zone.

The North Mongol type also

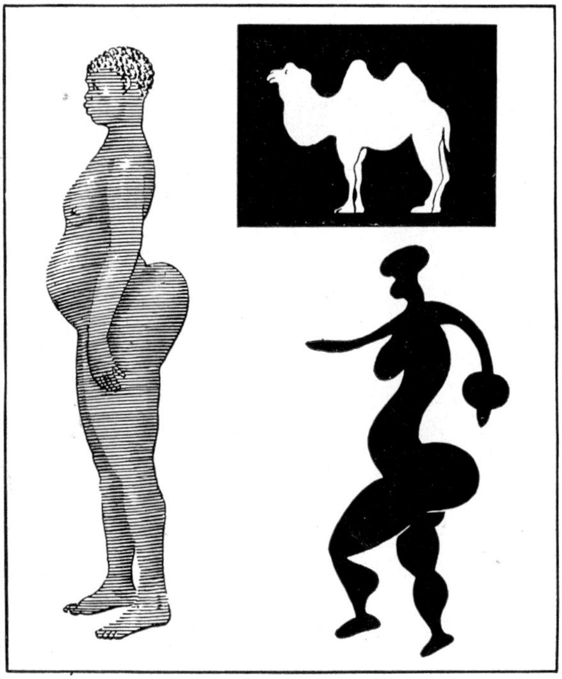

Specially drawn for this work.

HOW FAT IS STORED IN THE DESERT

Fat is necessary in hot climates, too, but it is often put on in parts. Camels have humps of storage fat and many Hottentot women are steatopygous (stee-a-top-e-gus). The condition is frequently shown in Hottentot cave art and is still regarded as a mark of beauty.

meets the tall, long-faced, round-headed pastoral people who range across the steppes of southern Russia from Lake Balkhash and Kirghizia to the Black Sea. This Turkic type links the Alpine and North Mongol types, thus forming the central section of a zone of roundheads stretching right across Eurasia.

The Central Mongol type occupies most of China, for it extends from Korea through the rich agricultural lands of the Huang-ho and the Yangtse-kiang to Tibet, Burma and Siam. The people of this type are the tallest in eastern Asia, their skins are yellower than the other Mongoloids, and their heads are mesocephalic—that is to say they are intermediate between long-headed (dolichocephalic) and round-headed (brachycephalic).

South Mongols and Polynesians

In contrast the people of the South Mongol type are almost as short as the Siberians, and they are dark, round-faced and very round-headed. They occupy South China and extend to Burma, Indo-China and Siam, whence they continue into Malaya.

The Malaysians are dominantly Mongoloid and the presence of large numbers of Chinese, mostly from South China, ensures that they will remain so. But in the interior there are shorter, darker, intermediate to long-headed, wavy-haired people of the Indonesian or Proto-Malay type. They are something of a problem, for they have traits in common with the Mediterraneans as well as the Veddas.

The Polynesians are also largely Mongoloid now, though they began as Caucasoids from Asia. They are as tall as Nordics, inclined to be fat, olive to brown skinned, oval-faced and large-eyed, but they are round-headed. Their ancestors began to reach the islands that dot the Pacific from the Carolines to Easter Island, Samoa to Hawaii, and Tahiti to New Zealand, a thousand years or so ago; and it is generally thought that they were Mongoloid Malays, made a little less Mongoloid by mixture with the Proto-Malays, from Sumatra. These Malays, who invaded Madagascar in large numbers before 500 B.C., are known for seafaring exploits as remarkable as those of the Vikings.

Another view is that Polynesia was populated by purer South Mongols who sailed from the Canton coast to the Philippines and Carolines. And there is the theory, advanced by Thor Heyerdahl of *Kon-Tiki* fame, that waves of immigrants reached Polynesia from Peru. It is also possible that Polynesia was populated in all three ways; but, whatever the way, the Mongoloid background of the Polynesian type is certain.

Negroid Types

There are many distinctive tribes in Africa south of the Sahara, but all of them can be grouped in eight connecting types. The " typical Negroes " are the tall, ebony black, moderately long-headed inhabitants of the forest and savannah lands from Senegal almost to the Blue Nile. They belong to the Sudanese type.

The Nilotic type, which extends from Khartoum to Lake Victoria, more or less begins where the Sudanese type ends. The Nilotics, represented by the Dinka, Nuer and other pastoral tribes, are among the tallest people in the world: they average 6 feet and many reach 6 feet 6 inches. They are also very slender, long-headed, long-faced, black and spiral-haired.

The South African or Bantu follow the Nilotic type and continues down south-eastern Africa to the Cape. The peoples along this belt, such as the Swahili, Zulu, Kaffirs and Basuto, bear some resemblances to Caucasoids, in spite of their deep chocolate brown skins and wide noses.

The Guinean type includes many tribes, such as the Ashanti of the Gold Coast and the Yoruba of Nigeria, who inhabit the area between the Ivory Coast and the Cameroons. They resemble the Sudanese peoples, but their skin colour is a dark chestnut with a reddish tint.

The tribes of the Congolese or " Forest Negro " type extend from French Equatorial Africa around the bend of the Congo, and then through the Congo region to

Angola. They approach the Nilotics and South Africans in the vicinity of Lake Victoria, touch the Khoisan type beyond Angola, and fraternise with the Congo pygmies. In appearance they are shorter than the Guineans, blackish-brown in colour, large-mouthed and thick-lipped; and they increase their distinctiveness by the remarkable raised scars which they produce in their skins.

The Ethiopians, Somalis, Masai, and some other tribes around the Abyssinian plateau, form the Ethiopian type. They are reddish-brown to brownish-black in colour, their hair is curly, " fuzzy " or wavy (not woolly), and their oval faces are much more Mediterranean than Negroid. Altogether they are more Caucasoid than Negroid, as we should expect from their origins and exposure to Mediterranean and Semitic mixture, but Negroid influences from the west and south are evidently strong.

The blackish-brown, flat-nosed, straight or wavy-haired Dravidian type of South India and Ceylon also has traits in common with Caucasoids as well as Negroids. But, as in the case of the Veddas and Australian aborigines (together called Veddoids or Australoids), their characteristics are probably derived more from the ancient pre-Negroids than from contacts with North Indians and East Africans.

The Melanesians, on the other hand, can be regarded as the Negroes of Oceania. They have the brownish-black skins, long heads, flat noses and woolly hair typical of most African Negroes; and we can only conclude that they evolved in much the same way from mixtures with Negritos.

The Amerasians

We do not know the routes followed by the Mongoloids when they first arrived in Alaska, but many of them reached the Canadian North-west, east of the Mackenzie river. Then they proceeded south to the Great Plains, turned into the Eastern Woodlands and moved up into the North Atlantic States and Eastern Canada. Others—perhaps later when the ice had lifted—found themselves in southern Alaska and wandered west of the Rocky Mountains towards Mexico.

The New World was as bountiful for the Amerasians as it was for the colonists who followed the Spanish adventurers. They multiplied rapidly in the rich Plains, divided into many tribes, and developed into the tall, well-built, big-nosed, coppery-brown North Atlantic type—the feathered Redskins we have all pretended to be since the days of Fenimore Cooper and Buffalo Bill.

They appeared from " nowhere " to surround the covered waggons, they glided down the rivers and shot rapids in their canoes, they ran incredible distances; but the main reason why they became a part of the boyhood of the world is that they borrowed the notion of riding horses from the Spaniards—and the horses as well. Thus they soon changed their whole way of life to a " horse culture " bent on widespread conquest, in much the same way as their first riding lessons gave the Mongolians the vision of empire.

Their tribal names are echoes of romance for most of us: Mohican, Delaware, Crow, Sioux, Cheyenne, Iroquois and many others. The Iroquois of New York State are perhaps the best known, for they formed the famous League of Five Nations, inspired partly by the legendary Hiawatha of Longfellow and Coleridge Taylor, to secure the Great Peace by methods which were as warlike as those of earlier and later peacemakers.

We know them, too, for their loyalty to the English during the War of Independence, though they faced disaster if the colonists won. And disaster was not long in coming. General Sullivan burned their villages and destroyed their crops in 1779. The shock was so great that they still refer to the President of the United States as *Ranadagaryas*, " The Destroyer of the Settlements." Is the word vaguely familiar? That is because the first three syllables give us C(R)anada, " The Settlement."

The peoples of the North Pacific type are of medium height, with round heads, broad faces and coppery but not very dark

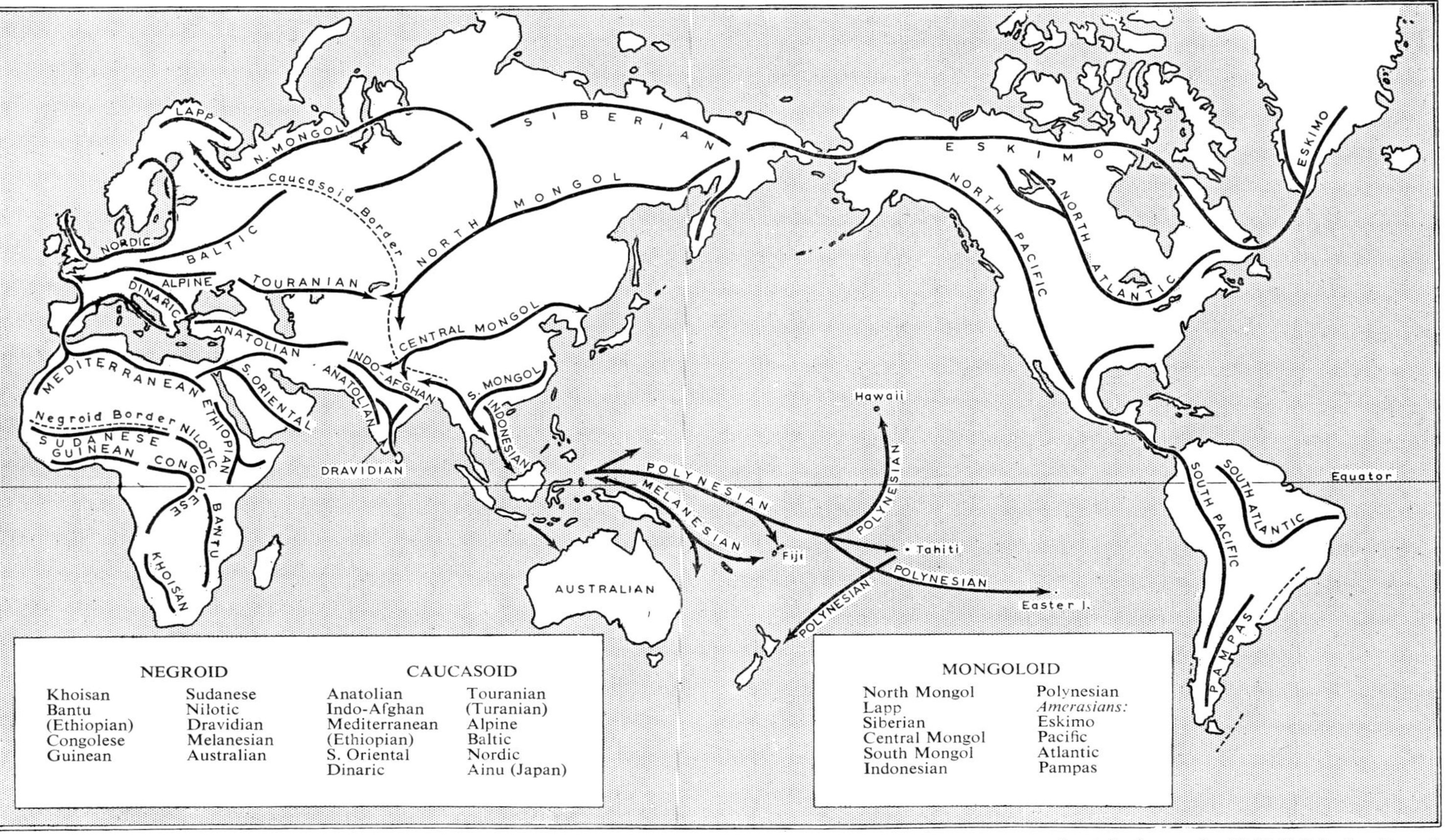

Specially drawn, after H. V. Vallois, for this work.

THE CHIEF ETHNIC GROUPS

Ethnic groups developed, as languages did, through the wanderings of man. Popularly called " races," they were once distinctive populations which kept their peculiarities as they grew. We can still distinguish ethnic characteristics, though they range through several populations instead of being typical of whole groups. Thus the Mediterranean belt encloses many populations within which other ethnic types are also found. In Britain, for example, Mediterraneans, Nordics and Alpines – and mixtures of these and other types – are all common.

Royal Anthropological Institute.

TOTEM POLES OF THE PACIFIC NORTH-WEST

This photograph, taken in Queen Charlotte Islands off southern Alaska by G. M. Dawson, shows a totem pole village in its heyday nearly a century ago. These elaborately carved structures became common in the Pacific North-west after 1830, when native craftsmen had mastered European tools and the fur trade established patrons who could afford such advertisements of their prestige.

complexions. They include the coastal Indians of British Columbia, whose natural resources are so plentiful that they have built the most advanced of the surviving hunting and food-gathering cultures. Abundant wood has made them experts in putting it to every kind of use. Their constructional and artistic skill is shown in their famous communal houses, 40 ft. long and 30 ft. wide (one prehistoric house was 520 ft. long and 60 ft. wide), with great totem poles rising from the front doors; in the variety of their decorated canoes, little and large; and in their carved and painted masks, utensils, ornaments and toys.

The wealth of these people is further indicated by the *potlatch*, an extravagant ceremonial feast when property is displayed, given away, and even destroyed. It is not an expression of a rich man's senseless vanity, nor is it an insurance for feasts and gifts to come. It is a means of upholding status and of conferring social position upon one's children—a man who has not given a *potlatch* is regarded as one who " never did anything for his children." In other words, it is not so very different from an extravagant christening party, wedding reception or house-warming.

Continuing from the North Pacific and North Atlantic types are the tribes whose ancestors built the great Aztec, Maya and Inca civilisations of Central and South America. They belong to the shorter, darker, more round-headed, thick-lipped and often beak-nosed South Pacific type.

Among them are large numbers of barrel-chested, large-lunged, surefooted " high altitude men " who have adapted themselves closely to living on the peaks of the Andes range. Some Chileans spend

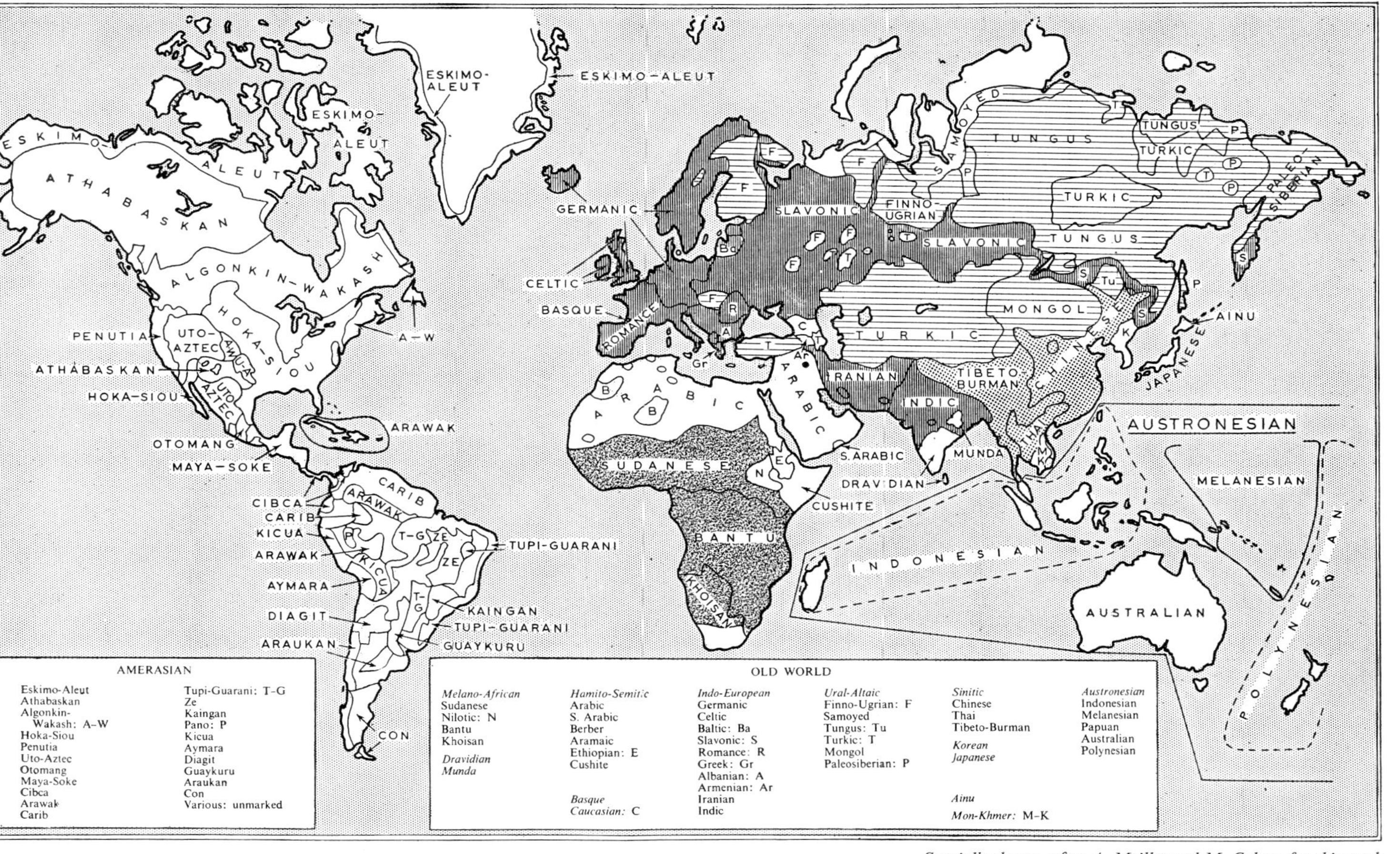

Specially drawn, after A. Meillet and M. Cohen, for this work.

LANGUAGE STOCKS OF THE WORLD

Languages grew as men wandered—in the New World their southwards increase is very striking. Some changed and many disappeared, but there are still nearly 3,000 languages, although hundreds of them are spoken by small numbers of people. It should be remembered, too, that they belong to relatively few language stocks. Eurasia, for example, is practically covered by the Caucasoid Indo-European stock and the Mongoloid Ural-Altaic and Sinitic stocks. The spread of European languages since Columbus is not shown here.

their working lives in the tin mines 17,000 feet up, where a white man from the plains would quickly die of oxygen starvation. But the cost is high. Mountain sickness or *saroche* kills many and incapacitates many more; and in some regions two out of three babies are dead soon after they are born.

The South Atlantic type extends from the Gulf of Venezuela to Pernambuco, but is concentrated in the interior of Brazil. Far from their origins in time and place, and often mongrelised by Europeans and Negroes, these very short forest dwellers bear little resemblance to Mongoloids. Their heads are intermediate, their faces oval, their noses straight and, uniquely amongst Mongoloids, their hair is often wavy. They belong to many tribes and clans, speaking a variety of languages, which include the remnants of the once proud and man-eating Caribs of the Caribbean shores and islands. The word "cannibal" is derived from *Caribales*, slightly corrupted to *canibales* by the Spaniards and English of the sixteenth century.

The Caribs were the first Amerasians to meet the pioneer builders of the New World. Within a few years they were dying out and, in an effort to save them, a Jesuit priest suggested that Negro slaves would supply more suitable labour. Later massacres and mongrelisation of Amerasian tribes continued into this century. For example, the Witotos of the dripping Amazonian jungle between the Yapura and Putumayo rivers were almost eliminated during the frantic demand for Brazilian rubber during the reign of Edward VII.

They were saved by an American, W. C. Hardenburg, who reported their plight to the Royal Anthropological Institute in 1909. An outcry on the "Putumayo Atrocities" followed which revealed that every ton of the 4,000 tons of Putumayo rubber produced between 1900 and 1911 had cost an average of eight Witoto lives. The man who provided the British Government with this information later became better known for other reasons—he was Sir Roger Casement.

The massacres have now stopped, but the mongrelisation continues. The "giants" of the Argentinian heartlands, to whom travellers' tales from Patagonia attributed enormous feet (*Patagones* means "Big Feet") and heights of about 10 feet, are fast disappearing. They belong to the tall (almost as tall as the Nilotics), well-built, very round-headed, thick haired, prominent nosed Pampas type, from which the part-Spanish Gauchos have emerged.

The Melting Pot

All the other Amerasians, including even the Eskimo, have also been extensively mongrelised; and in most of Latin-America a dominant Mestizo type and culture, unknown before A.D. 1500, can be recognised. The peoples of this type resemble those of southern Eurasia, and most of all the Mediterraneans, for they are white-Amerasian mixtures, with touches of Negroid, in which the white element is chiefly Mediterranean.

A mulatto type, too, has emerged in the Americas, which is naturally conspicuous in those countries with large Negroid populations: Haiti almost 100 per cent., West Indies over 90 per cent., Colombia 30 per cent., Puerto Rico 30 per cent., Cuba 20 per cent., Panama 20 per cent., Brazil 15 per cent., Venezuela 10 per cent., United States 10 per cent., and Ecuador 5 per cent. This type is also moving in the direction of a southern Eurasian or Eurafrican appearance brought about by the dominance of the Mediterranean element and the hair-straightening effects of continuing intermarriage with the Mongoloid Amerasians.

Obviously, we can no longer restrict Israel Zangwill's "Melting Pot" to the United States. The entire New World is a melting pot in which the Old World history of continuous mixture between the three great stocks of mankind is repeating itself in a concentrated way. Indeed, the whole world is a melting pot, for men are moving and mingling as never before—and not only white men but black men, brown men and yellow men. But that is another story.

AN OUTLINE OF EXPLORATION

IN this age of swift air travel and rapid radio communication, it is hard to imagine those days of long, long ago when man knew little of the world beyond his own locality. The ancient Greeks, and many people after them, believed the world to be flat, with the ocean as its rim and the unknown parts inhabited by strange and terrifying monsters. They believed that great serpents lurked in the distant seas, ready to devour at a gulp the ship of any foolhardy mariner who ventured their way. The remote and misty lands which no-one had visited, were said to be the home of dog-headed men and other hideous creatures.

Despite such stories, the desire to trade was strong enough to overcome the fears and make explorers of the ancient peoples. The urge to sell their goods in other lands and bring back whatever riches they might find was irresistible.

The Land of Punt

It was trade in spices which sent the ancient Egyptians voyaging down the Red Sea to the Land of Punt (the modern Somaliland). Sixteen hundred years before the Birth of Christ, five trading vessels belonging to Queen Hatshepsut made the voyage, returning triumphantly after two months' absence with rich cargoes of ivory, myrrh, resin, cinnamon wood and ebony. But although the Egyptians built up a knowledge of the nearer lands and much of the Mediterranean, it was left to other nations—the Minoans, the Phœnicians and the Greeks to clear the mists and broaden the horizons of the inland sea by their trade and colonisation.

From their island base of Crete, the Minoans sailed boldly to Egypt and Italy. The Phœnicians, keener traders and more daring sailors, went from their great home ports of Tyre and Sidon to found cities in North Africa, Sicily and Southern Spain. Their ships ventured into the Atlantic and, if legend is true, as far north as Great Britain (the Cassiterides or Tin Islands). From Carthage in 450 B.C., their great sea-captain Hanno sailed through the Pillars of Hercules (Gibraltar) and then resolutely southwards, probably reaching the Gulf of Guinea before he was driven back by lack of food. It is possible that even earlier Phœnician sailors had circumnavigated Africa.

Long before this, maps had been made by both the Babylonians and Egyptians. But it was the Greeks who took the lead in map-making and geography. About 580 B.C., Anaximander of Miletus made what was probably the first map of the ancient world. And eighty years later, Hecataeus wrote his *Tour of the World.* Herodotus, "the Father of History," has left us accounts of his travels to Assuan in Egypt, through Asia Minor and to the shores of the Black Sea.

In the fourth century B.C. another Greek named Pytheas made a memorable voyage northwards, sailing from the Greek colony of Massilia (Marseilles) to Brittany and Cornwall, where he traded in tin, and thence to the North Sea and one of the Shetland Islands.

Warriors also served the cause of exploration. Xenophon, a Greek volunteer in the army of Cyrus, the rebel brother of Ataxerxes of Persia, led the Greek contingent home across Asia Minor after the defeat of Cunaxa (401 B.C.), giving a full account of the hazardous march in his *Anabasis*. Julius Cæsar's expeditions in France, Britain and Germany at a much later date (60–54 B.C.) were explorations as well as military conquests.

But pride of place as conqueror-explorer must go to Alexander the Great (356–323 B.C.), the son of King Philip of Macedon. In carving out for himself a mighty empire, he shed fresh light on south-west Asia and by his famous expedition to India showed that the Mediterranean world was in reality but a fraction of the whole. His armies marched across Persia to the Caspian, over the Hindu Kush and through the Khyber Pass to the valley of the Indus and the Punjab. Eventually forced to turn back by the weariness of his troops, Alexander chose an arduous coastal route for the return march, leaving his fleet, under Nearchus, to sail along the northern shores of the Indian Ocean, and up the Persian Gulf to Babylonia.

Some Early Geographers

His sudden illness and death brought an end to Alexander's plans for fresh conquests and explorations, and we must turn now to one of the cities he founded—Alexandria, at the mouth of the River Nile, which became a world-famous centre of learning. Its librarian for more than forty years (240–196 B.C.) was a Greek named Eratosthenes, who may justly be called " the originator of Scientific Geography." Not only did he bring together

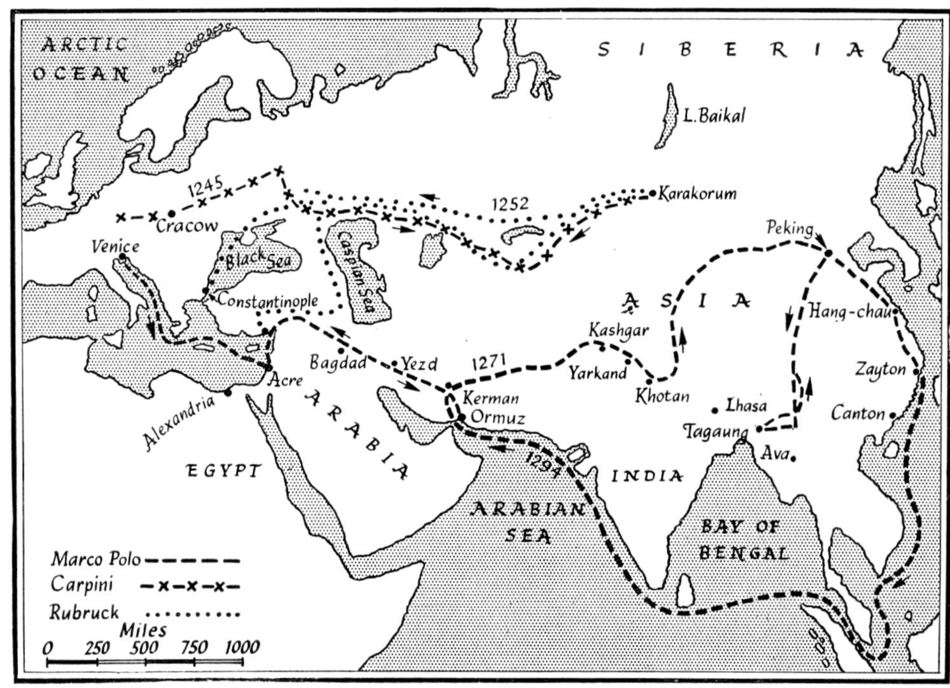

Specially drawn for this work.

EARLY EUROPEAN TRAVELLERS IN ASIA

Although large numbers of Nestorian Christian missionaries went to Asia, reaching the Malabar Coast of India as early as the sixth century, it was left to much later travellers to bring knowledge of the East to Europe. Among these was Juan de Piano de Carpini (1182–1252), also known as Friar John. Later came William de Rubruquis (1215–70), or Friar William. But most famous of all was the Venetian, Marco Polo (1254–1324).

Hulton Picture Library.

THE POLOS SET OUT FROM VENICE

This is part of a fourteenth-century manuscript of the travels of Marco Polo. It shows the Piazzetta at Venice, with the Polos embarking. In the foreground are indications of the strange lands they visited. Marco Polo was only seventeen years old when he set out with his father, Nicolo, and his uncle Maffeo. When he returned twenty-five years later, he wrote his famous account of the Court of Kublai Khan and of the many wonders he had seen.

in his library all the available books and records of voyages and travels; by solar observation and careful calculation, he arrived at a surprisingly accurate figure for the circumference of the earth. It measured, he said, 25,000 miles; which is not so very far off to-day's actual measurement of 24,902 miles. Unfortunately, his map of the world and other precious records of this famous seat of learning have been lost to us.

Another celebrated geographer of ancient times was Strabo (born *c.* 63 B.C.) who, like Herodotus, was himself a traveller. His *Geography*, a work in seventeen volumes, was a notable summary of the world of his day. Even more remarkable was Claudius Ptolemy, a Greek who was geographer, mathematician and astronomer. His eight books and twenty-six maps (the first maps to show lines of latitude and longitude) make possible a detailed reconstruction of the known world of A.D. 159. His general Map of the World was one of the most important made.

Christianity brought pilgrims and missionaries upon the scene. From the fourth century A.D. comes an unusual guide for travellers, an *Itinerary from Bordeaux to Jerusalem*, painstakingly compiled in the best Baedeker fashion by some unknown pilgrim. There was exploration of Ireland by St. Patrick (432–493), the arrival of

Hulton Picture Library.

PRINCE HENRY THE NAVIGATOR

The fourth son of King John I of Portugal and the great-grandson of King Edward III of England, he was the organiser of a whole succession of Portuguese voyages down the coast of West Africa and the inspiration of those who sought the sea route to India. He built ships, trained sailors, made many improvements in navigation, and financed expedition after expedition, so preparing the way for the great discoveries of later years.

St. Columba in the Orkney Isles (563), and the seven-year voyage of St. Brandon on an unknown sea that can only have been the Atlantic Ocean (sixth century). From this same century dates the *Christian Topography* of Cosmas, an Egyptian merchant turned monk, who travelled widely before he settled down to produce the oldest Christian maps to survive.

The Vikings

The collapse of the Roman Empire was followed by a sad decline in standards of learning. Much classical knowledge was forgotten and as one authority says, "geography and exploration were the reverse of scientific." Our story of discovery therefore moves on to the Baltic, whose grey waters were being swept by the black-sailed "long dragons" of the Vikings or Northmen. It was they who discovered Iceland (861) and Greenland (985) and in the year 1000 reached the coast of North America which Lief, their leader, called Vin-land. But Viking attempts to colonise the wooded shores of what may well have been Newfoundland and Labrador were unsuccessful, and thus it was left to Columbus to rediscover the great continent 500 years later.

The Brave Friars

The Christian world knew little or nothing of the eastward journeys of Arab travellers, but alarm at the expansion of the Mongol Empire reawakened interest in the East and led the Pope to send an envoy to the Great Khan of the Mongols. The man chosen for this perilous mission was a Franciscan named Carpini, or Friar John, and in 1245 he set off eastwards with Brothers Benedict and Stephen and after more than a year's hard travel reached the Khan's splendid encampment at Karakorum. With no more than a letter to offer the Mongol ruler, the travellers were hardly welcome. After some delay, they were given a reply and summarily told to be on their way.

A few years later another friar was sent to the Great Khan, on this occasion with letters from the King of France inviting the Khan to become a Christian, an invitation which the friar (William de Rubruquis, or William Rubruck) duly delivered, only to discover that the Khan was far more interested in finding out whether France might be conquered easily!

Stronger than any fear of the Mongols was the desire of certain Venetian merchants to build up trade with the East. Among them were the brothers Polo, Maffeo and Nicolo, who made the long journey overland to the court of Kublai at Peking, returning to Venice after an absence of fifteen years. In 1271 they set off again for China, but this time they were accompanied by Nicolo's son, the famous Marco Polo, and two friars. From Venice they sailed to the Holy Land and travelling by way of Jerusalem, Ormuz (on the Persian Gulf) and the Gobi Desert, they at length reached Peking. Not until twenty-five years had passed did they see Venice again, and then their old friends found it hard to believe that they were indeed the Polos. Stranger still were the tales told by the long-absent travellers —of stones that burned (coal), of water that could be set alight (petroleum), of strange animals (rhinoceros and alligator). But the descriptions given by the Polos were, for the most part, quite correct.

One of the last great travellers of medieval times was an Arab named Ibn Batuta, who from 1324 (the year of Marco Polo's death) until 1348 travelled extensively in Asia and, on his return, wrote an account of all he had seen. But it was not until centuries later, when his writings came into French hands, that his remarkable travels became generally known. Instead of the accuracy of Ibn Batuta, the world had to be content with the fantastic fiction of Sir John Mandeville, who

Hulton Picture Library.

THE STUDY OF A SIXTEENTH-CENTURY NAVIGATOR

With his instruments, charts, tables and terrestial globe to hand, this wise old navigator plans some new voyage of exploration. By this time navigation was becoming a science. The days were long since past when sailors hugged the coast and relied upon recognised landmarks. Sheepskin charts and a simple compass had been used in the Mediterranean since about 1200; and by the fifteenth century, the cross-staff was the accepted means of measuring the angle of the Pole Star with the horizon and thus determining the latitude of the ship.

used his imagination to cover up his ignorance.

Medieval Maps

One of the most interesting maps of the period is to be seen in the British Museum. It is the Cottoniana, or Anglo-Saxon map, which was probably the work of an Irish monk about A.D. 990. Its distortions are many, at one point it carries the quaint warning "Here lions abound," and, like all the maps of its period, it places Jerusalem in a central position. But, with all its oddities and shortcomings, it shows a remarkable degree of knowledge.

With the Hereford Mappa Mundi of 1280, pictorial geography begins to come into its own. The work of Richard of Haldingham, this large map of the world is embellished with representations of the Crucifixion, the Last Judgment, Adam and Eve, and no end of strange humans and animals.

Of considerable importance were the *Portulano*, a map of the Mediterranean and surrounding countries compiled in Catalonia between 1266 and 1291, and the *Portolani*, or Compass Charts of the Venetians. These were the first maps to be made with the aid of the compass, which had been brought to the Mediterranean by the Arabs, probably from the Chinese. Such accurate maps, improved and added to, played their part in the voyages of the Great Age of Discovery.

Prince Henry the Navigator

It was at Sagres, in the early fifteenth century, that Prince Henry of Portugal (1394–1460) built his famous naval arsenal, turned to the study of astronomy and mathematics, built ships and trained his sailors in the art of navigation. The outcome was not only the establishment of a Portuguese colonial empire, but an inspiration of explorers and mariners that long outlived the prince. Although he died before his greatest dream (finding the sea route to India) could be realised, Portuguese ships ventured for some 2,000 miles down the West African coast in his lifetime—the prelude to a succession of voyages and discoveries which have not been equalled to this day.

In 1484 Diego Cam discovered the mouth of the River Congo. Two years later, Bartholomew Diaz rounded the Cape of Storms (Good Hope), reaching Algoa Bay and the Great Fish River before his discontented crew forced him to turn, and thus pointed the way for Vasco da Gama, who in 1497 sailed the Cape route to the long-sought goal of India. In July of that year he set out from Lisbon with four small ships, doubling the Cape in tempestuous seas to make safe anchorage off a new coast on Christmas Day, 1498. To honour the day, Vasco called this territory Natal, a name which it still bears. After voyaging some way up the east coast of Africa, he made the crossing of the Arabian Sea and on May 21st, 1498, dropped anchor in the Indian port of Calicut. The sea way to India had been found. His achievements brought honour and riches to Vasco da Gama, who was given the proud titles of "Admiral of the Indies" and "Viceroy of India."

Columbus discovers the New World

Some years before this a Genoese navigator had made a voyage that was to become the most famous of all. His name was Christopher Columbus, and his discovery of the New World of the Americas in 1492 was to open a new period of exploration and expansion.

His voyages sprang from that familiar impulse of the times—the urge to find new sea routes to India. Columbus was convinced that such a route could be found to the *west* across the "Sea of Darkness." The Portuguese were not impressed by his theories, so he turned to Spain where he won the support of King Ferdinand and Queen Isabella.

On August 3rd, 1492, the newly-created "Admiral of the Ocean Sea" set out with three small ships from Palos, and six days later arrived at the Canary Islands, where the final preparations were to be made. On September 6th, the three ships (*Santa Maria*, *Pinta* and *Niña*) set course for the west. Day after day they sailed on.

ACROSS UNKNOWN SEAS

About five hundred years before Columbus made his first voyage, the Vikings or Northmen sailed across the Atlantic in their "long dragons" to the coast of North America, called Vin-land by Lief Erikson their leader. This was not a single bold voyage, however, but a stage-by-stage advance by way of the Faroes, Iceland and Greenland. No lasting results, however, came from their brief contact with the New World.

Illustrations : Hulton Picture Library.

In 1519 Ferdinand Magellan sailed from Seville with five small ships to search for a passage to the Southern Ocean and a westwards route to the Spice Islands. A ship was lost and a mutiny suppressed before he navigated the straits named after him, and it took him five weeks to pass through the storm-racked waters into the calm of the Pacific.

Hulton Picture Library.

THE MEETING OF CORTÉS AND MONTEZUMA

Hernando Cortés, the conqueror of Mexico, was one of the *conquistadores* who ruthlessly carved out an empire for Spain in the New World. The picture shows his first meeting with Montezuma II, the Aztec emperor, who believed the Spaniard to be a messenger of the gods and welcomed him with gifts, while Cortés in return presented him with a chain of coloured crystal—a strangely peaceful prelude to events that culminated in the death of Montezuma and the destruction of his empire.

Would their food last? Would they ever set eyes on land again? Columbus confidently laughed away such fears.

Then, in the second week of October, their spirits were raised by unmistakable signs that land was near—branches and vegetation floating in the water, birds that must have come from the shore they were seeking, a piece of wood that seemed to have been shaped and smoothed by man.

On October 12th they anchored off an island, which Columbus named San Salvador (the present Watling Island in the Bahamas) and whose natives he called *Indians*, for he was still convinced that he had reached "the Indian Sea." After visiting Cuba (which Columbus thought to be part of Japan or China) and other islands, he set course for home, reaching Spain on March 15th, 1493.

Columbus made three more voyages to his New World for Ferdinand and Isabella. He died, ill and poverty-stricken, after his last return in 1504 without even leaving his name to the lands he had revealed. The New World was named America, after Amerigo Vespucci (1451–1512), the Florentine explorer of the American coast to whom we owe the name Venezuela ("Little Venice") and who first realised that these lands were not part of Asia, but a new continent.

The Portuguese and the Spice Islands

It was westwards that Pedro Alvarez Cabral (*c.* 1467–*c.* 1520) sailed in 1500 with a powerful fleet to carve out for his royal master, the King of Portugal, an empire in Asia. He landed in Brazil, but not realising the importance of his discovery, took ship again to the Cape of Good Hope and Calicut, where he established a

MAPS OF YESTERDAY

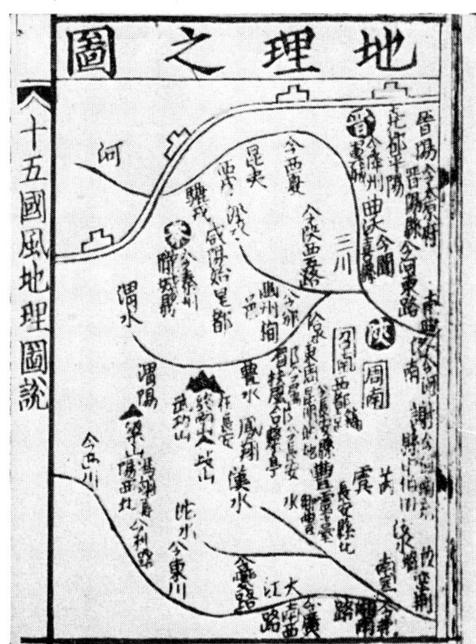

British Museum *Copyright*

The lower part of the clay tablet (*top left*) is a Babylonian map of the world of the seventh century B.C. The oldest map in the world, it is probably a copy of a much older tablet, for its text describes the campaigns of Sargon of Akkad, who reigned about 2300 B.C. The broad band running north to south is the river Euphrates, Babylon itself being the strip running across the river. Other details, such as the mountains at the source, and the swamps at the mouth of the Euphrates, are also shown. The oldest printed map in the world (*top right*) shows Western China and comes from the *Liu Ching T'u* of about A.D. 1130. The heading means " Geographical Map "; the words down the left side, " Description of the Places and Customs of the Fifteen Provinces." Running along the top of the map is the Great Wall of China. The upper river is the Yellow River; the lower, the Yangtze. Mountains are indicated by black symbols. The names of provinces are printed white on black. The Chinese sailing chart (*below*) was made about A.D. 1420. At the top of the chart is the western coast of India; at the bottom, the coast of Arabia and Africa. Sailing directions, including the compass points to be used, are marked alongside the tracks crossing the Indian Ocean.

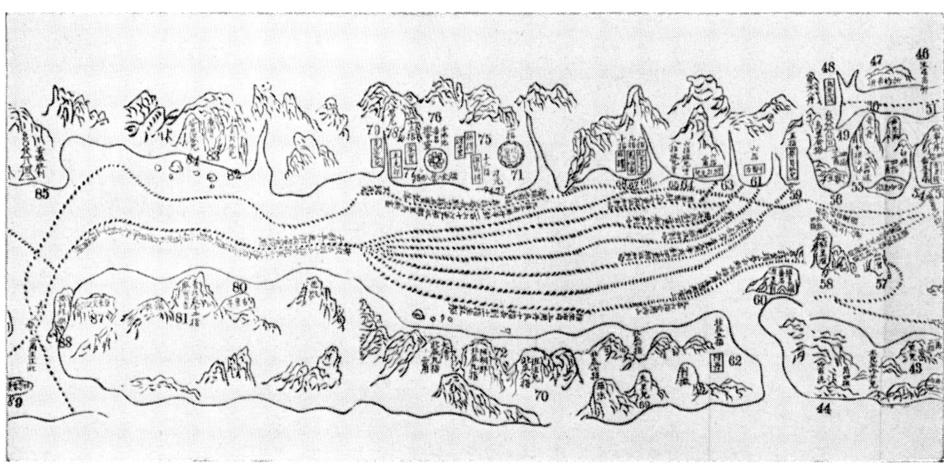

Copyright

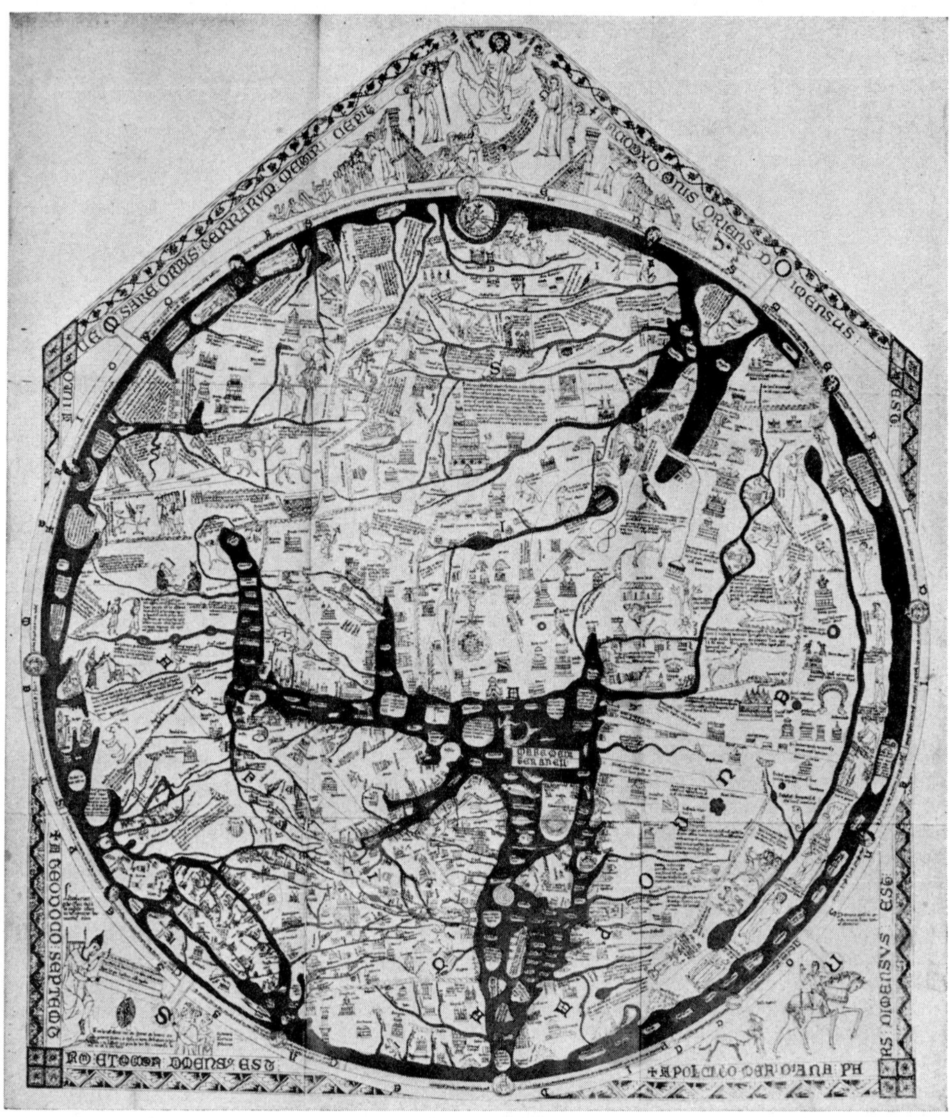

Radio Times/Hulton Picture Library

This is the Hereford Mappa Mundi of 1280, which was drawn by Richard de Haldingham and Lafford, sometime Prebendary of Lincoln and later (1305) Prebendary of Hereford. Jerusalem forms the centre of the map (the Crucifixion is depicted above the circular representation of the city). The design at the top of the map represents the Last Judgment, with the good on one side and the evil-doers on the other. The deep, double indentation (*top right*) is the Red Sea. The British Isles are shown out of all proportion to the rest of Europe (*bottom left*). This map, which may have been copied from one by Henry of Mainz, marks the beginning of medieval pictorial geography. The original is preserved in the Chapter House Library of Hereford Cathedral.

This delightful map is part of the world-map drawn by Fra Mauro about 1460. His ideas of the Far East were based upon the exploits of Marco Polo and he has obviously been inspired by that explorer's description of the palaces of the Great Khan: "wondrously beautiful and marvellously decorated." He draws them accordingly, but after the architectural styles of the Venetian Renaissance. Shown centrally in our illustration is "the Imperial City of Chambalech." Fra Mauro's map is the earliest on which "Chipangu" (the modern Japan) is named. Chambalech was the capital of the Great Khan. Its name was derived from *Khan-baliq* (City of the Khan) which was the Mongol name for the capital. Chambalech is known to us now as Peking. The Khan in Marco Polo's time was the famous Kublai (1216–94) the subject, many centuries later, of Coleridge's fragmentary dream-poem.

British Museum

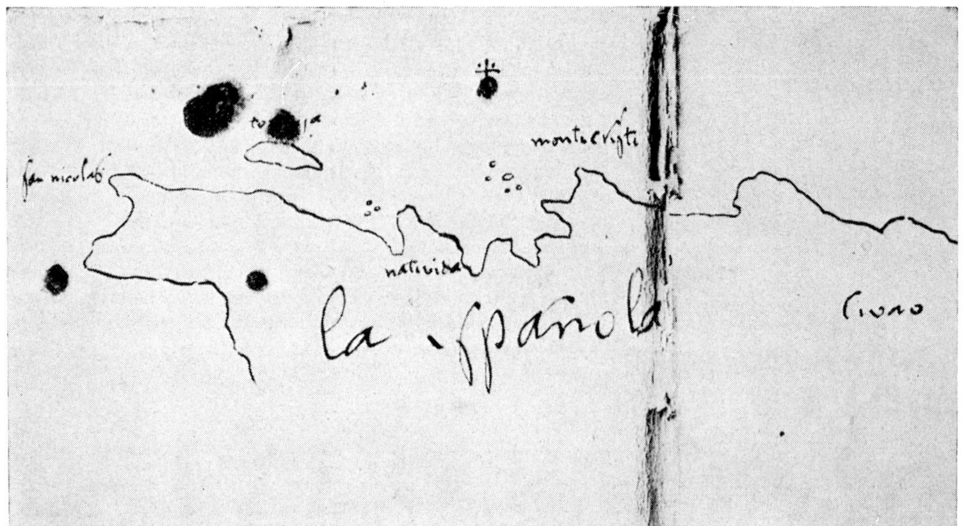

British Museum

British Museum

The upper illustration is indeed the work of an explorer. A sketch of north-eastern Hispaniola, it was drawn by Columbus during his voyage of 1492–93 and bears his cypher. His ship, the *Santa Maria,* struck a reef during this voyage and its timbers were used in the building of Natividad, the first European settlement in the Americas. The lower illustration shows the *Santa Maria* in the Bahamas in 1492 and was published, with other woodcuts, in the first edition of Columbus' letter to the Treasurer of Aragon reporting his great discoveries. The islands here depicted were named by him and include Hispaniola and his first landfall, San Salvador (Watling Island).

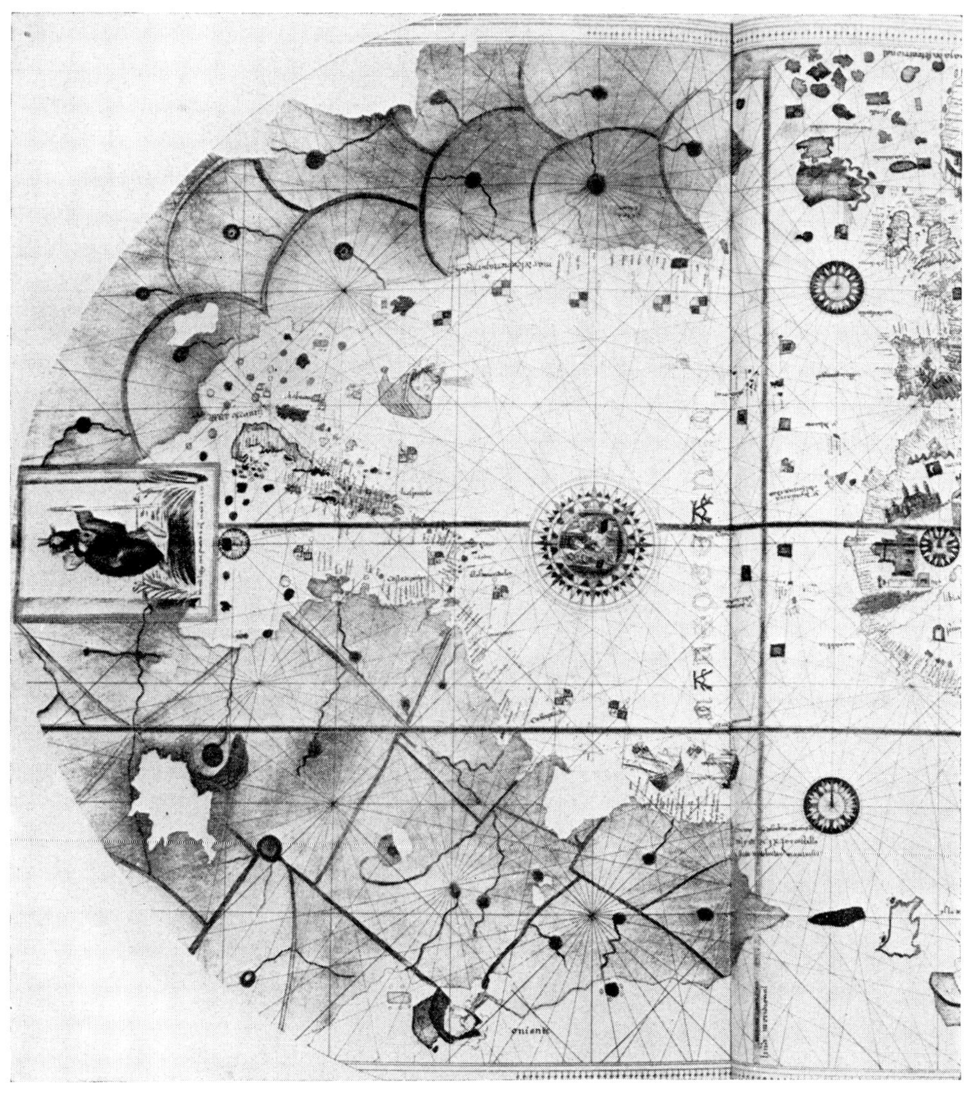

British Museum

One of the shrewdest of Columbus' pilots was Juan de la Cosa, the owner and commander of the *Santa Maria*. This celebrated map-maker made several later voyages to the New World. His world-map, of which this is the western part, was drawn in 1500 and shows both North and South America, divided only by a representation of St. Christopher at a point where Columbus sought a strait (1502–03). The Central and South American parts of the map are to a larger scale, since it was desired apparently to give emphasis to this region of the New World. Cuba is shown as an island, although it was not circumnavigated until 1508—which suggests that the map was revised or completed about this time. The presence of the English flag on the northern coast shows that de la Cosa was well aware of the Cabot discoveries. Drawn for Ferdinand and Isabella of Spain, this world map was kept a secret from Spain's rivals in trade and exploration.

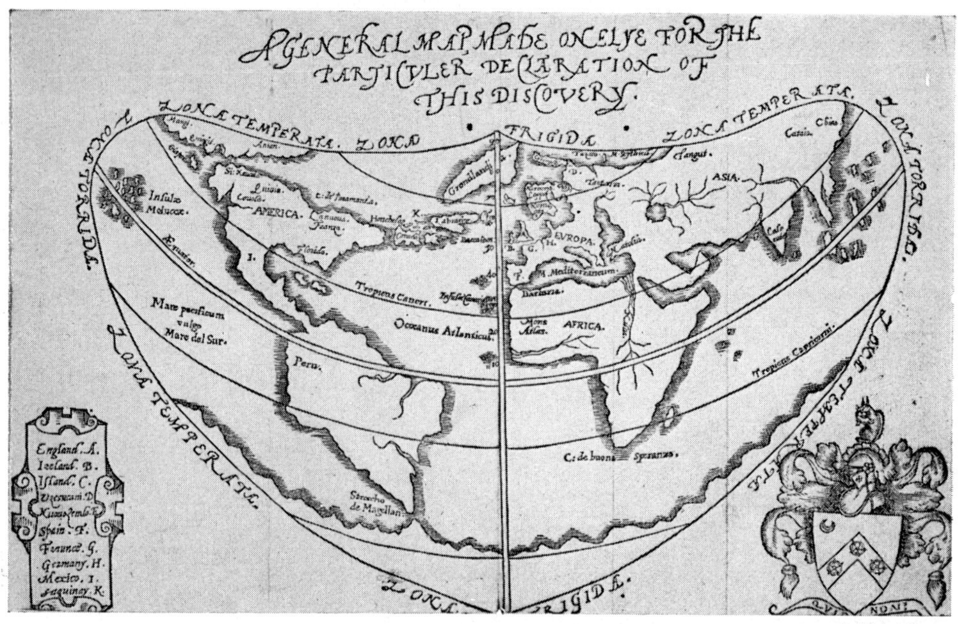

British Museum

The maps on this page illustrate the search for the North-West Passage. Sir Humphrey Gilbert's map (*above*) was published in 1576 and envisages a comfortably short north-west route to the Moluccas, or Spice Islands, through temperate latitudes. By contrast the Cape and Magellan Strait routes appear the much longer and arduous.

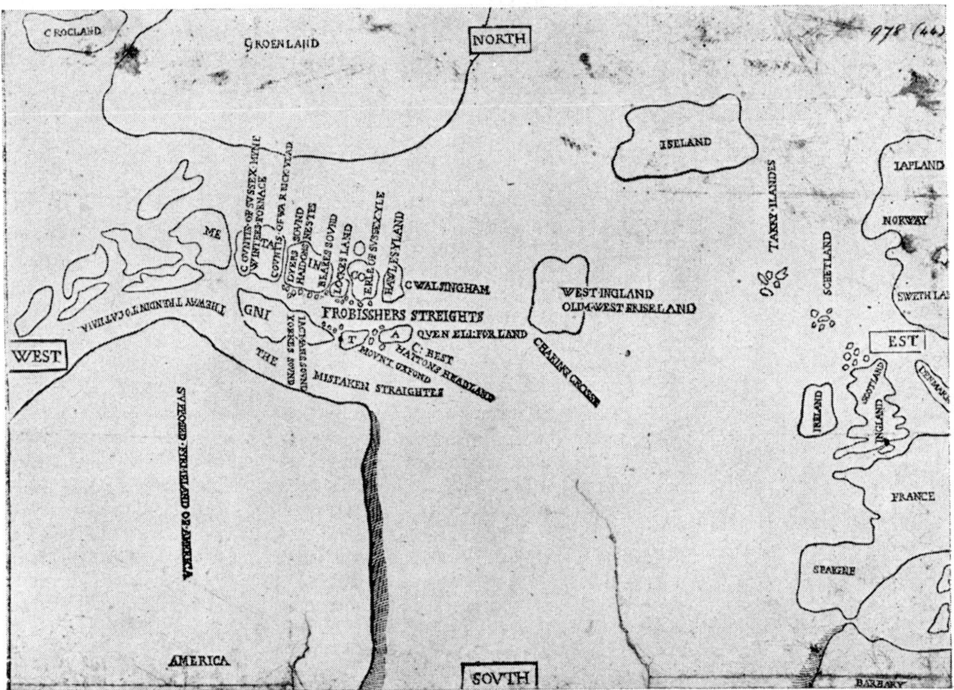

British Museum

This chart illustrates the voyages of Martin Frobisher in 1576–78 and shows the routes which, he thought, opened " the way trendin to Cathaia." The coast of Baffin Land is drawn as an archipelago named " Meta Incognita " (the Unknown Shore). The " Mistaken Straightes " are really Hudson Strait, which Frobisher penetrated in 1578, during his third voyage.

Essex Record Office

This is the south-west corner the MS map of Essex made in 1594 by the celebrated English topographer, John Norden the elder (1548–1625) and intended for presentation to Lord Burghley. It was discovered quite recently and is considered to be a mature example of his cartographic technique. The borders of the map are graduated in a 2-mile scale, lettered at the sides and numbered along the top and bottom, so that map references can be given to places listed in the accompanying " Description." John Norden was among the greatest of the early English map-makers and was responsible for many original improvements in county mapping. His fame rests securely on his *Speculuæ Britanniæ*, the series of county " Descriptions " and maps, some parts of which have unfortunately been lost to us.

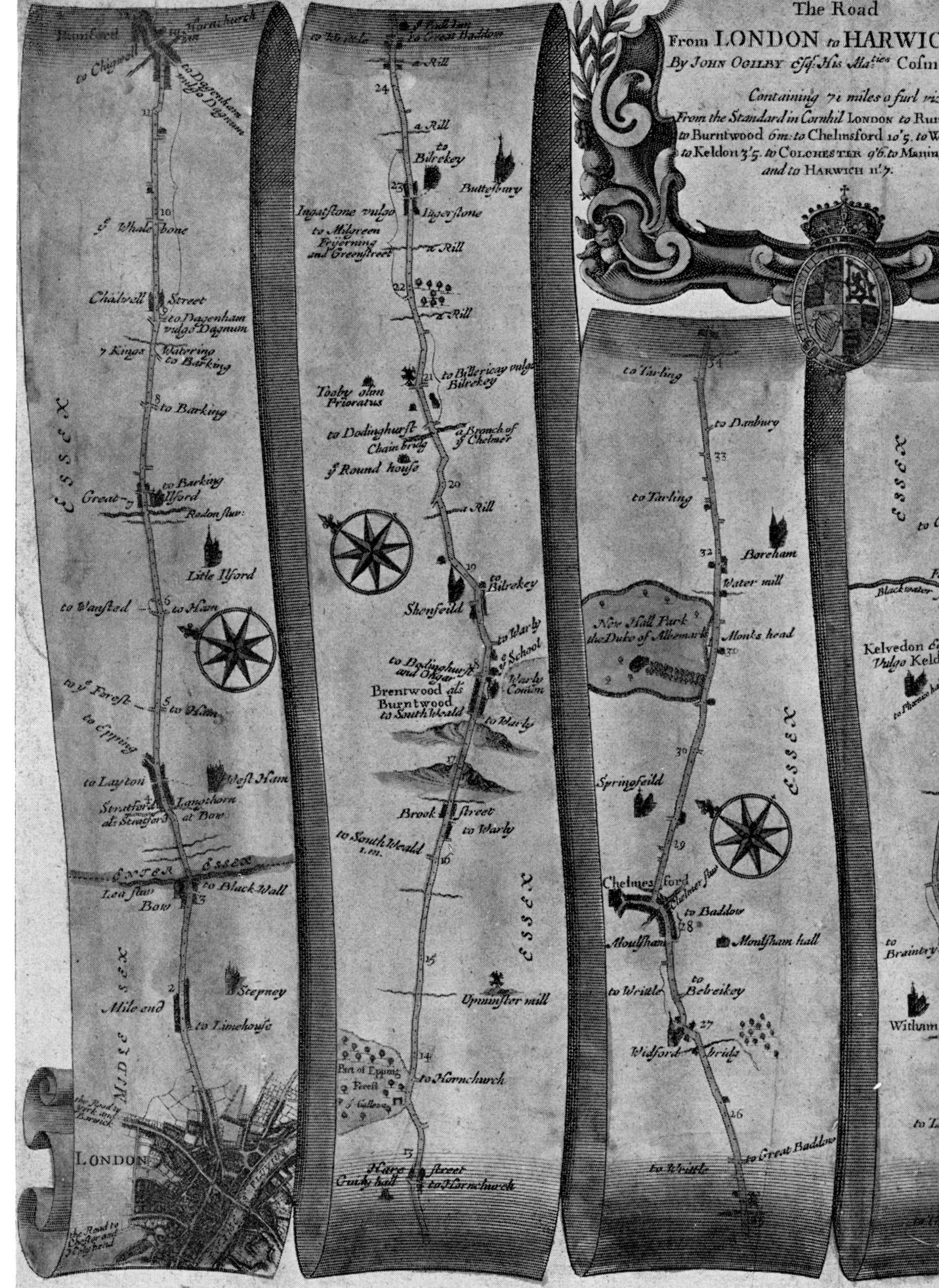

The Road
From LONDON to HARWIC
By JOHN OGILBY Esq. His Ma.ties Cosm
Containing 71 miles 0 furl viz
From the Standard in Cornhil LONDON to Rum
to Burntwood 6m: to Chelmsford 10'5. to W
to Keldon 3'5. to COLCHESTER 9'6. to Maning
and to HARWICH 11'7.
Rumford
Hornchurch
to Chigwell
to Dagenham vulgo Dagnum
Whale bone
Chalwell Street
to Dagenham vulgo Dagnum
7 Kings Watering
to Barking
to Barking
to Barking
Great Ilford
Rodon fluv:
Litle Ilsford
to Wansted
to Ham
to ye Forest
to Ham
to Epping
to Layton
West Ham
Stratford Langthorn
als Stratford at Bow
ENTER ESSEX
Lea fluv
Bow
to Black-Wall
Stepney
Mile end
to Limehouse
MIDDLESEX
LONDON
ESSEX
to Great Baddow
Rill
Rill
to Bilrekey
Buttesbury
Ingatstone vulgo Ingerstone
to Milgreen Frijerning and Greenstreet
Rill
Rill
to Billericay vulgo Bilrekey
Tooby olim Prioratus
to Dodinghurst
a Branch of ye Chelmer
Chain brig
ye Round house
Rill
to Bilrekey
Shenfeild
to Warly
ye School
to Dodinghurst and Ongar
Brentwood als Burntwood
to South Weald
Warly Comon
to Warly
Brook street
to Warly
to South Weald
Upminster mill
Part of Epping Forest
to Hornchurch
Hare street
Guidy hall
to Hornchurch
ESSEX
to Tarling
to Danbury
to Tarling
Boreham
Water mill
New Hall Park the Duke of Albemarle
Monks head
Springfeild
Chelmesford
Chelmer fluv
to Baddow
Moulsham
Moulsham hall
to Writtle
to Bebreikey
Widford Bridg
to Writtle
to Great Baddow
ESSEX
Blackwater
Kelvedon &c Vulgo Keld
to Braintry
Witham

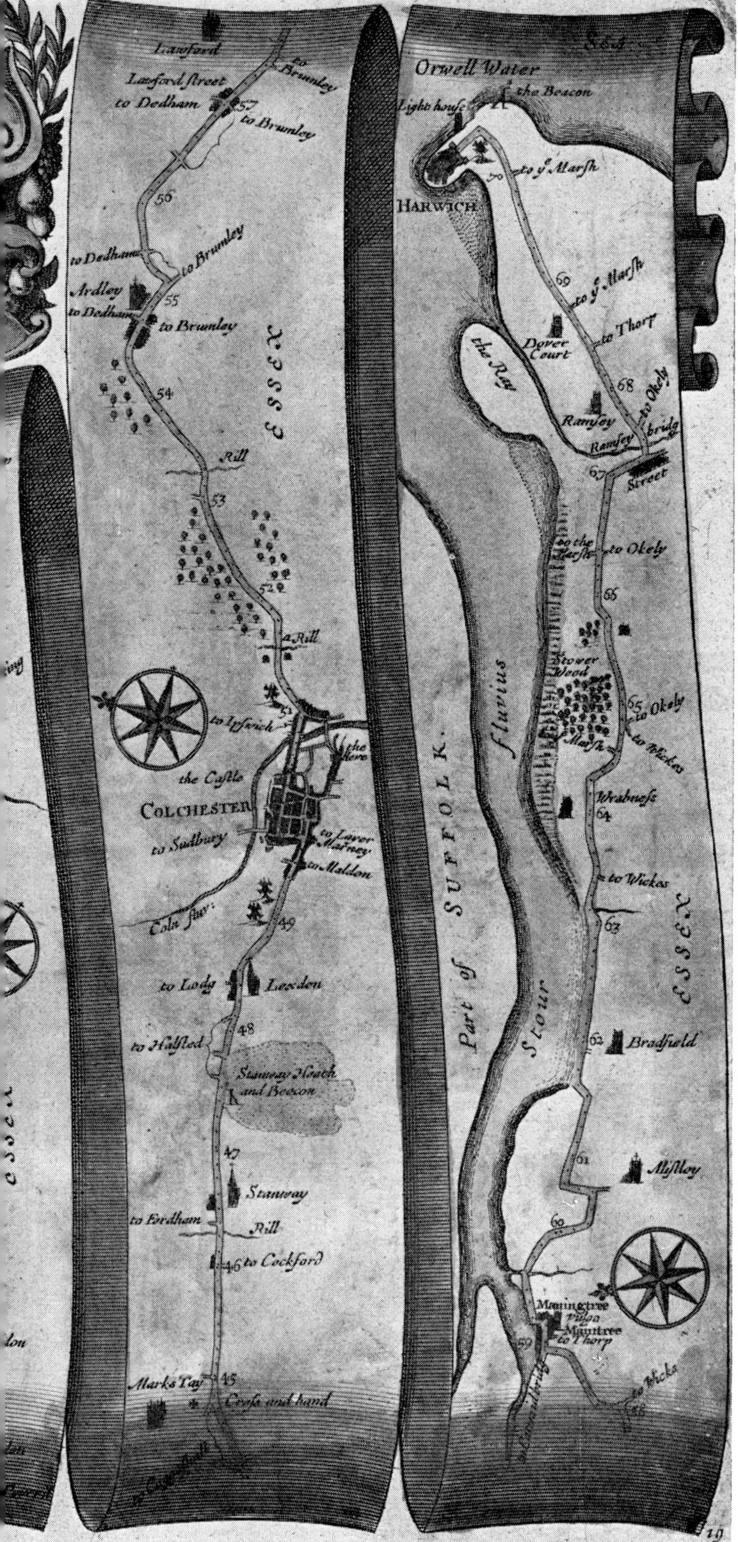

Essex Record Office

Norden's maps are the earliest printed maps of England to show roads and to provide a graduated marginal scale for reference. John Ogilby (1600–76) went a step further in meeting the shortcomings of earlier maps. He showed not only where places were, but how they might best be reached. This "ribbon" map is typical of those which he printed and published as "His Majesty's Cosmographer" at his house in Whitefriars, London. It shows the 71 miles of main road from London to Harwich *via* Colchester and was one of a series, based on his perambulations of the roads (*c.* 1671–75), which Ogilby published in his ***Britannia**, Volume the First: or an Illustration of the Kingdom of England and the Dominion of Wales: by a . . . Description of the Principal Roads thereof*, 1675. On the title-page Ogilby describes himself as "His Majesty's Cosmographer and Master of His Majesty's Revels in the Kingdom of Ireland." His survey was the first to be made of British roads. It is in Ogilby's strip-maps that the statute mile of 1,760 yards takes the place of the old British mile of 2,428 yards. Ogilby's other works include a plan of London, made for the city corporation after the Great Fire of 1666 and published by his partner William Morgan in 1677, and several completed volumes of his ambitious *Geographical Description of the Whole World.*

coste of her egipte
cost of affrik
the sey mediterrany
coste of Joude
cecill
Italy
The sey callit pontus euxinus

British Museum

To further his plans to make England a leading maritime power, Henry VIII employed many foreigners, among them John Rotz (Jehan Roze), whom he appointed Hydrographer Royal. As "sarvant to the Kingis most excellent Majeste," Rotz published in 1542 a "Book of Hydrography" which he dedicated to his royal master. The work is in English on vellum and contains instructions on the use of the compass, elevation of the pole, latitude, etc., and a number of charts with richly illuminated borders and lavish ornamentation in gold and colours. The chart here reproduced shows the Black Sea, Mediterranean and coasts of Europe, with the North Sea and the Baltic. Great Britain is clearly shown (bottom right). It was once thought that Rotz was a Fleming who came to England in the entourage of Anne of Cleves, but it now seems certain that he was a Frenchman from Dieppe; indeed, his "Book of Hydrography" contains a long explanation of why he did not dedicate the work to his lawful sovereign, the King of France. Apparently he worked in England for a number of years, only under compulsion. A further point of interest arises from his representation of Australia as "Terre de Java." Australia is similarly shown in the Dieppe world maps, and some scholars consider this evidence that the French (or more probably the Portuguese) knew something of the eastern and western shores of the island continent even at this early date (*c.* 1536).

British Museum

On this page, and the page opposite, is reproduced a manuscript map of the New World drawn about the year 1535. Fifteen years previously Magellan had sailed through his Strait and so revealed the westward route to the South Pacific. His voyage also showed that the westward route to Asia, the discovery of which had been the prime purpose of earlier endeavours was much longer than anyone had imagined. Even so, it was still thought possible to reconcile the Asia of Ptolemy with what had been discovered of the Americas.

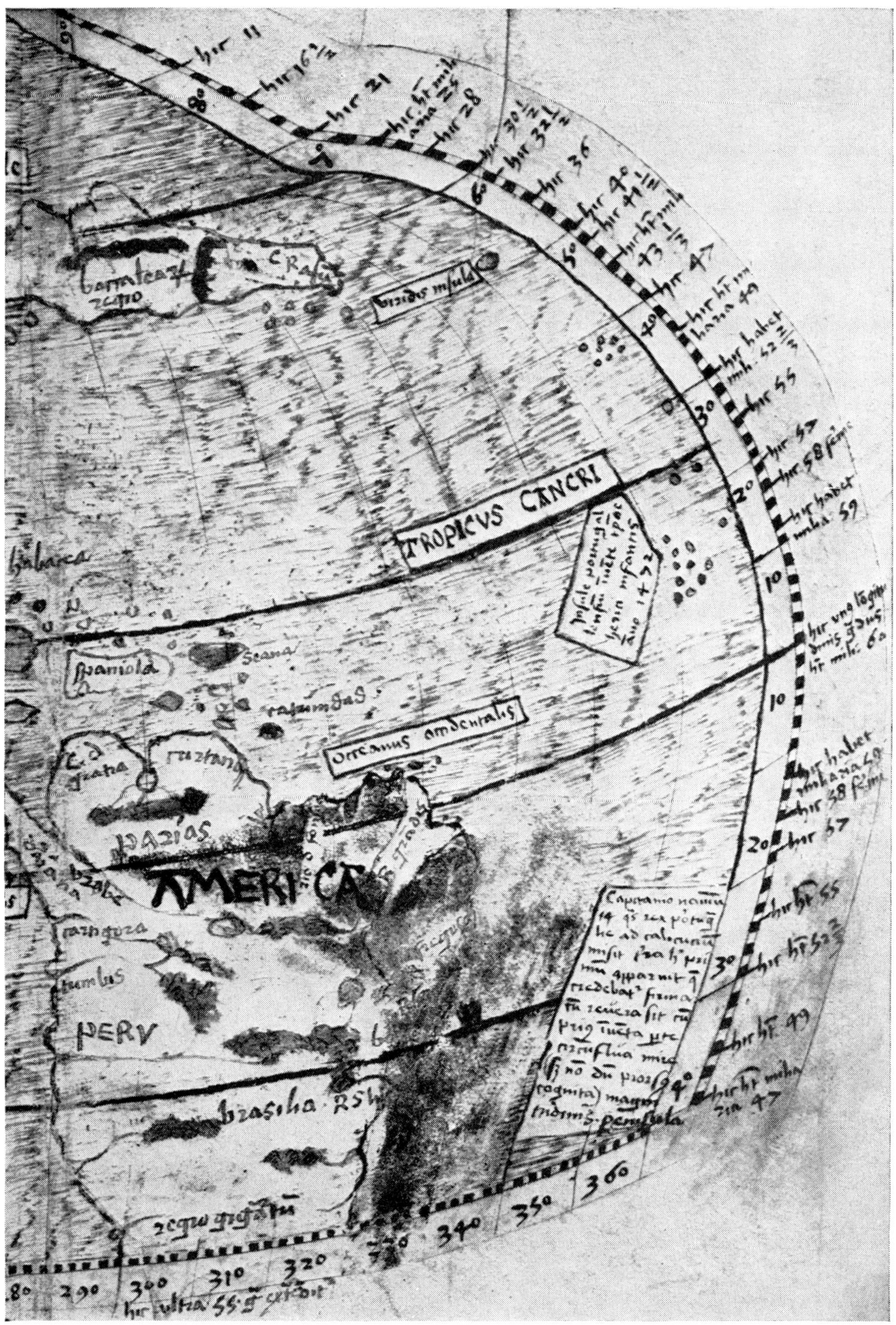

British Museum

So we find that while the map gives a reasonable representation of the American continent, it shows the Spice Islands ten degrees west of the Mexican coast. Ciamba, Thebet and other Ptolemaic names have been added subsequently, in darker ink, on the mainland of North America. Like his contemporaries, the cartographer has followed the fashion set by Waldseemüller in 1507 and given the name America to South America exclusively. The first map-maker to apply the name to both North and South America was Mercator in his world-map of 1538.

The maps on this page, and the page opposite, illustrate the opening of the sea-way to the East by the Portuguese. Running across the top of both pages is an intriguing view of Goa, published in the city-atlas *Civitates Orbis Terrarum* in 1573. This splendid collection of plans and views was the work of two Flemings, G. Braun and F. Hogenberg. Goa, which was taken by the Viceroy Afonso de Albuquerque in 1510, became the principal Portuguese colony in the East and enjoyed special privileges. The world map of Henricus Martellus (below) was drawn about thirty years before this, *i.e.*, shortly after the triumphant return of Bartholomew Diaz from his voyage round the Cape of Good Hope to the Great Fish River. The names on the map mark the limits of Portuguese exploration at this time. The Indian Ocean is no longer shown as landlocked, but the representation of southern Asia is still based upon Ptolemy's maps and geography. The first atlas of the whole world to be published after that of Ptolemy was the *Theatrum Orbis Terrarum* which appeared in 1570. It was the work of Abraham Ortelius of Antwerp (1527–98) and contained seventy maps (some by Ortelius himself) engraved by F. Hogenberg. It enjoyed instant success and was followed by many enlarged editions in a variety of languages.

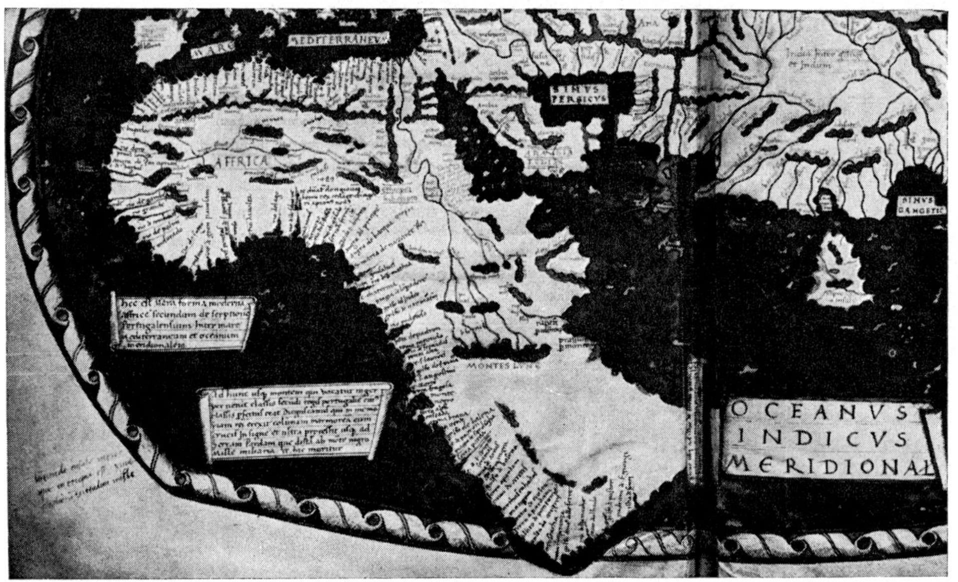

British Museum

British Museum

Goa (above) was the capital of a Portuguese commercial empire of well-defended posts and factories on the trade routes of the Indian Ocean, and is still the largest and most important part of Portuguese India, despite the claims laid to this territory by the Union of India. Portugal did her best to keep her new-found lands a closely-guarded secret and this is probably why comparatively few early original maps of the Portuguese discoveries have come down to us. The woodcut reproduced below is from the title-page of a collection of voyages published in Venice in 1507. It is of special interest because it is the first separate map of the continent of Africa.

British Museum

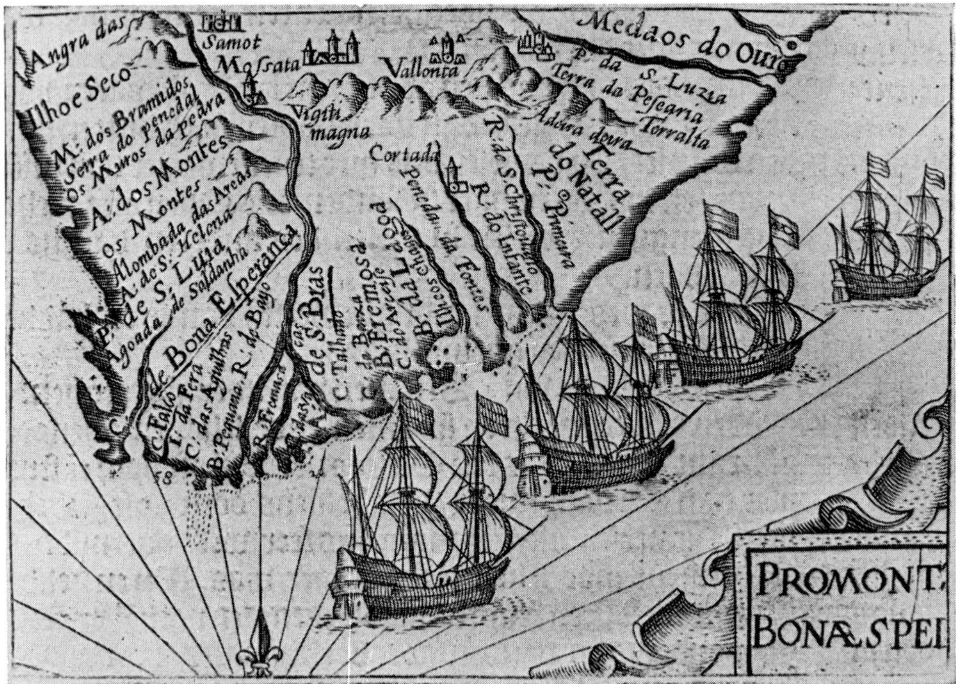

British Museum

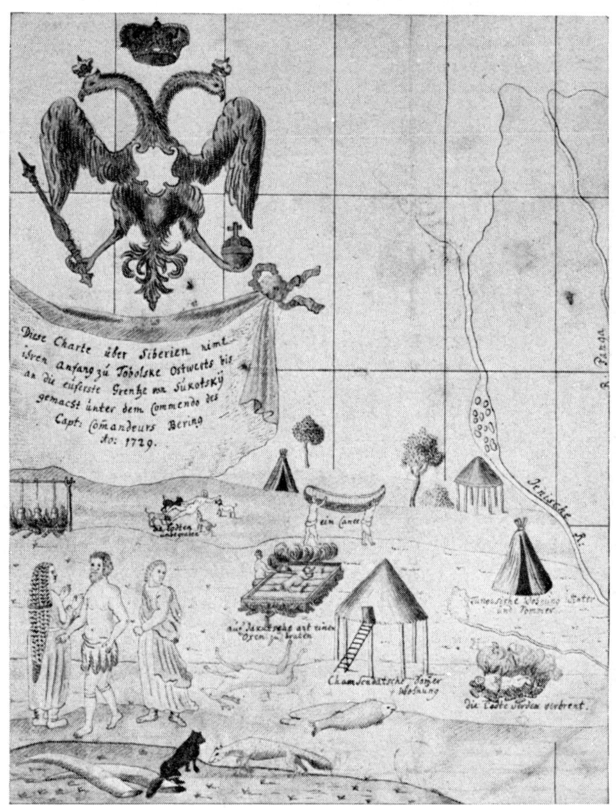

British Museum

For the layman, one of the most attractive features of the maps and atlases of yesterday is their decoration. More than a century separates the two examples given on this page. At the top is a representation of the first passage of the Cape of Good Hope by Dutch ships under the command of Cornelis Houtman (1596). Below is part of a map of Siberia "made by order of Captain Commander Bering Ao: 1729" and recording the customs of certain Siberian tribes. This map is now in King George III's collection in the British Museum.

trading depot. This was his nearest approach to founding an empire, but his adventures were enough to inspire other Portuguese expeditions (1502), which left forts and trading posts in their wake as far afield as Ceylon and Malacca. The fall of Malacca to Alphonso d'Albuquerque, the conqueror of Goa and Viceroy of India, in 1511 gave the Portuguese the key to the fabulous Spice Islands (the Moluccas).

Meanwhile news of Columbus' first voyage and the constant lure of the spice countries had touched off an expedition from the English port of Bristol. Bearing the commission of King Henry VII, a Genoese sailor named John Cabot and his son Sebastian set sail westwards in 1497; their goal was Cathay (China), but their achievement was the discovery of Newfoundland, later claimed for Queen Elizabeth I by Sir Humphrey Gilbert (1583).

Six years after Vasco Nuñez de Balboa, the Spanish venturer, stood " silent upon a peak in Darien " to gaze down upon the Pacific Ocean as it lapped the isthmus of Panama (1513), there began an epic voyage, the memorable first circumnavigation of the world. Its leader was Ferdinand Magellan (*c.* 1480–1521), a Portuguese navigator who saw Balboa's great " Southern Ocean " as the route to the Spice Islands.

An experienced navigator, he enlisted the support of King Charles V of Spain, and in 1519 sailed from Seville with five small ships. Storm and mutiny characterised his crossing of the Atlantic and the southwards search for a passage to the Southern Ocean. The way was found in October, 1520, when Magellan passed through the Straits that bear his name, seeing on the southern shore the fires of so many native villages that he called the land " Tierra del Fuego " (Land of Fire). The new ocean that he sailed was so calm that he called it the " Pacific."

His fleet was now reduced to three ships, and shortly after they had left the Philippines, one of these was found to be so leaky that she had to be burned. Only one completed the voyage round the world—the *Victoria*, which safely reached Seville in September, 1522. Magellan himself did not see the end of the expedition; he had been mortally wounded by a poisoned arrow in the Philippines. Not until some fifty-three years had passed was the Pacific crossed again, on this occasion by Sir Francis Drake (*c.* 1540–96), the first Englishman to sail round the world in a single voyage (1577–80).

In the wake of the navigators came the conquerors and land explorers. Mexico was conquered by Hernando Cortés, the Spanish adventurer (1519); another Spaniard, Francisco Pizarro, the erstwhile companion of Balboa, discovered and conquered Peru (1531); yet another, Francisco de Orellana, became the first European to travel down the great river Amazon. Far away to the north Jacques Cartier explored the Gulf of St. Lawrence (1534–35) so pointing the way to French settlement of this part of Canada.

The Northern Route

The riches of the East still beckoned compellingly, especially to the merchants of England, who found themselves late in the race for new trade routes. Surely, they reasoned, there was some convenient northern route to India and the Spice Islands? And in 1553, three small vessels under Sir Hugh Willoughby and Richard Chancellor slipped down the Thames bound for the North Cape and whatever lay beyond. Willoughby reached Nova Zembla (Novaya Zemlya) and met his end in the cold north; Chancellor won through to Archangel and visited Moscow. But though a profitable trade was established with Russia, the Far East was as remote as ever—and remained so, despite Anthony Jenkinson's attempt to find an overland route (which took him to Bokhara in 1558).

Was there, then, a North-West Passage? Sir Martin Frobisher believed so and made three voyages (1576–79) in vain efforts to seek it. The three voyages of John Davis (1585–87) were made with the same purpose, and failed.

Now the Dutch took a hand. William

In 1595, some years after his unsuccessful attempts to establish a colony in Virginia, Sir Walter Raleigh sailed on a voyage to Trinidad and the Orinoco. During this expedition he attacked and burned the city of San Joseph in Trinidad. This picture showing the Spanish governor being led to the English boats comes from the de Bry collection and was published in 1599.

Illustrations : Hulton Picture Library.

Samuel de Champlain (1567–1635) was one of the greatest pioneers of French rule in Canada and the hero of many voyages and journeys of exploration. He founded the city of Quebec (1608) and, after establishing friendly relations with the Huron and Algonquin Indians, defeated the savage Iroquois at Ticonderoga (1609). This contemporary drawing shows de Champlain leading the attack on the Iroquois stockade.

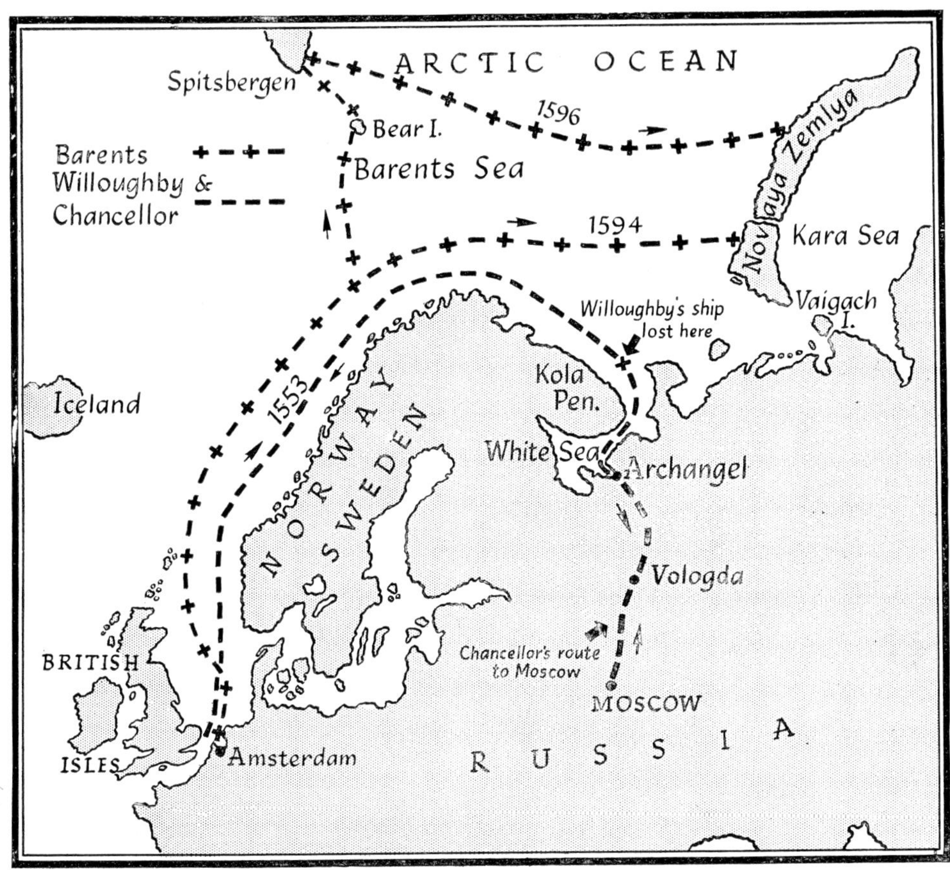

Specially drawn for this work.

SEEKING THE NORTH-EAST PASSAGE

Many attempts were made to find a North-East Passage from Europe to the riches of the Orient. Early voyages included the expedition of Sir Hugh Willoughby and Richard Chancellor. Poor Willoughby died of starvation and cold, but Chancellor won through to Moscow. Barents was the chief pilot of an expedition sponsored by the merchants of Amsterdam which discovered Spitsbergen and reached Novaya Zemlya.

Barents sailed northwards, discovering and circumnavigating Spitsbergen (1596), crossing the sea which bears his name and dying a prisoner of the winter ice. In vain Henry Hudson cruised these cold waters on behalf of the Muscovy Company and then, in 1609, set off in the little *Half Moon* on behalf of the Dutch East India Company, who had commissioned him to try where Frobisher and his successors had failed.

He safely reached Newfoundland and, cruising along the coast, came to and explored the great river named after him, the mouth of which had been discovered by Verrazano in 1524. In 1610 Henry Hudson returned thither, on this occasion at the behest of English noblemen and merchants, voyaging by way of Iceland and Greenland. He discovered Hudson Strait and Bay and after a grim winter in these inhospitable parts, with near-starvation and disease always at hand, was ready to make for home. But mutiny broke out; and the explorer, his son, and loyal and sick members of the crew were cast adrift in a small open boat and must have perished miserably.

Yet within two years another attempt was made, this time by William Baffin. Like earlier ventures, his voyages failed in their prime purpose, although it was Baffin who named Lancaster Sound, which was later to prove the seaway to the West.

The Pacific and Australia

We must quickly pass over Sir Walter Raleigh's ill-fated exploration in Guiana (1595 and 1617) and the discovery of Lake Ontario (1615) by Samuel de Champlain (1567–1635), the founder of Quebec, and turn to the southern seas, where the mists surrounding the great island continent of Australia were slowly to be cleared.

Many an explorer had sailed the Pacific since the first crossing of the great ocean. There was Pedro Fernandez de Quiros, who reached the New Hebrides in 1606 convinced that he had found the mysterious Southern Continent. On this same expedition a ship commanded by his friend, Luis Vaez de Torres, passed through the Torres Strait; and in this same year a small Dutch ship named the *Duyfken* entered the Gulf of Carpentaria. Other parts of the western and northern coasts of Australia were later visited by other Dutch navigators; but never, it seems, did they make landfall in the more favoured regions and so the great continent remained in vague and inscrutable outline.

By far the most famous of the Dutchmen who shared in the discovery of Australia was Abel Tasman (1602–59). In 1642, at the command of Anthony Van Diemen, the Governor-General of the Dutch East Indies, he undertook an expedition which led to the discovery of Tasmania. On a further voyage, Tasman charted the coast from Cape York to the Ashburton River (Western Australia).

Next upon the scene were Captain Swan and his buccaneers, among whom was that strange mixture of a man, William Dampier (1688). In 1699, proudly bearing the King's commission, Dampier returned

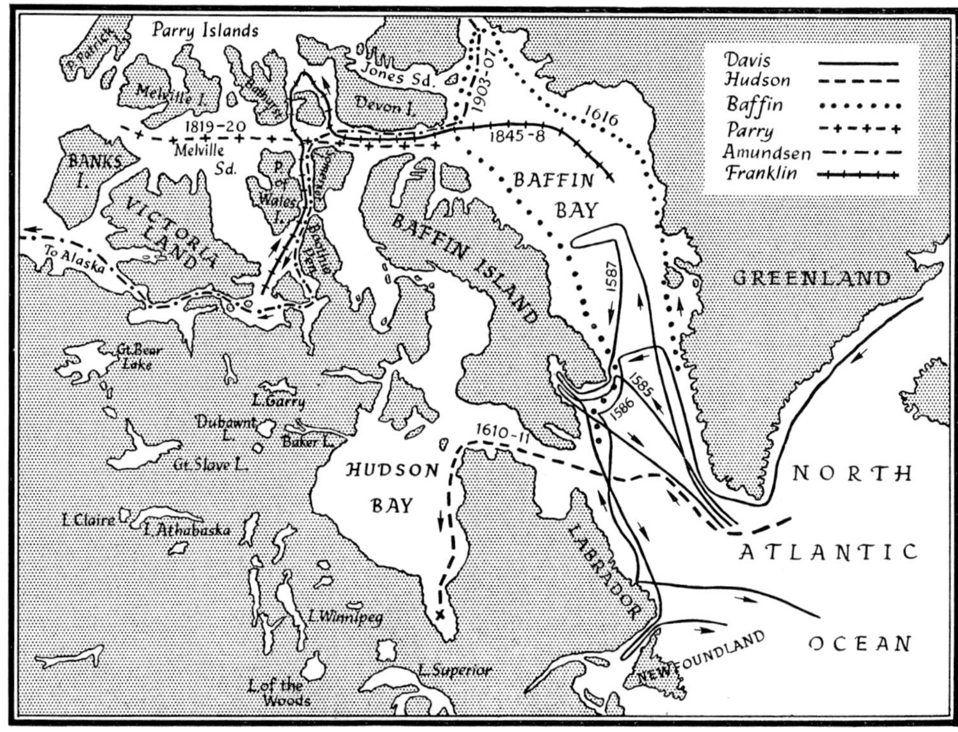

Specially drawn for this work.

THE NORTH-WEST PASSAGE

Generation after generation of explorers was baffled by the north-western route to the Far East. The way was eventually discovered by Sir John Franklin, but at the cost of his life, and the passage made (partly by water and partly across the ice) by M'Clure. The first vessel to sail the North-West Passage was the *Gjöa* commanded by Amundsen.

TWO FAMOUS CAPTAINS

The settlement of Australia began in 1788 when Captain Arthur Phillip reached New South Wales with the First Fleet. The picture shows Sydney Cove, where Captain Phillip hoisted the British flag on January 26th, and is a reproduction of a sketch made by John Hunter, the second captain of H.M.S. *Sirius* and later governor of the young colony.

Illustrations : Hulton Picture Library

Sandwich Islands was the name given to the Hawaiian islands of the Pacific by Captain James Cook. The great explorer, seen in this picture receiving a present from the islanders, discovered the group in 1778 during his third and last voyage. Returning to Hawaii after vainly probing the Arctic Ocean, he was clubbed and stabbed to death by the islanders on February 14th, 1779.

to Australian waters in the *Roebuck*, but once again saw only a barren part of the continent. Seventy years were to pass before the more inviting eastern shores were discovered by a Yorkshire naval officer named James Cook.

Captain James Cook

Cook had been given command of the *Endeavour*, which left England in 1768 with a party of scientists to observe a transit of Venus from a favourable point in the Pacific. This work done, Cook turned to exploring the great ocean in which he found himself. After visiting the Society Islands, he sailed completely round the North and South Islands of New Zealand, then continuing westwards to sight Cape Everard on the Australian mainland. He reached and named Botany Bay, landing there to carve a record of his visit on one of the trees and then cruising northward to the Great Barrier Reef, on whose jagged coral the *Endeavour* was nearly wrecked. So to Cape York and Possession Island, where Cook hoisted the flag and took possession of the eastern coast " in the right of His Majesty King George the Third."

This first voyage occupied him from 1768 until 1771. His second voyage (1772–75) not only revealed more of the vast Pacific, but took him nearer to the South Pole than any earlier navigator had been. On his third and last voyage (1776–80) he probed the North Pacific for the back door to the elusive North-West Passage, penetrating the Arctic Ocean before he turned southwards again to meet his death in Hawaii. His discoveries, his work of mapping and naming in the Pacific, place him in the forefront of British sea-explorers.

The major part of sea-exploration was now complete. Leaving aside for the moment the great field of Polar exploration, we can see that subsequent voyages were principally concerned with filling in the details on the broad canvas marked out by earlier navigators. Notable voyages included those of Jean François de Galaup La Pérouse (1741–88) in the Pacific; the survey of the coast of British Columbia (1792) by Captain George Vancouver, a brother officer and companion of the great Cook; the circumnavigation of Tasmania by Matthew Flinders and George Bass (1798); the survey of much of the Australian coast by Flinders (1801–03) on his—the first—circumnavigation of the island continent; and the four voyages of Captain Phillip Parker King off the northern and north-western coasts of Australia (1817–22).

Opening up the Continents

The continents were defined; much of their interiors remained a challenge to the adventurous. In North America, where Étienne Brulé (*c.* 1592–1632), the Sieur de La Salle (1643–87) and Samuel Hearne (1745–92) had pioneered so bravely, a hardy young Scot named Alexander Mackenzie (1763–1820) had traced the great river that bears his name (1789) and, while Vancouver was charting the western coast of the continent, was forcing his way over the formidable Rockies to the Pacific coast, which he reached in July, 1793. Another pathway across North America was later opened by two American explorers, Captain Meriwether Lewis (1774–1809) and William Clark (1770–1838), who in 1804 set off up the Missouri, crossed the Rockies and reached the coast at the mouth of Columbia River (1805). Another noteworthy American explorer was Zebulon Montgomery Pike (1779–1813), who investigated the headwaters of the Mississippi.

Valuable work was done in South America by Baron von Humboldt (1769–1859), a German naturalist and traveller, who explored the Orinoco and made other expeditions to the interior and whose compatriots, von Martius and von Spix, travelled extensively in Brazil (1817–20). Charles Darwin (1809–82) devoted nearly five years to travels in South America, which was also to be the hunting ground of Henry Walter Bates (1825–92) and Alfred Russel Wallace (1823–1913).

At the close of the eighteenth century Africa was still " the Dark Continent."

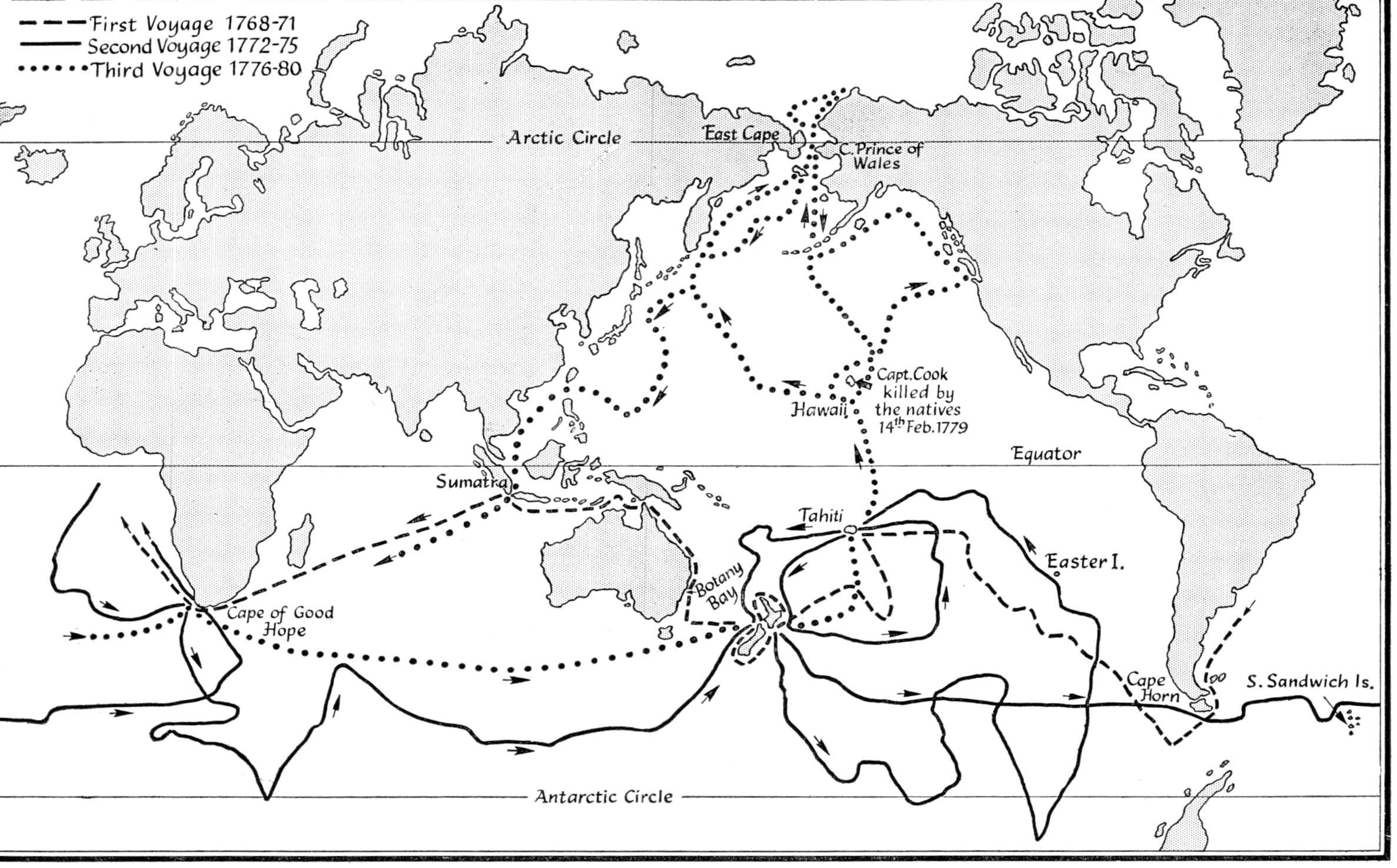

Specially drawn for this work.

THE VOYAGES OF CAPTAIN COOK

Captain Cook was probably the greatest of all English explorers and navigators. His three famous voyages revealed Australia and New Zealand and the islanded Pacific—discoveries which he painstakingly charted to an unprecedented standard of accuracy. His first voyage was made in the *Endeavour* and was officially a scientific expedition to observe the transit of the planet Venus, but took him to New Zealand and Australia. His second, with the *Resolution* and *Adventure*, included the first crossing of the Antarctic Circle. His third, with the *Resolution* and *Discovery*, took him through the Bering Strait in search of a North-West Passage. A stern but just officer, Cook was popular with his men. Cleanliness and proper diet were his weapons against dysentery and scurvy.

Specially drawn for this work.

SOME NORTH AMERICAN EXPLORERS

The map shows some of the principal voyages and journeys of discovery from the times of the early Spanish adventurers to the early nineteenth century. Canadian pioneers included Samuel de Champlain, the founder of Quebec; Samuel Hearne, whose journeys were made on behalf of the Hudson's Bay Company; and Alexander Mackenzie, who was knighted for his work as an explorer and official of the fur companies. Lewis and Clark, Pike of the famous peak, and much earlier travellers shared in the work of opening up the United States.

James Bruce, an enterprising Scot with a thirst for travel, had penetrated Abyssinia and located the source of the Blue Nile (1770). His fellow-countryman, Mungo Park (1771–1806) faced the challenge of another African river—the Niger, which, although hinted at in ancient times, was yet undefined. When he sailed for the Gambia in 1795, four explorers sent out by the African Association had already perished. Mungo Park, however, survived all hardships and perils, and returned to England in 1797 to report the direction and flow of the Niger and give the first

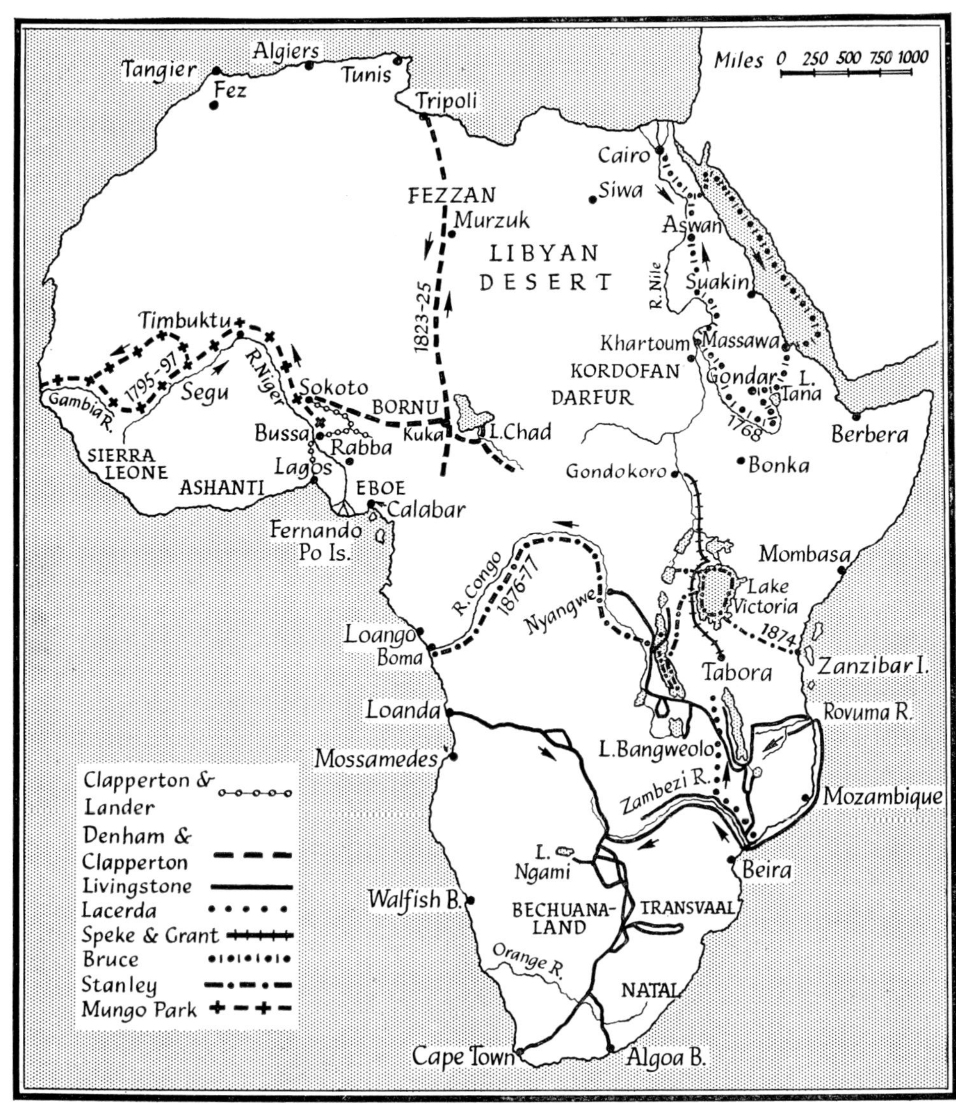

Specially drawn for this work.

THE UNVEILING OF AFRICA

The map shows some of the principal explorations of the "Dark Continent." Among the early travellers was the Portuguese engineer Lacerda, who died during his expedition of 1797. Not until the remarkable travels of Dr. Livingstone was the veil withdrawn from Central Africa. It will be noted what a great part was played by the rivers in challenging the explorers who opened up the continent.

detailed account of the interior of West Africa. But his second expedition (1805–06) ended in his death, probably in the turbulent Bussa rapids on the lower Niger.

Some sixteen years later the expedition of Denham, Clapperton and Oudney tried to reach the river from Tripoli. After crossing the Sahara and finding "the great Lake Chad, glowing with the golden rays of the sun," they pressed on to Kuka, and Clapperton himself got through to Kano and Sokoto before weakness compelled him to turn back (1823). In 1825 Clapperton and Richard Lander won through to the Niger, but Landor alone survived—to return to Bussa in 1830 with his brother John and follow the river to its mouth.

What of the Nile? Its sources were the

goal of Richard Burton (1821–90) and John Hanning Speke (1827–64) who in 1857 left Zanzibar for the great lakes so often mentioned by tribesmen and traders. Both were tortured by fever, Speke being almost blind at times, but it was he who eventually pushed on alone to reach the great lake which he named Victoria Nyanza after his Queen (1858). In 1860 Speke returned to the region of the lakes with a new companion, James Augustus Grant. The Ripon Falls were discovered and named; and while following the Nile northwards, they met Samuel Baker, who had come upstream with a relief party to search for the explorers. " Could they be Speke and Grant? " wrote Baker in his journal. " Off I ran and soon met them in reality. Hurrah for Old England! They had come from the Victoria Nyanza, from which the Nile springs . . . the mystery of the ages solved."

Speke and Grant returned to England, but Baker stayed on to discover and name Lake Albert and the Murchison Falls.

The Greatest of African Explorers

Rivers were the keys to the African continent. So we turn now to the Zambesi and the Congo, and to Dr. David Livingstone (1813–73) the great missionary-explorer, the friend and champion of the peoples of Africa, who did more than any other man to tear the veil from the heart of the Dark Continent. Between 1849 and 1856 he travelled through central Africa, crossing the southern part of the continent from the Atlantic to the Indian Ocean. In 1855 he discovered the Victoria Falls—that " stream of a thousand yards broad " which " leaped down a hundred feet and then became suddenly compressed into a space of fifteen or twenty yards." From 1858 to 1864 he was engaged in further exploration, during which he discovered and explored Lake Nyasa; and between 1866 and 1873, he made his third and last journey (to the Great Lakes and the upper Congo).

It was during this last period that fears for his safety resulted in the relief expedition led by Henry Morton Stanley (1840–1904) and the memorable meeting of the two explorers at Ujiji in 1871. Only two more years of travel remained to the " Great White Doctor." He died on April 30th, 1873, at a village in the Ilala district. Stanley, however, returned to Africa in 1874 as leader of an Anglo-American expedition, which largely completed the work of the explorers of the Great Lakes and followed the Congo down to Boma, near the river's mouth (1877). He also had a share in founding the Belgian Congo and was the discoverer of the Ruwenzori Mountains (" Mountains of the Moon ").

Travellers in Asia

Some of the most interesting and adventurous journeys ever undertaken by European explorers were made across the great land routes of Asia, or from Asian ports reached by ship via the Cape route to the East. There was the daring Duarte Barbosa, who travelled in parts of India, Ceylon and Malaya; fought at Malacca in 1511; and wrote one of the earliest guide-books about the places he visited. There was Ludovico di Varthema, an Italian adventurer who set off in 1502, travelled through the Holy Land and Arabia and eventually got as far afield as Java. The enterprise of Anthony Jenkinson was equalled in the early seventeenth century by Thomas Coryat, William Hawkins, Peter Mundy and other English travellers and traders. From Francisco Pelsaert, a servant of the Dutch East India Company, came an early account of the Vale of Kashmir. The German Kaempfer, not content with travels in Ceylon and the East Indies, went to Japan and lived there for two years. Jesuit missionaries were active in China.

Meanwhile Russia had been advancing eastwards across Siberia and by 1638 had reached the Pacific and founded Okhotsk. Seeking trade, her envoys crossed Manchuria and reached Peking (1676) only to be rebuffed by the suspicious Chinese. In 1725, an expedition led by Vitus Bering (1680–1741), a Danish officer in the Russian Navy, left St. Petersburg for the

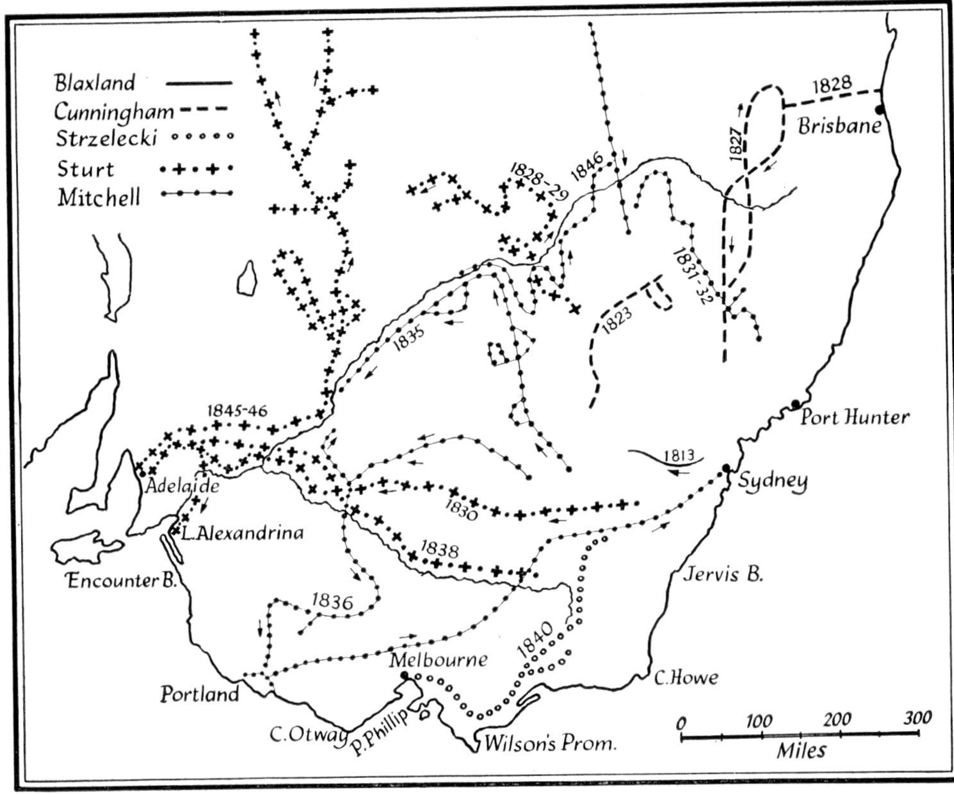

Specially drawn for this work.

EARLY TRACKS ACROSS SOUTH-EAST AUSTRALIA

In the early days of settlement, the Blue Mountains west of Sydney were thought to be a barrier that could not be forced. Then, in 1813, a party led by Gregory Blaxland found a way across to the fertile Bathurst Plains. The Darling Downs, another fertile region, were discovered by Cunningham. The mystery of the rivers was solved by Sturt, while Mitchell and Strzelecki did much to open up South Australia and Victoria.

Kamchatka peninsula, where the ship was built that took Bering through his strait to East Cape and the Chukchi lands. During a further voyage (1741), Bering reached Alaska, but died with several of his men as they starved the stormy winter through in crude hovels on Bering Island. His voyages prepared the way for the Russian trading posts which Captain Cook found in Alaska on his last voyage.

By the middle of the nineteenth century interest had revived in mysterious Central Asia and Christian missionaries were active there. Abbé Huc and Abbé Gabet travelled through Mongolia and eventually reached Lhasa, the capital of " forbidden " Tibet. But it was the Russians who undertook more scientific exploration, especially Nicholas Prjevalsky (1839–88) who crossed the Gobi Desert to Peking and from there followed the great caravan route westwards to the borders of Tibet. Englishmen and Indians concerned with the Survey of India also did valuable work in the mountainous heart of Asia; and at the turn of the century archæologists were playing their part, especially Zven Hedin, the Swedish discoverer of the buried cities of the Takla-Makan desert, and Sir Aurel Stein, who triumphantly brought back from one expedition twenty-nine cases of priceless manuscripts and relics from the wondrous Caves of the Thousand Buddhas on the edge of the Gobi desert.

The greatest of Arabian explorers was

Charles Doughty (1843–1926), who went into the desert country east of the Holy Land (1875) and travelled southwards, stopping here and there to live with one Arab tribe or another. Later travellers in Arabia included H. St. J. B. Philby, Miss Freya Stark and Sir Percy Sykes.

The Exploration of Australia

After the establishment of the First Settlement in 1788, the emphasis was upon coastal exploration. But in 1813, Blaxland, Wentworth and Lawson discovered a way over the barrier of the Blue Mountains west of Sydney and so made possible the development of the fertile plains around Bathurst. The Lachlan and Macquarie Rivers, discovered by G. W. Evans, a government surveyor, were explored by John Oxley, the Surveyor-General, until his way was blocked by swamps (1818). Hamilton Hume and William Hovell travelled overland from Lake George, crossed the Murray and eventually reached Port Phillip Bay (1824). Allan Cunningham, a keen young botanist from Kew Gardens, explored the rich Darling Downs (1827).

These beginnings revealed a number of westward flowing rivers and so led to speculation about the existence of an inland sea. The problem was solved by one of the greatest figures in Australian exploration, Captain Charles Sturt (1795–1869), who discovered the Darling River (1829) and traced the great Murray River down to the sea at Lake Alexandrina (1830).

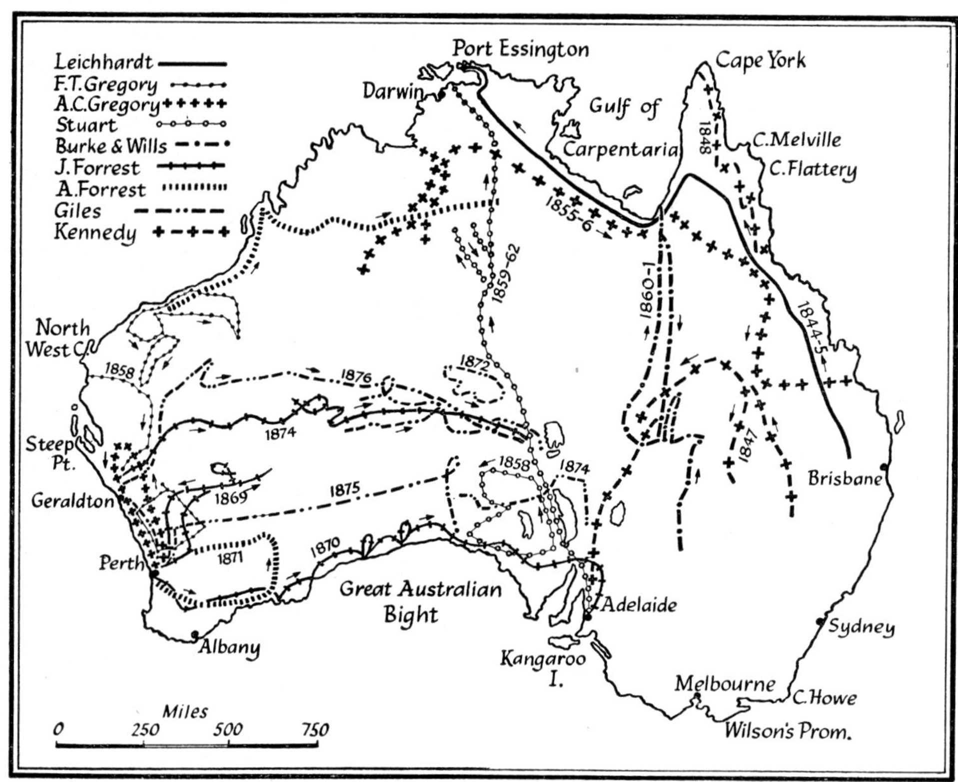

Specially drawn for this work.

LATER EXPLORERS OF AUSTRALIA

This map continues the story of the exploration of Australia from the expeditions of Leichhardt to those of the Forrest brothers. Especially noteworthy were the two south-north crossings of the continent by (i) the tragic Burke and Wills expedition; and (ii) John MacDouall Stuart, who found success on his third attempt. By 1875 the pioneer exploration of the continent was practically complete, although much remained to be done by minor expeditions and, of course, scientific survey.

Picture Post Library.

IN MEMORY OF A TRAGIC EXPEDITION

This reproduction of an old print shows the inauguration of the Burke and Wills memorial at Melbourne, the capital city of Victoria, Australia, in 1865. Burke and Wills were the leaders of the ill-fated expedition of 1860–61, which crossed Australia from south to north and ended with the death of the two explorers at Cooper's Creek in the " dead heart " of the island continent.

Sir Thomas Mitchell (1792–1855), the Surveyor-General of New South Wales, was the leader of several expeditions, the most famous being his overland journey through south-eastern Australia (1836), a region which was later travelled by McMillan (1839) and Strzelecki (1840).

Meanwhile, a number of new settlements had been established and these provided fresh starting points for Australian explorers, who were now more concerned with the interior of the continent. In 1840 Edward John Eyre (1815–1901) set out from Adelaide to reach the centre of Australia, was turned back at Mount Hopeless by lack of water, made for the coast and set about finding an overland route to Albany, a hazardous undertaking which took a year to accomplish.

Another who tried to reach the desert heart was Sturt. His expedition left Adelaide in 1844 and actually got to within 150 miles of the centre of Australia before it was driven back by lack of water and the burning heat of the desert—" so hot that the dogs lost the skin off their paws; the men had their backs blistered and their shoes were burnt as if by fire."

At this time a Prussian scientist named Ludwig Leichhardt (1813–?48) was making his memorable journey from the Darling Downs, in Queensland, to Port Essington, in the Northern Territory. His last expedition (1848) was an attempt to cross the continent from east to west. Leichhardt and his companions did not return from this venture. The mystery of their fate, which was a spur to many later expeditions, remains unsolved. In this same year Edmund Kennedy, the Assistant-Surveyor of New South Wales, lost his life on an expedition in the Cape York Peninsula.

The Burke and Wills expedition across the continent (1860–1) also ended in tragedy. The estuary of the Flinders

River was reached by an exhausting trek from the depot at Cooper's Creek, but only one of the party survived the terrible return journey.

The first man to reach the heart of the continent was John McDouall Stuart (1815–66), who set out from Adelaide in 1859 and reached Central Mount Sturt (a name afterwards changed to Central Mount Stuart). His second expedition (1861) nearly won through to the northern coast. Undaunted, he tried again (1862) and at last reached the sea at Chambers Bay, near Darwin, over a route now followed by the famous Overland Telegraph.

Notable explorers of Western Australia included A. C. (later Sir Augustus) Gregory, whose expedition of 1855–56 ventured far into the north-western desert lands; the Forrest brothers, John and Alexander, the first of whom travelled from Perth to Adelaide (1870) and later found an overland route from Perth to South Australia (1874); and Ernest Giles (1836–97) who made several remarkable inland journeys and in 1875 travelled from Adelaide to Perth—a journey of some 5,000 miles, mostly across dry, barren regions. John Forrest (1847–1918), it should be noted, was even greater as a statesman than he was as an explorer; he later became Baron Forrest of Bunbury, the first Australian to be raised to the peerage.

Polar Exploration

What of the Arctic and Antarctic? For many centuries Arctic exploration had been limited to the search for the North-West and North-East Passages to India. Sir John Ross (1777–1856) reached Lancaster Sound in 1818; and a year later Sir William Edward Parry (1790–1855) probed the Sound with his ships *Griper* and *Hecla*. Although he returned to these waters in 1821 and 1824, the secret of the North-West Passage escaped him. In 1827 Parry, travelling across the ice by sledge from Spitsbergen, reached 82° 45′ N. And in 1830 Ross, having discovered Boothia Land, located the North Magnetic Pole.

The discoverer of the North-West Passage was Sir John Franklin (1786–1847), a distinguished explorer who was for a time governor of Tasmania. In 1845 he set out from England with the ships *Erebus* and *Terror*, which had served so well in the Antarctic with Ross (1840–42), and provisions for three years. But these stout vessels were caught in the ice in Victoria Strait and abandoned by Franklin and his men, who perished in their attempt to reach the mainland. This much of the sad story was pieced together from evidence gathered by the many relief expeditions which went in search of the explorers. The most notable of these expeditions was that of Captain (Sir Robert) M'Clure, which actually made the North-West Passage, partly by water and partly across the ice (1853). The first ship to sail through the Passage was the *Gjöa*, commanded by Captain Roald Amundsen (1872–1928), one of the greatest Polar explorers, which left Oslo in 1903 and sailed through the Passage and Bering Strait to Nome, in Alaska.

The North-East Passage was eventually achieved by Baron Nils Nordenskiöld (1832–1901) in the *Vega* (1878–80).

The Quest for the North Pole

Commercial motives had led to the search for the Passages; after the discovery of the North-West route, Arctic exploration became purely scientific in its purpose. Fridtjof Nansen (1861–1930), the great Norwegian explorer who had made the first crossing of Greenland (1888), took his ship *Fram* and let her become locked in the ice in latitude 78° 50′ N., 133° 37′ E. Specially built for the expedition, the sturdy vessel resisted the pressure and, as Nansen hoped, drifted with the ice across the Polar basin. In March, 1895, Nansen and Lieut. Johansen left the ship and made for the Pole, but had to turn back at 86° 14′ N.—the "farthest north" at that time.

The North Pole was first reached in 1909 by Commander (later Admiral) Robert E. Peary (1856–1920) of the United States Navy. Sailing in the

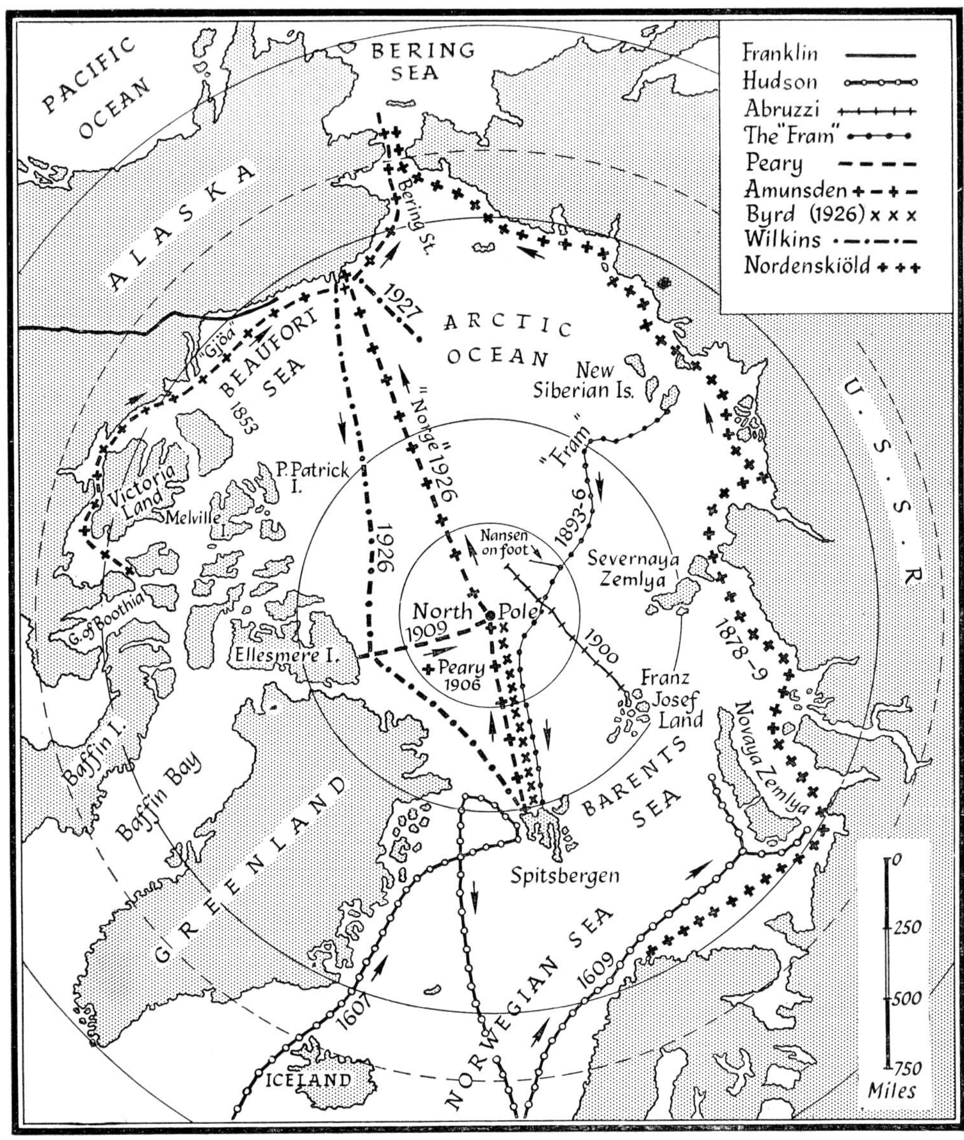

Specially drawn for this work.

ARCTIC EXPLORATION

Discovery of the North-West Passage cost Franklin his life, and not until Amundsen's voyage in the *Gjöa* was this route achieved completely by sea. The North-East Passage was discovered by Nordenskiöld in his ship *Vega*. Among those who attempted to reach the North Pole were Fridtjof Nansen in the *Fram*, the Duke of Abruzzi's expedition, and Robert Peary. Amundsen crossed over the Pole in the Italian airship *Norge*, and Byrd circled it in his monoplane *Josephine Ford*.

Roosevelt to the ice off Cape Sheridan in Grant Land (1908), Peary landed stores and established a depot at Cape Columbia. In the spring of 1909 he made his dash for the Pole, which was reached at 10 a.m. on April 6th.

The history of Arctic aviation begins with Salomon Andrée (1854–97) who lost his life in an attempt to reach the North Pole by balloon. The Americans, Commander (later Admiral) R. E. Byrd and F. G. Bennett, were the first airmen to look down on the Pole. Their flight was made in the Fokker monoplane *Josephine*

Ford in 1926, and in this same year the Italian airship *Norge*, with Amundsen aboard, crossed the Pole and landed safely in Alaska. Two years later the Pole was crossed by Hubert (afterwards Sir Hubert) Wilkins, the intrepid Australian explorer, on his third Polar flight. Umberto Nobile, who had piloted the *Norge*, now took the sister-ship *Italia* to the Pole (1928). But on the return flight the airship crashed and during the successful rescue operations, the gallant Amundsen lost his life.

The Soviet Union has taken a prominent part in scientific study of the Arctic. In May, 1937, four Soviet aircraft made a successful landing at the Pole; in June, the large Soviet monoplane *ANT*–25 made a trans-Polar flight from Moscow to Portland, U.S.A. Other flights followed.

Notable expeditions after the Second World War included the flight of the R.A.F. Lancaster *Aries* in 1945, " Operation Icicle " of the U.S. Alaskan Air Command in 1952, and the training flight of two Hastings aircraft of the R.A.F. to the North Pole in 1953. The first commercial air service across Polar regions was inaugurated in 1954 by Scandinavian Airlines and linked Copenhagen with Los Angeles.

The Remote Antarctic

Exploration of " the Seventh Continent " may be said to begin with Captain Cook, who reached the edge of the pack ice during his second voyage. Bellingshausen, Weddell, D'Urville and Wilkes later made Antarctic expeditions, but of far greater importance was the work of Sir James Clark Ross (1800–62) during the period 1840–43. He discovered and named Victoria Land and Mounts Erebus and Terror (named after his ships), reached the Great Ice Barrier and did not put about until he had made a " farthest south " record (Lat. 78° 10′ S.).

Pre-eminent among Antarctic explorers are Captain Robert Falcon Scott (1868–1912) and Sir Ernest Shackleton (1874–1922). They sailed together in the *Discovery* (1902) and established a new "farthest south " record by a great sledge journey to 82° 17′ S., some 380 miles from their winter base at Ross Island. This record was broken by Shackleton on his own expedition of 1908, when he reached Lat. 88° 23′ S., *i.e.* less than 120 miles from the Pole.

This brings us to a memorable period in the history of Antarctic exploration; the years 1911 and 1912. During the first, the South Pole was reached by Amundsen; during the second, Captain Scott and his comrades met death in the icy wastes as they returned from the Pole. Scott's venture has been described as " the most tragic of Antarctic expeditions." With Wilson, Oates, Bowers and Evans, he reached the Pole on January 18th, 1912, only to find that Amundsen had snatched the prize from him little more than a month earlier. On the return, Evans had a bad fall which gave him concussion of the brain; Oates, reaching the limit of his endurance, gallantly walked out to his death in the night rather than burden his failing comrades any longer; and then, the final blow, when they were but eleven days from their supply depot, a blizzard held them prisoner. When at last the cold and roaring gale died down, all of the gallant band were dead.

Shackleton returned to the Antarctic in 1914, hoping to make an overland crossing of the Antarctic continent. His ship, *Endurance*, caught in the remorseless grip of the ice, was crushed and sank in November, 1915, but Shackleton and his men escaped to Grytviken, a whaling station on South Georgia.

In 1928 Sir Hubert Wilkins took two monoplanes to the Antarctic. About this same time Commander Byrd reached the Ross Shelf, set up his base of " Little America " and claimed Marie Byrd Land for the United States. Later ventures included the British Graham Land Expedition (1934–37) led by John Rymill; the flight across Antarctica of Lincoln Ellsworth and Hollick-Kenyon; the American expedition of 1940 ; and the huge U.S. Navy Antarctic Expedition of 1946–47, which, led by Admiral Byrd, comprised five vessels manned by about 4,000 men.

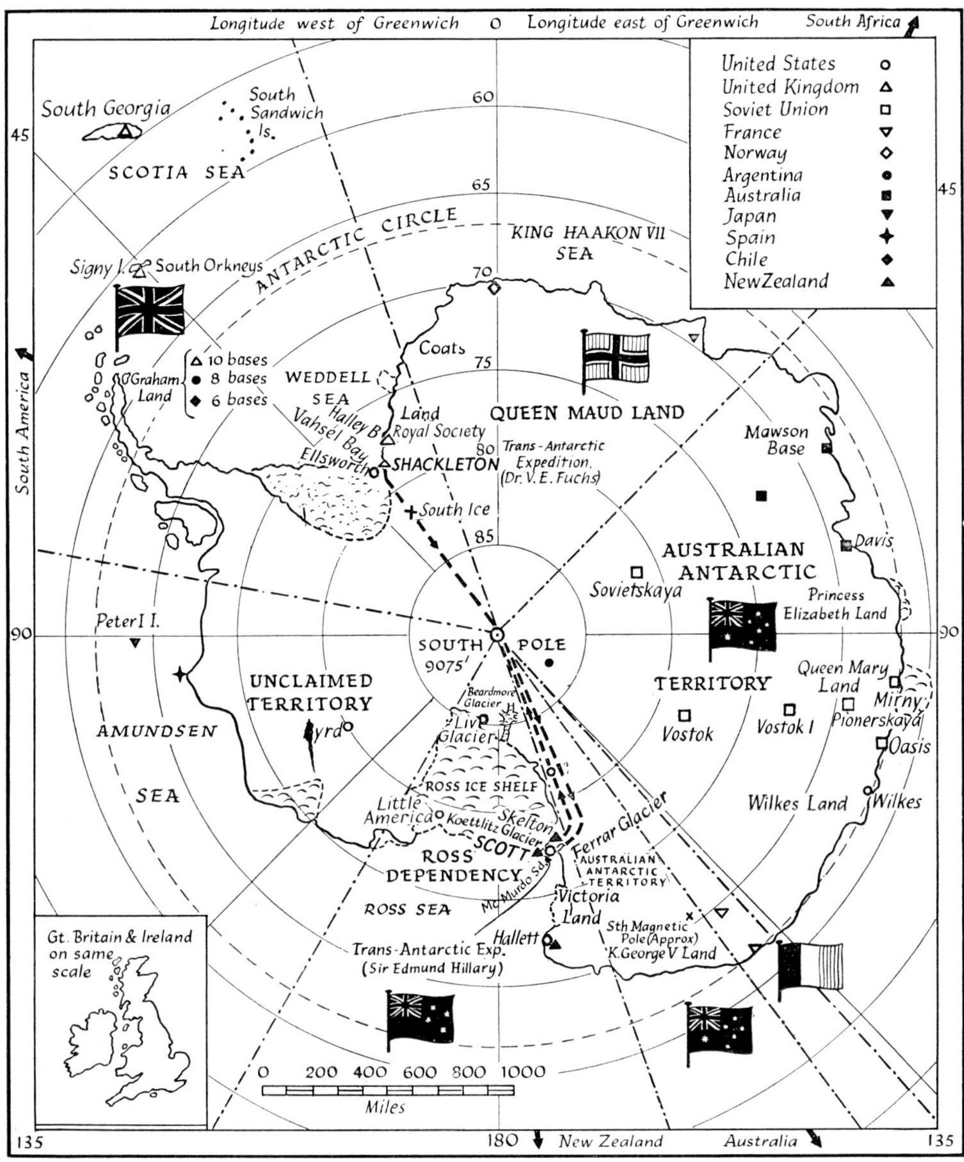

Specially drawn for this work.

THE ASSAULT ON ANTARCTICA

The map shows the principal bases in Antarctica during the International Geophysical Year. Of particular interest are the bases and route of the British Commonwealth Trans-Antarctic Expedition, and the base of the Royal Society's expedition. In weight of numbers and equipment, the American expedition with twelve ships and four thousand men was most impressive, but by far the most imaginative and daring was the British endeavour, led by Sir Vivian Fuchs.

The first international expedition took place in the period 1949–52; the co-operating nations were Norway, Sweden and Great Britain, and their base was the hutted camp of " Maudheim " built in 1950 in Queen Maud Land.

Australia has taken a prominent part in recent Antarctic exploration. The Australian National Antarctic Research Expedition, after establishing weather stations of Heard and Macquarie Islands, set up the first permanent station on the

Antarctic mainland (1954). It was called Mawson in honour of the great Australian explorer, Sir Douglas Mawson.

Antarctica and the Geophysical Year

It has been said that Antarctica is the last remaining challenge to the explorer. This challenge has now been met boldly and successfully; for the period 1955–58 will surely be remembered as one when man made his greatest assault upon the mysteries of Antarctica.

The International Geophysical Year (July, 1957–December, 1958) brought about co-operation on an unprecedented scale between scientists throughout the world. Some of the most interesting work has been done in Antarctica by national expeditions from several countries including the United Kingdom, New Zealand, Australia, the Soviet Union, the United States, France, Norway and Japan.

The United Kingdom's contribution included the Royal Society's expedition, based on Halley Bay and commanded by Lieut.-Commander David Dalgleish, R.N. and subsequently by Colonel Robin Smart, R.A.M.C. and Mr. Joseph McDowell. Its main concern during I.G.Y. was the study of the upper air.

A notable British achievement during I.G.Y. was the first non-stop flight across Antarctica by a single-engined aircraft (an R.A.F. *Otter*), which was made on January 6th, 1958 by Sqdn.-Leader John Lewis with a crew of three. This flight was part of the air reconnaissance for the British Commonwealth Trans-Antarctic Expedition — the principal and most dramatic British contribution to I.G.Y.

Led by Dr. Vivian Fuchs, with Sir Edmund Hillary in command of the supporting New Zealand party, the Trans-Antarctic Expedition made the first overland crossing of the " Seventh Continent," completing the 2,200-mile journey from its Shackleton Base to Scott Base on McMurdo Sound in 99 days.

Shackleton Base had been established by an advance party in January, 1956, and it was from here during the first half of 1957 that reconnaissance flights were made over vast uncharted areas to help Dr. Fuchs in planning his route from Shackleton to the South Pole. Meanwhile Sir Edmund Hillary and other New Zealanders were establishing Scott Base, reconnoitring the route that Dr. Fuchs would use from the Pole to McMurdo Sound and establishing supply depots.

On November 24th Dr. Fuchs and his party left Shackleton with three Sno-Cats, two Weasels and a Muskeg tractor. Many dangerous crevasses barred their way, and

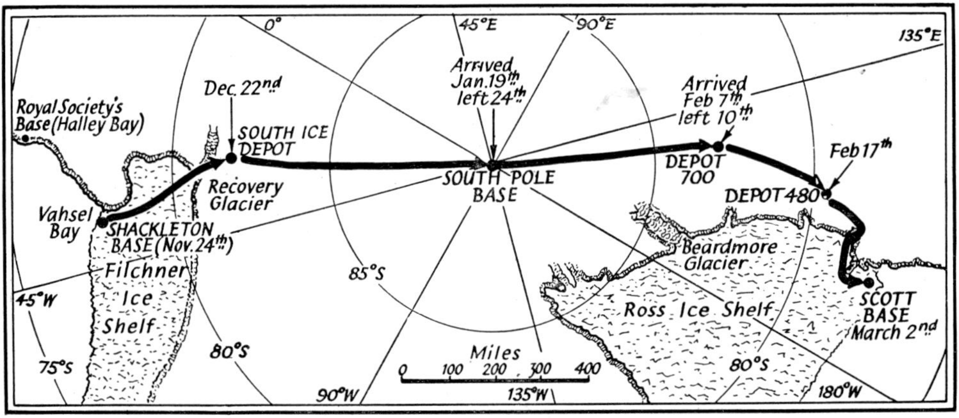

Specially drawn for this work.

THE FIRST OVERLAND CROSSING OF ANTARCTICA

This map shows the route taken by Dr. Fuchs and his party on their 2,200-mile journey from Shackleton Base to Scott Base by way of the South Pole. Crevasses, blizzards, and a formidable ice barrier some 800 feet high were encountered and at times progress was very slow and exhausting. But Scott Base was triumphantly reached ninety-nine days after the party had set out from Shackleton.

LEADERS IN ANTARCTICA

The Times.

Chosen to lead the British Commonwealth Trans-Antarctic Expedition was Dr. Vivian Fuchs. A geologist, he had been since 1950 Director of the Falkland Islands Dependencies Scientific Bureau.

The Times.

The New Zealand party was led by Sir Edmund Hillary who, with Sherpa Tensing, successfully climbed Everest in 1953. His task was to establish Scott Base and to reconnoitre part of the route which Dr. Fuchs would use.

Planet News.

The end of an epic. Proudly flying flags, the Sno-Cats of Dr. Fuchs and his party approach Scott Base at the end of their gruelling journey across Antarctica. Note the " GB " plate on the tractor in the foreground. The Queen recognised Dr. Fuchs' achievement by conferring a knighthood on him, and he also received the special gold medal of the Royal Geographical Society. Another Trans-Antarctic Expedition **photograph will be found on p. 199.**

at one, the leading Sno-Cat nearly plunged to destruction. Intense cold, blizzards and general bad weather also slowed down the party and it was not until December 22nd that the South Ice Depot was reached. Three days were spent in changing vehicle tracks, taking on stores and resting. Then, on December 26th, Dr. Fuchs set off on the 500-mile stretch to the South Pole.

By this time, Sir Edmund Hillary and his party had been at Depot 700 (the pre-arranged rendezvous for his meeting with Dr. Fuchs) for some days. On his own initiative, Hillary decided to make a dash for the Pole—" God willing and crevasses permitting." With four tractors and a caboose sledge, he set out across unexplored territory, doggedly pressing on through deep snow and bad weather to reach the Pole on January 3rd, 1958. This dramatic and successful dash made Hillary the first man to reach the Pole overland since Captain Scott.

Meanwhile Dr. Fuchs had met with serious difficulties. " Whiteout " blizzards, vast fields of ridged and frozen ice (*sastrugi*), and steep precipices made progress desperately slow. The terrible conditions produced mechanical breakdowns and damage to runners and tow-bars on the vehicles, and eventually his Muskeg tractor had to be abandoned. But at last the South Pole was reached (January 19th).

There was time for the warm welcomes of Sir Edmund Hillary, Rear-Admiral George Dufek (leader of the American expedition), the American scientists at the Pole, and the newspapermen and photographers who had flown in to see the arrival. When the party had rested and vehicles had been repaired, they set off (January 24th) on the route which Hillary had reconnoitred to Scott Base. Depot 700 was reached on February 7th; McMurdo Sound on March 2nd.

For the last mile of the journey Dr. Fuchs and his four Sno-Cats were escorted by vehicles and sledges from Scott Base. The end of the long adventure was the foot of Observation Hill below the Cross commemorating Captain Scott and his companions, and bearing the famous words from Tennyson's *Ulysses;* " To strive, to seek, to find, and not to yield." The National Anthem was played. The flags of the United Kingdom and New Zealand flew proudly from Scott's historic flagstaff.

Dr. Fuchs was the first man to complete an overland crossing of Antarctica. Congratulations reached him from many parts of the world. His great achievement was recognised by a knighthood and by the award of the special gold medal of the Royal Geographical Society.

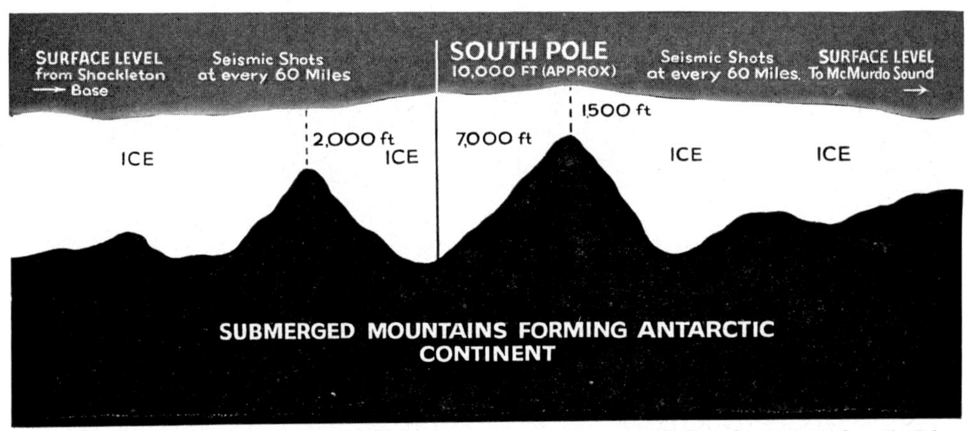

Redrawn by permission from The Sphere.

THE SHAPE OF THE SOUTH POLE

This sketch, based upon information from the geologists in Dr. Fuchs' party, provides confirmation that Antarctica is a continent. It shows the situation of the South Pole, high above a valley of ice dividing two submerged mountains. Dr. Fuchs' team made regular seismic shots and gravimetrical surveys throughout their journey.

THE MAP TO-DAY

IN the days of the ancient Greek and mediaeval cartographers, the preparation of a map was a leisurely and individual occupation. With so little precise information of the world, the difficulties the map-maker might meet with on that account were overcome by the inclusion of dragons and other artistic designs; cherubim with puffed cheeks and escaping breath would be drawn to depict " the Four Winds of the Heavens." In brief, the cartographer of old was also a complete craftsman and artist and might spread himself as his fancy and artistic ability dictated.

To-day, by contrast, the making of maps is a varied work which proceeds from one stage to another in a definite manner, each stage nicely dependent and balanced on the previous one. Throughout map making, the accuracy required in each part of the work has to be worked out and related to the accuracy of the whole. For instance, it is a waste of time and money, in the later stages of map-making, to draw a map very elaborately and carefully, if in the earlier stages great accuracy has been neglected and the framework for the drawing is wrong.

Survey and Mapping

The work is divided into two principal parts (1) survey in the field, (2) mapping from air photographs, compilation, drawing and printing in the office and factory.

1. *Survey in the Field.* This is outdoor work amounting to visiting, observing and measuring every part of the country to be mapped, using for this purpose a variety of instruments, the chief of which are theodolites, levels, plane-tables, chains and tapes, compasses and special cameras mounted in aeroplanes. The surveyors have to climb the mountains, churches and other high buildings to observe all parts; they have to walk the hills, woods, fields and coasts, measuring and recording, and drawing; or they fly, systematically photographing the country beneath until they have taken hundreds or thousands of pictures to be used later for measuring and recording and drawing by draughtsmen instead of, or to supplement, the land surveyor's method of walking over the actual ground.

2. *Mapping from Air Photographs, Compilation, Drawing and Printing.* Draughtsmen working in office or factory take the surveyors' records, drawings and pictures, and by exacting and painstaking hours of calculating, drafting, selection, interpretation, drawing, checking and cross-checking produce first the final drawings and then, after photography and other processes, the prints of the map on metal plates, which are put in the printing machines and there used to print as many copies of the map as are required.

SURVEY IN THE FIELD

Triangulation

The outdoor work starts with the observing of the position of a number of points so chosen that, if you imagine them joined by lines, they would cover the whole country to be mapped with a framework of large, evenly sized and shaped triangles. Fixing these points is, therefore, called *triangulation,* and the object is to use these points as controllers of the accuracy of the later detailed stages of the survey work. The points are chosen

FIG. 1. Triangulation.

after a reconnaissance of the whole area has been made using a plane-table (see p. 100).

As it is not possible to measure with a chain or tape between, say, two mountain peaks several miles apart, or between these peaks and the top of a church tower several miles from either peak, trigonometry is called to the surveyor's aid.

If the length of one side of a triangle is known, then the length of the other two sides can be calculated provided two angles of the triangle are known. It is necessary then to measure the length of one side only, and observe the size of every angle in the framework of triangles, in order to be able to calculate the length of the other sides of all the triangles.

All angles are observed as a check on accuracy and for final small adjustments which have to be made to the whole framework. To be able to measure all the angles, all adjoining points must be intervisible. This explains why triangulation points (stations) are mostly on high ground thus avoiding interference from hills, trees and buildings.

The instrument used for measuring the angles is called a *theodolite*. It is a precise instrument with many refinements for measuring angles accurately (say to one-tenth of one second of arc); in essentials, it is a telescope for viewing the distant point and attached horizontally to the telescope is a circular scale of degrees (minutes and seconds), with a pointer and a magnifying glass to read off the angle. There is also a similar scale attached vertically for reading angles of elevation or depression, and both scales are placed precisely horizontally and vertically by bubble levels.

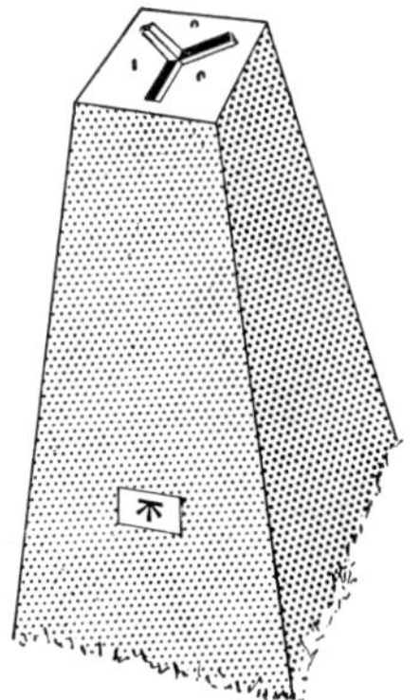

FIG. 2. A Triangulation Pillar.

Measuring the Base

The one side which is measured is called the *base*, and as the accuracy of length of all the other sides of the framework and, therefore, of the whole survey and maps is dependent on the length of thc base, it is measured with the greatest care.

A piece of reasonably flat country is chosen and special steel or invar (an alloy of nickel and steel) tapes are used for measuring the length, all kinds of precautions being taken to obtain an accurate result—comparing with a standard tape, temperature of the tape (as metal expands with heat), holding the tape under a constant tension (as tapes stretch when pulled), measuring several times in case someone has made an error and so on.

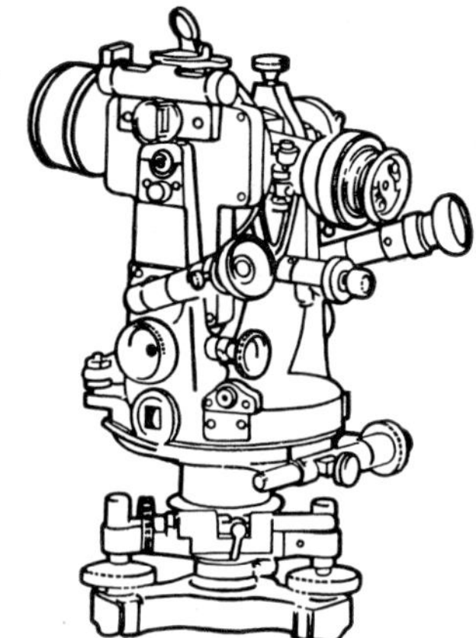

FIG. 3. A Theodolite.

For a survey which needs the greatest accuracy possible, the base of say, 10 miles would be so measured that any error would be less than ½ inch. Even more accurate methods of measuring bases are being developed, such as measuring the time taken for light to travel from one end of the base to the other, and then computing the length from the time taken and the known speed of light. Measuring by low-frequency radio waves may prove to be yet another alternative. As a further check, a side of one of the triangles at the other end of the country from the base is measured and the result compared with that calculated by trigonometry right through the framework from the base.

At the same time as the horizontal angles are being observed at the triangulation points, the vertical angles of elevation or depression are recorded and used to calculate, again by trigonometry, the heights of adjoining points. It was when making observations for the triangulation of India that the summit of Mt. Everest was observed by theodolite, and its angle of elevation from known heights enabled

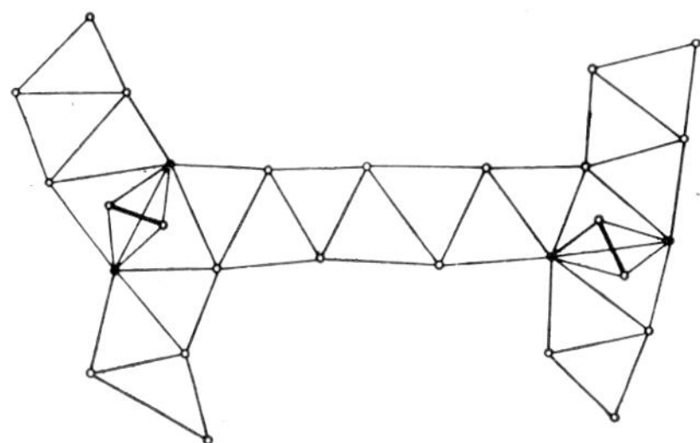

FIG. 4. A Triangulation Framework.

the height of the mountain to be calculated to a high degree of accuracy nearly 100 years before it was climbed (29,002 feet compared with the latest observations, which give 29,028 feet).

Fixing Latitude and Longitude

The position of the framework of triangles on the earth's surface has also to be found, so that the latitude and longitude of each point can be fixed. This is done by using a theodolite at one end of the base to observe certain stars, and from their position in the sky at the moment of observation (like the sun, the stars appear to travel through the sky) it is possible to calculate the position of that end of the base, and also the direction (bearing) of the other end of the base. Knowing the bearing and distance between points, the latitude and longitude of all the points in the triangulation framework can be calculated.

As it is a very long and therefore expensive task to travel all over a country and fix a framework of points and triangles, as described above, it sometimes happens that another cheaper but less thorough way of fixing a number of central points is used. This is called *traversing*. The start is made from a known point and the distance is measured by tape to the next point, and the bearing by theodolite, and so on in lines across the country where control points are needed.

Detail Survey

Using the framework of points fixed accurately by the triangulation, the detailed features of the region are surveyed and their position and shape plotted. This work is carried out in different ways depending on how accurate the final maps are to be.

In countries such as Great Britain, where accurate maps are essential in the plotting of railways, roads, gas mains, electricity grid lines, aqueducts, factories and mines and all the other features of a highly developed land, precise traversing is used to make a further framework of more control points within each and every part of the triangulation framework.

Then in each small portion of country

FIG. 5. Observing heights by Theodolite.

between the control points steel chains and tapes are used to measure every hedge, wood, road, street, building, etc. Of recent years, the same work has been carried out between the control points by measuring the detail (hedges, etc.) on large-scale air photographs on which the control points have been identified.

In less highly developed lands, for which less accurate maps would suffice, such as parts of Africa, air photographs are used to fill in the details of the country

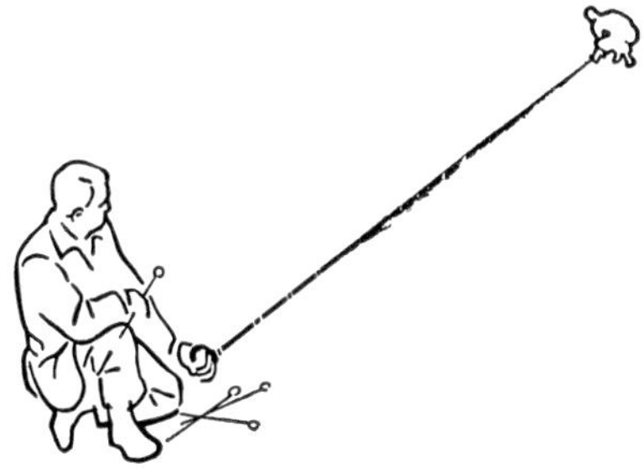

FIG. 6. Detail Survey: chaining.

using only the triangulation control points, and save all the great expense of laboriously traversing and measuring on the ground.

For exploratory surveys, and in pioneer lands, an instrument called a *plane-table* can be used to fill in the detail. The plane-table is simply a drawing board mounted on a tripod with a swivel head so that the board can be rotated. The control points are plotted on the board at the scale of the required map and a north point marked.

The plane-table is set up on a hill top from which at least three of the plotted control points can be seen. The plane-table is then rotated until a box compass set along the north point points north. The plane-table is then said to be "oriented," and any line drawn on the

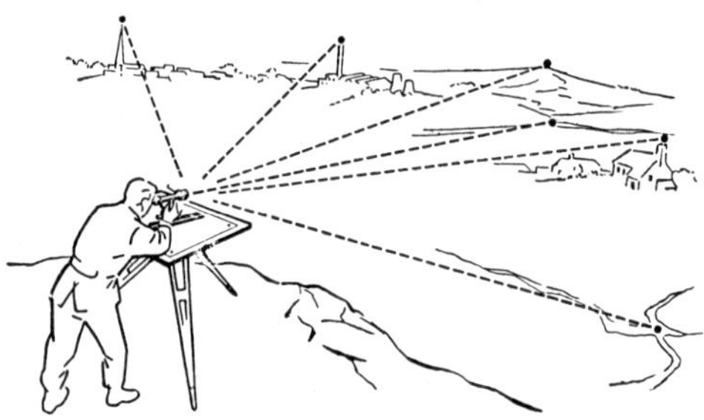

FIG. 7. Plane-table and alidade.

plane-table will be parallel to a corresponding line on the ground.

A sighting rule or alidade is now laid on the plane-table and pointed at each of the control points (probably hill tops or high buildings) in turn, a line being drawn along the rule through the corresponding control points on the board.

If the table is perfectly oriented, the lines will meet at a point, and this point on the board will correspond with the actual spot on which the surveyor has set up his plane-table. Fixing a point in this way is called *resection.*

The surveyor now proceeds to use his sighting rule to draw lines from his point towards other points of detail around and, having labelled each line (*e.g.*, white cottage, road junction, factory chimney, etc.) he goes to another vantage point, fixes his position again, and by taking further sights at the white cottage, etc., he is able to draw a second set of lines which will intersect the first and thus give the position of the points of detail.

Other features are then paced out and drawn, or sketched in by eye. Contour

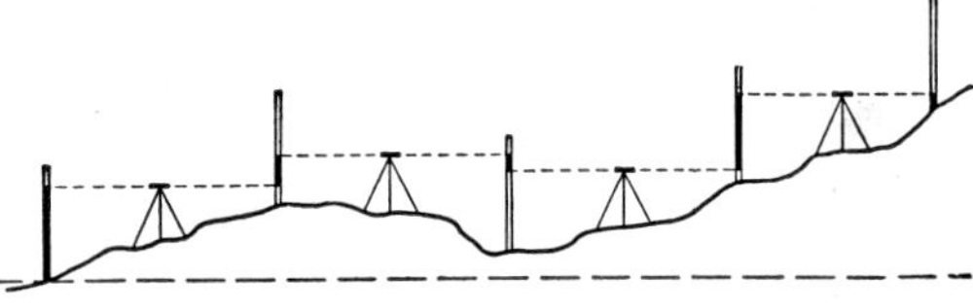

FIG. 8. Levelling: use of level and staff.

lines giving the shape and height of hills may also be drawn in by eye, after using an instrument called a *clinometer* to find the height of a sufficient number of points.

The clinometer is stood on the plane-table, levelled by a screw and bubble, and the angle of elevation, or depression read off the scale (marked in degrees on one side and tangents on the other). Knowing the distance to the point sighted, by measuring on the plane-table plot, the difference of height is obtained by simple trigonometry (difference = distance × tangent of angle).

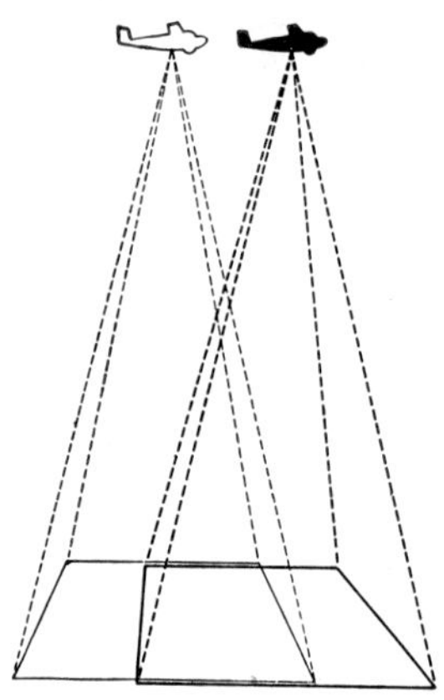

FIG. 9. Aerial photography.

Explorers in unmapped country always try to fix the position, size and shape of as much detail as time will allow. For this they often use a prismatic compass, which is an accurate compass with a scale of degrees for measuring bearings relative to magnetic north. The explorer starts from a known point, takes the bearing to the first point on his route, notes the distance travelled when he arrives there (in paces or miles, etc.) takes the bearing to the second point, and so on. At the same time he fixes points, in similar manner to the plane-tabler, on either side of his line of march by intersecting bearings.

MAPPING FROM AIR PHOTOGRAPHS, COMPILATION, DRAWING AND PRINTING

Mapping from Air Photographs

The detailed and laborious surveying in the field by plane-table, theodolite, chain and tape can be performed with much less effort, more quickly and cheaply by measuring air photographs in the office. Control points fixed by triangulation or precise traversing are however still needed to give the framework into which the information from air photographs must be adjusted.

The photographs are taken by a camera pointing downwards in the aircraft, which flies systematically over the country until the whole area is covered by strips of photographs. The camera is operated every few seconds, the actual interval being so arranged that the photographs overlap by 60 per cent. Each point of detail has then been " seen " by the camera from two viewpoints and appears on at least two photographs. A slight overlap is also arranged between strips to make sure that no gaps are left.

The photographs must be taken on clear days—surprisingly few, perhaps only four or five days in a year in some countries, as even the smallest clouds mask out the ground beneath.

There are various methods of making the map from air photographs. A simple way is by graphical methods, which are very similar to the resection and intersection method used in plane-tabling. Vertical, or nearly vertical photographs are required, as the method uses the fact that the angle subtended at the centre of the photograph by any two points of detail is the same as the corresponding angle on the ground. Vertical photographs are obtained by pointing the camera vertically downwards in the aircraft, and

FIG. 10. An air photograph taken with the camera pointing vertically downwards.

by the pilot taking great care to fly on an even keel.

The control points are identified on the photographs, and lines drawn from them to the centre of the photograph. The control points are also plotted on a board (as for plane-tabling) at the scale required; the centres of the photographs are then resected and plotted on the board. Next, other points of detail are identified on adjoining photographs and lines drawn from them to the centres.

With the photographs correctly oriented, the lines from the centres are transferred to the board and their intersections fix the position of the points of detail. (A refinement of the graphical method is to cut templates for each photograph, slotting them radially; hollow dowels are placed through the intersecting slots and pins driven through them to mark the points.) The shape of roads, railways, buildings, rivers, hedges, coastlines, etc., can then be drawn from the photographs through the plotted points of detail.

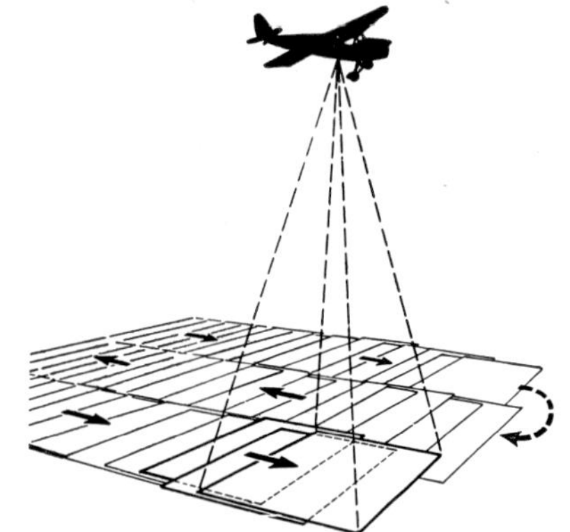

FIG. 11. Covering an area by overlapping photographs.

Interpreting correctly the wealth of detail shown is one of the greatest difficulties in attempting to do all detail survey from air photographs. Trees and shadows conceal roads and paths and settlements; the same surfaces photograph differently under different light conditions, *e.g.*, water can appear white, light grey, dark grey, or black; a sandy track reflects light and can look like a principal road. This difficulty can only be overcome by checking the uncertainties of interpretation on the ground.

Calculating Heights

In the same way as the clinometer is used in plane-tabling to find from a few known heights several spot heights around hills in order to assist drawing contours showing their shape and height, so on air photographs can several points be calculated from the heights of a few control

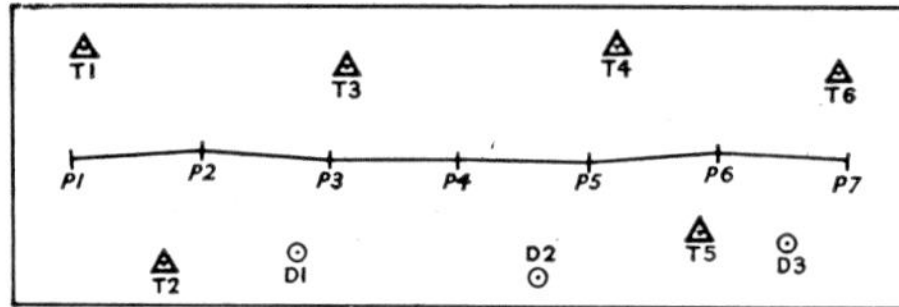

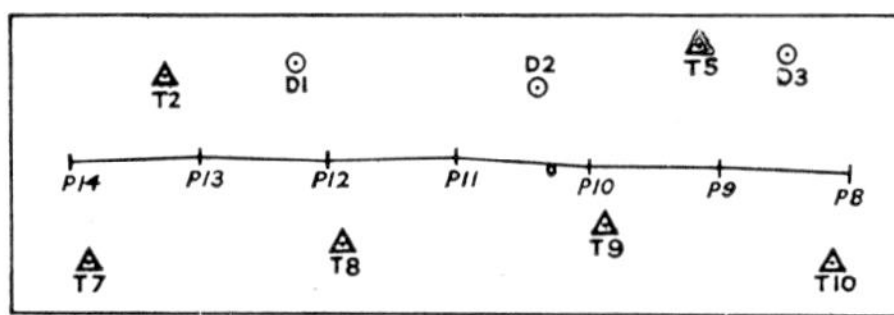

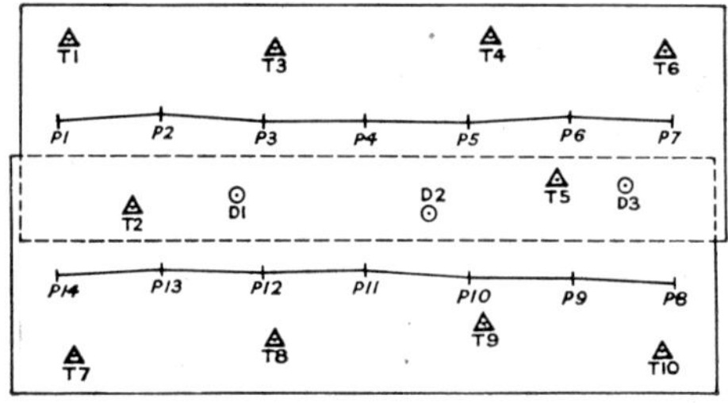

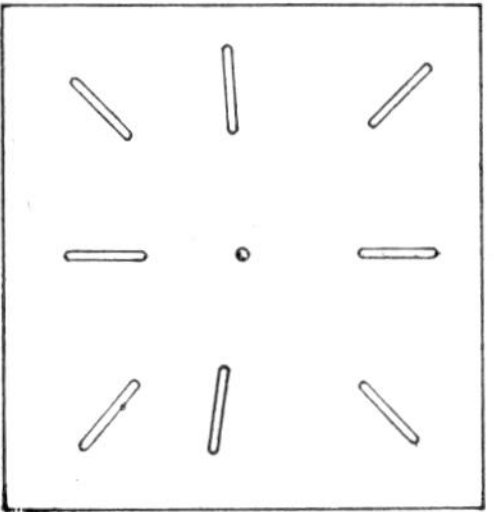

FIG. 12. Air photo control plotting by graphical methods and slotted template. P1, P2–14 are the principal points of the photographs. T1, T2, etc., are triangulation points and D1, etc., the points of detail fixed by intersection.

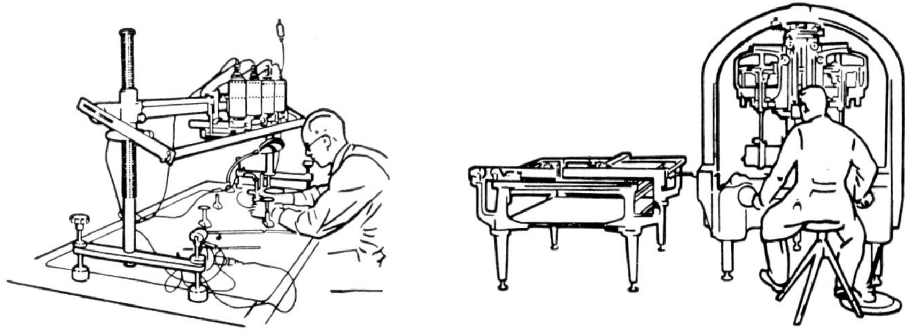

FIG. 13. Two types of air photo plotting machines.

points by an instrument called a *parallax bar*.

This instrument measures the displacement on the photograph of the top of a hill or building from the position of the foot of the hill, or building. As the amount of displacement is directly related to the height of the hill, and as the displacement for a known height can be observed, the displacement for other points can be compared and converted into heights.

More complicated and precise ways of plotting detail and heights from air photographs exist, using a variety of plotting machines. Some of these machines take miniature slides of the air photographs and project them from a line of projectors set up to represent exactly the positions of the aircraft camera when it took the photos. The pictures are projected downwards on to a long map table on which the triangulation control points have been plotted at the scale required for mapping, and the projectors adjusted until the control points on the picture lie exactly over their plotted positions.

As the projected pictures from two adjoining projectors intersect in space just above the table surface a perfect model of the country is formed in space, and can be seen standing out in relief before one's eyes, when use is made of red and green filters on the projectors and corresponding red and green spectacles. The detail (roads, etc.) which can be seen in the model is then traced on to the table top by using a pencil fixed under the centre of a miniature round table (about 4 inches high) adjustable for height, which is moved about on the surface of the large map table; and which, when the intersection of the light rays from a point is seen on its surface and at its centre, gives the position of that point on the map being compiled beneath.

By noting on a scale the height of the top of the miniature table required for rays from a point to intersect on its surface, the height of that point can easily be calculated, as with the parallax bar, by reference to the reading for a known height. All that is required to draw contours is to set the miniature table at a height representing, say, 500 feet, and move it only where rays intersect on its surface—the table can then only be moved along a line joining points of equal altitude, *i.e.*, a contour.

Owing to the comparative newness of mapping from air photographs, better methods are fast being developed in flying, photography and plotting. For example, it is possible that radar, which has already been used for fixing the positions above the ground of the camera at the instant of taking the photographs, may remove the need for the present plotting methods of fixing the centres of photographs mentioned above.

Compilation

The records and sketches obtained in the field are now used to plot accurately all detail of the country required for the map. The first task is to consider how the positions of points and shape of detail surveyed on the earth's curved surface should be plotted on the paper which is flat; this inevitably involves distortion of some kind.

The network of lines of latitude and longitude is called a map projection; there are several projections in common use and usually they are not projections in the geometrical sense. Each has special properties, and the choice of projection depends upon the scale and purpose of the map. The projection can represent distances correctly along the meridians and on one or two selected parallels ; or distances from the centre of the map; it may represent areas correctly; or it may preserve correct bearings and shapes over small areas.

FIG. 14. Various map projections are illustrated on this page, showing variations in the shape and scale of an area according to the choice of projection. Here, for example, is Europe on a conical projection based on two parallels of latitude. Compare the shaded area with its counterpart in Fig. 15.

On large-scale maps it may be difficult to tell which projection is used as the small errors in the representation of a very small part of the earth's curved surface are less than the stretch of the paper on which the map is printed. Nevertheless, the choice of projection is important in the length of computation it entails, the ease or difficulty in drawing the network, and in its accuracy for such purposes as siting and firing of artillery, railway or road construction.

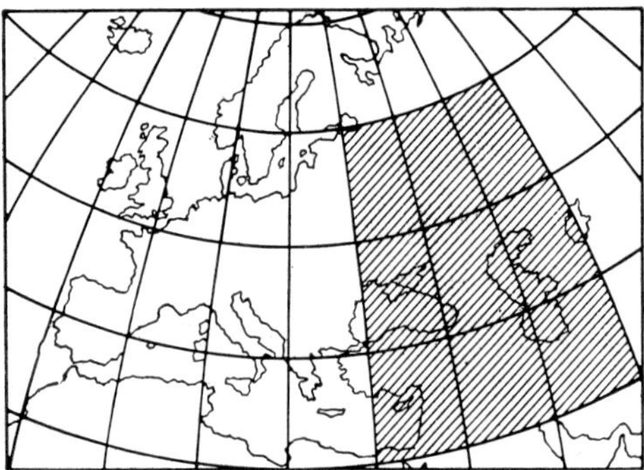

FIG. 15. Europe is here seen on Bonne's Projection. This is a modified conical projection ; distances are made true along each parallel. It shows areas correctly.

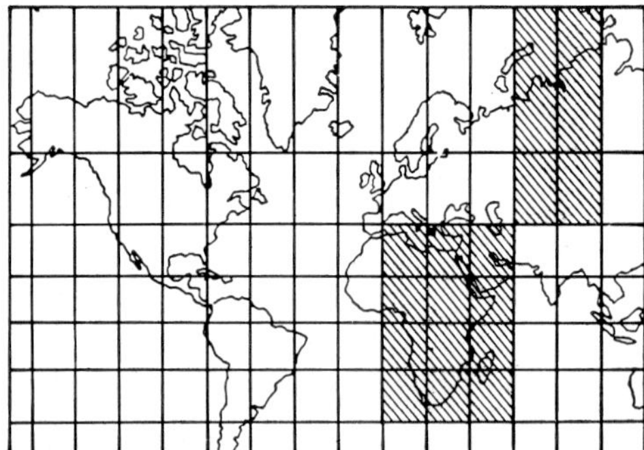

FIG. 16. Mercator's Projection agrees in scale with the globe at the Equator, but the scale becomes increasingly greater to north and south. Since longitude has been increased proportionately, the shape of the land is not locally distorted. The projection is commonly used for navigation because it is the only one which shows the true direction of one point from another.

FIG. 17. The Globular Projection has the Prime Meridian, Equator and Circumference divided into equal parts. It is easy to construct but has no special properties. Compare the shape and scale of the shaded areas with those of the same areas in Fig. 16.

Scale: 1:25,000 (2½ inches = 1 mile).

Scale: 1:63,360 (1 inch = 1 mile).

Scale: 1:253,440 (¼ inch = 1 mile).

Scale: 1:1,000,000 (16 miles = 1 inch).

FOUR EXAMPLES OF SCALE

Here we see part of Central London as it would appear on maps of four different scales. Rectangles indicate the area covered by the preceding larger scale map. The larger the scale of the map, the greater the amount of detail that can be shown. The process of selection and generalisation for small-scale maps is a task requiring much skill and judgment.

On small-scale maps covering large areas of the earth's surface—as in atlas maps—the variety and special properties of the projection can be seen.

Into the network are plotted rivers, coastline and railways, roads, woods, outlines, buildings, contours and all other information such as place names, county boundaries, names of hills, rivers and other features. If the scale of the map is small, much minor detail and names of small places have to be omitted. Also, shapes of roads, contours, coastline and towns can only be shown clearly in a generalised way. These processes of selection and generalisation are tasks in the compilation of small-scale maps requiring much skill and judgment.

Accuracy of position is here all-important as the draft map which results is the basis for the finished drawing. It is, therefore, checked meticulously before being passed as correct. If the survey has been carried out from photographs, the compilation consists of adding to the air survey draft map all the information not obtainable from the photographs—final interpretation made on the ground, names, boundaries, road and rail classifications, etc.

Finished Drawing

The draft maps are now used as the basis for the finished drawing. As each colour on the map required has to be printed separately, separate finished drawings are usually made for each colour. As each colour must fit the others perfectly, the draft is reproduced in a non-photographic blue on a material suitable for

BY CAMERA AND MAP

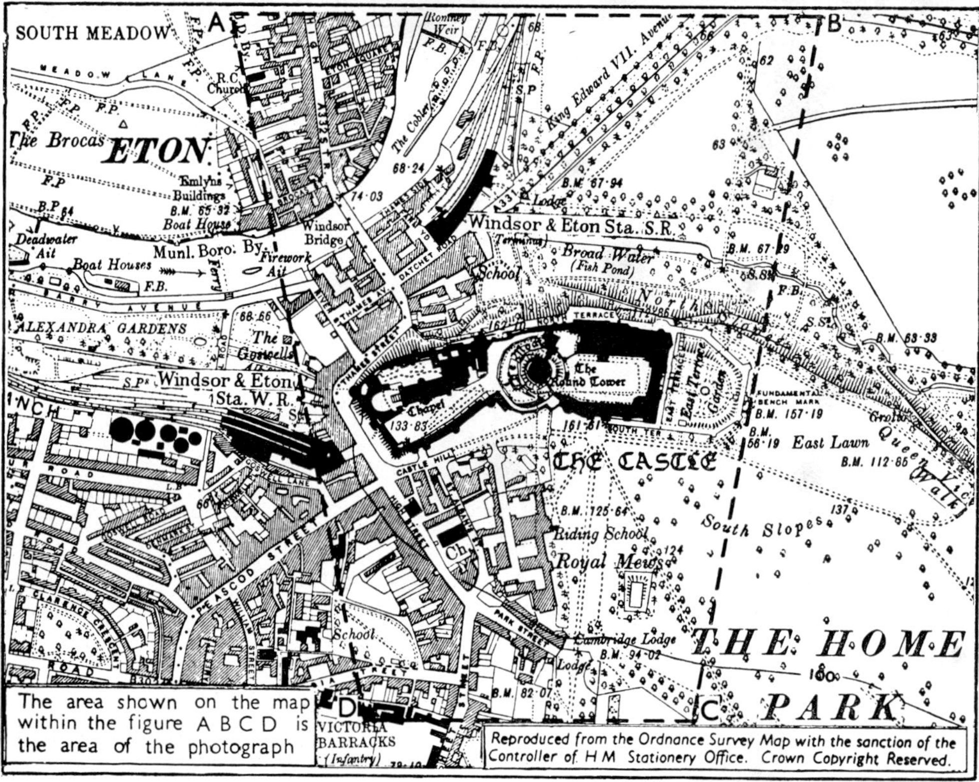

Photoflight Ltd. and George Philip & Son Ltd.

What the camera sees has been faithfully recorded by the map-maker. The map is to the scale of six inches to one mile and shows very clearly the detail of Windsor Castle and its surroundings. Among the many points that can be identified quite readily on both photograph and map are the Round Tower and Chapel of the Castle, the East Terrace Garden, and the Riding School and Royal Mews. Beyond the Castle are the Thames, the Windsor and Eton railway station, and the tree-lined King Edward VII Avenue.

drawing and which is also lasting and stable in size despite changes from dry to wet days; use is made of thin metal sheets coated with white enamel or paper, or thin plastic sheets specially prepared to keep size, or glass.

Unless the draft has been prepared at a larger scale than the final map, the draft is enlarged to give blue prints for drawing at a large scale in order that the drawings can benefit from a reduction to the final scale required for the map. The reduction gives finer lines, reduces imperfections in the drawing, and enables the draughtsmen to draw and letter larger and therefore more easily.

Draft maps were once used as the guide for engraving in copper and fine quality was achieved. Difficulties of correction have led to discarding this method and substituting drawing on the materials above-mentioned. Of recent years, however, engraving has returned as an alternative to drawing; coated glass or plastics are now used instead of copper and even finer quality of mapping is now possible. As the new engraving is also faster than drawing and more suited to later processes, the method is rapidly gaining favour.

The first drawing may contain the border, lines of latitude and longitude, the coastline and rivers. It is drawn, like all the other drawings also, in black as this is best for photography. Four small crosses, called register marks, are drawn most carefully just outside the borders and centrally on each side of the drawing; they are used for easy yet exact fitting of drawings to one another.

Then on the second blue print, railways, names, town symbols and everything eventually wanted to be printed in, say, black is drawn. The four register marks are repeated in exactly the same positions

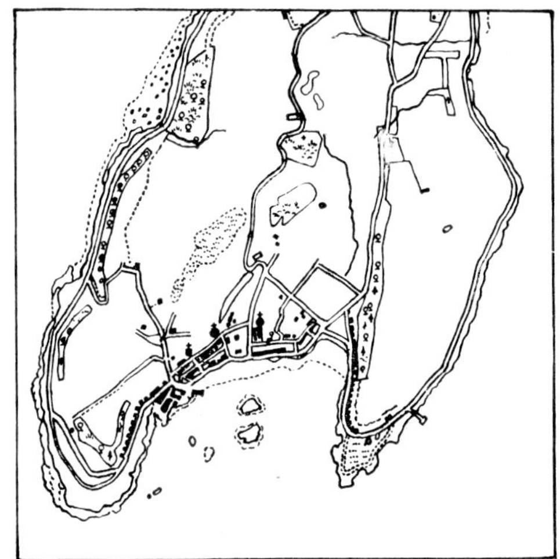

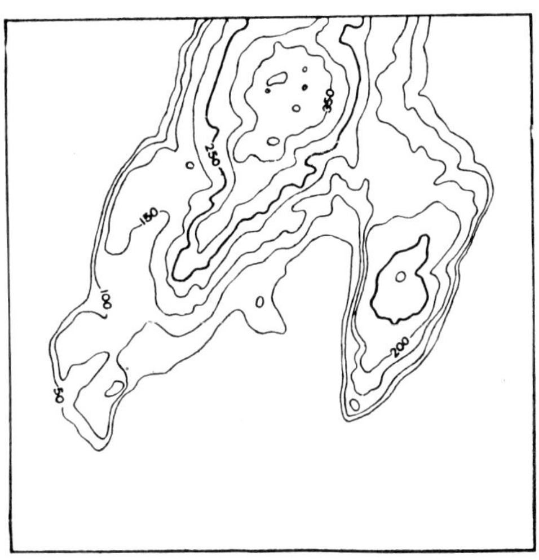

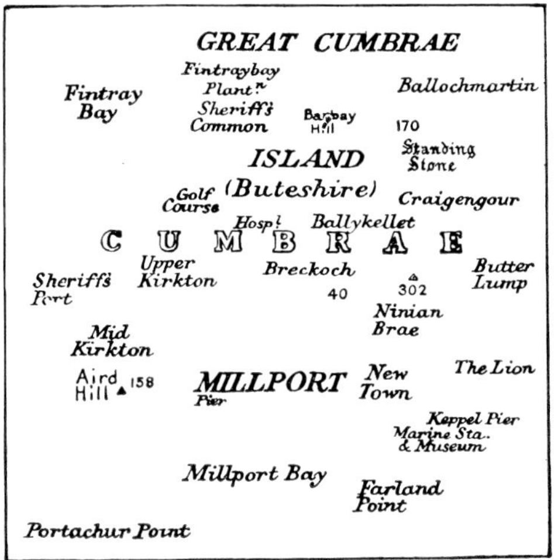

EXAMPLES OF FINISHED DRAWINGS

A separate finished drawing is required for each colour on the map. The uppermost of these examples is the basic outline. Next we have a drawing showing the contours and, lastly, the lettering. Register marks are used to ensure that one drawing fits exactly to the next.

as on the first drawing. Instead of writing the names, these are now more usually set in type by machine, printed on thin paper or on film and each name is cut out with a sharp-pointed knife and stuck on to the drawing in its correct position.

On the third blue print, contours only would be inked in. When all the required drawings are made, they are carefully checked to see that no errors have been made in drawing, or that there are any mistaken departures from the draft.

Reproduction Photography

The finished drawings now go to the Studio, where they are placed one by one in a copy board and photographed by a large and precise camera. The required reduction is set by adjusting the distance of the lens from drawing, and the glass or film from the lens, and by measuring the size of the image on a ground glass screen.

Care is taken to see that the image is "square." The negatives taken can be up to 40 by 30 inches, or even 60 by 40 inches, and often they are glass rather than film as the size and scale must be kept exact. Only the black ink of the drawings photographs; the portions of the draft blue print not drawn over do not record on the negative.

The negatives are developed and fixed, and then carefully examined for weaknesses, which are repaired by spotting with an opaque paint. If required for later processes, the negatives are contact printed to another glass plate so that a positive image is obtained.

Plate Preparation

Each negative or positive is then ready for placing in position on a thin metal plate, the surface of which has been coated with a light-sensitive emulsion. A powerful light is shone through the glass negative, or positive, on to the metal plate with which it is held in close contact in a printing-down frame. The light acts on the emulsion, so that when the plate is removed from the frame and developed, the coating is washed away except where the detail of the map has allowed the light to penetrate. A separate plate is made in this way for each colour to be printed.

Printing, Folding and Mounting

The maps are now printed from the plates, and finally folded; if required for heavy use, they are mounted on linen.

FIG. 18. A studio camera used for map reproduction. The required reduction is set by adjusting the distance of the lens from the drawing, and the glass or film from the lens, and by measuring the size of the image on a ground glass screen.

THE EXTENSION OF EUROPEAN INFLUENCE

This special Transart Supplement is complementary to the section *An Outline of Exploration* and illustrates the extension of European influence over other parts of the world. It comprises six maps, and notes on each of these will be found on page 2 of the Supplement. A summary of the principal dates and events in the history of exploration will be found on pages 3, 4 and 6.

THE MAPS

1. The Roman Empire under the Emperor Trajan, compared with the Empire of Alexander the Great.
2. Exploration and Expansion from 867 to 1490.
3. The Great Age of Discovery.
4. Expansion and Exploration from Drake to Tasman.
5. European Expansion and Contraction to 1830.
6. The World in 1914.

How to use the maps

FIG. 1

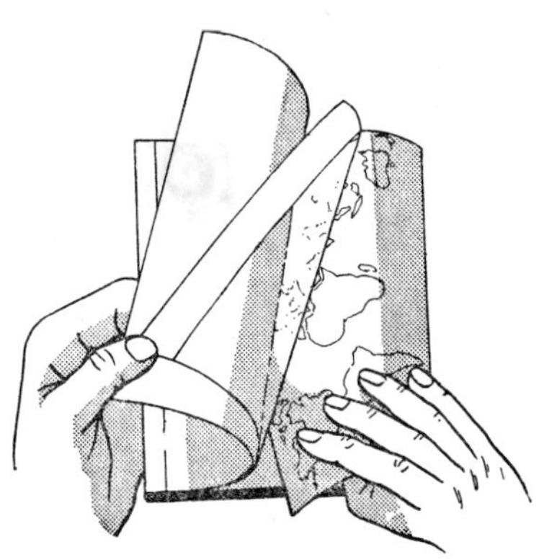

FIG. 2

The master map of the world, which forms the background to the six Transart maps, is on page 5 of the Supplement (*Fig. 1*). The Supplement can be opened and the master inserted so that it falls immediately behind any map or maps in the series (*Fig. 2.*).

1. THE EMPIRES OF ROME AND ALEXANDER THE GREAT

Alexander the Great carried Greek influence as far as the Indus valley and the Punjab in distant India, but the empire that he built so quickly collapsed with equal speed. Rome's was a different story. Her territories were greatest under the Emperor Trajan and although the great empire contracted and eventually gave way before the assaults of the barbarians, the foundations survived.

It has rightly been said that Western civilization was based upon Greek thought and Roman law and, of course, upon Christianity which rapidly spread through the lands where Rome ruled. Later, the Moslem, Eastern and Frankish Empires exerted their influence on the shaping of Europe, but the time had still to come when Western civilization and power would reach out beyond the bounds of the Old World.

2. EXPLORATION AND EXPANSION FROM 867 TO 1940.

After the fall of Rome contact with Asia was preserved only by the trickle of trade along the caravan routes. But interest revived by the Crusades and by the expansion of the Mongol empire brought about several memorable journeys, *e.g.* the famous exploits of Marco Polo. The discovery of America by the Northmen was a stage by stage advance, as the map shows, but had no lasting results. Evidence for their brief penetration of the heart of the continent is the ancient stone, inscribed with runic characters, discovered near Kensington, Minnesota, in 1898. Pointing the way to the great Age of Discovery were the voyages of Bartholomew Diaz (1486–88) and earlier Portugese venturers inspired by Prince Henry the Navigator.

3. THE GREAT AGE OF DISCOVERY

Voyagers of many nations shared in the great revealing of the world which now took place. The search for a westwards route to India led to the voyages of Columbus and the re-discovery of America (1492 onwards). Honour for the first circumnavigation of the world (1519–22) goes to Magellan, although this famous navigator did not live to see the end of the voyage. The vertical herring-bone lines on the map show the claims of Spain and Portugal, which received Papal approval. The Atlantic line was laid down in 1494 and gave dominion in the west to Spain, and in the east to Portugal. A similar line, dividing interests in the Pacific, was laid down in 1529. The Spanish conquest of Portugal (1580), the challenge of other nations, and the defeat of the Armada made such arbitrary divisions meaningless, however.

4. FROM DRAKE TO TASMAN

The challenge to Spanish power found a striking expression in Drake's voyage round the world, which also contributed to the knowledge of the west coast of America and the east coast of Asia. The great continents had now been defined, except for Australia, which was later revealed by Dutch and other explorers, particularly Tasman, whose voyages also embraced New Zealand (1642–44). The Dutch made no attempt, however, to colonise these new-found lands, but rested content with their control of the East Indies and the profits of trade.

5. EXPANSION AND CONTRACTION TO 1830

Dampier gave England news of the less-favoured parts of Australia, which he visited in 1688 and 1699. But British settlement there did not begin until 1788, *i.e.*, eighteen years after the discovery of New South Wales by Captain James Cook, whose three great voyages are shown in *An Outline of Exploration*, and not upon this Transart map. Note the changing fortunes of the imperial powers during the " Era of Revolution " (1765–1830). The United States has come into being. In North America, Britain is now concerned chiefly with Canada; but elsewhere she is building a new empire. The countries of Central and South America have freed themselves from Spain and Portugal.

6. THE WORLD IN 1914.

The rivalry of the colonial powers reached its final stages in Africa, the Pacific and the Far East. By 1914 the process of expansion was virtually complete and the scene was set for the Great War (1914–18)—the first which had an impact, direct or indirect, upon all the peoples of the world. The effect of more recent events—the Second World War (1939–45), the emergence of new nationalisms and the formation of new power blocs—is illustrated by the main map section of this Atlas.

Great dates in Exploration (continued)

Date	*Event*
1825.	Clapperton reaches the Niger, but dies at Sokoto (1827). Lander, his companion, survives.
1827.	Cunningham explores the Liverpool Range and Darling Downs in Australia. Parry attempts to reach the North Pole from Spitsbergen.
1828.	Réné Caillié reaches Timbuktu and crosses the Sahara to Tangier.
1828–31.	In Australia, Sturt discovers the Darling River and explores the Murray River.
1829.	John Ross discovers Boothia Land.
1830.	John and Richard Lander find the mouth of the Niger River. James Ross locates the North Magnetic Pole.
1831–36.	Voyage of *H.M.S. Beagle* with Charles Darwin as naturalist of the expedition.
1836.	Mitchell explores south-eastern Australia.
1837–40.	George Grey explores in Western Australia.
1838–45.	John Frémont travels and surveys in the western United States.
1840.	Discovery of Victoria Land by Ross.
1840–43.	Ross discovers Victoria Land, Mts. Erebus and Terror and the Ice Barrier in Antarctica.
1840–41.	John Eyre, having failed in his attempt to reach the centre of Australia, makes a perilous overland journey to Albany, Western Australia. Strzelecki travels through Gippsland in south-eastern Australia.
1844.	Sturt's expedition to the interior of Australia. Leichhardt's expedition to Port Essington.
1847.	Franklin discovers the North-West Passage.
1848.	Leichhardt's last expedition in Australia. Bates and Wallace set out for the Amazon. Wallace returned to England in 1852, Bates in 1859.
1849–56.	Livingstone travels in central Africa. He visits Lake Ngami, discovers the upper Zambesi and the Victoria Falls (1855), and crosses southern Africa from the Atlantic to the Indian Ocean.
1853.	M'Clure makes the North-West Passage, partly by water and partly across the ice.
1854.	Burton and Speke explore Somaliland.
1855–56.	Gregory's expedition in north-eastern Australia.
1857.	Burton and Speke discover Lake Tanganyika.
1858.	Speke finds and names Lake Victoria Nyanza.
1858–64.	Further explorations by Livingstone.
1860–63.	Speke and Grant in East Africa. Speke finds and names the Rippon Falls. The Nile followed to Gondokoro.
1860.	Stuart reaches the centre of Australia.
1860–61.	Burke and Wills expedition across Australia.
1862–63.	Stuart crosses Australia to Port Darwin.
1864.	Sir Samuel Baker finds Lake Albert.
1866–73.	Livingstone's last journey.
1869–72.	Stanley leads the Livingstone relief expedition.
1869.	John Forrest tries to solve the mystery of Leichhardt's end.
1870.	John Forrest goes from Perth to Adelaide.
1871–88.	Explorations of Nicholas Prjeválsky in Mongolia and other parts of inner Asia.
1874–89.	Stanley's expeditions in tropical Africa.
1874.	John Forrest's journey from Geraldton to the Lake Eyre district of South Australia.
1875–76.	Giles crosses and recrosses the Gibson Desert in Western Australia.
1875–77.	Charles Doughty travels in north-western and central Arabia.
1878–80.	Nordenskiöld conquers the North-East Passage.
1888.	Fridtjof Nansen makes the first crossing of Greenland.
1893.	Sven Hedin journeys through Tibet and China.
1893–96.	Nansen's expedition in the *Fram*. Nansen's dash for the North Pole takes him to 86° 14′ N. (1895).
1900.	Cagni, one of the Duke of Abruzzi's expedition, beats Nansen's " Farthest North."
1901–04.	Scott reaches 82° 17′ S.
1903–06.	Amundsen sails the North-West Passage in the *Gjöa*.
1909.	Peary reaches the North Pole.
1911.	Amundsen reaches the South Pole.
1912.	Scott reaches the South Pole, but perishes with his companions on the return journey.
1914–1917.	Shackleton's expedition in *Endurance* He fails in his attempt to cross Antarctica.
1926.	Byrd and Bennett fly to the North Pole and back from Spitsbergen. Amundsen and Ellsworth in the Italian airship *Norge* fly from Spitsbergen to Point Barrow, Alaska via the North Pole.
1927–35.	Sven Hedin's expeditions in China and central Asia.
1928.	Wilkins flies across the Polar Sea. The airship *Italia* reaches the North Pole but crashes on the return journey. Wilkins flies over Graham Land.
1928–30.	Byrd's expedition to Antarctica. He discovers Marie Byrd Land and flies to the South Pole.
1934–37.	British Graham Land Expedition.
1933–35.	Byrd explores Marie Byrd Land.
1939–41.	Byrd's third expedition to Antarctica.
1943–46.	Secret British All-Services Expedition to Graham Land.
1947–48.	Australian expeditions under Campbell to Heard and Macquarie Islands, Balleny Islands and Adelie Land.
1949–52.	First international (British-Norwegian-Swedish) expedition to Antarctica.
1957–58.	*International Geophysical Year*. British Commonwealth Trans-Antarctic Expedition and the Royal Society's Geophysical Year Expedition.
1958.	First voyage under the North Pole by the U.S. atomic submarine *Nautilus*.

MAJOR REGIONS OF THE WORLD

THE world, like mankind, has many faces. We call them *regions* and distinguish them according to their structure, climate, plant and animal life (biogeography), economic resources, or human activities (human geography). A classification based on any of these groups of characteristics would, of course, tell us a great deal about the others.

It is easy to see why: climate not only affects the nature and activities of all living things, and is in turn specially affected by plants, but also influences, and is influenced by, physical features. Again, if we study biogeography we have incidentally begun to study economic geography, since most of our basic resources come from animals and plants, including those that lived millions of years ago.

Camera Press.

A GREAT GLOBE

The Great Globe at Durlston Castle, Swanage, Dorset, sets an example which should be widely followed, for large globes are as necessary to geographical studies as maps and pictures.

Man and Nature

It follows that, no matter how we study the regions of the world, our studies will overlap into human geography. For mankind lives according to climate and regional peculiarities; and men have wandered, changed and developed in response to various geographical influences.

For thousands of years, we have been changing the world, too, by destroying, digging, building and rearranging life on the land according to our needs and extravagances. Even when we talk of "the country," we are usually talking of man-made country.

Indeed, human activities have altered nature so much, and the pace is increasing so rapidly, that we often read about "Man's Conquest of Nature." The truth is less romantic: the highest peaks and the coldest latitudes have been "conquered" but not productively colonised. At the same time, we already have the knowledge for controlling, altering and resisting natural phenomena to a much greater extent. We can remove the deserts from the geographies of tomorrow.

Sunshine and Climate

Climatic conditions are the effects of many interlinked causes, but geographers are fond of saying that latitude determines climate. More simply this means that, on the whole, temperature decreases, because the Sun's rays have farther to travel, as the breadths (latitudes) of the Earth decrease from the equator to the poles.

Thus, temperature is the first cause of regional differences in climate. Seasonal differences in temperature, and consequently in the total climate, follow the Earth's movement round the Sun with its axis tilted at $66\frac{1}{2}°$; and daily differences in weather are associated with the changes in temperature that occur as the spinning Earth takes us away from the warming rays of the Sun.

Indeed, weather and climate, like life itself, exist because the Earth receives one two-millionth of the enormous energy radiated by the Sun. This energy, travelling at 186,000 miles a second until it reaches the atmosphere, comes as short and invisible ultra-violet waves (12 per cent.), longer visible or light waves (37 per cent.), and much longer infra-red or dark waves (51 per cent.).

All these waves leave the Sun in one " bundle," but are separated and scattered when they reach the atmosphere. The ultra-violet rays are absorbed by the ozone layer, those that remain being so scattered that they reach sea-level more from the blue sky than direct sunlight.

The Importance of Ultra-violet Rays

Nevertheless, ultra-violet rays are an important element of climate which affects regional geography. They assist in the making of rain as they can convert water vapour into droplets of water. And wherever there is enough rain, plants grow quickly and abundantly providing there is warmth and plenty of ultra-violet radiation. For the same reasons, cultivation tends to be concentrated in sunny lands to the point of giving them definite regional characteristics.

The chief fruit-growing centres, for example, are in countries with the Mediterranean type of climate, while in those less blessed the areas of most sunshine, such as Kent, Norfolk and Devon in England, produce the most fruit.

In animals, the interaction between ultra-violet rays and a fatty substance in the skin makes vitamin D—the " sunshine vitamin " essential to the growth and health of the bones and teeth. Therefore, according to season and place, we either get " sunshine milk " or milk with very little vitamin D.

The amount can be increased by artificial irradiation, and we can get vitamin D from other sources, but it is best to make it ourselves as animals do. In the process germ-diseases of the skin are avoided or cured, for ultra-violet rays are fatal to germs: and we acquire a " healthy tan " because the rays stimulate the dark pigment in the skin as a protection against their dangerous effects. But the risk of sunburn remains, especially on bright days in the mountains, and fair people naturally suffer more than those who are dark.

In some countries sunstroke is greatly feared, but in many parts of the tropics there is so much moisture in the air that sun-helmets are a convention rather than a need. In fact, the growing danger everywhere is insufficient ultra-violet radiation. For, in addition to being screened according to the contents of the atmosphere, it is kept from us by clothing and the increasing habit of living and working indoors. The sun often shines pleasantly enough through our glass windows, but without its ultra-violet rays. Iron-free glass, however, lets them through and will undoubtedly be used when homes, offices and factories are designed with respect for the importance of sunshine.

The Nature of Light

Sir Napier Shaw (1854–1945), a great British meteorologist, thought we might respect it more by realising that if really scientific electric lighting and heating could be devised and supplied at a penny a unit, an hour's sunshine on a square yard of ground would give us the equivalent of a pennyworth of electricity. At this rate an hour's sunshine all over England is worth about £509,000,000.

We see the visible rays of sunshine as " white light," but when it is passed through a prism it splits into the rays that give the spectrum its seven colours—violet, indigo, blue, green, yellow, orange, and red.

The scattering of these rays begins in the upper atmosphere by the diffusion of violet, indigo and blue. Therefore, at high altitudes the sky is a rich violet-blue, as mountain-climbers and travellers by air know; but at sea-level, where there is little violet, the colour of the sky ranges from blue to a deep indigo-blue.

The longer light waves—yellow, orange and red—are scattered mostly by the water vapour and impurities of the lower atmosphere; and so we get the bright glows of sunset. The Sun itself is then a deep red ball, for scattering has taken all but the deeper reds from its rays.

The Dark Heat Rays

The infra-red, like the ultra-violet, rays are invisible, but we feel them immediately as heat. They are intercepted by water and water-vapour, as we know when sunshine is suddenly obscured by a cloud, the screening effects of the lower atmosphere being so great that even on clear days the strength of the sun's rays in the uppermost atmosphere is reduced to 75 per cent. at 6,000 feet and 50 per cent. at sea-level.

At 10,000 feet a third of the atmosphere, and most of the impurities, is left behind and the Sun's rays can be strong enough, though the air temperature is low, to boil and burn. Water has actually been boiled in a bottle exposed to the Sun, since the reduced pressures of high altitudes lowers the sea-level boiling point, at Leh (11,500 feet) in the Ladakh Range of Kashmir.

The Earth adds to its supply of surface warmth by converting the light rays into infra-red rays, for they are largely radiated back to the atmosphere as long heat waves.

Greek Embassy, London.

THE TOWER OF THE WINDS

Many ancient monuments testify to man's age-old attempts to cope with the weather. The Tower of the Winds (built before 35 B.C.) in Athens paid homage to the eight wind-gods, while serving the practical purpose of housing sundials and a water-clock. You can see Skiron, the North-wester, in front, with an inverted fire-pot in his hands symbolising cold; and to his right there is Zephyrus, the famous West wind of the Mediterranean.

Camb. Univ. Press.

AN OLD RAIN-GAUGE

The importance of measuring rainfall has also been understood from early times and in China, where rainfall is heavy and floods common, accurate rain-gauges were in use before the thirteenth century. Our picture, taken from Joseph Needham's *Science and Civilization in China*, shows a rain-gauge of 1770 in Taiko, Korea. The large Chinese characters mean "rain-measuring platform."

Usually they do not go right through the atmosphere, to be lost in space, as they strike the water vapour and droplets of water in the air and are reflected back to the Earth.

Thus, a "blanket" of low clouds helps to keep the Earth warm at night and protects crops and animals against destructive frost. Since clouds and dust particles scatter the Sun's rays, a red sky at sundown is practically a promise that there will be no frost that night and the morrow will be fine. Hence the old saying "Red sky at night is the shepherd's delight."

In dry cloudless areas, the heat rays pass freely to and from the Earth—and so one can roast in the day and freeze at night in such different places as Siberia and the Sahara. Siberia, incidentally, boasts of lower temperatures than the North Pole, for the polar air is relatively moist.

Temperature, then, is much more than heat from sunshine. It is the result of earthwards radiation from the Sun and spacewards radiation from the Earth, with latitude influencing the incoming supplies and the atmosphere acting as a regulator which regulates differently from day to day. So the regulator itself is a cause of variations in temperature and is in turn affected by those variations.

In fact, this pattern of interwoven influences continues throughout the study of temperature. Consider, for example, how variations in temperature affect, and are affected by, the endless movements of conduction, circulation, evaporation and precipitation.

Temperature and Circulation

Upwards or vertical circulation of a column of air above the land is a convenient starting point. The heat and light rays received by the land are both radiated into the atmosphere as heat; and, as the lower margin of the column is in contact with the surface of the land, it receives heat by conduction as well.

The warmed column rises and cool air from above descends to replace it; but it is not merely an up and down process, for cool air at low levels in the neighbourhood will also flow into the zone of low pressure. In warm coastal areas this sideways flow can usually be felt as an incoming sea-breeze during the day because, as you know, the land heats more rapidly than the sea. At night, as the land cools rapidly while the temperature of the sea does not change considerably, a slighter breeze blows seawards.

These land and sea breezes are miniatures, so to speak, of the continental winter winds which blow from the high pressure atmosphere over the cold lands to the warm seas, and the summer winds which speed towards the low pressure atmosphere above the warm lands. For the causes of all air-movements, including the great wind systems initiated by the intense heating of the equatorial region, are the same—differences in pressure through differences in temperature.

Now let us add evaporation and precipitation to our glimpse of the effects of temperature. The oceans supply the air with most of its water, but every body of water, from puddles to vast lakes, adds to the primary source; and so do animals and plants. Much heat is required for separating from water the particles that rise invisibly as vapour—and so the rate of evaporation varies according to the temperature and dryness of the air.

The Making of Rain

Consequently, the capacity of the air for holding moisture also varies according to temperature. At 30° F. a cubic foot of air cannot hold more than 1·9 grains of water vapour; at 60° F. it will hold 5·7 grains of water vapour; and at 90° F. it will not be saturated until it has taken up 14·7 grains of water vapour.

The amount of moisture actually in the air is its absolute humidity. The difference between this amount and the saturation point, expressed as a percentage, is the relative humidity. Thus, if you will work the sum out for yourself, when air at 60° F. contains 4 grains per cubit foot the relative humidity is 70 per cent., since the saturation point is 5·7 grains.

Heating the same air will reduce the relative humidity, as the saturation point will increase; cooling it will increase the relative humidity and eventually decrease the absolute humidity. At 30° F., the air which contained 4 grains per cubic foot at 60° F. will have to get rid of 2·1 grains per cubic foot, because it can only hold 1·9 grains per cubic foot at the reduced temperature.

The amount of vapour thrown out when warm saturated air is cooled is much more striking. Saturated air at 90° will lose 9 grains per cubic foot if its temperature drops to 60° F., but only 2·9 grains from 60° to 30° F.

What happens to the " lost " vapour? It condenses—that is, it is converted into droplets of water that may eventually fall as dew, frost, rain, sleet, snow or hail. This is *precipitation.*

Dust and other particles in the air help

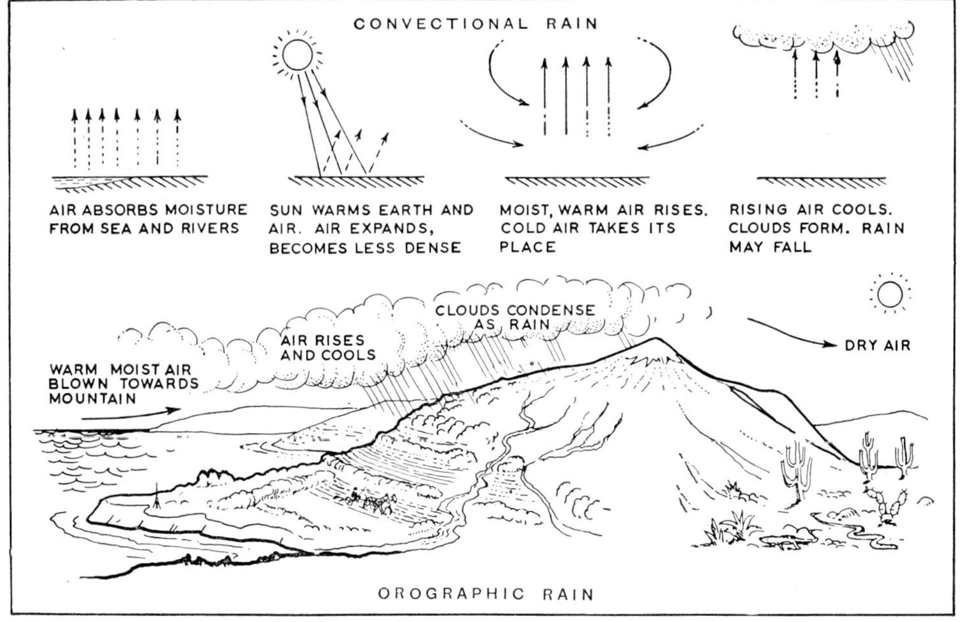
CONVECTIONAL RAIN
AIR ABSORBS MOISTURE FROM SEA AND RIVERS
SUN WARMS EARTH AND AIR. AIR EXPANDS, BECOMES LESS DENSE
MOIST, WARM AIR RISES. COLD AIR TAKES ITS PLACE
RISING AIR COOLS. CLOUDS FORM. RAIN MAY FALL
CLOUDS CONDENSE AS RAIN
AIR RISES AND COOLS
WARM MOIST AIR BLOWN TOWARDS MOUNTAIN
DRY AIR
OROGRAPHIC RAIN

Specially drawn for this work.

AIR CIRCULATION AND RAINFALL

In this diagram we try to show how the circulation of air may carry water vapour to levels where it condenses and falls as convectional rain; or push clouds against and up the sides of a mountain, thus causing orographic rain. On the other side, in the "rain shadow," the descending winds are dry and warm.

the formation of the droplets by providing microscopic centres around which the droplets form as the solid particles cool; but vapour can also be converted, as we have said, into water by the effects of ultra-violet radiation. So sunshine shares in the process of converting into water the vapour it has evaporated; and pollution itself is used to rid the sky of pollution.

Kinds of Precipitation

Now we can see how water, supplied primarily by the seas, returns from the sky to the land. The condensed vapour floats as mist, fog and cloud, or lies on the ground as dew.

Dew is formed on clear nights (when the land is not warmed by a blanket of cloud) by the chilling of vapour near the ground. Low-lying mists collect if this chilling extends upwards for some distance; and frost if the ground temperature is below freezing point (32° F.).

Mists, in fact, are "suspended dew" and fogs are thick mists. Smoke and dust share with low ground temperature the responsibility for some of our worst land fogs, but impenetrable fogs on land and sea are also caused by the condensation of the lower levels of vapour when warm saturated air passes over cold surfaces. This happens so frequently as the air warmed by the Gulf Stream flows over the cold waters of the Labrador Current that the seas around Newfoundland are fog-bound for more than seventy days in the year.

Clouds can be called "high fogs". They consist, like mists and fogs, of droplets of water squeezed out of the atmosphere by cooling below the saturation point; but they ride the high skies and usually ascend, while mists and fogs lie heavily near the surface and always descend.

The "lift" of upwards currents keeps clouds aloft and this updraught naturally has a tendency to oppose rainfall. Small droplets may be evaporated as they drift slowly down against a slight updraught, though they may fall as gentle rain. Or a strong current may carry them upwards, where they will grow, by merging with other droplets, until they are large enough to fall through the updraught as rain—or snow, if the temperature is cold enough.

But the larger the drops are the more likely they are to be broken up and blown higher when the updraught is very strong: they are always broken up when they reach a diameter of ¼-inch if the rising current exceeds 16 miles an hour. In the zone where water exists only as ice they freeze and start falling again; and, on reaching the level where water drops are found, they freeze a layer of water around themselves. Then they may fall as small hailstones; or they may rise and descend several times, acquiring layers of ice in the process, until they eventually fall as large hailstones.

Hailstorms, often associated with thunderstorms, are common in many countries. They do much damage, for the stones are usually in the neighbourhood of ½ to 1 inch in diameter, and are sometimes large enough to kill men and animals.

How Rain Falls

You may have concluded, from what we have said, that rain falls because vertical circulation carries water vapour up to levels where it condenses, forms clouds, and returns to the surface, if conditions are favourable, as rain. But, though all rainfall depends essentially on the cooling of rising saturated air, this is only one of three main ways of making rain.

Rain so produced is known as *convectional rain*. Typically it falls as showers that are most frequent and heavy, since they are initiated by rapid heating of the land, in tropical countries and during hot summer afternoons elsewhere.

Convectional rain often falls in torrential downpours, but *orographic rain* (*oros* is the Greek word for " mountain ") greatly exceeds it in total quantity. Its name is a clue to its cause: a mountain barrier

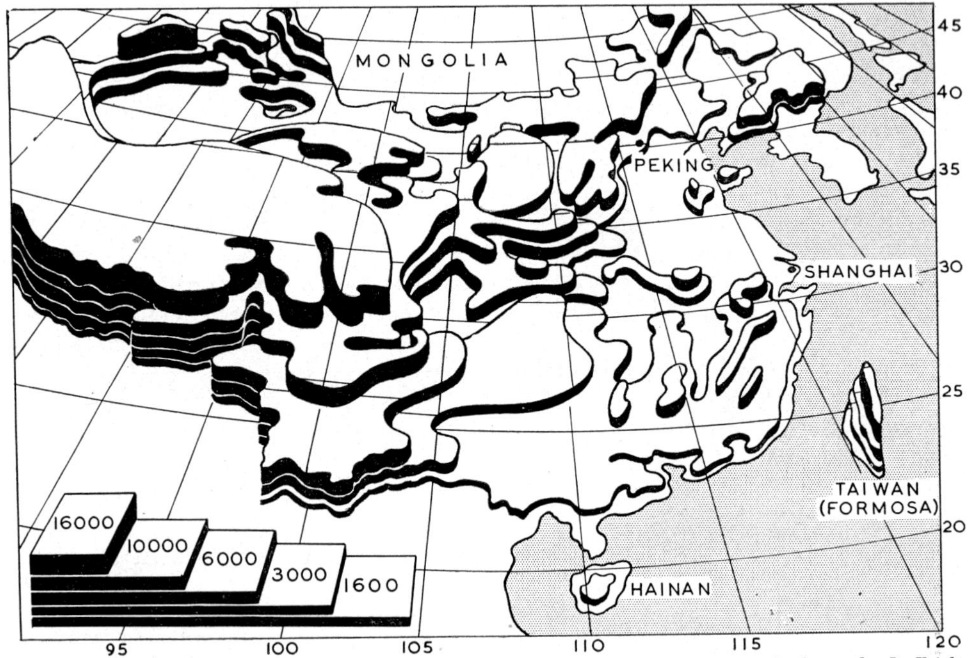

Re-drawn after Lo Kai-fu.

A LAND STEPS DOWN TO THE SEA

This modelled map of the stepwise descent of China from the western highlands to the eastern plains shows how the topography of a country affects climate, drainage and the development of hydro-electric power in the many places where the waters fall with torrential strength.

standing in the way of moisture-laden air blowing in from the sea. Therefore, the air is forced to rise and condensation and precipitation follow—which is why the tops of mountains are usually shrouded by clouds and mists.

On the other side of the mountain the air becomes progressively drier and warmer, sometimes reaching the foothills as a hot dry wind which raises the temperature appreciably. The Föhn of the Alpine valleys and the Chinook of the eastern Rockies are winds of this type. The effects of air descending along the leeward side of a mountain are not usually so dramatic, though in some places there is drought on the dry side and excessive rainfall on the windward side.

Masses of cold dense air also act as effective obstacles in the path of warm damp winds, for different densities prevent mixing. So the warm air rises, clouds are formed, and *cyclonic rain* results—a cyclone is the name given to a moving area of low pressure which attracts the inflow of air of various kinds and origins.

In these and other ways, including the driving force of the winds on ocean currents, the movements of air keep water in life-giving and relief-changing circulation from the oceans to the skies, and from the skies to the lands on its journey back to the oceans. And, urging these movements is the ceaseless interplay of radiated energy in which water itself takes a prominent part. For, apart from the vast reservoirs of heat and cold in the seas and glaciers, the release of stored heat in water vapour provides much of the power that keeps air in continuous circulation.

Many common phrases express the fact that sunshine, water and the nature of the land are the makers of climate. We speak of hot and cold countries, dry and wet seasons; and so recognise the climatic types that experts have classified.

Types of Climate

Broadly, they are grouped as *hot* when the mean annual temperature is above 70° F.; *subtropical* when the mean temperature does not go below 43° in any month; *temperate* when there is a cold season of one to five months below 43°; *cold* when there is a long cold season of six or more months below 43°; *arctic* when it is always below 50°; and *desert* when there is less than ten inches of rain in the year. *Mountain* climates are added to these types, for altitude creates special peculiarities.

The hot regions, extending on either side of the Equator to beyond the Tropics of Cancer and Capricorn, occupy half the total surface of the Earth. They are often called "the tropics," but they divide

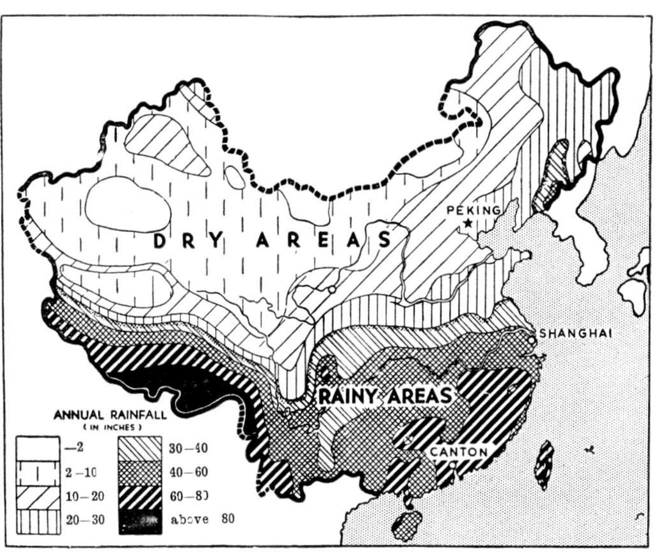

Re-drawn after Liang Yi-jou.

RAINFALL IN CHINA

Rainfall in China is largely the result of its structure and south-eastern seaboard. During the warm monsoon season, vapour-laden winds blow to the low pressure area over the land where, blocked by the highlands, they give eastern China 90 per cent. of its rainfall. Cyclones are created when these winds come into conflict with the westerlies blowing along the edges of the Tibetan plateau.

naturally into an inner *equatorial* climate, with *tropical* climates north and south of this belt.

The equatorial climate is hot and moist throughout the year, but the temperature drops considerably at night. Much of the rainfall, as you would expect, is convectional.

The tropical climates are of three kinds: marine, continental (or interior) and monsoon. In the marine type, owing to the nearness of the sea, there are no dry periods as there are in the hotter interior regions exposed to the dry trade winds. The monsoon countries also have a marked dry season, but the rainfall is extremely heavy during the summer.

The basic causes of monsoon climates are easily understood. The cooling of great land masses (those of Asia equal half the land of the world) creates high pressure areas from which dry winds blow towards the sea. This situation is strikingly reversed during the summer. Heating then sets up enormous low pressure areas into which the moisture laden trade winds flow, deluging the thirsty soil with cyclonic or orographic rain as they pass.

The subtropical (or " warm temperate ") climates are of two main types: the *Mediterranean* or *Western Margin*, and the *China* or *Eastern Margin*. Both have hot summers and mild winters, but in the Mediterranean type winter rain is brought by the warm west winds blowing from the sea. The same winds are comparatively dry by the time they reach the eastern margins, where the summers winds, that bring dryness to the western margins, provide generous rain.

The temperate (or " cool temperate ") regions differ from the subtropical in having definite winters, but their temperatures are often extreme, as in Mongolia. In fact, temperate climates can only be called temperate where marine influences are strong, but in such areas it rains fairly heavily throughout the year and often most heavily in the winter. Away from the sea, the total rainfall decreases and the peaks occur in the summer—conspicuously so when the monsoons are responsible.

The cold, like the temperate, climates are influenced by the westerly winds and the nearness or otherwise of the sea. Consequently, the differences between them are of degree, the cold climates having longer and more severe winters. Indeed, the severest winters occur in parts of the cold continental interiors and not in the Arctic. They are natural " frigidaires " in which the bodies of prehistoric elephants, frozen thousands of years ago in Siberia, have kept fresh enough for " mammoth steaks " to be served to distinguished visitors.

The subdivisions of the Arctic climate are the *tundra*, with summer temperatures above 32° F., and the perpetually frozen *ice cap*; those of the desert climate are the *hot* deserts where the mean temperature never drops below 43°, and the *cold* deserts which have four or five months of sharp winter.

Kinds of Vegetation

The diversity of plants, upon which even flesh-eating animals ultimately depend, is brought about by adaptations to the climatic and other conditions in which they live, including the need to live with each other. Those dominate which are best adapted to their situation; and those are best adapted which can make the fullest use of circumstances favourable to growth.

In fact, the behaviour of plants arises from the nature and extent of their adaptations and not as simple responses to climatic factors. At the same time, climate has influenced their adaptations and limits their spread; and for this reason we can draw maps that roughly fit vegetation zones into a climatic scheme.

We do this more effectively with trees because they have a long growing period when they need warmth and plenty of moisture, and their deep roots require water well below the surface of the soil. Dry winds greatly increase their need for water and in the winter the amounts evaporated cannot be made good from the chilled soil. Therefore, trees have to be specially adapted to deal with the climatic conditions so vital to their growth; and

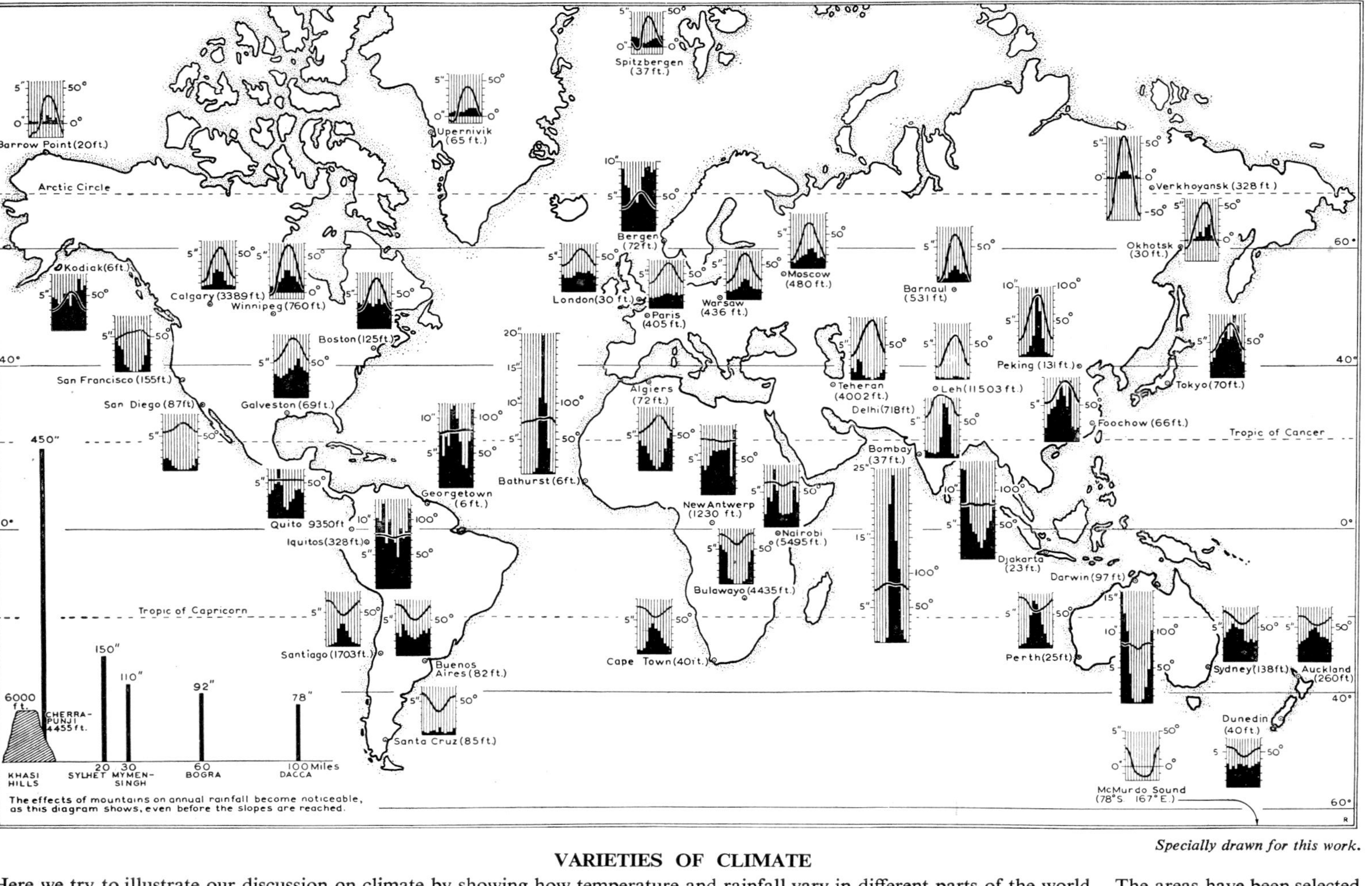

Specially drawn for this work.

VARIETIES OF CLIMATE

Here we try to illustrate our discussion on climate by showing how temperature and rainfall vary in different parts of the world. The areas have been selected to show the effects of altitude, western and eastern margins, and situation in the continental heartlands ("continentality"), as well as those of latitude.

Forestry Commission, London.

BROADLEAVED AND CONIFEROUS TREES

A broadleaved evergreen tree, the Holm or Holly Oak, is shown in the picture on the left; next to it is a winter photograph of a deciduous English Oak; and on the right is a typical conifer—the noble Silver Fir.

so we can broadly classify forests according to adaptations to climatic zones.

Thus, in the *broadleaved evergreen* forests of the equatorial, and many tropical, regions the trees are of a kind that can enjoy perpetual abundance: their leaves are broad and remain evergreen because they can go on drinking in sunshine and giving out moisture throughout the year. They grow tall, close together and in great variety, their spreading crowns meeting to form a canopy beneath which smaller plants struggle towards the light.

Beyond the equatorial belt broadleaved trees of the *deciduous* type (*decidous* means " fall " in Latin) begin to appear. They grow vigorously during the warm wet season and rest, shedding their leaves to do so, when winter or drought sets in; but some species have acquired this habit more successfully than others. For this reason, deciduous forests, unlike broadleaved evergreen forests, are dominated by a few species—a characteristic helpful to the timber industry.

The hardiest of these dominant species can survive in fairly high latitudes and altitudes, but the cold eventually defeats them and they give way to cone-bearing trees with needle-like leaves that are not, as a rule, shed when winter comes. Thus, they can take the fullest advantage of the short growing season, for they do not have to wait for their leaves to appear when the temperature increases.

These cone-bearing trees make up the bulk of the *coniferous* forests of the cold lands. They also occur with deciduous trees in cool climates, but are too highly specialised to go much below 40° N. at sea-level and are not specialised enough to establish themselves in the tundra—the reindeer desert of mosses and lichens, relieved sometimes by dwarfed trees and carpets of such familiar flowers as

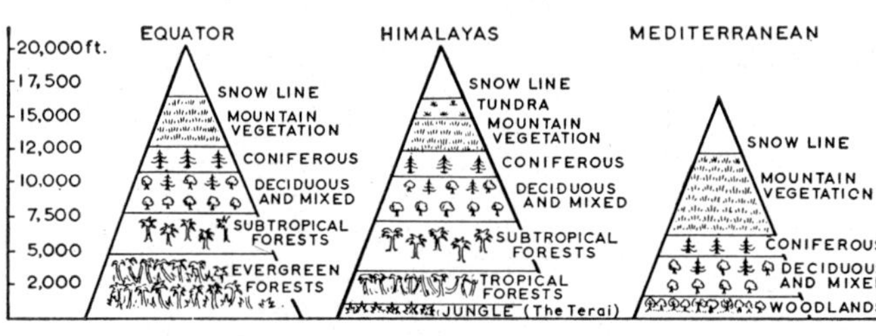

ALTITUDE AND VEGETATION

High altitudes affect vegetation in much the same way as high latitudes. This diagram shows the succession of vegetation according to height at the equator, in the tropics, and in the Mediterranean region.

Campion, Forget-Me-Not and Willow-herb.

Winds push the tundra higher up on the west as they benefit the trees. Western Europe gains so much from their gifts that the natural forests are conspicuously deciduous, but below 40° N. rainfall decreases and the forests thin out and finally disappear as the Sahara, with its prevailing dry winds, is reached. South of the Sahara, the rainfall again increases and the desert passes into short, and then tall, grass which persists to the edge of the equatorial belt.

Elsewhere, too, the *grasslands* begin where the forest ends; for grasses grow quickly when the little water they need is available. Their extent in the interiors of the temperate regions—the steppes of Eurasia and the prairie of North America are familiar examples—are striking evidence of the effects of climate in the continental heartlands; but in northern Africa it can almost be said that the dry winds blow the savanna, as the tall tropical grasslands are called, from coast to coast on either side of 10° N. There the sequence of tall and short desert grass, as dryness increases, is unusually clear.

The climax of the forest-grasslands sequence is water-conserving desert shrub and vast expanses of plantless rock and sand. Woodcutters who fell trees without replacing them, and nomads who let their animals graze on saplings, share the responsibility for these great waste lands. They cover more than a quarter of the world's land.

The Hot Lands

We come now to the major geographical regions.

Beginning with the Hot Lands, the first regional type is the *Equatorial.* It extends to about 10° on either side of the Equator and, as the name suggests, its climate changes little throughout the year. It is always hot (around 80° F.) and humid,

Swedish Travel Bureau.

THE TUNDRA

With reindeer grazing and flowering plants in bloom, the tundra at its best certainly presents an idyllic scene. But for the Lapps, who depend on the reindeer for almost all the necessities of life, from food, clothing and sewing thread to tents and sledges (called *pulka*), life is seldom easy.

CONGO AND SELVAS

Hulton Picture Library.

The gorilla is among the largest equatorial animals: strong males reach 6 ft. and 600 lb. or more. Their intelligence is humanlike, but they look stupid and ferocious because of their low foreheads, beetling brows and flattened chinless faces. Even so, they are friendly in captivity.

H. Goldstein (Congopresse).

This picture, typical of the African equatorial region, was taken in the Stanleyville District of the Belgian Congo. The men are hunting for gorillas, for there is always a good market for these rare apes. They seem too intent on the chase to bother with lesser quarry.

Paul Popper.

The density of the typical *selvas* of the Amazon region puts it beyond good photography, but we can get an idea of its character from this clearing inhabited by a small group of forest dwellers. Even here the tall slender trees grow close together and are of many different kinds.

Paul Popper.

The tree-sloth is the characteristic animal of the *selvas*. It is an odd, leaf-eating creature, related to the equally odd anteaters and armadilloes, which lives entirely in the trees, moving slowly among the branches or hanging slothfully upside down from them. With its food at hand, there is no need for it to waste energy in being active.

SNAPSHOTS FROM THE TROPICS

Cedric Dover.

A hillside forest scene in Malaya is shown above. *Right:* The edge of a Burmese forest. The suspension bridge was built by the Nung tribe.

Paul Popper.

Camera Press.

Camera Press.

Large animals are common. *Above:* A trained elephant clearing rubber trees in Ceylon. *Left:* A Fijian village—palms are typical of the tropical coasts.

Camera Press.

Paul Popper.

In India, where monkeys are sacred, the common *Macacus* and the Black-faced Langur, have poured out of the jungles into the villages and towns. Fortunately, the spotted Leopard and other " big cats," remain rare visitors.

Australian News Bureau.

THE AUSTRALIAN BOTTLE-TREE

The swollen and pithy trunks of the baobabs or bottle-trees help them to resist drought. They are also renowned for the fresh water found in hollows in their branches, but they are locally appreciated mostly for the useful timber and fibre they provide.

though there are usually two wet seasons when most of the average annual rainfall of 50–80 inches, often more than 100 inches, occurs. Its forests, especially the *selvas* of Brazil, are tall, dense and canopied, but the perpetual twilight is brightened by shafts of sunshine and the rich colours of its plants and animals. The animals are small and highly adapted to life in the treetops and to the difficulties of negotiating the tangled undergrowth. The people are small too—pygmies are equatorial folk.

In these circumstances human enterprise is continuously challenged. Everyday living is a ceaseless struggle, agriculture is forbiddingly difficult, and trade might seem to us impossible. Yet the region is being increasingly controlled and worked: rubber, sugar, and palm oil are among the chief equatorial contributions to world resources.

The *Sudan* type includes the savanna lands between the Tropics of Cancer and Capricorn. They occupy a broad belt across North Africa which turns south-east from the Sudan and Ethiopia; in Venezuela, where they are known as *llanos*, they flourish in the basin of the Orinoco; in Brazil, where they are known as *campos*, they extend from the south-eastern lowlands to Paraguay; and in Australia they distinguish the Northern Territory and bend southwards, behind the eastern ranges, to Victoria. The name *savanna* is a Spanish-American corruption of a Carib Indian word for grasslands or plains.

Scattered trees, growing singly or in clumps, give the savanna some resemblance to neglected parklands, but they are not forest trees. Representative species are the famous water-storing baobab and the hard and thorny acacias with reduced leaves. Gum arabic is an important Sudanese product obtained from certain acacias split by the heat and drought.

The animals, naturally, are mostly small and swift grass-feeders, such as the graceful antelopes and gazelles of Africa, the deer of South America, and the ungainly kangaroos and wallabies of Australia; and they are hunted by the larger carnivores, such as the African lion, which prey on them. More dangerous, however, than the fierce flesh-eaters is the tiny tsetse fly, which carries the dreaded sleeping-sickness from man to man and destroys whole herds of wild and domestic animals. But tsetse fly is being controlled: this is a token of the new techniques that are coming to the tropical grasslands and changing their pastoral economy to cattle raising and large-scale agriculture, with such important crops as millet, maize, cotton and tobacco.

The *Monsoon* lands, favoured when it is not too excessive by a season of high rainfall, are also limited by the Tropics of Cancer and Capricorn. Their forests are dense but never quite equatorial. Species are fewer and some dominate: teak is an important timber in Burma and sal in India. Animals, often similar to those of the Equatorial region, are abundant and varied; and include the large species, such

THE AFRICAN GRASSLANDS

Camera Press.

The African grasslands support great herds of swift hooved animals, such as antelopes, gazelles, wildebeeste, zebras and giraffes. This unusual picture shows sable antelopes, which are seldom found in company with other animals, herding with wildebeeste. It also illustrates the parkland character of the savanna.

Paul Popper.

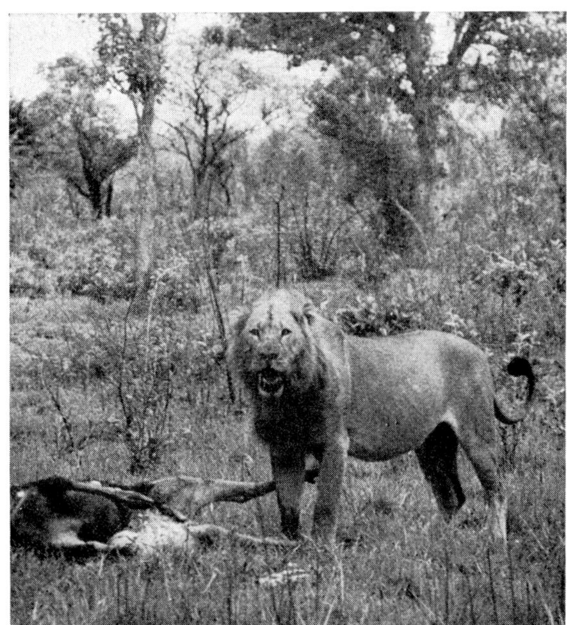

Camera Press.

The picture on the left shows a watering place in the veldt favoured by Blue Wildebeeste and Chapman's Zebra—their friendly orderliness is noticeable. The speed of these animals does not always save them from the carnivorous animals whose natural prey they are. The picture of the lion with his kill was taken in a game reserve in Northern Rhodesia.

MONSOON RICE AND PRAIRIE WHEAT

H. Armstrong Roberts.

Rice and wheat are staple grains that grow in very different climates. Rice is a major crop of the wet, and especially monsoon, lands; wheat is a product of the cold steppes and prairies. The scene above, taken in the Indonesian island of Bali, is an excellent example of the terraced cultivation of rice

High Commissioner for Canada.

This aerial picture, showing the marks of contour ploughing to prevent erosion, was taken near Lethbridge, Alberta, in the great wheatfields of the Prairie Provinces. We couple it with the photograph of rice terraces because both show good use of the land.

THE CHALLENGING DESERTS

Chinese Embassy, London.

During the last few years thousands of miles of trees have been planted in Asian countries to hold shifting soil, to prevent floods, and to protect newly-cultivated land against destructive winds. This picture shows one of many new shelterbelts in China.

S.C.R.

Detailed scientific studies are an essential part of all land reclamation projects. Here we see samples of sand being collected in the Kara Kum desert for analysis of their moisture content.

S.C.R.

Arid lands cannot be reclaimed without extensive irrigation. Many water channels are cut through soft earth; but some, as we see in this picture from Daghestan, have to be cut through hard stone.

E.N.A.

Trees have been planted on the fringes of the Sahara, but the vast shifting sands of the greatest and richest desert in the world still challenge world co-operation and scientific skill. Experience in America, Asia and Israel suggests that cultivation and industry is not impossible in the Sahara.

as elephants and rhinoceroses, excluded by the true equatorial forest.

Valuable timber has been an added incentive in clearing the forests and converting them into plantations of timber trees, palms, bamboos and bananas or extensive crop-lands yielding such well-known products as rice, maize, sugar, tea, cotton and jute. Agricultural products are, in fact, plentiful and diverse and are supplemented by fish-cultivation and fruit-growing. Yet life in the monsoon countries is not a paradise. The climate is difficult, hurricanes are frequent, diseases are numerous, populations are large, and famines kill millions. Therefore scientific cultivation and industrialisation determine much of the planning in the " new nations " of monsoon Asia and the Caribbean.

The *Sahara* type of region contains, on either side of the Tropic of Cancer, the great belt of Afro-Asian desert which extends from the west coast of North Africa to Sind, as well as the deserts of Mexico and the south-western United States. Similar deserts, on both sides of the Tropic of Capricorn, form a long strip in Chile and Peru and cover about half of Australia. The Sahara alone accounts for four million square miles of this largely unproductive region. It is forty-five times the size of Great Britain and could accommodate the whole of the United States with more than a million square miles to spare.

The people of this " Empty Space " (*El Khela*), as the Arabs call it, number barely over a million and leave nine-tenths of the area uninhabited. Some remain by their oases, but the majority are kept on the move by the need to keep alive. Yet the Sahara is potentially one of the richest territories of the world. It has about half as much oil as the Middle East and the

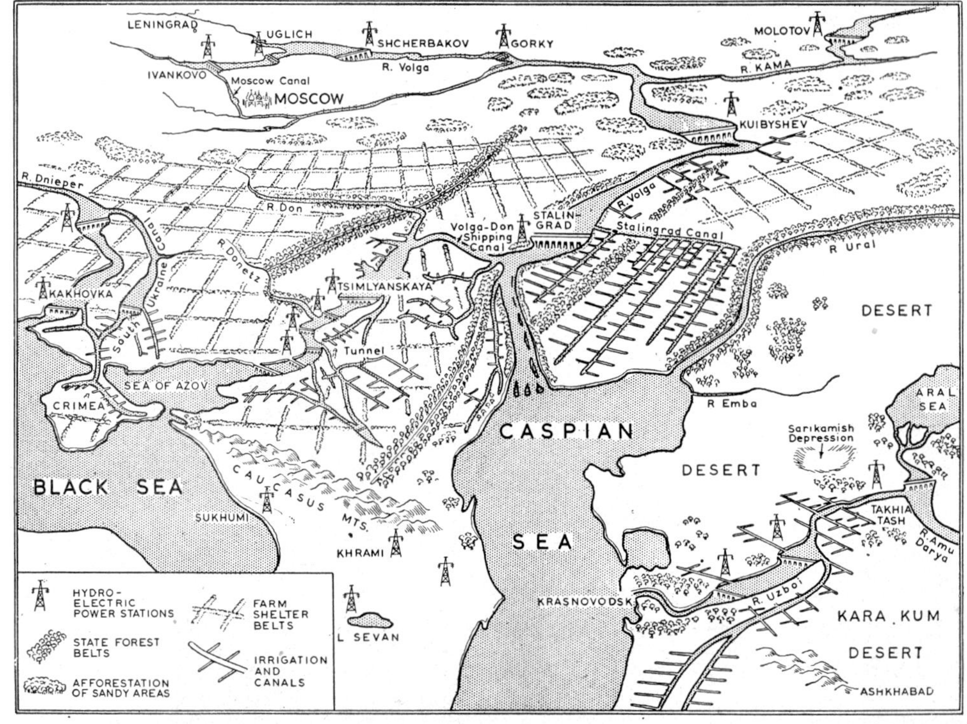

Re-drawn after S. M. Manton.

THE CHANGING GEOGRAPHY OF ASIA

Increasing population, the demand for more food, and the need to exploit all the resources of minerals and power, is rapidly changing the regional characteristics of many parts of Asia. An indication of the planning and effort required is shown in this map—and it should be remembered that the great deserts are much larger than those of Soviet Asia.

" MEDITERRANEAN " SCENES

Hulton Picture Library.

Terraces of vines, with olive and almond trees dotting the hillsides, are familiar sights in Mediterranean lands. The river is the Douro in the famous Port wine district of Portugal.

Paul Popper.

Scenes like this, photographed in the outskirts of Cagnes, south of France, are also familiar to those who know the Mediterranean countries. The olive trees, the goat, the health-giving work in the sunlit fields, are typical of the region.

Yugoslav Tourist Office.

The beautiful Adriatic coast of Yugoslavia shares the Mediterranean blessings. The city gleaming in the sun is the centre of Korcula, an island near Dubrovnik. The olive trees in the foreground testify to its Mediterranean character.

Camera Press.

This is a Mediterranean scene too, but the photograph was taken in Pershing Square, Los Angeles, Calfornia. Much of California enjoys a Western Margin or Mediterranean type of climate.

Society for Cultural Relations with the U.S.S.R.

THE IRAN TYPE OF COUNTRY

Daghestan is typical of the dry and forbidding interior plateaux described as the *Iran* type of geographical region. This picture was taken in the Gunib District, where much building, extending up the slopes, and planting has been done.

United States put together; and coal, natural gas, iron and other basic minerals in plenty. But these resources cannot be fully exploited without an all-African plan for reclaiming the land itself and giving it the real wealth that is founded on cultivation.

In the *Ecuador* region, which continues into Colombia, altitude brings " perpetual spring " to the Equator. The mean temperature at Quito (9,350 feet), the capital of Ecuador, is 54–55° F. throughout the year; at Bogota it varies between 57° and 59° F. Thus, the days are pleasantly warm, but the nights are chilly and the mornings misty. The people are engaged largely in the trade of a capital town and the business of their country, which depends much more on the products of the steaming lowlands than on the wheat, maize, potatoes and temperate fruits of the highlands.

The Warm Temperate Lands

The Mediterranean type of region is found on the western margins of the continents above the Tropic of Cancer and below the Tropic of Capricorn. The climate favours the cultivation of cereals and fruits, for the assured summer dryness is ideal for harvesting cereals and ripening and drying fruits. Olives, figs and grapes are the characteristic Mediterranean fruits, though introduced fruits, such as oranges, lemons and peaches, are exported on such a large scale that they are now regarded as equally if not more characteristic. Mixed forests furnish valuable timber, especially pine, cedar and evergreen oak; and it was a happy thought on the part of Nature to grow the vine and the cork oak in the same areas.

The *Iran* type of region contains the dry interior plateau country from Iran to Soviet Georgia and the flat highlands in and around Mongolia, in Mexico and the south-western United States, and in south-eastern Africa. The range of temperature, both seasonally and daily is extreme, and in Asia the vegetation is not much more

CONTRASTS IN THE ANDES

Llamas, a domesticated breed of the wild guanaco, are the sure-footed pack animals of the Andes. Their flesh is good to eat and they provide clothing too.

Giant cacti are the " trees " of the arid western Americas. These are growing in the " rain shadow " of the Andes.

Photos: Paul Popper.

Quito, the plateau capital (9,350 feet) of Ecuador, is typical of the *Ecuador* type of region. Dominated by the Pichincha volcano, the enjoyment of its " perpetual spring " is frequently marred by earthquakes; but its devout citizens, secure in their religion and Spanish traditions, if not in their adobe houses, quickly return to their agriculture, craft industries and governmental business.

French Govt. Tourist Office.

A WEST EUROPEAN SCENE

In Europe the chief natural characteristics of the *West European* type of region are its deciduous forests, healthy climate, and fairly dense populations pressing on to the edges of the forests. This photograph of Bec Hellouin, Eure, France, illustrates the region as well as one picture can.

than a plateau variation of the desert shrub of the surrounding lowlands, but it supports the small herds of the pastoral people.

North of the Iranian Plateau, and cut off from moisture-bearing winds, are the Turanian Plain and the vast flatlands around the Aral Sea; and we call this type of region, which also occurs in the United States, Argentina and south-eastern Australia, the *Turan* type. The vegetation is largely desert shrub, with considerable expanses of short grass in the United States on which cattle are set loose to graze.

In Asia this desert shrub is an extension of the poor lowlands of Iran, which begin the enormous north-easterly continuation of the Afro-Asian desert, and within it there are large islands of plantless sand deserts and salt flats. The largest lie below and to the east of the Aral Sea, but they are being transformed by irrigation, tree-planting and other reclamation services on a gigantic scale.

The *China* type of region, in contrast to the Mediterranean type, is confined to the eastern margins of the land masses. Its characteristics are summer rain, frequent storms, no marked drought and fertile soil supporting a variety of trees and crops. In the Chinese river valleys agriculture has supported a highly advanced culture for some five thousand years.

The Colder Lands

The *West European* type of region is the extension of the Mediterranean type into high latitudes. Its summers are warm, its winters not very cold; and there is rain throughout the year, though most of it falls in the autumn and winter. In western Europe itself the major natural vegetation is deciduous forest (in British Columbia it is coniferous), but centuries of cultivation have made it almost entirely a man-made region with much beauty that has survived the spread of ugliness since the Industrial Revolution.

The *Central European* type of region is unique. Its summers are warm and wet, its winters cold. Deciduous and mixed forests grow in the lowlands, conifers on the slopes. Stock-raising, dairy farming and agriculture have behind them the traditional knowledge of long settlement on the land without the sea calling to adventure abroad.

The *St. Lawrence* type of region occurs in eastern Canada and north-eastern Asia; and in the south-eastern tip of Argentina. In the north its forests are coniferous or mixed, for it is colder in the winter than the West European type and warmer in the summer, and the timber industry is the mainstay of the economy. Fisheries are also extensive. The Argentinian part of this region shares its climatic characteristics, but not its productivity.

The *Prairie* type of region is confined to the prairie of interior North America

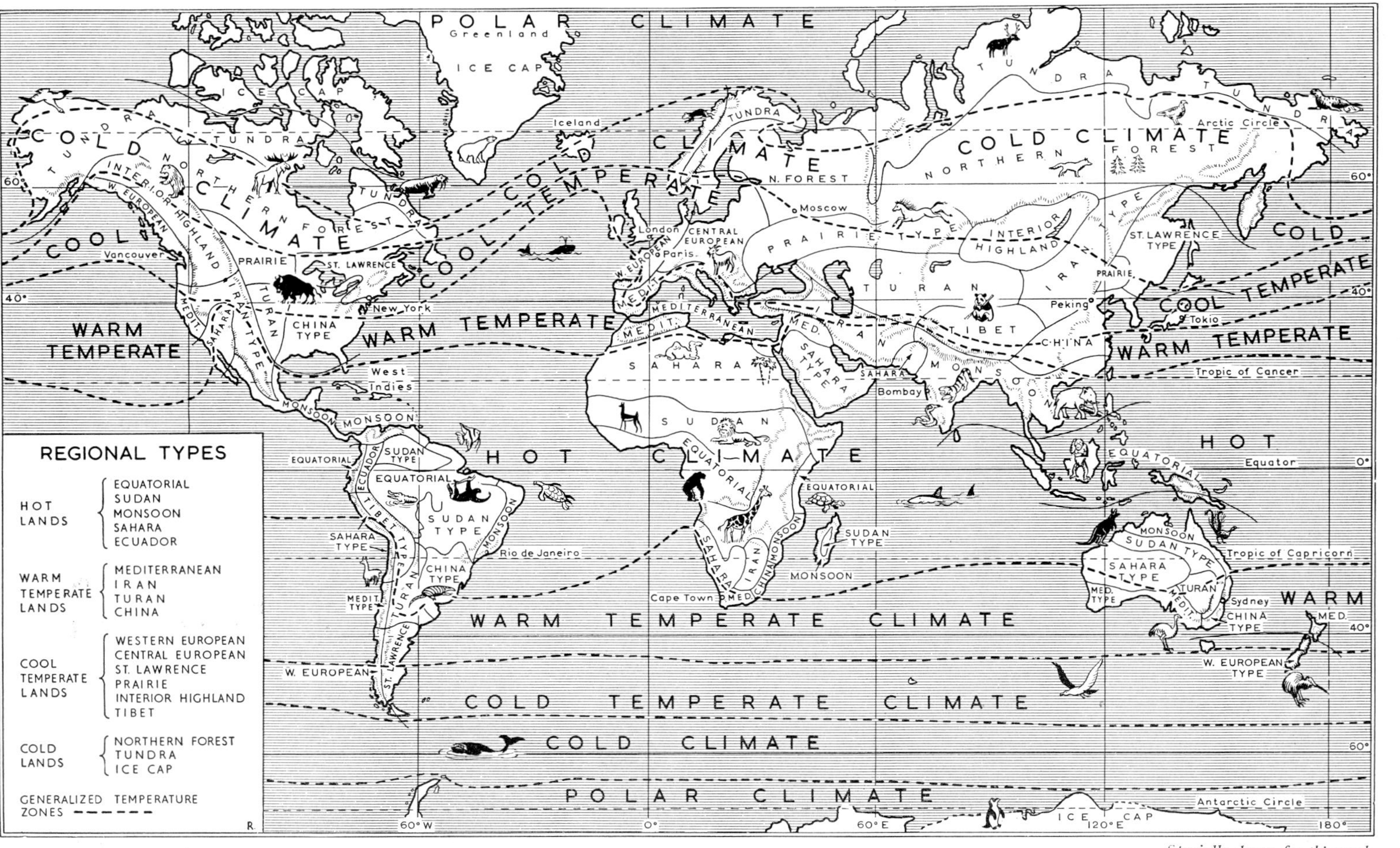

Specially drawn for this work.

THE MAJOR GEOGRAPHICAL REGIONS

This map plots the regions discussed, places them in temperature zones, indicates (by hatching) the influencing mountains, and shows some of the typical animals. It is intended for study—and to assist comparisons it has been drawn to the same scale as the map of the world elsewhere in this work.

WHEN MAN BUILDS HIS HOME—

The yurt and the igloo (p. 55) are striking examples of regional influences on human dwellings. The sloping-roofed cottage is no less interesting because it is more common, for it varies greatly according to climate and the building materials available—from the palm-thatched mud huts of the tropics (*left*) to slate-roofed stone cottages that defy the centuries in colder countries.

But blocks of stone are more suitable for building castles than cottages. Therefore, when engineering progress made them possible, massive houses (limited in height by the weight of the blocks) became typical of towns where suitable stone is abundant. Our picture (*right*) comes from Soviet Armenia, where multi-coloured tufa adds charm to the heaviness of homes and offices.

A general view of Tsingtao, a popular holiday resort on the Yellow Sea, is shown below. It looks more southern European than Chinese, because the natural tendency of subtropical coastal towns to have rather similar characteristics was intensified by German, but culturally very French, domination.

(*Photos: C. Dover, S.C.R., and Camera Press.*)

—GEOGRAPHY TAKES A HAND

Tsingtao is not unique. For westernisation, and with it the use of new building resources and techniques, has created widely spread resemblances in housing. But regional characteristics remain important. Bermuda, for example, depends on rainfall for its freshwater—and rainwater will be required there even when the sea itself provides cheap power for converting sea-water into domestic supplies. Methods of storing and distributing rainwater will doubtless improve, while relying basically on using the roofs as water traps. At present (*right*) this is done by laying and plastering square slices of limestone in such a way that rainwater passes along rows of parallel channels to a main pipe leading to a reservoir.

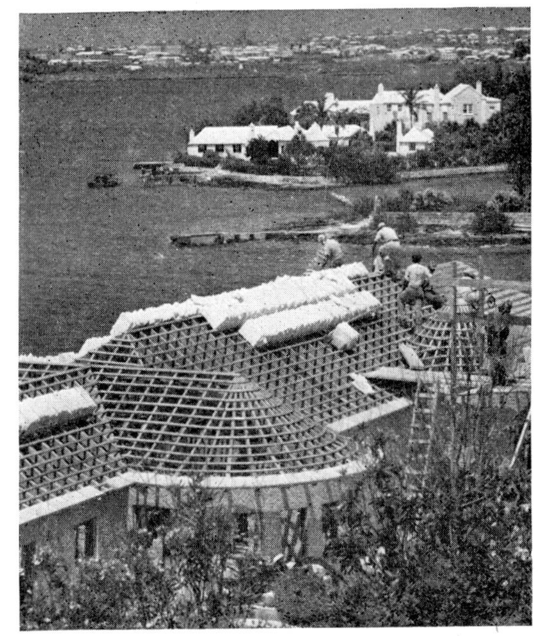

In Chandigarh, the growing showpiece capital of the East Punjab designed by Le Corbusier, Maxwell Fry, Jane Drew and leading Indian architects, the emphasis is on ventilation, protection from the sun, and quiet community living. The plan allows for twenty-six self-sufficient units, walled in to exclude noise and fast traffic and well supplied with shopping, educational, health, recreational and other facilities.

The homes are graded according to thirteen income scales, those for better paid officials (*left*) being lavishly spacious and much cooler than the arrangement of windows might suggest. Below we see a combined residential and shopping section. The *jali* (net-like) frontage of the living quarters, which increases ventilation and breaks up the sun's rays, is a feature of Chandigarh's architecture.

(*Photos: Bermuda News and the High Commissioner for India.*)

TRADITIONS SURVIVE—

The Chandigarh adventure has been criticised for its strangeness in the Indian scene. Arising from a sudden political situation (the division of the Punjab into Indian and Pakistani territories) and gifted drawing-board work, it ignores tradition completely; and dramatic breaks with tradition always excite criticism. Styles must change, of course, in accordance with changing demands and conditions, but traditionalists maintain that they should evolve with regard for history and surroundings.

These pictures illustrate this viewpoint. Stokesay Castle (*top left*), Shropshire, was built (1240, enlarged 1291) when more settled conditions in England were removing the need to fortify great houses. Consequently, it is much more of a house than a castle, but it remains a partly fortified manor house.

Three centuries later, home building on the grand scale, which benefited from the skilled knowledge previously concentrated on building churches and monasteries, was altogether free from older considerations of defence, for the use of gunpowder had altered methods of warfare. Nevertheless, battlement copings and similar survivals from castle architecture were often retained —very pleasantly, as our picture (*right*) of the E. Gateway, Leighs Priory (1536), Essex, shows.

In China the feeling for tradition is also deeply rooted; and there the straight-ridged curved roofs, turned up at the corners, have existed since antiquity. Made of cylindrical tiles, in glazed blue, green, golden-yellow and purple, and decorated with symbolic motifs, their purpose is to relieve the vertical straightness of walls and pillars. The same purpose is served by topping otherwise westernised houses with Chinese roofs (*left*)—a custom that has extended even to the boxlike public buildings and apartment houses erected during the last few years. Some critics find this practice incongruous, but the most that can be said against it is that it is expensive.

(*Photos: National Buildings Record and Camera Press.*)

—BUT STYLES CHANGE

In Mexico's long and turbulent history, a great city, rich in the fruits of struggle, has always flourished where the capital now stands; and in each of its phases architecture and the arts succeeded in harmonising the old with the new. This tradition was consciously developed by the renaissance in Mexican art rooted since 1917 in efforts to transform the country into a modern state. The artists, by expressing historical and folk themes in striking ways, fostered the feeling of national unity; and found in return the satisfactions of acclaim and official support for the decoration of public buildings. Thus, an interesting reconciliation was brought about between the severity of unadorned functionalism in architecture and the urge to embellish. An impressive recent example (*right*), in which a daring concentration of external symbolic design declares the purpose of the building in a nationalistic way and breaks the monotony of large flat surfaces, is the Library in University City, Mexico, D.F.

(*Photos: H. Armstrong Roberts and U.S. Information Service.*)

Functionalism in architecture is concerned with building efficient " machines for living, work and other purposes." It began in America with the work of Frank Lloyd Wright. Designed so that " the inside went outside and the outside flowed inside," his spreading houses were conceived with imaginative understanding of their surroundings, the nature of the materials used, the techniques by which they were made, and above all the essentials of gracious living. Each had the beauty of a total pattern in which everything—gardens, lighting, heating, furniture and even the hangings—was an architectural part of the whole.

His Imperial Hotel, Tokyo, was a triumph of functionalism, " respectfully bowed to Japanese traditions," which astonished the world by surviving the Great Earthquake of 1923; and many of his American houses are contemporary classics. " Falling Water," Bear Run, Pennsylvania, partly shown in our picture (*left*), is famous for the surprising manner in which it is supported by concrete slabs cantilevered from piers of stone.

and the steppes of the Eurasian heartlands. Its winters are long and bitter, but good summer grazing compensates for its rigours. In the United States the prairie remains the raising ground of the meat industry, but scientific ranching and the advance of agriculture have made it very different from the country of the famous Plains Indians. The steppes, too, are being transformed in accordance with modern needs and techniques.

The *Interior Highland* type of region includes the high plateaux above 45° N. in north-western America and central-eastern Asia. The valleys are fertile in the American part of the region, and the wet western slopes are densely forested. Mining adds to the variety of the economy, which not so long ago was based entirely on hunting and trapping. Timber extraction and mining are also features of the eastern part of the region, but it is still extensively pastoral.

The plateaux of Tibet and the High Andes of Bolivia and Peru constitute the *Tibet* type of region. Altitude gives these lofty mountain tables a climate similar to that of the northern Interior Highlands; and altitude has adapted both men and animals to the peculiar difficulties, mentioned elsewhere in this work, of living on them. Altitude has been isolating, too, but the urges and technical resources of modern civilisation have already reached Tibet and the High Andes on a considerable scale. Their mineral wealth is a decided attraction.

The Cold Lands need little comment. The *Northern* (coniferous) *Forest*, which gives the world much of its timber and paper pulp, merges into the *Tundra*; and beyond is the *Ice Cap*. Eskimos and Danes have colonised the tundra to its furthermost edges, but men have so far shared with plants the inability to occupy the Ice Cap. Perhaps we shall use it some day as a frigidaire for storing food reserves.

Paul Popper.

THE UNIQUE LOOK OF CENTRAL EUROPE

Central Europe represents a unique type of geographical region well illustrated by this photograph from the Vorarlberg, Austria. Dense coniferous forests ascend the slopes and in their shelter age-old communities live gracefully according to the traditions of a " farm and forest " economy.

COUNTRIES AND TERRITORIES OF THE WORLD

This section of the Atlas provides basic information about the countries and chief territories of the world. The small marginal sketch maps are intended only as reminders, and the main map section should be consulted for more accurate and detailed presentation of any country or territory.

ABYSSINIA

See ETHIOPIA.

ADEN

BRITISH COLONY AND PROTECTORATE

The colony and protectorate of Aden occupies an area of about 112,000 square miles on the south-west coast of Arabia east of the Bab-el-Mandeb (Gate of Tears) strait which gives entrance to the Red Sea. The colony includes the islands of Perim and Kamaran, and the Kuria Muria Islands. The western part of the protectorate includes the island of Socotra; the eastern part, the Hadhramaut.

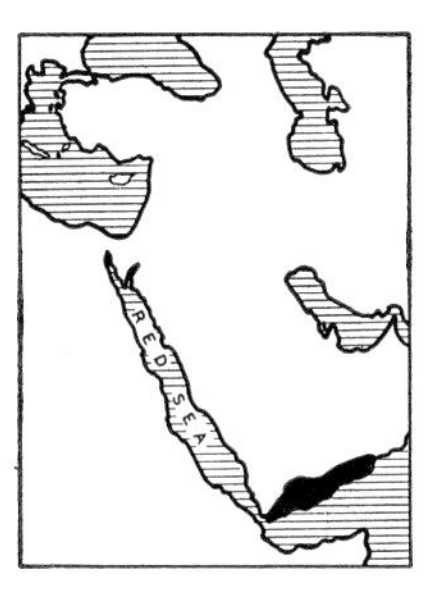

Population: Colony: 138,441 (mostly Arab, but including many Pakistanis, Somalis and Hindus); Protectorate: probably about 700,000 (but no census has ever been taken in its numerous sultanates and sheikhdoms). Aden and Sheikh Othman are the principal towns.

Production and Trade: Aden is best known as a refuelling point on important sea and air routes and as a trading port (cotton goods, coffee, grain, hides and skins). Its new oil refinery has a yearly capacity of five million tons of crude oil. There is a local salt industry. The unit of currency is the East African Shilling (divided, not into pence, but into 100 cents).

AFGHANISTAN

ISLAMIC CONSTITUTIONAL MONARCHY

An inland country bordered by the U.S.S.R. to the north, Persia to the west and Pakistan to the east and south. It has an area of about 250,000 square miles, which is mostly dry and mountainous. The north-east is dominated by the Hindu Kush range. There are considerable variations of climate from the harsh winters of the highlands to the intense dry heat of the south-west. Trees and shrubs are few, although vegetation is plentiful in the spring.

Population: Estimated at about 11,500,000, including wandering tribes (about two million). Besides the true Afghans, there are Tadjiks (hard-working farmers), Hindkis and Jats (traders of the towns), the educated Kizilbashes and the nomadic Hazaras. Kabul, the capital, has a population of over 206,000. Other important centres are Kandahar, Herat, Mazar-i-Sharif and Jalalabad. Pushtu and Persian are the official languages.

Production and Trade: Although cultivation is found only in the valleys and fertile plains, good crops of fruit, cereals and vegetables are raised. The asafoetida and castor-oil plants are found in all parts, and good tobacco is grown in some areas. Sheep-rearing is an important industry, both wool and skins (especially Persian lamb-skins) being exported. Cotton, too, is grown for export. Coal, chrome and salt are mined, but the considerable mineral wealth has still to be fully developed. Hydro-electric power is aiding the development of some industry and manufactures. Since 1949, irrigation has been developed in the provinces of Kandahar and Herat. The principal imports include machinery, textiles, rubber, tea and petrol. Much of Afghanistan's trade is conducted with the Soviet Union. The unit of currency is the Afghani.

Communications: There are no railways and the roads generally are poor. Camels and ponies form the chief means of transport.

ALBANIA

REPUBLIC

A mountainous country of the Balkan peninsula bounded by the Adriatic Sea on the west, Yugoslavia on the north-east, and Greece on the south-east. Area: 10,629 square miles.

Population: 1,394,310 (1955 census). Tirana, the capital, has a population of about 50,000. Most of the people are Moslems.

Production and Trade: The most fertile parts of this rugged land are the coastal areas, which enjoy a Mediterranean climate, and the central lowlands. Maize, wheat, olives, tobacco and sugar-beet are important crops. Large numbers of goats and sheep are raised. Oil is produced at Kuçovë, near Berat, but copper and other minerals have still to be developed fully. Exports of petroleum, farm produce, hides and skins go by sea from Shëngjin, Durrës (Durazzo) and other ports to the U.S.S.R. and other Soviet countries. Manufactured goods and machinery form the main imports. The Albanian unit of currency is the Lek.

ALGERIA

A FRENCH GOVERNMENT-GENERAL

Occupying an area of 847,550 square miles on the southern shore of the Mediterranean between Morocco and Tunisia, Algeria is divided into (i) Northern Algeria; and (ii) the Southern Territories. The northern departments are regarded as part of metropolitan France and are represented in the National Assembly, but there is also an Algerian Assembly of 120 members at Algiers.

Other important centres are Oran, Constantine, Bône, Sidi-Bel-Abbès, Tlemcen and Philippeville.

Population: Northern Algeria: 8,429,700. Southern Territories: 835,900. About 1,000,000 of the population are European, especially French, the remainder being Arab, Berber, Kabyle or a mixture of these three. Algiers, the capital, has 361,285 inhabitants.

Production and Trade: Cereals, wine and fruit are produced on the fertile coastal Tell. The high plateau to the south supports large numbers of sheep, goats and camels. Algeria has considerable cork-oak forests, esparto grass is grown, and phosphates, iron ore and other minerals are mined. More than 75 per cent. of trade is with France and French overseas territories. The unit of currency is the French franc.

ANDORRA

REPUBLIC

A tiny mountainous state (area, 191 square miles) in the Pyrenees with a population of about 5,000. Andorre-la-Veille (Andorra-la-Vieja) is the capital. Pastoral farming and tourism are the chief industries. The Andorrans speak Catalan and use both French and Spanish currency.

ANGOLA

PORTUGUESE OVERSEAS PROVINCE

Angola, or Portuguese West Africa, is a colonial territory with an area of 481,351 square miles, comprising a long coastal plain backed by a healthy tableland. Its natural resources have still to be fully developed.

Population: about 4,145,000, mostly Bantu people but including about 50,000 Europeans. S. Paulo de Luanda is the present capital, but Nova Lisboa (Huambo) will eventually be the capital.

Production and Trade: Coffee, sugar, palm-oil and sisal are the chief export crops; maize, the chief food crop. Diamonds are mined. Most of the trade is with Portugal. The unit of currency is the Angolar, the equivalent of the Portuguese escudo.

Communications: Luanda and Lobito are the chief ports, the latter being linked by the Benguela Railway with the Belgian Congo, the Rhodesias and Mozambique (Portuguese East Africa), etc.

ANTARCTICA

The ice-covered land mass about the South Pole, with an area of more than 5,000,000 square miles, nearly half of which is administered by Australia whose outpost of Mawson was the first permanent research base to be set up on this " seventh continent." New Zealand is responsible for the Ross Dependency. The United Kingdom and other nations hold Antarctic territory or lay claim to it (see the map on p. 97).

ARABIA

This peninsula of south-west Asia has an area of some 1,200,000 square miles, containing a number of Arab states and territories. See *Aden, Bahrein, Kuwait, Muscat and Oman, Qatar, Saudi Arabia, Trucial States, United Arab Republic, Yemen.*

ARGENTINA

REPUBLIC

The second largest country in South America, Argentina has an area of about 1,080,000 square miles. Its western frontier runs along the backbone of the Andes, where Aconcagua, the highest peak in the continent, rises to more than 23,000 feet. The north-west generally is mountainous plateau, but the north-east is the hot swampland of the Gran Chaco. Much of the remainder is rolling natural grassland (the famous *pampas*) which extends 700 miles from north to south and 400 miles from east to west. Patagonia, in the south, is largely dry plateau. In the north the rivers Paraguay, Paraná and Uruguay unite to form the Plate River (Rio de la Plata).

Population: About 19,857,700. The capital and chief port, Buenos Aires, has a population exceeding 3,367,000. Other important towns are Rosario (over 761,000), Cordobá (351,000), La Plata (known for a time as Eva Perón), Tucumán, Santa Fé, and Mendoza. Spanish is the language of the country and Roman Catholicism the established church.

Production and Trade: Agriculture is the most important industry. Cattle number over 45,260,000 and sheep over 54,600,000. Great quantities of meat are shipped from the *frigorificos* (freezing plants) along the Plate River and Argentina is the world's leading meat exporter. Wheat, the principal crop, is also grown for export and so are maize, linseed, sugar, cotton and various grain crops. Flour-milling and the refining of both oil and sugar are important industries.

Although some coal is produced at Rio Turbio and other centres, and there are deposits of iron ore, uranium and other minerals, mining is not important. Zapla is the centre of the small steel industry. The chief local source of oil is Comodoro Rivadavia (where natural gas is also tapped and piped to Buenos Aires).

The chief exports are grain, meat, wool, hides, dairy products and linseed oil; the chief imports, machinery, vehicles, manufactured goods and fuel oil. The United States heads the list of countries supplying Argentina. The United Kingdom, the United States, West Germany and Brazil are the leading markets for Argentinian exports. The unit of currency in the Argentine is the Peso.

AUSTRALIA

CONSTITUTIONAL MONARCHY

The Commonwealth of Australia, a member of the British Commonwealth of Nations, is a federation of states and an island continent with an area of 2,974,581 square miles. The states and territories, with areas in square miles, are: New South Wales (309,433), Victoria (87,884), Queensland (670,500), South Australia (380,070), Western Australia (975,920), Tasmania (26,215), Northern Territory (523,620), and the Australian Capital Territory (939). Tasmania is an island state separated from the main continental mass by Bass Strait. From east to west across the continent is approximately 2,400 miles; from north to south, about 2,000 miles.

Much of the continent is plateau and its heart contains dry and stony deserts and extensive salt marshes (" lakes "). The vast grasslands support a flourishing pastoral industry. The principal highlands are in the east where the Great Dividing Range runs along the coasts of Queensland and New

South Wales, turning westwards in Victoria; the highest peak, Mt. Kosciusko (7,328 feet) is in the south of New South Wales.

The chief river is the Murray (1,600 miles long) which with the Darling, Murrumbidgee, Lachlan and other tributaries forms the main river system of Australia. Plentiful artesian water and imaginative irrigation schemes have transformed large areas which would otherwise have been unsuitable for settlement.

Rainfall conditions go a long way to explaining the distribution of population in Australia and the progress of settlement. Along the south-eastern shorelands and in Tasmania there is good rainfall all the year round. The north has heavy rains in the summer (November to April); the south and south-west have most of their rain during the Australian winter (April to August). Generally the rainfall decreases as distances from the coast increase. The " dead heart " has little rain at any season of the year.

Nearly half Australia lies within the tropics; more than half, within warm temperate regions. It is indeed a continent of contrasts where practically every type of scenery can be found, from steaming jungle to snow-capped mountains. A remarkable feature of the eastern coast is the Great Barrier Reef, some 1,200 miles in length; renowned for its beautiful corals, exotic vegetation, unusual fish and birds, it is one of the natural wonders of the world. Australia generally is noted for its unique flora (especially eucalypts, acacias, jarrah and karri), and fauna (including the kangaroo, koala, dingo and platypus).

Population: 9,747,471 (this excludes some 46,638 Aborigines or " blackfellows "). Canberra, the Federal capital, has a population of 35,827. The population of the state capitals is given below:

Sydney (*New South Wales*)	1,975,020
Melbourne (*Victoria*)	1,677,100
Brisbane (*Queensland*)	543,000
Adelaide (*South Australia*)	529,000
Perth (*Western Australia*)	376,000
Hobart (*Tasmania*)	103,570

Darwin, the seat of administration of the Northern Territory, has just over 9,390 inhabitants; Alice Springs, also in the Northern Territory, has a population of 2,785.

Production and Trade: Australia is the world's chief wool-producing country, maintaining more than 139,000,000 sheep (of which nearly half are in New South Wales). She is also a prodigious producer of mutton, lamb and beef; cereals and fruit; and dairy products. There are extensive vineyards (table grapes, raisins and sultanas) and South Australia especially is noted for its wine industry. Sugar cane, bananas, pineapples

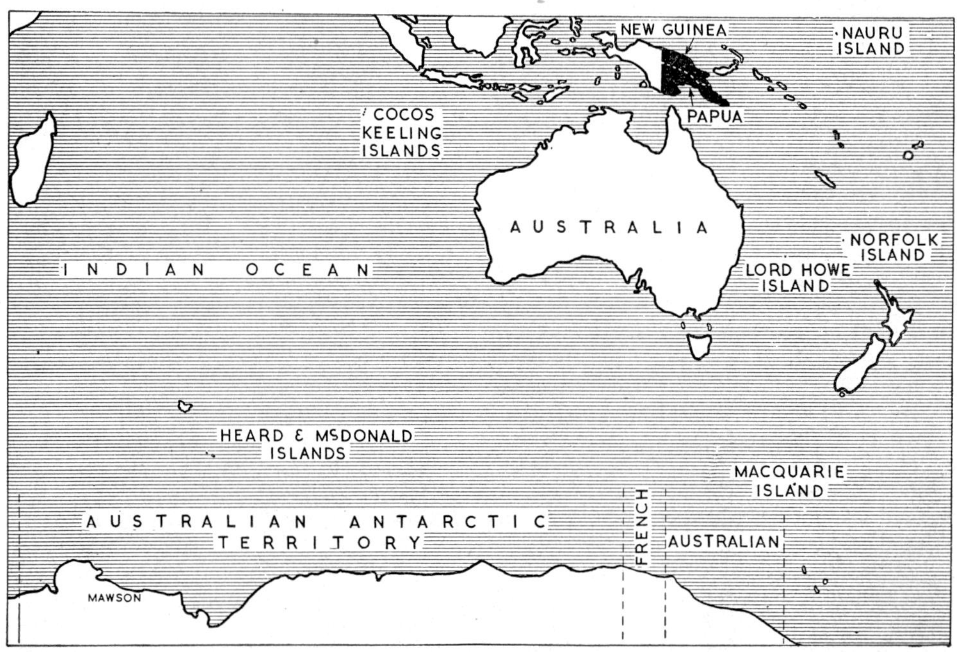

Principal Australian Overseas Territories

and other tropical fruits are grown in suitable regions, especially northern New South Wales and Queensland.

There is considerable mineral wealth, including *gold* (especially in Western Australia, where Kalgoorlie is the chief centre); *coal*, provided by the Newcastle coalfield (New South Wales), lesser fields in Queensland and other states, and by the large brown coal deposits of Victoria and South Australia; *iron ore* (Iron Monarch, South Australia and Yampi Sound, Western Australia); *uranium* (Rum Jungle, Mary Kathleen and other centres); *silver–lead–zinc* (especially Broken Hill, New South Wales); and copper, tin, nickel, bauxite and mica. In recent years high-grade oil has been discovered in Western Australia. Hydro-electric power is being developed on a very large scale in the Snowy Mountains.

These resources have led to considerable industrial development and manufacturing has also made rapid progress, many items which were once imported now being made in Australia. But the chief imports are still machinery, vehicles and manufactured goods; and the chief exports, pastoral, dairy, orchard and farm products. The United Kingdom is Australia's leading customer. The unit of currency is the Australian pound.

Communications: Australia is unfortunate in having railways of three different gauges and long "through" journeys across the continent are thus not possible. Plans are now in hand to establish a standard gauge throughout the continent. The country is covered by a large network of air services.

Overseas Territories, etc.: (1) *Papua–New Guinea*, which comprises the Trust Territory of New Guinea and the Territory of Papua, with an area of about 183,000 square miles. Port Moresby is the seat of administration. *Population:* Native, about 1,669,000; European and others, about 19,300. Copra, rubber, timber and gold are the chief products. There is extensive prospecting for oil. (2) *Nauru*, a South Pacific island administered by Australia under U.N. Trusteeship and an important source of phosphates. (3) *Norfolk Island*, in the Pacific. (4) *Lord Howe Island*, a dependency of New South Wales in the Pacific. (5) *Ashmore Islands*, a dependency of the Northern Territory in the Indian Ocean. (6) *Cocos-Keeling Islands*, Indian Ocean. (7) *Macquarie*, *Heard* and *McDonald Islands*, Southern Ocean. (8) *Christmas Island*, Indian Ocean (since 1958). (9) *Australian Antarctic Territory*, some 2,472,000 square miles, *i.e.*, about half Antarctica. The Australian base of Mawson was the first permanent research station established on the Antarctic continent.

AUSTRIA

REPUBLIC

This country of Central Europe has an area of 32,369 square miles. It is a very mountainous country, with peaks reaching heights of more than 12,000 feet and extensive forests. The Danube is the chief river.

Population: 6,933,905. Vienna, the capital, has a population of over 1,616,000. Other large towns include Graz, Linz, Salzburg, Innsbruck and Klagenfurt. German is the language of the country. Most of the people are of the Roman Catholic faith.

Production and Trade: Agriculture is the chief industry, although foodstuffs have to be imported. There is considerable production of iron ore and steel, and the manufacture of motor-cycles, tractors and goods vehicles is important. There are large deposits of oil and reasonable supplies of coal. The country provides much of the world's high-grade graphite. The beautiful mountain scenery makes tourism a thriving industry. Hydro-electric power is being developed and the potential is considerable. The river Danube is an important commercial waterway. Manufactures include textiles, glass, jewellery, paper, millinery and leather goods. The unit of currency is the Schilling.

BAHAMAS

BRITISH COLONY

A chain of islands, about twenty of which are inhabited, off the south-eastern coast of Florida, U.S.A. The total area of the group is about 4,400 square miles. More than 80 per cent. of the population of

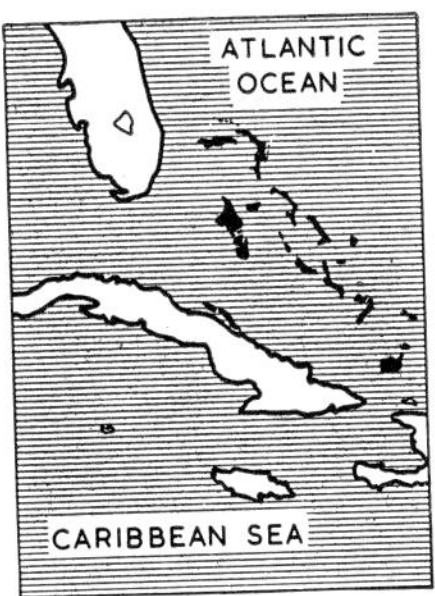

some 116,530 are coloured people, many of them being the descendants of freed slaves. Nassau, the capital, stands on New Providence, the chief island of the group. Watling Island (San Salvador) was the landing-place of Christopher Columbus (1492).

Tourism is an important local industry and the chief source of income. The famous sponge fisheries were brought to a halt by disease, but revived successfully in 1956. Crawfish, lumber, pit props and tomatoes are exported. Some United Kingdom currency is accepted and local notes of various denominations are also used. Both the American and Canadian dollar are accepted.

BAHREIN

INDEPENDENT SHEIKHDOM

Bahrein (also spelt Bahrain) is a group of islands in the Persian Gulf and off the Qatar peninsula. Their total area is approximately 213 square miles. Manama, the capital, is on Bahrein Island. The population numbers about 125,000 and includes about 3,000 British and Americans. Once famous for its pearl fisheries, Bahrein now owes its importance to its oilfield and refinery. Oil from Saudi Arabia, as well as local oil, is processed. In 1958 Manama was made a "free transit port." The unit of currency is the Indian rupee.

BARBADOS

BRITISH COLONY

The easternmost island of the West Indies, it has an area of 166 square miles and a population of about 229,100. Bridgetown is the capital. The chief products and exports are sugar, rum, molasses and cotton. Various currencies are in circulation, including British coinage, Canadian and Eastern Caribbean Territories dollars, and currency notes issued by British Guiana and Trinidad. Barbados was one of the inaugural members of the Federation of The West Indies.

BASUTOLAND

BRITISH HIGH COMMISSION TERRITORY

This South African territory of 11,716 square miles is mostly high plateau, bordered on the east by the lofty Drakensberg mountains. There are only about 2,000 Europeans in the population of 631,396, and it is thus virtually an African territory, the home of the Basuto people of the Bantu. Maseru is the administrative headquarters and "capital." Wheat, maize, sorghum and other crops are grown; large numbers of sheep are reared, as well as goats, cattle and other livestock. Many Basuto labourers are employed in the gold mines in the Union of South Africa. The unit of currency is the South African pound.

BECHUANALAND

BRITISH PROTECTORATE

The protectorate occupies an area of about 275,000 square miles between the Zambesi and Molopo rivers in South Africa. It is dry plateau land, with the Kalahari Desert in the south.

Population: About 294,000, of whom more than 292,000 are African. The principal tribes include the Bamangwato, who have their capital at Serowe; and the Bakgatla, Bakwena, Bangwaketse and Batawana. The administrative headquarters of the protectorate are at Mafeking, in the Cape Province of the Union of South Africa.

Production and Trade: Stock-breeding and dairy farming are the chief occupations. Some gold is mined. Food crops are grown where the rainfall permits. The unit of currency is the South African pound.

BELGIUM

CONSTITUTIONAL MONARCHY

Belgium, one of the "Low Countries," lies between the Netherlands and France and has an area of 11,755 square miles. It is largely a low-lying country, protected from the sea by dykes (but not to the same extent as the Netherlands). In the south-east the ground climbs to the wooded heights of the Ardennes, which, however, do not rise above 2,100 feet. The most important river

is the Scheldt, which with the Lys, Meuse, Sambre and lesser streams, and an extensive canal network, forms a valuable commercial waterways system.

Population: 8,951,443. Brussels, the capital, has a population of 985,793. Other important places are Antwerp (the chief port and commercial centre), Ghent, Liège and Mechelen. The country is the most thickly populated in Europe. There are two distinct types of Belgian: the Walloons, who speak French, and the Flemings, who speak Flemish and are found mostly in the north.

Production and Trade: Belgium is a land of modest farms and small-holdings, which are cultivated intensively and provide large crops of cereals, flax, hops and vegetables. The considerable mineral wealth includes coal, iron, lead and zinc. The centres of industry include Courtrai and Tournai (linen), Liège (metal-working and engineering), Ghent and Verviers (textiles), Charleroi (glass), Mons coal), Namur (iron and steel). The Netherlands, Western Germany, France, the United Kingdom and the United States are the leading countries with which Belgium trades. She is linked in a Customs union (Benelux) with the Netherlands and Luxemburg. The unit of currency is the Belgian franc.

Overseas Territories: Belgium has benefited considerably from her rich overseas colony of the Belgian Congo (*q.v.*). She also holds under United Nations' trusteeship the territory of Ruanda-Urundi. The capital of this territory is Usumbura, but it is joined economically and administratively with the Belgian Congo. It has an area of nearly 21,000 square miles and a population exceeding 4,450,000 (but including only some 6,500 Europeans).

BELGIAN CONGO

BELGIAN COLONY

Extending over the basin of the river Congo, this territory has an area exceeding 909,000 square miles, much of it either dense forest or tropical grassland.

Population: the African peoples number more than 12,800,000. The European population of 107,413 is mostly Belgian. The capital is Léopoldville. Other important centres are Elisabethville and Stanleyville.

Production and Trade: There is much mineral wealth, especially in the Katanga province, where copper and uranium ore are mined. Kasai province is one of the chief world sources of diamonds. Gold, silver, tin, cobalt and other minerals are also obtained. Palm-oil, timber, cotton, coffee and rubber are produced for export. More than half the exports go to Belgium, which also provides a sizeable share of the imports, but both the United Kingdom and the United States share in the trade of the Belgian Congo. The unit of currency is the Congolese franc.

Communications: The principal port is Matadi, on the estuary of the Congo.

BERMUDA

BRITISH COLONY

The Bermudas, also known as Somers Islands, are a group of about 100 islands in the west Atlantic about 600 miles from Cape Hatteras. Only about twenty of them are inhabited. The total area of the colony is 21 square miles. The population exceeds 42,000 and includes about 26,000 coloured people. The capital is Hamilton, on Main Island. Although there is some agriculture and flowers and bulbs are exported, the chief business of the colony is the tourist trade. Large numbers of Americans visit the islands every year. The unit of currency is the Pound sterling.

BHUTÁN

INDEPENDENT STATE

This mountainous country of the eastern Himalayas has an area of about 18,000 square miles. It is ruled by a maharaja. Estimates of the population vary from 300,000 to 700,000. Nearly all are Buddhists. The fortress capital is Punakha, but Trashichödzong (or Tashi-Cho-Dong) is sometimes described as the "summer capital." Rice,

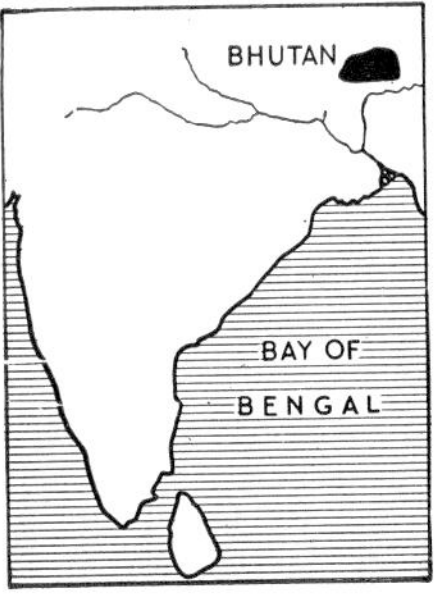

maize, millet, silk, leather and goods cloth are among the chief products. Swords and muzzle-loaders are made. There are valuable forests. There are neither roads nor railways, all loads being carried by porters or animals. The unit of currency is the Indian rupee.

BOLIVIA

REPUBLIC

Named after the famous liberator, Simon Bolivar (1783–1830), this land-locked South American country has an area exceeding 415,000 square miles. Running across the mountainous western part of the country are the Western and Eastern Cordilleras of the Andes, and between these two mountain chains lies the Altiplano—a great central plateau some 12,000 feet above sea level and about 65,000 square miles in area. On the plateau are lakes Titicaca and Poopó. The eastern part of Bolivia is tropical lowland.

Population: 3,273,000. La Paz, the seat of government, has a population of 321,063. Other important centres are Cochabamba, Oruro, Santa Cruz and Sucre (the legal capital), Spanish is the official language, but more than half the population is South American Indian, and thus both Quechua and Aymara are spoken. The established church is Roman Catholic.

Production and Trade: Although most of the population depend upon agriculture, the chief industry is mining. The tin output is one of the largest in the world. Wolfram, copper, lead, zinc, antimony, silver and gold are also mined. The rich oilfields are now being developed. Rubber is an important crop. There are splendid tropical forests awaiting development. More than half of Bolivian trade is conducted with the United States, but Britain is a good customer for her exports (of which tin usually accounts for about 70 per cent.). Foodstuffs, vehicles and machinery are among her main imports. The unit of currency is the Boliviano.

BRAZIL

REPUBLIC

The United States of Brazil occupy nearly half of South America. Brazil has an area of 3,289,440 square miles, *i.e.*, one-seventeenth of the land surface of the world. It is larger than the U.S.A. and four-fifths the size of Europe. About one-third of this area forms the basin of the great river Amazon, with its dense tropical forest (the *Selvas*) and hot, wet climate. In the east and south are other rivers—the São Francisco, Paraguay, Paraná and Uruguay. On the Iguassu, which joins with the upper Paraná, are the beautiful Iguassu Falls. The most fertile and thickly-populated lands lie along the east coast, behind which lies the vast Brazilian Plateau, crossed by mountain systems.

Population: 61,268,000. Rio de Janeiro, the chief port and capital, has a population of more than 2,303,000. São Paulo, too, exceeds 2,017,000. The many other large centres include Recife, Salvador (Bahia), Porto Alegre, Belo Horizonte, Belem (Pará) and Santos (the second port). Portuguese is the official language. Roman Catholicism is the religion of nearly all Brazilians. *N.B.* The capital will shortly be transferred to the new city of Brasilia in the state of Goiás.

Production and Trade: Brazil is a rich agricultural country, although the actual area under cultivation is comparatively small. She is the world's leading producer of livestock, coffee, and one of the chief sources of castor beans, sugar and tobacco. Most of the coffee is grown on very large *fazendos* (plantations) of upwards of 100,000 trees. Oranges, bananas, cotton and rice are other important crops. Rubber is produced in the states of Amazonas and Pará, and in the Acre territory. Brazil has overtaken Argentina in stock-breeding; in 1956 she had nearly 67,000,000 cattle, 19,000,000 sheep, 41,400,000 pigs, as well as many millions of goats, horses and mules. There are valuable forests.

The country has considerable mineral wealth. At Itabira, in the state of Minas Gerais, are fabulously rich deposits of iron ore (probably the largest in the world), and a large steel plant operates at Volta Redonda, in the state of Rio de Janeiro. Manganese, bauxite and diamonds are also mined in Minas Gerais, which also has the chief Brazilian gold mine. Chrome, mica, zirconium, beryllium, quartz crystal and coal are also mined in Brazil. Santa Catarina and Rio Grande do

Sul are the coal-mining centres, but the quality of the coal is not good. Oilfields and hydro-electric power are being developed.

Cotton spinning and weaving is the chief manufacturing industry. Other manufactures include paper, flour, leather goods and processed foods.

Coffee accounts for more than half the total value of Brazilian exports, which also include raw cotton, cocoa, iron ore and timber. Fuel oil, grain and vehicles are the chief imports. About 37 per cent. of the overseas trade is conducted with the United States. The unit of currency is the Cruzeiro.

BRITAIN

See UNITED KINGDOM.

BRITISH CARIBBEAN FEDERATION

See WEST INDIES.

BRITISH COMMONWEALTH OF NATIONS

This is a unique and voluntary association of ten independent nations, together with their dependencies. The nations are: the United Kingdom, Canada, Australia, New Zealand, South Africa, India, Pakistan, Ceylon, Ghana and Malaya. They are " autonomous communities . . . equal in status, in no way subordinate one to another, but united by a common allegiance to the Crown and freely associated as members of the British Commonwealth of Nations " (*Statute of Westminster*, 1931). At the head of the Parliament of each member-nation is the Queen (except in the case of the Republics of India and Pakistan which, however, recognize the Queen as " the Head of the Commonwealth ").

Many variations are found in the status of other countries and territories within the Commonwealth, *i.e.*, those described loosely (above) as " dependencies." For example, the Federation of Rhodesia and Nyasaland is on the brink of becoming a fully-fledged member, and the Federation of Nigeria is on the verge of independence. Dependencies in the West Indies already enjoy a large measure of self-government and the Federation of The West Indies which was inaugurated in 1958, takes them another step along the road to independence.

Other lands are colonies, protectorates, protected states or territories held under U.N. Trusteeship; those for which the United Kingdom is responsible include the following: Aden (colony and protectorate), Bahamas (colony), Barbados* (colony), Bermuda (colony), British Guiana (colony), British Honduras (colony), Cyprus (colony), Falkland Is. (colony) and dependencies, Fiji (colony), Gambia (colony and protectorate), Gibraltar (colony), Hong Kong (colony), Jamaica* (colony) and dependencies, Kenya (colony and protectorate), Leeward Is.* (group of four colonies), Malta (colony), Mauritius (colony), North Borneo (colony), St. Helena (colony) and dependencies, Sarawak (colony), Seychelles (colony), Sierra Leone (colony and protectorate), Singapore (colony), Somaliland (protectorate), Tanganyika (Trusteeship territory), Trinidad and Tobago* (colony), Uganda (protectorate), Western Pacific High Commission (comprising the Gilbert and Ellice Is. colony, the British Solomon Is. protectorate, the Southern Line Is. and the New Hebrides Condominium), Windward Is.* (group of four colonies), and Zanzibar (protectorate).

Territories marked * are parts of the Federation of The West Indies (*q.v.*). The British Virgin Islands, in the Leeward group, however, did not accept the plan for federation and are thus excluded.

The Gilbert and Ellice group includes Canton and Enderbury Islands, which have been administered as an Anglo-American Condominion since 1939 under the terms of a 50-year agreement.

The land area occupied by the British Commonwealth is about 14,435,000 square miles and its total population has been estimated at 660,000,000. It thus extends over about one-quarter of the land surface of the earth and contains about one-quarter of the total world population.

BRITISH EAST AFRICA

See KENYA, TANGANYIKA, UGANDA, ZANZIBAR.

BRITISH GUIANA

COLONY

This colony, the only British territory in South America, has an area of 83,000 square miles. It is bordered by Dutch Guiana (Surinam) on the east and Venezuela on the west, with Brazil to the south and west. From the high plateau of the north-west, hilly jungle falls down to the coastal plain where most of the population of about 508,000 live. This population includes 238,000 East Indians, more than 170,000 people of African descent, some 53,000 coloureds (mixed) and about

19,000 Amerindians, as well as Europeans and Chinese. The capital and chief port is Georgetown, at the mouth of the Demerara river.

Agriculture (especially sugar-cane) is the chief industry, but the mining of bauxite (for the Canadian aluminium plants), gold and diamonds is important. The bulk of trade is conducted with the United States, Canada and the United Kingdom. The unit of currency is the Eastern Caribbean Territories dollar.

BRITISH HONDURAS

COLONY

The only British colony in Central America, it looks out over the Gulf of Honduras and is bordered by Guatemala and Mexico. The colony has an area of 8,867 square miles, *i.e.*, it is just a little larger than Wales. Behind the low, swampy coastlands the colony rises to the mountains of the south and the flat uplands of the north. The population exceeds 80,000. Belize is the capital and chief port. The forests are rich in mahogany, cedar and other woods and account for nearly three-quarters of the colony's exports. Citrus fruit (especially grapefruit and oranges) is grown for export. Chicle (for chewing gum) is collected during the season. The chief trading partners of the colony are the United Kingdom and the United States. The unit of currency is the British Honduras dollar.

BRITISH ISLES

See IRISH REPUBLIC, UNITED KINGDOM.

BRITISH NORTH BORNEO

COLONY

As its name suggests, this colony occupies the northern part of the island of Borneo. It includes the island of Labuan. It has an area of about 29,389 square miles. Dusuns, Muruts, Suluks and other tribes form more than two-thirds of the population of over 389,000, which also includes more than 74,000 Chinese. The capital is Jesselton. The growing of food crops is the main occupation. Rubber, timber and copra are exported. Foodstuffs are the principal import. Most of the trade is handled by Singapore (*q.v.*). The unit of currency is the Malayan dollar.

BRITISH SOMALILAND

PROTECTORATE

This territory in north-east Africa looks out over the Gulf of Aden and has an area of 68,000 square miles. Behind the coastal plain is a dry, elevated plateau where the nomadic people follow a pastoral life with their camels, goats and sheep. Estimates of the population vary from 500,000 to 700,000. Hargeisa is the seat of government, and Berbera the chief port. The unit of currency is the East African shilling.

BRITISH WEST AFRICA

See GAMBIA, NIGERIA, SIERRA LEONE.

BRITISH WEST INDIES

See BAHAMAS, BARBADOS, JAMAICA, LEEWARD ISLANDS, TRINIDAD, WEST INDIES, WINDWARD ISLANDS.

BRUNEI

BRITISH PROTECTORATE

This ancient sultanate has an area of about 2,226 square miles and a population exceeding 65,000, which includes some 31,000 Malays. The capital is Brunei, on the river of the same name. Its rich Seria oilfield provides crude oil for export and for refining at Lutong. Rubber, too, is produced for export. There are valuable forests still to be exploited. The unit of currency is the Malayan dollar.

BULGARIA

REPUBLIC

This Balkan country is largely rugged and mountainous. The greater part of its northern frontier with Rumania is formed by the Danube; and between the southern bank of this great river and the Balkan mountains are fertile lowlands. Beyond the Stara Planina is the plain of Rumelia, warmer than the northern lowlands, which is isolated from Greece by the forested Rhodope Mountains.

Population: 7,629,254. Sofia, the capital, has an estimated population of 726,000. Other important centres are Plovdiv, Varna, Ruse (Rustchuk), Burgas and Dimitrovo (formerly Pernik). Most Bulgarians are members of the Orthodox Church, but there are many Moslems. About 88 per cent. of the people have Bulgarian as their language; about 10 per cent. Turkish, the remainder being accounted for by various minorities.

Production and Trade: Bulgaria is an overwhelmingly agricultural country, with cereals, fruit, sugar-beet, potatoes, cotton, tobacco and grapes as the main crops. The famous rose-oil industry (" attar of roses ") is directed by the state, and there are a number of large state farms and co-operative farms. Irrigation areas are being developed with the help of the Soviet Union. Large numbers of cattle and sheep are raised in the north. Industry is slowly being developed, *e.g.*, the " Stalin " chemical combine at Dimitrovgrad and various hydro-electric stations; iron and steel; engineering and mining. By far the greater part of Bulgarian trade is with the Soviet Union and other east European countries. The unit of currency is the Lev (*plural*, Leva).

BURMA

REPUBLIC

This country of south-east Asia has an area of about 261,610 square miles. A tropical monsoon land, it is shut in on three sides by mountains. Thickly forested ranges and deep river valleys run from north to south. It is in the fertile valleys and deltas of the great Burmese rivers, the Irrawaddy, Salween and Chindwin that most of the people live.

Population: About 19,250,000. About 9,000,000 of these are Burmans, 1,000,000 Indians, 300,000 Chinese. Most of the remainder are people of the hill tribes, *e.g.*, Shans, Karens, Chins and Was. The capital and chief port of the Union of Burma is Rangoon, which has an estimated population of 737,000. Most of the people in Burma are Buddhists.

Production and Trade: Agriculture is the chief industry, great quantities of rice being produced every year. Cotton, millet, groundnuts and rubber are also produced. Chauk, Yenang-yuang and other centres provide oil. Tin is mined in the Tavoy region and the Salween highlands, silver at Bawdwin and rubies at Mogok. Rice, teak and petroleum are the chief exports. Burma's principal trading partners are India and the United Kingdom. The unit of currency is the Kyat.

Communications: The forested ridges running from north to south determine the natural flow of traffic. East–west traffic is obviously difficult. The famous natural highway of Burma is the river Irrawaddy, which is navigable as far as Bhamo. The main railway system links the north with Mandalay and Rangoon, and Prome with Rangoon.

CAMBODIA

MONARCHY

Once a French protectorate, Cambodia was recognised in 1949 as "an independent Associate State." Subsequently military, financial and economic ties with France were severed and the country now enjoys sovereign independence. Its area is some 70,000 square miles, the chief features of which are the plain of the river Mekong and Lake Tonlé Sap.

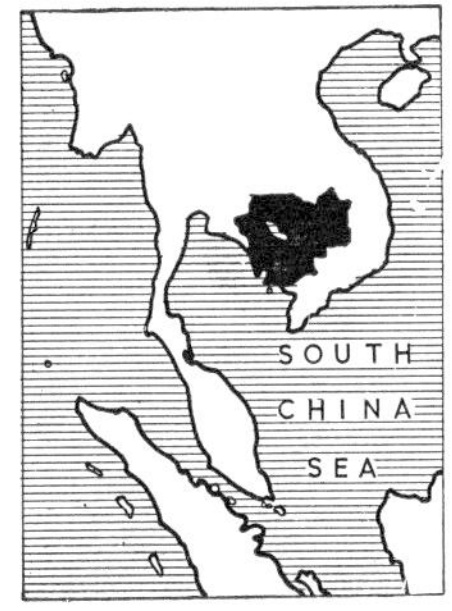

Population: About 4,500,000, including 250,000 Chinese, 220,000 Vietnamese and Laotians, and 85,000 Chams. Primitive peoples live in the forests of the north-east. Phnôm-Penh, the capital, has a population of about 500,000.

Production and Trade: Rice is the chief crop, but maize, pepper and rubber are also important. The valuable forests have still to be exploited. The lake fisheries are important. Much of Cambodia's trade is conducted with Japan and Hong Kong. The unit of currency is the Riel (formerly the Cambodian piastre).

CANADA

CONSTITUTIONAL MONARCHY

The Dominion of Canada is a member of the British Commonwealth of Nations and comprises ten provinces and two territories with a total area of 3,845,774 square miles, *i.e.*, more than half the North American continent. The provinces and provincial capitals are: Alberta (Edmonton), British Columbia (Victoria), Manitoba (Winnipeg), New Brunswick (Fredericton), Newfoundland (St. John's), Nova Scotia (Halifax), Ontario (Toronto), Prince Edward Island (Charlottetown), Quebec (Quebec) and Saskatchewan (Regina). The capital of the Yukon Territory is Whitehorse; the Northwest Territories (divided into the three districts of Mackenzie, Keewatin and Franklin) are administered from Ottawa, the Dominion capital.

More than half the Dominion falls within the area known as the Canadian, or Pre-Cambrian, Shield—a wide area of old, hard rock spread horseshoewise round Hudson Bay and characterised by rivers, lakes, muskeg and forest. Roughly bordering this area are two great waterway systems: the St. Lawrence and the lakes in the south, and the Mackenzie in the west.

Running from north to south down the western side of Canada are the Rocky Mountains, which form part of the great North American system of mountain ranges, plateaux and valleys known as the Western Cordillera. Between the mountains and the Canadian Shield lie the forests and prairies of the Interior Plains.

The deep forest belt stretches across the Dominion south of the Arctic lands and tundra. Still farther south are the wheat and cattle lands of the prairies. The sea coast has many inlets and islands; much of it is ice-bound during the winter.

Population: The Census of 1951 showed a total population of 14,009,429. This included 4,319,167 people of French origin (most of them in the province of Quebec), 155,874 Indians and 9,733 Eskimos. In 1958 the population numbered 17,085,000. The chief cities and towns include: Montreal (1,109,439), Toronto (667,706), Vancouver (365,844), Winnipeg (255,093), Hamilton (239,625), Edmonton (226,002), Ottawa (222,129), Quebec (170,703), Windsor (121,980), London (101,693), Halifax (93,301), Regina (89,755), Verdun (78,262), Saskatoon (72,858), Kitchener (59,562), Sherbrooke (58,668), St. John's (57,078), Victoria (54,584), Saint John (52,491), Brantford (51,101), Three Rivers (50,483). Both English and French are official languages.

Production and Trade: Agriculture is a leading industry. Enormous yields of wheat come from the prairies, and there too, on the hillier and drier parts, large-scale cattle-raising is carried on. Dairy farming is especially important in the St. Lawrence lowlands; fruit farming, in the Niagara peninsula and in parts of Nova Scotia and British Columbia. The great forests provide lumber, pulp and paper (especially newsprint). The cod fisheries of the Grand Banks of Newfoundland and the salmon fisheries of British Columbia have long been famous. Trapping is another historic industry, but many pelts now come from the special farms devoted to fur animals.

Mining is of great importance. Mineral wealth is being rapidly exploited, especially in the remoter parts of the Dominion. It includes oil (Alberta and Northwest Territories), which, with its refineries and great pipelines, ranks as a major industry; natural gas (Alberta), coal (Alberta, British Columbia and Nova Scotia), iron ore (British Columbia, Newfoundland and northern Ontario; the newly-developed deposits on the Quebec–Labrador border are of prime importance), gold, silver, cobalt, copper, asbestos, titanium ore, zinc and uranium. Port Radium (Northwest Territories), Beaverlodge (northern Saskatchewan) and Blind River (Ontario) are among the chief sources of uranium ore; Chalk River, Ontario, is the main centre of atomic research.

Recent industrial developments include the huge aluminium plant at Kitimat, about 400 miles north of Vancouver, and its hydro-electric scheme. The Dominion will derive hydro-electric power in abundance from the St. Lawrence Seaway project (see next page).

There is a considerable manufacturing industry of great variety, centred mostly in the Great Lakes–St. Lawrence lowlands region; Canada is now making ships, aircraft, cars, machinery, processed foods, leather goods, textiles, metal goods, etc. But her principal exports, except metal ores, are based on her traditional farm and forest industries, *e.g.*, paper, timber and cereals. The United States and, to a much lesser extent, the United Kingdom are her chief trading partners. The unit of currency is the Canadian dollar.

Communications: There are two major trans-continental railway systems, the Canadian National Railways and the Canadian Pacific. Air services have been developed vigorously and have played a leading part in opening up the more inaccessible parts of the country. Nearing completion is the Trans-Canada Highway, a coast-to-coast scenic route and the most ambitious civil engineering project of its kind ever undertaken in Canada.

Montreal is one of the leading ports, but with the completion of the St. Lawrence Seaway it may be succeeded in importance by Toronto. The Seaway provides a new deep-water canal, by-passing the rapids on the St. Lawrence, and numerous hydro-electric power stations. It is a joint Canadian-American undertaking designed to open the natural waterway of the Great Lakes to ocean shipping.

CEYLON

CONSTITUTIONAL MONARCHY

Ceylon, a member of the British Commonwealth of Nations, is a beautiful island off the southern tip of India and has an area of 25,332 square miles. Much of it is covered with forest and jungle. Beyond the coastal plains and at the heart of the island, in the south, is a mountainous core, with Pidurutallagalla (Pedrotallagalla) and other high peaks. The climate generally is warm and humid, and the island enjoys a generous rainfall. The principal river is the Mahaveliganga.

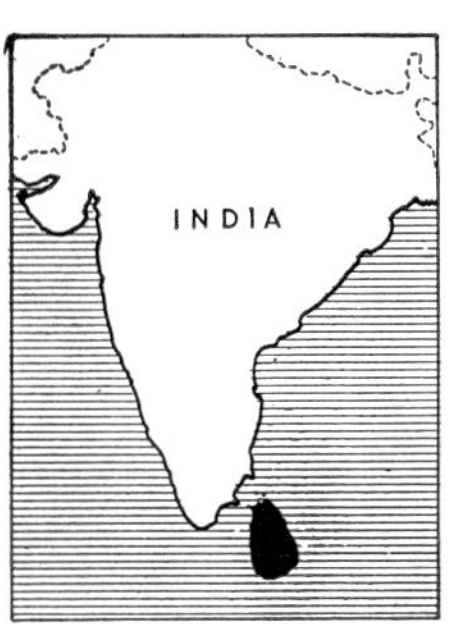

Population: 8,103,648. This figure includes more than 5,600,000 Sinhalese, nearly 1,000,000 Tamils from Southern India, 474,000 Moors, and numbers of Burghers, Eurasians, Veddas, Malayans and Europeans. Sinhalese, Tamil and English are the principal languages spoken, but there is a strong movement for making Sinhalese the only official language of the country. The capital and chief port, Colombo, has a population of 424,816.

Production and Trade: Agriculture is the principal activity, with tea and rubber as the leading export crops. Rice, coconuts and spices are also important, but considerable quantities of foodstuffs have to be imported. Sapphires, rubies and other gems are mined. Plywood, leather and other manufactures are being developed. The leading trading partners are the United Kingdom, India, the United States, Burma and China. The unit of currency is the Ceylon rupee.

CHILE

REPUBLIC

This long, narrow country of South America lies between the Andes and the South Pacific. From north to south it measures nearly 3,000 miles and its average width is about 100 miles, the total area being some 290,000 square miles. There are high peaks exceeding 20,000 feet in the Andes, some still active volcanoes. The north is a dry desert region; the south, wet and thickly forested but with rich pastures. Most Chileans live in the central Mediterranean-type region.

Population: Estimated at 6,941,000. Most of the people are *mestizo*, *i.e.*, of mixed Spanish-Indian blood. Spanish is the official language. The capital, Santiago, has a population of 1,350,409. Other important towns are Valparaiso (the chief port), Concepción, Viña del Mar and Antofagasta.

Production and Trade: Chile is one of the world's leading producers of copper; the ore is mined in the northern mountains, nearly all of it by American companies. There are rich deposits of iron and manganese. Huachipato, near Concepción, is the centre of the Chilean steel industry. Gold, a little silver, some coal, and lead are also mined. Finds of uranium have been reported in Coquimbo and Atacama. Oil and natural gas are produced in Tierra del Fuego. The famous nitrate industry of the Atacama Desert is not so profitable these days owing to the development of synthetic nitrates, but it does provide (as a by-product) much of the world's iodine. Generally speaking, Chilean mineral wealth accounts for nearly 80 per cent. of the total value of her exports.

The best agricultural land is in mid-Chile, where stock-raising is carried on. Cereals, vines and citrus fruits are also grown, but Chile has to import food. Patagonia provides large amounts of wool and mutton for export. There are valuable forests, especially in Valdivia and Cautin, which have still to be fully exploited.

Manufacturing is becoming more important, and includes food processing, textiles, metal goods and chemicals. Nearly half of Chile's trade is conducted with the United States. The unit of currency is the Chilean peso.

CHINA

REPUBLIC

The People's Republic of China has an area of about 4,300,000 square miles. This vast country may be divided into (i) *China proper*, from mountainous Tibet (a "special territory") to the Pacific, and from the Great Wall to Indo-China; (ii) *Outer China*, which includes the provinces of Heilungkiang, Jehol and Kirin, and Inner Mongolia, Sinkiang and Tibet. *China proper* falls into three main regions, each of which corresponds roughly to the basin of one of the great rivers: (i) the north, the Hwang-ho ("Yellow River") basin; (ii) central China, the basin of the Yangtse-kiang ("Blue River"); and (iii) south China, the basin of the Si-kiang ("West River"). Dividing the regions are the east-west mountain masses. The north, much of which is covered by the wind-borne brown-yellow *loess*, has severe winters and hot, dusty summers; central and southern China enjoy plenty of rain and sunshine, and the land can provide two or three harvests each year (compared with the single harvest of the north).

Population: 601,938,035. The estimated population of Peking, the capital, is 5,420,000. Other large centres include Shanghai (6,204,417), Tientsin (2,693,831), Shenyang (formerly Mukden, 2,290,000), Wuhan (1,800,000), Chungking (1,620,000), Sian (1,500,000), Canton (1,496,000) and Port Arthur—Dairen (1,054,000).

The Chinese language has many dialects, but its most important form is known as Mandarin. The three main religions are Confucianism, Taoism and Buddhism.

Production and Trade: China is predominantly an agricultural country. Most of her farmers now work co-operatively, but about 20 per cent. still have smallholdings worked as family ventures. In the north the main crops are wheat, millet (*kaoliang*) and soya beans; in the centre, wheat, rice, cotton and tea; in the south, rice, tea and fruit. Both silk and cotton are products of the centre and south. Other important crops are sweet potatoes, sugar-cane and tobacco. Literally millions of pigs, sheep, goats, oxen and poultry are raised. There are valuable forests in Heilungkiang, Szechwan and Yunnan.

In recent years there has been remarkable large-scale industrial development, often with technical assistance from the Soviet Union. There are rich coal deposits, plentiful iron ore, tungsten, antimony, tin, manganese, mercury, gold, copper and zinc. Oilfields are being exploited (especially in Sinkiang) and hydro-electric power developed. Among the important centres of industry are Fushun and Penshi (coal and iron ore), Anshan (steel), Tayeh and Hanyang (iron ore), and Mengtse (tin).

Manufactures are of increasing importance. There are large textile concerns at Shanghai, Canton and other centres, and Shanghai in particular is being developed as the leading manufacturing and commercial city. About three-quarters of China's trade is conducted with countries of the Soviet bloc. The Chinese unit of currency is the *Jen Min Piao*, the People's dollar, or Yuan.

Communications: Shanghai, Canton (Yhampoa) and Tientsin are the chief ports. In recent years much has been done to extend the railway system. New trunk lines have been laid, providing better links with the Soviet Union and the remoter parts of "Outer China." There are extensive air services.

Special Territories: *Inner Mongolia*, *Sinkiang-Uighur*, *Kwangsi-Chuang*, *Ningsia-Hui* and *Tibet* are "autonomous regions" enjoying some measure of self-government. Tibet was once entirely independent (but was always claimed by China). It is clearly now regarded as an integral part of the country, although it too has a measure of self-government under its priestly rulers, the Dalai Lama and the Panchen Lama, whose capital is Lhasa. *Formosa* (Taiwan), defined recently as territory " yet to be liberated," is the island stronghold of the Chinese Nationalists under General Chiang Kai-shek, the President of the " National Republic of China." The island has an area of 13,890 square miles and a population of about 9,409,886. Taipei (759,200) is the capital. The unit of currency in Formosa is the New Taiwan Yuan.

COLOMBIA

REPUBLIC

This country occupies an area of some 439,520 square miles in the north-west of South America. The Andes here divides into the Western, Central and Eastern Cordilleras, the Central being the highest with peaks rising to 18,000 feet and more. Much of the interior of the country is thickly forested, but to the east are the *llanos* (grasslands). The high plateaux and the temperate valleys of the Eastern Cordillera are the most densely populated part of the Republic. The principal rivers are the Magdalena and its tributary, the Cauca. Colombia has shores on both the Pacific and the Caribbean.

Population: About 13,227,480. Bogotá, the capital, has a population exceeding 648,000. Other important towns are Medellín, Cali, Barranquilla (seaport and international airport), Cartagena and Manizales. Most of the people are *mestizo*, but there are numbers of Europeans, American Indians and Negroes. Spanish is the official language.

Production and Trade: Although a comparatively small part of the country is under cultivation, there is great variety in the crops produced—tropical crops (sugar, rice, bananas) on the lowlands, wheat and other temperate-region crops on the high plateau. Colombia is second only to Brazil as a coffee producer. Large numbers of cattle, sheep and pigs are raised on the *llanos*.

Colombia has long been famous for its emeralds and is also rich in gold, silver, platinum and copper. Coal and iron ore are available and a steel industry has been established in the Paz de Rio. There are unusual salt mines in Zipaquirá. Oil is of growing importance. Colombia's chief trading partner is the United States. The unit of currency is the Colombian peso.

COSTA RICA

REPUBLIC

A Central American state with an area of 19,653 square miles. Volcanic mountains dominate the heart of the country, with tropical forest and swamp on the east and grasslands on the west.

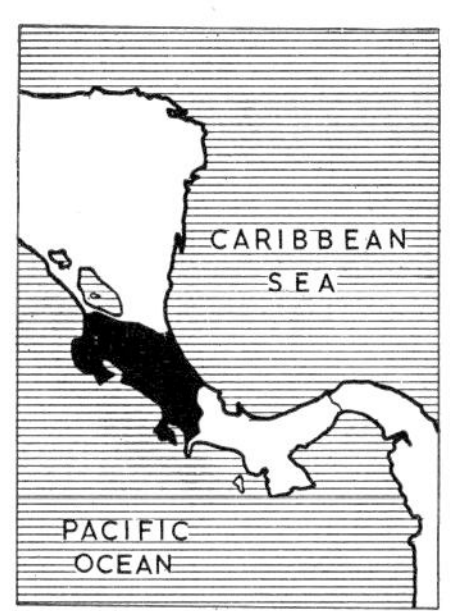

Population: About 1,055,200. San José, the capital, has a population of about 128,000. Many of the people are of pure Spanish descent. Roman Catholicism is the established religion.

Production and Trade: Agriculture is the chief industry, with coffee and bananas as the chief crops. The valuable forests have still to be exploited. Gold and silver are mined. The chief trading partner of Costa Rica is the United States. The unit of currency is the Colón.

CUBA

REPUBLIC

Cuba is the largest island in the West Indies. Its area, including adjacent islands, is 44,206 square miles. The south-east is mountainous and wooded, with the Sierra Maestra reaching a height of 8,400 feet. Most of the island is very fertile.

Population: 5,807,057. Havana, the capital and chief port, has a population of 787,765. Other important centres are Holguín, Camagüey, Santa Clara, and Santiago de Cuba, all of which have populations exceeding 144,000.

Production and Trade: More than half the area under cultivation is devoted to sugar; more sugar is produced in Cuba than in any other country in the world. Tobacco is the second export crop. Mahogany, cedar and other woods are provided by the rich forests. Large numbers of cattle and horses are reared on the central grasslands. There are vast deposits of iron ore, which have still to be exploited by the American interests which control them. Most Cuban trade is conducted with the United States. The unit of currency is the Peso.

CYPRUS

BRITISH COLONY

A mountainous island of the eastern Mediterranean with an area of 3,572 square miles. Its estimated population is 528,879. Nicosia, the capital, has a population of about 48,900. More than 80 per cent. of the people are Greek Orthodox; about 18 per cent. are Moslem. Greek and Turkish are the languages most commonly used, but French and English are also favoured.

Agriculture is the chief industry with cereals, olives, grapes and citrus fruits among the principal crops. Iron ore, copper, asbestos, gypsum and chrome ore are mined. The main trading partners of Cyprus are the United Kingdom and other countries of the British Commonwealth, and West Germany. The chief seaport is Famagusta. The unit of currency is the Cypriot pound.

CZECHOSLOVAKIA

REPUBLIC

A country of Middle Europe with an area of 49,355 square miles. The western part of this land of rich forests and fertile plains and valleys has the river Elbe and its tributary, the Vltava (Moldau), as the chief features, with the Erzgebirge ("Ore Mountains") marking the frontier on the north-west. Dividing this western part from the Moravian plateau and the western Carpathians is the valley of the Morava river, a tributary of the Danube.

Population: 13,420,000. Prague (Praha), the capital and an important railway centre, has a population exceeding 978,000. Other important towns are Brno, Bratislava (an important railway centre and river port on the Danube), Ostrava, and Plzen (Pilsen). The Czech and Slovak languages are used.

Production and Trade: Agriculture is a leading industry and is organised on Soviet lines with state farms and collective farms. Cereals, potatoes, sugar-beet and hops are among the principal crops. Coal, iron, graphite, copper, uranium and other minerals are plentiful. But manufacturing is perhaps the most important activity and embraces textiles, chemicals, timber products, glass, fine china, leather goods and shoes. Pilsen has long been famous for its breweries (and its armaments works).

At one time Czechoslovakia enjoyed a thriving trade with Germany and other Western countries. In recent years, however, by far the greater part of her trade has been with countries of the Soviet bloc. The Czech unit of currency is the Koruna (crown).

DENMARK

CONSTITUTIONAL MONARCHY

Denmark is a low-lying peninsula of north-western Europe; the highest point is only some 564 feet above sea level. There are sand dunes and marshes along the western coast, and also Limfjord and other deep inlets. The central and eastern parts of the mainland and the Danish islands in the Baltic (except Bornholm) are fertile and well cultivated. The climate is not unlike that of eastern England, but the winters are colder and the rainfall heavier. The country has an area of 16,608 square miles.

Population: 4,476,000. Copenhagen ("Merchants' Haven"), the capital and chief port, has a population of 753,361. Other important towns include Aahus, Odense, Aalborg and Esbjerg (the chief fishing port). The established Church is Lutheran Protestant.

Production and Trade: Although nearly half the population is employed in manufactures and trading, agriculture is the leading industry.

Cereals and vegetables are grown, but pride of place goes to dairying, for which Denmark has long been famous. There are many co-operative buying and selling establishments for the farmers. Large quantities of eggs, bacon and butter are exported to the United Kingdom, which is Denmark's principal trading partner. Fisheries and ship-building are important. The country has a considerable merchant fleet and is one of the world's prominent carrying countries. The unit of currency is the Krone.

Overseas Territories: *The Faröe Islands* (capital Thorshavn) have an area of 540 square miles and a population of 32,380. They enjoy a measure of self-government and are important for their fisheries. *Greenland* has an area of about 835,000 square miles, some 132,000 square miles being ice-free. The population numbers 27,101. The island is divided into three " inspectorates ": West Greenland (capital Godthaab), North Greenland (capital Godhavn) and East Greenland. Cod-fishing is the chief industry, but the island has deposits of coal, lead and zinc.

DOMINICAN REPUBLIC

REPUBLIC

Formerly known as Santo Domingo, the republic has an area of 19,332 square miles and occupies the eastern part of the West Indian island of Hispaniola. The tropical lowlands are very fertile. The forest-clad mountains are the highest in the West Indies, Pico Trujillo reaching a height of 10,319 feet.

Population: 2,593,325. Ciudad Trujillo, the capital, has a population exceeding 272,000. Spanish is the language of the country, and Roman Catholicism its religion.

Production and Trade: Agriculture is the principal industry, and sugar-cane the leading crop. Cocoa, coffee, tobacco and rice are of increasing importance. Gold is mined and deposits of copper, iron, silver and platinum have been found. The United States is the chief trading partner of the republic, but the United Kingdom takes a large share (about 46 per cent.) of the exports. The unit of currency is the Peso oro.

ECUADOR

REPUBLIC

Ecuador (" state of the Equator ") is crossed from north to south by the Western and Eastern Cordilleras of the Andes. In the north there are peaks more than 19,000 feet in height, some of which are volcanic. Chimborazo, the highest peak in the country, rises to 20,551 feet, while Cotopaxi, the highest active volcano in the world, reaches a height of more than 19,340 feet. The upland valleys of the Andes are the home of more than half the population. Along the Pacific coast there are fertile lowlands; in the east the country falls away to the tropical forests of the upper Amazon. The exact area of the country has still to be determined, but an official estimate is 275,855 square miles.

Population: 3,619,345. Quito, the capital, has a population of 237,103. Other important towns are Guayaquil (the chief port and commercial centre), Cuenca, Ambato and Riobamba. Most of the people are *mestizo*, speaking Spanish. Quechua is the language of the Indians, who form about 27 per cent. of the population.

Production and Trade: Agriculture is the chief industry. Cocoa, coffee, bananas and rice are the principal export crops. Toquilla palm fibre (which is made into " Panama " hats) and ivory nuts are obtained from the forested Pacific slopes. Cereals, fruits and vegetables are grown in the upland valleys, where there is also a pastoral and dairying industry. The vast forests provide balsa and other woods. Gold, silver, copper and lead are mined. Oil production has increased in recent years, but petroleum still has to be imported. More than half of Ecuador's trade is conducted with the United States. The unit of currency is the Sucre.

EGYPT

A " REGION " OF THE UNITED ARAB REPUBLIC (see p. 190)

Egypt is the land of the Nile. It is on this great river that the fertility and prosperity of the country depend. The Region has an area of 386,198 square miles, but by far the greater part of this is desert with occasional

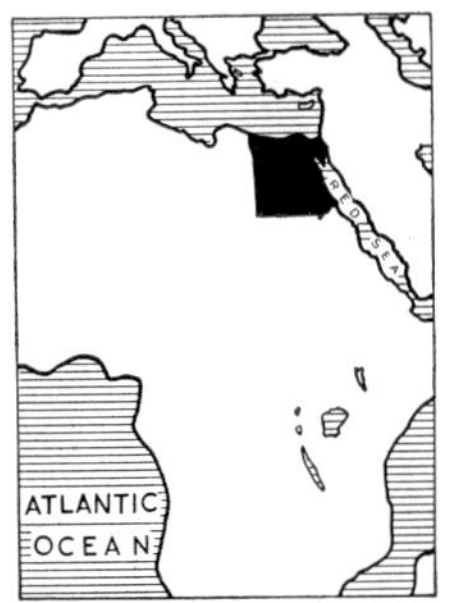

oases; it is the area watered by the Nile (estimated at 13,500 square miles) which is important. Large dams and barrages have been built to control the precious flood waters.

Population: 23,240,000. Cairo, the chief city, and capital of the United Arab Republic, has more than 2,090,600 people and is the largest city of the African continent. Alexandria, the second city and chief port of Egypt, has a population exceeding 919,000. Port Said has more than 177,000 inhabitants. Arabic is the official language.

Production and Trade: Agriculture is the chief industry and is largely undertaken by peasant proprietors. Irrigation is of prime importance. Wheat and other cereals are grown, but the principal cash crop is fine quality cotton—the most valuable export. Rice and sugar-cane are also grown. There are good fisheries. Manufactures include textiles, perfume and cigarettes. Phosphate rock and petroleum are the chief mineral resources. Textiles, coal, petroleum, machinery, vehicles and various manufactures are imported. The Soviet Union, France, Italy, Western Germany, the United Kingdom and the United States are the principal trading partners. The unit of currency is the Egyptian pound.

Communications: In the north-east, linking the Mediterranean with the Red Sea, is the Suez Canal, 101 miles in length. The controlling organisation of this vital waterway, the *Compagnie Universelle du Canal Maritime de Suez*, was nationalised by Egypt in 1956.

EIRE

See IRISH REPUBLIC.

EL SALVADOR

See SALVADOR.

ENGLAND

See UNITED KINGDOM.

ERITREA

See ETHIOPIA.

ETHIOPIA

MONARCHY

Ethiopia, or Abyssinia, has an area of 395,000 square miles (including Eritrea, which has been a federated autonomous region of the country since 1952). It is a country of high plateaux, cut by streams and deep valleys which make communications difficult. There are good grasslands and forest in the central and south-western parts; desert in the north and east.

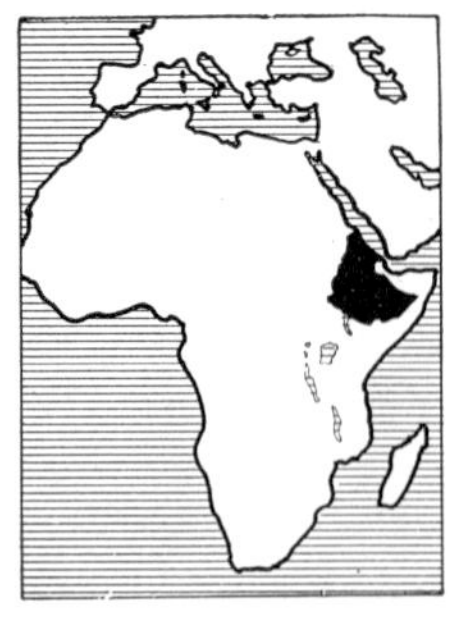

Population: Estimates vary from 8,000,000 to 18,000,000, the latter being the most recent official figure. The ruling people are the Amharas, who number about 2,000,000 and live in the central highlands. Other races of Hamitic and Semitic origin, as well as Somalis and Nilotic tribes, make up the population. The estimated population of Addis Ababa, the capital, is 400,000. Other important centres are Dire-Dawa, Harar, Jimma, Dessie and Asmara (the capital of Eritrea). The Amharic, English and French languages are used; many tribal tongues are also spoken. Most of the people are Coptic Christians, but Moslems are numerous.

Production and Trade: Agriculture is mostly primitive. Large numbers of cattle, sheep and goats are reared. Coffee is the chief cash crop, and is exported with hides, oilseeds and wax to adjacent countries. Gold is mined and deposits of other minerals (including iron, coal and copper) have been found. The unit of currency is the Ethiopian dollar.

Communications: Addis Ababa is linked by railway with Jibuti (Djibouti), the seaport capital of French Somaliland, but mules and other pack animals are the chief means of transport.

FALKLAND ISLANDS

BRITISH COLONY

This island group lies in the South Atlantic, the chief islands being East Falkland (2,580 square miles) and West Falkland (2,038 square miles). The chief town is Stanley, on East Falkland, with a population of 1,135. The estimated total population of the group is 2,294. Sheep-farming is the principal activity and wool, tallow, sheepskins, etc., are exported. United Kingdom currency is used.

Dependencies include South Georgia, important for seasonal whaling; the South Shetlands and South Orkneys; the South Sandwich Islands; and Graham's Land (an Antarctic peninsula).

FIJI

BRITISH COLONY

A group of some 320 islands in the West Pacific of which more than 100 are uninhabited. The principal islands are mountainous, volcanic, forested and fertile; there are many coral atolls in the group. Viti Levu, the largest island, has an area of just over 4,000 square miles, the total area of the group being some 7,000 square miles.

Population: 345,737. It includes about 6,400 Europeans, 148,100 Fijians and 169,400 Indians, as well as Chinese, Rotumans, Polynesians and others. Suva, the capital (on Viti Levu), has an estimated population of 37,000. English, Fijian, Hindustani and other languages are in use.

Production and Trade: Coconuts, bananas, sugar cane, rice, pineapples and yams are cultivated, sugar being the leading export. Gold, silver and manganese are mined. Most Fijian trade is conducted with the United Kingdom, Australia, New Zealand and other countries of the British Commonwealth. The local unit of currency is the Fijian pound.

Communications: Fiji is of considerable importance as a place of call on the main trans-Pacific air routes and as a base for South Pacific air services. It is an important centre of radio-telephone, cable and wireless communications.

FINLAND

REPUBLIC

This low-lying country of Northern Europe is noted for its thousands of lakes, the largest of which is Saimaa, and for its extensive conifer forests which cover about 70 per cent of its total area of 130,127 square miles. The coastline is rocky and indented and is fringed by numerous islands. The winter is harsh (but not so severe as the north Russian winter), the summer is short and sometimes very hot.

Population: 4,315,140, composed of Finns, Swedes and Lapps. Finnish is the language of more than 90 per cent of the population. Helsinki (Helsingfors), the capital, has a population of over 425,000. Other important towns are Turku (Abo), Tampere (Tammerfors), Lahti and Pori (Björneborg).

Production and Trade: Only a comparatively small area is cultivated and the true wealth of the country lies in its forests. Wood pulp, paper, cellulose, furniture and prefabricated houses are manufactured, and timber and paper are the chief exports. There is no coal in Finland, but hydro-electric power is well developed. The Finnish unit of currency is the Markka (divided into 100 penni).

FORMOSA

See CHINA.

FRANCE

REPUBLIC

France has an area of some 213,100 square miles and lies between the Atlantic and Mediterranean, with the Pyrenees marking her frontier with Spain and other considerable mountain ranges (Alps, Juras and Vosges) on her east and south-east borderlands. The outstanding physical feature of the country is the Central Plateau (Massif Central) with its highest points in the Auvergne Mountains. This Central Plateau, which is bordered on the east by the Cevennes, contains the headwaters of the great rivers Loire and Garonne. Eastwards, between the Cevennes and the Alps, is the fertile valley of the river Rhône, into which the Saône flows at Lyons. The Central Plateau has long, hard winters and hot summers, *i.e.*, a " Continental " climate.

The fertile lowlands of the north-west, like the United Kingdom, enjoy a " West European " climate, with mild winters, cool summers and most rainfall during autumn and winter. Rugged Brittany is not unlike Devon and Cornwall. In the north-east (but mostly in neighbouring Belgium) are the Ardennes. In the extreme south is the Mediterranean shore with its long, hot summers and mild winters; here is the famous Riviera with its chain of fashionable resorts.

Population: 44,289,000 (including more than 1,400,000 foreigners). Paris, the capital, has a population of 2,850,189. French, of course, is the language of the country, but Basque, Breton and Provençal may be encountered in certain districts. The many other important cities and towns include

Marseilles (second city and chief commercial port), with a population of 661,492, and Lyons (the headquarters of the French silk industry) with a population of 471,270. Some twenty-one other cities have more than 100,000 inhabitants.

Production and Trade: Agriculture is the leading industry, most of the cultivated land being in the hands of small peasant proprietors. Leading crops include wheat (especially in the Paris and Aquitaine Basins), maize, barley, oats, rye, potatoes, flax and sugar-beet. Wine is produced in practically all parts of the country except the north-west, and the vineyards of Bordeaux, Burgundy and Champagne are world-famous. Fruits of many kinds are grown and on the Mediterranean shorelands the mulberry and olive are cultivated. Cattle, sheep and other livestock are numerous. There are valuable forests and profitable fisheries.

The chief source of coal is the rich Northern Coalfield, which extends into Belgium. The mines of Lorraine provide iron ore in abundance. Other minerals include copper, lead, silver and uranium. In recent years there has been remarkable development of hydro-electric power (especially along the Rhône). Leading industrial and manufacturing centres and their products are: Lille (iron and steel, textiles, foodstuffs, chemicals, brewing, metal-work), Roubaix and Tourcoing (textiles), Lyons (silk), Cambrai (linen), Paris (cars, clothing, furniture, jewellery), Grenoble (gloves), Besançon (clocks and watches).

The chief exports are manufactured goods, iron ore, silk, steel and wine. Foodstuffs, tobacco and petroleum are among the leading imports. A considerable part of French trade is conducted with French overseas territories, but the United States and the United Kingdom are important trading partners. The unit of currency is the French franc.

Overseas Territories: (1) The Government-General of Algeria (*q.v.*) and the Overseas Departments of Martinique, Guadeloupe, Réunion and French Guiana (*q.v.*), all of which are represented in the National Assembly; (2) The Overseas Territories—French West Africa and French Equatorial Africa (*q.v.*), Madagascar (*q.v.*), French Somaliland (*q.v.*), and other territories (Comoro Archipelago, New Caledonia, settlements in Oceania, St. Pierre and Miquelon); (3) Trusteeship Territory—Cameroon; (4) the Anglo-French Condominium of the New Hebrides.

FRENCH EQUATORIAL AFRICA

FRENCH OVERSEAS TERRITORY

Occupies more than 977,000 square miles and extends from the Atlantic in the west to the Sudan in the east, and from the Congo and Ubangi rivers in the south to Libya in the north. It comprises the Gabun (capital, Libreville), Middle Congo (capital, Brazzaville), Ubangi-Shari (capital, Bangui) and Chad (capital, Fort Lamy). Brazzaville is the capital of the whole. The African population exceeds 4,853,000; Europeans number less than 26,000.

The resources have still to be developed. Products include palm-oil, coconuts, cotton,

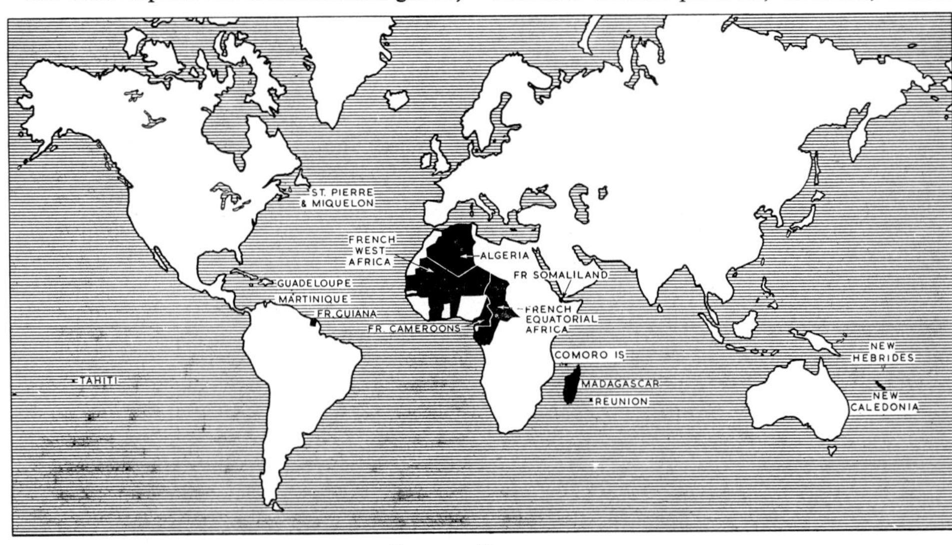

France Overseas

ivory, gold, diamonds and jute. The unit of currency is the Franc CFA.

FRENCH GUIANA

FRENCH OVERSEAS DEPARTMENT

French Guiana, in north-east South America, has an area of about 34,750 square miles. It has a population of approximately 28,000. Cayenne, the capital, was the site of a notorious penal settlement. Its resources include gold and valuable forests.

FRENCH SOMALILAND

FRENCH OVERSEAS TERRITORY

This territory occupies an area of some 9,000 square miles in the Gulf of Aden. The population of about 63,700 includes only 3,132 Europeans. Capital and chief port is Jibuti.

FRENCH WEST AFRICA

FRENCH OVERSEAS TERRITORY

This territory has an area of about 1,800,000 square miles and a population exceeding 19,000,000 (but only about 92,000 are Europeans). The capital and chief port is Dakar.

The territories of French West Africa and their capitals are: Senegal (St. Louis), French Sudan (Bamako), Mauritania (administered from St. Louis, Senegal), Ivory Coast (Abidjan), Upper Volta (Ouagadougou), Dahomey (Porto Novo) and Niger (Niamey).

Agriculture is the chief occupation, with coffee, cocoa, groundnuts and bananas as the chief export crops. The unit of currency is the Franc CFA.

GAMBIA

BRITISH COLONY AND PROTECTORATE

This territory occupies an area of about 4,000 square miles along the lower reaches of the Gambia river in West Africa. The population numbers about 276,000. Bathurst, the capital and port, has about 20,000 inhabitants.

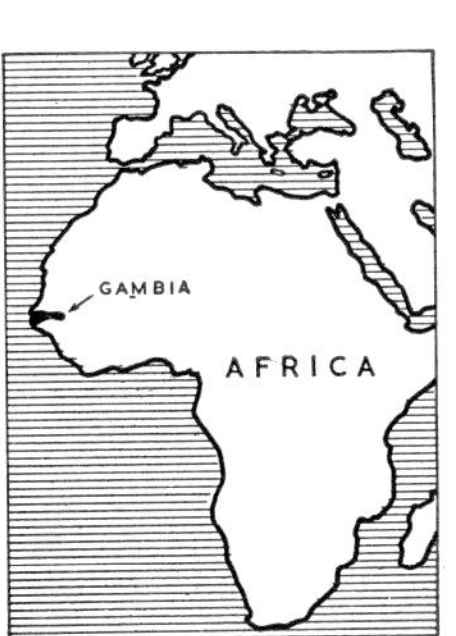

Groundnuts and palm kernels are the chief products and exports, with the United Kingdom as the dominant trading partner. The local unit of currency is the West African pound.

GERMANY

That part of Europe now occupied by the Federal Republic of Germany (see *Germany, Western*, p. 162) and the German Democratic Republic (see *Germany, Eastern*, below) is characterised by (1) the Northern Plain, whose sandy, low-lying heath extends from the Netherlands in the west to Poland in the east; (2) the forested and mountainous country of the centre and south-west; (3) the great rivers—Rhine, Elbe and Danube—which with their network of canals provide a splendid waterways system.

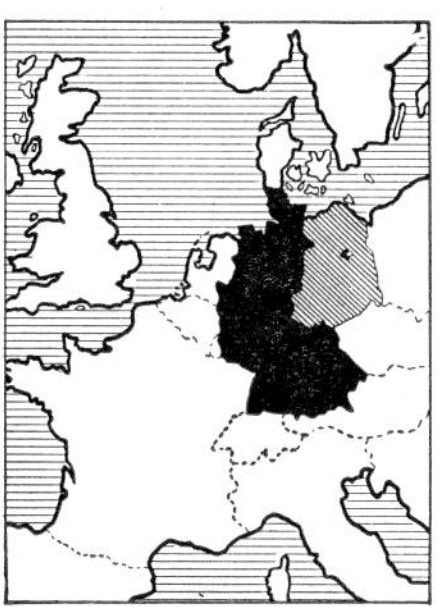

At the end of the Second World War, Germany was divided into Zones of Occupation by the Allies, from which sprang the present political divisions of the former German Reich, the Western Zones becoming the Federal Republic of Germany and the Eastern, the German Democratic Republic. Berlin, the German capital, was likewise divided. Its Western Sectors, though isolated, became a part of the Federal Republic; its Eastern Sector, the capital of the German Democratic Republic.

The Saarland was separated from Germany after the war and, for a time, constituted an independent republic. It was reunited with Western Germany on January 1st, 1957.

Another outcome of the Second World War was the drastic revision of the eastern frontier, which was redrawn on the line of the rivers Oder and Neisse. Northern East Prussia was absorbed by the Soviet Union, and the remaining German lands east of this line by Poland.

GERMANY, EASTERN

GERMAN DEMOCRATIC REPUBLIC

The republic has an area of 41,380 square miles and a population estimated at 17,832,200. Eastern Berlin, the capital, has about 1,120,000 inhabitants. Other important cities and towns include Dresden, Leipzig, Magdeburg and Karl-Marxstadt (formerly Chemnitz).

Production and Trade: Agricultural production is considerable, but while Eastern Germany is wellnigh self-sufficient in this respect she is not so fortunate as Western Germany in the raw materials for industry. Important industrial centres include Dresden (on the

Saxon coalfield), Karl-Marxstadt and Zwickau (textiles and railway machinery), and the new iron and steel centre of Stalinstadt. There are large uranium mines in the Erzgebirge operated under Soviet direction. Although much of Eastern Germany's trade is with other countries of the Soviet bloc, trade with the nations of Western Europe has been developed. The unit of currency is the Deutsche Mark (DM) East.

GERMANY, WESTERN

FEDERAL REPUBLIC OF GERMANY

The Federal Republic has an area of 95,725 square miles and a population exceeding 52,798,000. Bonn, the capital, has about 136,000 inhabitants. Other important cities and towns include Western Berlin (with a population exceeding 2,200,000), Hamburg (the chief port and a flourishing shipbuilding centre), Munich (the capital of Bavaria) and the great industrial centres of the Ruhr.

Production and Trade: Although agricultural production is high, food has to be imported. Grain, potatoes and sugar-beet are leading crops. The Rhineland vineyards are world-famous. There are valuable forests. The Ruhr basin is one of the most important coalfields in Europe and is the Republic's chief industrial area (iron and steel, engineering, textiles and chemicals), its largest city being Essen (population: 699,000). The Saarland, also, is rich in coal. The textile industry has such important centres as Wuppertal (woollens and silks), Krefeld (silks and velvets) and Aachen (woollen cloth).

The many other important manufactures include machine tools, optical instruments, clocks and watches, china, leather goods and toys, and it is not surprising that manufactured goods account for nearly 90 per cent. of the foreign trade of the Federal Republic. Much of this trade is conducted with other Western European countries; but the United States also ranks as a major trading partner, and many other countries have a share.

The unit of currency in Western Germany is the Deutsche Mark (DM).

GHANA

CONSTITUTIONAL MONARCHY

Formerly known as the Gold Coast, Ghana took this name on March 6th, 1957, when it achieved full independence as a member of the Commonwealth. Its area is 91,843 square miles. Behind the hot, wet coastal region are the tropical forests, and then the savanna country and grasslands. The principal river is the Volta, which it is hoped to harness for hydro-electric power for an aluminium industry based on the rich local deposits of bauxite.

Population: Estimated at 4,691,000, of whom only some 7,000 are non-Africans. Accra, the capital, has more than 135,000 inhabitants.

Other places of importance include Kumasi, Sekondi-Takoradi and Cape Coast.

Production and Trade: Ghana is the world's leading cocoa producer. Other important products are gold, manganese ore, diamonds and timber. More than 34 per cent. of the overseas trade is conducted with the United Kingdom. The local unit of currency is the West African pound.

N.B. In November 1958 Ghana and Guinea provisionally agreed to come together " as the nucleus of a union of West African states."

GIBRALTAR

BRITISH COLONY

A fortress rock and important fueling and naval base dominating the western entrance to the Mediterranean. Its area is 2¼ square miles and it is linked to Spain by a low-lying neck of land. The Rock itself rises to a height of some 1,400 feet. Its population is nearly 25,000.

GREECE

CONSTITUTIONAL MONARCHY

This mountainous country with its many islands (which include the Dodecanese) has an area of 51,246 square miles. Dividing Thessaly and Macedonia in the north-east from Epirus in the north-west are the Pindus Mountains, whose spurs partly enclose sheltered fertile basins. In the south the great peninsula of the Morea, or Peloponnese, is severed from the mainland by the Corinth Canal.

In the north and in the mountainous regions farther south winters are very cold, and very snowy or rainy for several months; but summers are dry and hot. The coastal regions have short, mild winters and warm summers; interior lowlands are very hot in the dry summers. On the whole, rainfall is heavier in the western half of the country, because the wet winter winds come from the west.

Population: 8,031,000. Athens, the capital, has a population of 565,084. But the population of Greater Athens (which includes the port of the capital, Piraeus) is about 1,368,000. Modern Greek is the language of the people, except in Western Thrace where there is a Turkish minority. The state religion is the Greek Orthodox Church.

Production and Trade: Greece is an agricultural country. Tobacco the most important export crop, is grown mainly in Macedonia, Thrace and Thessaly. Currants, olives, figs, cotton, cereals and sugar are also grown. But less than a third of the country is cultivatable and food has to be imported. Minerals include iron, bauxite, copper, zinc, lead and marble. Wine, olive-oil, textiles, chemicals, leather goods and carpets are among the principal manufactures, one of the chief manufacturing centres being Piraeus. Electrification, irrigation and land reclamation schemes are now being carried out.

Tobacco, currants, olive oil, wine and sponges are the main exports. Western Germany, the United States, the United Kingdom and Italy are the chief trading partners. The Greek unit of currency is the Drachma.

GREAT BRITAIN

See UNITED KINGDOM.

GUATEMALA

REPUBLIC

This Central American country has an area of 42,042 square miles. Behind the fertile Pacific coastal plain is a high mountain chain, with volcanic peaks of more than 12,000 feet. Earthquakes are not uncommon. The central plateau has forested slopes towards the Atlantic. The higher parts of the country are temperate, but the lowlands are hot and malarious.

Population: About 3,302,000, of whom more than half are of pure Indian descent, most of the remainder being *ladinos* (mixed Indian-Spanish). Guatemala City, the capital, has a population of about 294,000. Spanish is the language of the country, but Indian tongues are also spoken. Roman Catholicism is the religion of most of the people.

Production and Trade: Agriculture is the principal activity, with coffee as the main crop. Bananas, chicle and vegetable oils are also produced for export, while cereals and sugar-cane are the chief domestic crops. Mahogany and other woods are obtained from the forests of the Petén. The chief trading partner is the United States. The unit of currency in Guatemala is the Quetzal.

GUINEA

REPUBLIC

In the French referendum of September 28th, 1958, Guinea (then a French overseas territory) voted against the proposed changes and thus claimed her independence. The country has an area of 106,178 square miles. Beyond the mangrove estuaries and sandy coastal plain are the rugged scarps and forested valleys of the Fouta Djalon, and (to the south-east) the Guinea highlands. Light savanna is the chief characteristic of the Niger and Milo plains in the east.

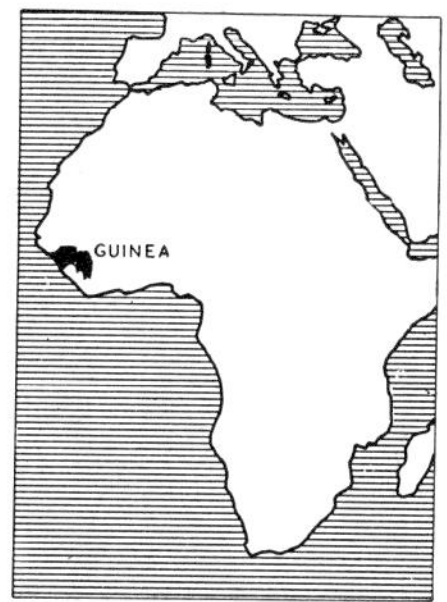

Population: About 2,492,000 (including about 8,700 Europeans). The principal tribes are the Fullah, Malinké and Soussou. Conakry, the island capital and largest town, has a population of 38,500. Other important places include Kankan (24,000) and Kindia (13,000).

Production and Trade: Agriculture, in great variety, is the chief industry. There are important banana plantations. Large numbers of cattle are raised, especially on the Fouta Djalon grasslands. Coffee, fruit, rice, cassava, groundnuts and millet are widely grown. There is some mining of gold (Siguiri), diamonds (Macenta), bauxite (the Los islands) and iron ore (the Kaloum peninsula). Bananas, coffee, palm-kernels, bauxite and iron ore are the chief exports. France is the principal trading partner. The unit of currency is the Franc CFA.

N.B. In November 1958 Guinea and Ghana provisionally agreed to come together " as the nucleus of a union of West African states."

HAITI

REPUBLIC

This country occupies an area of about 10,700 square miles, forming the western part of the island of Hispaniola in the West Indies. The name "Haiti" means "Land of Mountains," and is indeed appropriate, two forested mountain ranges dominating the countryside.

Population: About 3,500,000. Most of the people are Negroes, but mulatto Haitians (descended from French settlers) are also numerous. The official language is French, but a dialect (Creole French) is commonly spoken. Most Haitians are Roman Catholics. Port-au-Prince, the capital and chief port, has a population of about 200,000 (that of the Port-au-Prince area exceeds 424,000).

Production and Trade: Agricultural industries predominate, although only about one-third of the country is cultivated. Coffee (the leading export crop), sugar, rice, sisal, tobacco and bananas are grown. Much use is made of irrigation. The bulk of Haitian trade is carried on with the United States. The unit of currency is the Gourde.

HOLLAND

See NETHERLANDS.

HONDURAS

REPUBLIC

This mountainous country of Central America has an area of more than 43,200 square miles. There are narrow plains on both coasts, where the climate is hot and wet. There are valuable mahogany forests, particularly in the north-east.

Population: Exceeds 1,700,000, most of whom are *mestizos* (Spanish-Indian). Spanish is the language of the country and Roman Catholicism its religion. Tegucigalpa, the capital, has a population of 99,948. Amapala and La Ceiba are the chief ports.

Production and Trade: Honduras is an agricultural country, with bananas as the main crop (60 per cent. of exports). Other crops include coconuts, coffee and rice. Cattle-breeding is of growing importance. Besides mahogany, the forests yield pine and cedar. There is said to be much mineral wealth, but only gold, silver and lead are being mined. More than 65 per cent. of the trade of Honduras is handled by the United States. The unit of currency is the Lempira.

HONG KONG

BRITISH COLONY

The colony comprises certain islands off the south-eastern coast of China, part of the Kowloon peninsula of the mainland, and the adjoining New Territories leased from China in 1898. Hong Kong island itself has an area of 32 square miles, the total area of the colony being 391 square miles. The population, mostly Chinese, is about 2,500,000. The population of Victoria, the capital, exceeds 700,000. Hong Kong is one of the great trading ports of Eastern Asia. But manufacturing of cotton goods and all kinds of small items has greatly increased. Shipbuilding and repairing are also important. The local unit of currency is the Hong Kong Dollar.

HUNGARY

REPUBLIC

Hungary has an area of 35,912 square miles. It is a landlocked country, drained by the river Danube, to the east of which lies the Great Hungarian Plain. The deep gap through which the Danube flows before reaching Budapest is known as the Hungarian Gate and stands between the Bakony Forest and the spurs of the Carpathians. Lake Balaton, in Western Hungary, has an area of 245 square miles and is the largest lake in Central Europe.

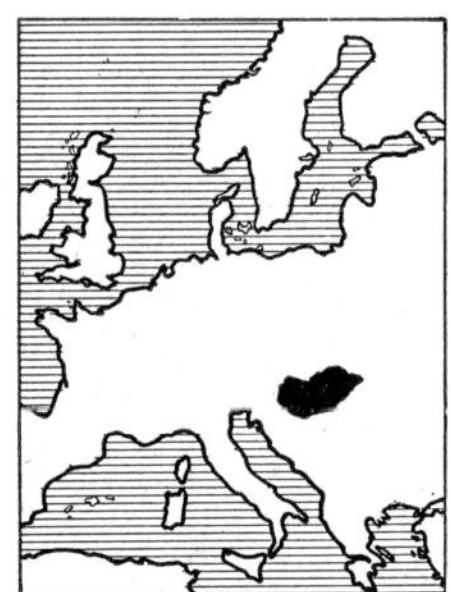

Population: About 9,840,000. More than 90 per cent. of the people are Magyars, but there are German, Slovak, Croat, Rumanian and Serb minorities as well as some 18,600 Gipsies. More than 60 per cent. of the people are Roman Catholics and about 27 per cent. Protestant. Budapest, the capital, has a population of about 1,757,000. Other important places are Miskolc, Szeged, Debrecen, Pécs and Györ.

Production and Trade: Hungary is essentially an agricultural country producing large crops of grain, potatoes and sugar-beet and raising cattle, horses and other livestock. The famous Tokaj wines come from the vineyards of the north-east. There are important fisheries in the rivers Danube and Tisza, and in Lake Balaton. Coal is mined at Pécs, in the south, and there are oil wells in the west. The new town of Sztalinvaros (" Stalin town ") has been built on the Danube about 35 miles south of Budapest as the centre of the iron and steel industry. In recent years more than 70 per cent. of Hungarian trade has been conducted with the Soviet Union. The unit of currency is the Forint.

ICELAND

REPUBLIC

This island republic in the North Atlantic has an area of 39,758 square miles. Iceland is of volcanic origin and large areas are uninhabited. There are great snowfields and glaciers, beds of lava, more than 100 volcanoes (including Hekla, Askja and Laki) and remarkable geysers. The rivers are swift-flowing and have magnificent waterfalls.

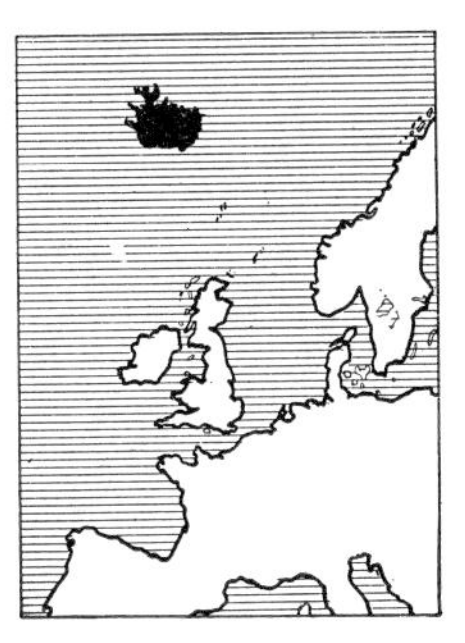

Population: 162,700. Reykjavik, the capital and chief port, has 65,305 inhabitants. Icelandic is the language of the people, but Danish and English are used commercially. The established Church is Evangelical Lutheran.

Production and Trade: The rich fishing grounds along the shores of the country provide the main industry, but there are good pastures which support large numbers of sheep. Fish and fish products are the chief exports; coal, petrol, vehicles, machinery and textiles the chief imports. Many nations share in Icelandic trade, including the United Kingdom, the United States, Denmark and Italy. The unit of currency is the Króna.

INDIA

REPUBLIC

Although a republic, India is a member of the Commonwealth. This Union of 14 States (including disputed Kashmir) and 6 Union territories has an area of 1,269,640 square miles and thus extends over by far the greater part of the huge sub-continent which is still called " geographical India " —even though it includes Pakistan (*q.v.*). This sub-continent projects into the Indian Ocean, with the Arabian Sea to the west and the Bay of Bengal to the east; it is shut off from the heart of Asia by the rampart of the Himalayas. The northern Great Plain is crossed by the Indus and its tributaries, and by the Ganges and its tributaries. The central plateau known as the Deccan, drops sharply to the coastal plains on the west and east (Western and Eastern Ghats). The tropical monsoon climate provides (i) a cool season with little or no rain from November to February; (ii) a hot season with little or no rain from March until mid-June; and (iii) a rainy season, from mid-June to November.

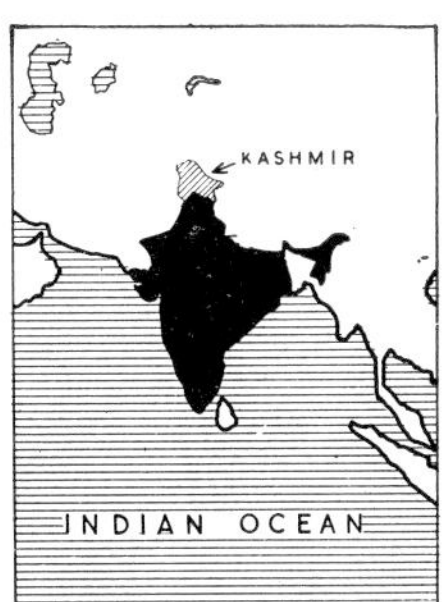

Population: 386,500,000. There are many different religions, racial and social groupings. Hinduism is the chief religion and has more than 303,180,000 followers. There are more than 6,219,000 Sikhs and 1,000,000 Jains, some 35,400,000 Moslems and 8,157,000 Christians, as well as Buddhists and others. Hindi is the official language, but English is also recognised officially for the time being. About fourteen other regional languages are recognised.

There are many large cities and towns. Delhi, the capital, has a population of 1,191,104. Greater still are Bombay (2,839,270), the largest city in India and an important manufacturing centre (especially cotton) and seaport; Calcutta (2,548,677), an even greater port and a leading industrial centre; Madras (1,416,056), a commercial and manufacturing centre; and Hyderabad (1,085,722).

Production and Trade: Agriculture has long been the most important industry, although most of the farms are of 5 acres or less. Rice, wheat and other cereals, oil-seeds, cotton, sugar-cane, tea (especially in Assam), coffee, cotton, jute and tobacco are the principal crops. Irrigation is of prime importance. There is more irrigated land in India than in any other country, and large new irrigation schemes are still being carried out, *e.g.*, the Damodar Valley Scheme. India has about 25 per cent. of the world's cattle. Buffaloes, sheep and goats can also be counted in tens of millions.

India is one of the world's leading coal-producers, her principal mines being in West Bengal and Bihar. Iron ore is plentiful (especially in the Singhbhum district of Bihar) and so is manganese (especially in Madhya Pradesh). Gold, mica, monazite, tungsten and chromite are among the other minerals worked.

The chief centre of the iron and steel industry is Jamshedpur. Manufactures include textiles, especially cotton (Bombay, Cawnpore, Nagpur) and jute (Calcutta). Cotton and jute, with tea, are the chief exports. The United Kingdom and the United States are the leading trade partners. The Indian unit of currency is the Rupee. 100,000 Rupees = 1 Lakh. 100 Lakhs = 1 Crore.

INDO-CHINA

See CAMBODIA, LAOS, VIETNAM.

INDONESIA

REPUBLIC

This Asian republic occupies the maze of islands which once constituted the Dutch East Indies. There are four large islands (Java, Sumatra, Borneo and Celebes), fifteen lesser islands and thousands of smaller islands. Most of these are forested, mountainous and volcanic. The total area of the republic is 735,865 square miles.

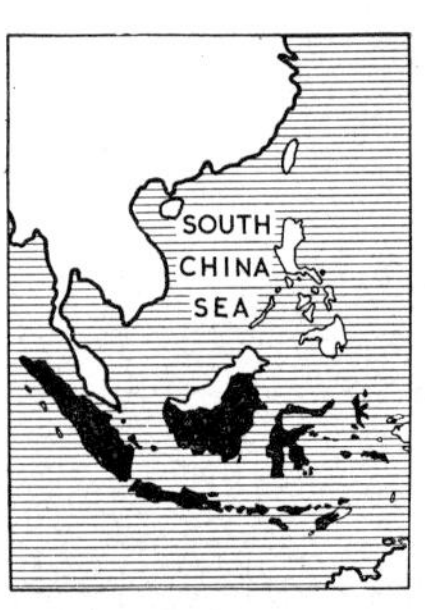

Population: About 83,500,000. Java, on which stands Djakarta (about 3,000,000 people), the capital and chief port, is the most densely populated island. The people are Javanese, Balinese and other races. Most of them are Moslems, but there are many Christians, Hindus and Buddhists.

Production and Trade: More than two-thirds of the people are employed in agriculture. Leading crops are copra, kapok, spices, rubber, tea, coffee, tobacco, sugar, palm oil, cinchona, rice and cassava. Tin, bauxite and coal are mined. Oil is produced in Sumatra, Borneo and Java. Rubber, petroleum, tea and sugar are exports. The Netherlands, the United States and Japan head the list of trading partners. The Indonesian unit of currency is the Rupiah.

IRAN

See PERSIA.

IRAQ

REPUBLIC

Iraq is largely a country of the rivers Tigris and Euphrates. From the highlands of the north-east, the land drops sharply to the plains and great river valley, and finally to the desert of the south and west. Irrigation is vital. Iraq has long, dry, hot and dusty summers, and cold winters with only a limited rainfall. Estimates of the area of Iraq vary from 116,600 to 172,000 square miles.

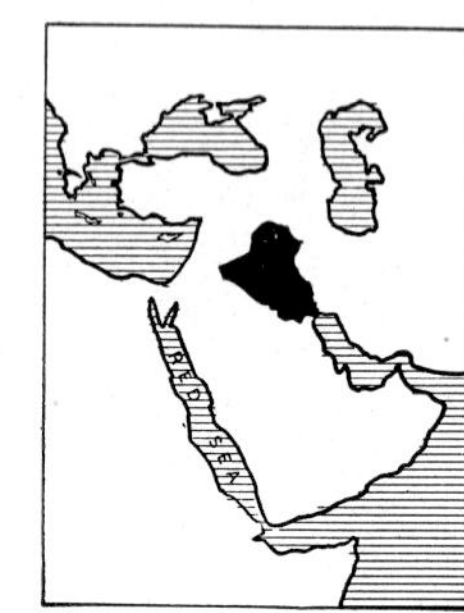

Population: About 6,538,000. Baghdad, the capital, has a population exceeding 1,080,000. Other important towns include Mosul and Basra. Most of the people are Arabs, and Islam is the principal religion. There are Kurd, Turkoman and Persian minorities.

Production and Trade: The oilfields of the Mosul region and Kirkuk are the chief source of wealth. Agriculture depends on irrigation (which is being modernised); wheat, rice, cotton and maize are important crops. Dates are cultivated extensively around Basra. Crude oil is the chief export. The leading partners in trade are the United Kingdom, the United States and France. The Iraqi unit of currency is the Iraqi dinar.

IRELAND

See *Irish Republic*. Northern Ireland forms part of the United Kingdom and is considered under this heading.

IRISH REPUBLIC

The republic comprises the whole of Ireland except for the counties of Antrim, Armagh, Down, Fermanagh, Londonderry and Tyrone, which form Northern Ireland (see *United Kingdom*). The area of the republic is 26,600 square miles. The dominant feature is the Central Plain, bordered by coastal highland. There are a number of isolated mountain ranges, Carrantuohill (3,414 feet, the highest point) being in Macgillycuddy's Reeks.

The principal river, and the longest in the British Isles, is the Shannon. There are extensive peat bogs.

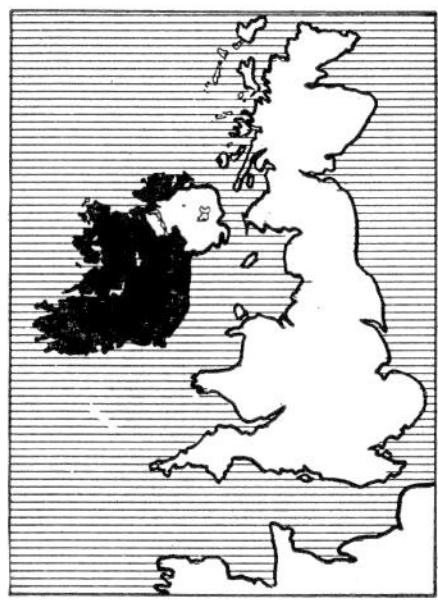

Ireland has a milder climate than Great Britain and enjoys a higher rainfall in the west.

N.B. Eire, the former name of the republic, is still in common use. Since 1949 the republic has not been a member of the British Commonwealth.

Population: 2,898,264. Dublin (*Baile Atha Cliath*), the capital, has a population of 539,476. Both Irish and English are official languages. Roman Catholicism is the predominant religion.

Production and Trade: Agriculture is the chief industry, with cereals, potatoes, turnips and sugar-beet as the main crops. Dairy-farming, pig-breeding, horse-breeding and distilling are important. More than three-quarters of the export trade is in livestock and foodstuffs. The United Kingdom is the republic's dominant trading partner. The unit of currency is the Irish pound.

ISRAEL

REPUBLIC

The republic was proclaimed in 1948 and occupies an area of 8,048 square miles of the former mandated territory of Palestine.

Behind the long coastal plain are the highlands of Acre and Galilee in the north, separated by the Plain of Esdraelon from the highlands of Samaria and Judaea, which run southwards to the desert region of the Negev. Parts of the valley of the river Jordan, and the south-western part of the Dead Sea, come within Israel.

Population: Now exceeds 1,975,000, of whom more than 1,759,000 are Jews, many of them originally immigrants from other parts of the world. Most of the remainder are Arabs. The official language is Hebrew, but Arabic is also used. The Jewish religion predominates. The largest city in Israel is Tel-Aviv/Jaffa (371,000). Haifa has about 160,000 inhabitants; and the Israeli part of Jerusalem about 150,000. Jerusalem was named as the capital in 1950.

Production and Trade: Agriculture is the principal activity, the main crops being cereals, citrus and other fruits, olives and vegetables. Irrigation is important. Stock-breeding is being developed. Potash and other valuable chemicals are produced from the salt deposits of the Dead Sea. Oil has recently been found in the Negev. Manufactures of many kinds have been developed in recent years. About half of the trade of Israel is conducted with the United States and the United Kingdom. Citrus fruits are the chief export. The unit of currency is the Israeli pound.

ITALY

REPUBLIC

This Mediterranean country comprises a long boot-shaped peninsula and a number of islands (including Sicily and Sardinia). Its total area is about 131,000 square miles.

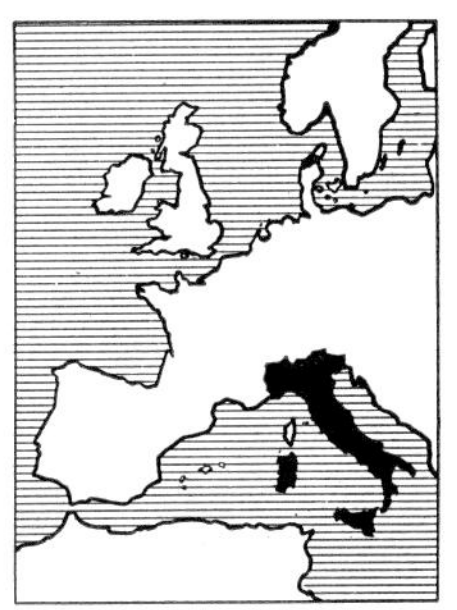

Below the arc of the Alps in the north is the fertile Plain of Lombardy, the most thickly-populated part of the country, through which flows the river Po. The Apennines form the mountain backbone of the peninsula. Italy has three notable volcanoes: Vesuvius (near Naples), Etna (Sicily) and Stromboli (Lipari Islands).

Population: Exceeds 48,500,000. Rome, the capital, has a population of 1,701,913. Other important cities include Milan (1,276,521), Naples (1,024,543), Turin (721,795) and Genoa (687,480). The country is predominantly Roman Catholic.

Production and Trade: Nearly half the population depends upon agriculture. Leading crops are wheat, fruits, rice, olives, sugar-beet, vegetables, chestnuts and tobacco. Many famous wines are produced. Silkworm cultivation is extensive in Alpine Italy. Except for mercury, mineral resources are limited, but some coal, iron ore and other deposits are worked. Hydro-electric power has been greatly developed. Important industries include textiles, especially silk and cotton (Milan and Turin), engineering and car manufacture (Milan and Turin), shipbuilding (Genoa and Venice) and chemicals. There is a large tourist trade.

About 60 per cent. of Italy's imports are raw materials and manufactured goods. Cotton goods, machinery, fruit and vegetables are the principal exports. Western Germany, the United Kingdom, Switzerland and the United States are the main trading partners. The Italian unit of currency is the Lira.

Overseas Territory: Italy is responsible for the U.N. Trusteeship territory of Somalia in East Africa. The territory has an area of about 220,000 square miles and an estimated population of 1,263,500. The capital and chief seaport is Mogadishu.

JAMAICA

BRITISH COLONY

Jamaica (4,411 square miles) is the largest island in the Federation of The West Indies. (But the colony also includes administratively the Turks and Caicos Islands and lesser islands, some 202 square miles.) The eastern part is dominated by the Blue Mountains, from which many small streams descend to the coast.

Population: About 1,580,000. Kingston, the capital and chief port, has a population of 158,702.

Production and Trade: Sugar, coffee, citrus fruit, cocoa, pimento, bananas and other tropical crops are grown. Jamaican rum is world famous. Large quantities of bauxite are mined. The United Kingdom, Canada and the United States handle the greater part of Jamaican trade. The currency is legally British and Jamaican, but various other currencies are also accepted.

JAPAN

MONARCHY

Japan consists of four large islands (Hokkaido, Honshu, Shikoku and Kyushu) and many smaller islands, the total area being about 142,275 square miles. Most of the islands are mountainous and volcanic. The highest and most famous peak is Fujiyama, the sacred mountain on Honshu. Earthquakes are frequent. There are many small rivers and one large lake (Biwa). A temperate monsoon climate prevails.

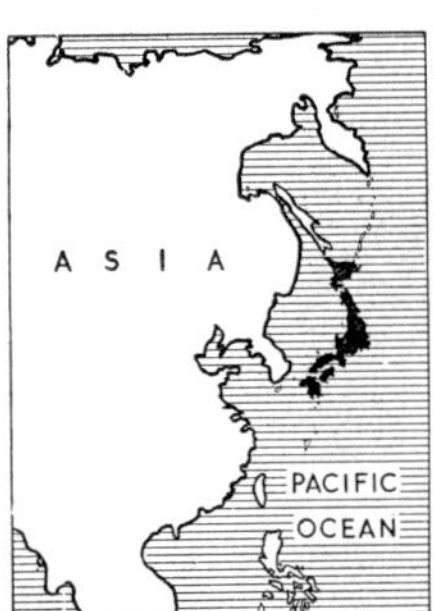

Population: 90,017,000. Tokyo, the capital, has a population of 8,638,000. Other cities with a population exceeding 1,000,000 are Osaka, Kyoto, Nagoya, and Yokohama. Japanese is spoken, except in the north, where Ainu is spoken by the aboriginals. English is used commercially. The principal religions are Shinto and Buddhism, but there is some Christianity.

Production and Trade: Although only one-sixth of the country can be cultivated, agriculture (especially rice growing) is important. Most farms are very small. There are rich fishing grounds. Japan is highly industrialised. Of particular importance are textiles (cotton, silk, rayon, wool), iron and steel, engineering, shipbuilding, paper and toys. Both coal and petroleum are produced locally—and also imported. Water power is abundant.

Manufactures, especially of cotton and rayon, account for a large percentage of Japanese exports. Many nations trade with Japan, but her biggest customer is the United States. The unit of currency is the Yen.

JORDAN

MONARCHY

The Hashemite Kingdom of the Jordan has an area of 34,750 square miles, much of which is dry, desert plateau. West Jordan is the most fertile region, but has suffered greatly from erosion.

Population: Estimated at 1,500,000 (including more than 400,000 refugees from Israel). Arabic is the language of the country, and Islam its religion. Amman, the capital, has a population of about 250,000.

Production and Trade: Agriculture is the main activity, especially on the terraced highlands. Cattle, goats, sheep and camels are reared. Industry is limited to the production of raw phosphate. The unit of currency is the Jordan dinar.

KENYA

BRITISH COLONY AND PROTECTORATE

The land area of Kenya measures 219,730 square miles (total area, including water, 224,960 square miles). The low coastal lands are hot and wet, but a large part of Kenya belongs to the East African plateau and boasts some of the highest mountains in Africa, *e.g.*, Mount Kenya. Crossing the plateau from north to south is the Great Rift Valley. European settlers have found the "white highlands" of the south-west most suitable climatically, for here altitude offsets the effects of latitude, and here large-scale farming of the rich, red volcanic soil has been developed. Forming part of Kenya's western frontier is Lake Victoria, or Victoria Nyanza, the largest lake in Africa.

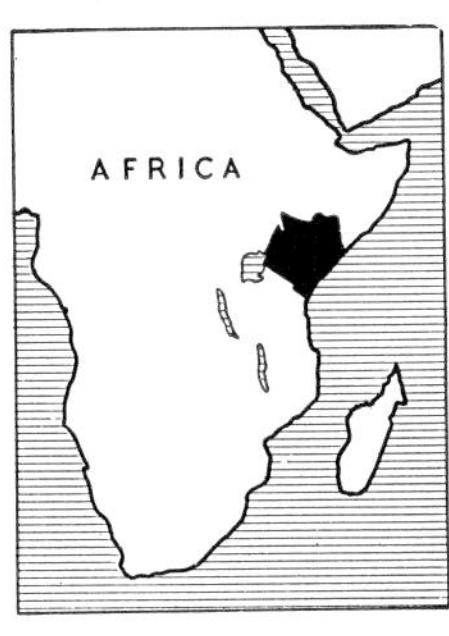

Population: exceeds 6,048,000 (including more than 5,815,000 Africans). Arabs are the chief inhabitants of the coast. Nairobi, the capital, has an estimated population of 186,000, of whom about 18,000 are Europeans and 65,000 Asians.

Production and Trade: Agriculture is the dominant industry and a wide variety of crops is made possible by the range of altitude. Among the more important are coffee, sisal, pyrethrum, maize, tea, wattle, sugar and cotton. There are large herds of cattle, and dairy farming is of growing importance. The valuable forests provide cedar and other woods. Mineral wealth includes gold, silver and soda-ash. The United Kingdom is Kenya's chief trading partner, but considerable trade is also carried on with Western Germany, the United States and other countries. The unit of currency is the East African shilling.

KOREA, NORTH

REPUBLIC

The Korean People's Democratic Republic occupies an area of 46,814 square miles, between China (the frontier being the Yalu river) and South Korea.

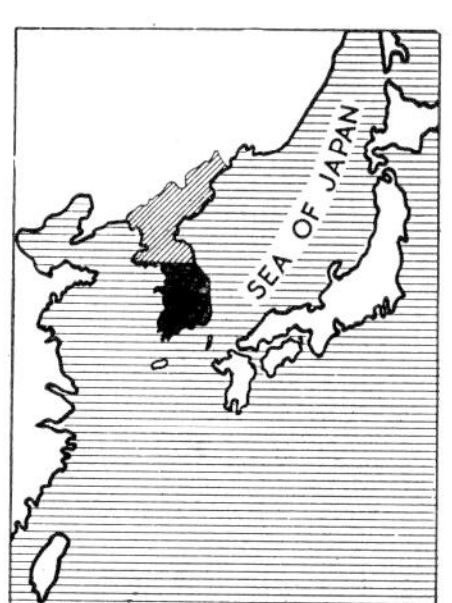

Population : about 9,000,000. Pyon-Yang, the capital, has an estimated population of 286,000.

Production and Trade: Rice, millet, wheat, soya beans and barley are the chief crops. Coal, iron and other mineral wealth, together with hydro-electric power, have given North Korea well-developed industry (including iron and steel, chemicals and textiles). Trade is conducted with China and the Soviet Union. The North Korean unit of currency is the Won.

KOREA, SOUTH

REPUBLIC

The Republic of Korea has an area of 38,452 square miles. Like North Korea the country is mountainous, especially along the eastern coast.

Population: 21,526,374. Seoul, the capital, has 1,574,868 inhabitants; the port of Pusan, 1,045,183. Confucianism and Buddhism are the dominant religions, but there are more than 500,000 Christians. Korean is the language of both northern and southern republics.

Production and Trade: South Korea is predominantly an agricultural country with rice as the main crop. Industry does not compare with that of North Korea, although coal and other minerals are mined. One of the world's richest deposits of tungsten is at the Sangdong mine. Textile manufacture (especially cotton) is being expanded. The United States and Japan are the main trading partners. The South Korean unit of currency is the Hwan.

KUWAIT

INDEPENDENT SHEIKHDOM

Kuwait occupies an area of about 5,800 square miles at the north-western end of the Persian Gulf. It is a British Protected State. The estimated population is 207,000, of whom about 180,000 live in the port of Kuwait, which is the capital.

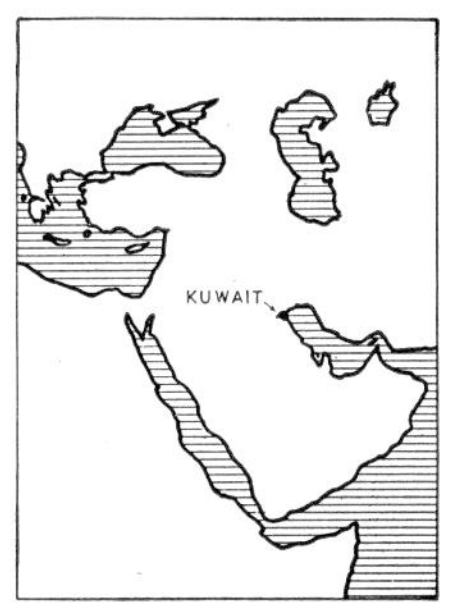

Kuwait's traditional role is a trading port for the interior and centre for pearl fisheries. But its present importance springs from its Burgan oilfield, connected by pipeline to the port of Mina al Ahmadi. The Kuwaiti unit of currency is the Indian rupee.

LAOS

MONARCHY

Once part of French Indo-China, Laos became an "independent Associate State" in 1949 and now enjoys sovereign independence.

The country has an area of about 90,000 square miles and is mountainous and thickly forested.

Population: Estimated at 2,000,000. The seat of administration is Vietiane; estimates of its population vary from 20,000 to 60,000. The royal capital is Luang Prabang (about 12,000 inhabitants). The Thai people are most numerous, but there are also Indonesians and peoples of Chinese origin (Ho, Yao and Meo). Buddhism is the principal religion.

Production and Trade: Rice, maize, coffee, citrus fruits and tobacco are the chief crops. Teak and other valuable woods are obtained from the northern forests and floated to the south on the Mekong river. Some tin is mined. Thailand, France and Japan are the chief trading partners. The currency unit is the Kip (formerly the Piastre).

LEBANON

REPUBLIC

This narrow, mountainous and coastal country of the eastern Mediterranean has an area of about 3,400 square miles. The coastal region and the deep valley between the Lebanon and Anti-Lebanon mountains are very fertile.

Population: Estimated at 1,400,000. Beirut, the capital (and one of the great trading ports of the Levant), has about 400,000 inhabitants. The people are mostly Arabs, but there are Armenian, Turkish, Kurd and other minorities. Just over half the population is Christian, the remainder being Islamic. Arabic is the official language, but French is often used commercially.

Production and Trade: Agriculture provides a livelihood for about three-quarters of the working population, despite the serious problem of soil erosion. Wheat, barley, maize, citrus fruits, olives, water-melons and grapes are important crops. Silk and cotton yarns and piece-goods are produced. Iron ore is mined on a modest scale. Both Tripoli and Saida are important as oil pipeline terminals, and both possess refineries. Tourism is a growing industry.

Lebanon benefits from Beirut's standing as " the market of the Levant " and from a large transit trade with her neighbours. Fruit, textiles and vegetables are among her exports. Syria, the United Kingdom, France and the United States are among her principal trading partners. The unit of currency is the Lebanese pound.

LEEWARD ISLANDS

BRITISH COLONIES

This group in the West Indies comprises four colonies: Antigua (with Barbuda and Redonda); St. Christopher-Nevis (St. Kitts, Nevis, Anguilla); Montserrat; and the Virgin Islands. All, except the Virgin Islands, are part of the Federation of The West Indies. The total area of the group is about 420 square miles; the total population, about 126,000. St. John's, on Antigua, is the principal town and has 12,000 inhabitants. Products of the group include sugar, cotton, molasses, rum, coconuts, limes, fruits, vegetables, salt, charcoal and livestock. The United Kingdom, Canada and the United States handle the bulk of the trade. The unit of currency is the ECT dollar.

LIBERIA

REPUBLIC

This Western African country has an area of about 43,000 square miles. Its coastal region is fertile, but a large part of the republic is tropical forest and jungle. There are also extensive swamps.

Population: Estimates vary from 1,000,000 to 2,000,000. The estimated population of Monrovia, the capital and chief port, is 41,000. Liberia was founded by the American Colonization Society as a settlement for freed slaves, and the present-day population is entirely African. English and various African languages are spoken. Although there are some pagan tribes, Christianity prevails, several denominations being represented.

Production and Trade: Liberia is comparatively undeveloped. Rice, sugar cane and other crops are grown for local consumption.

Piassava, palm oil and other forest products are exported, but rubber accounts for about 90 per cent. of exports. The mining of gold and iron ore is of growing importance. The dominant trading partner is the United States. The unit of currency is the United States dollar, but there is a local coinage.

LIBYA

KINGDOM

This hereditary kingdom of Mediterranean Africa became independent in 1951. It comprises the three provinces of Tripolitania, Cyrenaica and the Fezzan, estimates of the total area ranging from 679,000 square miles to 810,000 square miles. Much of the kingdom is desert, with scattered oases, but the coastal regions are fertile.

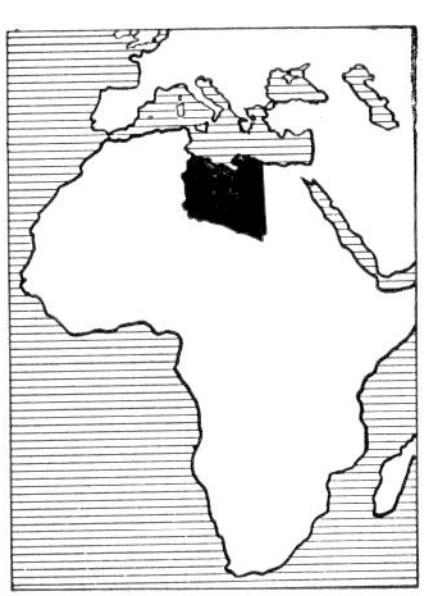

Population: 1,091,830, mostly Arabs. Both Tripoli (about 140,000) and Benghazi (about 60,000) rank as capitals. A new " administrative capital " is being built at Beida. Arabic is the official language, and Islam the predominant religion.

Production and Trade: Olives and oranges are grown in the coastal regions, which also provide wheat, almonds and dates. Sheep, goats and camels are reared. Such pastoral and agricultural produce as can be spared is exported. Food and manufactured goods are imported. The volume of trade fluctuates and is handled principally by the United Kingdom, Italy and Eastern Mediterranean countries. The unit of currency is the Libyan pound.

LIECHTENSTEIN

PRINCIPALITY

Liechtenstein is one of the little states of Europe, occupying an area of only 62 square miles between Switzerland and Austria. The population numbers 14,757; Vaduz, the capital, has a population of about 3,000. German is the language of the people, most of whom are Roman Catholics. Agriculture (especially fruit-growing, stock-breeding and wine-growing) is the principal activity, but there is also considerable small-scale manufacturing. The unit of currency is the Swiss franc.

LUXEMBOURG

CONSTITUTIONAL GRAND DUCHY

Wedged between Belgium, France and Germany, this small country has an area of 1,000 square miles. The country is fertile, hilly and well forested.

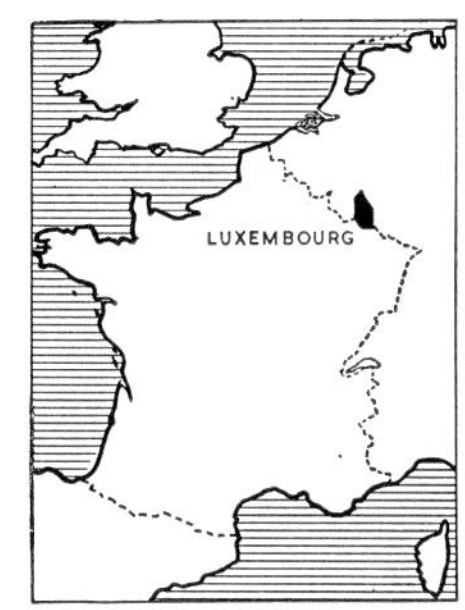

Population: 311,633. Luxembourg, the capital, has 68,032 inhabitants. French is the official language, but Letzeburgesch is common. Most of the people can speak German, and many of them English.

Production and Trade: Potatoes, wheat, oats, apples and pears are the chief crops. But far more important than agriculture is the flourishing iron and steel industry. Iron ore is abundant and the annual production of steel tops 2,500,000 tons. Engineering and textiles are important. The unit of currency is the Belgian franc.

MADAGASCAR

FRENCH OVERSEAS TERRITORY

This island off the south-east coast of Africa has an area of about 228,000 square miles. Its dependencies include the Comoro Islands. The climate is tropical, but more temperate on the savanna lands of the central plateau, which has an average height of about 4,000 feet. The hot, wet parts of the island are densely forested.

Population: 4,939,000, including 79,000 French and over 21,000 Asians, but for the most part Malagasy. Tananarive (formerly Antananarivo), the capital, has 193,000 inhabitants. Missionary societies are active, but many remote tribes are still pagan.

Production and Trade: Agriculture is the main industry, the chief crops being coffee, oilseeds, tobacco and sisal. Stock-breeding is important. Coal, mica, graphite and gold are mined. The bulk of Madagascar's trade is carried on with France and other overseas territories of France. The unit of currency is the Franc CFA.

MALAYA

FEDERATION

An independent and fully-fledged member of the British Commonwealth since August 31, 1957, the Federation of Malaya comprises eleven Malay States: Johore, Perak, Selangor, Negri Sembilan, Pahang, Kedah, Kelantan, Trengganu, Perlis, Penang and Malacca. It does not include Singapore (*q.v.*). The total area is about 50,690 square miles.

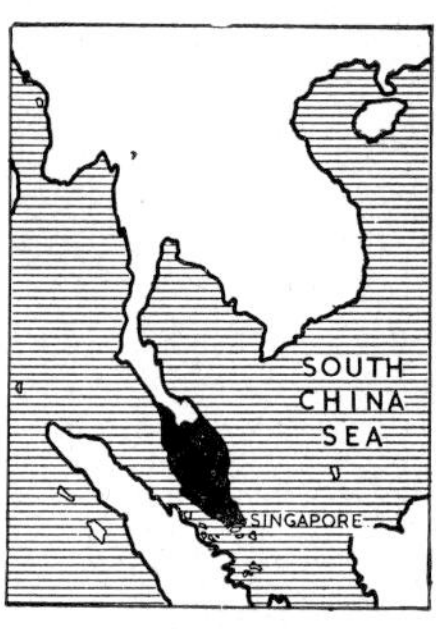

Mountainous ranges run from north to south, with peaks exceeding 7,000 feet in height and deep valleys. The climate is hot and wet, and there is luxuriant evergreen forest.

Population: Over 6,363,000, including nearly 3,093,000 Malays and 2,413,000 Chinese, as well as more than 759,000 Indians and 12,800 Eurasians. The Sakai and other primitive peoples live in the forest depths. Kuala Lumpur, the federal capital, has about 300,000 inhabitants; Ipoh, the chief tin-mining centre, has more than 100,000.

Production and Trade: Rice, coconuts and vegetables are grown. Malaya is one of the world's chief sources of rubber and tin. Oil-palms, pineapples (and associated canneries) and fisheries are also important. Rubber, tin and copra are the chief exports; petroleum, manufactures and foodstuffs, the chief imports. The bulk of Malayan trade is handled by Singapore (*q.v.*), with the United Kingdom, Indonesia and the United States as the leading partners. The unit of currency is the Malayan dollar.

MALDIVE ISLANDS

BRITISH PROTECTORATE

This sultanate is an island group to the south-west of Ceylon, its total area being about 115 square miles. Coconut palms grow in profusion on the principal atolls. The population exceeds 81,900 and is overwhelmingly Moslem. Malé, the capital (on King's Island) has about 8,000 inhabitants. Millet, fruit and nuts are produced. Fishing is an important industry. The unit of currency is the Ceylon rupee.

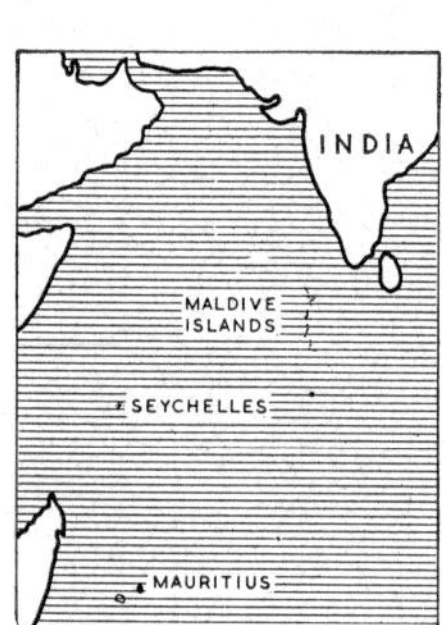

MALTA, G.C.

BRITISH SELF-GOVERNING TERRITORY

This island group in the central Mediterranean comprises the islands of Malta, Gozo and Comino, and a number of uninhabited islets. Malta (95 square miles) is the largest island, the total area of the group being 122 square miles.

In 1942, to acknowledge the bravery and endurance of the people during the Second World War, the island was awarded the George Cross. In 1956 a referendum produced an overwhelming vote in favour of the integration of Malta with the United Kingdom.

Population: About 316,239. Valletta, the capital and chief harbour, has about 19,000 inhabitants. Maltese and English are the official languages; Roman Catholicism is the predominant religion.

Production and Trade: Wheat, barley, vegetables (especially potatoes, onions and tomatoes for export) are grown. Small items of various kinds are manufactured. Craft industries include the making of Maltese lace and filigree-work. Malta is a leading naval base (headquarters of the Mediterranean Fleet and of N.A.T.O. Mediterranean Command), known for its dockyard and arsenal, and an important port of call on the Suez route. Government of Malta currency and British coinage are used.

MAURITIUS

BRITISH COLONY

This volcanic island in the Indian Ocean has an area of 720 square miles. Its climate is principally sub-tropical. Including its dependencies, the population numbers more than 596,000. Port Louis, the capital, has a population of nearly 98,000. Sugar is the main crop, and sugar-processing the principal industry. Nearly all trade is with the United Kingdom and other Commonwealth countries. The unit of currency is the Mauritius rupee.

MEXICO

REPUBLIC

The United States of Mexico consists of twenty-nine states, a federal district and two territories, and has a total area of about 760,375 square miles. Most of the country is high plateau, with hot wet shorelands (especially on the Gulf of Mexico). Running down towards the narrow Isthmus of Tehuantepec are the ranges of the Sierra Madre, which end in a series of volcanic peaks running across the country. In the south-east is the lowland peninsula of Yucatán. The principal river is the Rio Grande.

Population: About 31,454,000. Some are of mixed Indian-Spanish descent, and some are American Indians (about 30 per cent.). Spanish is the official language, but various Indian languages are used by some 10 per cent. of the population. The country is predominantly Roman Catholic. Mexico City, the capital, has a population of 2,234,795. Other important places with more than 100,000 inhabitants are: Guadalajara, Monterrey, Puebla, Mérida, Torreón, San Luis Potosi, León, Ciudad Juárez and Vera Cruz.

Production and Trade: Agriculture is a leading industry, more than half the cultivated land being devoted to maize. Irrigation is important. About half the world's sisal crop is grown in Mexico (especially in Yucatán). Sugar, wheat, cotton, coffee, tobacco and fruit are also grown. The forests provide mahogany, rosewood and other timbers. Mexico has great mineral wealth, especially silver, gold, copper, lead, zinc and petroleum. Nearly 60 per cent. of the world's silver comes from Mexico. There are large deposits of coal and iron ore.

The chief items of export include silver and other metals, oil, coffee and sisal. Vehicles, machinery and wheat are among the main imports. More than three-quarters of Mexican trade is handled by the United States. The unit of currency is the Peso.

MONACO

PRINCIPALITY

This tiny Mediterranean state on the French Riviera has an area of about 368 acres taken up by the towns of Monaco (the capital), Monte Carlo and La Condamine. The population numbers about 20,400, but there are tens of thousands of visitors every year. Monte Carlo is world-famous as a fashionable pleasure resort and for its casino. French is the language of the Principality, and French currency is used.

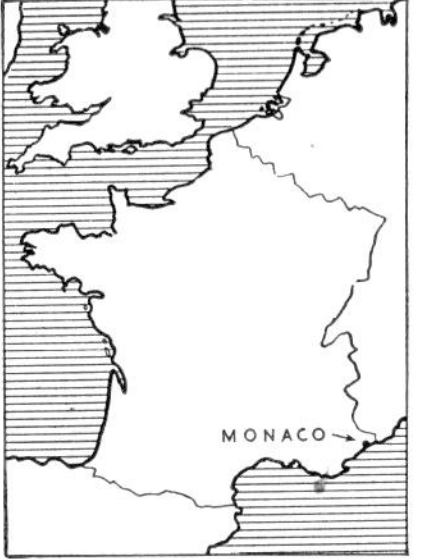

MONGOLIA

REPUBLIC

The Mongolian People's Republic was at one time the Chinese province of Outer Mongolia. Its independence was recognised in 1945. Its area is estimated at about 590,000 square miles; its population at about 1,000,000. Turkic languages are spoken by the Mongols, most of whom are Buddhists (Lamaist). The capital, Ulan Bator (formerly Urga) has a population of 100,000.

Mongolia is a country of high plateaux, steppe and desert (the Gobi). Most of the people are nomadic, with stock-breeding (sheep, cattle and camels) as their main interest. Some gold, coal and uranium are mined. Some oil is produced. Livestock, wool, hides, etc., are exported, mostly to the Soviet Union. The unit of currency is the Tughrik.

MOROCCO

SULTANATE

Until 1956, this Barbary State was divided into three zones: French, Spanish, and the International Zone of Tangier. In March of that year, France recognised the independence of Morocco, and Spain did likewise a month later. Ceuta and Melilla, two towns which have been Spanish for many centuries, were not

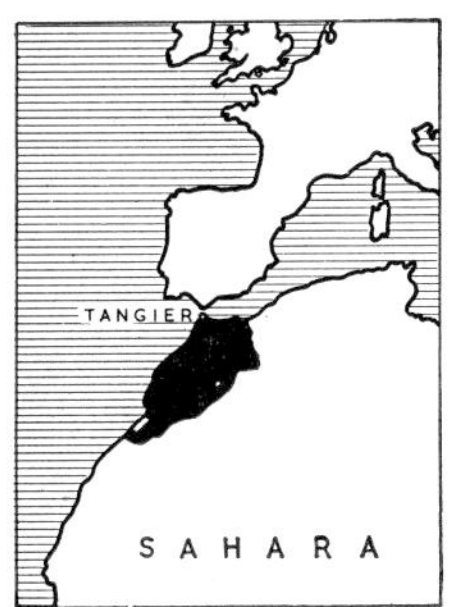

mentioned in the Madrid agreement, however; the international status of Tangier was abolished in 1956. Behind the Mediterranean coastlands is the mountainous Rif region; even more prominent are the Atlas Mountains, rising to heights of more than 13,000 feet, separating coastal Morocco from the Sahara Desert, and protecting the country from the hot desert winds.

Population: About 10,000,000, most of whom are Berbers or Arabs. Islam is the predominant religion. Both Arabic and Berber dialects are spoken, but French and Spanish are also in common use in the towns. Rabat, the capital, has a population of 160,000. (But Fez, Marrakesh and Meknès are also traditionally capitals of the Sultanate.) Other important places include the seaport of Casablanca (700,000), Tangier (180,000), Tetuan (85,000), Oujda (85,000) and Safi (56,750).

Production and Trade: Agriculture is the chief industry; wheat, barley, citrus fruits, vegetables, esparto grass, wool, skins and hides are produced for export as well as for local use. Phosphates, manganese, iron ore, zinc and lead are mined; other minerals include coal, petroleum, cobalt and copper. France is the principal trading partner, but the United States, United Kingdom and other countries have a share in Moroccan trade.

Hitherto the Moroccan franc has been the unit of currency in the south (formerly French Morocco) and the Peseta in the north (formerly Spanish Morocco), both being accepted in Tangier. The effect of independence in this matter has not yet been resolved.

MOZAMBIQUE

PORTUGUESE OVERSEAS PROVINCE

Mozambique, or Portuguese East Africa, is a colonial territory with an area of about 298,000 square miles. The coastal lowlands contain the deltas of the rivers Zambesi and Limpopo, and rise inland towards the South African plateaux. The climate is tropical.

Population: 5,738,911, of whom only some 30,000 are Europeans. Lourenço Marques, the capital and chief port, has a population of 48,000.

Production and Trade: Agriculture is the chief industry and provides large crops of sugar-cane, maize, cotton, copra, sisal and cashew nuts. Gold, beryl, bauxite and coal are mined. A considerable amount of the trade of the interior (especially the Transvaal and the Rhodesias) is handled by the ports of Lourenço Marques and Beira, by virtue of their important railway links with South and Central Africa. The unit of currency is the Escudo.

MUSCAT AND OMAN

SULTANATE

This Arabian sultanate bordering the Gulf of Oman has an area of some 82,000 square miles and an estimated population of 550,000 (mostly Arab). Parts of the coastal plain are fertile, the Batinah being famous for its dates. Sugar-cane is grown in the coastal province of Dhofar. Inland cultivation is mainly confined to isolated oases, and the main activity is camel-breeding. Dates, fish and fruit are the chief exports. The capital is Muscat (about 4,000), but Matrah (the chief port, 8,500) is the main commercial centre. The people of these towns are mostly Indians, Baluchis and Negroes. The official unit of currency is the Indian rupee, but the Maria Theresa dollar is also in use.

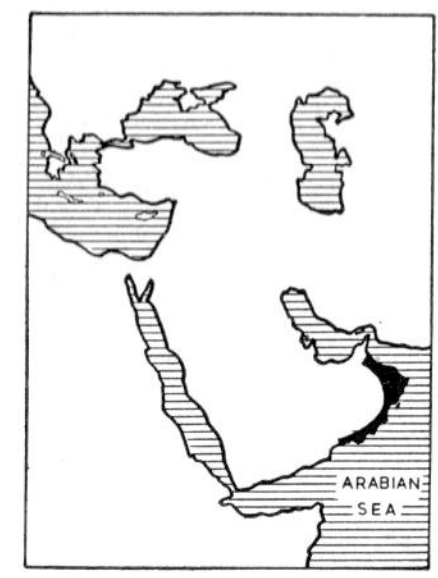

NEPAL

KINGDOM

This Himalayan kingdom has an area of about 54,000 square miles. It is a land of great mountain peaks and fertile valleys. In the north are Everest (partly in Tibet), Kanchenjunga (partly in Sikkim) and other giants. The south of the country includes a part of the hot, marshy jungle of the Terai.

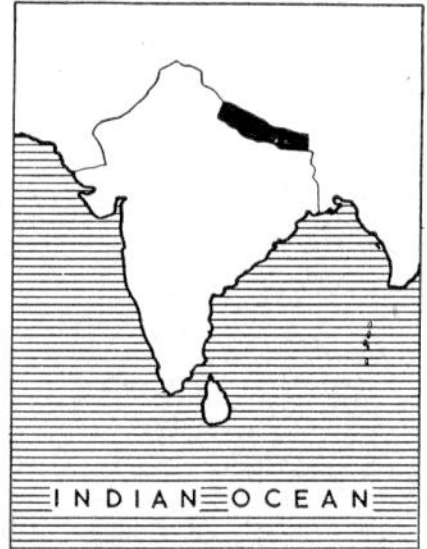

Population: 8,337,537. Katmandu, the capital, has an estimated population of 175,000. Most of the people are Gurkhas, but the ruling family is Hindu Rajput. Nepalese is the language of the country. Buddhism and Hinduism are the predominant religions.

Production and Trade: Cereals, tobacco, vegetables and other crops are grown on the terraced and irrigated hillsides. Timber is obtained from the southern forests, and large quantities of medicinal herbs from the slopes of the Himalayas. Coal and mica are mined.

Nepal trades mostly with India. The unit of currency is the Nepalese rupee.

NETHERLANDS

CONSTITUTIONAL MONARCHY

The Netherlands, or Holland, is a low-lying country of north-western Europe with an area exceeding 13,500 square miles, of which about a quarter is land reclaimed from the sea (*polder*). Crossing the country are the rivers Rhine, Waal, Maas, Ijssel and Scheldt—Holland is virtually a large delta formed by the silt of these rivers. Canals are numerous.

Population: 10,957,040. Amsterdam, the capital (and a leading seaport, manufacturing and commercial centre) has 871,188 inhabitants. Rotterdam, the chief port and a leading industrial city, has a population of 722,718. Other important centres are: Utrecht (247,816), Haarlem (167,264) and Eindhoven (157,621). The Hague (606,728) is the seat of government. Dutch is the language of the people, but Frisian is spoken in some parts. The principal denominations are Dutch Reformed Church (Protestant) and Roman Catholic.

Production and Trade: Holland is renowned for its agriculture (especially dairy-farming and stock-breeding) and for its flower bulb industry (centred on Haarlem). Wheat, rye, vegetables, flax and sugar-beet are produced in quantity. There is extensive heavy industry and manufacturing, including steel, engineering, ship-building, textiles, radio and electrical equipment, chemicals, china, glass, leather, clothing, and paper. Amsterdam has been the world headquarters of the diamond industry for many years. Coal is mined and there is some production of crude oil. Fisheries are important and there is a large merchant fleet.

Holland's main exports are dairy produce, textiles, vegetables, coal, oil, and flower bulbs. Cereals, raw materials for industry, and machinery are among the principal imports. Western Germany, Belgium and Luxembourg, the United Kingdom, United States and Indonesia head the list of countries with which trade is conducted. The unit of currency is the Guilder.

Overseas Territories: (1) *Surinam*, or Dutch Guiana, on the north-east coast of South America, with an area of about 54,000 square miles and an estimated population of 230,000. Paramaribo is the capital. Sugar, rice, coffee, citrus fruits, gold and bauxite are the chief products. (2) *Netherlands Antilles*, comprising two groups of Caribbean islands, the largest and most important island being Curaçao, noted for its oil refining and the oranges from which the Curaçao liqueur is made. Total area of the Netherlands Antilles is about 400 square miles; the population numbers about 186,600. The capital is Willemstad (45,000). (3) *Netherlands New Guinea*, a territory of some 160,000 square miles forming the western part of the island of New Guinea, with a population (mainly Papuan) of about 700,000. Hollandia, the capital, has about 13,700 inhabitants. Oil (from the Vogelkop district) and forest products are the principal exports. The territory contains some of the largest swamps in the world, as well as lofty mountains.

NEW GUINEA

See *Overseas Territories* under AUSTRALIA and NETHERLANDS.

NEW ZEALAND

CONSTITUTIONAL MONARCHY

The Dominion of New Zealand is a member of the British Commonwealth of Nations.

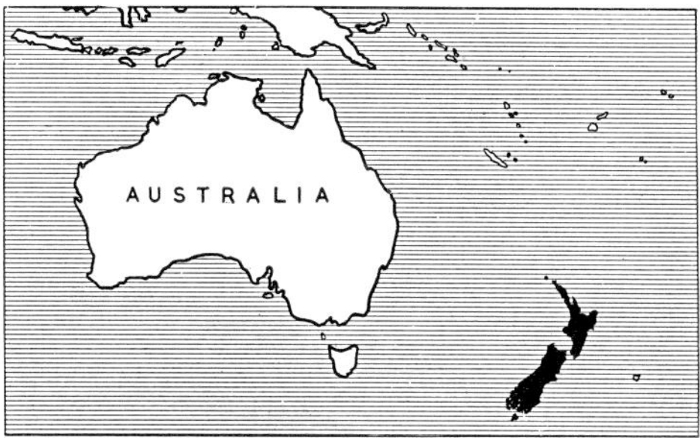

The total area of 103,736 square miles embraces the following: North Island (44,281 square miles), South Island (58,093 square miles), Stewart Island (670 square miles), Chatham Islands (372 square miles) and certain minor islands (320 square miles).

The dominant feature of the major islands is a mountain chain running from north-east to south-west and culminating in the great peaks of the Southern Alps. In the centre of North Island a volcanic plateau is topped by Ruapehu and Ngauruhoe, both active volcanoes. The main lowland areas are the Waikato Plain in North Island and the Canterbury Plains of South Island. The coastline of the south-west of South Island is deeply indented by beautiful fjords. Both lakes and rivers are numerous, the largest lake being Taupo in North Island, and several rivers have been harnessed for power. North Island has its hot springs and geysers (Rotorua); South Island, its glaciers (Tasman, Franz Josef, etc.) and glacial lakes. The climate is equable; rain is plentiful and sunshine abundant.

Population: 2,246,093, including 147,118 Maoris. Wellington, the capital, has 141,300 inhabitants. Larger still are Auckland (401,500) and Christchurch (205,500). Other important centres include Dunedin (101,600), Hutt (90,600), Hamilton (43,700), Palmerston North (39,800), Invercargill (37,000) and Wanganui (33,000).

Production and Trade: New Zealand is primarily a pastoral country. Dairy produce, meat and wool account for more than 90 per cent. of the exports. The pastures of the Auckland peninsula and the Wanganui Plains are noted for their dairy cattle. The Canterbury and Otago Plains in South Island, and the eastern and southern coastal plains in North Island, support large numbers of sheep. Such ports as Lyttelton, Dunedin, Invercargill, Wellington, Auckland and Napier have large freezing plants.

Fruit farming is important (especially apples and plums) around Nelson and Hastings. There are rich forests. Coal and some gold are mined. Uranium has been found. Hydro-electric power is plentiful and geothermal power is now being developed.

Dairy produce, meat, wool and canned foodstuffs are the chief exports. Machinery, textiles, vehicles and manufactured goods are the chief imports (although there is now much small-scale manufacture within the Dominion). More than 50 per cent. of New Zealand's trade is with the United Kingdom, and some 10 per cent. with the United States and Australia. The unit of currency is the New Zealand pound.

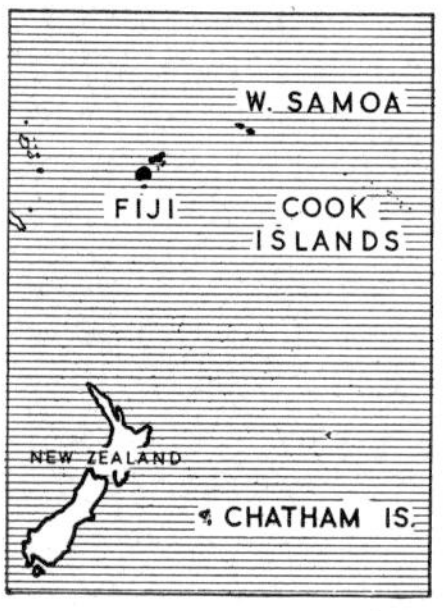

Island Territories: (1) *Cook Islands*, with an area of about 90 square miles and some 16,680 inhabitants, the principal island being Rarotonga. (2) *Niue Island*, one of the Cook group but administered separately. Area: 100 square miles. Population: about 5,000. (3) *Tokelau Islands*, of some four square miles extent, with nearly 1,700 inhabitants. (4) *Western Samoa.* A territory of about 1,130 square miles comprising two large and mountainous islands and numerous smaller isles, and held under U.N. Trusteeship. Apia, on Upolu, is the administrative centre and chief port. The population numbers 97,327 (including more than 92,400 Samoans). The chief products are copra, cocoa and bananas.

Other Territories: New Zealand shares with Australia and the United Kingdom responsibility for the island of Nauru (administered by Australia). She is also responsible for the Ross Dependency in Antarctica.

NICARAGUA

REPUBLIC

With an area of 57,145 square miles, Nicaragua is the largest of the Central American republics. The Atlantic coast is bordered by extensive lowlands, behind which are the plateaux and mountain ranges of the central highlands. The lowlands of the south-west contain two large lakes, Nicaragua and Managua. The most fertile parts of the country (nearly half of which is thickly forested) are along the Pacific coast.

Population: About 1,245,000. Most of the people are of mixed Spanish-Indian descent. Others are pure Spanish or pure Indian, or Negro. Spanish is the official language, but Indian tongues are also in use. Roman Catholicism is the predominant religion. The population of Managua, the capital, exceeds 176,500.

Production and Trade: Most of the people are employed in agriculture, the principal crops being coffee, cotton, sugar, rice, maize and bananas. Sesame is also an important crop. Wild rubber, gums and medicinal plants are obtained from the forests. Gold and silver are mined. More than half of Nicaraguan trade is conducted with the United States. Corinto is the chief port. The unit of currency is the Córdoba.

NIGERIA

FEDERATION

The Federation of Nigeria, which also includes the U.N. Trusteeship territory of the

Cameroons, was formed from British colonial and protected territory. It has an area of some 373,250 square miles. Mangrove swamp and forest fringe the coast, but inland there is tropical forest and, as the country rises, savanna. The extreme north is desert. The chief mountains are in the east. The principal rivers are the Niger, Benue and Cross. A tropical climate prevails.

Population: Exceeds 31,170,000, and is almost wholly African. Lagos, the Federal capital, has 272,000 inhabitants. Other large towns include Ibadan (459,000), Ogbomosho (140,000), Kano (130,000), Oshogbo (123,000), Ife (111,000) and Iwo (100,000). The people of the Sultanates and Emirates of the north are predominantly Moslem. A number of missionary societies are active in Nigeria generally, but there are only some 7,000,000 Christians in all, many of the people clinging to their old gods and fetishes. Prominent linguistic groups include the Hausas, Ibos and Yorubas.

Production and Trade: Agriculture is the leading activity and provides five major export crops (palm-oil, cocoa, cotton, bananas and groundnuts) as well as subsistence crops, piassava, rubber, tobacco, and gum arabic. Large numbers of cattle are raised, especially in the Northern Region, and there are many goats and sheep; hides and skins are a major export. Timber also is exported. Tin-mining (around Jos, on the Bauchi tableland) and coal-mining (at Enugu) are important. Most of the world's columbite comes from Nigeria, and gold and tantalum are also produced. Manufactures of many kinds are being developed.

More than half Nigeria's trade is conducted with the United Kingdom. Kano, as a focal point of caravan routes, has been a renowned trading centre for centuries and remains so to this day. The chief Nigerian ports are Lagos, Port Harcourt, Sapele, Calabar and Tiko. The unit of currency is the West African pound.

NORTHERN IRELAND

See UNITED KINGDOM.

NORWAY

CONSTITUTIONAL MONARCHY

This Scandinavian country of mountains and deep, fertile valleys has a long, jagged fjord-indented coastline looking out towards the Arctic and Atlantic. The Kiölen Mountains, which virtually separate the country from Sweden, divide in the south, where there is a mountain knot including Glittertind and other high peaks. Nearly a quarter of the country is forest. The rivers are small and swift, the longest being the Glommen. If some 1,000 square miles of water are included, the total area of Norway is 124,556 square miles. The climate generally is cold, but would be much more severe if it were not for the Gulf Stream. The North Cape is noted for its "Midnight Sun" (see *Glossary*); the north generally for its displays of the Aurora Borealis (see *Glossary*) during the long winter nights.

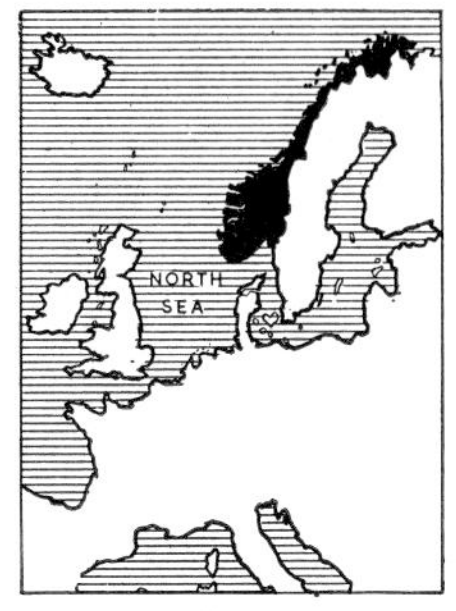

Population: 3,445,673. Oslo, the capital and chief port and manufacturing centre, has 451,247 inhabitants. Bergen, a fishing port and industrial and tourist centre, has 114,720. Both Trondheim and Stavanger have populations exceeding 52,000. Norwegian is the language of the country, but Lappish is spoken in some parts of the north. Nearly all the people are members of the Lutheran Church.

Production and Trade: Agriculture is limited by the barren and mountainous nature of the country. The wealth of the country comes mainly from its fisheries (including whaling), forests and large merchant navy. Iron ore is mined at Kirkenes and other northern places; copper at Roros. Hydro-electric power has been developed on an impressive scale. Zinc, lead, silver and molybdenum are also produced. The chemical industry is important.

Paper, wood pulp, canned fish products and minerals are the chief exports; machinery, fuel oil, metal goods and textiles are the chief imports. Norway carries on trade with many countries, including the United Kingdom, Sweden, the Netherlands, Western Germany, and the United States. The unit of currency is the Krone.

Overseas Territories: (1) *Svalbard* (*Spitsbergen*). An Arctic archipelago with an area of about 24,300 square miles, where there are rich coalfields mined by both Norway and the Soviet Union. (2) *Jan Mayen Island*, a desolate place about 300 miles north of Iceland with a radio and meteorological station, visited by whalers and sealers. (3) *Bouvet Island*, in the South Atlantic—uninhabited. (4) *Peter I Island* and *Queen Maud Land*, in Antarctica.

NYASALAND

See RHODESIA AND NYASALAND.

OMAN

See MUSCAT AND OMAN.

PAKISTAN

ISLAMIC REPUBLIC

A member of the British Commonwealth of Nations, Pakistan is divided into two parts: *West Pakistan* (provincial capital, Lahore) and *East Pakistan* (provincial capital, Dacca), with areas of 309,424 square miles and 54,501 square miles respectively. Karachi stands in its own Federal Capital Area (812 square miles) in West Pakistan. The total area of the republic is thus 364,737 square miles.

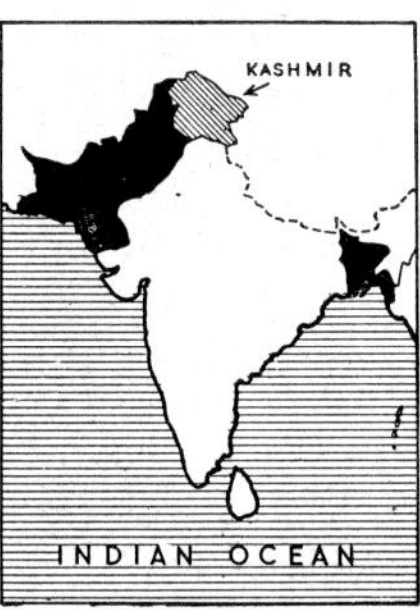

N.B. Plans have been prepared for a new federal capital at Gadap, about 24 miles north-east of Karachi.

A large part of West Pakistan is mountain and desert, but there is much fertile, irrigated land in the valley of the Indus and its tributaries. Some parts of the province are well-forested. The dominant feature of East Pakistan is the Ganges-Brahmaputra delta.

Population: About 81,000,000. More than 80 per cent. are Moslems. Karachi, the Federal capital (and main sea and air port of West Pakistan), has 1,126,417 inhabitants (Federal capital area). Other important centres are Lahore (849,476), Hyderabad (241,801), Rawalpindi (237,219), Multan (190,122), Lyallpur (179,144) and Peshawar (151,776); and in East Pakistan, Dacca (411,000) and Chittagong (294,000), the chief port of this province. The official language of Pakistan is Urdu, but English and Bengali (in East Pakistan) are also used.

Production and Trade: Agriculture is the chief industry (especially rice, cotton, wheat, sugar, tea, and jute). More than three-quarters of the world's jute comes from East Pakistan. Irrigation is of prime importance to West Pakistan, where the Lloyd, Jinnah and Ghulam Mohammed barrages have been built across the Indus. Forest products of East Pakistan include timber, bamboos, gums and resins. Coal and chromite are mined in West Pakistan; iron ore and oil have been discovered. Kot Addu is the site of a large new iron and steel works. Hydro-electric power is being developed. Natural gas is piped from Sui to Karachi and Multan. There is a growing textile industry. Cottage industries are important, especially in East Pakistan.

Raw cotton, jute, wool, hides and skins, tea and fish are the chief exports; imports include petroleum, machinery and manufactured goods. India, Japan and the United Kingdom are the chief trading partners. The unit of currency is the Pakistani rupee.

PANAMA

REPUBLIC

This mountainous country has an area of about 30,000 square miles. It is thickly-forested and very fertile, but little more than half the land is cultivated. The climate is tropical, and often unhealthy.

Population: Estimated at 934,400. Some are of Spanish and some of Negro descent; but nearly 75 per cent. are of mixed blood. Spanish, English and Amerindian languages are in use. The people are overwhelmingly Roman Catholic. Panama City, the capital, has a population of 127,874.

Production and Trade: The chief crop is bananas, grown for export to the United States. Rice, coffee, cocoa, coconuts and abacá fibre are also produced. The unit of currency is the Balboa.

Panama Canal Zone: Comprising a strip ten miles wide (five miles on each side of the Canal), the Zone was given over to the sovereignty of the United States by the treaty of 1903. Its chief town is Balboa, at the Pacific end of the Canal. The cities of Panama and Colón are not included in the Zone, however, but remain under Panamanian sovereignty. Population of the Zone (excluding American service personnel): 38,953.

PAPUA—NEW GUINEA

See *Overseas Territories* under AUSTRALIA.

PARAGUAY

REPUBLIC

This land-locked South American republic has an area of some 157,000 square miles, divided by the river Paraguay which is joined by the river Paraná at the south-western tip of the country. East of the river Paraguay are grassy, well-forested highlands; to the west are the plains and Gran Chaco lowlands and swamps. The northern regions are sub-tropical; the climate in the south is temperate.

Population: About 1,601,000, overwhelmingly *mestizo* (mixed Spanish-Indian descent). About 25,000 Guarani Indians live in the Chaco. Both Spanish and Guarani languages are in use. The established religion is Roman Catholicism. Asunçion, the capital, has 205,605 inhabitants.

Production and Trade: Agriculture (especially cattle-breeding) is the main activity. Maize, cotton, sugar-cane, peanuts, rice and *yerba maté* (Paraguayan tea) are important crops. The forests provide cedar, quebracho and other woods. The minerals, said to be abundant, have still to be fully exploited. Cotton, timber, quebracho extract (tannin), tobacco, hides, and canned meat are the main exports. Imports include foodstuffs, textiles, metal and other manufactures. Argentina and the United States are the leading trade partners. The unit of currency is the Guarani.

PERSIA

MONARCHY

Also known as Iran, Persia has an area of 628,000 square miles, much of which is salt desert tableland, locked in by mountains which reach their greatest heights in the north where the Elburz ranges rise to more than 18,000 feet in Mt. Demavend. Parts of the north and west are well-forested.

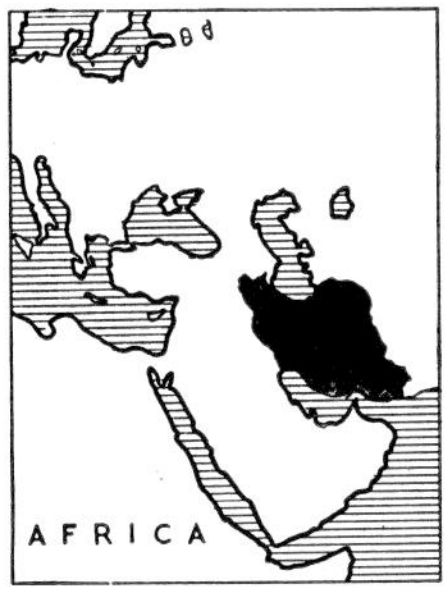

Population: Estimated at 18,944,000, including many nomads. Tehran, the capital, has about 1,513,000 inhabitants. Other important towns, with population figures, are: Tabriz (290,195), Isfahan (254,876), Mashad (242,165), Abadan (226,103), Shiraz (169,088) and Kermanshah (125,181). The language of the country is Persian (Farsi). Shia Islam is the official religion, but there are 900,000 followers of the Sunni branch of Islam.

Production and Trade: The most important product is oil (Karun valley and Kermanshah). Abadan has one of the world's largest oil refineries. But despite the desert nature of much of the country, most of the people depend on agriculture for their livelihood. Irrigation is important. The leading crops include wheat, rice, sugar, fruit, cotton, dates and tobacco. Large numbers of sheep and goats are reared.

Manufactures include textiles (silk, wool and cotton), carpet-weaving and many small-scale enterprises. Coal is mined, but the reputedly rich mineral wealth of the country has still to be fully developed.

Oil accounts for more than 75 per cent. of export trade. The leading partners are the United States, Western Germany, the United Kingdom, France and the U.S.S.R. The unit of currency is the Rial.

PERU

REPUBLIC

Estimates of the area of this South American state range from 482,000 square miles to 534,000 square miles. Crossed by the Andes, it is a land of lofty peaks, high plateaux and deep valleys, bordered on the west by a narrow coastal strip and on the east by the Amazon lowlands. In the south-east is Titicaca, the largest lake in South America. The high Andean peaks include Huascaran (over 22,000 feet).

Population: Estimated at 9,923,000, more than half of whom are Indians speaking Qũechũa or Aymara (although Spanish is the official language), the remainder being mostly *mestizos*. Roman Catholicism is the established religion. Lima, the capital, has over 1,133,000 inhabitants. Other important centres are Callao, the chief port (125,598), Arequipa (117,208) and Cuzco (68,483).

Production and Trade: Agriculture is the

chief industry and irrigation is important. Cotton, sugar and rice are produced in the more temperate coastal strip. Grain and fruits are grown in the valleys and foothills; tobacco, cocoa, coffee, bananas and sweet potatoes on the eastern slopes of the Andes (the *Montaña*). There are large ranches on the *puna* (high plateaux) where cattle, sheep, alpacas and llamas are reared. There are valuable fisheries (and associated canneries).

Copper, silver, lead, zinc, coal, petroleum and other minerals are worked. Peru is the world's leading producer of vanadium. Guano, a valuable fertiliser, is obtained from certain coastal islands. Industry includes steel, textiles and many small-scale enterprises. Cotton, sugar, petroleum, copper and wool are leading exports, the chief imports being foodstuffs, machinery, vehicles, metal and other manufactures. Trading partners include the United States, Chile, the United Kingdom and Western Germany. The unit of currency is the Sol.

PHILIPPINES

REPUBLIC

This country comprises eleven large islands and more than 7,000 smaller with a total area of 114,830 square miles, the two largest being Mindanao (36,538 square miles) and Luzon (40,422 square miles). They are largely mountainous, richly forested and fertile; some have active volcanoes. There is a tropical monsoon climate.

Population: Over 22,000,000. Manila, the old capital, has 1,200,000 inhabitants, Quezon City, the new capital nearby, has a population of over 107,900. More than 80 per cent. of the Filipinos are Roman Catholics, about 10 per cent. belong to the Philippine Independent Church, and the remainder are Moslem Moros or Pagans. There are Chinese, Spanish and American minorities. Tagalog, English and Spanish are official languages.

Production and Trade: Agriculture is the chief industry, providing rice and fruits for home consumption, and coconuts, sugar-cane, pineapples and Manila hemp (abacá) for export. The forests yield cabinet and other woods, gums, oils and canes. Gold, silver, lead, chromite, iron ore, manganese and copper are mined. Uranium has been discovered at Larap. Sugar, copra and hemp are the chief exports; machinery, textiles and manufactured goods, the chief imports. More than 75 per cent. of trade is conducted with the United States. The unit of currency is the Peso.

POLAND

REPUBLIC

This country of east central Europe has an area of some 121,000 square miles, bordered in the south by the Carpathian Mountains, in the west by the rivers Oder and Neisse, and in the north by the Baltic Sea. In general, Poland is part of the North European Plain, through which flow the Vistula, Bug and other important rivers. There are extensive forests.

Population: 28,535,000. Warsaw, the capital, has 1,069,000 inhabitants. Other important centres are: Lodz (683,000), Krakow (461,000), Wroclaw (*Breslau*) (389,000), Poznan (379,000), Gdansk (*Danzig*) (242,000), Szczecin (*Stettin*) (229,500) and Bydgoszcz (202,000). The language of the country is Polish and its religion, Roman Catholic.

Production and Trade: Traditionally an agricultural country, Poland has rye, oats, potatoes, sugar-beet, tobacco and flax as her leading crops. But in recent years there has been much industrialisation. Coal is abundant (especially Silesia). Iron ore, zinc, natural gas, petroleum and salt are produced. The iron and steel industry (Nowa Huta), textiles, chemicals and engineering are important. The Soviet Union and associated countries predominate in Polish trade. The unit of currency is the Zloty.

PORTUGAL

REPUBLIC

This country of the Iberian Peninsula has an area of some 34,450 square miles. It is long and narrow, mountainous in the north, with the plateau of the *Meseta* (cut by the rivers Douro, Tagus and Guadiana) in the east, and dry plains in the south.

Population: 8,654,436 (including Madeira and the Azores). Lisbon, the capital and chief port, has a population of 790,434. Important

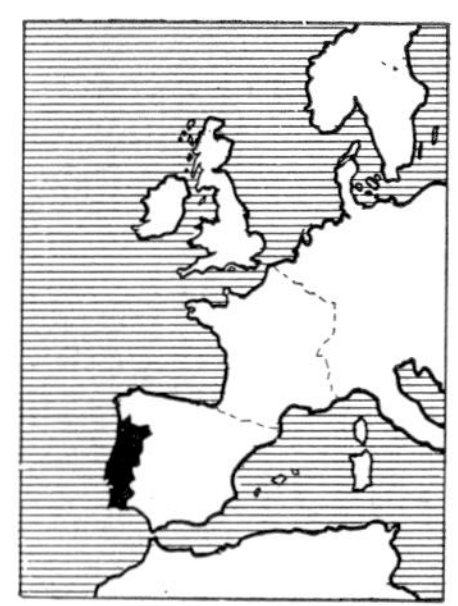

centres include Oporto (284,842), the second city and port, and Setubal and Coimbra (both with populations exceeding 40,000). Portuguese is the language of the country and Roman Catholicism its religion.

Production and Trade: Agriculture is the leading activity, with cereals, fruit, vegetables and almonds as the most important crops. Port wine is one of the principal exports, which also include cork and tinned fish (especially sardines). Wolfram, lead, tin, iron ore, coal, manganese and other minerals are worked, but the deposits have still to be fully exploited. Hydro-electric power is being developed. Portugal trades chiefly with her own overseas territories (see below), the United Kingdom, the United States, and Western Europe generally. The unit of currency is the Escudo.

Overseas Territories: For administrative purposes both Madeira (capital, Funchal) and the Azores (capital, Angra) are regarded as part of metropolitan Portugal. Other overseas territories are: (1) *Cape Verde Islands* (capital Praia); (2) *Portuguese Guinea* (capital, Bissau); (3) the islands of *S. Tomé* and *Principe*; (4) *Portuguese West Africa* (see ANGOLA); (5) *Portuguese East Africa* (see MOZAMBIQUE); (6) *Portuguese India* (Gôa); (7) *Macao*; and (8) *Portuguese Timor.*

QATAR

SHEIKHDOM

Qatar, which is under British protection, occupies the peninsula of the same name on the Persian Gulf and has an area of about 8,000 square miles. The estimated population is 35,000, of whom some 25,000 live in Doha, the capital. Most of the country is desert, and pearling and fishing are the traditional activities. But the oil deposits provide the main source of income. The local unit of currency is the Indian rupee.

RHODESIA AND NYASALAND

FEDERATION

The Federation comprises the self-governing territory of Southern Rhodesia and the protectorates of Northern Rhodesia and Nyasaland and is part of the British Commonwealth and Empire. The total area exceeds 485,000 square miles, the units and their areas in square miles being: Southern Rhodesia (150,333), Northern Rhodesia (287,640) and Nyasaland (about 49,000, including 12,000 square miles of water).

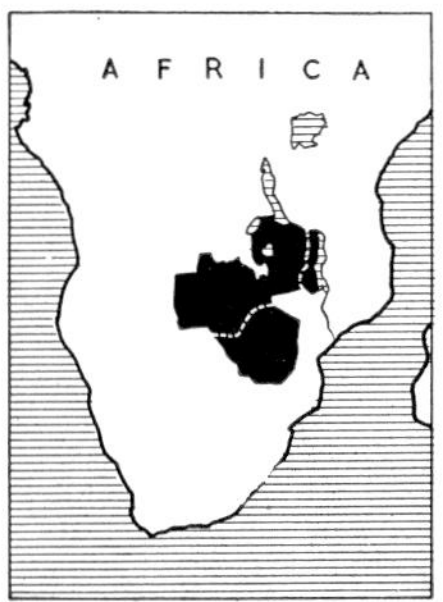

The whole Federation lies within the tropics, but most of it is at altitudes between 3,000 and 5,000 feet above sea level and is thus climatically suitable to European settlement. Dividing Southern and Northern Rhodesia is the Zambesi River (Victoria Falls), which is now being harnessed for hydro-electric power at Kariba Gorge. Lake Nyasa marks the southern end of the Great Rift Valley.

Population: Estimated at 7,450,000 (274,000 Europeans, 7,140,000 Africans and 32,000 other races). *Southern Rhodesia* (capital, Salisbury): 2,560,000 (193,000 Europeans, 2,350,000 Africans and 13,900 other races); *Northern Rhodesia* (capital, Lusaka): 2,240,000 (73,000 Europeans, 2,160,000 Africans and 7,500 other races); *Nyasaland* (capital, Zomba): 2,650,000 (7,500 Europeans, 2,630,000 Africans and 10,400 other races). The Federal capital is Salisbury, which is also the capital of Southern Rhodesia (see above).

Production and Trade: Agriculture is of prime importance, the main cash crops being tobacco, tea and cotton. Maize, millets and other crops are grown for local consumption. Stock-breeding is of growing importance. The valuable mineral deposits include copper (Northern Rhodesia), coal (Wankie), iron ore, asbestos (Shabani), chrome ore (Selukwe), gold, lead, zinc and cobalt. In recent years there has been remarkable development in heavy industry and manufacturing, especially in Southern Rhodesia. Iron and steel (Que Que), textiles, metal and wood manufactures, cigarettes, cement and processed foodstuffs are among the most important products.

Metals (particularly copper) and tobacco provide more than 60 per cent. of the export trade. Machinery, vehicles, clothing and fuel oil are among the chief imports. The United Kingdom and South Africa are the main trading partners. The unit of currency is the Rhodesian pound.

RUMANIA

REPUBLIC

This south-east European country has an area of 91,671 square miles. The heart of Rumania is dominated by mountains, the Carpathians swinging down from the north-west to link with the Transylvanian Alps running to the west. Eastwards, broad plains run out to the Black Sea coastline. Forming the greater part of the southern frontier is the river Danube. There are extremes of climate.

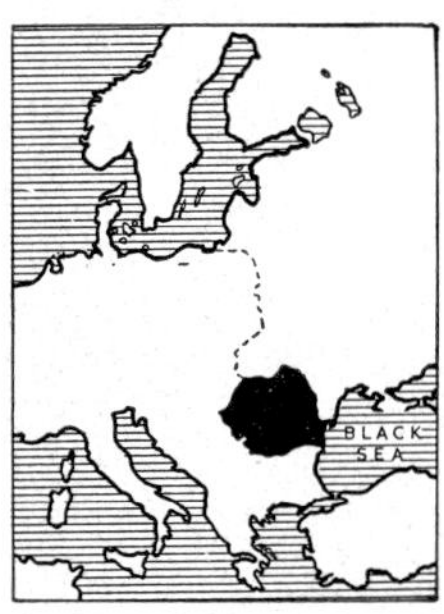

Population: 17,489,794. Bucharest, the capital, has 1,236,905 inhabitants. Cluj, Timisoara, Stalin, Ploesti, Iasi, Arad and Braila all have populations exceeding 100,000. There are Magyar, German and other minorities. The Rumanian Orthodox Church has nearly 14,000,000 adherents.

Production and Trade: The plains of Moldavia and Wallachia are among the finest grainlands in the world. Vines, fruit, flax and tobacco are other important crops in this predominantly agricultural country. Stock-breeding is also important. Good timber is abundant.

The chief mineral is oil, the main fields being in the Ploesti district. Gold, mica, lignite and uranium are mined. Oil-refining, chemicals and ship-building are of increasing importance. About 85 per cent. of Rumanian trade is conducted with the Soviet Union and associated countries. The unit of currency is the Leu (*plural*, lei).

Communications: Rumania operates the largest fleet on the river Danube and exercises many of the powers of the former European Commission of the Danube.

RUSSIA

See UNION OF SOVIET SOCIALIST REPUBLICS.

ST. HELENA

BRITISH COLONY

A South Atlantic island with an area of 47 square miles, and a population of 4,652. Jamestown is the chief centre and port. Flax-growing and lace-making are the main local industries. The island has an important cable station. Ascension Island and Tristan da Cunha are dependencies of St. Helena. The unit of currency is the Pound sterling.

SALVADOR

REPUBLIC

With an area estimated at about 8,250 square miles, El Salvador is the smallest of the Central American republics. It is mostly high plateau, topped by volcanic peaks, with narrow Pacific shorelands.

Population: Exceeds 2,300,000, mostly of Spanish descent. The official language is Spanish and the predominant religion, Roman Catholicism. San Salvador, the capital, has a population exceeding 203,000.

Production and Trade: Agriculture is the main industry and coffee the predominant crop. Other crops include cotton, rice, maize, tobacco, cacao and sugar. Gold and silver are mined. Coffee accounts for about 80 per cent. of exports. The main trading partner is the United States. The unit of currency is the Colon.

SAN MARINO

REPUBLIC

This tiny state, enclosed by Italy, has an area of about 38 square miles and a population of 13,500. Its capital is the city of San Marino. Sheep and cattle raising, and the production of wine and ceramics, are the main activities. Italian currency is in use.

SARAWAK

BRITISH COLONY

Sarawak occupies an area of about 48,000 square miles on the north-west coast of Borneo. The population is estimated at

626,223 and includes Sea Dyaks, Chinese, Malays, Land Dyaks and several other races. Numerous Christian missions are active. The capital is Kuching. Miri is the centre for a rich oilfield. There are valuable coal deposits and gold is mined. Oil, rubber and timber are the chief exports, the bulk of trade going through Singapore. The unit of currency is the Malayan and British Borneo dollar.

SAUDI ARABIA

MONARCHY

Saudi Arabia, occupying the greater part of Arabia, has an area estimated at 927,000 square miles, most of which is desert. It is really a union of two countries, the Sultanate of Nejd and the Kingdom of Hejaz.

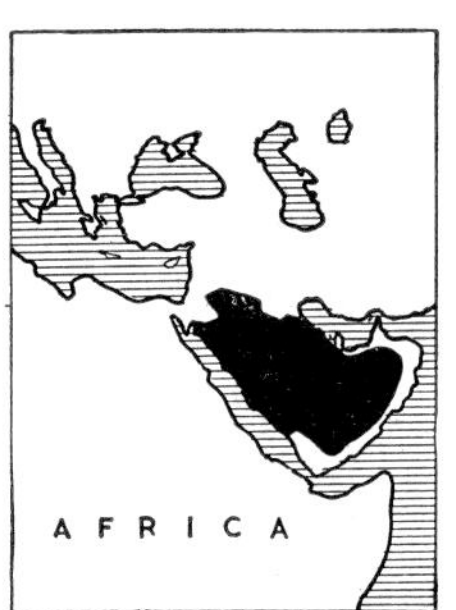

Population: About 6,000,000, most Arab, but some nomad Bedouin. Arabic is the language of the country and Islam, its religion. Mecca, capital of Hejaz, has probably not more than 150,000 inhabitants; Riyadh, capital of Nejd, not more than 100,000.

Production and Trade: By far the most important product is oil, the main field being at Abqaiq. Other oilfields include Ain Dar, Dammam, Ghawar, and Safaniya (offshore). A large refinery has been built at Ras Tanura, but oil is also refined at Bahrein (*q.v.*), and a vast amount is carried by the Trans-Arabian Pipeline to the port of Saida in the Lebanon.

There is some production of dates, fruit, wheat, honey and coffee. Horses, donkeys, sheep and camels are reared. Large numbers of pilgrims visit the cities of Mecca and Medina, holy to Islam.

Oil is the prime export and has made the United States the supreme trading partner. The official monetary unit in Saudi Arabia is the Rial, a silver coin; paper currency is in use, but is not officially recognised.

SCOTLAND

See UNITED KINGDOM.

SEYCHELLES

BRITISH COLONY

This island group in the Indian Ocean has a total area of 156 square miles, the principal island being Mahé, and a population of about 40,400. Victoria, the capital (on Mahé), has about 9,500 inhabitants. Coconuts, cinnamon and other oils are the chief products. Copra is the main export. The United Kingdom and India are the principal trading partners. The unit of currency is the Rupee.

SIAM

See THAILAND.

SIERRA LEONE

BRITISH COLONY AND PROTECTORATE

Sierra Leone has an area of about 28,000 square miles in West Africa. Behind the low coastland the ground rises to the Fouta Djalon plateau and to tropical rain forests and the savanna plateau beyond. There is heavy rainfall from May to October, and the territory is subject to the dust-laden Harmattan during the dry season.

Population: about 2,500,000 (of whom only 1,000 are Europeans). The Africans include descendants of liberated slaves, Limbas, Korankos and other tribes. Freetown, the capital and one of the finest harbours in West Africa, has 100,000 inhabitants.

Production and Trade: Agriculture is the main activity, the chief crops and products being palm-kernels and palm-oil, cocoa, coffee, kola-nuts, piassava and ginger—all of which are produced for export. Iron ore, diamonds and chrome ore are mined for export. Imports include foodstuffs, textiles, machinery, vehicles, fuel oil, building materials and manufactured goods. Trade is mostly with the United Kingdom. The unit of currency is the West African pound.

SINGAPORE

BRITISH COLONY

Although Singapore stands at the tip of the Malay Peninsula, from which it is separated by the narrow Johore Strait, and handles the bulk of Malaya's trade, it is not part of the Federation of Malaya. Christmas Island (Indian Ocean), a former dependency, is now the responsibility of Australia. The area of Singapore Island is about 225 square miles. Its population of 1,290,493 includes more than 987,000 Chinese, 157,000 Malaysians and 101,000 Indians and Pakistanis. It is one of the world's great trading ports. The unit of currency is the Malayan dollar.

SOUTH AFRICA

CONSTITUTIONAL MONARCHY

The Union of South Africa is a member of the British Commonwealth of Nations. It comprises four provinces and also administers South-West Africa, which is represented in the Union House of Assembly. The total area of the Union is 472,359 square miles (not including South-West Africa, 318,099 square miles). The provinces and their areas in square miles are: Cape Province (278,465), Natal (33,578), the Transvaal (110,450), and the Orange Free State (49,866).

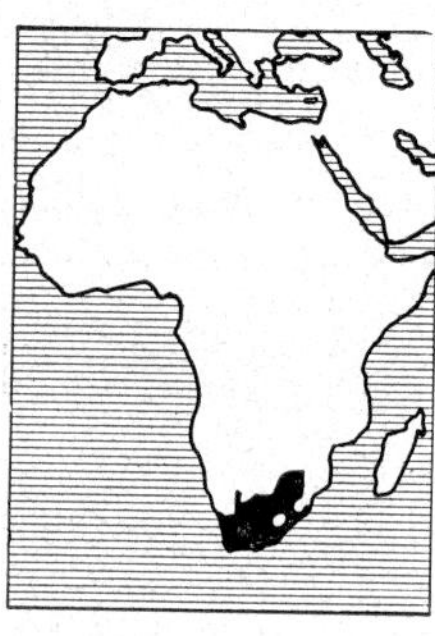

From the coastal lowlands the ground rises in a series of plateau " steps " (Little Karroo and Great Karroo) to the high plateau which forms most of the country and which is bordered by high mountains, such as the Drakensberg and the Nieuwveld Mountains. Flowing across the plateau are (i) the Limpopo river, forming much of the northern boundary of the Transvaal, and (ii) the Orange river, whose tributary the Vaal forms the boundary between the Transvaal and the Orange Free State. The Limpopo flows eastwards, the Orange westwards. Climate varies from the Mediterranean type at the Cape and the regions of good rainfall in south and east to the dry, semi-desert conditions of the Kalahari in South-West Africa. The climate generally is one of the sunniest in the world, but the heat is not excessive since so much of the country is plateau.

Population: 14,167,000, composed of 2,957,000 Whites and 11,210,000 Non-Whites. The Non-Whites comprise 9,460,000 Bantu, 1,319,000 Coloureds, and 431,000 Asians.* The largest cities and towns, and their populations, are: Johannesburg (over 884,000); Cape Town, the chief port of the Union, the seat of the Legislature, and the capital of Cape Province (578,000); Durban, the chief port of Natal (480,000); Pretoria, capital of the Union (285,000); Port Elizabeth (189,000); Germiston (168,000); Bloemfontein, capital of the Orange Free State (109,000); East London (91,264); Benoni (110,000); Pietermaritzburg, capital of Natal (74,500); Springs (119,300).

The official languages are Afrikaans and English, many people speaking both. The Bantu also use their own languages and dialects. Tamil, Hindi, Gujerati and Telegu are used by the Asiatics. There are numerous Christian denominations, the largest being the Dutch Reformed Church.

**N.B.* These figures do not include South-West Africa, which has a population of 418,104, the White population being 49,612. Windhoek, the capital, has 11,363 White inhabitants and some 18,300 Coloureds and Bantu.

Production and Trade: Mining is of prime importance, especially gold (Johannesburg and Welkom), diamonds (Kimberley), coal, copper, iron ore, tin, asbestos, manganese, platinum, chrome and uranium. Industrial development, which has been proceeding rapidly, includes iron and steel, textiles, chemicals, and manufactures of all kinds.

Agriculture has many aspects. Nearly half of the arable land is devoted to maize (" mealies "); wheat, barley, oats, cotton, tobacco, potatoes and other vegetables are also grown. Cape Province is noted for wine and table grapes, citrus and other fruits; Natal for its sugar-cane and tropical fruits. The Union has more than 37,000,000 sheep, 11,600,000 cattle and 5,400,000 goats, and is one of the leading producers of wool and mohair.

The chief exports include wool, gold, uranium, diamonds, maize, textiles, asbestos, fruits, copper and bark extract. Imports include machinery, vehicles, fuel oil, drugs and fertilisers, and many manufactured items. The chief trading partners are the United Kingdom and other Commonwealth countries, the United States, Belgium, Italy, Germany and France. The unit of currency is the South African pound.

SOUTH-WEST AFRICA

See SOUTH AFRICA.

SPAIN

NOMINAL MONARCHY

Spain occupies most of the Iberian Peninsula, the central feature of which is the plateau or *Meseta* bordered and ridged by mountain ranges. In the north are the Pyrenees, which form the border with France, and the Cantabrians; in the south are the Sierra Nevada and Sierra Morena. The Montes de Toledo, Sierra Guadarrama and Sierra de Gredos isolate the rivers which run down from the *Meseta*. Among these are the Douro, Tagus, Guadiana, Guadalquivir and Ebro. Much of the country is dry and barren. There are extremes of climate. The total area exceeds 195,000 square miles (including the Balearic and Canary Islands, and Ceuta and Melilla, all of which are regarded as part of metropolitan Spain).

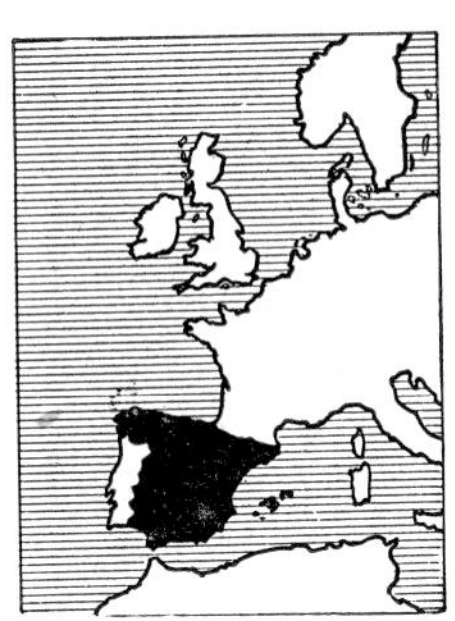

Population: 29,130,499. Madrid, the capital, has over 1,843,000 inhabitants. Other large cities include Barcelona, a leading port and commercial centre (1,403,000), Valencia (511,400), Seville (405,800), Malaga (277,800), Zaragoza (274,200), Bilbao (248,500), Murcia (235,700) and Córdova (182,200). Spanish is the official language, but there are also Basque, Galician and Catalan dialects. The established church is Roman Catholicism.

Production and Trade: Spain is predominantly agricultural, despite the dry climate. Irrigation has long been practised in some areas, *e.g.*, the *huertas* of Valencia. Large crops of cereals, olives, vegetables and fruit are grown; Valencia and Castellon are noted for oranges. There are many vineyards, the most famous of the many Spanish wines being sherry. Other important products include esparto grass and cork. Much of the land is pasture, supporting large numbers of sheep, goats and cattle. There are valuable sardine, tunny and cod fisheries.

Mineral deposits are plentiful and include iron ore (Viscaya, Santander, Murcia and Almeria), coal (Asturias), copper (Rio Tinto), lead and silver (Linares), and mercury (Almaden). Manufactures include textiles (especially Barcelona), paper-making, many kinds of leather goods, ceramics, bicycles, sewing machines and chemicals.

Wine, oranges, olive oil, cork, iron and other ores, and textiles are the chief exports. Imports include raw materials, machinery, vehicles, coal, petroleum and tobacco. The United States, United Kingdom, Western Germany and France are the leading trade partners. The unit of currency is the Peseta.

Overseas Territories: The Balearic Isles (capital, Palma), the Canary Islands (chief towns, Las Palmas and Santa Cruz), Ceuta and Melilla (Morocco) are regarded as part of metropolitan Spain. *Colonies:* (1) Spanish Guinea; (2) Ifni; (3) Spanish Sahara (Rio de Oro and Sekia el Hamra).

SUDAN

REPUBLIC

Formerly an Anglo-Egyptian Condominium, the Sudan was proclaimed an independent republic on 1st January, 1956. Its area exceeds 967,000 square miles and is drained by the Nile and its tributaries. The north is dry, stony desert; the south is tropical grassland, with areas of "sudd" swamp (floating vegetation).

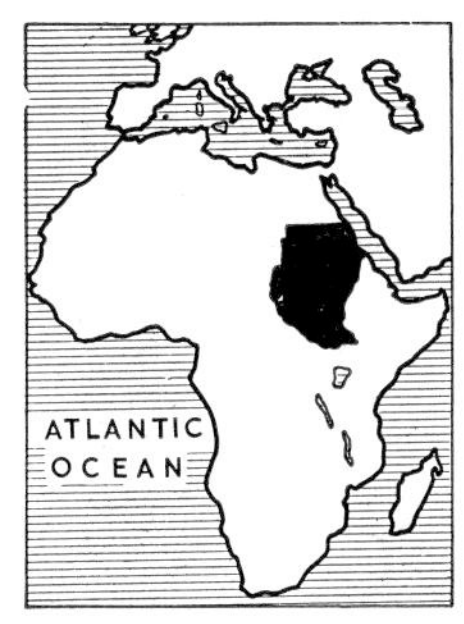

Population: About 10,000,000. Khartoum, the capital, has about 83,000 inhabitants. The largest town is Omdurman, which has 125,000 inhabitants. The population includes Arabs and Nubians (Moslems) and Negroes, mostly pagan but some have been converted to Christianity. Arabic (the official language), English and various Sudanese tongues are in use.

Production and Trade: Cattle, sheep, camels and other livestock are reared in large numbers. Dura and dukhn (both forms of millet) are the chief grain crops. Cotton is the predominant cash crop, providing 75 per cent. of the exports, the highest quality coming from the Gezira irrigation scheme. Most of the world's gum arabic comes from the Sudan. The forests of the south contain mahogany and other valuable woods. The United Kingdom, India, Pakistan and Egypt are the chief trading partners. The unit of currency is the Sudanese pound.

SWAZILAND

BRITISH HIGH COMMISSION TERRITORY

This South African territory occupies an area of 6,705 square miles between the Transvaal, on the west, and Natal and

Mozambique on the east. There are mountains on both sides, and between these lie the Middle and Low Veld, fertile and well-watered. The population numbers about 237,000, but includes fewer than 6,000 Europeans, of whom nearly 2,000 live in Mbabane, the seat of administration.

Cattle-breeding is important. Maize, cotton, tobacco, sorghum, groundnuts and other crops are grown. Asbestos is mined in quantity, but other mineral wealth (including coal) has still to be exploited. The territory is joined in a customs union with the Union of South Africa. British currency and South African coinage are in use.

SWEDEN

CONSTITUTIONAL MONARCHY

Sweden occupies the eastern part of Scandinavia and is divided from Norway by the Kiölen mountains. The north has dense conifer forests and small, swift rivers, and is thinly populated. The central lowland region has many lakes, linked by rivers and canals. The most fertile parts are the southern plains. The area of the country is 173,436 square miles.

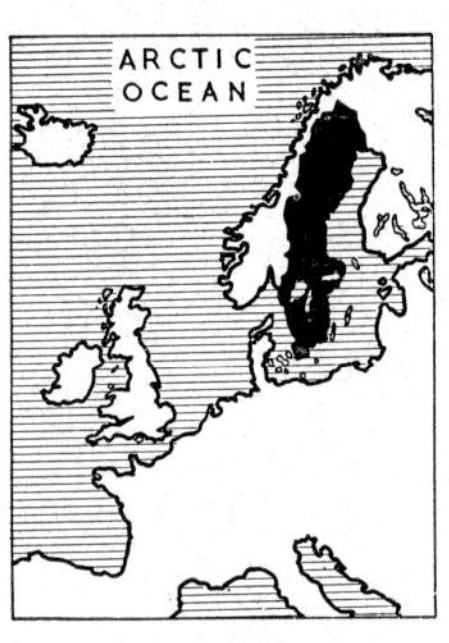

Population: 7,341,122, most of whom are members of the Evangelical Lutheran Church. Swedish is the language of the country, but some Lappish is spoken in the north. Stockholm, the capital, has 794,113 inhabitants. Other important towns include Göteborg, the chief commercial port (387,061) and Malmö (213,260).

Production and Trade: Nearly one-third of the population is employed in agriculture, forestry and fisheries. Dairy-farming is especially important. The forests provide timber, pitch, fuel and wood-pulp. The rich mineral deposits include iron ore (Gällivare and Kiruna), zinc, sulphur, manganese, coal and uranium. There is industry and manufacturing of many kinds, including machinery, electrical equipment, textiles and glassware. Hydro-electric power is plentiful.

Trade is carried on with many countries, especially the United Kingdom and Western Germany. Wood-pulp, timber, paper, machinery, iron and steel, matches and foodstuffs are the chief exports; coal, vehicles, oil, chemicals and fertilisers the main imports. The unit of currency is the Krona.

SWITZERLAND

CONFEDERATION (FEDERAL REPUBLIC)

This land-locked country comprises twenty-two cantons and has an area of 15,950 square miles, of which nearly 75 per cent. is extremely mountainous (Alps and Jura Mountains). There are fertile mountain valleys, rich Alpine pastures and many beautiful lakes. The climate is mainly Continental, with temperatures ranging widely according to altitude.

Population: 5,045,000. Berne, the capital, has some 157,000 inhabitants. Of greater size are Zürich, the leading commercial and cultural city (390,000), Basle (195,000) and Geneva (160,000). Other important towns include Lausanne, St. Gallen, Winterthur, Lucerne, Biel and La Chaux de Fonds. Four languages are spoken: German (more than 70 per cent.), French (about 20 per cent.), Italian (about 6 per cent.) and Romansch. More than half the people are Protestant and most of the remainder, Roman Catholic.

Production and Trade: The country is still mainly agricultural (especially dairying and stock-breeding). Grain and root crops, fruits and vines are grown; wine is made in all but four cantons. Industry, which has increased rapidly, includes machinery, textiles, chemicals, tools and instruments, processed foodstuffs, forest products, clocks and watches. The tourist industry is most important. Hydro-electric power is highly developed. Coal, oil, steel, machinery and vehicles are the chief imports. The main partners in trade are Western Germany, the United States, France and the United Kingdom. The unit of currency is the Swiss franc.

SYRIA

A " REGION " OF THE
UNITED ARAB REPUBLIC (See p. 190)

This country of the Eastern Mediterranean has an area of 72,234 square miles, much of which is desert plateau. Between the western mountain ranges and the sea is a fertile and

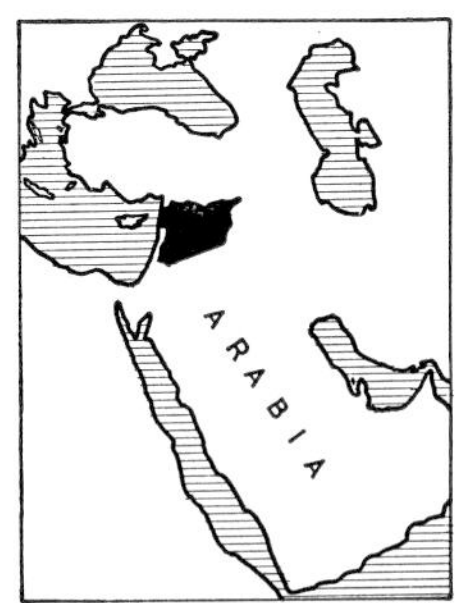

thickly-populated region. Crossing the country in a south-easterly direction is the Euphrates, the largest river in Western Asia. The climate generally is hot and dry.

Population: About 3,906,000, including Syrians of mixed descent and other peoples, but overwhelmingly Moslem. Arabic is the predominant language, but French and Aramaic may also be encountered. Damascus, the principal city, has 395,124 inhabitants. Other important towns are Aleppo (398,461), Homs (293,643), Hama (172,988) and Latakia (109,216), the chief port.

Production and Trade: Agriculture (cereals, cotton, fruits and tobacco) is the principal activity. Sheep, goats, camels, cattle and other livestock are numerous. Banias is the terminal of an oil pipeline from Kirkuk (Iraq); the TAPline from Saudi Arabia also crosses Syria on its way to Saida (Sidon) in the Lebanon.

Animals, skins and hides, fruit, cotton and cereals are exported. Textiles, foodstuffs, vehicles, machinery, tools and chemicals are the chief imports. The United Kingdom, Lebanon, France, Italy and the United States are the main trading partners. The unit of currency is the Syrian pound.

TANGANYIKA

TRUSTEESHIP TERRITORY

Administered by the United Kingdom under U.N. Trusteeship, Tanganyika has an area of 362,688 square miles (including some 20,000 square miles of water). Most of Tanganyika is plateau (Central African Plateau) and here, too, are Kilimanjaro (the highest mountain in Africa) and other high peaks. The unhealthy coastal strip is comparatively narrow.

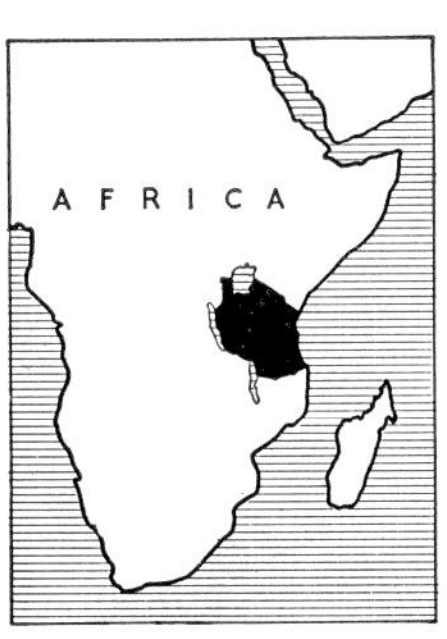

Population: The African peoples, numbering more than 100 tribes, are mostly Bantu and exceed 7,400,000 (the present figure is probably nearly 8,330,000). There are also some 20,600 Europeans, and more than 65,800 Indians and 19,000 Arabs. The population of Dar es Salaam, the capital and chief port, is 107,709 (including 72,330 Africans). Swahili is used and understood throughout the territory.

Production and Trade: Agriculture is the main industry and sisal the chief export crop. Coffee, cotton, groundnuts, and sunflower, castor and sesame seed are also produced for export. Mining (diamonds, gold, lead, mica, tin, tungsten and silver) is of growing importance. The United Kingdom is the dominant trading partner. The unit of currency is the East African shilling.

THAILAND

CONSTITUTIONAL MONARCHY

Thailand, or Siam, has an area of 198,247 square miles. The north and west of the country are hilly and densely forested, and the rivers flow southwards to join the Menam Chao Phraya, in whose fertile basin most of the people live. The eastern part of the country is drained by the River Mekong.

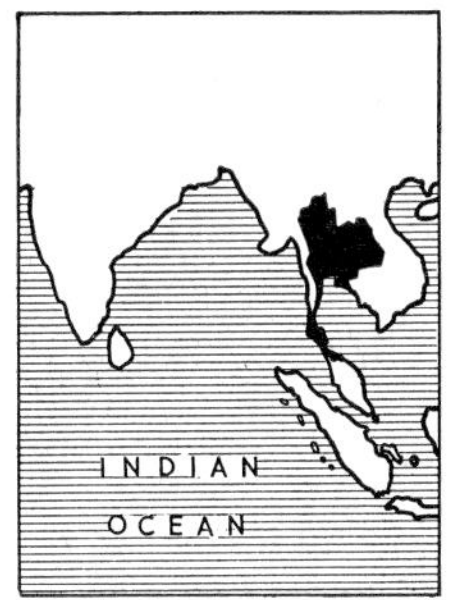

Population: Estimated at about 22,800,000. Bangkok, the capital and chief port, has more than 1,208,000 inhabitants. Thai is the language of the country and Buddhism the principal religion.

Production and Trade: Agriculture and fishing provide a livelihood for nearly all the population. Rice is the outstanding crop and large quantities are exported. Rubber, tin, wolfram and teak are important products. Foodstuffs, textiles, metal goods and oil are the chief imports. The United States, Japan, Malaya and Singapore, Hong Kong and the Netherlands handle the bulk of Siamese trade. The unit of currency is the Baht.

TIBET

See *Special Territories* under CHINA.

TONGA

KINGDOM

Tonga, or the Friendly Islands, is a group in the Southern Pacific constituting an independent kingdom under British protection.

There are some 150 islands in the group, the total area being 270 square miles. Nukualofa, the seat of Government, is on Tongatapu, the largest island. The population numbers 56,838; more than 55,000 of these are Tongans. The people are Christian, Wesleyans being the most numerous. Copra and bananas are the chief products.

TRINIDAD AND TOBAGO

BRITISH COLONY

The area of Trinidad is 1,864 square miles and it is the second largest of the islands in the Federation of The West Indies. Tobago (116 square miles) forms part of the colony administratively. Trinidad is very fertile and, like Tobago, is popular with tourists. Its "Pitch Lake" of natural asphalt is famous.

Population: Estimated at 742,500, including Tobago. Most of the people are West Indians of African descent, but there are some East Indians and Chinese as well as people of mixed blood and Europeans. Port of Spain, the capital and chief port, has 120,000 inhabitants. Scarborough (about 15,000) is the chief town of Tobago.

Production and Trade: Oil and asphalt are leading products of Trinidad. No less important are sugar, molasses, rum, cocoa, coconuts and citrus fruit. Copra and cocoa are produced in Tobago. The unit of currency is the West Indian dollar, but British currency is also accepted. The principal trading partners are the United Kingdom, Venezuela, Canada and the United States.

N.B. Trinidad has been selected for the capital of the Federation of The West Indies (*q.v.*).

TRUCIAL STATES

SHEIKHDOMS

These comprise seven states on the Persian Gulf, *viz.*, Abu Dhabi, Dubai, Sharjah and Kalba, Ajman, Umm al Qaiwain, Ras al Khaimah, and Fujairah. The area of the whole is probably about 40,000 square miles and estimates of the population vary from 60,000 to 80,000. Oil concessions provide the chief source of revenue.

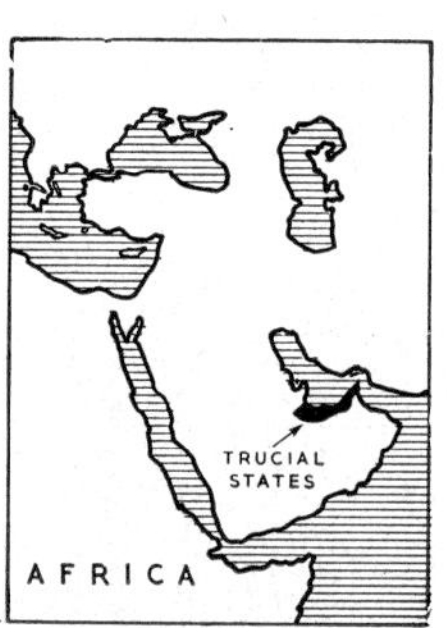

TUNISIA

REPUBLIC

Once a French protectorate, Tunisia was granted independence in March 1956. The country has an area of about 48,000 square miles and comprises: the mountainous north, with the Medjerda and other fertile valleys; the Cape Bon peninsula, noted for its citrus fruits; the Sahel lowlands in the east, where olives are cultivated; the pastures of the central plateau; and the desert south, with its oases and date gardens.

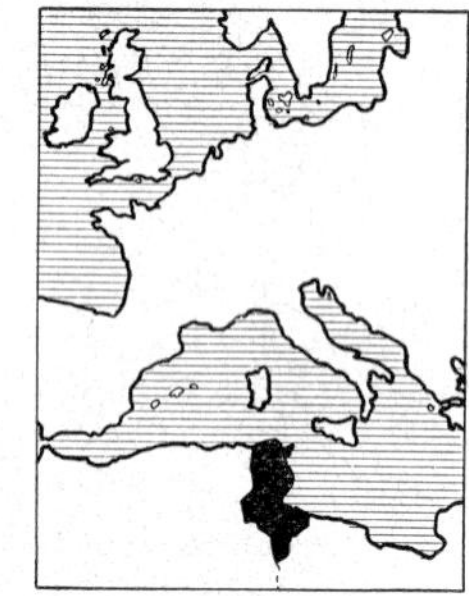

Population: 3,800,000, of whom more than 3,400,000 are Tunisians. Tunis, the capital, has 410,000 inhabitants. Other important towns are Sfax, Sousse, Bizerta and Kairouan. Islam is the dominant religion; Arabic, the official language.

Production and Trade: Agriculture is the chief activity. The leading crops include wheat, barley and oats, vines and olives, citrus fruits and dates. Sheep, goats, camels, cattle and other livestock are numerous. Minerals include phosphates, iron, lead and zinc. More than 75 per cent. of Tunisian trade is conducted with France and Algeria. The unit of currency is the French franc.

TURKEY

REPUBLIC

Turkey has an area of some 296,000 square miles, the area of European Turkey being 9,256 square miles. The principal feature of Turkey in Asia is the Anatolian plateau, bordered in the north by the Pontic Mountains and the Black Sea and in the south by the Taurus Mountains. The highest point of the eastern mountains (bordering Armenia) is Mt. Ararat. The coastal regions are the most fertile.

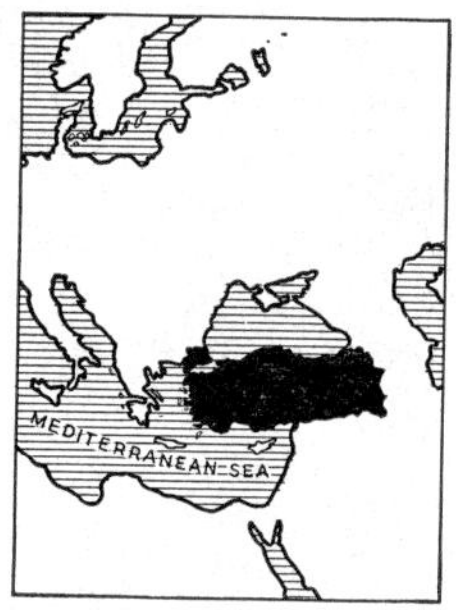

Population: 24,111,778. Turkish is the language, and Islam the religion, of nearly all the people. The largest city is Istanbul

(1,214,616), formerly known as Constantinople and once the capital. The modern capital, Ankara (Angora), has 453,151 inhabitants. Other important centres are Izmir, Adana, Bursa, Eskisehir, Gaziantep, Konya, Kayseri and Erzerum.

Production and Trade: Agriculture is the main activity, although the area under cultivation seems comparatively small. The chief crops include wheat, barley, cotton, tobacco, fruit, figs and sultanas, sugar beet and opium. Large numbers of sheep, goats, cattle, buffaloes and camels are reared. There are valuable forests. The considerable mineral wealth includes coal, iron ore, copper, manganese and chrome (Turkey is a leading producer of this last), but has still to be fully exploited. Industrialisation of the country is proceeding and has provided an iron and steel industry (Karabük), textile and paper-making factories and manufactures of many kinds. Tobacco, cotton, dried fruits and minerals are the chief exports; iron and steel, machinery, petroleum, vehicles and locomotives are among the chief imports. Western Germany, the United Kingdom, the United States, Italy and France are the principal trading partners. The unit of currency is the Lira, or Turkish pound.

UGANDA

BRITISH PROTECTORATE

Uganda has an area of 93,981 square miles (including 13,680 square miles of water). This is divided into the Eastern, Western and Northern Provinces, and the Kingdom of Buganda. Most of the Protectorate has an average elevation of 4,000 feet, but on its eastern border Mount Elgon rises to more than 14,000 feet, while the Western Province is overlooked by the lofty Ruwenzori range. Despite the elevation of the country, temperatures are generally high, and the climate as a whole is not kind to Europeans.

Population: Estimated at 5,593,000 and including 8,400 Europeans and over 54,400 Indians. The Africans include nearly 1,000,000 of the Baganda tribe, speaking Luganda (a Bantu tongue). Ki-Swahili and other languages are also in use. Entebbe is the seat of administration; Kampala and Jinja are the chief commercial towns.

Production and Trade: The most valuable export crop is cotton, grown by countless small farmers. Coffee, hides and skins are also valuable exports. The principal food crops are maize, millet and bananas. Mineral wealth includes copper (Kilembe), tin and wolfram, but has still to be fully exploited. Industrial development is being helped by the Owen Falls hydro-electric scheme. The United Kingdom, India and Western Germany are the chief trading partners. The unit of currency is the East African shilling.

UNION OF SOVIET SOCIALIST REPUBLICS

FEDERAL REPUBLIC

The U.S.S.R., or Soviet Union, embraces much of Europe and the great land mass of north and central Asia; the total area, some 8,700,000 square miles, is about one sixth of the total land area of the earth. Its most striking feature is the Great Russian Plain, which is divided by the Ural Mountains into the East European Plain and the West Siberian Lowlands. To the north is the Arctic Ocean; the Caucasus, Pamirs and other massive mountain systems stand guard in the south. The many long, navigable rivers include the Volga (the longest river in Europe), Don, Dnieper, Dvina, Dniester, Ob, Yenesei and Amur. There are large inland seas and lakes, and numerous canals.

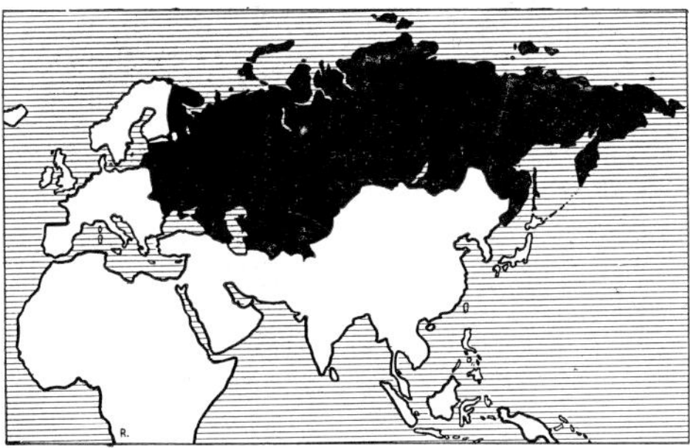

The Soviet Union

So great a land mass naturally has a wide range of climatic variation, and of vegetation and ways of life. The main types range from the Tundra in the north, through Taiga, Forest and Steppe, to the Desert of the south.

The fifteen Union republics (some of which incorporate certain Autonomous Republics and Regions) are given below, with their capital cities in brackets: Russian Soviet Federated

Socialist Republic (Moscow), Ukrainian S.S.R. (Kiev), Byelorussian S.S.R. (Minsk), Turkmen S.S.R. (Ashkhabad), Uzbek S.S.R. (Tashkent), Kazakh S.S.R. (Alma-Ata), Armenian S.S.R. (Yerevan), Georgian S.S.R. (Tbilisi, or Tiflis), Azerbaijan S.S.R. (Baku), Kirghiz S.S.R. (Frunze), Lithuanian S.S.R. (Vilnius), Latvian S.S.R. (Riga), Esthonian S.S.R. (Tallinn), Tadzhik S.S.R. (Stalinabad), Moldavian S.S.R. (Kishinev).

Population: There has been no census since 1939, but in 1956 an official statement gave the population as 200,200,000. Moscow, the capital of the Soviet Union, has an estimated population of 4,847,000. Nearly half the total population is Russian, the next largest group being Ukrainians (about 30,000,000). There are numerous other peoples. Russian is the principal language, but each republic decides its own official tongue and more than 100 languages are in use. The Russian Orthodox Church survived its disestablishment in 1918, and other Christian denominations are represented; Islam predominates in Soviet central Asia.

Production and Trade: Once predominantly agricultural, the Soviet Union is now one of the great manufacturing and industrial countries of the world. Mineral wealth of all kinds abounds, *e.g.*, coal (especially the Donetz and Kuznetz Basins), iron ore (Krivoi Rog and Urals), oil (Grozny and Maikop in the Caucasus, and the Ural-Volga area), copper, uranium, platinum, and many other minerals.

Among the many industrial and manufacturing centres are Chelyabinsk (iron and steel), Sverdlovsk (machinery and machine-tools), Nizhne Tagil (railway rolling stock), Leningrad (engineering, paper, chemicals, vehicles, textiles) and Moscow (vehicles, electrical equipment, engineering, machine-tools). Hydro-electric power has been developed on the Volga and other rivers.

Like industry, agriculture is in the hands of the State and is characterised by the Collective Farms (*Kolkhoz*) and the much larger State Farms (*Sovkhoz*): there are now about 75,000 of the former and some 5,800 of the latter. Crops of all kinds are grown, wheat being especially important (about 30 per cent. of total world production). Livestock includes more than 70,000,000 head of cattle and 129,900,000 sheep. The vast forests, covering about 40 per cent. of the Soviet Union, are an important source of wealth.

Full details of foreign trade are not available, but by far the greater part is conducted with countries of the Soviet bloc. The Soviet unit of currency is the Rouble.

Communications: Spanning the Soviet Union is the Trans-Siberian Railway completed in 1903, the longest direct line in the world. Great use is made of rivers and waterways, the five seas of European Russia (White, Baltic, Caspian, Azov and Black Sea) being linked in a single canal-river system.

UNITED ARAB REPUBLIC

On February 1st, 1958, Egypt and Syria were merged into a single country, the United Arab Republic, with Cairo as its capital. Subsequently Colonel Nasser was elected President. On March 8th, a federal union (the United Arab States) was established between the United Arab Republic and the Yemen (*q.v.*). See also *Egypt, Syria.*

UNITED KINGDOM

CONSTITUTIONAL MONARCHY

The United Kingdom of Great Britain and Northern Ireland, the motherland of the British Commonwealth of Nations (*q.v.*), has an area (including inland waterways) of 94,207 square miles. This area comprises: England (excluding Monmouthshire), 50,329 square miles; Scotland, 30,411 square miles; Wales (including Monmouthshire), 8,016 square miles; Northern Ireland, 5,451 square miles.

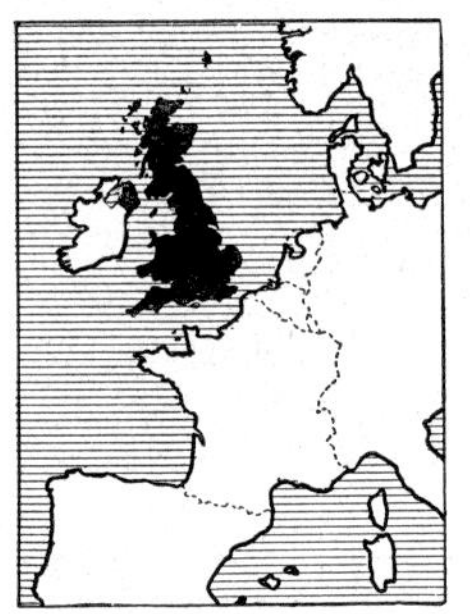

The most mountainous part of the United Kingdom is Scotland, whose north-west Highlands contain Ben Nevis (the highest peak in the British Isles). Most of Britain's hydro-electric power is produced here. Running southwards from the Southern Uplands of Scotland and the Cheviots is the Pennine Chain. But most of England is lowland, hills and mountains being mainly confined to the north and west. Snowdon, the highest range south of the Tweed, is in North Wales. The principal English river is the Thames, but the longest in the United Kingdom is the Severn. The Clyde is the most important of Scotland's rivers.

Generally speaking, the climate is mild and equable, though perversely fickle at times. The prevailing Westerlies bring considerable rain to the higher western regions.

Population: 50,225,224 (1951 census); current estimate: 51,209,000, excluding Service personnel overseas. Estimated population by countries: (i) England and Wales, 44,667,000; (ii) Scotland, 5,145,000; (iii) Northern Ireland, 1,397,000.

London, the capital of the United Kingdom and of the British Commonwealth, has 8,348,023 inhabitants (" Greater London "). Figures for the other capital cities are: (i) Edinburgh (Scotland), 467,000; (ii) Cardiff (Wales), 249,800; (iii) Belfast (Northern Ireland), 443,671. Among the many other important cities are: Birmingham (1,103,000), Glasgow (1,089,000), Liverpool (768,700), Manchester (682,000), Leeds (510,100), Sheffield (498,500), Bristol (439,600), Nottingham (312,600), Hull (300,500), Bradford (287,000) and Coventry (277,300).

At the 1951 Census more than 715,000 persons in Wales and Monmouthshire were able to speak Welsh; about 48,000 could speak Welsh only. In Scotland more than 95,000 persons were able to speak Gaelic; some 2,100 could speak Gaelic only.

Production and Trade: The United Kingdom is one of the world's great manufacturing countries. Mineral wealth includes large deposits of coal and iron ore. The chief coalfields are: (i) in *England*, Cumberland, Northumberland and Durham, South Lancashire, West Riding, Derby and Nottingham, the Midlands, Bristol and Somerset; (ii) in *Scotland*, Lanark, Ayrshire, Firth of Forth; (iii) in *South Wales*, Cardiff, Swansea, Llanelly, Merthyr Tydfil, Ebbw Vale, and Tredegar.

The many industrial centres include Barrow in Furness, Belfast, the Clyde, and Sunderland (shipbuilding); the Black Country, Darlington, Middlesbrough (iron, steel and metals); South Wales (iron and steel, tinplate, chemicals, nylon); Manchester and many Lancashire towns, and Paisley in Scotland (cotton); Bradford, Leeds and West Riding towns, and Kilmarnock in Scotland (woollens); Belfast, Dundee, Dunfermline and Manchester (linen); Leicester and Nottingham (hosiery); Macclesfield, Congleton, Brighouse, Coventry (silk and artificial silk); Bristol, Leicester, Northampton, Norwich (leather goods); Sheffield and Rotherham (cutlery); Birmingham (hardware and vehicles); the Potteries (china); Coventry, London, Oxford (vehicles)—these are but a few examples. London itself is one of the chief and most diverse manufacturing centres in the kingdom.

Of great significance is the present swift development of atomic energy; Calder Hall, the first atomic power station of its kind in the world, has been followed by others.

Agriculture, however, remains a leading industry and is highly mechanised. Wheat, barley and sugar-beet are found mostly in eastern England; fruit in Kent, East Anglia, the Vale of Evesham, Hereford and the West Country; cattle in the Midlands and south-west; sheep on the Downs, Cheviots, Southern Uplands of Scotland, and in Wales; market gardening near many of the great centres of population. Grimsby, Hull, Yarmouth, Lowestoft, Milford Haven, Aberdeen and Fleetwood are the chief ports of the important fishing industry.

The United Kingdom has many sea gates. London itself is a great port; others include Liverpool, Bristol (Avonmouth), Southampton, Glasgow, Belfast, Hull and Leith. Although it may be said that the United Kingdom trades with the world, more than half her trade is conducted with the countries of the Sterling Area. These comprise all the countries of the British Commonwealth, except Canada, together with Burma, Iceland, Iraq, the Irish Republic, Jordan and Libya. The British unit of currency is the Pound sterling.

Overseas Territories: See *British Commonwealth of Nations*.

UNITED STATES OF AMERICA

FEDERAL REPUBLIC

Extending over a great part of the North American continent, the U.S.A. has a land area of 3,545,791 square miles. Running down the western part of the country are the Rocky Mountains and other ranges of the Western Cordillera. Between the Cordillera and the Appalachian Highlands and eastern coastal plain are the vast prairie-lands. The main river system is the Mississippi-Missouri, the longest in the world, which flows into the Gulf of Mexico. The overall climate of the country is temperate.

There are 49 states in the federal republic, the 49th state being the former territory of Alaska which entered the Union with the signing of the Alaskan Statehood Bill on July 7th, 1958. The federal capital is Washington, in the District of Columbia.

Population: 150,697,361 (1950); current estimate, 172,554,000. These figures include more than 15,000,000 Negroes, 343,000 North American Indians, 142,000 Japanese and 118,000 Chinese. Washington, D.C., has some 802,178 inhabitants. The largest city in the U.S.A. is New York, which has a population of 7,795,471. Other important cities (and they are numerous) include Chicago (3,620,962), Los Angeles (2,243,901), Philadelphia (2,071,605), Detroit (1,849,568), Baltimore (949,708), Cleveland (941,103) and St. Louis (856,796).

Production and Trade: Most human activities are carried on in the U.S.A., which enjoys great fertility and mineral wealth. Agriculture ranges from the Corn Belt, stretching from Nebraska and Kansas to Lake Michigan and the Ohio River, and the rich dairying area to the north, to the cotton, tobacco and sub-tropical crops of southern States, the irrigated valleys of the south-west, and the cattle lands of Texas and the western prairies. There are vast areas of pine and other valuable timber.

Mineral wealth includes coal (especially western Pennsylvania and eastern Ohio), iron ore (especially Minnesota), oil (Texas, California, Oklahoma, Louisiana, Kansas and Illinois), uranium, gold, silver, copper, lead and zinc. Noted industrial centres include Pittsburgh (iron and steel), Detroit (vehicles), and Chicago (meat-packing and flour-milling). Hydro-electric power has been developed on an impressive scale. In a small space it is not possible to give details of the huge volume and variety of manufactures (some 35 per cent. of the world's total) which place the U.S.A. in the leading position in the world. This same volume and variety characterise the exports of the Republic, which trades with many countries, with Canada topping the list. The unit of currency is the Dollar.

Overseas Territories: These comprise the *Territory of Hawaii; the Commonwealth of Puerto Rico;* the Panama Canal Zone (see *Panama*); *Guam; American Samoa; Virgin Islands* of the U.S.A.; and a number of Pacific islands, including certain former Japanese possessions now held by the U.S.A. under U.N. trusteeship. The Territory of Hawaii has an area of 6,423 square miles and a population of 551,537; Honolulu, the capital and chief port (and a popular tourist centre) is on the island of Oahu.

URUGUAY

REPUBLIC

Uruguay has an area of about 72,170 square miles and is the smallest of South American republics.

Most of the country is rolling grassland and the climate is mild and with little variation.

Population: Estimated at 3,000,000. Montevideo, the capital and chief port, has about 838,000 inhabitants. Other important centres include Salta (60,000), Paysandu (60,000) and Mercedes (24,000). The country is predominantly Roman Catholic and Spanish is its language.

Production and Trade: Agriculture is the principal industry, the grasslands supporting great numbers of cattle and sheep. Meat and meat products, leather and wool are the chief exports. The United States, Brazil, United Kingdom, the Netherlands and Western Germany are the main trading partners. The unit of currency is the Peso.

U.S.A.

See UNITED STATES OF AMERICA.

U.S.S.R.

See UNION OF SOVIET SOCIALIST REPUBLICS.

VATICAN

The Vatican City State, which is under Papal sovereignty, has an area of 109 acres and a population of 940. It has its own railway and broadcasting stations, coinage and postal service.

VENE7UELA

REPUBLIC

The northernmost country in South America, Venezuela has an area of about 352,143 square miles. Andean ranges cross the north-west to the Caribbean coast; other thickly-forested ranges enclose the eastern and Brazilian borders. The main river is the Orinoco, and its basin forms the *llanos*, or tropical grasslands. The Venezuelan coast has many lakes and lagoons, the chief being Lake Maracaibo. The climate is tropical.

Population: 6,129,700, including about 57,000 tribal Indians. Spanish is the language of the country and Roman Catholicism the predominant religion. Caracas, the capital, has 1,102,230 inhabitants. Other important towns include Maracaibo (290,000), Barquisimeto (165,000), Valencia (124,000) and Maracay (64,535).

Production and Trade: Venezuela has much mineral wealth. She is the second largest oil-producer (Lake Maracaibo) in the world and the leading oil exporter. Gold, manganese, coal, phosphates, tin, iron ore and other minerals are also produced. Nevertheless agriculture employs about 40 per cent. of the population. Wheat, maize, high quality coffee, cocoa and sugar are leading crops. Stock-breeding is of great importance. There are valuable forests.

The United States and the Netherlands Antilles are the dominant trading partners. The unit of currency is the Bolivar.

VIETNAM

REPUBLIC

Since the Geneva Conference of 1954, Vietnam has been virtually two countries: the Northern Zone (63,000 square miles) being a "People's Republic," the Southern Zone (66,000 square miles) being the Republic of Vietnam. The capital of the former is Hanoi; and of the latter, Saigon. Reunification is presumably dependent on the general elections called for by the Geneva conference (still to be held).

Northern Vietnam is mountainous, and most of its people live on the coastal plain and the delta of the Red River. The chief feature of Southern Vietnam is the extremely fertile valley of the Mekong River. The country has a tropical monsoon climate.

Population: *Northern Zone;* estimated at 13,000,000. Hanoi has about 298,000 inhabitants. *Southern Zone;* estimated at 12,000,000, this figure almost certainly includes a large number of refugees from the north. Saigon-Cholon has about 1,800,000 inhabitants. The Annamite and Siamese languages are used; Taoism and Buddhism are the main religions.

Production and Trade: Agriculture is the main activity, large crops of rice being grown in both north and south. Rubber is an important product of the south; coal, of the north. Other southern products include tea, cinnamon, quinine, coffee and timber. Coffee, tea, tobacco and sweet potatoes are grown in the north.

France is the leading trade partner of the Southern Zone. China and other Soviet countries predominate in the trade of the Northern Zone. The unit of currency in the Southern Zone is the Piastre; in the Northern Zone, the Vietminh piastre, or Dong.

WALES

See UNITED KINGDOM.

THE WEST INDIES

FEDERATION

The Federation of The West Indies came formally into existence on January 3rd, 1958.

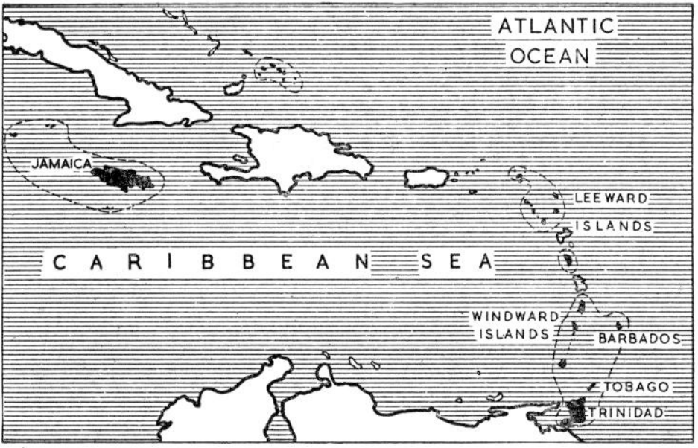

The Federation, which is in the Commonwealth, consists of the following: (1) Jamaica; (2) Trinidad and Tobago; (3) Barbados; (4) Antigua, St. Kitts-Nevis-Anguilla, Montserrat—colonies of the Leeward Islands (*q.v.*); the Virgin Islands elected to remain outside the Federation; (5) Grenada, St. Vincent, St. Lucia, Dominica, *i.e.*, the islands of the Windward group (*q.v.*).

Trinidad was chosen as the seat of government but the site for the capital has still to be decided.

Population: The total population of the widely-scattered islands forming the Federation is about 3,000,000, and is multi-racial

(African, Carib, Chinese, East Indian and European). The following table shows the area and population of each federating unit.

	Area (sq. miles)	*Estimated Population*
Antigua (including Barbuda and Redonda) . .	171	54,228
Barbados . . .	166	229,100
Dominica . . .	305	64,415
Grenada . . .	133	89,068
Jamaica . . .	4,411	1,580,000
Montserrat . . .	33	14,321
St. Kitts-Nevis-Anguilla .	168	55,335
St. Lucia . . .	238	89,262
St. Vincent . . .	150	78,594
Trinidad and Tobago .	1,864	742,500
Totals	7,639	2,996,823

British territories in the area which remain outside the Federation are: the Bahamas, British Honduras, British Guiana and the British Virgin Islands.

WINDWARD ISLANDS

BRITISH COLONIES

This group in the Federation of the West Indies has a total area of some 826 square miles and comprises the colonies of Grenada, St. Vincent, St. Lucia and Dominica; responsibility for the Grenadines is shared between St. Vincent and Grenada. St. George's, the chief town of Grenada, is the normal residence of the Governor. The total population numbers more than 321,000. The chief products are cocoa, spices, copra, cotton, sugar and rum. The unit of currency is the ECT dollar.

YEMEN

MONARCHY

This country of south-west Arabia has an estimated area of 75,000 square miles and an Arabic-speaking population numbering about 4,500,000. The capitals are San'a and Tai'zz. The country is mostly fertile plateau and is noted for its coffee (exported from Hodeida). Hides, raisins and dates are also exported.

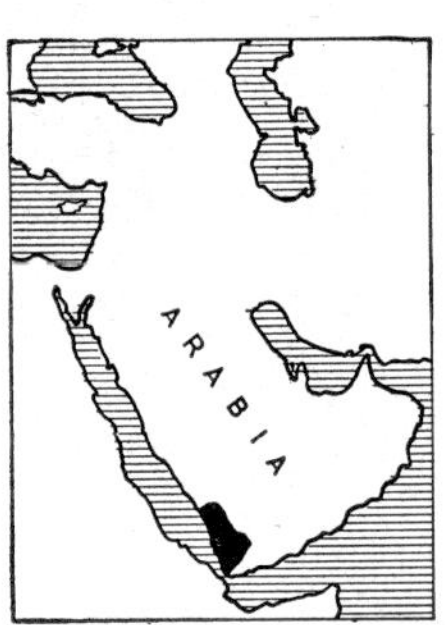

On March 8th, 1958, the Yemen federated with the United Arab Republic (*q.v.*) to form the United Arab States.

YUGOSLAVIA

FEDERAL REPUBLIC

Yugoslavia has an area of some 99,000 square miles and is a federation of the following units: Serbia (including Vojvodina, Kosovo and Metohija), Croatia, Slovenia, Montenegro, Bosnia and Hercegovina, and Macedonia. The north-west of this Balkan country is well forested and has numerous lakes; the north-east contains the fertile plain of the River Danube; the south is mountainous. Hot summers and cold winters are usual in the north, but the Adriatic coast has a Mediterranean climate.

Population: 18,234,000 Serbs, Croats, Slovenes, Macedonians and Montenegrins; and including Albanian, Magyar, Rumanian and other minorities. The languages of the country are Serbo-Croat (the most common), Slovenian and Macedonian. Nearly half the population belongs to the Orthodox Church, about 37 per cent. are Roman Catholic, and there are also Protestant, Islamic and Jewish communities. Belgrade, the capital, has 522,000 inhabitants. Other important centres include Zagreb (350,400), Ljubljana (138,000), and Sarajevo (136,000).

Production and Trade: The country is largely agricultural (peasant co-operatives), although there has been much industrial development recently. Wheat and maize are the most important crops and there is considerable stock-breeding. Mineral wealth is plentiful and includes coal, copper and iron.

Timber, lead and copper ore, fruit, tobacco and livestock are exported. Textiles, manufactures and machinery are the chief imports. The United States, U.S.S.R., United Kingdom, Italy and Western Germany are important trading partners. The unit of currency is the Dinar.

ZANZIBAR

SULTANATE (BRITISH PROTECTORATE)

This comprises the islands of Zanzibar and Pemba, with their dependencies, the total area being about 1,020 square miles. The population numbers about 264,100 and includes some 45,000 Arabs, 200,000 Africans and 16,000 Indians. Zanzibar town, the capital, has about 45,300 inhabitants. Most of the people are Moslems. By far the greater part of the world's supply of cloves comes from Zanzibar and Pemba. The unit of currency is the East African shilling.

GLOSSARY OF GEOGRAPHICAL TERMS

Aborigines. People believed to be the original inhabitants of a region or found there when it was discovered, *e.g.*, the " Blackfellows " of Australia.

Abrasion. The wearing away of rocks by the action of water, wind (carrying sand particles) or ice.

Adret. A mountain slope facing towards the equator and so often a hollow sun-trap. The term is used principally of the Alps.

Æolian Deposits. Rock particles which have been transported by the wind, *e.g.*, the sand-dunes and the loess soils of China.

Air Pressure, or Atmospheric Pressure. Air is a gas and has weight which is its pressure. This is greatest at sea level and least on the tops of the highest mountains. Air pressure varies continuously through the effect of heat or cold and these variations give rise to the winds (the movement of air from high pressure regions to low pressure regions). At sea level the pressure is about 15 lbs. to the square inch. It can be measured by a barometer; and since it decreases as height becomes greater, it provides a means of measuring altitude. At sea level, the pressure is equal to approximately 30 in. on a mercury barometer. The rate of decrease for each 1,000 ft. of ascent is about 1 in., but this rate itself decreases at higher altitudes.

Alluvial Fan or Cone. Sediment deposited by a river where it suddenly enters a plain (and so loses its speed). A large fan or cone formed by several adjoining streams or rivers is known as a *Piedmont Alluvial Plain.*

Alluvial Plain. A level area formed by the deposition of alluvium (*q.v.*) along the lower reaches of a river.

Alluvium. Sand, silt, clay or mud carried by fast-flowing streams and rivers from harder, higher ground and laid down when the stream slows down at lower levels, to form fertile flood-plains, river-flats and, on reaching a lake or the sea, deltas.

Alps. The collective name for one of the greatest mountain masses in Europe centred mainly in Switzerland, but extending also into France, Italy, Austria and Germany. In the Alps is Mont Blanc (15,781 ft.), the highest mountain in W. Europe. The word *Alp* is used by Swiss farmers to describe a summer pasture on the flatter shelves of the mountain slopes, to which they take their cattle when the snows melt. The term has also been adopted in other parts of the world, where it is used to describe great mountain masses, *e.g.*, the Australian Alps.

Altitude. Another word for height. Used chiefly in respect of high land (measured vertically from mean sea level) or of levels of the atmosphere (above the horizon).

Antarctic Circle. The line of latitude 66° 30′ South which bounds the Antarctic regions around the South Pole. Seasonal conditions are the opposite of those prevailing within the Arctic Circle (*q.v.*), *e.g.*, the Antarctic midsummer occurs about December 22nd, which is the Arctic midwinter. The nearer one approaches to the Pole, the longer are the winter nights, the shorter the winter days. At the Pole itself, the winter night lasts for some six months. The summer day is equally long, although at no time is the Sun more than 23½° above the horizon.

Anticline. Rock bent upwards into a

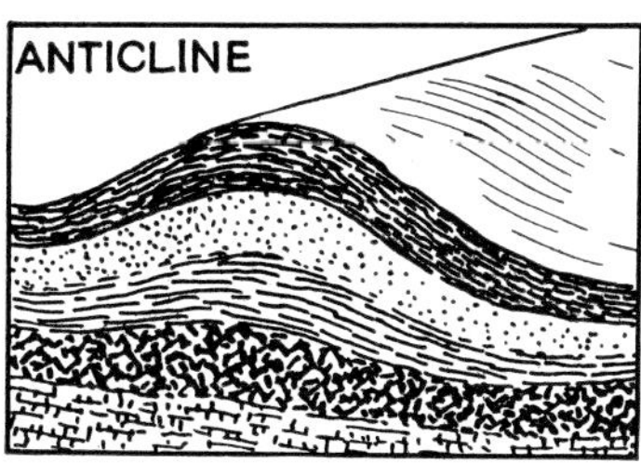

long saddle-shaped structure, the older rocks remaining in their position. When the rocks are pushed up into a mound shape, it is called a *Dome.* An *Anticlinorum* is an anticline in which the rocks have numerous secondary folds as well.

Anticyclone. An area in which air pressure is higher than in surrounding areas. The isobars (or lines of equal pressure) are usually circular or oval in shape, those of highest pressure being within and at the centre. Winds therefore move outwards from an anticyclone into areas of lower pressure. These winds blow clockwise around the anticyclone in the Northern Hemisphere and anti-clockwise in the Southern and are thus deflected owing to the rotation of the Earth. The weather in areas covered by an anticyclone is usually sunny and fine, yet sometimes foggy. The Horse Latitudes (*q.v.*) are permanent anticyclonic belts.

Antipodes. Places on the globe in exact opposition to each other. London, England and Antipodes Island to the south-east of New Zealand are almost exact antipodes to each other, *i.e.*, 180° of longitude apart and equidistant from the Equator. Antipodes are opposites also in day and night and summer and winter. The word means " feet opposite."

Anti-trades. The name given to the westerly winds which prevail in the belt north of the tropical belt of high pressure in the Northern Hemisphere, and south of the tropical belt of high pressure in the Southern. Their direction is opposite that of the respective Trade Winds (*q.v.*) and they are sometimes called *Counter-Trades.*

Archipelago. An island-studded sea, after the name once given to the Aegean Sea between Greece and Asia Minor, and hence a group of islands.

Arctic Circle. The line of latitude 66° 30′ North which bounds the Arctic regions around the North Pole. Seasonal conditions are the opposite of those prevailing within the Antarctic Circle (*q.v.*), *e.g.*, the Arctic midsummer occurs about June 21st, which is the Antarctic midwinter. The nearer one gets to the Pole, the longer are the winter nights, the shorter the winter days. At the Pole itself, the winter night lasts for some six months. The summer day is equally long, although the Sun is never more than 23½° above the horizon.

Artesian Well. More than merely a deep well. It taps water in permeable rock sandwiched between two impermeable layers of a syncline. Thus when the boring reaches the water which is under pressure (the level of the well-top being below the topmost level of the source of the water) the water rises to the surface without pumping. The first Artesian Wells were sunk at *Artois* in France (hence

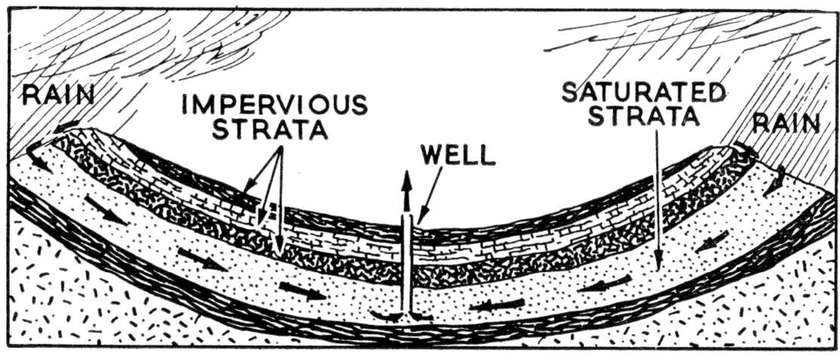

Sectional Diagram of an Artesian Well.

the name). There are large numbers in Australia.

Atmosphere. The layer of air which envelopes the earth. It is a mixture mainly of the gases oxygen (21 per cent.), nitrogen (78 per cent.), argon (1 per cent. nearly) and carbon dioxide (·03 per cent.). There is helium (·01 per cent.) in dry air and water vapour or moisture in varying quantities. Soot and dust are some of the solid impurities in the atmosphere. This envelope of air thins out to almost nothing with increasing height above the surface of the Earth.

Atmospheric Pressure. See *Air Pressure.*

Atoll. A ring-shaped coral reef now above sea-level and found in hot latitudes. Inside is the lagoon, and palm trees often grow on the atoll. A well-known example is Bikini, in the Pacific Ocean, where atomic bombs have been tested.

Aurora Australis. A display of light seen under certain conditions over the south polar regions and corresponding to the *Aurora Borealis* of the Northern Hemisphere.

Aurora Borealis, or **Northern Lights.** A display of light seen under certain conditions over north polar regions. It is caused by an electrical discharge in the atmosphere and is sometimes seen as far south as Britain.

Avalanche. A mass of snow and ice which has accumulated on a mountain side above a valley and becomes detached for some reason, then thunders down causing great damage to villages, trees and roadways and often burying houses and people.

Axis. Similar in meaning to axle but used to describe the imaginary line around which the Earth rotates, at the ends of which are the North and South Poles.

Bad Lands. A high, dry region deeply cut into by the rain of thunderstorms. It does not support vegetation and soil erosion is unchecked. The harder rocks stand up above their surroundings. Named after the Bad Lands of South Dakota, U.S.A.

Bar. A bank of sand and rock often formed across a river mouth or indented bay. It occurs at the slowing down of the river when it enters the sea or when shore currents come into calmer, deeper waters. The solids in suspension are then deposited to form a bar, spit, or *Nehrung.*

Barometer. The instrument by which air or atmospheric pressure is measured. The mercury barometer is 30 in. high and the level is expressed either in inches or millibars. An aneroid barometer registers air pressure by means of a needle set on a sealed metallic box, inside which is a partial vacuum. It is not so accurate as a barometer using liquid.

Barrier Reef. A coral reef which has formed parallel to a shore leaving an expanse of water between it and the mainland, *e.g.*, the Great Barrier Reef of Australia.

Basin. The area which is drained by a river and all its tributaries, or other large hollows in the Earth's surface, *e.g.*, the Thames Basin. The term is also used in geology to describe the reverse of a dome; that is, when the strata are dipped in the shape of a basin.
See *Anticline.*

Beaufort Scale. This is used to indicate the relative speeds of winds, thus:
No. 0. Calm. Less than 2 miles per hour.
Nos. 1 to 3. Light breezes. 2 to 12 miles per hour.
Nos. 4 to 5. Moderate winds. 13 to 23 miles per hour.
Nos. 6 to 7. Strong winds. 24 to 37 miles per hour.
Nos. 8 to 9. Gale force. 38 to 55 miles per hour.
Nos. 10 to 11. Storms. 56 to 75 miles per hour.
No. 12. Hurricane. Above 75 miles per hour.
The scale was first devised in 1805 for the use of sailing ships, by Admiral Sir Francis Beaufort and has since been adopted internationally.

Bench Mark. A sign used on Ordnance Survey maps. It is a broad arrow, point uppermost against a horizontal bar, and is an indication of altitude.

Bergschrund. The gap often formed where a glacier or icefield parts from the rock at the head of the valley or high hollow in which it has formed. It is also called a *Crevasse* and the French name for it is *Rimaye.*

Bight. A sort of bay which is less deeply indented into the land, curves more gently and is of greater extent than the usual bay, *e.g.*, the Bight of Benin in West Africa, the Great Australian Bight.

Bise. A cold, drying northerly wind that sometimes blows in Switzerland and southern France. It often carries heavy clouds with it.

Block Mountains. Mountains formed when the strata fracture in straightish lines; faults occur, and then parts are pushed up or others let down so that block-like mountain masses are formed above the surrounding land. These, of course, suffer from erosion by the weather; but their flattish tops can usually be discerned. An example in Britain is the Pennine Chain.

BLOCK MOUNTAIN

Bog. A soft, peaty hollow, badly drained by rivers, in which vegetation, mainly mosses, has accumulated over the years. A bog is often formed in what was once a shallow lake. A well-known example is the Bog of Allan in Ireland.

Bora. The dry, cold northerly or north-easterly wind which blows in northern Italy and in the Adriatic Sea and on its eastern shores in winter. It usually occurs when there is high air pressure over the continent of Europe and low pressure over the Mediterranean Sea. It sometimes reaches No. 12 on the Beaufort Scale (*q.v.*).

Bore. The wall-like edge of the tide wave entering some rapidly narrowing estuary or gulf where it meets shallow water or advancing river water as well. Well-known examples are the Bores of the estuaries of the Severn (England), the Seine (France), the Yangtse-Kiang (China), and the Hooghly (India). There is also a noted bore in the narrow Bay of Fundy (Canada). Other names for a bore are *Eagre* or *Eger.*

Boulder Clay. The material, or "ground moraines," which was dragged along the underside of a glacier and left there when the glacier melted. It is often finely ground in places to form a clay, but usually also contains masses of unsorted stones. See *Glacier.*

Bourne. A seasonal stream which flows intermittently in wet weather and is usually found in limestone or chalk areas, so that when the flow is small the water drains through and proceeds underground. Bournes have given their names to several places in England, *e.g.*, Sittingbourne and Hollingbourne in Kent, and Bournemouth in Hampshire.

Broad. A wide sheet of water formed in the course of a slow-moving river in flat country, *e.g.*, the Norfolk Broads.

Buran. A winter wind of Siberia and Central Asia, often reaching gale force, which blows from the north or north-east. It brings with it sharp particles of ice and snow just like the *Blizzard* of Canada and the Polar Regions. The summer north-easterly is also called the Buran, and to distinguish it the winter Buran is sometimes called the *Purga.*

Bush. A region still covered with forest or scrub which has not been cultivated. The term also is used for wildernesses or any rough region even without many trees. The name is most common in Australia, New Zealand and South Africa.

Butte. A hill, usually flat on the top, produced where a cap of harder rock has protected softer layers below it so that erosion has left the hill standing well above the surrounding country. It is pronounced like *beaut* in *beauty.* See also *Mesa.*

Canal. A man-made waterway for ships and barges linking important towns or rivers, or by-passing rapids on a navigable river. Changes of level along a canal are effected by locks. The most famous canals in the world are Suez and Panama. Notable canals in the United Kingdom include the Manchester Ship

S.C.R.

At one time it was thought that there could never be any agriculture in the Arctic. But at Igarka and other small Siberian towns along the Arctic Circle (*q.v.*) methods of " Polar agriculture " have been successfully developed, and crops of grain and vegetables are being grown from special seed. Similar small-scale experiments were tried in Antarctica by the Soviet scientists there during the International Geophysical Year (July, 1957—December, 1958).

Irish Tourist Board.

Bogs (*q.v.*) are numerous in Ireland; in fact, there are no fewer than two and a half million acres of peat in the Irish Republic alone. The picture shows a typical peat bog in County Kerry. Stacked peat from the cuttings in the foreground is being removed by pony cart for use as fuel. Peat fuel is also used in certain of the electricity generating stations and the bogs are being reclaimed for agriculture.

Canal and the Forth and Clyde Canal. Canals are sometimes built for irrigation.

Canyon or **Cañon.** A gorge cut by a river deep into the soft rocks, usually in an arid region where the sparse rainfall is insufficient to cause the extensive denudation or wearing down of the precipitous walls. The best known example is the Grand Canyon of the Colorado river, U.S.A.

Cape. Land on the coast that projects out into the sea. If it is high it is sometimes called a head, headland, promontory, ness (or nose), bill or foreland.

Cardinal Points. North, South, East and West, the four chief points of the compass.

Cataract. A waterfall which comes down in successive steps, *e.g.*, the Cataracts of the Nile, the Cataract of Lodore. A small cataract is called a cascade.

Catchment Area. Similar to a basin, it is the area whose rain drains into one river system or lake. Its boundaries are watersheds or water partings.

Cave. An opening in the rocks of the Earth's crust. Caves are commonest in limestone rock where, in course of time, percolating water has dissolved the rock away.

Channel. A river bed; the deep-water route into a harbour or along an estuary; or, like the English Channel, a narrow belt of water joining two larger areas of sea.

Chinook. A westerly wind which blows over the prairies of western Canada and the United States. It is of *Föhn* type, dry and warm, having lost its bulk of moisture on the way over the Rocky Mountains and been raised in temperature through compression during its descent to the plains. In early spring this wind can raise the temperature of a place 30° to 40° F. in less than half an hour and, being so warm and dry, it can melt the snows of the winter very quickly, thus enabling cattle to graze and early wheat to be sown.

Cirrus Clouds. See *Clouds.*

Climate. The general weather conditions of a region taken over the year. Weather is the particular occurrence at any specific time, while climate is the average of all such occurrences. The climate of a region is determined by its latitude or distance from the Equator, its elevation, its nearness to the sea, whether it is near the western or the eastern margins of a land mass, its prevailing winds and whether it is far within a continent or not. Local variations may be caused by the shelter of mountains, the collection of cold or damp air in hollows and other factors. See *Weather.*

Clouds. The familiar masses of water vapour, water or ice particles seen in our skies. They are formed by the evaporation of water on the Earth's surface which returns to Earth again, usually elsewhere, in the form of rain, hail, sleet or snow. Clouds rise to great heights or they may touch the ground as mists or fogs. Low clouds are those up to about 8,000 ft., medium clouds 8,000–15,000 ft., and high clouds above this level. Clouds take many forms or shapes:

Cumulus—white and billowing, often rising in the sky.

Cirrus—high feathery wisps in a long mass, yet separate.

Nimbus—heavy black or dark grey rain clouds.

Stratus—layers of grey cloud rather low in the sky.

And there are, of course, various combinations of these types. See pictures on pp. 204 and 205.

Col. The saddle-shaped gap or pass in a range of hills at the watershed where the head-waters of rivers on either side have cut back almost to meet each other, and so lower the level at this point. The term is also used in weather reports for areas between two anticyclones or two cyclones.

Cold Front. The line of the surface of the Earth where a mass of advancing colder air meets one of warmer air and, being denser and heavier, displaces or pushes the warmer (and therefore less dense) air up to higher levels. Here the warmer air is cooled and its moisture becomes cloud or rain.

Compass, Magnetic. An instrument in which a needle swings to point to the north Magnetic Pole. Tables of

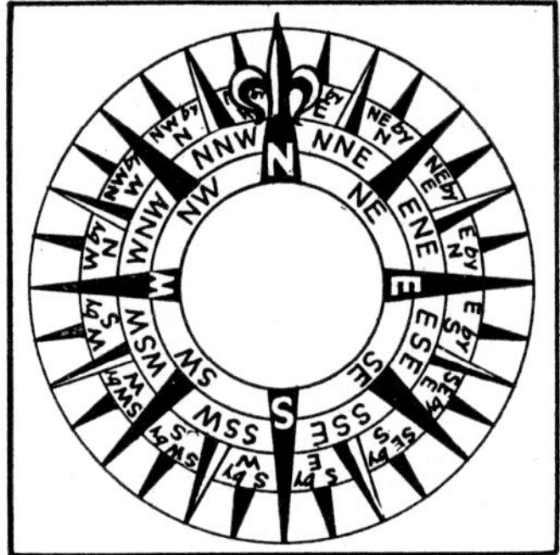

corrections for various longitudes are applied to obtain the correct reading for the Geographical or True Pole. The compass card is divided into thirty-two divisions which indicate directions away from the north.

Confluence. The point where two streams join. Each stream is thus a confluent.

Coniferous Forest. Forests of cone-bearing trees like pines, larches, firs and so on. Their leaves are needle-shaped and, except for the larch, the trees are evergreen. These forests are found in the colder parts of the Temperate Zones, such as northern Canada and Siberia, and on higher land in warmer latitudes, such as on the Alps and the Rockies. They form the most valuable sources in the world for soft woods for timber and wood-pulp for paper-making.

Continent. One of the five great portions of the land mass of the world, *i.e.*, Europe, Asia, Africa, America and Australia. Sometimes the land mass around the South Pole, Antarctica, is called "the seventh continent," while North and South America are often regarded as two. In the United Kingdom the phrase "the Continent" is usually taken to mean Europe.

Continental Drift. The name of the theory first put forward by Wegener that the continents once formed one joint land mass on the surface of the globe. They then broke apart and drifted into their present positions. Evidence to support the theory is found, for example, in the way that Africa seems to fit into the opposite coast of South America.

Continental Shelf. The sea bed on the edge of the continents up to about 100 fathoms in depth. This may be narrow and sloping rapidly to 100 fathoms, or it may be up to 100 miles in width with a gentle slope from the land. Beyond the edge of the Continental Shelf the sea bed plunges down to far greater depths. The Continental Shelf, with the lower levels of the continents themselves, forms what is known as the Continental Platform.

Contour. The line on a map or plan which joins places of equal altitude or height above sea level. The interval of altitude may range from perhaps 50 ft. on a large-scale map to thousands of feet on the small-scale map. Sometimes the area between the contours is coloured from shades of green in the lowlands to browns in the uplands, all deepening in tone with increase in height, and then, for lands of even greater altitude, to red and, lastly, white. Contours can also be used to show depths of the sea bed; in this case deepening shades of blue are often used.

Convection Currents. Convection relates to the movement of heat from one part of a gas or liquid to another. When the lower portion of a gas or liquid is heated, it expands and is reduced in density so that the cold or denser part displaces it upwards. Thus air heated at the Earth's surface moves upwards, this movement being a convection current. In tropical regions the displaced air is cooled so much as it rises to higher altitudes, and moves so suddenly, that its moisture falls in heavy *Convectional Rains.* See also *Monsoon.*

Coral. The coral polyp is a small creature which inhabits hot tropical seas at certain shallow depths and temperatures. Its skeleton is made of lime extracted from the sea water; and when the polyp dies the skeleton remains as coral "rock." It is the build-up of millions of coral polyp skeletons that creates coral islands and reefs, the most famous of which is the Great Barrier Reef of Australia. See also *Atoll* and *Barrier Reef.*

Cordillera. Mountain ranges, roughly parallel, grouped into one long system, *e.g.*, the Andes of South and the Rockies of North America.

Corrie. A chair-shaped hollow formed in a mountain side by ice action. Corries often have lakes left in the "seat" of the chair, with moraines

A SNO-CAT IN PERIL

British Commonwealth Trans-Antarctic Expedition.

Crevasses (*q.v.*) were among the hazards encountered by the British Commonwealth Trans-Antarctic Expedition during the memorable crossing of the " Seventh Continent." Spanning the crevasse and partly submerged in snow, this Sno-Cat was eventually hauled to safety by other tractors in the expedition. Five of the eight vehicles with which Sir Vivian Fuchs left Shackleton Base reached the Pole and four (all Sno-Cats) completed the 2,200-mile journey to Scott Base.

Polar Photos.

The calm waters of this by-pass canal (*q.v.*) are a sharp contrast to the angry rapids (*q.v.*) at Long Sault on the St. Lawrence River in Canada. More canals of this type have been made to form the St. Lawrence Seaway (see overleaf). When this is complete Toronto and not Montreal will be the head of ocean navigation on this important river.

THE ST. LAWRENCE SEAWAY

INTERNATIONAL RAPIDS SECTION

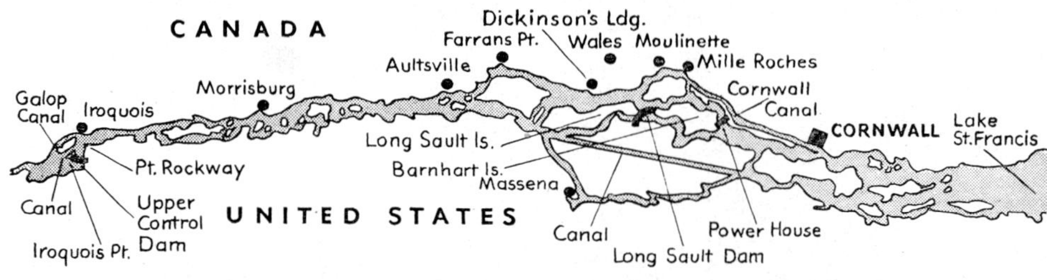

SOULANGES AND LACHINE SECTION

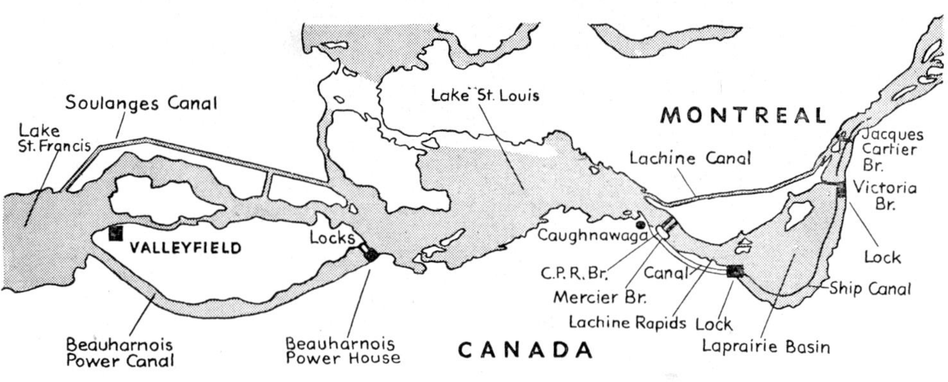

WATER LEVEL PROFILE OF THE GREAT LAKES AND ST. LAWRENCE DEEP WATERWAY

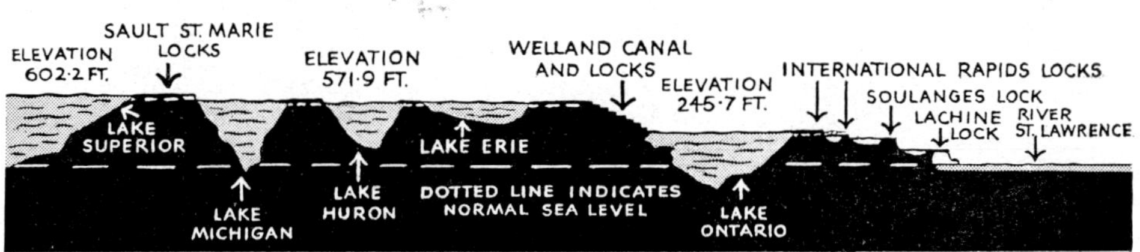

These diagrams show how clever engineering has made the St. Lawrence Seaway, a route for ocean-going ships from the Atlantic to the heart of the North American continent. Canals (*q.v.*) provide a way round the various rapids, locks overcome the differences in the levels of the Great Lakes and the St. Lawrence River. The drops in water-level form a means of creating hydro-electric power. At Barnhart Island, for example, in the International Rapids Section, the drop in water-level of about 90 feet will be used to provide about 2,200,000 horse power for Canada and the United States jointly. The power production will also be increased at Beauharnois, in the Soulanges and Lachine Section, and about 1,200,000 horse power will be available for the Montreal industrial area. This seaway/hydro-electric power project is a joint Canadian and American undertaking.

FROM OCEAN TO GREAT LAKES

The pictures on this page show sections of the St. Lawrence Seaway during construction. This aerial view shows (right foreground) the bridge linking Barnhart Island with the American bank of the river and, beyond, the curving Long Sault Dam. On the left (foreground) are the Eisenhower Lock and Long Sault Canal.

Photos: Planet News

Here we are looking downstream in the International Rapids Section, where a dyke has been built round a large area of Toussaint's Island (foreground) for the land to be excavated to below water-level, to allow the passage of ocean-going ships. In the background can be seen the Iroquois Dam and by-pass canal and lock.

in front. They are also called *Cirques*.

Crater. The opening at the top of a volcano through which the lava, smoke, fumes and other erupted material escape. The crater is usually in the form of a hollow cone or funnel. See *Volcano*.

Crevasse. A deep crack worn through and usually across the ice of a glacier, which forms when there are changes of level in the valley floor, or of direction of the glacier. When it forms where the glacier becomes detached from the rock slope at the head of the valley, it is also called a *Bergschrund*.

Cumulus Clouds. See *Clouds*.

Cyclone. Now usually called a *depression* in the weather reports. It is an area of low atmospheric or air pressure with the isobar figures lowest on the inner side of the depression. Winds blow inwards towards a cyclone, anti-clockwise in the Northern Hemisphere and clockwise in the Southern. Contrast this with the anticyclone. When cyclones or depressions approach land from over the sea, they usually bring rain.

The term "cyclone" is now more often given to a *tropical cyclone*, which covers a smaller area, and with more steeply-graded falls in air pressure. This means very violent winds around the cyclone as it moves quickly over the surface of the land or sea.

Date Line. The International Date Line, fixed by international agreement and following the meridian of 180° (except for certain detours made to accommodate island groups such as the Aleutians), determines where one day begins and another ends according to its date, and so compensates for the time lost or gained (one hour per 15°) when travelling round the world. See map on pp. 228 and 229.

Datum Level. The mean or average level of the sea from which all heights are measured and stated. In the case of the British Isles, the datum level on Ordnance Survey Maps is the mean sea level at Newlyn in Cornwall.

Deciduous Forest. Forests in which most of the trees drop their leaves once a year. In the temperate or cooler regions this takes place in the autumn, or the "Fall," as a defence against the cold of winter. Monsoon forests in wet tropical regions are deciduous in the hot season to avoid excessive loss of water by evaporation from the leaves.

Defile. A gorge, ravine or steep-sided valley.

Degree. The measuring unit of temperature, latitude and longitude.

Delta. The fan-shaped alluvial tract formed at the mouth of a river when it deposits more alluvial material there than can be removed by tides or other currents. The name was first applied to the delta of the Nile by the Greeks, since the fan-shaped deposits resembled their letter D (or delta, Δ). One delta often causes a number of smaller ones fanning out towards the open water. A good example of this is the delta of the river Congo.

Denudation. The work done by the sea, frost, rain, ice, wind, heat and water in wearing away the rocks which form the land surface of the earth.

Deposition. The opposite of denudation, that is the carrying away of particles of rock by wind or water or ice and laying them down or "depositing" them elsewhere.

Depression. See *Cyclone*.

Desert. A rainless or almost rainless area which may be in hot or cold regions. Because of the lack of rain, vegetation may be absent or scarce. Deserts may be (1) of rock type where the wind has carried away the soil and sand particles and laid bare the rock; (2) stony deserts where the rock surface has been broken up by temperature changes and the ground covered by the fragments; (3) sandy deserts where the land is covered by sand plains and dunes. See also *Oasis*.

Detritus. Fragments broken off the larger rocks by the action of rain, frost and heat.

Dew. The moisture formed and deposited on the earth's surface when the land cools rapidly on a calm clear night and so lowers the temperature of the air in contact with it that water vapour in suspension is condensed and forms on grass or under stones. The dew point is the temperature at which in any particular situation the air becomes saturated and dew is deposited.

Diatom Ooze. A slimy deposit on a deep, cold ocean bed, formed of dead siliceous plants.

Dike. See *Dyke*.

Dip. The slope of a bed of rock inclined from the horizontal. Dip may also mean the angle between the direction of the Earth's magnetic field and the horizontal at a point on the Earth's surface.

Displacement Theory. See *Continental Drift*.

Dissected Plateau. A mass of high land once levelled by erosion and now cut into by river valleys of later formation.

Doldrums. A belt of low atmospheric pressure in equatorial regions where the north-east and south-east Trade Winds converge on each other and move upwards so as to cause a calm. The Doldrums move north and south about 5°, slowly following the Sun, and are subject to occasional violent storms. See also *Wind*.

Dolmen. A very large horizontal stone resting on three or more upright ones. Dolmens were erected, usually as tombs, by Neolithic man. Also known as a *Cromlech*.

Dolomite. A rock composed of calcium and magnesium carbonate. This rock is found especially in the Dolomites and mountains on the eastern shores of the Adriatic Sea.

Down. An area of open, almost treeless hills, mainly used as sheep pasture. The chalk downs of south-east England are a good example.

Drowned Valley. An inlet of the sea or a lake formed by the land sinking and the water filling what had previously been a valley.

Drumlin. An oval-shaped hill, or ridge, of boulder clay. Drumlins are usually found lying in large numbers along the path cut by a glacier a long time ago.

Dry Farming. A method of farming, without irrigation, in an area of low rainfall. The land is usually treated to prevent excessive evaporation of moisture from the ground. The term is mostly applied to arable farming.

Dry Valley. A valley without a river or stream except, perhaps, in extremely wet weather. A dry valley is usually found in porous limestone or chalk rock or may have been caused by river capture (*q.v.*).

Dune. A sand hillock in a sand desert or on a sandy shore which has been formed by the movement of large masses of sand by the wind. Plants and trees of a suitable kind are often sowed to prevent further movement of sand dunes over fertile land.

Dyke, or Dike. A sheet of vertical igneous rock formed long ago when molten material forced its way up from the interior of the Earth, often through fissures, to the surface and there cooled and solidified. Because of its extreme hardness, erosion has not taken place and the rock, therefore, stands above the level of the surrounding, softer, sedimentary rocks. Such a sheet, when horizontal, is called a *sill*. The name is also applied to a long bank of earth and also to a straight drainage ditch.

Eagre. See *Bore*.

Earth. The fifth in size of the nine planets, which with their satellites revolve round the Sun. The greatest distance of the Earth from the Sun is about 93 million miles and the least, 90 million miles. The Earth rotates on its axis once per day and takes nearly 365¼ days to revolve round the Sun, the quarters being included as an extra day in February once every fourth or "leap" year. In shape the Earth is very nearly a sphere, in fact, an "oblate spheroid," which is orange-shaped, pressed in at the North and South Poles—the ends of the axis on which it rotates. The diameter is 7,926·7 miles at the Equator compared with the polar diameter of 7,900 miles. The total area of the Earth is estimated at 196,836,000 square miles of which roughly 56 million square miles are land areas and 141 million square miles are water. The solid surface of the Earth is known as the lithosphere, the water surface as the hydrosphere and the air all around it as the atmosphere.

Earth Pillar. A pillar of earth capped by a larger and harder rock or boulder which has protected the strata immediately below it from the effects of rain erosion. Earth pillars can be seen in the valleys of the Tyrol.

Earthquake. A trembling of the Earth's crust caused by the movement of strata downwards or forwards. Earthquakes are usually

CARVED OUT BY NATURE

H. Armstrong Roberts.

The best known example of a Canyon (*q.v.*) is seen in this picture. It is the Grand Canyon of the Colorado river in the United States. It has a length of about two hundred miles, and its upper section is from five to fifteen miles in width. In places it is a mile deep.

Crown Copyright.

This cave (*q.v.*) is at Watermouth, near Ilfracombe, Devon. It has been eroded along a fault (*q.v.*) by the waves, the soft fault-material being washed out so that a roof has been formed.

Swiss National Tourist Office.

A glacier (*q.v.*) is a " river of ice." The picture shows the Fiescher Glacier, Switzerland, in its descent from the Finsteraarhorn. The dark "tracks" are lateral and medial moraines (*q.v.*).

A SHORT GUIDE—

1. CUMULUS

Cumulus clouds, as the picture shows, resemble heavyish blobs of cotton-wool with flat bases. They surmount ascending convection currents formed by the warming of air near the earth's surface. With other types of Low Cloud, *e.g.*, nimbostratus, stratus and stratocumulus, they are found at heights up to 10,000 feet, but usually below 7,000 feet.

2. CUMULONIMBUS

These are large cumulus clouds whose tops have frozen. Some of the ice crystals develop into hail and rain, and the remainder spread out into a crown of snow which gives the cloud an anvil shape. Cumulonimbus reaches a greater height than cumulus cloud and often brings with it thunder and lightning.

3. STRATOCUMULUS

This is fair weather cloud of small thickness which may spread over hundreds of miles of sky. Such cloud is maintained by turbulent mixing in moving air-streams and heat-exchanges by radiation. Compare this picture with Nos. 6 and 7 on the opposite page. Altocumulus is really a higher and lighter form of stratocumulus.

4. NIMBOSTRATUS

This name is given to any extensive layer cloud from which rain or snow falls. The layer is usually at least several thousands of feet thick and hangs low and threatening in the sky.

5. STRATUS

This is the lowest type of cloud. It is formed when damp air is chilled near the earth's surface. It often covers small hills, but a little wind prevents it from resting on the lower ground. Climbers and hikers have good cause to dislike this type of cloud and the persistent fog or drizzle which it often brings.

—TO CLOUDY SKIES

6. ALTOCUMULUS

Altocumulus and Altostratus are medium-level clouds, found at heights between about 1½ and 4 miles. The Altocumulus seen here is in globular cloudlets which are due to a pattern of convection currents in a shallow layer of air. Cloud of this type is often seen in the early morning and late evening in summer.

7. ALTOCUMULUS

Here the size of the individual clouds suggests that they lie low in the medium-cloud zone, and they might equally well be called high strato-cumulus. Compare with picture No. 3 on the previous page.

8. ALTOCUMULUS CASTELLATUS

These medium-level clouds reveal instability in the upper air and are often the heralds of thundery weather. They are also known as " turret clouds," and are here seen quickly growing upwards into cumuliform towers.

9. ALTOSTRATUS

These veil-like, detailless clouds are composed of ice crystals or snow and usually soon thicken into rain-clouds. They are formed by widespread slow ascent of air near depressions and give this typically " watery sky " effect.

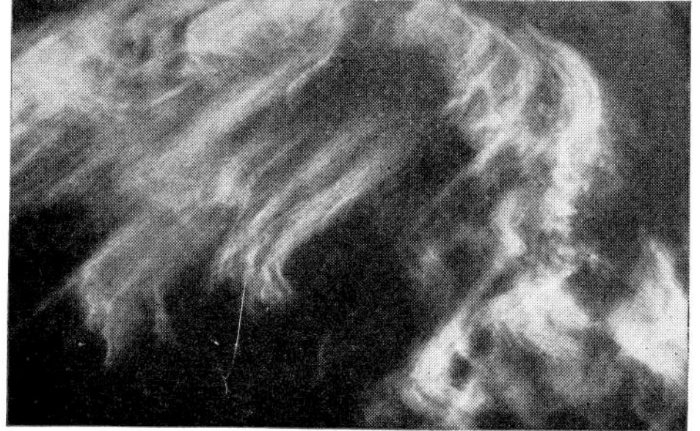

10. CIRRUS

These plumed and whispy clouds are found at heights which usually exceed four miles and at which the temperature is invariably below freezing-point. The cloud is thus composed of ice crystals, formed by the wind into " Mares' Tails " that are often the first sign of approaching storms. This series of pictures is from the Clarke Collection and is reproduced by permission of the Royal Meteorological Society.

commonest in areas of volcanic activity and these areas are often along lines of weakness in the Earth's crust. See also *Fault*.

Eclipse. The cutting off, or obscuring, of the light of the Sun or of the Moon by the occasional intervention of some heavenly body, the Moon between Earth and the Sun for a *Solar Eclipse*, and the Earth itself between the Moon and the Sun for a *Lunar eclipse*. The light of the Moon is, of course, reflected sunlight. Eclipses may be *partial* or *total*.

Ecliptic. The annual path of the Sun through space as seen from the Earth. Actually it is the Earth that moves round the Sun and not *vice versa*, and the ecliptic is only the *apparent* track.

Elevation. A raised portion of the Earth's surface, or the raising of a part of the Earth's crust in relation to the rest. (See also *Subsidence*.) The term is also used to express the height or altitude, expressed usually in degrees, of an object above a lower ground level or of a heavenly body above the horizon.

Enclave. An area belonging to one country or region outlying from it and surrounded, or almost surrounded, by the territory of another.

Entrepôt. Usually a seaport or great market centre to which goods are brought from a wide area for redistribution. Examples are London, Hong Kong, and Singapore.

Equator. The imaginary line around the circumference of the globe, midway between the North and South Poles. It is a " Great Circle " which is set at right angles to the axis of the Earth and its centre is also the centre of the sphere which is the Earth. From the Equator, latitudes north and south are calculated.

Equatorial Calms. See *Doldrums*.

Equatorial Forests. These grow in regions of heavy and continuous rainfall around the Equatorial belt. The great heat of the Sun causes air movements which displace the warm air of these areas rapidly upwards causing it to be cooled and so to lose its moisture in frequent torrential rains. The heat, intense sunlight and the heavy rainfall give rise to dense and luxuriant Tropical Forests.

Equatorial Rains. See *Equatorial Forests*.

Equinox. The time, occurring twice in each year, when all places on the Earth have equal days and nights and the Sun appears vertically overhead at all places on the Equator. The Spring or *Vernal* Equinox is about March 21st and the Autumnal Equinox about September 22nd.

Equipluve. The line on a map joining places of equivalent rainfall—usually expressing monthly totals. Compare with *Isotherm*, *Isobar*.

Erg. The sandy areas in the Sahara Desert.

Erosion. The action of water, ice, wind, heat and cold in wearing away the rocks forming the Earth's surface.

Erratic. A rock transported from its source by a glacier and, when the glacier melted, left stranded often on a different type of rock.

Escarpment. The steeply inclined edge of a tilted stratum or rock bed which appears high above the surrounding countryside. Usually this rock slopes away more gradually on the opposite side to the escarpment. A good example is the western edge of the Cotswolds. See also *Dip* and *Strike*.

Esker. The bed of a river which once flowed beneath a glacier and which now appears as a long narrow ridge of sand or gravel. The Scandinavians call it an *Asar*.

Estuary. The wide mouth of a river and sometimes the " Drowned Valley " part of its lower course. Estuaries are tidal and often decide the situation of great seaports. An example is London which stands almost at the head of the tidal waters of the Thames, sixty miles from the open sea.

Etesian Winds. Northerly and constant, dry summer winds of the eastern Mediterranean Sea: also known as *Meltemi*.

Evaporation. The changing of water from a liquid into water vapour held in suspension in the air. Evaporation is constantly going on over water surfaces and wet areas. Thus clouds are formed and the winds carry the moisture to fall later as rain.

Exfoliation. The weathering of rock surfaces by the peeling off of layers. This is usually caused by the expansion of the rock surface in the Sun's heat during the day and its contraction in the clear, cold night. Ice and running water sometimes have the same kind of effect.

Fall Line. The line joining the waterfalls on a number of rivers which run approximately parallel to one another. Along the Fall Line the rivers leave the uplands for the lowlands. The term is especially applied to the line running along the sudden increase of slope (where the waterfalls occur) from the Atlantic coastal plain in the eastern U.S.A. to the Appalachian Mountains. There are also many Fall Lines in Africa.

Fault. A fracture in the rock beds forming the Earth's crust. It is generally vertical but may incline in one direction or the other. Where two faults, roughly parallel, cause the subsidence of a long area of the rock bed, this may form a Rift Valley like that of the Dead Sea area. Faults mean that the rocks on one side of the fracture do not match those on the other and these changes of level may be small or very considerable. Faults occur in areas of *folding* and *thrust* of subterranean volcanic disturbances. See *Escarpment* and *Rift Valley*.

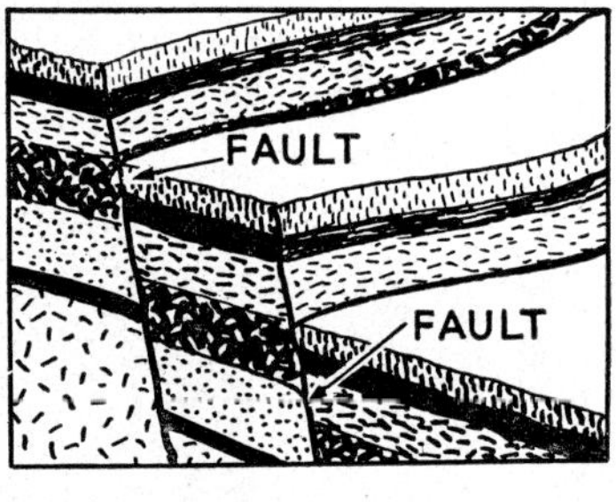

Fell. A high, bare hillside which is uncultivated and generally grazed by sheep. This is a term used particularly in the Lake District of England.

Fen. An area of marshland, low lying usually such as that around the Wash in eastern England. Drained, the alluvium of fenlands is often highly fertile.

Firth. Not unlike a fjord (*q.v.*) but usually less steep-sided. This is a Scottish term.

Fjord (*pron.* Fee-ord). A narrow drowned valley with steep sides. Such valleys were usually deepened and straightened somewhat by glaciers in one of the Ice Ages, and the material (or Moraines) scooped out often forms bars at the mouth of the fjord so that the deeper waters are within it. Fjords are frequent along the coasts of Norway and Greenland. Also spelt *fiord*.

Flood Plain. The flat valley floor of a river in its lower reaches which has been levelled mainly by the deposition of alluvium by the river when it has flooded. The deposits are usually highest near the present bed of the river. See *Levee* and *Meander*.

Fog. A mist which is thick enough to interfere seriously with visibility. It is caused by the condensation of moisture in stagnant air cooled for some reason and it is thickest when this moisture forms in minute droplets around small soot or dust particles.

Föhn. A warm, dry wind which blows down from a mountain mass or ridge. This name is used especially in the Alps. See also *Chinook*.

Fold Mountains. Mountains formed by the pushing up of the Earth's crust into ridges or anticlines long ago. The Rockies, Andes and Himalayas are examples of mountains which have been produced by folding.

Ford. A shallow place in a river where it can be safely crossed, except in times of flood.

Fosse. Another name for a long ditch or dyke.

Frigid Zones. The coldest areas on the Earth's surface which are around the North Pole (North Frigid Zone) and the South Pole (South Frigid Zone). See *Antarctic Circle* and *Arctic Circle*.

Front. See *Cold Front*, *Occluded Front*.

Frontier. The border line between the territories of one state or country and another.

Fumaroles. Holes in the Earth's crust, usually in a semi-extinct volcanic region, from which steam and other gases are erupted from levels deep below the surface. See also *Geyser* and *Volcano*.

Gale. See *Beaufort Scale*.

Geoanticline. Arched strata on a large scale and the opposite of a Geosyncline (*q.v.*). The ridge thus

Aerofilms Ltd.

Here is a typical coral island (*q.v.*) guarded by its characteristic ring-shaped coral atoll (*q.v.*). Coral islands are built up from the skeletons of countless numbers of coral polyps. These creatures live only in warmer waters, and most coral islands are therefore found in the warmer parts of the Indian and Pacific Oceans. The picture was taken at Aitutaki in the Cook group.

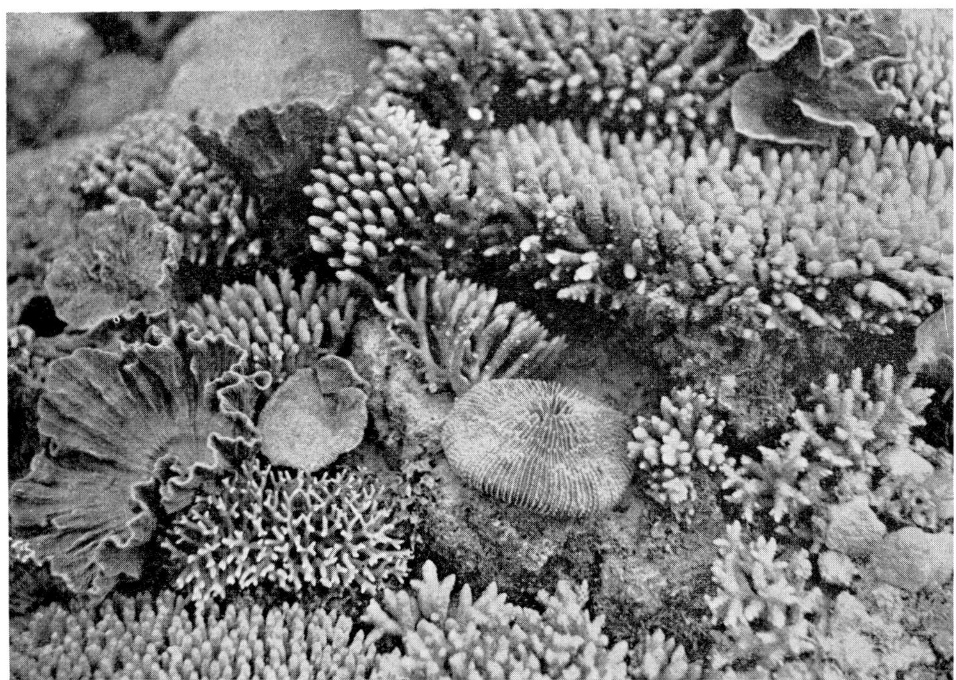

Queensland Government Tourist Bureau.

The most remarkable mass of coral in the world is the Great Barrier Reef of Australia, which stretches along the coast of Queensland for some 1,250 miles. The picture shows some of the many lovely corals which go to make the Reef. In the centre of the picture is an easily-identified mushroom coral. Below it, and to the left, is the common staghorn coral. Above it is a mass of branching coral.

Aerofilms Ltd.

By means of dams and hydro-electric power stations man makes the great rivers work for him. The picture shows the Kariba dam under construction across the Zambesi River, part of an impressive hydro-electric scheme for the Rhodesias. Its purpose is to hold back water in a vast artificial lake so that a steady flow can be maintained through the seasons and an even output of power obtained.

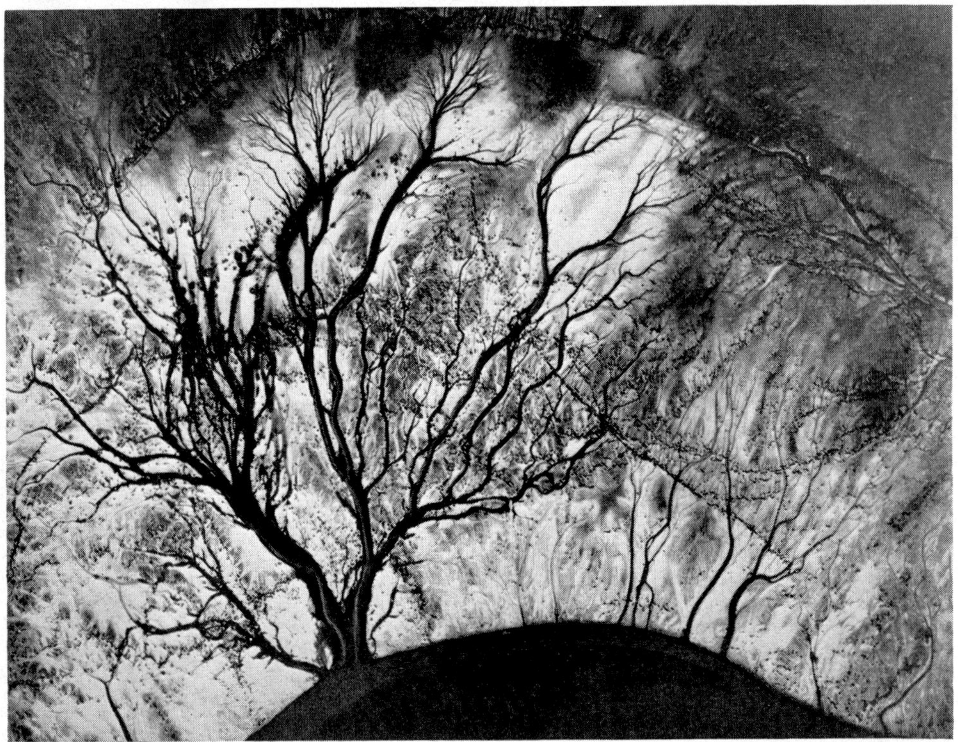

Fairchild Aerial Surveys Inc.

This remarkable aerial picture shows part of the delta (*q.v.*) of the Colorado River and is appropriately called " the Burning Tree." The branch-like drainage was formed as the river successively choked itself off in forming a delta. The " flames " are really brilliant sands and light-coloured deposits through which the river has forced its way.

ENCROACHING SANDS

Ministerio de Fomento, Dirección de Turismo, Venezuela.

Dunes (*q.v.*) are formed by the movement of large masses of sand by the wind and will relentlessly encroach upon fertile land if their development is not checked. Dunes are usually crescent-shaped and steeply sloped on the side facing away from the wind. The sand dunes in this picture are near the town of Coro, at the neck of the Paraguaná Peninsula in Venezuela.

Crown Copyright.

This is the flood plain (*q.v.*) of the River Towy above Carmarthen in South Wales. The dark projecting knoll in the middle distance (left centre) is a faulted outlier (*q.v.*) In the distance can be seen the stepped scarps (escarpments) of the Black Mountains. The Towy rises in Cardiganshire and enters the sea at Carmarthen Bay.

WON FROM THE SEA

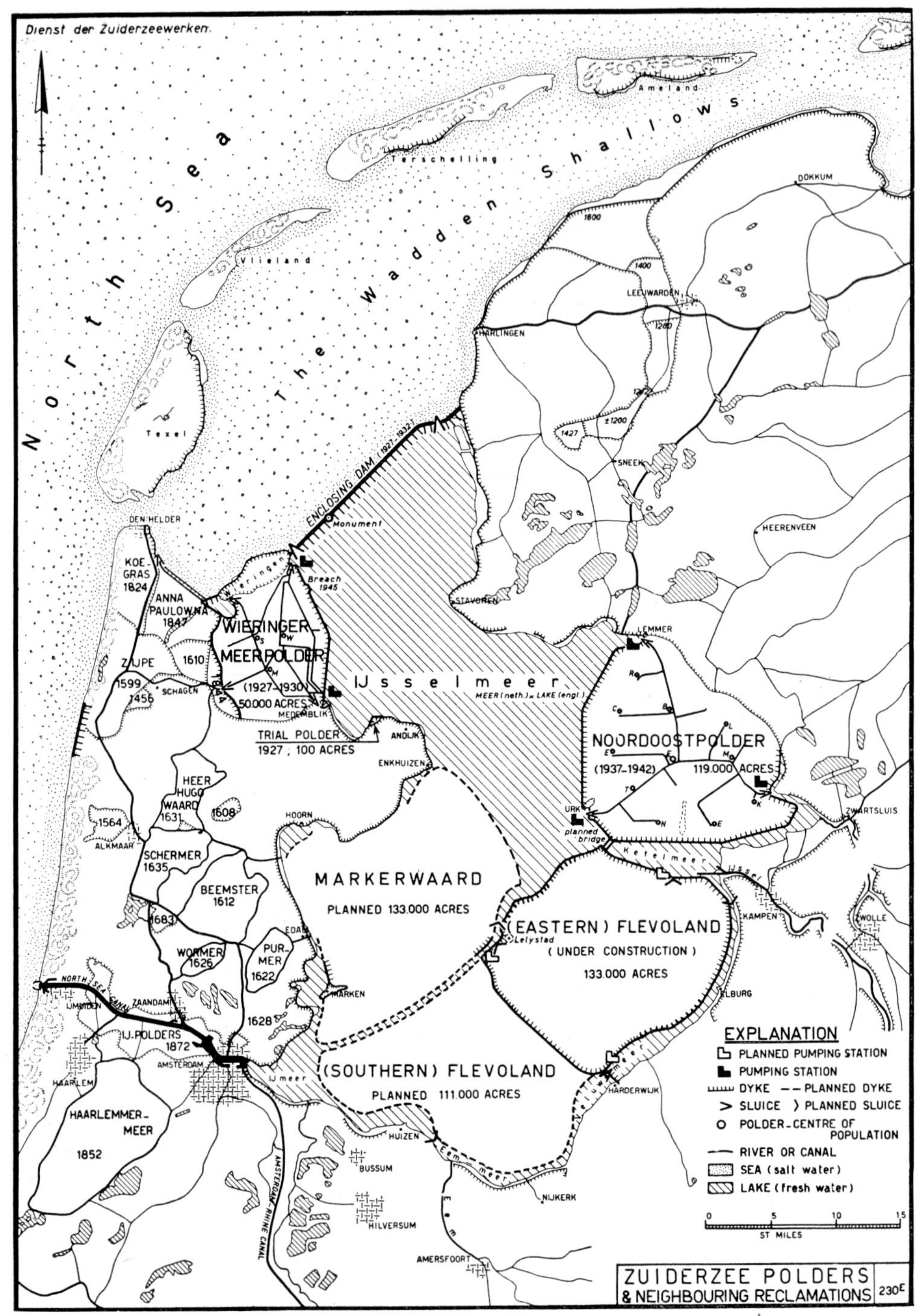

Copyright.

The Dutch are famous as builders of dykes (*q.v.*) and for the amount of land which they have reclaimed, and are still reclaiming, from the sea. This map shows the polders (*q.v.*) which have been created from the former Zuider Zee (now much reduced in size and known as the Ijsselmeer). Reclamation is slow work and even when the land has been won from the sea about seven years must pass before it is fit for cultivation. Note the new town of Lelystad on the edge of the East Flevoland Polder.

formed may suffer progressive erosion, and the geoanticline may not be visible to the eye; but it can be surveyed by special "geodetic" or Earth-measuring instruments. Buried accumulations of crude oil are sometimes found on each side of such geoanticlines. See also *Anticline*.

Geosyncline. A syncline or a trough-shaped bending of rock layers on a large or "world-sized" scale. In this trough great thicknesses of sedimentary rocks may have been deposited at a later period in time. See also *Syncline*.

Geyser. A spring of hot water which erupts intermittently as a jet from a hole in the Earth's crust in a volcanic region which is still sub-active. The action is caused by water from the Earth's surface accumulating in a narrow rock cavern over hot volcanic rocks, changing at its lower end into steam, which periodically blows out the rest of the water above it in a great jet. Well-known geysers are the Great Geyser of Iceland (which is the origin of the name) and Old Faithful Geyser, in the Yellowstone National Park in the U.S.A. There are many geysers in New Zealand.

Glacier. A "river of ice" which moves slowly down a valley after its formation in the mountain heights above the snowline. Its underside is partly liquid owing to the pressure and this allows the mass of snow and ice to move downwards through its own weight. Glaciers are thick above the snowline, but become thinner through melting as they push down into the warmer valleys and usually have streams emerging from their lower ends. Glaciers bring down with them masses of soil and rock; they grind the rocks beneath them so as to form *Moraines* and *Boulder Clay*. A well-known example of a glacier is the Mer de Glace (Sea of Ice) in the Alps.

Gorge. See *Defile* and *Canyon*.

Grand Banks. A famous cod-fishing ground stretching from Newfoundland in a south-easterly direction for about 300 miles. It is a *continental shelf* only about 15–90 fathoms deep. The Gulf Stream passes over the southern area and brings ample food supplies to cod and other fish.

Grasslands. Areas where the rainfall is sufficient for grass to grow, but not for many trees. They form the natural sheep- and cattle-raising areas, such as the Steppes (of Russia), the Prairies (of North America) and the Pampas (of South America).

Great Circle. A circle around the earth which bisects it, *e.g.*, the Equator or two opposite meridians. The shortest distance between two points on the Earth's surface is along a Great Circle, and this is why Great Circle routes are favoured by ships and aircraft.

Greenwich Mean Time. This is the actual time, in relation to the sun, on Longitude Zero, which passes through Greenwich and is accepted as the Standard Time of the British Isles and Western Europe. See also the map on pp. 228 and 229.

Grotto. A cave dissolved out of limestone rock by water with carbon dioxide in solution.

Gulch. The name given in the west of the United States to a deep ravine formed by torrents during the wet season.

Gulf Stream or **Gulf Stream Drift.** See *Ocean Currents*.

Gully. A narrow valley or small water-course on high ground—often the start of a river.

Hachures. Shading lines on a map, drawn perpendicular to the contours, representing relief. Gentle slopes are shown by thin lines rather far apart, abrupt slopes by shorter and thicker lines close together. The tops of mountains, plateaux and level areas appear white. A hachured map thus gives a kind of picture in relief of the area covered by the map.

Hade. The angle between the plane or fracture line of a fault and the perpendicular.

Haff, or Nehrung. The lagoon set in a bay outside the mouth of a river where currents have drifted the silt to form a bar or spit which almost shuts the river off from the open sea. *Nehrungs* are frequent along the Baltic coast of Eastern Germany.

Halo. The ring of light that sometimes seems to surround the Sun or Moon when it is seen through the ice crystals of Cirrostratus Clouds.

Harmattan. A north-easterly or easterly wind blowing off the Sahara over parts of West Africa. Being very hot but also dry, it absorbs the moisture in the air of these areas very quickly and makes conditions cooler and more pleasant; but it often carries clouds of dust and may dry up crops and trees. It is sometimes called "The Doctor."

Hemisphere. One-half of the sphere which is the Earth. The plane through the Equator divides the Earth into the Northern and Southern Hemispheres. Roughly the Northern contains most of the land and so approximates to the *Land Hemisphere*, and the Southern approximates to the *Water Hemisphere*. Eastern and Western Hemispheres are sometimes shown on certain world maps.

Hinterland. The "land behind" an important seaport from which it derives its exports and to which it distributes most of its imports. For example, west Glamorgan and east Carmarthenshire, with their metal working, oil refining and anthracite mines, form the hinterland to the port of Swansea.

Hook. A curved *spit* at the end of a projection into the sea caused by currents laying down sands and gravels. Examples are at the Hook of Holland, in the Netherlands, and Cape Cod, in Massachusetts, U.S.A.

Horizon. The line of extreme visibility in the clearest weather from one particular point on sea or land. This forms a circle around the observer which, on land, is broken into by mountains, etc. The horizon is more extended when the point of observation is raised, *e.g.*, from the top of the mast of a ship. At the height of 100 ft. the horizon is about fourteen miles away.

Horse Latitudes. The sub-tropical belts of high air pressure in the Northern and Southern Hemispheres, between the North-east Trades and the Westerlies around 30° N. Lat. and the South-east Trades and the Westerlies about 30° S. Lat. Calms, light winds and cloudless skies are characteristic of the Horse Latitudes. See diagram on p. 221.

Horst. The opposite of a trough in faulted rock beds. It is the raised mass between two roughly parallel *Faults*.

Hot Spring. Water emerging from among heated rocks in a volcanic or once volcanic area. Hot springs are common in New Zealand. See *Geyser* and *Fumarole*.

Huerta. Areas in Spain where high temperatures and ample sunshine, with the aid of *Irrigation*, enable two crops every year of fruit, sugar-cane, cotton, etc., to be produced. These areas are mainly in Valencia, Granada and Murcia.

Hum. A harder limestone block standing above the surrounding land level in a *karst* or limestone district, or left lying above a mass of other kinds of rock which it has protected from *erosion*. See *Outlier*.

Humidity. The level of moisture absorption present in the air at a particular place or time. *Absolute humidity* is the state when the air at that temperature is unable to absorb more moisture. *Relative humidity*, expressed as a percentage, is the relation between the actual moisture present in the air and the total amount it could absorb to reach absolute humidity at that particular temperature. *Relative humidity* is measured by a *hygrometer*, which consists of a wet-bulb and a dry-bulb thermometer.

Humus. That part of the soil which is composed of decayed vegetable and animal matter. It contains myriads of bacteria, many of which are of assistance to plant life.

Hurricane. See *Beaufort Scale*, Force 12. The name is also given to tropical cyclones in the Gulf of Mexico and the West Indies, which often cause great devastation on the islands and the mainland.

Hydrophyte, or **Hygrophyte.** A moisture-loving plant of wet or humid regions, *e.g.*, the banana plant.

Hydrosphere. The water layer surrounding the Earth and through which the continents (or the lithosphere) project.

Hygroscope. A mechanism which, through changes in itself owing to dampness, can indicate roughly changes of humidity in the air. Examples are the piece of seaweed used to foretell the weather and the "John and Joan" weather house, in which a piece of twisted catgut expands or contracts as humidity changes, so that Joan is out in fine and poor John in wet weather.

Ice Ages. Periods, many millions of years ago, when glaciers and ice fields spread over great areas of the land surfaces of the world. Glacial moraines, eskers, boulder clay, erratics, etc., were left on much of the land surface in the northern areas and affected the flow of rivers, formed lakes and gouged out V-shaped valleys. The ice sheets of Greenland and the ice fields of the high Alps and Norway are examples of the remnants of the Quaternary or Fourth Ice Age.

Iceberg. A floating mass of ice which has broken away from an Arctic or Antarctic ice field, or from the end of a glacier which has reached the sea. Eight-ninths of the ice is under water, and the iceberg is constantly changing its shape and often its position because of melting by Sun and water and by pieces "calving" off from the main mass. Icebergs are a great danger to ships, especially in early summer, and "ice patrols" are organised to warn ships when there is danger. Flat pieces of ice floating in the sea are called icefloes.

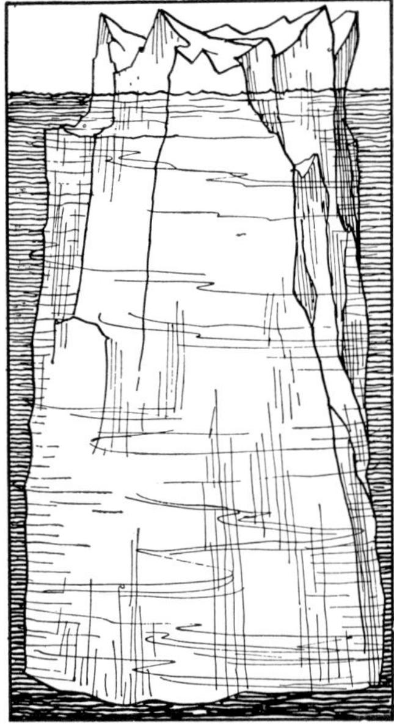

Igneous Rocks. Rocks which were not laid down under shallow water like the sandstones and shales, or in deep seas like chalk and limestone, but solidified out of molten magma or lava formed deep within the crust of the Earth. Examples are the granite of Cornwall and the basalt of the Giant's Causeway. See *Volcano* and *Dyke*.

Impermeable Rocks. Rock beds which do not allow water to pass through them easily, such as granite (except through the cracks) and clay. The description *impervious* is sometimes used to describe such rocks. See *Artesian Well*.

Insolation. The amount of sunshine reaching any part of the Earth's surface on any particular day or during a season.

Insular Climate. The climate of islands as affected by the moderating effects of the sea around them upon what otherwise might be extremes of heat or cold.

Intensive Cultivation. The intense and continuous use of fertile land to produce heavy crops, leaving none of it uncultivated or unused for any period.

Interior Drainage. A river basin or basins with outlets only into an inland sea or lake. Examples are the Dead Sea, in Asia Minor, and the Caspian Sea and the Volga River, in the Soviet Union.

International Date Line. See *Date Line* and map on pp. 228 and 229.

Invisible Exports. These are not goods but services, such as transport, interest on foreign loans and investments, insurances and tourist traffic. They help to adjust the balance of trade.

Irrigation. The artificial storage of water and its distribution over deserts and other areas of low rainfall to make the land suitable for cultivation. Irrigation schemes usually call for large dams or barrages, *e.g.*, the Assuan Dam on the River Nile, by which the water can be conserved for controlled distribution through irrigation canals to the area under cultivation. Quite often the dam operates in conjunction with a hydro-electric power station, power as well as irrigation thus being provided.

Island. Land surrounded by the waters of a sea, lake or river.

Isobars. Lines on a map which are drawn to join places having equal air pressure at a particular time. To allow for the lower pressures on high ground, the isobars are corrected at such places to what the pressure would be at sea level. Isobars can be drawn to show average pressure over a period as well as for particular days and times, as in the daily charts of the Meteorological Office.

Isobaths. Lines drawn on a map of the sea bed (or of a lake) joining points of equal depth. They are really underwater *contours*.

Isohalines. Lines drawn on a map joining points in the sea of equal saltiness or *salinity*.

Isohyets. Lines drawn on a map joining places of equal rainfall over a season.

Isoseismal Lines. Lines drawn on a map joining places which suffer earthquake shocks of equal force or intensity.

Isotherms. Lines on a map drawn joining places of equivalent temperature at a particular time, corrections being made to sea-level temperatures in respect of the cooler land heights. Isotherms, like isobars, can be specific to a particular day and time or averages for a season.

Isthmus. A narrow piece of land which joins together two larger areas. Examples are the Isthmus of Corinth, the Isthmus of Panama.

Joints. Cracks in the bed of a rock or across it and along which the stone will split or laminate. They are usually present only in sedimentary rocks like sandstone and slate, although some igneous rocks have a jointed columnar structure with transverse breaks across.

Jungle. Area of thick tropical vegetation in a hot, wet, uncultivated region.

Kanats. The underground irrigation channels of Persia.

Karaburan. The north-easterly wind that blows in the hot season in Sinkiang in China. It brings in fine dust from the desert which settles in the valleys as *Loess*. Over the desert it also carries sand, which then darkens the sky and blocks the river courses.

Karroo. The karroo beds of South Africa are composed of sedimentary rocks lying on a very hard and older mass of rock rich in minerals. Towards the south-east the formation descends in successive steps towards the sea (Indian Ocean), while in the south-west the beds have been folded to form a small mountainous area. The plateaux of the karroo form the two intermediate steps between the coast line of South Africa and the greater plateau in the interior. The Little Karroo is the plateau nearest the Cape, and the Great Karroo is the next great "shelf" farther north. The dry karroos are suitable mainly for the raising of sheep and goats.

Karst. A barren region of limestone rocks through which the rain percolates quickly to an impervious rock below which it forms underground streams and lakes. The surface rocks are much eroded by the chemical action of the carbon dioxide dissolved in the rain, and the soil of a karst area is usually thin and even absent at the higher levels. An example, the parent one, is the karst limestone area in the Dinaric Alps, Yugoslavia.

Katabatic Wind. A wind caused by the movement of cool air down the slopes of mountains or ice-caps, particularly at night.

Kettle Hole. Caused in moraines and outwash plains of ice sheets where a block of ice buried in the boulder clay or gravel has since melted so as to leave a hollow.

Khamsin. The name given in Egypt to the Sirocco (*q.v.*).

Knoll. A rounded hill usually standing on its own. Compare with *Kopje* and *Butte*.

Kopje (*pron.* Koppie). The South African name for a butte (*q.v.*) or low hill. There are many kopjes on the Karroo plateaux.

Lagoon. An area of the sea, usually shallow, separated from the rest by a coral barrier reef or the ring of an atoll. The term is used sometimes for any stretch of shallow water separated from the main water area by spits, sandbanks or beds of shingle. See *Atoll, Barrier Reef*.

Lake. An area of water, usually fresh, surrounded by land and occupying a depression in the land surface or a widened area in the course of a river. Salt lakes usually have no

RICHES FROM THE DESERT

These pictures illustrate the development of the rich oil deposits in the Sahara Desert. The uppermost picture shows one of the drilling rigs at Hassi Messaoud, about 500 miles south of Algiers and to the north-west of Edjélé. This field contains an estimated 1,500 million tons of oil. The centre picture shows the ever-growing camp at Hassi Messaoud. Note the sun awnings, made of horizontal sticks, which protect the living quarters. In the foreground have been marked out flower beds made from soil brought in from Algiers. The bottom picture shows some of the oil men gazing admiringly at the first completed Saharan well-head. In June, 1958, agreement was reached with Tunisia for the construction of a pipeline from the Edjélé oilfield to the Gulf of Gabès which, it is hoped, will take 14,000,000 tons of oil to the coast every year. Large deposits of natural gas and iron ore have also been found in the Sahara.

Photos: Camera Press.

HARNESSED TO SERVE MAN

H. Armstrong Roberts.

The Niagara Falls provide a magnificent spectacle for visitors to this part of North America and are a valuable source of hydro-electric power. They occur on the Niagara River and comprise the Horseshoe Fall, on the Canadian side, and the American Fall. This picture shows the falls from Rainbow Bridge.

Uganda Electricity Board.

Opened by the Queen in 1954, the Owen Falls Dam harnesses the Nile below Jinja, where this great river of Africa leaves Lake Victoria. The construction of the dam raised the level of the river and submerged the Ripon Falls, discovered by the explorer John Hanning Speke (1827–64) in 1862. The dam provides hydro-electric power for both industrial and domestic use in Uganda.

LAKE AND JUNGLE

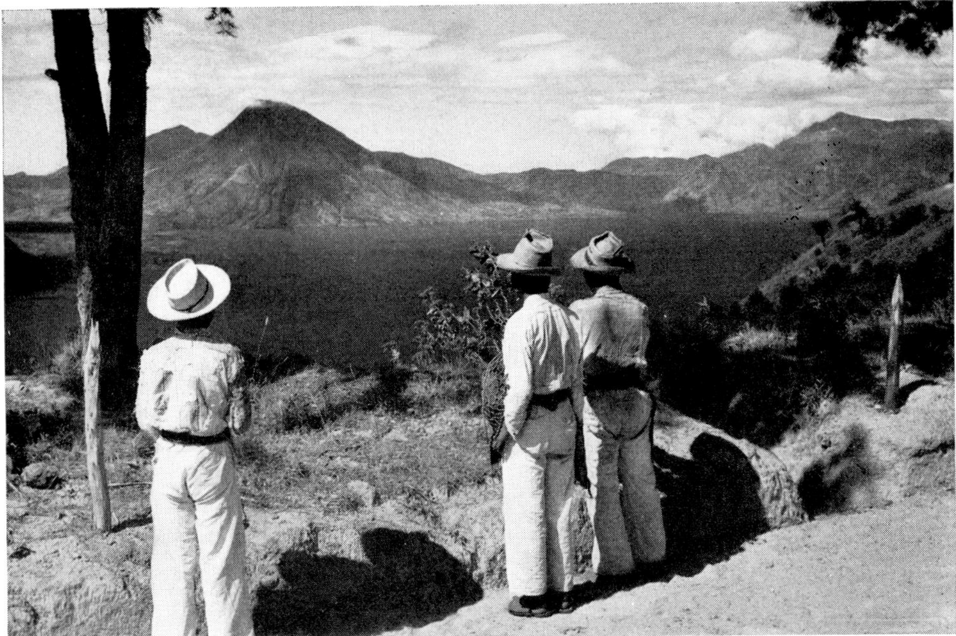

H. Armstrong Roberts.

One of the most beautiful lakes (*q.v.*) in the world is Atitlan in Guatemala. High volcanic cones stand guard over its blue and emerald waters, and on its shores are more than a dozen picturesque Indian villages, some of which are named after the Apostles. The lake stands 5,000 feet above sea level.

Camera Press.

The dense and tangled nature of jungle (*q.v.*) vegetation is well illustrated by this picture from Burma showing the members of an expedition hacking a way clear for their vehicle. Trees of great height and variety, lesser trees, festoons of rope-like creepers, ferns and other plants combine to form a strangely dark and impenetrable realm.

TWO KINDS OF EROSION

Erosion (*q.v.*) has several causes, and this photograph illustrates the work of the sea. It shows the cliffs and reefs in the Ilfracombe Beds, east of Ilfracombe, where marine erosion has picked out the soft from the hard beds along the strike of the interbedded shales and limestones.

Photos: Crown Copyright.

These peculiar formations are earth pillars (*q.v.*). The photograph was taken one mile north of Fortrose, Ross-shire. It shows glacial sands overlaying boulder clay in the old valley and now being eroded by Rosemarkie Burn and by the direct action of rain, giving rise to earth pillars. The protective remains of soil and vegetation on the earth pillars were once continuous with that seen in the background and serves as an index to the amount of material removed by denudation.

outlet and the hot Sun evaporates the water, leaving the mineral salts, brought by the rivers flowing into them, in solution, in the lake.

Landes. Land subject to the drifting of sand over it, usually in low-lying areas adjacent to the seashore. Special types of vegetation and trees are often planted in the path of the advancing sand to arrest its progress. The name is particularly applied to coastal regions of south-west France where forest industries have now resulted from the planting of the trees.

Land Hemisphere. See *Hemisphere.*

Laterite. A red soil, particularly of Central Africa, rich in iron and alumina. It is unfertile and becomes sticky in wet weather. It is also found in parts of India, Malaya and some East Indian islands.

Latitude. The position of a point on the Earth's surface north or south of the Equator. It is expressed as the degrees of the angle between the line from this point to the centre of the Earth and from the Equator to the centre of the Earth. The half-circle from Pole to Pole being 180°, there are thus 90° of north and 90° of south latitude marked off from the Equator which is 0° latitude. Each degree is divided into sixty minutes and each minute into sixty seconds. Each degree represents approximately sixty-nine miles of the Earth's circumference, except near the Poles, where this linear distance is slightly longer because of the flattening of these areas.

Lava. Molten rock emitted from the lower levels of the crust of the earth through cracks, volcanic craters, etc., at points of weakness in the crust. Usually this is associated with earthquakes, hot springs and other volcanic occurrences. See *Igneous Rock*, *Volcano*, *Dyke*.

Leaching. An agricultural term used to describe the washing away from the surface soil by rain of the mineral salts and organic matter contained in it thus reducing the fertility of the land.

Leap Year. The Earth's revolution of the Sun takes about 365¼ days so that every fourth year an extra day, February 29th, has to be added to the Calendar. This is done when the year number is divisible by four, except in the case of concluding years of centuries, of which only those divisible by 400 are leap years.

Leeward. The sheltered side from the wind of hills, mountains, cliffs, clumps of trees, etc.

Levee. Levees are banks formed by a river liable to overflow its Flood Plain (*q.v.*). They are formed by the river depositing at its edges, more silt, gravel and sand than farther out in the flood plain, due to the slowing down of the water carrying this material. Levees may be built up so much as to raise the river bed above the surrounding flood plain and they may be artificially raised and strengthened to contain the river when in flood. The term is especially used for the banks of the Mississippi.

Lithosphere. The land parts of the Earth's surface which project through the oceans or hydrosphere. See *Earth.*

Littoral. The land bordering a sea shore.

Llanos. The grass plains or tropical *Savanna* of Guiana, Venezuela and the Orinoco river basin in north-eastern South America. They are on high ground and dryer and cooler than the forested lowlands. They support large herds of cattle.

Loam. Soil, consisting of sand, clay, silt and humus.

Local Time. The " sun time " at any particular place on the Earth's surface. On the meridian concerned, the Sun reaches its highest point at noon local time. See map on pp. 228 and 229.

Loch, Lough. Loch in Scotland, and Lough in Northern Ireland, means a large lake or narrow inlet of the sea. Examples are Loch Lomond (a lake), Loch Fyne (an arm of the sea), Lough Neagh (the largest lake in Ireland), Lough Foyle (an arm of the sea).

Lode. A vein of mineral deposits in the fissures of rocks.

Loess. Fine, wind-blown dust or soil which has been deposited (particularly in western and northern China) as deep, compact beds through which the rivers flow between vertical walls. It sometimes blocks the rivers and causes them to change course. When irrigated, loess makes fertile soil. Loess with a high humus content forms the rich black earth of the Soviet Union and there are deposits in the central plains of North America, Hungary, etc.

Longitude. The angle, as measured along the Equator, between the Meridian upon which a place is situated, and the Standard or Zero Meridian which passes through Greenwich. Since the Earth is a globe, there are 180° west and 180° east of the Zero Meridian. The equivalent of a degree of longitude in miles decreases from sixty-nine miles on the Equator to nil at each Pole. By giving the longitude and latitude (*q.v.*) of a place, its exact position on the globe can be fixed.

Lough. See *Loch.*

Low. See *Depression* and *Cyclone.*

Lunar Month. The period, actually 29·5 days, which the Moon requires to make one complete circulation of the Earth.

Mælstrom. A whirlpool in the sea caused by twisting, fast-moving currents. The original mælstrom is between two of the Lofoten Islands off the west coast of Norway.

Mæstro. A central Mediterranean north-westerly wind experienced mainly in the Adriatic, Ionian and Tyrrhenian Seas.

Magma. The molten rock below the crust of the Earth which sometimes comes to the surface by volcano (*q.v.*).

Magnetic Poles. The Poles, North and South, to which the compass needle actually points, the Earth being a bi-polar magnet. They are approximate to the actual Poles and tables of corrections of the compass readings to give the true north from various points on the Earth's surface arc available to navigators.

Mallee. Scrub country in the drier regions of Australia, *i.e.*, in the south-west and south-east, in which bush eucalyptus is the predominant vegetation.

Mandated Territory. Territory transferred by the Versailles Treaty after the First World War, from the ownership of Germany and Turkey to the administration of one of the victorious powers. The modern equivalent is the " Trusteeship Territory," *i.e.*, a territory held under United Nations' trusteeship.

Maquis. Groves, mainly of wild olive and myrtle shrubs, on dry infertile uplands in the coastal regions of southern France and Italy (where it is called *macchia*). It is similar to the chaparral of California. The term is particularly used in Corsica, whose maquis is renowned for its fragrance which has given Corsica the title of " Scented Isle."

Maritime Climate. A climate influenced by the nearness of the sea. The effect generally is a cooling in the summer and a warming in winter of the lands concerned and also ample rainfall.

Marl. A kind of soil in which lime (calcium carbonate) and clay are combined.

Massif. A mountain mass which is grouped rather than range-like in character.

Meander. The swinging curves, to and fro, of the course of a river within its wide valley or flood plain, so

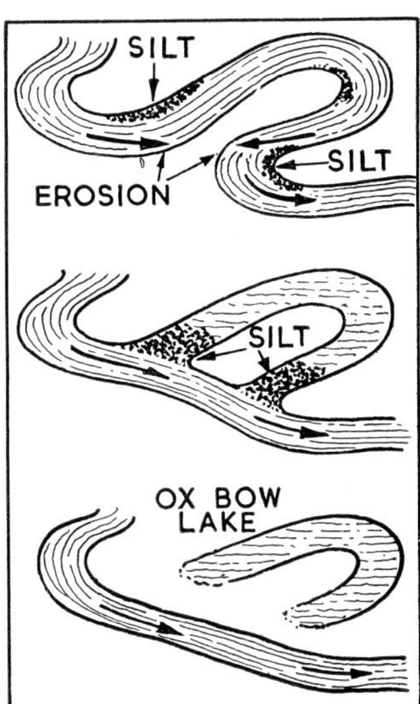

named after the River Meander in Asia Minor. Meanders have the highest banks on the concave side and flat shingle deposits on the convex side. The swing of the river tends to accentuate the meanders, and often the loops, in flood time, become cut off by straight channels leaving stagnant *Ox Bow Lakes* in the old meanders. Incised or entrenched meanders are deepened because of a new uplift of the river bed making the stream more active.

Mediterranean Climate. The kind of climate which western margins of continents between about 30° and 40° north and south latitudes enjoy. The apparent movement of the Sun (north in summer in the Northern Hemisphere, and south in the Southern) brings warm, dry, sunny weather, while the reverse in winter brings rain. Typical products are wine, olives, wheat and fruit. This type of climate is found particularly in the Mediterranean area of Europe, North Africa and Asia Minor; similar climates are found in South Africa, South Australia, Chile and California.

Meltemi. The Turkish name for Etesian Winds (*q.v.*).

Menhir. A large "Long Stone" set upright in the ground by Neolithic man to mark some sacred spot or burial place.

Mere. A large pond or small lake sometimes marshy in character.

Meridian. Half of one of the Great Circles which cross at the Poles. It is a line of longitude and its position on the globe is expressed in degrees east or west of the prime or zero meridian which passes through Greenwich. See *Greenwich Mean Time* and *Longitude.*

Mesa. A tableland with steep sides and horizontal rock beds. Such tableland is found especially in Spain and in Colorado.

Meseta. The high plateau forming much of the interior of Spain. It is cut into by river valleys and has mountain ranges. It has extremes of climate, being very cold in winter and very hot and dry in summer.

Metamorphic Rocks. Rocks which have been changed in their form and structure through the effects of heat, pressure, etc. For example, shale may be hardened under pressure and have its mica flakes levelled out to make highly laminated slate, while granite can have its crystals rearranged so as to form Gneiss. Marble is metamorphosed limestone.

Meteors. Solid masses from outer space which, striking the atmosphere of the Earth, are heated by friction with that air to incandescence and so dissipated into dust, although very large ones may fall to Earth as Meteorites which usually contain large proportions of iron. The popular name for Meteor is Shooting Star.

Midnight Sun. The Sun as seen at midnight when it shines for twenty-four hours of the day in the summer at places within the Arctic and Antarctic Circles.

Mile, Geographical and Nautical. The Nautical Mile is equivalent to the distance contained within one-sixtieth of a degree (*i.e.*, one minute) of any Great Circle around the Globe. It is 6,080 ft. in length. The Geographical Mile, which is equal to one minute of latitude, varies according to the latitude covered, but at the Equator is equivalent to the Nautical Mile. The Land or Statute Mile measures 5,280 ft. (1,760 yds.).

Millibar. The unit used to express the extent of atmospheric pressure as measured by a barometer. About 29½ in. of mercury (or 750 mm.) represent a bar, that is, 1,000 millibars. Therefore, one thousandth of 29½ in. would be the approximate length of a millibar on the barometer scale.

Mirage. The reflection of distant objects in the skies where, under certain atmospheric conditions, air layers act as a kind of mirror. Mirages are seen most frequently over hot deserts and in the polar regions. They also appear at sea.

Mistral. A cold, dry northerly wind from the Central Plateau of France which blows, chiefly in winter, down the Rhône Valley to the Mediterranean coasts. It can reach great force, as much as seventy-five to eighty miles per hour at times, and often brings hard frosts with it.

Mole. An artificially constructed pier, jetty, or breakwater made to shield a harbour from the full force of tides and storms.

Monadnock. A high mound of rock which has been able to resist erosion as compared with the surrounding country.

Monsoons. Seasonal winds of certain large land masses which are completely reversed at the end of a period. For example, the intense heating in summer of the land surface of south-eastern Asia causes the air over it to be greatly reduced in density and weight so that the colder air over the Indian Ocean flows in to displace it, bringing very heavy rains, which are increased in intensity by the height of the land. This is the south-west Monsoon and it lasts, as a rule, from April to September. When the land cools in autumn, the winds are reversed and they flow out as the north-east Monsoon, which is usually a dry, dusty and cold wind. This usually lasts from October to March. The name comes from the Arabic *Mausim*, meaning "a set time."

Montaña. The eastern sides of the Andes. They are heavily forested and subject to frequent rains.

Moon. Although this term may be used astronomically for the satellite of any planet, it is usually taken to mean the familiar satellite of the Earth. The Moon has a diameter of about 2,160 miles and is thus much smaller than the Earth. Its average distance from the Earth is about 239,000 miles and it makes one complete revolution of the Earth in every lunar month (29·5 days). Its light is reflected sunlight. It turns on its axis once during each revolution of the Earth and its phases are caused by changes in the relative position of Earth, Sun and Moon.

Moor. Wild, uncultivated upland covered with coarse vegetation and pasture for sheep.

Moraine. Rock fragments transported by the action of a glacier. Débris falling from the sides of the valley on to the edge of the glacier forms Lateral Moraines. The mass of material formed at the melting end of glaciers is called the Terminal Moraine. When two glaciers from side valleys meet, their Lateral Moraines will join to form Medial Moraines carried along the surface of the glacier. Ground Moraines and Boulder Clay are formed from rock débris dragged along on the under side of the glacier. See picture on p. 203.

Mountain. A land mass considerably higher than the surrounding area, and usually above 1,000 ft. in height. Isolated peaks are much less common than mountain ranges or massifs. Mountains may be formed by Earth movements (*e.g.*, fold mountains and block mountains), by erosion, or by volcanic action.

Natural Gas. Inflammable gas originating in buried oil fields or even coal seams or ancient decayed masses of organic (vegetable and animal) matter. It can be reached by borings and piped for use in towns.

Natural Regions. Large areas of the Earth's land surface in which conditions of climate, vegetation, geological structure, etc., tend to be generally similar. A natural region may approximate to a climatic region. See the special section on the MAJOR REGIONS OF THE WORLD in this Atlas.

Nautical Mile. See *Mile.*

Naze. A prominent cape or headland.

Neap Tides occur when the attraction of the Sun is at right angles to the pull of the Moon on the hydrosphere, or water envelope of the Earth. These gravitational pulls tend to average things out so that there is less difference between high water and low water than at other times. A neap tide does not "go out" so far or "come in" so much as other tides. This condition occurs twice a month.

Nebular Theory. The theory that the solar system was once a huge mass of hot gas rotating in space and that, when it cooled, it formed the solid masses (the planets and their satellites) that now revolve round the central mass (the Sun), which is still incandescent.

Nehrung. See *Haff.*

Nekton. The larger creatures of the sea; that is, the fishes. Contrast with the Plankton (*q.v.*).

Ness. Similar to Naze (*q.v.*).

Nevados. A Katabatic wind of the valleys in the mountains of Ecuador. See *Katabatic Wind.*

Névé (French). Snow in a glacier hardening into ice. The German term is *Firn.*

Nimbus. Low dark cloud usually accompanied by heavy rain. See *Clouds.*

Nitrogen. The inert gas which takes up 78 per cent. of the volume of dry air. See *Atmosphere.*

Nivation. The action of snow as an agent of erosion.

Nomads. Peoples who move about with their flocks and herds seeking good pastures. They do not, as a rule, cultivate the land.

Norte. A northerly winter wind of

THE MIDNIGHT SUN

Polar Photos.

This unusual picture of the Midnight Sun (*q.v.*) was obtained by making a series of exposures of the same photographic plate at regular intervals, thus giving this record of the apparent path of the sun during the polar midsummer when it never sets. The slight central dip in the line of suns is the nearest the sun gets to setting. The phenomenon, which is visible for days or even months (according to latitude), is caused by the tilting of the Earth's axis.

Crown Copyright.

These famous screes (*q.v.*) may be seen at Wast Water, Cumberland. They begin at a height of about 1,500 feet and descend at an angle of some 38 degrees to below the level of the lake. Wast Water is the deepest and wildest of the lakes of the Lake District.

Central America. Also the name of a cold northerly wind which blows out from the cold interior of Spain in winter towards the Mediterranean coasts of that country.

Norther. A cold wind from the north, sometimes violent, which blows in the southern parts of the United States. It often causes damage to fruit crops because of the sudden fall in temperature (30° to 40°) which can occur when it blows.

Northern Lights. See *Aurora Borealis.*

Nullah. A dry river bed which becomes flooded after heavy rain. It is a term used in India. Compare with *Wadi* and *Gulch.*

Nunatak. A large rock, usually the top of a mountain, which projects above the level of a surrounding ice sheet.

Oasis. An area in a desert region where the water table is sufficiently near the surface to provide wells or springs, or where a river from an area of high rainfall debouches on to the desert. Here life can be supported and crops such as date palms and clover can be raised. Irrigation is a method of making artificial oases.

Occluded Front. A meteorological term used to describe the contact of a cold front, or mass of cold air, with a warm front. The colder, and therefore heavier, air tends to displace the warmer and lighter air upwards. At this occlusion rain usually occurs owing to the cooling of the warm moist air as it is forced upwards. See also *Cold Front.*

Ocean. One of the larger divisions of the seas which cover about 71 per cent of the Earth's surface. The oceans are usually regarded as five in number—Atlantic, Pacific, Indian, Arctic and Antarctic. The deepest parts are termed Abyssal, the general area Pelagic, and the shore areas the Littoral. The greatest ocean depth is in the Pacific Ocean, where a depth of 35,640 feet was recorded in 1951. The Pacific Ocean is also the largest of the five oceans.

Ocean Currents. These are movements of the waters of the ocean. Surface currents are caused mainly by prevailing winds and by the reverse movements of water in condensation. Currents in the lower layers of the ocean are sometimes due to changes of temperature and also to difference in salinity, which affects water density. The flow of the currents is determined by winds, the shape of the coastline and the rotation of the Earth. One of the best-known currents, the Gulf Stream, gives an example of typical behaviour. It originates in the Gulf of Mexico and flows out north-eastwards across the Atlantic towards Europe. It is some 350 fathoms deep with a narrowest width of about fifty miles and it flows at about 5 miles per hour. On its way across the Atlantic it splits—one part (the Gulf Stream Drift, or North Atlantic Drift) carrying on to the British Isles and Western Europe and the other (the Canaries Current) moving southwards to rejoin the North Equatorial Current about the Equator. The Gulf Stream is a warm current, and the prevailing winds with which it travels bring warmth and moisture to Western Europe. Other important currents are the Brazil Current, the North Equatorial Current, the Equatorial Current and the Peru Current.

Oolite. A limestone of the Jurassic Age such as that found in the Cotswolds and similar hills in Britain. This rock often contains large beds of iron ore such as those worked near Corby, in Northamptonshire.

Ooze. The mud-like deposit on deep ocean beds, composed mainly of the remains of plankton (*q.v.*), and also of some volcanic dust.

Orbit. The path of a planet or other object in space. The Earth's orbit, for example, is an ellipse around the Sun which is a little to one side of the centre of the ellipse. The inclined axis of the rotating Earth is at right angles to the Sun's rays in spring and autumn, tilted towards them in summer, and away from them in winter.

Ore. A rock containing a metal in an impure form which can be worked to manufacture this metal. The metal is usually in chemical combination with other elements, *e.g.*, iron pyrites: iron combined with sulphur.

Orogenesis. The process of mountain building by folding of rock beds, by faulting or by volcanic action.

Outcrop. Where a rock-bed appears on the surface of the land. If this rock-bed is inclined it may appear as an escarpment.

Outlier. A piece of rock surrounded by rocks of earlier date and probably the remnant of similar rock-beds which have been removed by erosion. The opposite to this type of occurrence is called an inlier, that is, older rock-beds appearing within surrounding later ones.

Outwash Plain. A plain of alluvium deposited by the stream emerging from the melting terminal of a glacier, the materials being derived from the Moraines. An Alluvial Fan is formed when a river debouches from a narrow valley on to a plain and, losing its momentum, deposits the silt that it carries, the coarser and heavier materials first and the fine muds last.

Ox-bow Lake. See *Meander*. Ox-bow lakes are common in the lower reaches of the Mississippi, where they are called Bayous.

Oxygen. The active gas in the atmosphere which is necessary to life. It forms about 21 per cent. of the volume of the air when it is dry. It is present as oxides in the rocks of the Earth's crust. See *Atmosphere.*

Pack Ice. Ice blocks floating on Polar seas from a broken-up ice field. It is known as close pack when the blocks are close together, and open pack if there are spaces between them.

Pampas. The grasslands in the basin of the River Plate, in South America. They are similar to the steppes of the Soviet Union, the veld of South Africa and the prairies of North America. Though much of the pampas is only suitable for grazing, large areas are suitable for the cultivation of cereals, alfalfa and flax. The "cowboy" of the pampas is called a *gaucho.*

Pampero. A cold south or south-westerly summer wind that blows over the southern parts of South America from the South Polar regions.

Pancake Ice. The thin plates of ice which form when the polar seas begin to freeze.

Papagayo. The Norther wind of the United States continuing into Mexico. See *Norther.*

Paramos. The mountain areas in the Andes which extend from the *Puna* to the snowline. Here, stunted vegetation, similar to that of the *Tundra,* prevails.

Pass. A gap through which a mountain range can be crossed. When the headwaters of streams flowing down opposite sides of the mountain range have cut back towards each other far into each river bed, a pass is usually the result. Ice action long ago might also have caused a pass to be formed.

Peak. The sharp top of a mountain or volcano.

Peat. Decayed vegetation of great thickness found in bogs like those of Ireland. Cut out and dried, it can be used as a fuel.

Pelagic. This word means "pertaining to the open sea." See *Ocean.*

Peneplain. Almost a plain—a stretch of land worn down by erosion to be generally level, yet cut into by rivers and often dotted about with isolated hills of harder rock. It may also be spelt *Peneplane.*

Peninsula. An area of land which is almost entirely surrounded by water.

Permeable Rocks. Rocks through which water can soak, that is, rocks which are pervious.

Piedmont Glacier. Ice at the foot of a range of mountains derived from several valley glaciers which have joined up. The sheet is therefore very wide and slow moving. A good example is the Malaspina Glacier of Alaska.

Plain. Land, usually of low altitude, which is generally flat or with very slight undulations. There are plains caused by erosion; also alluvial, coastal and flood plains.

Planet. One of the many heavenly bodies, including the Earth, which revolve in regular orbits around the Sun. In order of size, the eight chief planets are: Jupiter, Saturn, Neptune, Uranus, Earth, Venus, Mars and Mercury. Pluto, the other major planet, is 3,666 million miles from the Sun. Planets are spherical in shape and their light is reflected sunlight, unlike the Sun and stars, which give out their own light. In addition to these major planets, there are a great many smaller bodies revolving round the Sun which are called asteroids and planetoids. Of the 1,000 asteroids discovered only one, Vesta, can ever be seen with the naked eye.

Plankton. The almost microscopic plants and animals floating in water, especially in the sea, which form the main food supply of many fishes and other creatures which live in water.

OCEAN CURRENTS AND WINDS

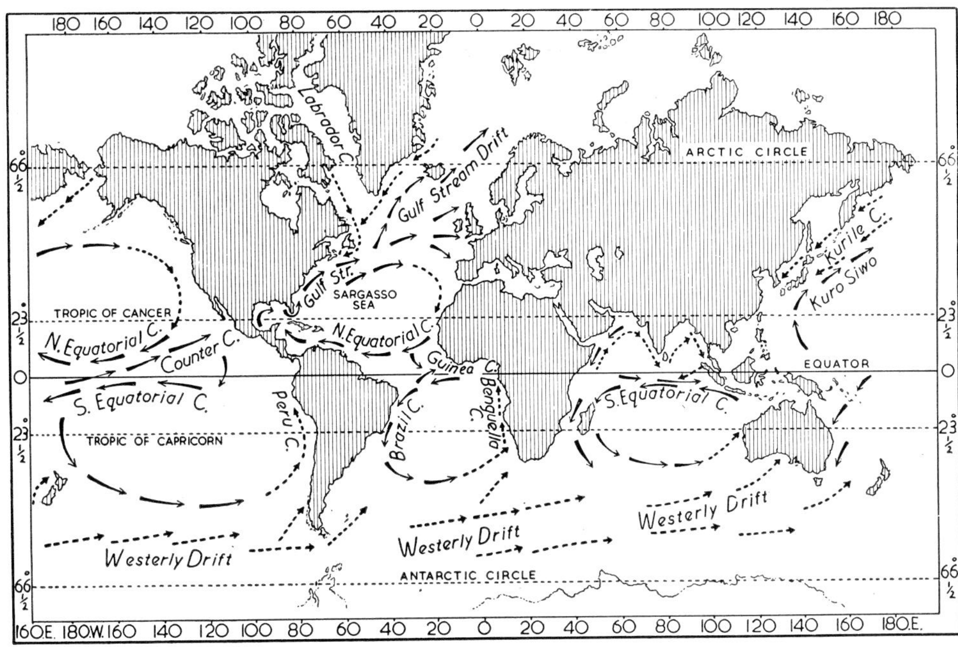

Specially drawn for this work.

This map shows the main ocean currents (*q.v.*) and drifts of the world and how these are affected by the great winds. In the upper layers of ocean the currents are, in fact, mainly caused by prevailing winds. Notice that ocean currents in Trade Wind latitudes run counter clockwise in the Southern Hemisphere and clockwise in the Northern Hemisphere.

Winds are air in motion and are mainly caused by differences in atmospheric pressure, the air currents tending to flow from areas where pressure is high towards areas where pressure is lower. The rotation of the Earth, however, may cause them to flow on a curved or indirect course—towards the right in the Northern Hemisphere and towards the left in the Southern Hemisphere. This diagram shows the prevailing winds of the world. The Trade Winds (*q.v.*) are so called because they follow a steady, or trodden course. At one time, ships carrying horses were often becalmed and ran out of water in the Horse Latitudes (*q.v.*), or so it is said, and had to throw their animals overboard. In the Doldrums (*q.v.*), sailing ships were often becalmed for weeks on end.

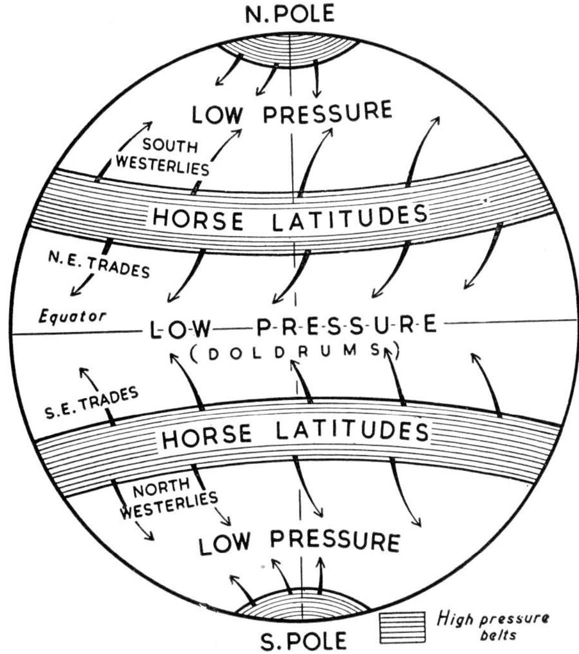

STALACTITE AND SWALLOW-HOLE

Bermuda News Photo.

The magnificent stalactites hanging from the roof of this cave (*q.v.*) were formed over thousands of years by deposits of lime left by the rainwater seeping through the porous aeolian sandstone. This is the Crystal Cave, near Harrington Sound, Bermuda. The subterranean lake is called Cahow Lake, because the skeletons of Cahow birds, once plentiful in Bermuda, but now almost extinct, were found here.

Crown Copyright.

The carboniferous limestone Mendips in Somerset are well-known for their swallow-holes (*q.v.*), or swallet-holes, and underground streams. Our picture shows the entrance to one of the largest caves, Wookey Hole, near Wells, through which the river Axe flows. Prehistoric implements and fossil bones have been found in the cave. Not far distant are the equally famous caves of Cheddar.

Plankton is commonest in the shallower waters of the sea, so that the Continental Shelves are usually the most important fishing grounds. See also *Nekton*.

Plateau. A high, generally level, piece of land. It may be a peneplane which has been raised in level by later Earth movements. It is usually cut into by river valleys. Examples are the Meseta of Spain, the coal measures of South Wales and the plateau of South Africa.

Playa. Shallow areas in Nevada and Utah, U.S.A., which after very heavy rains become marshes or muddy lakes.

Podzol, or Podsol. A highly leached soil of the Coniferous Forest areas of the world. It is poor soil for cultivation and may be acid in character.

Polder. Land in Holland reclaimed from the sea by the building of dykes and the pumping out of the enclosed water. See map p. 210.

Poles (North and South). The geographical poles are points at the northern and southern ends of the axis around which the Earth spins once in every twenty-four hours. The magnetic poles (to which the compass needle points) differ from the geographical by a varying angle (magnetic declination or variation).

Pole Star, or North Star. The star always seen in the Northern Hemisphere at the zenith of the heavens directly above the North Pole, and used therefore by mariners to give them the direction of true north and also, by its height from the horizon, the latitude of the place from which it is observed. The bright Pole Star may be located by extending a line joining the two stars at the square end of the group known as the Great Bear or the Plough. This line all but passes through the Pole Star. There is no similarly situated star above the South Pole. See *Southern Cross*.

Prairies. Grasslands in North America roughly situated between Longitude 88° West and the Rocky Mountains. The Canadian provinces of Manitoba, Saskatchewan and Alberta are therefore often referred to as " the prairie provinces." The rainfall is enough only to permit of grass, with a few trees in the wetter hollows. The area is now one of the greatest wheat-producing centres in the world. Compare with *Steppe*, *Pampas* and *Veld*.

Precipitation. The falling of water in the form of rain, hail, sleet or snow from the atmosphere upon the surface of the Earth.

Prevailing Wind. The wind that blows most frequently during the year at any particular place.

Projection, Map. The representation on a flat map of the curved surface of the Globe. Large areas of the Globe cannot be accurately represented at one time in the flat, although one kind of projection can show accurate directions, another kind correct areas and so on. See the special section in this Atlas on THE MAP TO-DAY.

Promontory. A prominent high cape or headland projecting from the mainland well out into the sea.

Pudding Stone. A rock composed of pebbles once rounded by water, but now fixed in a cement or matrix of hardened clay, mud or lime. Geologists call it *Conglomerate*.

Pumice. A solid type of lava which is extremely light and will float. This is because, when it was molten, it was frothed up by steam and gases and filled with small pockets or holes.

Puna. The high, very cold plateau of the Andes, between about 10,000 and 13,000 ft. in altitude.

Purga. The name given by inhabitants of the Tundra to the cold north-easterly Buran wind. See *Buran*.

Puy. A French term used in Auvergne, Central France, for the cone of a small volcano which has become extinct, *e.g.*, Puy de Dôme, 4,798 ft. high, in the department of the same name.

Quartz. A compound of silicon and oxygen which forms hard, glassy crystals, especially in the joints of certain other rocks, where it is often associated with metallic ores.

Quartzite. A rock in which small particles of quartz are mixed with the sand particles, resulting in a rock of extreme hardness.

Quicksand. An area of wet sand which might appear firm but is actually loose and not stable enough to carry the weight of a person walking over it. Some quicksands are deep enough to engulf men and animals.

Race. A fast tidal current in a narrow strait or off a headland.

Radiation. The movement of heat by rays into the atmosphere compared with the convection and conduction of heat.

Rain, Rainfall. Water which falls on to the surface of the Earth as raindrops. This precipitation may be *orographic*, *i.e.*, caused by the high land of a country pushing incoming clouds up into the colder upper air; *cyclonic*, due to areas of low pressure; or *convectional*, such as the equatorial rains.

Rainbow. This is caused by the reflection and refraction of the light in

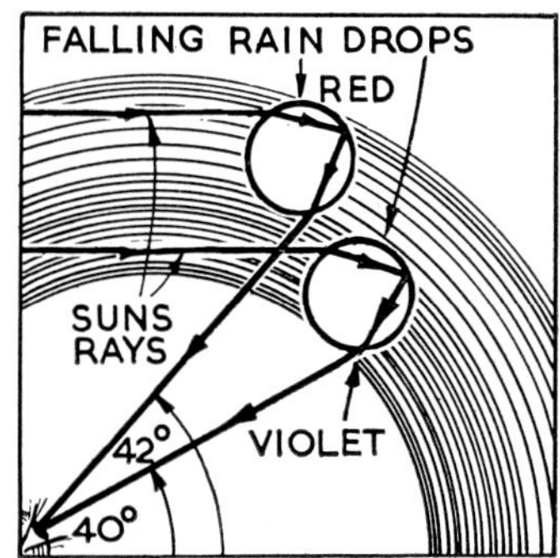

water drops, and it is seen when the Sun shines on a shower of rain. In a *primary* rainbow the white light of the Sun is broken up into red, orange, yellow, green, blue, indigo and violet, and these colours are seen in this order, the red being on the outside edge of the bow and the violet on the inside. Some light, however, may be reflected a second time, forming a *secondary* rainbow in which the order of the colours is reversed.

Rain Gauge. The instrument used for measuring the amount of rainfall in a particular period of time.

Rain Shadow. An area sheltered by a mountain range and receiving only a light rainfall. The prevailing winds drop their moisture on the windward side of the range as they approach the summit, so that by the time they reach the far side of the range they contain little or no moisture. Further, the descent to the rain shadow area warms and dries the air. See *Chinook*.

Raised Beach. An old sea or lake beach which, by uplift of the land, is now well above the level of the water. Raised beaches often have the old cliffs behind them on the landward side.

Rand. The name in South Africa for a ridge of low hills. "The Rand" refers to the Witwatersrand, in the Transvaal, famous for its gold mines.

Rapids. A stretch of river where the water flows more swiftly than normally. Rapids may often be strewn with boulders, and waterfalls are common. Hard rock beds cross the river; softer rocks between the outcrops are worn away by the continual flow of water; the result is a number of " sills " of small falls which together make the rapids. Rapids can also be formed by a sudden steepening of the course of a river. They are a great nuisance to navigation, often being almost impossible to traverse without considerable danger. Steep rapids are called *cataracts*. Where the harder rock-beds dip against the direction of the stream or are horizontal, waterfalls rather than rapids are formed.

Ravine. A deep, long and narrow valley with steep sides.

Reef. An outcrop of rocks occurring just below the surface of the sea except perhaps at low tide. The name is also used to describe a lode or mineral vein in rocks, particularly veins which are gold-bearing in character.

Rejuvenated River. A river which, after it has flattened its profile, is given a new lease of active life by the uplift of its basin or part of it.

Relative Humidity. The ratio between the amount of water vapour actually present in a certain volume of air at a given temperature and the total amount it could hold if fully saturated.

Relief. A term used to describe the differences of elevation between various areas of the land surface of the Earth.

Relief Map. See *Contours*, *Hachures*, etc.

Revolution of the Earth. The annual movement of the Earth in an ellipse around the Sun, which is placed at

TORNADO IN TEXAS

Planet News.

This remarkable picture shows a tornado (*q.v.*) bearing down upon the city of Dallas, Texas, U.S.A. The raging black column of wind and débris cut a 21-mile-long lane through the city, killing ten people and injuring more than 200 others. Roofs were sucked off buildings and walls damaged. At times cars and other heavy objects were picked up as though they were just toys.

Crown Copyright.

This more peaceful photograph comes from Perthshire, Scotland and shows part of beautiful Glen Lyon. Glen Lyon is a typical U-shaped valley (*q.v.*). Such valleys were formed during the Ice Age by glaciers or rivers of ice which cut back the slopes and spurs of the high ground, smoothing the sides of the valleys and flattening the valley bottoms. Many such valleys may be seen in the Scottish Highlands.

one end of the foci and not at the exact centre of the ellipse (see *Orbit*). This movement is the cause of the seasons.

Rhumb-Line, or Loxodrome. A line drawn on a globe or map so as to cut all lines of longitude or meridians at the same angle. Rhumb-line routes are longer than Great Circle routes.

Ria. A narrow, long inlet into the coast of a country caused by the lower reaches of a river valley being "drowned" by the sea due to the subsidence of the land. A ria differs from a fjord in that it is deepest at its mouth and not so narrow; moreover, its life as a river valley was shaped by water rather than ice erosion. Examples are found on the coasts of north-west Spain and south-west Ireland.

Rift Valley. A deep and long trough formed by two parallel faults which

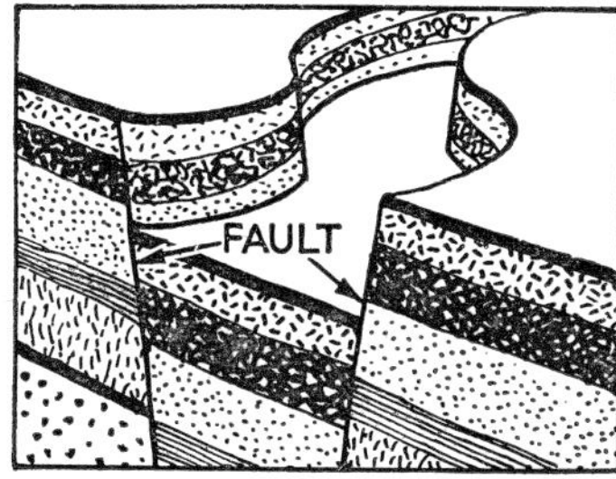

have dropped a long piece of the Earth's crust deep below the level of the surrounding rock-beds. The largest rift of this kind stretches through East Africa, Palestine and Syria. In this great Rift Valley are now found the long, narrow lakes of Tanganyika, Edward and Albert, and Lakes Nyasa and Rudolf. The rift caused the formation of the Red Sea and the Gulf of Akaba, also the Dead Sea, the Jordan Valley and the Sea of Galilee. Other examples are the Central Lowlands of Scotland and the Rhine Valley.

River. A large stream, often deep, wide and navigable, which flows from high ground into the sea, a lake or another river. Its source is where it begins, its course is the route it takes, its tributaries are other rivers that join it, and where it enters the sea or lake is its mouth. The area which the river drains is called its system or basin.

Rivers may be *Consequent*, that is, the direct result of the slope; *Subsequent*, as a tributary coming into the consequent stream along the softer rocks of the *Strike;* or *Obsequent*, as tributaries to the subsequent river and flowing opposite in direction to the parent consequent river. A vertical section following the bed of a river from its source to its mouth is called its *profile.*

River Capture. As the headwaters of a river eat away the soil and rock of the higher slopes, they may present an easier route for streams which until then escaped on the other side of the watershed. This cutting back enables the river to absorb these streams—a process which is known as River Capture.

River Terrace. A piece of an earlier flood plain of a river left as a "terrace" along the side of a valley after the river has been rejuvenated and has begun again to cut deeply into its bed. See *River, Rejuvenated River.*

Roadstead. A safe yet open anchorage for ships where sufficient shelter is provided by a headland, island or sandbank to protect them from stormy seas.

Roaring Forties. The name applied both to the winds and the latitudes 40° to 60° South approximately. The winds are the prevailing westerlies of the temperate regions of the Southern Hemisphere, and they gain their force by being unimpeded by land masses. The winds are also known as the Brave West Winds and, though mild, they bring storms and rain. They were much used by sailing ships on the Australian and New Zealand run.

Rock. The term applied to all the solid materials which make up the land surface of the Earth. It includes clay, mud, sand, etc., although the popular meaning of rock applies only to hard and larger portions of the Earth's crust.

Rotation of the Earth. The spinning of the Earth on its axis once in every twenty-four hours. This movement is the cause of day and night, the side of the Earth towards the Sun having daylight, and the other side darkness. The direction of rotation is from west to east.

Salinity. The saltness of the sea water usually expressed as parts per 1,000 of salt in relation to the water.

Salt Lake. A lake, usually without an outlet, situated in a hot arid region where there is a high degree of evaporation. This means that the salts dissolved in the rivers which enter the lake accumulate there and cause a very high degree of salinity in the waters of the lake. For example, the Dead Sea has about 250 parts per 1,000 of salt and is so dense and heavy as a result that bathers cannot sink in its waters. A dried up salt lake would result in an *Alkali Flat* or *Salt Pan.*

Samoon. A Chinook type of wind which blows down the mountains of Kurdistan into Persia (Iran).

Savanna. The grasslands of certain tropical regions which lie between the Equatorial forests and the rainless deserts. These grasslands are intermediate regions benefiting from the equatorial rains as they move north in the summer, and in winter are under the influence of the drier Trade Winds. The *Llanos* of South America are a good example of Savanna land. There is also much Savanna in Africa.

Scarp. See *Escarpment.*

Schist. A metamorphic rock consisting of many thin plates which have been formed by intense heat and pressure. The same process can take place in other kinds of rock if there is sufficient heat and pressure. An important mineral is found in schists—mica, which is able to stand great heat and is also a good electricity insulator.

Scree. The rock débris lying at the foot of a rock slope or cliff. The pieces are broken off the parent rock by the action of frost, heat and cold and other processes of erosion. Scree is also called *Talus.*

Scrub. An area covered by stunted bushes, usually evergreen in type. It results from inadequate rainfall in relation to the heat, which gives rise to excessive evaporation.

Sea Level. The level of the surface of the sea irrespective of tides and the effects of wind. See also *Datum Level.* Actually, from a global point of view, the "level" of the sea is the great curve of the Earth's surface.

Seasons. The changing seasons of the year are due to the tilt of the Earth's axis and its constant direction, and also to the revolution of the Earth around the Sun. In the temperate zones of the world the year can be divided into four seasons, Spring, Summer, Autumn and Winter. Each is some three months long. In the Northern Hemisphere, Spring consists of March, April and May; Summer of June, July and August; Autumn of September, October and November; and Winter of the remaining months. In the Southern Hemisphere, the same seasons occur at exactly the opposite times of year, *e.g.*, Spring in the Northern Hemisphere is Autumn in the Southern. Seasons in the temperate zones are clearly defined because of the considerable tilt of the Earth's axis towards or away from the Sun; in tropical regions, however, the seasons are not so noticeable and depend more on the rainfall than the tilt of the Earth's axis, which, in the equatorial belt, has little effect on the climate.

Sedimentary Rocks. Rocks formed from sediments laid under water, of sand, mud or gravel and also from chemically deposited substances like chalk and limestone. Because these rocks were formed in layers (strata), they are often called "stratified rocks."

Seiche. The banking up of the water level on the leeward side of a large lake. It may be caused by the wind, by Earth movements below the lake, or by changes in atmospheric pressure.

Selvas. The Equatorial forests of the basin of the River Amazon.

Séracs. A French word for the ice pillars formed when crevasses criss-cross a glacier when it goes down a steep slope—a sort of "Ice Rapids."

Shale. A soft sedimentary rock made of mud or clay. Shale metamorphosed by great pressure and heat may become slate. See *Metamorphic* and *Sedimentary Rocks.*

Shoal. A sandy or gravelly bank just below the surface of the sea, river or lake. Another meaning is a large group of fish.

Shotts. Salt lakes which, when dry,

form salt pans on the mountain plateau of Algeria and to the south of the Atlas Mountains.

Sierra. Mountain ranges with serrated edges and sharp peaks. So called in Spain and in those parts of America in which the Spaniards settled.

Sill. See *Dyke*.

Silt. Fine deposits in a lake, in the sea or in a river, which are not quite as coarse as sand or as fine as mud.

Sirocco. A wind blowing north, usually in spring, from the Sahara into North Africa, southern Italy and parts of southern Spain. While in North Africa the wind is hot and dry, but on crossing the Mediterranean it becomes moisture-laden and can be uncomfortably humid in Southern Europe.

Skerry. A small rock island.

Sleet. Precipitation in the form of a mixture of rain and snow.

Snow. Precipitation in the form of fine ice crystals which mass together into snowflakes. Snow is really rain that has passed through air whose temperature is below freezing point, that is, below 32° F.

Snow Line. The boundary of the lowest level of perpetual snow on a mountains lope. The altitude of the snow line varies with the latitude and the direction of the mountain slope.

Soil. Broken up particles on the surface of rocks enriched by humus or decayed vegetable and animal matter. Soils also may be derived from Boulder Clay and Moraines, or may have been transported by rivers (as silt) or by wind (as loess).

Solifluction. The sliding of masses of soil down slopes. It is usually caused by heavy rains or water seepage.

Solstice. The longest and shortest days of the year when the Earth is at one of the ends of the Eliptic, its axis sloping towards the Sun in the Summer Solstice and away from it at the Winter Solstice. The summer solstice of the Northern Hemisphere (June 21) occurs when the sun is vertical over the Tropic of Cancer; it is, of course, the winter solstice of the Southern Hemisphere. The winter solstice of the Northern Hemisphere (December 22) occurs when the sun is vertical over the Tropic of Capricorn, and is the summer solstice of the Southern Hemisphere.

Sound. Similar to *Strait*.

Southerly Buster. Also known as Southerly Burster. A heavy southerly gale experienced in southern and south-eastern Australia, especially in the spring and summer. It blows from Antarctic regions and can often cause a 20° F. or more drop in temperature. This wind corresponds with the *Pampero* (*q.v.*) in South America.

Southern Cross. A constellation of the Southern Hemisphere comprising four stars arranged in the form of a cross. The longer arm of the cross points almost directly towards the South Pole.

Spring. The point at which the overflow of the water table emerges out of the ground. The season of spring.

Spring Tides. The highest of the tides which occur twice a month when the Earth, Sun and Moon are more or less in a straight line and the gravitational force of Sun and Moon is combined. See *Tides*.

Squall. A short-lived sudden burst of wind.

Standard, or Zone, Time. The time based on a certain meridian and adopted for use within a specified zone or area. For example, Greenwich Mean Time, based on the Greenwich meridian, is the standard time for the British Isles and Western Europe. See map on pp. 228 and 229.

Steppes. Grasslands of the temperate regions of south-eastern Europe and the contiguous parts of Asia. Compare with *Prairies* and *Pampas*.

Strait. A narrow channel of the sea which joins two larger areas of water.

Stratified Rocks. Rocks which were laid down in layers and which tend to split along the planes of these layers or strata; for example, the Pennant sandstones of Yorkshire and South Wales. See also *Sedimentary Rocks*.

Stratosphere. The upper part of the envelope of air which encircles the Earth. The stratosphere begins about six or seven miles up, but this distance varies somewhat, especially over the Equator where it is at its greatest.

Stratum. A rock-bed. The plural is *Strata*.

Stratus. Stratified forms of low clouds. See *Clouds*.

Stream. A small river.

Strike. The level of a rock-bed at right-angles to the dip (*q.v.*).

Sub-polar Region. The cold temperate belt spreading from the edge of the Tundra over the Coniferous Forest (*q.v.*) areas and similar latitudes. Though rainfall within the continental areas is usually slight, evaporation is, in many places, low enough to allow the growth of trees.

Subsequent River. See *River*.

Subsidence. The subsiding or sinking of an area in relation to its surroundings. The word is also used to describe the falling to the Earth's surface of masses of air denser and heavier than the ground air layer. In its descent the air becomes compressed and warmer.

Subsoil. The material lying below the surface of true soil which is less enriched by humus.

Sub-tropics. The regions between the Equatorial Tropics and the temperate regions. The apparent movement of the Sun, north or south, gives rise to marked differences between Summer and Winter in the sub-tropics. The western subtropical margins of continents are the "Mediterranean" areas (see *Mediterranean Climate*), while their eastern sides usually have a higher rainfall, most of it being Summer rain.

Sudd. Masses of vegetable matter which break loose from the swamps of the Sudan to become large "floating islands" on the River Nile.

Sun. The centre of the solar system. It is a great star of burning gases with, perhaps an incandescent liquid interior. Its surface temperature is over 12,000° F. It is, on the average, 93,000,000 miles from the Earth and has a diameter of about 866,000 miles.

Sundarbans. The waste land on the seaward border of the delta of the Ganges. It is intersected by numerous channels which are some of the many mouths of the river. The country is a water-logged jungle which is the home of many wild beasts. Timber is the most important product of the area, and the name Sundarbans is, in fact, derived from the sundri tree (a hardwood) which is very common in the district.

Swallow-holes. Holes dissolved deep into limestone or chalk rocks, through which water flows to reach underground caves, lakes or streams. Swallow-holes are also known as *Sink Holes* or *Pot Holes*.

Swamp. A water-logged, hollow area of land, filled with water-loving vegetation. After heavy rains it may become a marsh and if the hollow is deep and completely filled with decayed vegetable matter, it may become a bog.

Syncline. Folded rock-beds which are in a concave trough often of considerable length. Within synclines,

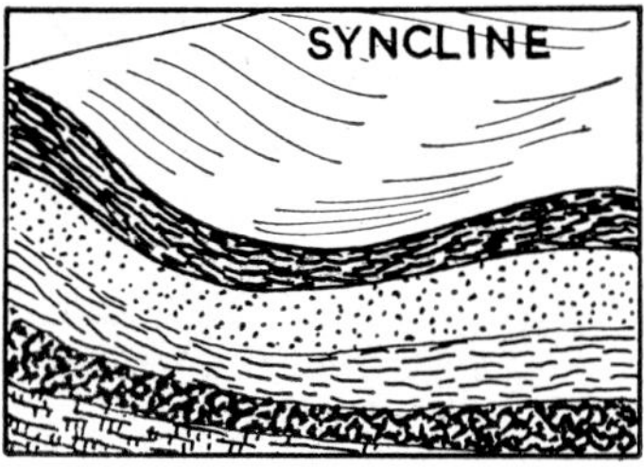

rocks like the coal measures are frequently protected from surface erosion and so preserved for subsequent mining. An example is the South Wales coalfield which is held in a deep syncline.

Tableland. A high, extensive, flat plateau which has steep sides. The Veld of South Africa is a good example.

Taiga. The name given to the Coniferous Forest areas, especially of Siberia.

Talus. See *Scree*.

Tarn. A small lake near a mountain top.

Temperate Zones. The zones round the Earth about the middle latitudes, north and south, between the Torrid Zones (Equatorial Regions) and the Frigid Zones (Arctic and Antarctic Regions). The Temperate Zones lie, in the north, between the Tropic of Cancer (23½° N. lat.) and the Arctic Circle (66½° N. lat.), and in the south between the Tropic of Capricorn (23½° S. lat.) and the Antarctic Circle (66½° S. lat.). The climate in these regions is, however, by no means uniform, and wide variations occur in relation to the physical conditions. For example, the western margins of the continents are

Associated Press.

A new volcano rises from the sea off the north-east coast of the island of Luzon. It is Didicas, formed by the eruption of March, 1952, which united the three Didicas rocks into an active cone 250 feet high and about five acres in extent. Within four months the cone had reached a height of 800 feet and had an estimated area of 600 acres. Many years previously steam had been observed in the vicinity of the rocks and it had rightly been assumed that they were really the peaks of a submarine volcano.

Aerofilms Ltd.

Here is an aerial view of a typical Norwegian fjord (*q.v.*). Notice the steep and rocky sides, and (in the foreground) the little village at the head of the fjord. Many such fjords are found along the coast of Norway. The longest and most branched is Sogne fjord, which has a length of more than 100 miles. One of the most beautiful is Hardanger fjord, about seventy miles in length.

TIME IN DIFFERENT LANDS

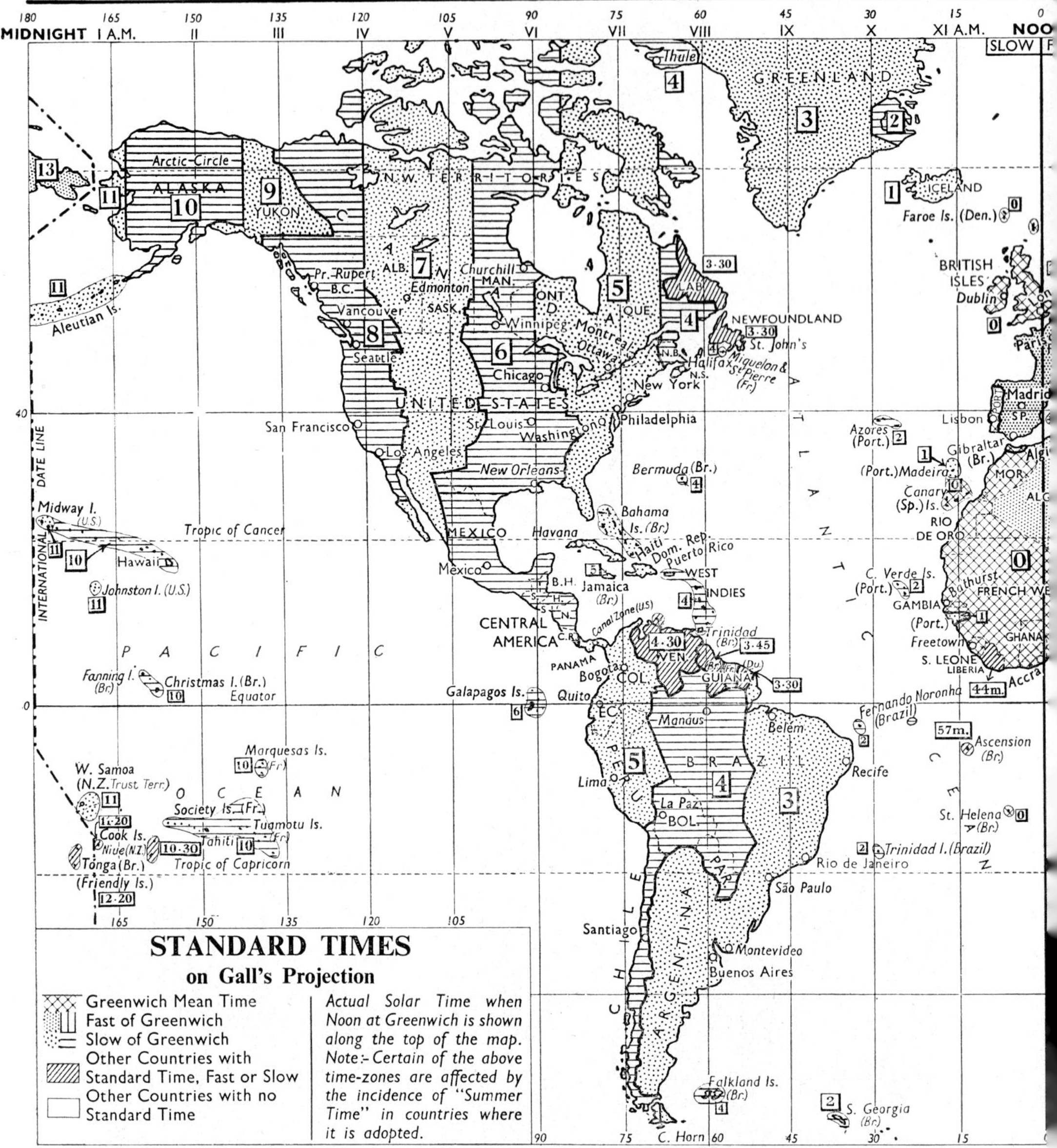

The Earth makes one complete rotation on its axis in twenty-four hours which is equal to 15 degrees in one hour. This rotation is from West to East; so the time in a place 30 degrees East of Greenwich will be two hours fast on British time, *e.g.*, in Cairo it is 2 p.m. at noon G.M.T. And while places East of Greenwich are so many hours or half-hours fast on G.M.T., places West of Greenwich are so many hours slow according to the Zone in which they lie.

As the map shows, this Standard Time by Zones is now general almost throughout the world and its basis is Greenwich Mean Time (*q.v.*). The standard meridians of the Zones have been chosen, for the most part, to differ by multiples of 15 degrees or 7½ degrees from the Greenwich meridian; the time variations thus occur by an exact number of hours or half-hours.

Europe has three standard times: Greenwich Mean Time (used throughout Western Europe), Central European Time, and Eastern European Time. Countries like Australia, Canada and the U.S.A., which extend to east and west over great distances, are divided into several Zones. Thus, Australia has Western, Central, and Eastern Times; and Canada and the U.S.A. share Atlantic, Eastern, Central, Mountain, and Pacific Times. If Local Time (*q.v.*) were used throughout the world instead of the Standard Time system, there would be endless confusion.

THROUGHOUT THE WORLD

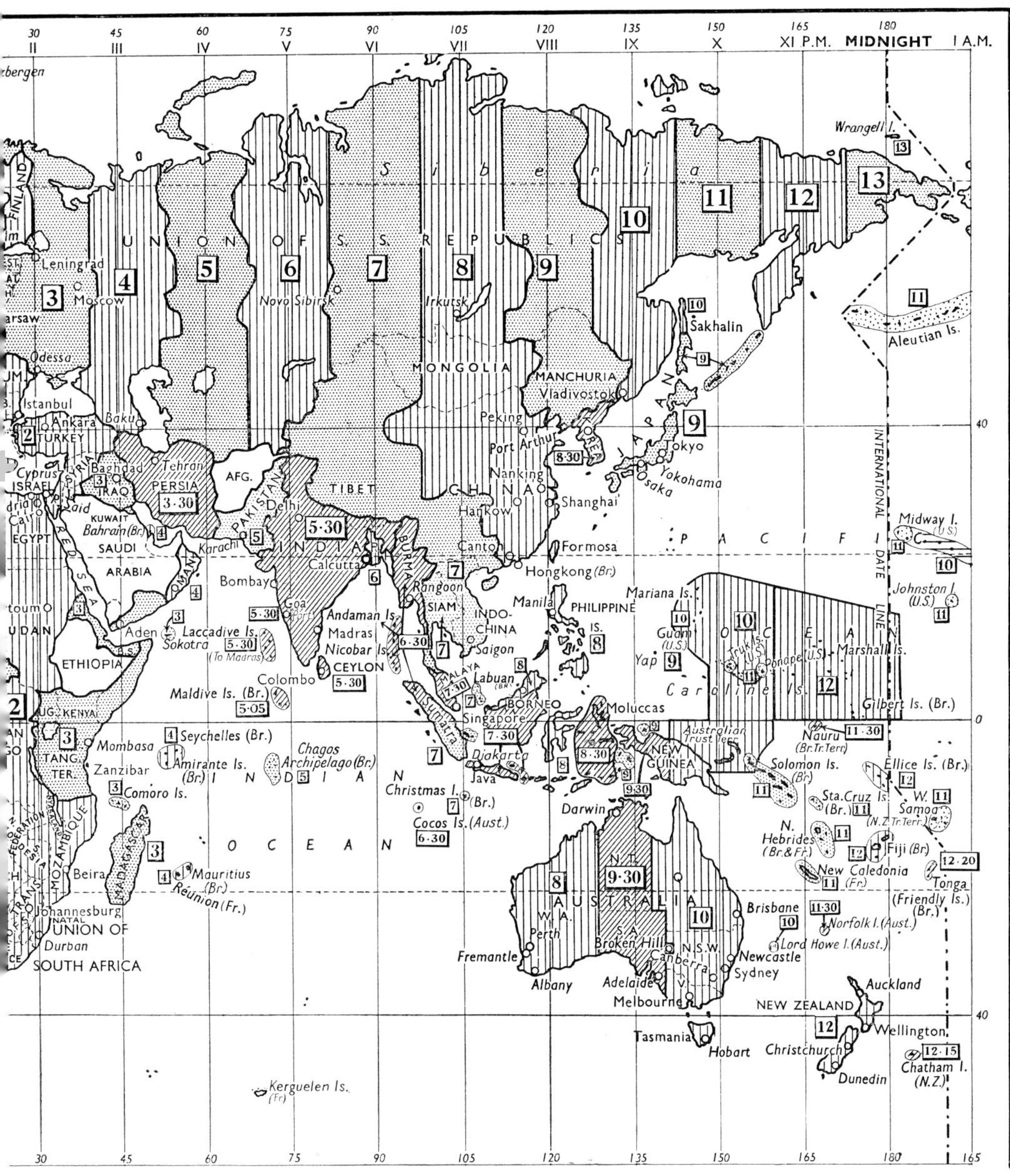

The map also shows the International Date Line. This is based by international agreement on the meridian of 180 degrees and has been established to compensate for the time lost or gained when travelling round the world. For example, a traveller setting off from London and travelling round the world without altering his time, would find (on reaching London again) that he had lost a day, if he had travelled westwards, or gained a day if he had travelled eastwards. So somewhere or other on the journey, the date has to be changed, and the most convenient place for this is along the meridian of 180 degrees, most of which lies in the ocean.

A ship approaching the International Date Line from the west drops a day, *e.g.*, going from Monday to Wednesday, if it crosses the Line. A ship approaching from the east repeats a day, *e.g.*, going thus, Monday, Monday, Tuesday, if it crosses the Line.

References to time will be found under the following headings in the Glossary: *Greenwich Mean Time*, *Local Time*, *Standard Time*. A further term that may be encountered is *Apparent Time*. This merely means " solar time " and is thus, for example, the time shown by a sundial.

British Summer Time (B.S.T.) was introduced by Act of Parliament in 1916 and places time in Great Britain during the summer period one hour in advance of Greenwich Mean Time. A similar system is operated in certain other countries, *e.g.*, Bermuda, Canada (except the Yukon), Hong Kong and Trinidad. In some countries, *e.g.*, the Dominican Republic, the variation takes place in winter and is known as Winter Time.

comparatively mild, while in the interiors and on their eastern margins there is usually an extreme climate. Summer and winter are well-marked seasons in the Temperate Zones.

Temperature. The degree, not the amount, of heat of a substance. It is measured usually by a thermometer in which the expanding and contracting mercury or alcohol indicates the changes in the heat level.

Terai. A narrow belt of hot, marshy jungle between the southern Himalayas and the Ganges plain.

Terrace Agriculture. The method of cultivation wherein the soil and the moisture are conserved by retaining walls or banks along the contours of the slopes of the hills.

Terrestrial Magnetism. See *Magnetic Poles.*

Territorial Waters. The belt of sea along the coast of a country which is regarded as part of its territory. This is usually three miles wide, but in recent years some countries have claimed wider belts as territorial waters.

Thalweg. This is the German name for river profile. See *River.*

Tidal Wave. The gigantic wave which usually follows an earthquake that has disturbed the level of the land bordering upon a sea. The water returns to its level in a great devastating wave.

Tides. The rise and fall, approximately twice in every twenty-four hours, of the level of the sea. Tides are caused by the attraction of the Moon, and to some extent of the Sun, affecting the fluid water envelope, or Hydrosphere, of the Earth and pulling it out of shape on opposite sides. These bulges move as gigantic waves over the seas of the Earth because of its daily rotation. In narrow estuaries and bays the rise can be up to 40 or 50 ft., in the seas over Continental Shelves up to 20 or 25 ft., but in the open ocean the rise is far less, being about 2 ft. at most. See also *Neap Tides, Spring Tides.*

Tierra. In South and Central America this word means " land ". Tierra Caliente is the region of hot, moist lowlands of the coastal regions up to about 3,000 ft. Tierra Templada is the more temperate region, between 3,000 and 7,000 ft. in altitude, and Tierra Fria is the cooler and colder region, above 7,000 ft.

Till. Another name for Boulder Clay (*q.v.*).

Timber Line. The line on mountain slopes above which trees cannot grow. Its altitude varies with the latitude, the aspect (the line is higher on south-facing slopes) and, to some extent, with the rainfall and the soil.

Time. See *Greenwich Mean Time, Local Time, Standard Time* and the map on pp. 228 and 229.

Tor. A mass of granite rock standing on its own. Such masses are very common in Devon and Cornwall.

Tornado. A very violent and sudden cyclonic wind storm. The African Tornado, frequent in parts of West Africa, is the result of the dry north-easterly Harmattan wind meeting moist air coming in from the south-west. A similar tornado develops in the Mississippi Basin on hot spring and summer days. This wind acts as a whirlwind and its speed at the centre may be as much as 200 miles per hour, resulting in great damage to the places over which it passes.

Torrid Zone. See *Tropics.*

Trade Winds. These blow from sub-tropical to equatorial regions; that is, from areas of high pressure to areas of low pressure. The rotation of the Earth causes the trade winds to be deflected towards the west, so that they become North-East Trades in the Northern Hemisphere and South-East Trades in the Southern. The regions affected by the trade winds move about 5° North and South in harmony with the apparent seasonal movement of the Sun. The trade winds are usually very regular, especially over oceans, and they were extremely valuable to the old sailing ships. In fact, their name is derived from the nautical expression " to blow trade," which means " to blow along a regular track." See diagram on p. 221.

Transhumance. The movement of pastoral peoples and their flocks and herds to the high pastures in the mountains in summer, and the reverse movement for the winter. There may be living quarters both in the uplands and in the valleys. It is still a feature of life in the Alps. Many pairs of hill farmhouses in Wales are called *Hafod,* or summer home, and *Hendre,* the permanent (or old) home.

Tributary. A stream or river which joins a larger one.

Tropical Cyclone. A whirlwind type of storm originating in a small tropical area of low atmospheric pressure; that is, in an acute depression. The cyclone is localised and may be only fifteen to thirty miles at the focus of the whirlwind, the cyclone as a whole being about 100 to 200 miles across. Around the centre winds are often of hurricane force (see *Beaufort Scale*), and they are associated with very dark thunder clouds, thunderstorms and torrential rains. These whirlwinds tend to move over similar tracks, the cyclones as a whole having speeds of about twelve to fifteen miles an hour. Tropical cyclones rotate in an anti-clockwise direction in the Northern Hemisphere, and clockwise in the Southern. They usually originate on the hot western margins of oceans where low-pressure hot spots develop on islands or continental shores; then into the very low-pressure areas thus caused cooler winds will move quickly off the sea, bearing much moisture. In the China Seas, the Tropical Cyclone is called a *Typhoon;* in the West Indies, a *Hurricane;* and in Western Australia, a *Willy-Willy.*

Tropics. (1) The area between the Tropic of Cancer and the Tropic of Capricorn, *i.e.,* the Torrid Zone, which is evenly divided by the Equator.
(2) The two actual parallels of latitude: 23½° N. (Tropic of Cancer) and 23½° S. (Tropic of Capricorn). On the Tropic of Cancer the Sun appears exactly overhead about June 21st, the Summer Solstice of the Northern Hemisphere. It appears directly above the Tropic of Capricorn about December 22nd, the Summer Solstice of the Southern Hemisphere.

Tuff. Rock composed of volcanic ash compressed by the weight of later rocks into a compact mass.

Tundra. The band of almost treeless country bordering the Arctic Circle in Siberia, Northern Europe and North America. Because the temperature for most of the year is below freezing point, the subsoil remains permanently frozen, so that in summer the surface of the Tundra is often swampy. The Tundra is the home of the Eskimo in America and the Samoyed in Eurasia, whose herds of reindeer have been domesticated. In summer the Tundra is often covered with flowers and berry plants, but its vegetation is mostly mosses and lichens. In summer the Tundra is often infested by clouds of mosquitoes.

Typhoon. See *Tropical Cyclone.*

Ubac. A French word used to describe land that slopes generally northwards and, in the Northern Hemisphere, away from the Sun. Such slopes are colder and less fruitful than those with southerly aspects.

Umbra. The shadow of the Moon on the Earth as seen in an eclipse.

Undertow. When a wave breaks on a shore there is below it a returning undercurrent of water. This is called the undertow and it can often be dangerous to bathers.

Uplands. The areas in a country which are well above the level of the lower valleys and lowland plains.

U-shaped Valley. A river valley in which a glacier of the Ice Age flattened the valley bottom and cut back the bottoms of the slopes and the projecting spurs. Such valleys when " drowned " by the sea form fjords. See *Fjord.*

Valley Wind. The wind that moves up a valley on clear summer days towards the hot mountain slopes. It may be reversed at night when the mountain slopes cool more quickly than the valley so that the air in contact becomes denser and heavier than the valley air, which it then displaces by gravity.

Veering. The change in the direction of a wind clockwise. An anti-clockwise change is known as Backing.

Vega. Irrigated land in Spain which is not so fertile as the Huerta (*q.v.*) and yields only one crop every year.

Vein. The ore deposits in the cracks of rocks. Coal seams also are sometimes called veins, as are beds of ironstone.

Veld. The high tableland grass country of the Transvaal, in South Africa. It is in three levels: the Low or Bush Veld, from about 1,000 to 3,000 ft.; the Middle Veld, about 3,000 to 5,000 ft.; and the High Veld, which

HIGHEST IN THE WORLD

Ministerio de Fomento, Dirección de Turismo, Venezuela.

The highest waterfall (*q.v.*) in the world occurs on a small tributary of the river Caroni in the south-eastern highlands of Venezuela. The height of these Angel Falls, as they are called, is 3,212 feet, the highest fall being 2,648 feet. They can be visited by air from Ciudad Bolivar, an important commercial and trading town on the southern bank of the Orinoco and some two hundred miles from the mouth of the river. Ciudad Bolivar is the headquarters of navigation on the Orinoco. The Caroni is a tributary of the Orinoco, which flows mainly in Venezuela and is one of the major rivers of South America.

is between 5,000 and 6,000 ft. above sea level.

Vendavales. The wet, winter, south-westerly winds of the Western Mediterranean. See *Mediterranean Climate*.

Volcano. An opening in the crust of the Earth through which from time

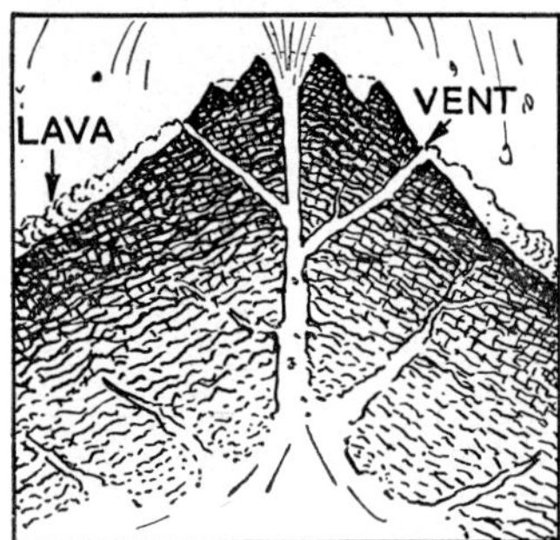

to time molten rock, hot ashes and cinders, flaming gases and steam are erupted to the surface. These come from, or are caused by, the *magma* which seems to form a molten layer below the Earth's crust. Through the accumulation of solids around the point of emission, a volcano tends to build up a cone-shaped mountain with the hollow crater in the top. The molten magma sometimes forces itself along and upwards through the joints of rocks to form, when cooled, sills and dykes or even a huge mass of igneous rock under the surface of the sedimentary rocks. Volcanoes may be active, dormant (sleeping) or extinct. See picture p. 227.

Wadi. A gully or nullah in desert regions which only has a stream in it after torrential rains or when the heat of summer melts the snow in adjoining mountains.

Warm Front. The line where an advancing mass of warm air meets colder air which, being heavier, causes the warm air to be pushed up at an acute angle over the cold mass. Temperatures rise and there is usually rain followed by bright intervals. See also *Cold Front*.

Waterfall. This is usually caused by a river wearing away softer rocks below a harder, level or backward-tilted rock-bed in its course. Changes in level due to faulting and in respect of tributary streams to main valleys deepened by ice erosion may form waterfalls which are likely, however, to be more short-lived.

Watershed. The high land which separates two or more river systems or basins. This is also known as a Divide which, however, does not follow the crests of the hills since the headwaters of opposite rivers tend to cut backwards into each others' basins. Water-parting is another term for watershed.

Waterspout. In the whirling centre of a tornado or tropical cyclone, with its extremely low air pressure, a heavy, dark rain-forming cloud descends to meet water sucked up in the form of a cone from the surface of the sea. The column, or waterspout, thus formed may reach a height of several hundred feet.

Water Table. The level of the water which has accumulated under the permeable rocks of a particular area above an impermeable layer. The level of the water table may rise and fall in relation to the precipitation, but usually there is a vast reservoir of underground water (see *Artesian Well*). Springs often occur where permeable and impermeable rocks outcrop together.

Weather. The conditions of temperature, rainfall, sunshine, winds, etc., of a particular place from day to day. The accumulated effect over a year would be the *climate* (*q.v.*).

Weather Chart. The map upon which are drawn the Isobars and Isotherms for a particular area, time and date. The information for these is sent to the Meteorological Office by observation stations scattered over a wide area of land and sea. From experience of how the distribution, shape and relation of, particularly, the Isobars have on past occasions affected the weather, fairly consistent forecasts of the weather likely to follow can usually be made.

Weatherings. The effects of weather upon the rocks of the Earth's crust. See *Erosion*.

Well. A hole dug or bored from the surface of the land to reach a water table. A shallow well would tap subsoil or water lying above the first impermeable layer; a deep well would pass through an impermeable layer to reach water lying above another impermeable layer farther down. *Artesian Wells* (*q.v.*) are deep wells in which the water is under sufficient pressure (or head) to enable it to surge to the surface at a boring.

Westerlies. These variable winds blow Polewards from sub-tropical high pressure areas in the Northern and Southern Hemispheres. In winter, the Westerlies move southwards in the Northern Hemisphere and bring rain to sub-tropical and Mediterranean regions. They are the prevailing west winds which blow over the British Isles and Western Europe, especially during the summer, when they are at their northern limit. In the Southern Hemisphere the winds blow strongly and regularly throughout the year in a belt known as the *Roaring Forties* (*q.v.*). See diagram on p. 221.

Wet Bulb Temperature. See *Humidity*.

Whirlpool. See *Mælstrom*.

Willy-Willy. A tropical cyclone experienced in Western Australia, especially in summer. The term is also applied to whirlwinds that occur over the Australian deserts.

Wind. See diagram on p. 221.

Windrose. A diagram recording, by lines proportioned to the times which each wind has prevailed over a period, the wind pattern of a particular place. The longest line indicates the prevailing wind. The number in the circle at the centre is a percentage of the instances of observation when the air was calm.

Windward. The direction from which the wind *comes*. Compare with *Leeward*.

Yardangs. Ridges of rock in the Central Asian deserts caused by the "sand blast" of the prevailing wind wearing out narrow "canyons" along the weaker vertical joints in the rock-beds. Harder beds of rock at the top resist this erosion so that the softer rocks below these beds are undercut.

Year. The time taken for the planet Earth to move in its orbit once round the Sun. The time actually taken is 365 days, 5 hours, 48 minutes and 46 seconds but, for convenience, this is regarded as 365 days. The lost time is then, once every 4 years, added together to make another day—the 29th of February in every Leap Year of 366 days. But this creates another, though small, error because Leap Year is 11 minutes 14 seconds longer than the true year (or 44 minutes, 56 seconds total every 4 years). This again is corrected in the new style Gregorian Calendar by the centuries being regarded as Leap Years only when they are divisible by 400 (not 4).

Young Stream. In the young stage the current flows briskly and cuts down its bed faster than the eroded materials from the valley sides are brought down. This makes the valley V-shaped and the stream eats back rapidly into the slope at its source. If a plain is raised, its rivers become rejuvenated and they will cut deep ravines in the plateau leaving flat-topped steep-sided heights between them, *e.g.*, the Glamorgan Plateau.

Youthful Topography. This results from comparatively recent Earth movements, folding and uplift. The physical features will then be sharp and well-marked. The mountain slopes will tend to be steep, and jagged mountain peaks will stand up rugged and uneroded. The rivers and streams will run fast and be busy at their work of wearing down the landscape. A good example of Youthful Topography is the Alps. But, ultimately, in millions of years, the landscape will become gentle and mature with rounded hills in which will run slow-moving streams.

Zonda. A very hot summer wind in the River Plate area (Argentina and Uruguay) which blows in from the tropical northern regions of South America, rather like the *Brickfields* wind in the southern parts of Australia.

Zones. The regions into which the Earth is sometimes divided are: the *Frigid Zones* (within the Arctic and Antarctic Circles), the *North* and *South Temperate Zones* (between the Tropic of Cancer and the Arctic Circle and the Tropic of Capricorn and the Antarctic Circle) and the *Torrid Zone* which is the Equatorial "Belt" (between the Tropics of Cancer and Capricorn.)

Zone Time. See *Standard*, or *Zone*, *Time*.

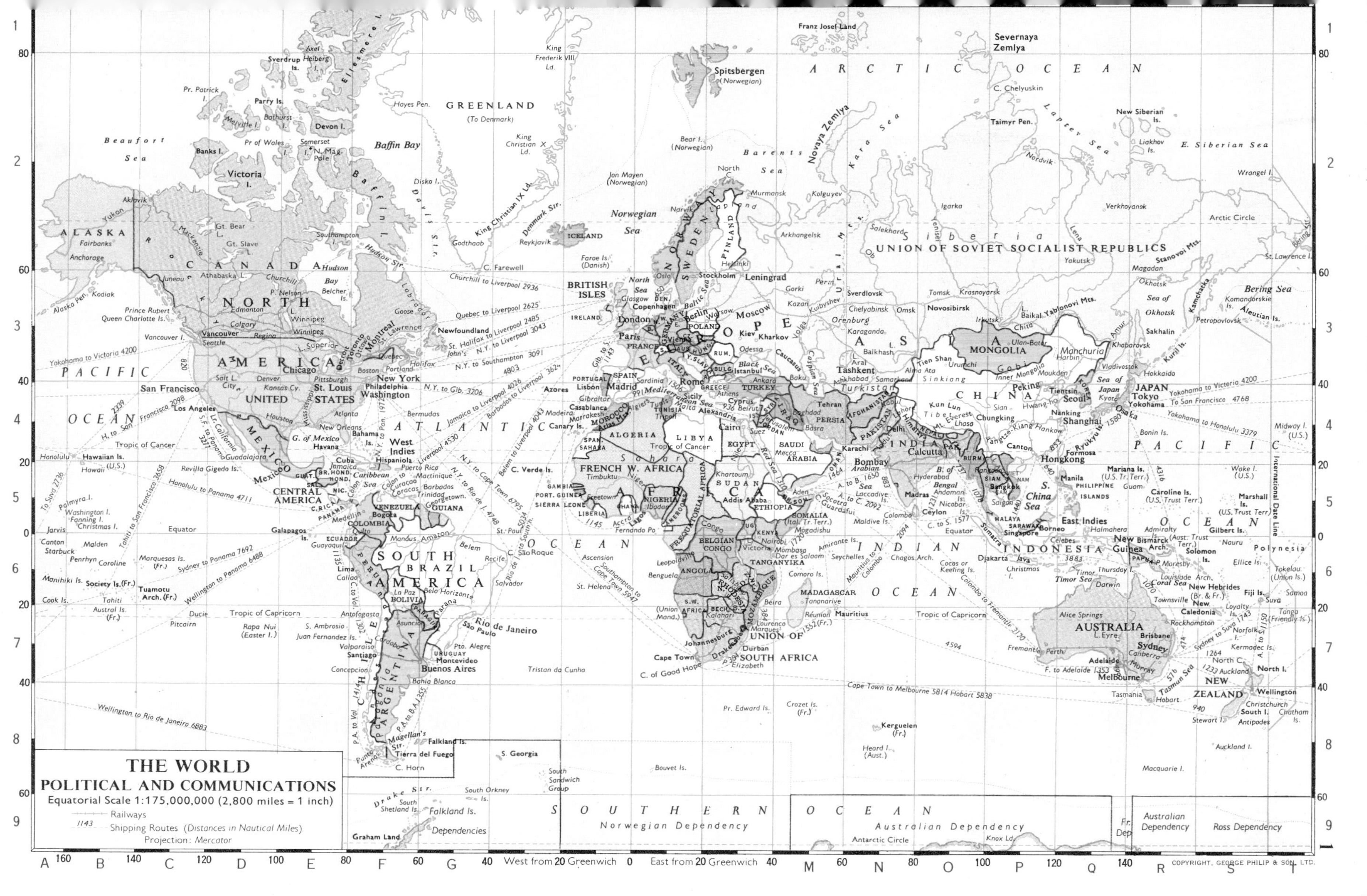

THE WORLD
POLITICAL AND COMMUNICATIONS
Equatorial Scale 1:175,000,000 (2,800 miles = 1 inch)
Railways
1143 Shipping Routes (Distances in Nautical Miles)
Projection: Mercator
COPYRIGHT, GEORGE PHILIP & SON, LTD.

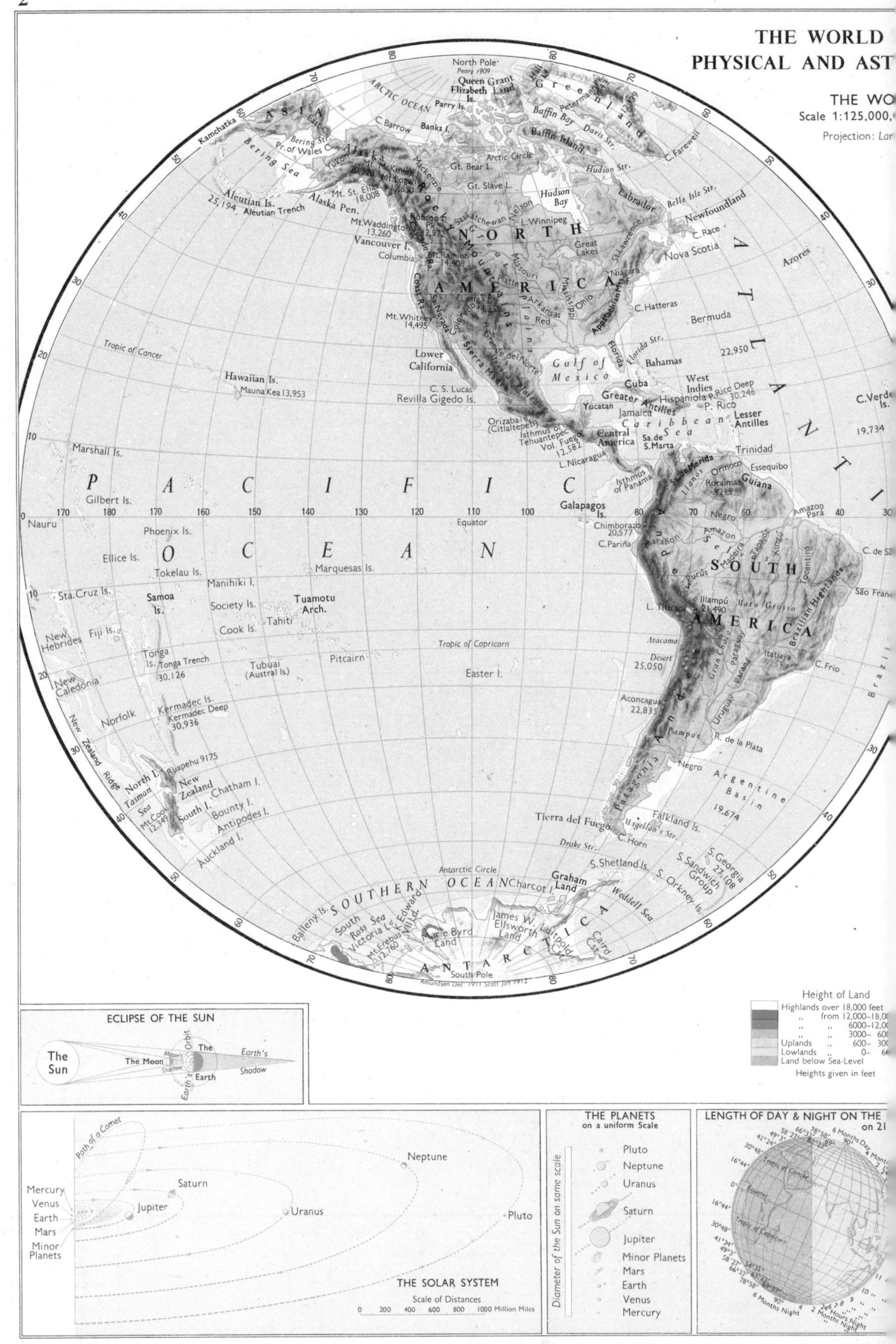
THE WORLD
PHYSICAL AND AST
THE WO
Scale 1:125,000,
Projection: Lar
North Pole
Peary 1909
ARCTIC OCEAN
Queen Elizabeth Is.
Grant Land
Parry Is.
Banks I.
Greenland
Baffin Bay
Davis Str.
Baffin Island
C. Farewell
Hudson Str.
Hudson Bay
Labrador
Belle Isle Str.
Newfoundland
C. Race
Nova Scotia
Azores
ASIA
Kamchatka
Bering Str.
Pr. of Wales C.
Bering Sea
Alaska
Yukon
Mt. McKinley 20,320
Mt. Logan 19,850
Mt. St. Elias 18,008
Alaska Pen.
Aleutian Is.
25,194 Aleutian Trench
C. Barrow
Mackenzie
Arctic Circle
Gt. Bear L.
Gt. Slave L.
Rocky Mountains
Robson Pk. 12,972
Mt. Waddington 13,260
Vancouver I.
Columbia
Mt. Rainier 14,408
Saskatchewan
Nelson
L. Winnipeg
NORTH AMERICA
Great Lakes
St. Lawrence
Niagara F.
Missouri
Platte
Mississippi
Ohio
Appalachian Mts.
Arkansas
Red
Coast Ra.
Sa. Nevada
Colorado
Leighs Pk. 14,255
Mt. Whitney 14,495
C. Hatteras
Bermuda
Great Plains
Florida
Florida Str.
Bahamas
22,950
Tropic of Cancer
Lower California
Gulf of Mexico
Rio Grande del Norte
Sierra Madre
Hawaiian Is.
Mauna Kea 13,953
C. S. Lucas
Revilla Gigedo Is.
Cuba
West Indies
Greater Antilles
Yucatan
Jamaica
Hispaniola
P. Rico Deep 30,246
P. Rico
Caribbean Sea
Lesser Antilles
C. Verde Is.
Orizaba (Citlaltepetl)
Isthmus of Tehuantepec
Vol. Fuego 12,582
Central America
Sa. de S. Marta
19,734
Trinidad
Marshall Is.
L. Nicaragua
Isthmus of Panama
Sa. de Merida
Llanos
Orinoco
Essequibo
Roraima 9219
Guiana
PACIFIC OCEAN
ATLANTIC
Gilbert Is.
Galapagos Is.
Amazon
Para
Nauru
Equator
Phoenix Is.
Chimborazo 20,577
C. Pariña
Negro
Marañon
Ellice Is.
Tokelau Is.
Marquesas Is.
Selvas
Madeira
Tapajóz
Xingú
Tocantins
C. de S
Purús
SOUTH AMERICA
Manihiki I.
Sta. Cruz Is.
Samoa Is.
Society Is.
Tuamotu Arch.
Tahiti
L. Titicaca
Illampú 21,490
Matto Grosso
Brazilian Highlands
São Fran
Fiji Is.
Cook Is.
New Hebrides
Tropic of Capricorn
Atacama Desert
25,050
Gran Chaco
Paraguay
Paraná
Itatiaya 9255
C. Frio
Tonga Is.
Tonga Trench 30,126
Tubuai (Austral Is.)
Pitcairn
Easter I.
New Caledonia
Kermadec Is.
Kermadec Deep 30,936
Norfolk
Aconcagua 22,835
Andes
Uruguay
Pampas
R. de la Plata
New Zealand Ridge
Ruapehu 9175
North I.
New Zealand
Chatham I.
Tasman Sea
Mt. Cook 12,349
South I.
Bounty I.
Antipodes I.
Auckland I.
Negro
Patagonia
Argentine Basin
19,674
Falkland Is.
Tierra del Fuego
Magellan's Str.
C. Horn
Drake Str.
S. Shetland Is.
S. Sandwich Group
S. Georgia 27,108
S. Orkney Is.
Antarctic Circle
SOUTHERN OCEAN
Charcot I.
Graham Land
Weddell Sea
Balleny Is.
South Victoria Ld.
Ross Sea
Edward VII Ld.
Mt. Erebus 12,760
Marie Byrd Land
James W. Ellsworth Land
Luitpold Cst.
Caird Cst.
ANTARCTICA
South Pole
Amundsen Dec. 1911 Scott Jan 1912
Height of Land
Highlands over 18,000 feet
from 12,000–18,0
6000–12,0
3000– 60
Uplands 600– 30
Lowlands 0– 6
Land below Sea-Level
Heights given in feet
ECLIPSE OF THE SUN
The Sun
The Moon
Moon's Shadow
Earth's Orbit
The Earth
Earth's Shadow
Path of a Comet
Mercury
Venus
Earth
Mars
Minor Planets
Jupiter
Saturn
Uranus
Neptune
Pluto
THE SOLAR SYSTEM
Scale of Distances
0 200 400 600 800 1000 Million Miles
THE PLANETS
on a uniform Scale
Diameter of the Sun on same scale
Pluto
Neptune
Uranus
Saturn
Jupiter
Minor Planets
Mars
Earth
Venus
Mercury
LENGTH OF DAY & NIGHT ON THE
on 21
6 Months Day
Tropic of Cancer
Equator
Tropic of Capricorn
6 Months Night
2 Months Night

MISPHERES
MICAL GEOGRAPHY
YSICAL
miles=1 inch)
ent Azimuthal
POINTS OF THE COMPASS
N
NNE
NE
ENE
E
ESE
SE
SSE
S
SSW
SW
WSW
W
WNW
NW
NNW
North Pole
ARCTIC OCEAN
Svalbard
Fr. Josef Ld.
Severnaya Zemlya
New Siberian Is.
Jan Mayen
Iceland
Arctic Circle
Novaya Zemlya
N.Cape
Kara Sea
Taimyr Pen.
Kamchatka
British Isles
Scandinavia
Finland
Kola
White Sea
Dvina
L.Ladoga
Baltic
North Sea
English Ch.
Loire
Bay of Biscay
Rhine
Pyrenees
Alps
Apennines
Carpathians
Vistula
Dnieper
Danube
Iberian Pen.
Tagus
Str. of Gibraltar
Sardinia
Sicily
Adriatic
Balkan Pen.
Mediterranean Sea
Black Sea
Anatolia
Caucasus
Elbrus 18,481
Ararat
Caspian Sea
Don
Volga
Ural Mts.
Ural
Kirgiz Steppe
Aral Sea
Ob
Yenisei
West Siberian Plain
Siberia
Irtysh
Khatanga
Lena
Aldan
Cr.Tunguska
Up.Tunguska
Sayan Mts.
L.Baikal
Yablonovy Ra.
Stanovoi Ra.
S. of Okhotsk
Sakhalin
Kuril Is.
Kuril Trench 31,458
Hokkaido
Amur
Altai
L.Balkhash
ASIA
Mongolia
Gobi or Shamo
Khingan Ra.
Sea of Japan
Honshu
Japan
Fujiyama 12,388
Korea
North China Plain
Yellow Sea
Hwang-ho
Lop Nor
Tien Shan
Tarim Basin
Pamirs
Kunlun
Tibet
Karakoram
Hindu Kush
Amu Darya
Syr Darya
Elburz
Demavend 18,380
Plateau of Iran
Tigris
Euphrates
Dead Sea
Sinai Pen.
Persian G.
Arabia
Rub 'al Khali
G. of Oman
Sulaiman Ra.
Indus
Thar
Himalaya
Mt. Everest 29,028
Ganges
Brahmaputra
Yangtse-kiang
China
Si-kiang
East China Sea
Ryukyu Is.
Bonin Is.
Formosa
Tropic of Cancer
34,038
Kutch
Narbada
India
Kistna
Godavari
W. Ghats
Deccan
E. Ghats
Bay of Bengal
Irrawaddy
Salween
Further India
Red
Mekong
Hainan
Luzon
South China Sea
Philippine Is.
22,400
Mariana or Ladrone Is.
Marianas
Guam
PACIFIC OCEAN
35,640 Trench
Mindanao Trench 34,578
Mindanao
Caroline Is.
Palau Is.
G. of Siam
Malay Pen.
Kinabalu 13,448
Str. of Malacca
Sumatra
Borneo
Celebes Sea
Halmahera
Celebes
Moluccas
East Indies
Java Sea
Banda Sea
Java
Sunda Is.
Sunda Str.
22,968
Christmas I.
Java Trench
Timor
Pt. Darwin
New Guinea
Bismarck Arch.
Solomon Is.
Mt. Victoria 13,363
Torres Str.
C. York
G. of Carpentaria
York Pen.
Gt. Barrier Reef
Coral Sea
AUSTRALIA
L.Eyre
Steep Pt.
C. Leeuwin
Great Australian Bight
Spencer Gulf
Darling
Murray
Australian Alps
Mt. Kosciusko 7328
C.Byron
18,204
Bass Str.
Tasmania
Madeira
Canary Is.
Tenerife 12,100
Atlas Mts.
Toubkal 13,661
Ahaggar Plat.
Sahara
Libyan Des.
Egypt
Nile
Red Sea
Tibesti
Senegal
Niger
L.Chad
Shari
Benue
Adamawa Highlands
AFRICA
Sudan
Volta
B. of Benin
Fernando Po
G. of Guinea
Cameroon Pk. 13,350
Uele
Bahr el Ghazal
Wh. Nile
Bl. Nile
Atbara
Ethiopian Highlands
G. of Aden
Somali Pen.
C. Guardafui
Socotra
Arabian Sea
Laccadive Is.
C.Comorin
Palk Str.
Ceylon 8295
Andaman Is.
Nicobar Is.
Maldive Is.
L.Rudolf
Congo
Ruwenzori 16,794
L. Albert
L. Victoria
Mt. Kenya 17,040
Juba
Kilimanjaro 19,340
Stanley Falls
Kasai
L. Tanganyika
Zanzibar
Seychelles
Amirantes
Aldabra Is.
Chagos Arch
Equator
Cuanza
L. Bangweulu
Nyasa
Comoro Is.
Zambesi
Mozambique Chan.
Madagascar
8674
Réunion 10,070
Mauritius
Tropic of Capricorn
Cocos or Keeling Is.
20,094
INDIAN OCEAN
St. Helena
Cunene
Cubango
Victoria Falls
L. Ngami
Matopo H.
Limpopo
Walvis Bay
Kalahari
Delagoa Bay
Vaal
Drakensberg
Orange
C. of Good Hope
C. Agulhas
Tristan da Cunha
Atlantic Ridge
ATLANTIC OCEAN
New Amsterdam
Crozet Is.
Kerguelen
Kerguelen Gaussberg Ridge
Bouvet I.
Atlantic - Indian - Antarctic Basin
Eastern - Indian - Antarctic Basin
Macquarie I.
SOUTHERN OCEAN
Antarctic Circle
Enderby Ld.
K. Wilhelm Ld.
Q. Mary Land
Wilkes Land
Adélie Ld.
Coats Ld.
ANTARCTICA
South Pole
Depth of Sea
0– 600 feet (100 fathoms)
600– 6000 ,, (1000 ,,)
6000–24,000 ,, (4000 ,,)
Below 24,000 ,,
Deeps given in feet
ECLIPSE OF THE MOON
Earth's Shadow
The Moon
The Earth
Earth's Orbit
The Sun
TERRESTRIAL ZONES
North Pole
NORTH FRIGID ZONE
Arctic Circle
NORTH TEMPERATE ZONE
Cancer
TORRID ZONE
Equator
Capricorn
SOUTH TEMPERATE ZONE
SOUTH FRIGID ZONE
Antarctic Circle
South Pole
THE EARTH'S ORBIT (THE SEASONS)
(NORTHERN HEMISPHERE)
Spring
Winter
Summer
Autumn
March 21st (Vernal Equinox)
June 21st (Midsummer)
Aphelion
The Sun
Perihelion
December 21st (Midwinter)
September 23rd (Autumnal Equinox)
THE PHASES OF THE MOON
New Moon
First Quarter
Last Quarter
Full Moon
Noon
Morning
Evening
Midnight
The yellow lines represent the rays of the Sun

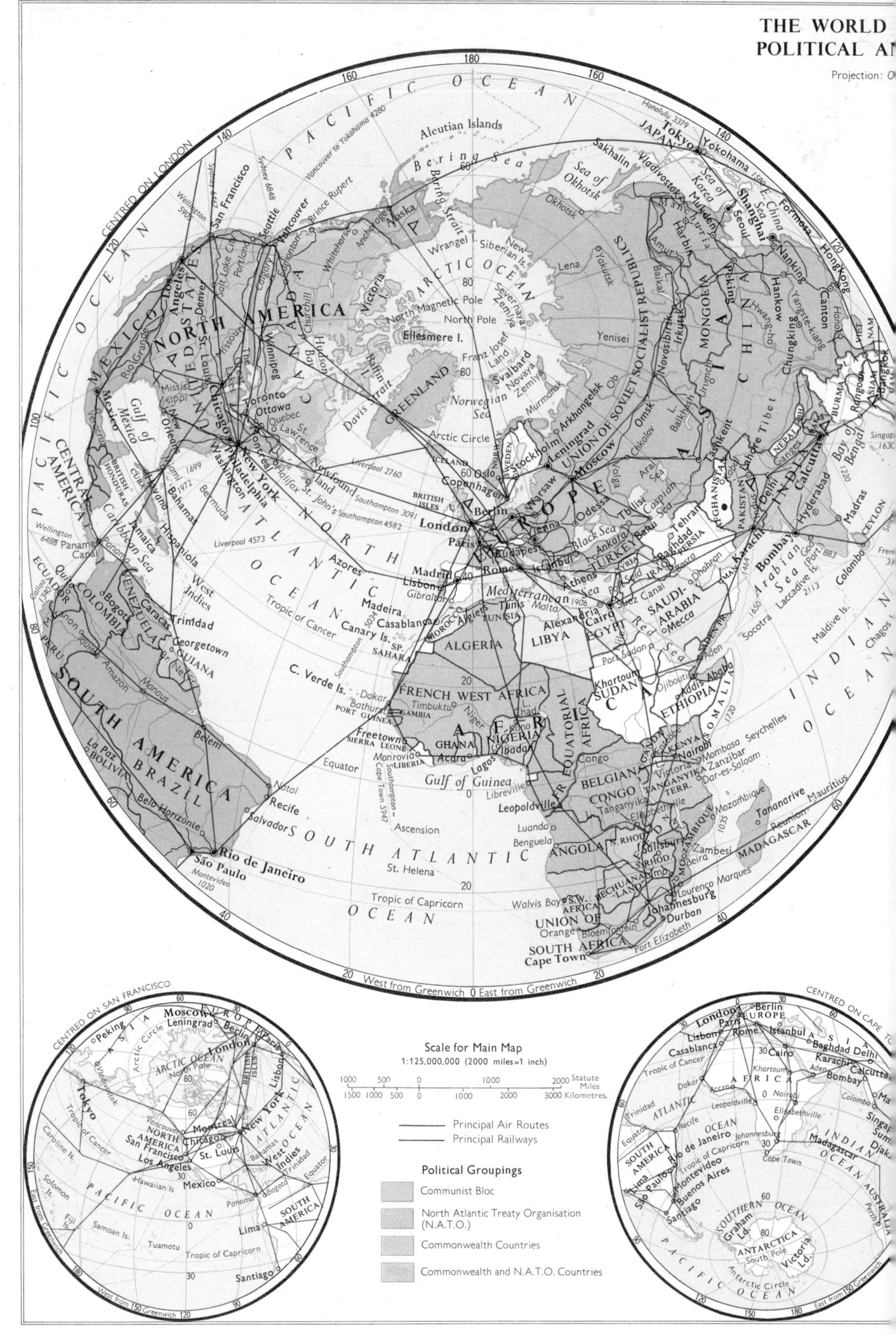
THE WORLD
POLITICAL AI
Projection: O
CENTRED ON LONDON
PACIFIC OCEAN
ARCTIC OCEAN
NORTH ATLANTIC OCEAN
SOUTH ATLANTIC OCEAN
INDIAN OCEAN
NORTH AMERICA
SOUTH AMERICA
EUROPE
ASIA
AFRICA
UNION OF SOVIET SOCIALIST REPUBLICS
UNITED STATES
CANADA
MEXICO
CENTRAL AMERICA
BRAZIL
GREENLAND
CHINA
INDIA
JAPAN
MONGOLIA
ALGERIA
LIBYA
EGYPT
SUDAN
ETHIOPIA
FRENCH WEST AFRICA
FR. EQUATORIAL AFRICA
BELGIAN CONGO
ANGOLA
UNION OF SOUTH AFRICA
MADAGASCAR
SAUDI-ARABIA
TURKEY
PERSIA
North Pole
North Magnetic Pole
Arctic Circle
Tropic of Cancer
Equator
Tropic of Capricorn
West from Greenwich 0 East from Greenwich
CENTRED ON SAN FRANCISCO
CENTRED ON CAPE TOWN
SOUTHERN OCEAN
ANTARCTICA
South Pole
Antarctic Circle
Scale for Main Map
1:125,000,000 (2000 miles=1 inch)
1000 500 0 1000 2000 Statute Miles
1500 1000 500 0 1000 2000 3000 Kilometres
Principal Air Routes
Principal Railways
Political Groupings
Communist Bloc
North Atlantic Treaty Organisation (N.A.T.O.)
Commonwealth Countries
Commonwealth and N.A.T.O. Countries

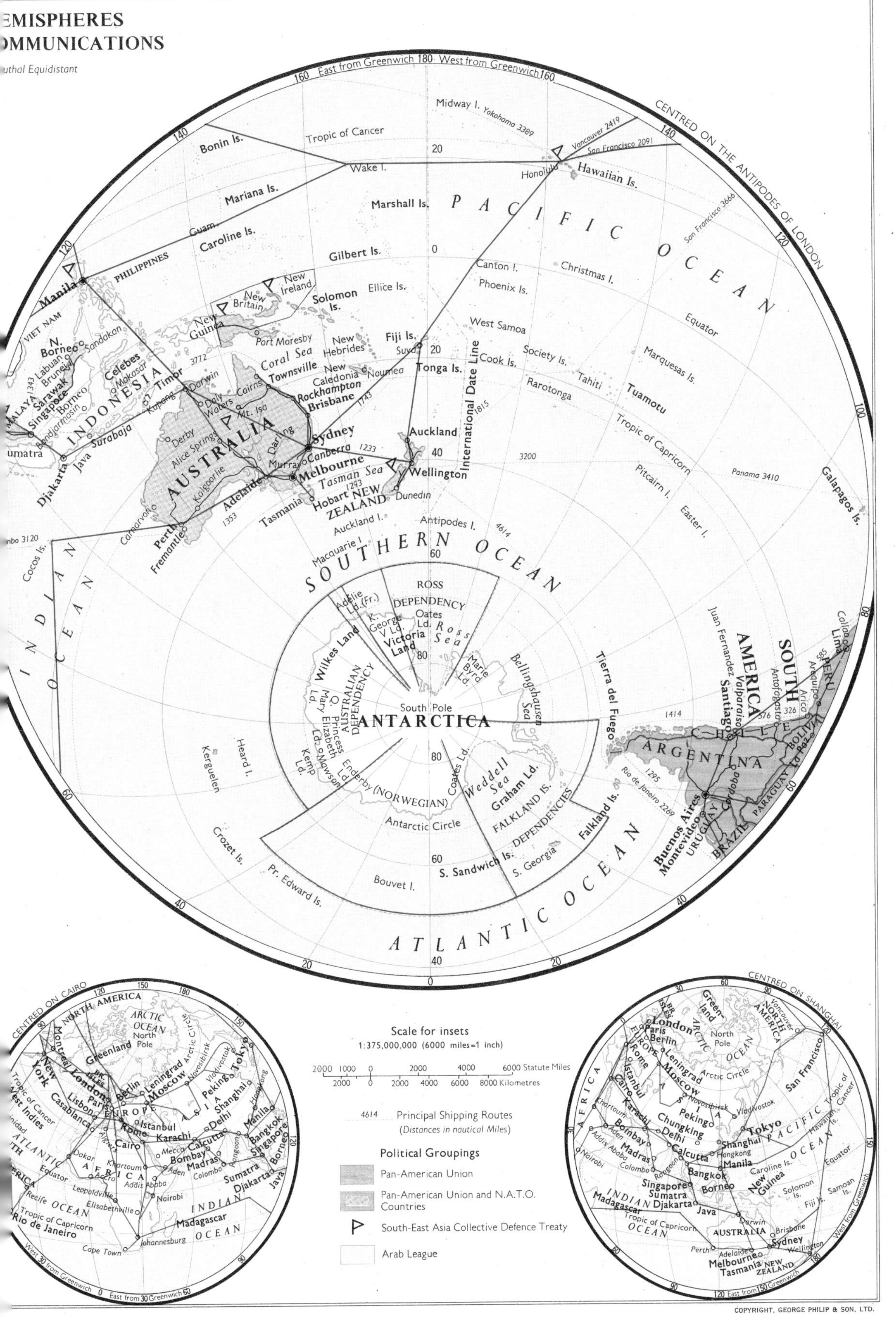
EMISPHERES
OMMUNICATIONS
uthal Equidistant
CENTRED ON THE ANTIPODES OF LONDON
East from Greenwich 180 West from Greenwich
PACIFIC OCEAN
SOUTHERN OCEAN
ATLANTIC OCEAN
INDIAN OCEAN
ANTARCTICA
South Pole
AUSTRALIA
INDONESIA
NEW ZEALAND
SOUTH AMERICA
ARGENTINA
CHILE
BOLIVIA
PERU
PARAGUAY
URUGUAY
BRAZIL
PHILIPPINES
ROSS DEPENDENCY
AUSTRALIAN DEPENDENCY
(NORWEGIAN)
FALKLAND IS. DEPENDENCIES
Tropic of Cancer
Equator
Tropic of Capricorn
Antarctic Circle
International Date Line
Manila
Sydney
Melbourne
Canberra
Brisbane
Adelaide
Perth
Auckland
Wellington
Honolulu
Hawaiian Is.
Buenos Aires
Montevideo
Santiago
Valparaiso
Djakarta
Singapore
CENTRED ON CAIRO
CENTRED ON SHANGHAI
Scale for insets
1:375,000,000 (6000 miles=1 inch)
2000 1000 0 2000 4000 6000 Statute Miles
2000 0 2000 4000 6000 8000 Kilometres
4614 Principal Shipping Routes
(Distances in nautical Miles)
Political Groupings
Pan-American Union
Pan-American Union and N.A.T.O. Countries
South-East Asia Collective Defence Treaty
Arab League

NORWEGIAN SEA
Iceland
Hekla 5095
Oraefa Jökull 6952
Arctic Circle
North Cape
Nordkinn
Vesterålen
Lofoten
L. Inari
Lapland
Kebnekaise 6965
Torne
Kjölen Mts.
Scandinavia
Ume
Indals
G. of Bothnia
Finland
Galdhopiggen 8097
Faroe Is.
Fisher Bank
Shetland Is.
Rockall
Hebrides
Orkney Is.
ATLANTIC OCEAN
British Isles
Ben Nevis 4406
Great Britain
Ireland
Irish Sea
Valentia I.
C. Clear
Snowdon 3560
Thames
Land's End
English Channel
NORTH SEA
Dogger Bank
Heligoland
Lindesnes
Skagerrak
Jutland
Kattegat
L. Vänern
L. Vättern
L. Mälaren
Gotland
BALTIC SEA
G. of Finland
Neva
L. Chudskoye
G. of Riga
W. Dvina
Niemen
North Europe
Netherlands
Weser
Elbe
Harz 3750
Oder
Vistula
Pripet
Pripet Marshes
Meuse
Ardennes
Eifel
Rhine
Westerwald
Taunus
Hunsrück
Seine
Brittany
Loire
Bay of Biscay
Gironde
Garonne
C. Finisterre
Erz Geb.
Sudetes
Jura
Vosges
Black For.
Danube
Bohemian For.
Moravian Heights
Inn
Carpathians
Tatra 8743
Dnestr
Prut
Central Massif
Mt. Dore 6190
Cevennes
Rhône
Mt. Blanc 15,780
ALPS
Bakony For.
Plain of Hungary
Danube
Drava
Tisza
Mures
Transylvanian Alps
Sava
Po
Dinaric Alps
Wallachia
Danube
Morava
Balkans
Rhodope
Balkan Peninsula
Pindus
Cantabrian Mts.
Pyrenees
Maladetta 11,168
Douro
Old Castile
Iberian Peninsula
C. da Roca
Tejo (Tagus)
Sa. da Estrela
Sa. de Guadarrama
New Castile
Sierra Morena
Guadalquivir
Andalusia
Sa. Nevada
Mulhacen 11,420
C. St. Vincent
C. Trafalgar
C. Spartel
Str. of Gibraltar
Er Rif
G. of Lions
Ligurian Sea
Corsica
Str. of Bonifacio
Sardinia
Balearic Is.
Apennines
ADRIATIC SEA
Gran Sasso 9560
Tiber
3890
Tyrrhenian Sea
Str. of Messina
Str. of Otranto
Calabria
Ionian Is.
Ionian Sea
Sicily
Etna 10,741
C. Bon
C. Blanco
MEDITERRANEAN
Malta
Maritime Atlas
Plateau of the Shotts
Saharan Atlas
Morea
C. Matapan
Aegean Sea
Ida
Crete
Gulf of Sidra
EUROPE: PHYSICAL
Scale 1:20,000,000 (320 miles = 1 inch)
Statute Miles
Kilometres
Canals
6190 Heights in feet
Projection: Bonne
West from Greenwich 0 East from Greenwich

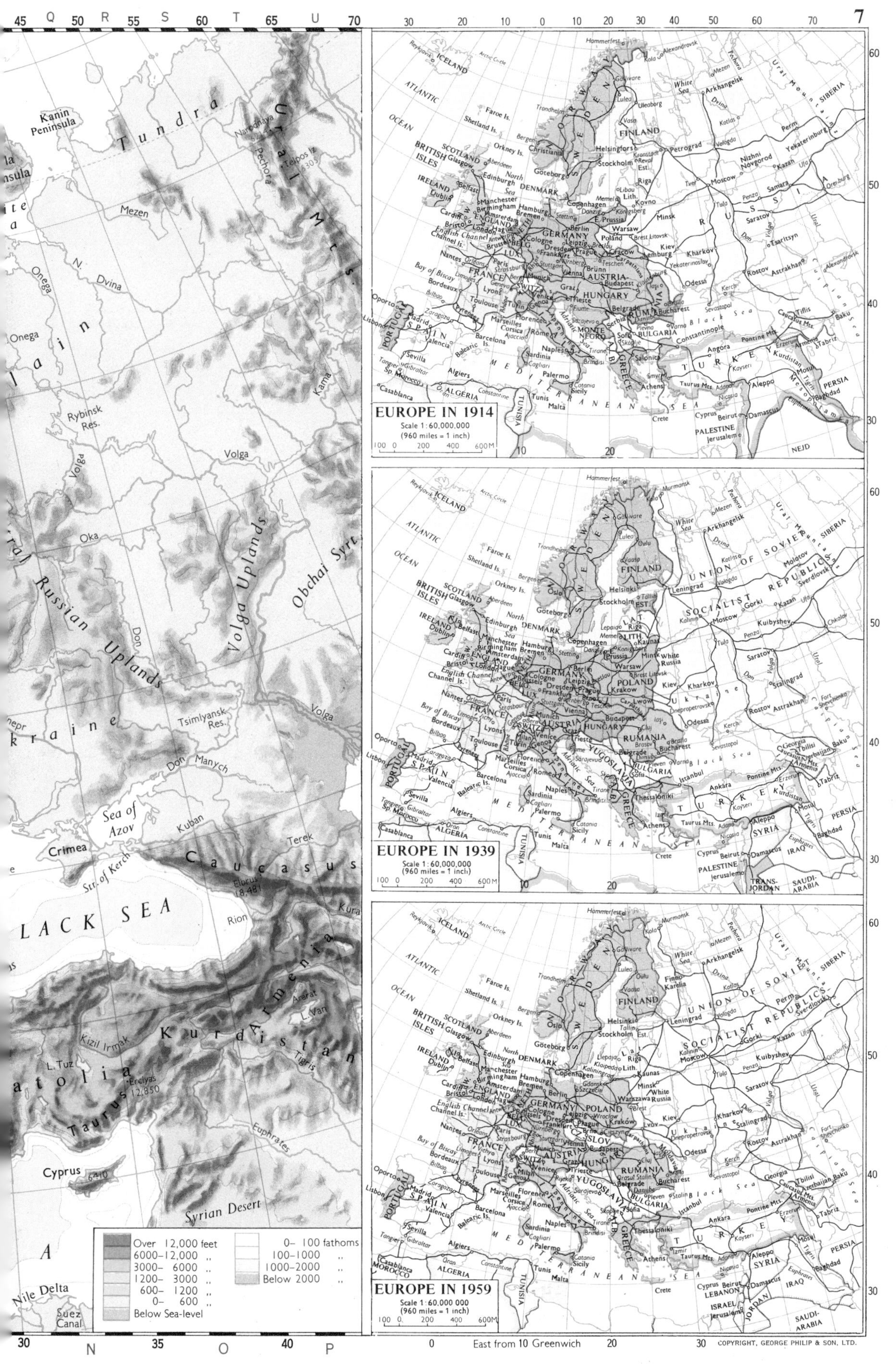

East from 10 Greenwich 20 30

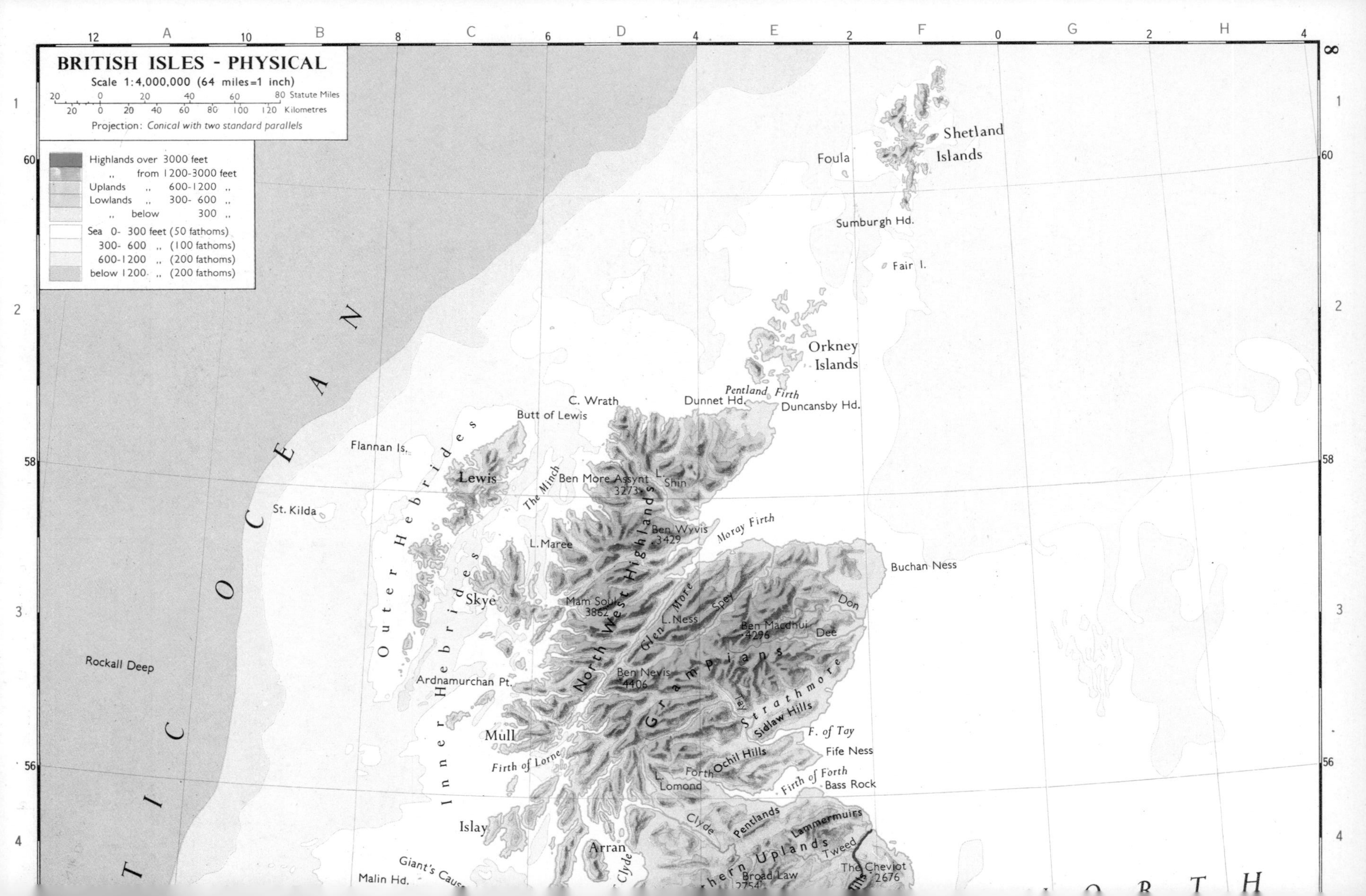
BRITISH ISLES - PHYSICAL
Scale 1:4,000,000 (64 miles=1 inch)
80 Statute Miles
120 Kilometres
Projection: Conical with two standard parallels
Highlands over 3000 feet
,, from 1200-3000 feet
Uplands ,, 600-1200 ,,
Lowlands ,, 300- 600 ,,
,, below 300 ,,
Sea 0- 300 feet (50 fathoms)
300- 600 ,, (100 fathoms)
600-1200 ,, (200 fathoms)
below 1200 ,, (200 fathoms)
Shetland Islands
Foula
Sumburgh Hd.
Fair I.
Orkney Islands
Pentland Firth
Dunnet Hd.
Duncansby Hd.
C. Wrath
Butt of Lewis
Flannan Is.
Lewis
The Minch
Ben More Assynt 3273
L. Shin
St. Kilda
Outer Hebrides
Ben Wyvis 3429
Moray Firth
L. Maree
North West Highlands
Buchan Ness
Skye
Mam Soul 3862
Glen More
L. Ness
Spey
Don
Ben Macdhui 4296
Dee
Grampians
Ben Nevis 4406
Ardnamurchan Pt.
Inner Hebrides
Tay
Strathmore
Sidlaw Hills
F. of Tay
Mull
Firth of Lorne
Ochil Hills
Fife Ness
Forth
L. Lomond
Firth of Forth
Bass Rock
Rockall Deep
Islay
Clyde
Pentlands
Lammermuirs
Arran
Tweed
The Cheviot 2676
Broad Law 2754
Giant's Caus
Malin Hd.
OCEAN
NORTH

IRISH SEA
SEA
English Channel
St. George's Channel
Bristol Channel
FRANCE
Dogger Bank
100 Feet
Flamborough Hd.
Spurn Hd.
Humber
Holderness
York Wolds
N. York Moors
Vale of York
Tees
Swale
Derwent
Ouse
Wharfe
Aire
Pennine Range
Cross Fell 2930
Eden
Cumbrian Mts.
Sca Fell 3210
St. Bee's Hd.
Solway Firth
Mull of Galloway
I. of Man
Snaefell 2034
Morecambe Bay
Formby Pt.
Liverpool Bay
Mersey
Cheshire Plain
Dee
The Peak 2088
Derwent
Don
Trent
Lincoln Wolds
Lincoln Heath
Witham
The Wash
Yare
Lowestoftness
Welland
The Fens
Nene
Gt. Ouse
Wrekin 1335
Severn
Avon
Cherwell
Stour
The Naze
Gt. Ormes Hd.
Anglesey
Holy I.
Menai Strait
Snowdon 3560
Cambrian Mts.
Cardigan Bay
Plynlimmon 2469
Wye
Towy
Brecon Beacons
St. David's Hd.
Milford Haven
Cotswold Hills
Thames
Chiltern Hills
Lea
Berks. Downs
Marlboro' Downs
Kennet
Thames
North Foreland
Medway
North Downs
The Weald
Strait of Dover
Dungeness
C. Gris Nez
South Downs
Beachy Hd.
Hampshire Downs
Salisbury Plain
Avon
Mendip Hills
R. Severn
Parrett
N. Dorset Downs
Avon
Lundy I.
Hartland Point
Exmoor 1707
Exe
Tamar
Yes Tor 2028
Dartmoor
Bodmin Moor
Start Pt.
Land's End
Lizard
Scilly Is.
Needles
Portland Bill
I. of Wight
C. de la Hague
Channel Isles
Guernsey
Somme
Seine
L. Neagh
Mourne Mts.
L. Erne
Erne
Donegal Bay
Erris Hd.
Achill I.
Mweelrea 2688
L. Mask
L. Corrib
Connemara
Galway Bay
Central Plain
Boyne
Liffey
Shannon
Bog of Allen
L. Derg
Sl. Bloom Mts.
Barrow
Wicklow Mts.
Loop Hd.
Shannon
Golden Vale
Suir
Galty Mts. 3015
Blackwater
Macgillicuddy's Reeks 3414
Lee
Dunmore Hd.
Carnsore Pt
Cork Harbour
C. Clear
West from Greenwich
COPYRIGHT, GEORGE PHILIP & SON, LTD.

ENGLAND AND WALES
Scale 1.2,500,000 (40 miles = 1 inch)
10 0 20 40 Statute Miles
10 0 20 40 60 Kilometres
Railways
Canals
2028 Heights in feet
Projection: Conical with two standard parallels
NORTH SEA
IRISH SEA
SCOTLAND
Southern Uplands
Pennines
Cheviot Hills
Cumbrian Mts.
N. York Moors
Yorkshire Wolds
Lincoln Wolds
Holderness
NORTHERN IRELAND
North Channel
Firth of Clyde
Firth of Forth
Firth of Tay
Firth of Lorne
Solway Firth
Sound of Jura
Mull
Iona
Colonsay
Islay
Jura
Gigha
Kintyre
Arran
Goat Fell 2866
BUTE
ARGYLL
PERTH
ANGUS
FIFE
KINROSS
CLMN.
DUNBARTON
STIRLING
RENFREW
LANARK
WEST LOTHIAN
MIDLOTHIAN
EAST LOTHIAN
BERWICK
PEEBLES
SELKIRK
ROXBURGH
AYR
DUMFRIES
KIRKCUDBRIGHT
WIGTOWN
Galloway
NORTHUMBERLAND
CUMBERLAND
DURHAM
WESTMORLAND
YORKSHIRE
NORTH RIDING
WEST RIDING
EAST RIDING
LANCASHIRE
CHESHIRE
DERBY
NOTTS
LINCOLN
LINDSEY
FLINT
DENBIGH
CAERNARVON
ANGLESEY
ISLE OF MAN
ANTRIM
DOWN
ARMAGH
LOUTH
MEATH
DUBLIN
Glasgow
Edinburgh
Dundee
Perth
Stirling
Dunfermline
Kirkcaldy
Leith
Falkirk
Paisley
Greenock
Port Glasgow
Dumbarton
Clydebank
Airdrie
Coatbridge
Motherwell
Wishaw
Hamilton
Kilmarnock
Ayr
Dumfries
Carlisle
Newcastle
Gateshead
Tynemouth
South Shields
Sunderland
West Hartlepool
Middlesbrough
Stockton
Darlington
Scarborough
York
Leeds
Bradford
Harrogate
Hull
Grimsby
Cleethorpes
Doncaster
Scunthorpe
Sheffield
Rotherham
Barnsley
Huddersfield
Halifax
Manchester
Salford
Oldham
Stockport
Bolton
Wigan
St Helens
Liverpool
Bootle
Wallasey
Birkenhead
Preston
Blackpool
Blackburn
Southport
Lancaster
Morecambe
Barrow
Lincoln
Mansfield
Chesterfield
Chester
Crewe
Belfast
Lisburn
Bangor
Ballymena
Coleraine
Dundalk
Drogheda
Dublin
Dun Laoghaire
Douglas
Ben Nevis
Ben More 3843
Ben Vorlich 3224
B. Lomond 3192
Ben Cruachan 3689
Broad Law 2754
The Cheviot 2676
Merrick 2764
Skiddaw 3054
Sca Fell 3210
Cross Fell 2930
Whernside 2414
Ingleborough 2373
Pen-y-Ghent 2273
Gt. Whernside 2310
The Peak 2088
Snaefell 2034
Trostan 1817

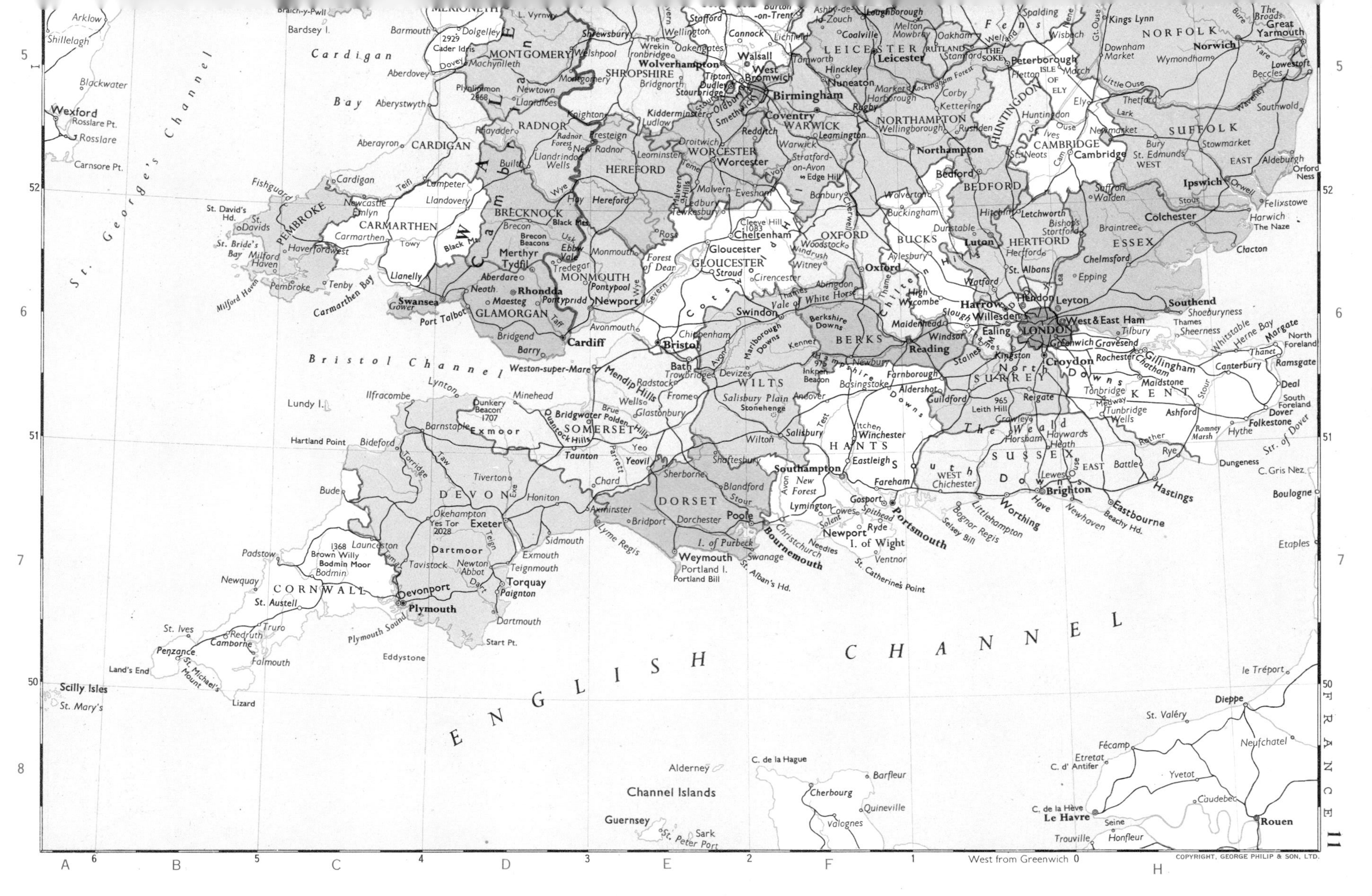
ENGLISH CHANNEL
Bristol Channel
St. George's Channel
Cardigan Bay
FRANCE
Channel Islands
Alderney
Guernsey
Sark
St. Peter Port
Scilly Isles
St. Mary's
Land's End
Lizard
Penzance
St. Ives
Camborne
Redruth
Truro
Falmouth
Newquay
Padstow
St. Austell
CORNWALL
Bodmin
Bodmin Moor
Brown Willy
1368
Launceston
Bude
Devonport
Plymouth
Plymouth Sound
Eddystone
Start Pt.
Dartmouth
Paignton
Torquay
Teignmouth
Newton Abbot
Tavistock
Dartmoor
Yes Tor
2028
Okehampton
Exeter
Exmouth
Sidmouth
Honiton
DEVON
Tiverton
Barnstaple
Bideford
Hartland Point
Lundy I.
Ilfracombe
Lynton
Exmoor
Dunkery Beacon
1707
Minehead
Taunton
Quantock Hills
Bridgwater
Polden Hills
SOMERSET
Mendip Hills
Weston-super-Mare
Wells
Glastonbury
Yeovil
Chard
Axminster
Lyme Regis
Bridport
Dorchester
DORSET
Weymouth
Portland I.
Portland Bill
I. of Purbeck
Swanage
St. Alban's Hd.
Poole
Bournemouth
Christchurch
Blandford
Sherborne
Shaftesbury
Salisbury
Salisbury Plain
Stonehenge
Wilton
WILTS
Devizes
Marlborough Downs
Swindon
Chippenham
Bath
Bristol
Trowbridge
Frome
Radstock
Avonmouth
Cardiff
Barry
Bridgend
GLAMORGAN
Port Talbot
Swansea
Gower
Neath
Maesteg
Rhondda
Pontypridd
Aberdare
Merthyr Tydfil
Newport
Pontypool
MONMOUTH
Monmouth
Tredegar
Ebbw Vale
Brecon
Brecon Beacons
BRECKNOCK
Black Mts.
Llanelly
Carmarthen
CARMARTHEN
Carmarthen Bay
Tenby
Pembroke
PEMBROKE
Milford Haven
Haverfordwest
St. Bride's Bay
St. David's Hd.
St. Davids
Fishguard
Cardigan
CARDIGAN
Aberayron
Aberystwyth
Aberdovey
Lampeter
Llandovery
Newcastle Emlyn
Builth Wells
Llandrindod Wells
RADNOR
Rhayader
New Radnor
Presteign
Knighton
Llanidloes
Newtown
Plynlimmon
2468
MONTGOMERY
Montgomery
Welshpool
Machynlleth
Cader Idris
2929
Dolgelley
Barmouth
Bardsey I.
Shrewsbury
SHROPSHIRE
Bridgnorth
Ludlow
Hereford
HEREFORD
Leominster
Ross
Forest of Dean
Gloucester
GLOUCESTER
Stroud
Cirencester
Cheltenham
Cleeve Hill
1083
Tewkesbury
Ledbury
Malvern
Worcester
WORCESTER
Droitwich
Kidderminster
Stourbridge
Dudley
Wolverhampton
Walsall
West Bromwich
Birmingham
Coventry
WARWICK
Warwick
Leamington
Stratford-on-Avon
Edge Hill
Banbury
Oxford
OXFORD
Woodstock
Witney
Abingdon
Vale of White Horse
Berkshire Downs
BERKS
Reading
Newbury
Hampshire Downs
Inkpen Beacon
975
Andover
Basingstoke
Winchester
HANTS
Eastleigh
Southampton
New Forest
Lymington
Fareham
Gosport
Portsmouth
Newport
I. of Wight
Ryde
Cowes
Ventnor
St. Catherine's Point
Needles
Chichester
WEST
SUSSEX
Worthing
Littlehampton
Bognor Regis
Selsey Bill
Brighton
Hove
Lewes
Newhaven
Eastbourne
Beachy Hd.
Hastings
Battle
Rye
The Weald
Horsham
Haywards Heath
Crawley
Leith Hill
965
Reigate
Guildford
Aldershot
Farnborough
SURREY
North Downs
Kingston
Croydon
LONDON
Ealing
Willesden
Harrow
Hendon
Leyton
West & East Ham
Slough
Windsor
Maidenhead
High Wycombe
Aylesbury
BUCKS
Buckingham
Wolverton
Chiltern Hills
Watford
St. Albans
Luton
Dunstable
Hitchin
Letchworth
HERTFORD
Hertford
Bishop's Stortford
Bedford
BEDFORD
Northampton
NORTHAMPTON
Wellingborough
Kettering
Corby
Rugby
Nuneaton
Hinckley
Leicester
LEICESTER
Loughborough
Coalville
Melton Mowbray
Oakham
RUTLAND
Stamford
Peterborough
THE SOKE
HUNTINGDON
Huntingdon
St. Ives
St. Neots
CAMBRIDGE
Cambridge
Ely
ISLE OF ELY
March
Wisbech
Spalding
Fens
Kings Lynn
NORFOLK
Norwich
Great Yarmouth
Lowestoft
Beccles
Thetford
SUFFOLK
Bury St. Edmunds
Stowmarket
Ipswich
Felixstowe
Aldeburgh
Orford Ness
Southwold
Harwich
The Naze
Clacton
Colchester
ESSEX
Chelmsford
Braintree
Saffron Walden
Epping
Southend
Shoeburyness
Tilbury
Gravesend
Rochester
Chatham
Gillingham
Maidstone
KENT
Tonbridge
Tunbridge Wells
Ashford
Canterbury
Whitstable
Herne Bay
Margate
Thanet
North Foreland
Ramsgate
Deal
South Foreland
Dover
Folkestone
Hythe
Romney Marsh
Dungeness
Str. of Dover
C. Gris Nez
Boulogne
Etaples
le Tréport
Dieppe
St. Valéry
Fécamp
Etretat
C. d' Antifer
Yvetot
Neufchatel
Caudebec
Rouen
C. de la Hève
Le Havre
Seine
Honfleur
Trouville
C. de la Hague
Cherbourg
Barfleur
Quineville
Valognes
Wexford
Rosslare
Rosslare Pt.
Carnsore Pt.
Blackwater
Arklow
Shillelagh
West from Greenwich 0
COPYRIGHT, GEORGE PHILIP & SON, LTD.

SCOTLAND
Scale 1:2,500,000 (40 miles = 1 inch)
Statute Miles
Kilometres
Railways
Canals
3429 Heights in feet
Projection: Conical with two standard parallels
CL. Clackmannan
DUN. Dunbarton
E.L. East Lothian
KIN. Kinross
ML. Midlothian
REN. Renfrew
STIR. Stirling
W.L. West Lothian
Shetland Islands
Unst
Yell
Fetlar
Hillswick
Burravoe
Papa Stour
ZETLAND
Lerwick
Scalloway
Bressay
Burra
Sumburgh Hd.
Fair Isle
North Ronaldsay
Westray
Sanday
Rousay
Stronsay
ORKNEY
Orkney Islands
Stromness
Kirkwall
Hoy
Burray
South Ronaldsay
Pentland Firth
Dunnet Hd.
John-o-Groats
Duncansby Hd.
Freswick
Castletown
Thurso
Halkirk
Watten
CAITHNESS
Wick
Noss Hd.
Ulbster
Latheron
Lybster
Dunbeath
Berriedale
Ord of Caithness
Helmsdale
Lothmore
Brora
Golspie
Dornoch
Dornoch Firth
Portmahomack
C. Wrath
Durness
Loch Eriboll
Kinlochbervie
Tongue
Farr
Strathy
Loch Laxford
Eddrachillis Bay
Scourie
B. Hope 3040
SUTHERLAND
Kildonan
L. Assynt
Inchnadamph
Loch Shin
B. More Assynt
Lairg
Rogart
Enard Bay
Butt of Lewis
Port of Ness
Barvas
Flannan Is.
Carloway
Stornoway
Broad Bay
Lewis
Balallan
Outer Hebrides
The Minch
Tarbert
Harris
Sound of Harris
North Uist
Lochmaddy
Little Minch
Uig
Skye
Portree
Kilmuir
Bracadale
L. Bracadale
Cuillin Hills
South Uist
B. More 1994
Broadford
Canna
Cuillin Sound
Barra
Castlebay
Barra Hd.
Rhum
Eigg
Muck
Inner Hebrides
L. Broom
Ullapool
Oykell Br.
Invershin
Bonar Br.
Ben Dearg 3547
Kincardine
Tain
ROSS AND CROMARTY
Melvaig
Poolewe
Gairloch
L. Maree
Kinlochewe
B. Wyvis 3429
Invergordon
Alness
Nigg
Dingwall
Cromarty
Fannich
Achnasheen
Torridon
Shieldaig
Strathpeffer
Kessock
Applecross
Lochcarron
Strome Ferry
Kyle of Lochalsh
Mam Soul 3862
Glen Affric
Glenelg
Kylerhea
Armadale
Sound of Sleat
Inner Sound
Moray Firth
Burghead
Findhorn
Elgin
Lossiemouth
Forres
Nairn
NAIRN
MORAY
Rothes
Keith
Huntly
Buckie
Fochabers
Findochty
Cullen
Portsoy
Banff
Macduff
Rosehearty
Kinnaird's Hd.
Fraserburgh
Peterhead
New Deer
Boddam
Ellon
ABERDEEN
BANFF
Dufftown
Insch
Inverurie
Oldmeldrum
Kintore
Newburgh
Alford
Dyce
Aberdeen
Girdle Ness
Portlethen
Inverness
Beauly
Dores
Cannich
Loch Ness
Carrbridge
Grantown
Boat of Garten
Strathdon
Aviemore
Findhorn
Monadhliath Mts.
Fort Augustus
G. Moriston
Caledonian Canal
Kingussie
Cairn Gorm 4084
B. Macdhui 4296
Badenoch
Dee
Ballater
Balmoral
Braemar
Banchory
Stonehaven
INVERNESS
Gl. Garry
Mallaig
Glenfinnan
Banavie
L. Lochy
Spean
Tulloch
Lochaber
Ft. William
Ben Nevis 4406
L. Eil
L. Shiel
Onich
Kinlochleven
Strontian
Salen
Kilchoan
Ardnamurchan Pt
Coll
Tobermory
Dervaig
Tiree
Mull
Morven
Lochaline
L. Linnhe
Ballachulish
Dalwhinnie
Dalnaspidal
Blair Atholl
Kinloch Rannoch
L. Rannoch
Ben Lawers 3984
Aberfeldy
Pitlochry
Ballinluig
Kirkmichael
Kirriemuir
Braes of Angus
Clova
Edzell
KINCARDINE
Fettercairn
Inverbervie
Laurencekirk
Brechin
Montrose
ANGUS
Forfar
Friockheim
Arbroath
Carnoustie
Alyth
Blairgowrie
Dunkeld
Sidlaw Hs.
Dundee
Monifieth
Broughty Ferry
Bell Rock
Breadalbane
PERTH
Grampian
Strathmore
Lochearnhead
Comrie
Crieff
Stanley
Perth
Newburgh
Newport
St. Andrews
Fife Ness
Anstruther
Ladybank
Leven
Elie
Methil
Buckhaven
Kirkcaldy
FIFE
Firth of Forth
Abernethy
Auchtermuchty
Kinross
KIN.
Ochil Hills
Muthill
Auchterarder
Callander
B. Vorlich 3224
Ben More 3843
Crianlarich
Tyndrum
Dalmally
Arrochar
Inveraray
Strachur
L. Fyne
Staffa
Iona
Bunessan
Lochdonhead
Firth of Lorne
Connel
Oban
L. Etive
Kilninver
ARGYLL
Orchy
Ardlui
B. Lomond 3192
L. Lomond
Dunblane
CL.
Alloa
Stirling
STIR.
Dunfermline
Cowdenbeath
Rosyth
Inverkeithing
Burntisland
N. Berwick
East Linton
Dunbar
Haddington
Cockburnspath
Eyemouth
ATLANTIC
OCEAN
Colonsay
Scalasaig
Ardlussa
Crinan
Lochgilphead
Jura
Garelochhead
DUN.
Helensburgh
Denny
Falkirk
Dumbarton
Clydebank
Glasgow
Airdrie
Bo'ness
Leith
Edinburgh
Dalkeith
Leadburn
Musselburgh
Prestonpans
Gifford
Lammermuir Hs.
E.L.
ML.
W.L.
Berwick
Duns
BERWICK
Coldstream
Tweed
Flodden
Otter Ferry
Dunoon
Gourock
Greenock
Port Glasgow
Renfrew
Paisley
Johnstone
REN.
Coatbridge
Motherwell
Wishaw
Hamilton
Pentland Hills
Carluke
Carstairs
Lanark
LANARK
Moorfoot Hills
Peebles
PEEBLES
Biggar
Innerleithen
Lauder
Galashiels
Melrose
Kelso
Roxburgh
Jedburgh
Selkirk
SELKIRK
Yarrow
Ettrick
Teviot
Hawick
ROXBURGH
Cheviot Hills
The Cheviot 2676
Coquet
Peel Fell 1964
Newcastleton
N. Tyne
Port Askaig
Islay
Craighouse
Tarbert
Skipness
Rothesay
Largs
BUTE
Dalry
Beith
Kilwinning
Irvine
Darvel
Kilmarnock
Ardrossan
Saltcoats
Fort Ellen
Gigha
Glenbarr
Mull of Oa
Kintyre
Brodick
Lamlash
Arran
Troon
Prestwick
Ayr
Mauchline
Muirkirk
Clyde
Tweed
Broad Law 2723
Moffat
Beattock
Cumnock
AYR
New Cumnock
Maybole
Sanquhar
Nith
Dalmellington
Moniaive
Thornhill
DUMFRIES
Esk
Langholm
Lochmaben
Dumfries
Ecclefechan
Campbeltown
Rathlin I.
North Channel
Mull of Kintyre
Firth of Clyde
Ailsa Craig
Girvan
Cairnsphairn
Ballantrae
Stinchar
Barrhill
New Galloway
Dalry
Ken
Maxwelltown
Corsewall Pt.
KIRKCUDBRIGHT
Galloway
New Abbey
Annan
Dalbeattie
Castle Douglas
Gretna
Bowness
Carlisle
Haltwhistle
S. Tyne
Hexham
New Luce
Newton Stewart
Glenluce
Wigtown
WIGTOWN
Stranraer
Portpatrick
Luce Bay
Whithorn
Wigtown Bay
Garliestown
Kirkcudbright
Solway Firth
Silloth
Mull of Galloway
Workington
Maryport
ENGLAND
Penrith
Keswick
Malin Hd.
Giant's Causeway
Portrush
Portstewart
L. Swilly
Buncrana
L. Foyle
Coleraine
Bann
Ballymoney
Ballycastle
Londonderry
LONDONDERRY
Main
ANTRIM
Ballymena
Larne
NORTHERN IRELAND
Strabane
Cookstown
Carrickfergus
Antrim
Moneymore
L. Neagh
Newtown Stewart
TYRONE
Mourne
Omagh
Dungannon
Belfast
Belfast L.
Bangor
Newtownards
Lisburn
West from Greenwich
A B C D E F G

IRELAND
Scale 1:2,500,000 (40 miles = 1 inch)
Statute Miles
Kilometres
Railways
Canals
3429 Heights in feet
Projection: Conical with two standard parallels
West from Greenwich
ATLANTIC OCEAN
IRISH SEA
North Channel
St. George's Channel
NORTHERN IRELAND
IRELAND
ULSTER
CONNACHT
LEINSTER
MUNSTER
DONEGAL
LONDONDERRY
ANTRIM
TYRONE
FERMANAGH
ARMAGH
DOWN
MONAGHAN
CAVAN
LEITRIM
SLIGO
MAYO
ROSCOMMON
LONGFORD
LOUTH
MEATH
WESTMEATH
DUBLIN
GALWAY
OFFALY
KILDARE
LAOIGHIS
WICKLOW
CARLOW
KILKENNY
WEXFORD
CLARE
TIPPERARY
LIMERICK
KERRY
CORK
WATERFORD
Islay
Port Askaig
Craighouse
Rothesay
Port Ellen
Glenbarr
Arran
Brodick
Campbeltown
Rathlin I.
Malin Hd.
Tory I.
Horn Hd.
Sheep Haven
L. Swilly
Bloody Foreland
Gweedore
Aran I.
Errigal 2466
Dungloe
Gweebarra B.
Loughros More B.
Glenties
Ardara
Rossan Pt.
Bluestack 2219
Killybegs
Rathlin O'Birne I.
Donegal
Donegal Bay
Ballyshannon
Bundoran
Ballintra
Letterkenny
Raphoe
Lifford
Stranorlar
Castlefinn
Rathmullen
Ramelton
Buncrana
Carndonagh
Moville
L. Foyle
Londonderry
Strabane
Newtown Stewart
Omagh
Limavady
Dungiven
Claudy
Sperrin Mts.
Draperstown
Moneymore
Cookstown
Dungannon
Portstewart
Portrush
Giant's Causeway
Coleraine
Bushmills
Ballycastle
Fair Hd
Ballymoney
Cushendall
Carnlough
Glenarm
Ballymena
Larne
Carrickfergus
Whitehead
Ballyclare
Antrim
L. Neagh
Belfast L.
Holywood
Belfast
Bangor
Newtownards
Lisburn
Ards Pen.
Portaferry
Strangford L.
Lurgan
Portadown
Banbridge
Downpatrick
Armagh
Keady
Tanderagee
Newry
Warrenpoint
Mourne Mts.
Newcastle
Dundrum Bay
Ardglass
Kilkeel
Carlingford
Greenore
Dundalk
Fintona
Augher
Clogher
Aughnacloy
Glasslough
Monaghan
Clones
Irvinestown
Kesh
Enniskillen
Lisnaskea
Upper L. Erne
Derrygonnelly
Ballybay
Castleblayney
Carrickmacross
Cootehill
Shercock
Kingscourt
Cavan
Belturbet
Killeshandra
Bailieborough
Ballyjamesduff
Virginia
Dunleer
Drogheda
Mornington
Gormanston
Balbriggan
Skerries
Rush
Lambay
Ireland's Eye
Howth
Swords
Dublin
Clontarf
Blackrock
Dun Laoghaire
Dalkey
Killiney
Bray
Kippure 2473
Poulaphouca Res.
Ceanannus Mor (Kells)
Navan
Tara Hill
Trim
Dunshaughlin
Slane
Mullingar
Athlone
Kinnegad
Summerhill
Enfield
Maynooth
Leixlip
Edenderry
Clane
Naas
Kildare
Droichead Nua
Granard
Longford
Edgeworthstown
Mohill
Drumlish
Newtown forbes
Lanesborough
Ballymahon
Ballynacargy
Rathowen
Athboy
Delvin
Castlepollard
Oldcastle
Moate
Clara
Tullamore
Daingean
Ferbane
Cloghan
Birr
Banagher
Portumna
Mountmellick
Portarlington
Monasterevin
Port Laoighise
Abbeyleix
Athy
Castledermot
Ballitore
Wicklow Mts.
Lugnaquillia
Laragh
Rathnew
Wicklow
Wicklow Hd.
Glenealy
Rathdrum
Aughrim
Arklow
Gorey
Shillelagh
Tullow
Carlow
Bagenalstown
Muine Bheag
Borris
Graiguenamanagh
Enniscorthy
Ferns
Camolin
Ballycanew
Cahore Pt.
Blackwater
Wexford
Rosslare
Greenore Pt.
Tuskar Rk
Carnsore Pt.
Kilmore Quay
New Ross
Inistioge
Thomastown
Kilkenny
Callan
Gowran
Durrow
Ballyragget
Castlecomer
Johnstown
Roscrea
Moneygall
Borris-in-Ossory
Castletown
Templemore
Thurles
Nenagh
Borrisokane
Cashel
Fethard
Clonmel
Carrick-on-Suir
Knocktopher
Slievenaman
Cahir
Tipperary
Cappawhite
Dundrum
Galtymore 3015
Galty Mts.
Knockmealdown Mts. 2478
Comeragh Mts.
Kilmacthomas
Waterford
Cheekpoint
Tramore
Dunmore East
Waterford Hr.
Dungarvan
Dungarvan B.
Bunmahon
Ring
Cappoquin
Lismore
Tallow
Youghal
Youghal Hr.
Ardmore
Piltown
Cloyne
Castlemartyr
Midleton
Cork
Cobh
Cork Harbour
Crosshaven
Kinsale
Old Head of Kinsale
Timoleague
Courtmacsherry
Clonakilty
Clonakilty B.
Ballinascarthy
Rosscarbery
Galley Hd.
Castletownsend
Skibbereen
Baltimore
Clear I.
C. Clear
Fastnet I.
Schull
Mizen Hd.
Dunmanus B.
Bantry
Bantry B.
Crow Hd.
Bere I.
Castletown Berehaven
Glengariff
Caha Mts.
Kenmare
Kenmare R.
Dunmanway
Bandon
Innishannon
Passage West
Macroom
Coachford
Blarney
Donoughmore
Boggeragh Mts.
Mallow
Rathcormac
Fermoy
Mitchelstown
Kanturk
Banteer
Millstreet
Rathmore
Charleville
Buttevant
Kilmallock
Newcastle
Abbeyfeale
Athea
Rathkeale
Adare
Croom
Hospital
Limerick
Newport
Killaloe
Tulla
Ennis
Quin
Clarecastle
Ennistymon
Lisdoonvarna
Lahinch
Liscannor
Liscannor B.
Miltown Malbay
Kilkee
Kilrush
Kildysart
Doonbeg
Carrigaholt
Loop Hd.
Foynes
Glin
Tarbert
Ballybunion
R. Shannon
Listowel
Lixnaw
Kerry Hd.
Tralee
Tralee B.
Brandon B.
Ardfert
Castleisland
Ballydesmond
Sl. Mish
Castlegregory
Annascaul
Dingle
Dingle Bay
Castlemaine
Killorglin
Killarney
Macgillicuddy's Reeks
Carrantuohill 3414
Kilgarvan
Knights Town
Valentia I.
Cahirciveen
Waterville
Skellig Rocks
Ballinskelligs B.
Parknasilla
Ballinasloe
Loughrea
Gort
Craughwell
Athenry
Oranmore
Galway
Galway Bay
Kinvara
Ballyvaughan
Aran Is.
Inishmore I.
Spiddal
Costelloe
Kilkieran B.
Connemara
Roundstone
Clifden
Slyne Hd.
Ballyconneely
Oughterard
L. Corrib
Headford
Tuam
Mount Bellew Bri.
Ahascragh
Kilconnell
Aughrim
Eyre court
Killimor
Mountshannon
Slieve Aughty
Cong
Shrule
Kilmaine
Ballinrobe
L. Mask
Muilrea 2688
Croagh Patrick
Killary Hr.
Inishbofin I.
Louisburgh
Westport
Clare I.
Clew B.
Castlebar
Newport
Balla
Claremorris
Ballyhaunis
Kiltamagh
Swinford
Charlestown
Foxford
Achill I.
Achill Hd.
Blacksod Bay
Mullet Peninsula
Belmullet
Erris Hd.
Broad Haven
Downpatrick Hd.
Ballycastle
Killala
Killala B.
Ballina
Crossmolina
L. Conn.
Nephin 2646
Ox Mts.
Inniscrone
Tubbercurry
Ballymote
Coolaney
Sligo
Sligo B.
Drumcliff
Manorhamilton
Dromahair
Ballintogher
Collooney
L. Allen
L. Arrow
Arigna
Boyle
Ballaghadereen
Ballanagare
Castlerea
Roscommon
Athleague
Ballymoe
Strokestown
Rooskey
Carrick-on-Shannon
Cliffoney
Bundoran
Mullinahone
Killenaule
COPYRIGHT, GEORGE PHILIP & SON, LTD.

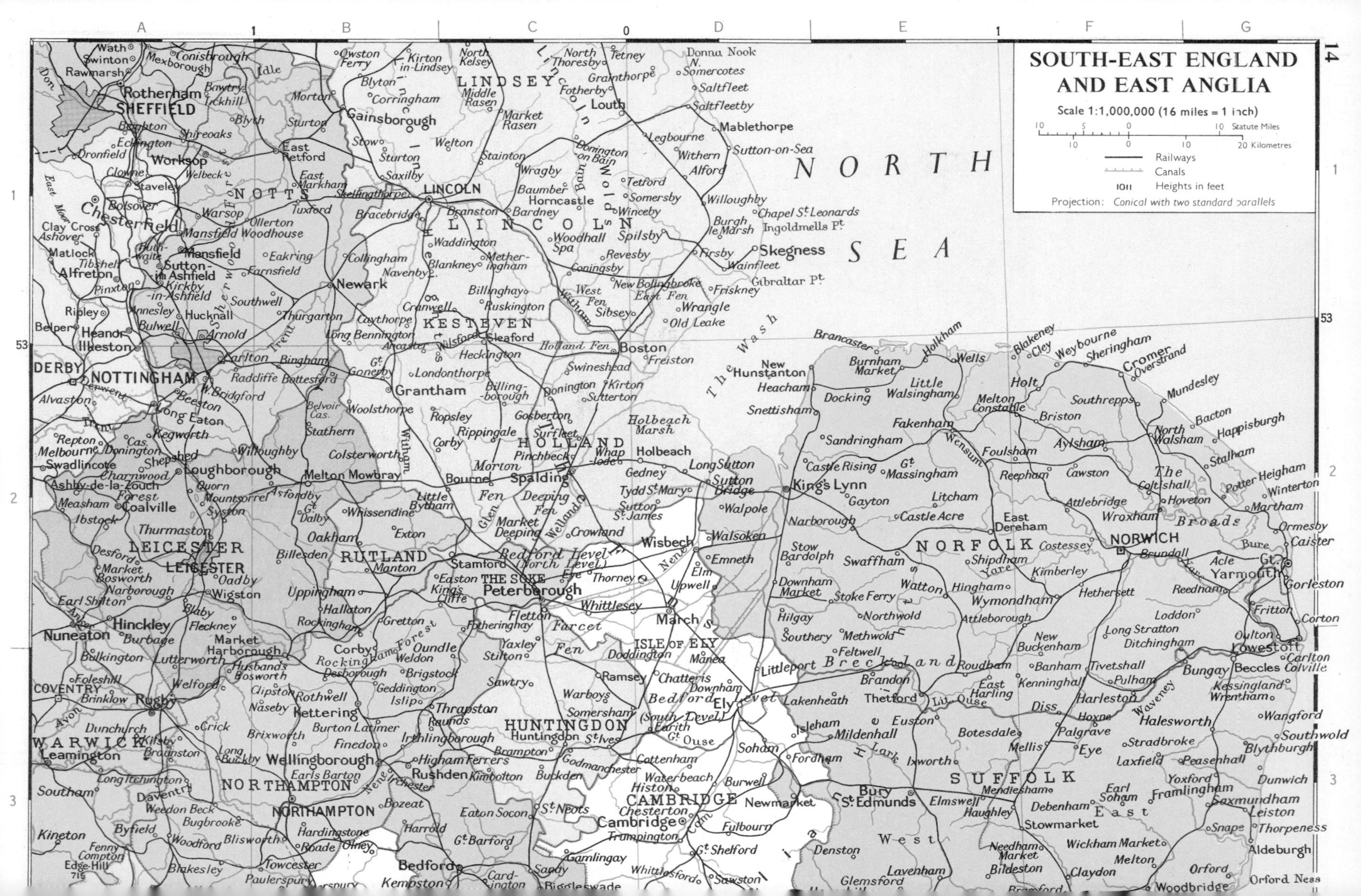

SOUTH-EAST ENGLAND AND EAST ANGLIA
Scale 1:1,000,000 (16 miles = 1 inch)
Statute Miles
Kilometres
Railways
Canals
Heights in feet
Projection: Conical with two standard parallels
NORTH SEA
The Wash
LINDSEY
LINCOLN
KESTEVEN
HOLLAND
NOTTS
RUTLAND
LEICESTER
NORTHAMPTON
HUNTINGDON
ISLE OF ELY
CAMBRIDGE
NORFOLK
SUFFOLK
WARWICK
THE SOKE
East Suffolk
West Suffolk
Breckland
Broads
Bedford Level
Sherwood Forest
Lincoln Wolds
SHEFFIELD
Rotherham
LINCOLN
NOTTINGHAM
DERBY
LEICESTER
Peterborough
Cambridge
NORWICH
King's Lynn
Boston
Grantham
Newark
Gainsborough
Louth
Skegness
Spalding
Wisbech
Ely
Great Yarmouth
Lowestoft
Cromer
Bury St. Edmunds
Northampton
Bedford
Coventry
Rugby
Kettering
Wellingborough
Huntingdon
Chesterfield
Mansfield
Loughborough
Melton Mowbray
Hinckley
Nuneaton
Leamington

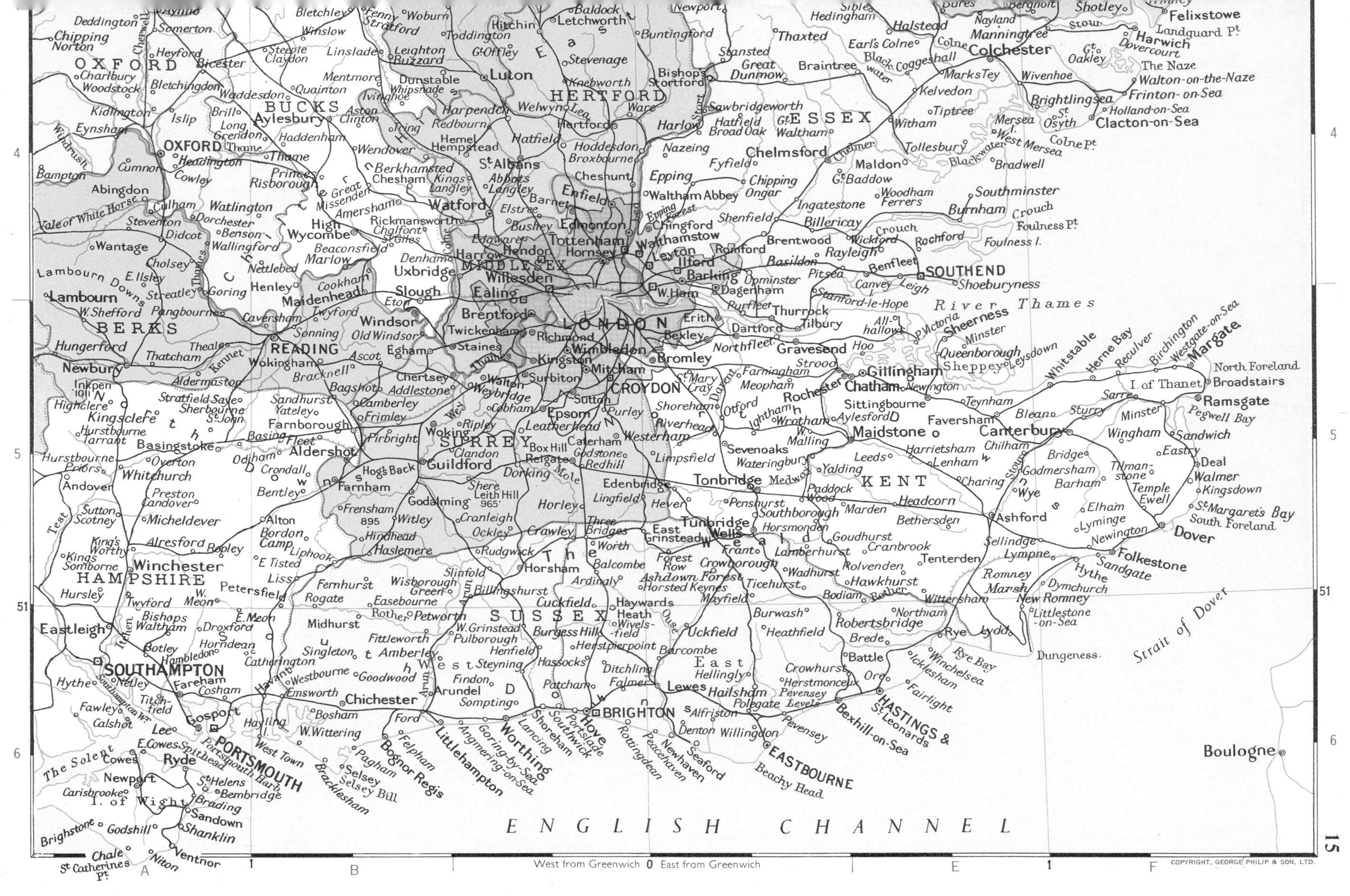
OXFORD
BUCKS
HERTFORD
ESSEX
MIDDLESEX
LONDON
BERKS
SURREY
KENT
SUSSEX
HAMPSHIRE
I. of Wight
ENGLISH CHANNEL
Strait of Dover
River Thames
The Weald
North Downs
South Downs
The Solent
Chipping Norton
Deddington
Somerton
Heyford
Bicester
Charlbury
Woodstock
Bletchingdon
Kidlington
Islip
Eynsham
OXFORD
Headington
Thame
Cumnor
Cowley
Bampton
Abingdon
Culham
Vale of White Horse
Steventon
Dorchester
Didcot
Benson
Wallingford
Wantage
Cholsey
Lambourn Downs
E. Ilsley
Lambourn
Streatley
Goring
W. Shefford
Pangbourne
Hungerford
Thatcham
Theale
Newbury
Inkpen
Highclere
Kingsclere
Aldermaston
Hurstbourne Tarrant
Basingstoke
Hurstbourne Priors
Overton
Whitchurch
Andover
Preston Candover
Micheldever
Sutton Scotney
King's Worthy
Kings Somborne
Alresford
Ropley
Winchester
Hursley
Twyford
Bishops Waltham
Eastleigh
Botley
SOUTHAMPTON
Hythe
Netley
Fawley
Calshot
Fareham
Cosham
Gosport
PORTSMOUTH
Hayling I.
Lee
E. Cowes
Cowes
Ryde
Newport
Carisbrooke
Brading
Sandown
Shanklin
Godshill
Brighstone
Chale
Niton
Ventnor
St Catherines Pt
Bletchley
Fenny Stratford
Woburn
Winslow
Steeple Claydon
Linslade
Leighton Buzzard
Toddington
Hitchin
Baldock
Letchworth
Stevenage
Luton
Dunstable
Whipsnade
Mentmore
Quainton
Waddesdon
Aylesbury
Aston Clinton
Tring
Wendover
Haddenham
Princes Risborough
Great Missenden
Amersham
Chesham
Berkhamsted
Harpenden
Redbourn
Hemel Hempstead
St. Albans
Hatfield
Welwyn
Hertford
Ware
Bishops Stortford
Buntingford
Knebworth
Watlington
High Wycombe
Marlow
Beaconsfield
Rickmansworth
Chalfont St. Giles
Watford
Henley
Nettlebed
Maidenhead
Cookham
Slough
Eton
Windsor
Old Windsor
Uxbridge
Denham
Harrow
Hendon
Willesden
Ealing
Brentford
Twickenham
Staines
Egham
READING
Caversham
Sonning
Twyford
Wokingham
Bracknell
Ascot
Sandhurst
Yateley
Farnborough
Fleet
Aldershot
Farnham
Hogs Back
Guildford
Godalming
Haslemere
Hindhead
Frensham
Woking
Weybridge
Chertsey
Addlestone
Camberley
Frimley
Pirbright
Leatherhead
Epsom
Dorking
Reigate
Redhill
Box Hill
Leith Hill
Cranleigh
Horsham
Crawley
Horley
Three Bridges
East Grinstead
Edenbridge
Tonbridge
Tunbridge Wells
Sevenoaks
Westerham
Croydon
Bromley
Wimbledon
Kingston
Richmond
Mitcham
Surbiton
Sutton
Purley
Enfield
Edmonton
Tottenham
Hornsey
Barnet
Walthamstow
Chingford
Epping
Waltham Abbey
Cheshunt
Hoddesdon
Harlow
Nazeing
Ongar
Chelmsford
Maldon
Witham
Braintree
Great Dunmow
Thaxted
Halstead
Colchester
Harwich
Felixstowe
Walton-on-the-Naze
Frinton-on-Sea
Clacton-on-Sea
Brightlingsea
Mersea
Burnham
Southminster
Foulness I.
Rochford
SOUTHEND
Shoeburyness
Leigh
Canvey
Rayleigh
Wickford
Billericay
Basildon
Brentwood
Romford
Ilford
Leyton
Barking
Dagenham
W. Ham
Upminster
Purfleet
Thurrock
Tilbury
Stanford-le-Hope
Erith
Bexley
Dartford
Gravesend
Northfleet
Rochester
Chatham
Gillingham
Sheerness
Queenborough
Sheppey
Sittingbourne
Faversham
Whitstable
Herne Bay
Margate
Broadstairs
Ramsgate
North Foreland
I. of Thanet
Sandwich
Deal
Walmer
Canterbury
Maidstone
Ashford
Tenterden
Dover
Folkestone
Hythe
Sandgate
New Romney
Romney Marsh
Lydd
Dungeness
Rye
Winchelsea
Hastings & St. Leonards
Bexhill-on-Sea
Battle
Eastbourne
Beachy Head
Pevensey
Hailsham
Lewes
Seaford
Newhaven
Peacehaven
Rottingdean
BRIGHTON
Hove
Shoreham
Lancing
Worthing
Littlehampton
Arundel
Bognor Regis
Chichester
Selsey Bill
Emsworth
Havant
Petersfield
Midhurst
Petworth
Pulborough
Steyning
Burgess Hill
Cuckfield
Haywards Heath
Uckfield
Crowborough
Ashdown Forest
Heathfield
Boulogne
West from Greenwich 0 East from Greenwich

A
5
B
C
4
D
ATLANTIC
OCEAN
Bristol Channel
PEMBROKE
CARMARTHEN
DEVON
CORNWALL
St. Dogmells
Cardigan
Blaenporth
Llanwnen
Lampeter
Llanwrtyd Wells
Newport B.
Dinas Hd.
Fishguard Bay
Strumble Hd.
Goodwick
Cilgerran
Llechryd
Llandyssul
Teifi
Llanbyther
Pumpsaint
Cilycwm
Nevern
Newport
Cenarth
Newcastle Emlyn
Pencader
Fishguard
Llanrian
Mathry
Puncheston
Mynydd Prescelly 1760
Crymmych Arms
Brechfa
Llanwrda
Llandovery
St. David's Hd.
Bishops & Clerks
Letterston
Cleddau
Conwil Elfed
Llanpumsaint
Talley
Llangadog
Trecastle
St. David's
Spittal
Clarbeston
Taf
Llanglydwen
Towy
Llandeilo
Black Mountain
2632
Fforest
Ramsey I.
Solva
Roch
Llandissilio
Carmarthen
Abergwili
Llanarthney
Whitland
Brynamman
St. Brides Bay
Haverfordwest
Narberth
St. Clears
Llanstephan
Ammanford
Ystalyfera
Coelbren
St. Brides
Johnston
Templeton
Laugharne
Ferryside
Glyn Neath
Skomer I.
Milford Haven
Neyland
Amroth
Kidwelly
Pontardulais
Pontardawe
Resolven
Grassholm
Skokholm I.
Dale
Milford Haven
Carew
Saundersfoot
Pendine
Clydach
Glyncorrwg
St. Ann's Hd.
Pembroke Dock
Tenby
Carmarthen Bay
Llanelly
Neath
Pembroke
Penally
Burry Port
Burry Inlet
Loughor
Gowerton
Castlemartin
Caldy I.
Llanrhidian
SWANSEA
Port Talbot
Linney Hd.
Manorbier
Rhossili B.
Rhossili
Gower
Swansea Bay
Maesteg
Bosherston
St. Gowan's Hd.
Worms Hd.
Oxwich
The Mumbles
Mumbles Hd.
Margam
Port Eynon
Pyle
Porthcawl
St. Bride's Major
Foreland Pt.
Lynton
Porlock B.
Combe Martin
Ilfracombe
Mortehoe
Lynmouth
Morte Pt.
Morte B.
Parracombe
Dunkery Beacon 1708
Exmoor
Lundy I.
Woolacombe
Simonsbath
Croyde
Braunton
Bratton Fleming
Bideford Bay
Barnstaple
Winsford
Hartland Pt.
Appledore
Westward Ho
Northam
Swimbridge
North Molton
Dulverton
Clovelly
Bideford
South Molton
Hartland
Monkleigh
Taw
Great Torrington
Langtree
Torridge
Chulmleigh
Bradworthy
Kilkhampton
Merton
Dolton
Lapford
Bude
Bude Bay
Stratton
Thornbury
Shebbear
Holsworthy
Hatherleigh
Sampford Courtenay
N. Tawton
Dizzard Pt.
Week St. Mary
St. Gennys
Halwill
Yeoford
Tedburn St. Mary
Newton St. Cyres
Boscastle
Ashwater
Okehampton
S. Tawton
EXETER
Otterham
Bridestowe
Yes Tor 2028
High Willhays 2039
Dunsford
Tintagel Hd.
Tintagel
Egloskerry
Teign
Chagford
Port Isaac B.
Delabole
Port Isaac
Camelford
Launceston
Lifton
Lydford
Moreton-hampstead
Pentire Pt.
Padstow Bay
Brown Willy 1375
Dartmoor
Postbridge
Bovey Tracey
Trevose Hd.
St. Kew
St. Teath
St. Tudy
Milton Abbot
Tamar
St. Minver
Bodmin Moor
Tavistock
Dart
Widecombe
Padstow
Wadebridge
Egloshayle
Gunnislake
Princetown
Newton Abbot
Callington
St. Cleer
Calstock
Holne
Yelverton
Ashburton
Watergate B.
St. Mawgan
Bodmin
Camel
Bere Alston
Newquay
Major
Fowey
Liskeard
Buckfastleigh
Torquay
Towan Hd.
St. Columb Minor
Roche
Menheniot
Cornwood
Totnes
Ligger B.
Luxulyan
Lostwithiel
St. Germans
Saltash
PLYMOUTH
Plympton
S. Brent
Churston
Perranporth
Newlyn E.
St. Dennis
St. Blazey
Par
Torpoint
Plymstock
Ivybridge
St. Agnes Hd.
Mitchell
St. Austell
Fowey
E. Looe
W. Looe
DEVONPORT
Antony
Yealmpton
Dartmouth
Stoke Fleming
Godrevy Pt.
Portreath
St. Agnes
Ladock
Charlestown
Polruan
Polperro
Cawsand
Modbury
Illogan
Fal
Grampound
St. Austell B.
Gribbin Hd.
Rame Hd.
Plymouth Sound
Slapton
St. Ives B.
St. Day
Truro
Wembury
Bigbury B.
Bigbury
Kingsbridge
Gurnard's Hd.
St. Ives
Redruth
Tregoney
Mevagissey
Newton Ferrers
Torcross
Pendeen Pt.
Phillack
Camborne
Veryan
Gorran Haven
Malborough
Start Pt.
Zennor
Hayle
Veryan B.
Dodman Pt.
Salcombe
Unv Leland
St. Erth
Penryn
Mylor
Penare Hd.
Eddystone
Prawle Pt.
Ludgvan
Falmouth
Gerrans B.
Portscatho
Bolt Head
St. Just
Penzance
Marazion
St. Mawes
Pendennis
Newlyn
St. Michael's Mount
Helston
Falmouth B.
Mousehole
Paul
Land's End
Sennen
St. Buryan
Porthleven
Gweek
Helford
Helford R.
Lamorna
Penryn
Falmouth
Pendennis
Falmouth B.
Helston
Helford R.
Gweek
Helford
Porthleven
St. Keverne
Mount's Bay
Mullion
Coverack
Black Hd.
Cadgwith
Kynance Cove
Lizard T.
Lizard Pt.
1
2
3
4
5
52
51

SOUTH-WEST ENGLAND AND SOUTH WALES
Scale 1:1,000,000 (16 miles = 1 inch)
Statute Miles
Kilometres
Railways
Canals
1760 Heights in feet
Projection: Conical with two standard parallels
COPYRIGHT, GEORGE PHILIP & SON, LTD.
3 West from Greenwich
E
F
G
H
J
ENGLISH CHANNEL
Lyme Bay
Bridgwater Bay
HEREFORD
Hereford
Malvern
Malvern Wells
Upton-on-Severn
Evesham
Honeybourne
Chipping Campden
Shipston-on Stour
Banbury
Middleton Cheney
Pains-castle
Clifford
Credenhill
Marden
Colwall
Ledbury
Eastnor
Bredon
Broadway
Blockley
Bloxham
King's Sutton
Aynho
Hay
Wye
Llyswen
Dorstone
Peterchurch
Madley
Holme Lacey
Dymock
Tewkesbury
Ashchurch
Moreton in-Marsh
Long Compton
Deddington
Somerton
Talgarth
Black Mountains
Llangorse
Llanthony
Abbey Dore
St Devereux
Long-town
Pontrilas
Linton
Ross
Staunton
Newent
Winchcombe
Cleeve Cloud 1070
Stow-on the Wold
Chipping Norton
Cherwell
Heyford
OXFORD
Bicester
Cheltenham
Charlton Kings
Bourton on-the-Water
Charlbury
Woodstock
Usk
Tretower
Pandy
Walford
Goodrich
Crickhowell
Whitchurch
Llangattock
Mitcheldean
GLOUCESTER
Andoversford
Shipton under Wychwood
Kidlington
Islip
Beaufort
Brynmawr
Abergavenny
Symonds Yat
Cinderford
Westbury on Severn
Birdlip
Northleach
Windrush
Eynsham
Tredegar
Rhymney
Ebbw Vale
Monmouth
Newnham
Forest of Dean
Blakeney
Painswick
Burford
Witney
Oxford
Blaenavon
Blaina
Abertillery
Abersychan
Raglan
Coleford
St Briavels
Awre
Stonehouse
Stroud
Bibury
Bampton
Cumnor
Cowley
MONMOUTH
Bargoed
Pontypool
Cwmbran
Crumlin
Abercarn
Tintern
Lydney
Sharpness
Dursley
Minchinhampton
Nailsworth
Cirencester
Fairford
Lechlade
Abingdon
Culham
Faringdon
Thames
Highworth
Vale of White Horse
Steventon
Didcot
Treharris
Chepstow
Berkeley
Wotton under-Edge
Kemble
Minety
Cricklade
Tetbury
Llantarnam
Caerwent
Beachley
Severn
Pontypridd
Risca
Thornbury
Malmesbury
Purton
Shrivenham
Wantage
Bedwas
Caerleon
NEWPORT
New Passage
Aust
Wickwar
Sherston
Avon
Badminton
Brinkworth
SWINDON
White Horse Hill 856
Lambourn Downs
Cholsey
E. Ilsley
Caerphilly
Taff
Whitchurch
Pilning
Almondsbury
Yate
Chipping Sodbury
Wootton Bassett
Wroughton
Lambourn
St Mellons
Westbury-on-Trym
Avonmouth
Mangotsfield
Marlborough Downs
Aldbourne
W. Shefford
Llandaff
Rhymney
CARDIFF
Portishead
Walton
Marshfield
Chippenham
Ogbourne
Ramsbury
BERKS
Penarth
Clevedon
Nailsea
BRISTOL
Corsham
Calne
Marlborough
Avebury
Hungerford
Thatcham
Barry
Dinas Powis
Barry I.
Keynsham
BATH
Box
Lacock
Bromham
Beckhampton
Newbury
Bathampton
Bradford-on-Avon
Melksham
Savernake
Vale of Pewsey
Gt Bedwyn
Inkpen 1011
Burbage
Highclere
Kingsclere
Weston-super-Mare
Worle
Yatton
Yeo
Pensford
Chew Magna
Twerton
Congresbury
Seend
Devizes
WILTS
Pewsey
Bleadon
Mendip Hills
Blagdon
Camerton
Radstock
Trowbridge
Potterne
Market Lavington
Upavon
Collingbourne Ducis
Ludgershall
Hurstbourne Tarrant
Axe
Axbridge
Midsomer Norton
Cheddar
Beckington
Edington
Westbury
Tidworth
Hurstbourne Priors
Overton
Brent Knoll
Burnham
Wedmore
Wookey Hole
Frome
Netheravon
Salisbury Plain
Weyhill
Whitchurch
Highbridge
Nunney
Warminster
Durrington
Bulford
Andover
Watchet
Nether Stowey
Wookey
Wells
Shepton Mallet
Heytesbury
Shrewton
Amesbury
Wherwell
Sutton Scotney
Micheldever
Williton
Brue
Pilton
Evercreech
Horningsham
Maiden Bradley
Codford
Wylye
Gt Wishford
Porton
Stockbridge
Test
King's Worthy
SOMERSET
Quantock Hills
Bridgwater
Polden Hills
Glastonbury
Street
Bruton
Mere
Hindon
Wilton
Salisbury
Winchester
HAMPSHIRE
Hills 1261
North Petherton
King's Sedge Moor
Castle Cary
E. Knoyle
Fovant
Mottisfont
Hursley
Bishops Lydeard
Norton Fitzwarren
Athelney
Somerton
Langport
Wincanton
Tisbury
Twyford
Sparkford
Gillingham
Donhead St Mary
Downton
Romsey
Bishop's Waltham
Milverton
Tone
Taunton
Curry Rivel
Ilchester
Marston Magna
Temple Combe
Shaftesbury
Redlynch
Breamore
W. Wellow
Eastleigh
Yeo
Martock
Milborne Port
Marnhull
Cranborne Chase
Fordingbridge
Avon
Botley
Wellington
1035
Hatch
South Petherton
Parrett
Yeovil
Stalbridge
Iwerne Minster
Cranborne
SOUTHAMPTON
Itchen
Bitterne
Blackdown Hills
Ilminster
W. Coker
Sherborne
Sturminster Newton
Shillingstone
Totton
Hemyock
Uffculme
Chard
Crewkerne
Yetminster
Blandford
Verwood
New Forest
Lyndhurst
Hythe
Netley
Southampton W.
Titchfield
Ringwood
Cullompton
Upottery
Dorset Heights .902
Witchampton
Brockenhurst
Fawley
Calshot
Broadwindsor
Evershot
Cerne Abbas
Spettisbury
Stour
Beaulieu
Lee
Otter
Beaminster
DORSET
Wimborne
Sopley
Lymington
E. Cowes
Honiton
Axminster
Powerstock
Maiden Newton
Sturminster Marshall
Puddletown
Broadstone
Milton
Cowes
Whimple
Charmouth
Lytchett Minster
Poole
The Solent
Ottery St Mary
Colyton
Bridport
Frome
Charminster
Bere Regis
Hamworthy
Christchurch
Milford
Newport
Sidbury
West Bay
Winterbourne St Martin
Dorchester
Poole Harb
BOURNEMOUTH
Boscombe
Yarmouth
Carisbrooke
Axmouth
Lyme Regis
Chideock
Portesham
Totland
I. of Wight
Seaton
Beer
Salcombe Regis
Abbotsbury
Upwey
Wool
Wareham
Studland
The Needles
Freshwater
Sidmouth
Osmington
I. of Purbeck
Corfe Castle
Swanage
Godshill
Budleigh Salterton
Chesil Bank
Weymouth
W. Lulworth
Durlstone Hd
Brighstone
Exmouth
St Alban's Hd
Chale
St Catherine's Pt
Niton
I. of Portland
Easton
Bill of Portland

NORTH AND CENTRAL WALES AND MIDLANDS
Scale 1:1,000,000 (16 miles = 1 inch)
Statute Miles
Kilometres
Railways
Canals
2263 Heights in feet
Projection: Conical with two standard parallels
A
B
C
D
4
3
1
2
3
4
53
52
IRISH SEA
Liverpool Bay
Cardigan Bay
ANGLESEY
CAERNARVON
DENBIGH
FLINT
MERIONETH
MONTGOMERY
CARDIGAN
RADNOR
BRECKNOCK
CHESHIRE
LANCASHIRE
SHROPSHIRE
HEREFORD
Cambrian Mts
Berwyn Mts
Clee Hills
Long Mynd
Wenlock Edge
Radnor Forest
Clun Forest
Mynydd Bach
Mynydd Eppynt
Holyhead
Holy I.
Amlwch
Beaumaris
Bangor
Caernarvon
Snowdon 3560
Carnedd Llewelyn 3484
Llandudno
Colwyn Bay
Conway
Rhyl
Prestatyn
Abergele
Denbigh
Ruthin
Flint
Mold
Holywell
Wrexham
Llangollen
Oswestry
Harlech
Barmouth
Dolgellau
Cader Idris 2927
Bala
Bala L.
Corwen
Ffestiniog
Pwllheli
Criccieth
Portmadoc
Lleyn Pen.
Bardsey I.
Aberdaron
Towyn
Aberdovey
Machynlleth
Aberystwyth
Plynlimmon 2468
Llanidloes
Newtown
Welshpool
Montgomery
Shrewsbury
Chester
Liverpool
Birkenhead
Blackpool
Preston
Blackburn
Bolton
Wigan
St. Helens
Warrington
Southport
Fleetwood
Crewe
Nantwich
Whitchurch
Wem
Ludlow
Knighton
Presteigne
Rhayader
Llandrindod Wells
Builth Wells
Newbridge-on-Wye
Tregaron
Lampeter
Aberayron
New Quay
Cardigan
Newcastle Emlyn
Llandovery
Brecon
Talgarth
Hay
Hereford
Leominster
Kington
Bromyard
Ledbury
Tenbury
Bishop's Castle
Craven Arms
Church Stretton
Bridgnorth
Much Wenlock
Wellington
The Wrekin 1335
R. Dee
R. Mersey
R. Ribble
Severn
Wye
Teme
L. Vyrnwy
Reservoirs
R. Dovey

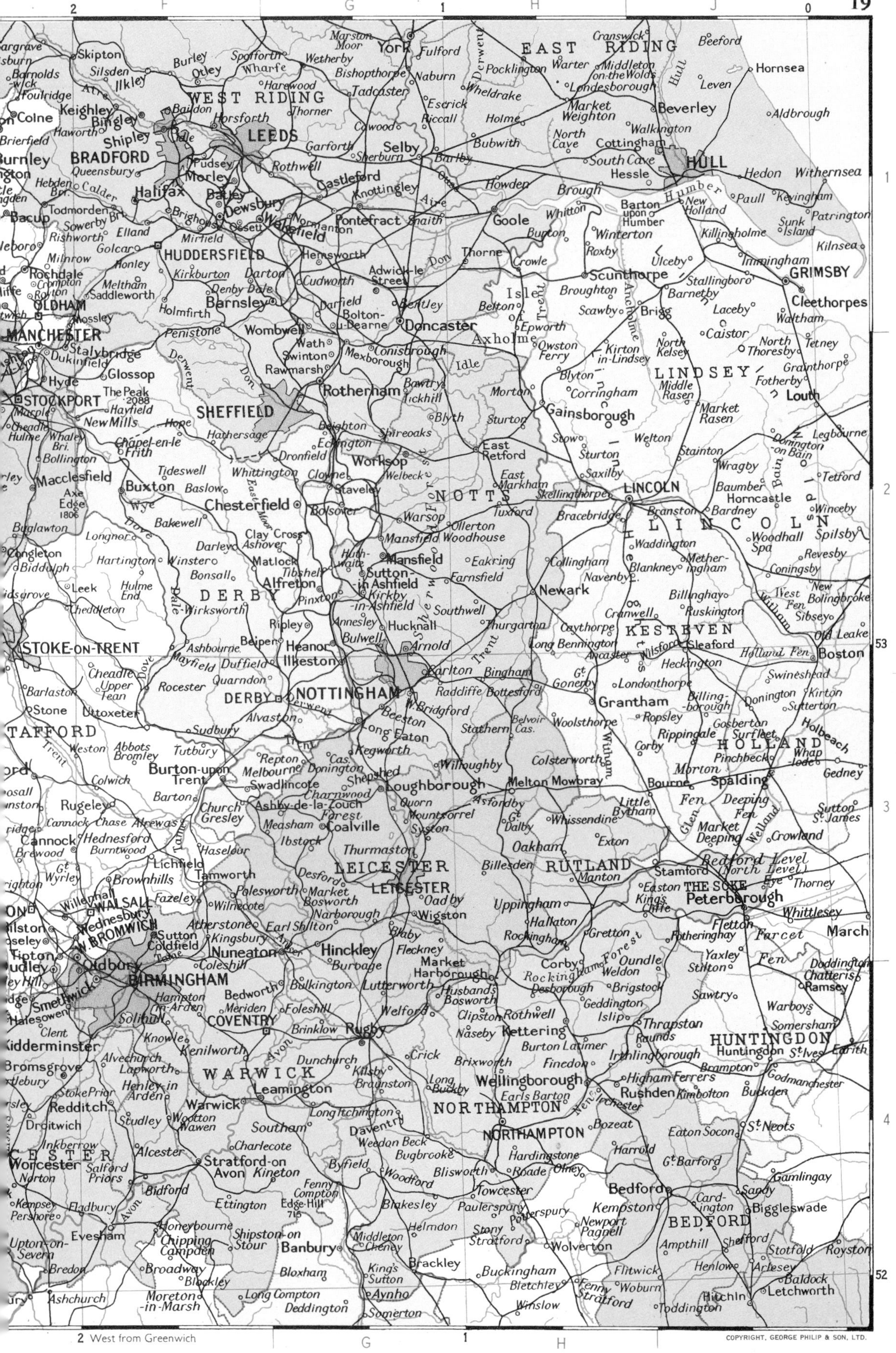

F
G
H
J
Skipton
Silsden
Ilkley
Burley
Otley
Spofforth
Wharfe
Wetherby
Marston Moor
York
Fulford
Bishopthorpe
Naburn
Derwent
Pocklington
EAST RIDING
Cranswick
Warter
Middleton on-the-Wolds
Londesborough
Beeford
Hornsea
Leven
Hull
Harewood
WEST RIDING
Tadcaster
Escrick
Wheldrake
Market Weighton
Beverley
Aldbrough
Keighley
Bingley
Baildon
Horsforth
Thorner
Riccall
Holme
Colne
Haworth
Shipley
LEEDS
Cawood
Walkington
BRADFORD
Idle
Garforth
Selby
Bubwith
North Cave
Cottingham
Burnley
Queensbury
Pudsey
Rothwell
Sherburn
Barlby
South Cave
HULL
Hessle
Hedon
Withernsea
Morley
Castleford
Howden
Brough
Halifax
Batley
Knottingley
Ouse
Calder
Paull
Keyingham
Barton upon Humber
Humber
New Holland
Bacup
Todmorden
Sowerby Br.
Dewsbury
Normanton
Wakefield
Pontefract
Snaith
Aire
Goole
Whitton
Winterton
Killingholme
Sunk Island
Patrington
Rishworth
Elland
Brighouse
Ossett
Mirfield
Burton
Golcar
HUDDERSFIELD
Hemsworth
Thorne
Crowle
Roxby
Kilnsea
Milnrow
Honley
Don
Ulceby
Immingham
GRIMSBY
Rochdale
Kirkburton
Darton
Cudworth
Adwick-le Street
Scunthorpe
Stallingboro'
Meltham
Saddleworth
Denby Dale
Barnsley
Darfield
Isle of Axholme
Broughton
Barnetby
Cleethorpes
OLDHAM
Mossley
Holmfirth
Bolton-u-Dearne
Bentley
Belton
Trent
Scawby
Brigg
Laceby
Waltham
MANCHESTER
Penistone
Wombwell
Doncaster
Epworth
Caistor
Ancholme
Stalybridge
Dukinfield
Wath
Swinton
Mexborough
Conisbrough
Owston Ferry
Kirton in-Lindsey
North Kelsey
North Thoresby
Tetney
Glossop
Rawmarsh
Idle
Grainthorpe
Hyde
The Peak 2088
Hayfield
Rotherham
Bawtry
Tickhill
Morton
Blyton
Corringham
LINDSEY
Middle Rasen
Fotherby
Louth
STOCKPORT
SHEFFIELD
Marple
New Mills
Hope
Beighton
Blyth
Sturton
Gainsborough
Market Rasen
Cheadle Hulme
Whaley Bri.
Hathersage
Eckington
Shireoaks
Stow
Welton
Legbourne
Chapel-en-le Frith
Dronfield
Worksop
East Retford
Sturton
Stainton
Donington on Bain
Bollington
Tideswell
Whittington
Clowne
Welbeck
Saxilby
Wragby
Bain
Tetford
Macclesfield
Buxton
Baslow
East Moor
Staveley
NOTTS
East Markham
Skellingthorpe
LINCOLN
Baumber
Horncastle
Axe Edge 1806
Chesterfield
Bolsover
Tuxford
Bracebridge
Branston
Bardney
Winceby
Bakewell
Warsop
Ollerton
LINCOLN
Woodhall Spa
Spilsby
Buglawton
Longnor
Clay Cross
Ashover
Mansfield Woodhouse
Waddington
Revesby
Congleton
Hartington
Winster
Darley
Matlock
Tibshelf
Huthwaite
Mansfield
Eakring
Collingham
Blankney
Metheringham
Coningsby
Biddulph
Bonsall
Alfreton
Sutton-in Ashfield
Sherwood Forest
Farnsfield
Navenby
New Bolingbroke
Leek
Hulme End
DERBY
Pinxton
Kirkby-in-Ashfield
Newark
Billinghay
West Fen
Sibsey
Kidsgrove
Cheddleton
Wirksworth
Dale
Southwell
Cranwell
Ruskington
Witham
Ripley
Annesley
Hucknall
Thurgarton
Caythorpe
KESTEVEN
Old Leake
STOKE-ON-TRENT
Ashbourne
Belper
Heanor
Bulwell
Arnold
Long Bennington
Ancaster
Wilsford
Sleaford
Holland Fen
Boston
Cheadle
Mayfield
Duffield
Ilkeston
Carlton
Bingham
Gt. Gonerby
Heckington
Swineshead
Upper Tean
Dove
Quarndon
Rocester
DERBY
NOTTINGHAM
Radcliffe
Bottesford
Londonthorpe
Billingborough
Donington
Kirton
Barlaston
Stone
Uttoxeter
Alvaston
Derwent
Beeston
W. Bridgford
Belvoir Cas.
Woolsthorpe
Grantham
Ropsley
Sutterton
STAFFORD
Sudbury
Long Eaton
Stathern
Rippingale
Gosberton
Surfleet
Holbeach
Weston
Abbots Bromley
Tutbury
Trent
Kegworth
Corby
HOLLAND
Repton
Melbourne
Cas. Donington
Willoughby
Colsterworth
Pinchbeck
Whaplode
Burton-upon Trent
Shepshed
Morton
Gedney
Colwich
Swadlincote
Loughborough
Melton Mowbray
Bourne
Spalding
Barton
Charnwood Forest
Asfordby
Little Bytham
Fen
Deeping Fen
Rugeley
Ashby-de-la-Zouch
Quorn
Mountsorrel
Sutton St. James
Cannock Chase
Alrewas
Church Gresley
Gt. Dalby
Whissendine
Glen
Welland
Cannock
Hednesford
Measham
Coalville
Syston
Market Deeping
Crowland
Burntwood
Ibstock
Exton
Brewood
Haseldur
Thurmaston
Oakham
Lichfield
LEICESTER
Billesden
RUTLAND
Stamford
Bedford Level (North Level)
Gt. Wyrley
Brownhills
Tamworth
Desford
LEICESTER
Manton
Easton
THE SOKE
Eye
Thorney
Fazeley
Polesworth
Market Bosworth
Oadby
Uppingham
King's Cliffe
Peterborough
Willenhall
WALSALL
Wilnecote
Narborough
Wigston
Hallaton
Whittlesey
Wednesbury
W. BROMWICH
Atherstone
Earl Shilton
Fletton
March
Sutton Coldfield
Kingsbury
Anker
Blaby
Rockingham
Gretton
Rotheringhay
Farcet
Tipton
Nuneaton
Hinckley
Fleckney
Yaxley
Stilton
Fen
Dudley
Oldbury
Coleshill
Burbage
Market Harborough
Corby
Rockingham Forest
Oundle
Doddington
Chatteris
BIRMINGHAM
Bedworth
Bulkington
Lutterworth
Weldon
Smethwick
Hampton in-Arden
Meriden
Husbands Bosworth
Desborough
Brigstock
Sawtry
Ramsey
Halesowen
Solihull
COVENTRY
Foleshill
Welford
Clipston
Rothwell
Geddington
Islip
Warboys
Clent
Brinklow
Rugby
Naseby
Kettering
Thrapston
Somersham
Kidderminster
Knowle
Kenilworth
Avon
Raunds
HUNTINGDON
Bromsgrove
Alvechurch
Lapworth
Dunchurch
Crick
Burton Latimer
Huntingdon
St. Ives
Earith
WARWICK
Kilsby
Brixworth
Finedon
Irthlingborough
Brampton
Henley-in Arden
Braunston
Long Buckby
Wellingborough
Higham Ferrers
Godmanchester
Stoke Prior
Leamington
Earls Barton
Rushden
Kimbolton
Buckden
Redditch
Warwick
Long Itchington
NORTHAMPTON
Irchester
Studley
Wootton Wawen
Southam
Daventry
NORTHAMPTON
Bozeat
Eaton Socon
St. Neots
Droitwich
Nene
Inkberrow
Weedon Beck
Alcester
Charlecote
Bugbrooke
Hardingstone
Harrold
Gt. Barford
Worcester
Salford Priors
Stratford-on Avon
Kineton
Byfield
Roade
Olney
Norton
Blisworth
Gamlingay
Fenny Compton
Woodford
Towcester
Bedford
Sandy
Kempsey
Bidford
Pershore
Fladbury
Ettington
Edge Hill 715
Blakesley
Paulerspury
Potterspury
Kempston
Cardington
Biggleswade
Avon
Honeybourne
Newport Pagnell
BEDFORD
Evesham
Shipston-on Stour
Helmdon
Stony Stratford
Upton-on-Severn
Chipping Campden
Banbury
Middleton Cheney
Wolverton
Ampthill
Shefford
Stotfold
Royston
Bredon
Broadway
Blockley
Brackley
Buckingham
Flitwick
Henlow
Arlesey
Bloxham
King's Sutton
Bletchley
Fenny Stratford
Woburn
Baldock
Ashchurch
Moreton-in-Marsh
Long Compton
Aynho
Winslow
Hitchin
Letchworth
Deddington
Somerton
Toddington
1
2
3
4
53
52

Cumbrae
Millport
Is.
Largs
Kilbirnie
Barrhead
Beith
Neilston
E. Kilbride
Motherwell
Wishaw
Wilsontown
Hamilton
Eaglesham
Dalry
Dunlop
W. Kilbride
Kilwinning
Stewarton
Larkhall
Stonehouse
Carluke
Strathaven
Carstairs
Carnwath
Pentland
Hills
W. Linton
Dolphinton
Moorfoot Hs.
Fountainhall
Lauder
Lauderdale
Stow
Earlston
Ardrossan
Saltcoats
Irvine
Kilmarnock
Lesmahagow
Lanark
Broughton
Biggar
Stobo
Peebles
PEEBLES
Innerleithen
Galashiels
Melrose
Selkirk
Darvel
New Milns
Galston
Irvine
Kyle
Coalburn
LANARK
Symington
Clyde
Tweed
Holy I.
Troon
Mauchline
Muirkirk
Douglas
2335
2433
Yarrow
Ettrick Wr.
Prestwick
Catrine
Cairn Table
1944
Roberton
2680
Broad Law
2754
Ettrick Forest
SELKIRK
Ayr
Ayr
Cumnock
Crawford
White Coomb
2695
Heads of Ayr
Alloway
AYR
New Cumnock
Leadhills
Elvanfoot
Hawick
ROXBURGH
Firth of Clyde
Dalrymple
Wanlockhead
Kirkconnel
2403
Daer
Hart Fell
2651
Ettrick
Teviotdale
Teviot
Turnberry Pt.
Maybole
Girvan
Doon
Dalmellington
2298
Sanquhar
Blackcraig Hill
Nith
Lowther Hills
2267
Moffat
Ettrick Pen
2270
Annandale
Girvan
New Daily
Cairnsmore
2612
Nithsdale
Queensberry
2285
Wisp Hill
1950
Riccarton Junc.
Peel Fell
L. Doon
The Glenkens
Thornhill
DUMFRIES
Eskdale
Black Esk
White Esk
Carrick
Stinchar
Pinwherry
Moniaive
Auldgirth
Liddesdale
New-castleton
Larriston Fells
Ballantrae
Barrhill
Merrick
2764
2668
Kells Range
Dalry
Dunscore
Lochmaben
Annan
Lockerbie
Langholm
Kershope-foot
Bewcastle Fells
Benerairđ
1435
Hightae
Canonbie
Eaglesfield
Ecclefechan
Riddings
Cree
2349
New Galloway
Maxwelltown
Dumfries
Loch Ryan
Kirkcolm
KIRKCUDBRIGHT
L. Ken
Crossmichael
Gretna
Gretna Green
Gretna
Annan
Lyne
Longtown
Galloway
New Luce
The Moors
Newton Stewart
Minnigaff
2329
New Abbey
Criffell
1866
Bowness
P. Carlisle
Irthington
Rockcliffe
Brampton
The Rhinns
Stranraer
WIGTOWN
Kirkcowan
Glenluce
Creetown
Castle Douglas
Dee
Dalbeattie
Nith
Moricambe B.
Eden
Hayton
Scotby
Wetheral
Carlisle
Portpatrick
Wigtown
Gatehouse of Fleet
Kirkcudbright
Southerness Pt.
Silloth
Abbey Town
Kirkbride
Waver
Thursby
Dalston
Ainstable
The Machers
Garliestown
Wigtown Bay
Solway Firth
Wigton
Caldew
Armathwaite
Aspatria
Mealsgate
Luce Bay
Port Logan
Whithorn
Kirkcudbright B.
Abbey Hd.
Allonby
Ellen
Ireby
Caldbeck
Hesket Newmarket
Lazonby
Maryport
Dearham
CUMBERLAND
Drummore
Burrow Hd.
Flimby
Seaton
Derwent
Cockermouth
2329 High Pike
Greystoke
Edenhall
Penrith
Mull of Galloway
Workington
Brigham
Bassenthwaite L.
Skiddaw
3053
Threlkeld
Clifton
Harrington
Gt. Clifton
Distington
Greta
Pooley Bridge
Keswick
Braithwaite
Askham
Parton
Lowes Water
Crummock Wr.
Derwent Wr.
Ullswater
Whitehaven
Frizington
Arlecdon
Buttermere
Ennerdale Wr.
Thirlmere
3118
Patterdale
Bampton
St. Bees Hd.
Cleator Moor
Borrowdale
Helvellyn
Haweswater
St. Bees
Cleator
Cumbrian Mts.
Egremont
Kirkstone Pass
Grasmere L.
WESTMORLAND
Rydal
Beckermet
Wast Wr.
3210
Sca Fell
Ambleside
Ehen
Seascale
Gosforth
Irt
Esk
Boot
Hawkshead
Windermere
Staveley
Pt. of Ayre
Jurby Hd.
Andreas
Bride
Coniston
Sulby
Ramsey B.
Ramsey
Ballaugh
Maughold Hd.
Maughold
Kirkmichael
Snaefell
2034
Drigg Pt.
Ravenglass
Coniston Water
Torver
Bowness
Kendal
Broughton-in-Furness
Bootle
Black Combe
1969
Lake Side
Peel
ISLE OF MAN
Laxey
Whicham
Millom
Greenodd
Newby Br.
St. Johns
Clay Hd.
Ulverston
Cartmel
Foxdale
Douglas
Douglas Hd.
Duddon R.
Conishead Pry.
Grange
Arnside
S. Barrule
1585
Furness Abb.
Dalton
Bradda Hd.
Colby
Santon Hd.
BARROW IN FURNESS
Aldingham
Carnforth
Port Erin
Derbyhaven
Calf of Man
Castletown
Langness
Scarlet Pt.
Port St. Mary
Spanish Hd.
Chicken Rk.
Vickerstown
Walney Island
Bolton le Sands
Morecambe
Heysham
Lancaster
IRISH
Hilpsford Pt.
Overton
Morecambe Bay
Sunderland Pt.
R. Lune
Glasson
Galgate
Lancaster Bay
Fleetwood
Rossall Pt.
Pilling
Knott End
Garstang
Wyre
LANCASHIRE
Thornton-Cleveleys
Poulton le Fylde
SEA
BLACKPOOL
Kirkham
A
B
C
D
E
1
2
3
4
5
54

NORTHERN ENGLAND
Scale 1:1,000,000 (16 miles = 1 inch)
10 5 0 10 Statute Miles
10 0 10 20 Kilometres
Railways
Canals
2329 Heights in feet
Projection: Conical with two standard parallels
F
G
H
J
K
2
1
55
54
3
4
5
NORTH SEA
NORTHUMBERLAND
DURHAM
NORTH RIDING
YORKSHIRE
EAST RIDING
WEST RIDING
Berwick-upon-Tweed
Spittal
Tweedmouth
Holy I.
Farne Is
Budle B.
Bamburgh
Seahouses
N. Sunderland
Beadnell
Embleton
Duns
Greenlaw
Coldstream
Norham
Ancroft
Beal
Cornhill
Ford
Flodden
Carham
Kelso
Roxburgh
Yetholm
Wooler
Belford
Lucker
Chathill
Chillingham
Ilderton
The Cheviot 2676
S. Charlton
Breamish
Howick
Longhoughton
Alnmouth
Glanton
Alnwick
Aln
Alwinton
Shilbottle
Warkworth
Amble
Coquet I.
Hauxley
Rothbury
Felton
Simonside 1447
Coquet
Rede
Rochester
Otterburn
Long-horsley
Druridge B.
W. Chevington
Ashington
Newbiggin
Morpeth
N. Seaton
Falstone
Cambo
Wansbeck
Cowpen
Blyth
Bellingham
Kirk-whelpington
Bedlington
Cramlington
Redesmouth
Stannington
Seaton Delaval
Wark
Birtley
Belsay
Seghill
Earsdon
Chollerton
Ponteland
Longbenton
Stamfordham
Gosforth
Tynemouth
ROMAN WALL
Pont
NEWCASTLE
Wallsend
Haltwhistle
Hexham
Heddon
SOUTH SHIELDS
Haydon Bri.
Corbridge
Tyne
Hebburn
Prudhoe
Ryton
Newburn
Blaydon
GATESHEAD
Whickham
Monkwearmouth
SUNDERLAND
Catton
Tanfield
Washington
Allendale Town
Slaley
Stanley
Chester le Street
Ryhope
Benfieldside
Leadgate
Consett
Annfield Plain
Seaham Harbour
Allen
Derwent
Houghton le Spring
Allenheads
Edmondbyers
Lanchester
Sacriston
Hetton le Hole
Alston
Collier Law 1692
Durham
Easington
Brandon
Sherburn
Peterlee
Wearhead
Stanhope
Tow Law
Brancepeth
Wheatley Hill
Wolsingham
Hartlepool
West Hartlepool
St John's Chapel
Wear Dale
Crook
Willington
Coxhoe
Wingate
Spennymoor
Seaton Carew
Ferryhill
Tees Bay
Witton le Wear
Bishop Auckland
West Auckland
Sedgefield
Grangetown
Redcar
Kirkleatham
Marske
Saltburn-by-the-Sea
Middleton in Teesdale
Tees Dale
Mickle Fell 2591
Shildon
Billingham
P. Clarence
Skelton
Brotton
Loftus
Staithes
Old Nab
Hinderwell
Kettle Ness
Mickleton
Cockfield
Newton Aycliffe
Bank
Eston
Appleby
Staindrop
Stockton -on-Tees
Cotherstone
Darlington
MIDDLESBROUGH
Guisborough
Easington
Warcop
Barnard Castle
Winston
Thornaby on Tees
Ormesby
Lythe
Whitby
Brough
Bowes
Gainford
Piercebridge
Yarm
1057 Roseberry Topping
Cleveland
Commondale
Hawsker
Kirkby Stephen
Stainmore Forest
Greta
Croft
Melsonby
Stokesley
Great Ayton
Castleton
Esk
Egton
North Cheek
Robin Hood's Bay
Dalton
Picton
Whorlton
Grosmont
Pendragon Cas.
Rogans Seat 2203
Arkle
Marske
Richmond
Cowton
Scorton
Welbury
Cleveland Hills
1489 Burton Head
North York Moors 1419
Goathland
Hayburn Wyke
Keld
Reeth
Swale
Muker
Catterick
Danby Wiske
Brompton
Osmotherley
Rosedale Abbey
Cloughton
Great Shunner Fell 2340
Swale Dale
Hornby
North-allerton
Levisham
Scalby
Scalby Ness
Hawes
Askrigg
Leyburn
Leeming
1225
Hambleton Hills
Hawnby
Kirby Moorside
Hackness
Wensley Dale
Bainbridge
Aysgarth
Middleham
Bedale
S. Otterington
Rievaulx Abb.
Normanby
Ayton
Scarborough
Dent
Snape
Thirsk
Helmsley
Pickering
Seamer
Cayton
Jervaulx Abbey
Cover
Whernside 2419
Langstrothdale Chase
Masham
Baldersby
Ampleforth
Vale of Pickering
Thornton Dale
Filey
Filey Bay
Topcliffe
Sessay
Derwent
Hunmanby
Ribble
Wharfe
Lofthouse
Kirkby Malzeard
Ripon
Melmerby
Vale of York
Gilling
Hovingham
Rye
Rillington
Sherburn
Speeton
Bempton
Ingleton
Horton
Pen-y-Ghent 2273
Gt Whernside 2310
Fountains Abbey
Helperby
Malton
Norton
Burton Fleming
Kirkby Lonsdale
Kettlewell
Easingwold
Settrington
Rudston
Flamborough
Bridlington
Malham Tarn
Grassington
Nidderdale
Pateley Bri.
Boroughbridge
Alne
Sheriff Hutton
Kirkham
Kilham
Giggleswick
Settle
Linton
Ripley
Whixley
Sutton on the Forest
Sledmere
Wolds
Burton Agnes
Long Preston
Killinghall
Nidd
Knaresborough
Goldsboro'
Ouse
Poppleton
Huntington
Fridaythorpe
Nafferton
Wetwang
Driffield
Bolton Abbey
Harrogate
Stamford Bridge
Hellifield
Marston Moor
York
Hutton Cranswick
Skipsea
Beeford
Gargrave
Gisburn
Bolton-by-Bowland
Skipton
Burley
Spofforth
Wetherby
Fulford
Pocklington
Warter
Middleton on-the Wolds
Hornsea
Silsden
Otley
Wharfe
Harewood
Bishopthorpe
Naburn
Londesborough
Leven
Barnoldswick
Foulridge
Ilkley
Aire
Tadcaster
Wheldrake
Hull
Pendle Hill 1831
Keighley
Baildon
Thorner
Escrick
Market Weighton
Beverley
Nelson
Colne
Bingley
Horsforth
Riccall
Holme
Walkington
Haworth
Shipley
Idle
LEEDS
Cawood
North Cave
Cottingham
Padiham
Brierfield
Burnley
BRADFORD
Pudsey
Garforth
Selby
Sherburn
Barlby
Bubwith
South Cave
HULL
2 West from Greenwich

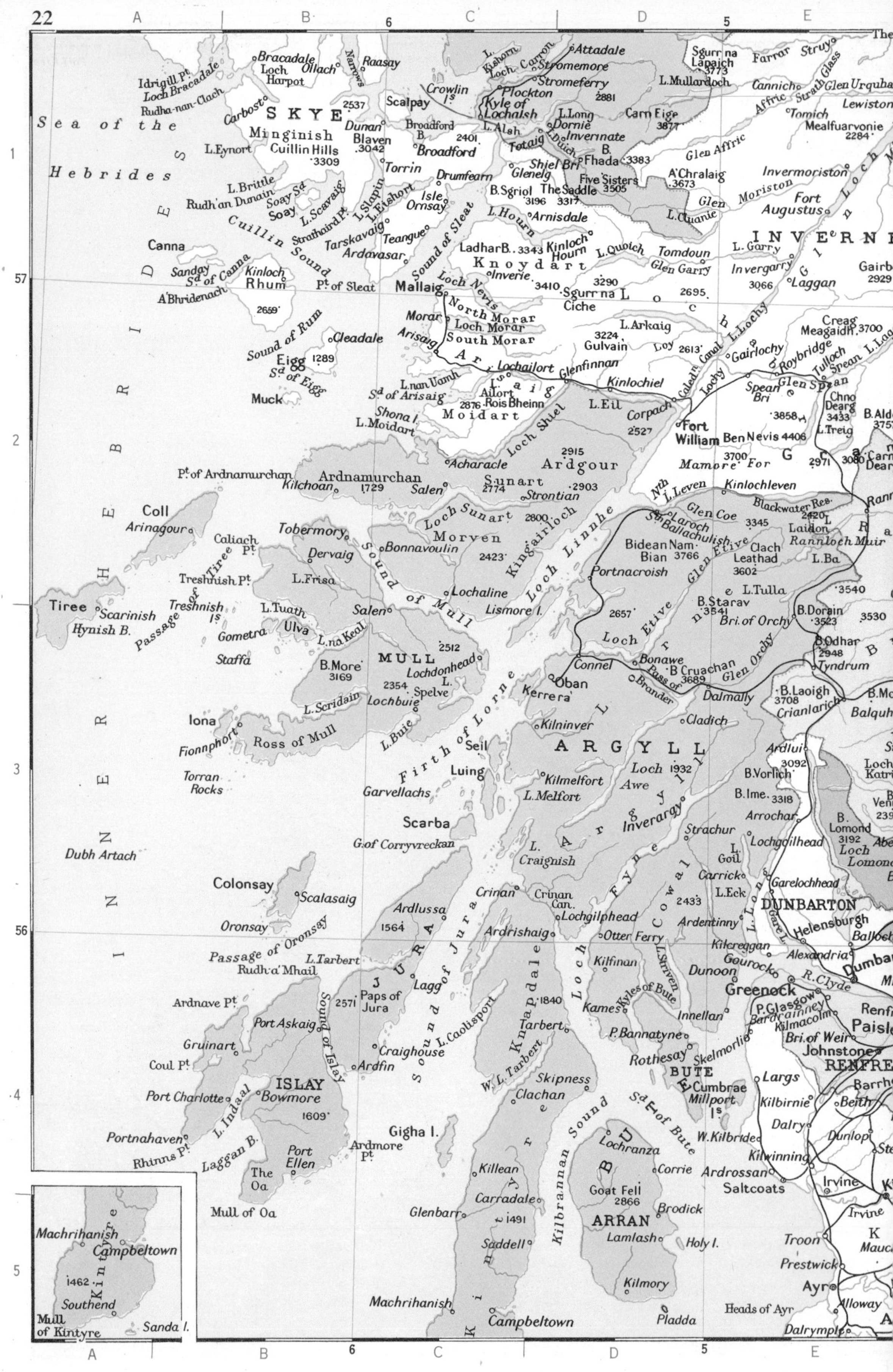
A
B
6
C
D
5
E
Sea of the
Hebrides
INNER HEBRIDES
SKYE
Idrigill Pt.
Loch Bracadale
Bracadale
Loch Harpot
Ollach
Narrows
Raasay
Rudha-nan-Clach
Carbost
2537
Scalpay
Crowlin Is.
L. Kishorn
Loch Carron
Attadale
Stromemore
Plockton
Stromeferry
Kyle of Lochalsh
L. Alsh
2881
Sgurr na Lapaich
3773
L. Mullardoch
Farrar
Struy
The
Cannich
Glen Urquhart
Strath Glass
Affric
Tomich
Lewiston
Mealfuarvonie
2284
Minginish
Cuillin Hills
3309
L. Eynort
Dunan
Blaven
3042
Broadford B.
Broadford
2401
Totaig
L. Long
Dornie
Invernate
L. Duich
Carn Eige
3877
B. Fhada
3383
Glen Affric
Torrin
Drumfearn
Shiel Bri.
Glenelg
Five Sisters
3505
A'Chralaig
3673
Invermoriston
L. Brittle
Rudh'an Dunain
Soay Sd.
Soay
L. Scavaig
L. Slapin
L. Eishort
Isle Ornsay
B. Sgriol
3196
The Saddle
3317
Glen Moriston
L. Cluanie
Fort Augustus
Loch Ness
Cuillin Sound
Strathaird Pt.
Tarskavaig
Teangue
Ardavasar
Sound of Sleat
L. Hourn
Arnisdale
Canna
Ladhar B.
3343
Kinloch Hourn
L. Quoich
Tomdoun
L. Garry
INVERNESS
Sanday
Sd. of Canna
Kinloch
Rhum
Pt. of Sleat
Mallaig
Loch Nevis
Knoydart
Inverie
3410
Glen Garry
Invergarry
3066
Laggan
Gairbe
2929
57
A'Bhridenach
2659
3290
Sgurr na Ciche
2695
Loch Lochy
Glen Gloy
North Morar
Morar
Loch Morar
South Morar
Arisaig
L. Arkaig
3224
Gulvain
Loy
2613
Creag Meagaidh
3700
Sound of Rum
Cleadale
Eigg
1289
Sd. of Eigg
Caledn. Canal
Gairlochy
Roybridge
Tulloch
Spean
L. Laggan
Lochailort
Glenfinnan
Kinlochiel
Spean Bri.
Glen Spean
Muck
L. nan Uamh
Sd. of Arisaig
Ailort
2876
Rois Bheinn
Moidart
L. Eil
Corpach
Lochy
Chno Dearg
3433
B. Alder
3757
Shona I.
L. Moidart
Loch Shiel
2527
Fort William
Ben Nevis
4406
3858
L. Treig
2
Acharacle
2915
Ardgour
Mamore For.
3700
2971
3080
Carn Dearg
Pt. of Ardnamurchan
Ardnamurchan
Kilchoan
1729
Salen
Sunart
2774
2903
Strontian
Nth. L. Leven
Kinlochleven
Blackwater Res.
Rannoch
Coll
Arinagour
Loch Sunart
2800
Glen Coe
Laroch
St. Ballachulish
3345
2420
Laidon
Rannoch Muir
Caliach Pt.
Tobermory
Dervaig
Sound of Mull
Bonnavoulin
Morven
2423
Kingairloch
Loch Linnhe
Bidean Nam Bian
3766
Glen Etive
Clach Leathad
3602
L. Ba
Passage of Tiree
Treshnish Pt.
L. Frisa
Portnacroish
L. Tulla
3540
Tiree
Scarinish
Hynish B.
Treshnish Is.
L. Tuath
Ulva
Gometra
Staffa
Salen
Lochaline
Lismore I.
2657
B. Starav
3541
B. Dorain
3523
Bri. of Orchy
3530
L. na Keal
Loch Etive
B. Odhar
2948
MULL
B. More
3169
2512
Lochdonhead
L. Spelve
2354
Connel
Bonawe
Pass of Brander
B. Cruachan
3689
Glen Orchy
Tyndrum
Oban
Kerrera
Dalmally
B. Laoigh
3708
Crianlarich
Balquh
B. Mo
Iona
Fionnphort
Ross of Mull
L. Scridain
Lochbuie
L. Buie
Firth of Lorne
Kilninver
Cladich
Seil
ARGYLL
Ardlui
3092
3
Torran Rocks
Luing
Kilmelfort
Loch Awe
1932
B. Vorlich
Loch Katri
Garvellachs
L. Melfort
B. Ime.
3318
Arrochar
Scarba
Inverarary
Strachur
B. Lomond
3192
Loch Lomond
Dubh Artach
G. of Corryvreckan
L. Craignish
L. Goil
Lochgoilhead
Colonsay
Scalasaig
Crinan
Crinan Can.
Carrick
L. Eck
Garelochhead
Ardlussa
1564
JURA
Lochgilphead
Loch Fyne
Cowal
2433
DUNBARTON
Oronsay
Ardrishaig
Otter Ferry
Ardentinny
L. Long
Gare L.
Helensburgh
56
Passage of Oronsay
L. Tarbert
Rudh'a'Mhail
Sound of Jura
Knapdale
Kilfinan
L. Striven
Kilcreggan
Alexandria
Gourock
Dunoon
Greenock
R. Clyde
Lagg
Paps of Jura
2571
Ardnave Pt.
Port Askaig
Sound of Islay
1840
Kames
Kyles of Bute
Innellan
P. Glasgow
Bardrainney
Kilmacolm
Renfr
Paisl
Gruinart
L. Caolisport
Tarbert
P. Bannatyne
Bri. of Weir
Johnstone
RENFRE
Craighouse
Ardfin
Coul Pt.
W. L. Tarbert
Skipness
Rothesay
Skelmorlie
BUTE
Largs
ISLAY
Bowmore
Port Charlotte
L. Indaal
1609
Clachan
Sd. of Bute
Cumbrae
Millport Is.
Kilbirnie
Beith
Dalry
Portnahaven
Rhinns Pt.
Laggan B.
Port Ellen
The Oa
Gigha I.
Ardmore Pt.
Kintyre
Kilbrannan Sound
Lochranza
BUTE
W. Kilbride
Dunlop
Kilwinning
Killean
Corrie
Ardrossan
Saltcoats
Irvine
Carradale
Goat Fell
2866
Brodick
Mull of Oa
Glenbarr
1491
ARRAN
Lamlash
Holy I.
Troon
Saddell
Prestwick
Kilmory
Ayr
Machrihanish
Campbeltown
Pladda
Heads of Ayr
Alloway
Dalrymple
Machrihanish
Campbeltown
Kintyre
1462
Southend
Mull of Kintyre
Sanda I.
5

CENTRAL SCOTLAND
Scale 1:1,000,000 (16 miles = 1 inch)
10 5 0 10 Statute Miles
10 0 10 20 Kilometres
Railways
Canals
4084 Heights in feet
Projection: Conical with two standard parallels
COPYRIGHT, GEORGE PHILIP & SON, LTD.
West from Greenwich
NORTH SEA
ABERDEEN
BANFF
KINCARDINE
ANGUS
PERTH
FIFE
KINROSS
CLACKMANNAN
STIRLING
DUNBARTON
W. LOTHIAN
MIDLOTHIAN
E. LOTHIAN
BERWICK
PEEBLES
SELKIRK
ROXBURGH
LANARK
Aberdeen
Dundee
Edinburgh
Perth
Leith
Firth of Forth
Firth of Tay
Cairngorm Mts
Monadhliath Mts
Grampians
Forest of Atholl
Braes of Angus
Sidlaw Hills
Ochil Hills
Pentland Hills
Moorfoot Hs.
Lammermuir Hills
Cheviot Hills
Strathmore
Strathspey
Strath Earn
Braemar
Balmoral For.
Lochnagar
Ben Macdhui 4296
Cairn Gorm 4084
Braeriach 4248
Cairn Toul 4241
Schichallion 3547
Ben Lawers 3984
Loch Tay
L. Leven
Girdle Ness
Fife Ness
Isle of May
Bass Rock
St. Abb's Head
Inchcape or Bell Rock
Buddon Ness
Holy I.
Montrose
Arbroath
Forfar
Brechin
Stonehaven
Kirkcaldy
Dunfermline
St. Andrews
Cupar
Stirling
Falkirk
Alloa
Motherwell
Hamilton
Lanark
Peebles
Galashiels
Hawick
Berwick-upon-Tweed
Dunbar
Haddington
Crieff
Pitlochry
Blairgowrie
Kingussie
Aviemore
Banchory
Ballater
Inverurie
Ellon

NORTHERN SCOTLAND
Scale 1:1,000,000 (16 miles = 1 inch)
10 5 0 10 Statute Miles
10 0 10 20 Kilometres
Railways
Canals
3066 Heights in feet
Projection: Conical with two standard parallels
Continuation Westwards on same scale
A B C D E F
1 2 3 4 5
7 6 5
Toe Hd.
S. Harris
Cluer
Pabbay
Sd. of Pabbay
Berneray
Sound of Harris
Leverburgh
Renish Pt.
Griminish Pt.
Sollas
NORTH UIST
L. Maddy
Sd. of Monach
Paible
L. Eport
Carinish
Eaval 1138
Monach Is.
Baleshare
Ronay
Gramisdale
Grimsay
Benbecula
Ardivachar Pt.
Wiay
L. Bee
Bagh nam Faoileann
Howmore
Hecla 1988
Rudha Ardvule
SOUTH UIST
B. Mhor 2034
L. Eynort
Daliburgh
Lochboisdale
L. Boisdale
Boisdale
Sound of Barra
S. of Eriskay
Eriskay
Greian Pt.
57
Barra
Bruernish Pt.
Heaval 1260
Castlebay
Vatersay
Sandray
Pabbay
Mingulay
Berneray
Barra Hd.
OUTER HEBRIDES
Little Minch
INNER HEBRIDES
Vaternish Pt.
Geary
Dunvegan Pt.
L. Dunvegan
Loch B.
Stein
Milovaig
Dunvegan
Healaval More 1538
Beg 1601
Roskhill
Moonen B.
Idrigill Pt.
Loch Bracadale
Sea of the Hebrides
Rona
Stack Sk
Butt of Lewis
Lionel
Dell
Ness
Borve
Cellar Hd.
Aird Barvas
Barvas
808
N. Tolsta
Tolsta Hd.
Muirnag
Shawbost
Bragor
Carloway
Back
Coll
Gt. Bernera
E. L. Roag
W. L. Roag
Gallan Hd.
B. Barvas 918
Broad B.
Tiumpan Hd.
Portnaguran
Garrabost
Eye Peninsula
Bayble
Chicken Hd.
Newmarket
Stornoway
Melbost
Camus Uig
Callanish
L. Roag
LEWIS
Aird Brenish
1885
Luerbost
Crossbost
Cromore
Loch Langavat
Braighe Mor
L. Erisort
Graver
Scarp 1011
58
L. Resort
Tirga More 2227
Park
Kebock Hd.
Husinish Pt.
N. Harris
Clisham 2622
1874 B. Mhor
L. Sheil
W. L. Tarbert
Taransay
Sd. of Taransay
Tarbert
L. Claidh
L. Seaforth
Sd. of Shiant
Shiant Is.
Scalpay
E. L. Tarbert
Toe Hd.
S. Harris
HARRIS
Cluer
Leverburgh
Renish Pt.
Sound of Harris
HEBRIDES
The Minch
Rudha Hunish
The Aird
Kilmaluag
Digg
Kilvoxter
Vaternish Pt.
L. Maddy
L. Eport
Geary
Loch Snizort
Uig
B. Edra 2003
Lealt
Trotternish
Dunvegan Pt.
L. Dunvegan
Loch B.
Stein
The Storr 2360
Milovaig
Edinbain
Skeabost Br.
Dunvegan
Roskhill
Healaval More 1538
Beg 1601
Moonen B.
Portree
Bracadale
Ollach
Sound of Raasay
Raasay
Rona
Inner Sound
Little Minch
INNER HEBRIDES
C. Wrath
Kyle of Durness
Faraid Hd.
Durness
Loch Eriboll
Kinlochbervie
L. Inchard
2630
L. Laxford
Foinaven 2980
Arkle 2580
Reay Forest
Strath More
Handa I.
Scourie
B. Stack 2364
Eddrachillis B.
L. More
B. Hee 2864
Clashnessie B.
Pt. of Stoer
Quinag 2653
Stoer
Assynt
L. Assynt
SUTH
Inver
Lochinver
Inchnadamph
2399
Canisp 2779
B. More Assynt 3273
Rhu Coigach
Enard B.
Elphin
Cromalt Hills
Oykell
Summer Isles
L. Lurgainn
Coigach
Inverc
Greenstone Pt.
Gruinard Bay
Oykell Bri.
Scoraig
L. Broom
Lit. L. Broom
Ullapool
Mellon Charles
Badrallach
Freevater For.
Carron
Rudh Re
Aultbea
Seana Bhraigh 3040
An Teallach 3483
Easter
L. Ewe
L. na Sheallag
3547
B. Dearg
B. a'Chaist 2404
Fionn L.
Poolewe
L. Gairloch
Gairloch
Sgurr Ban 3194
ROSS AND CROMAR
Loch Maree
3637 Sgurr Mor
Slioch 3217
L. Fannich
Wester
Highlands
Achanalt
Loch Torridon
Rudha na Fearn
B. Alligin 3021
B. Eighe 3309
Kinlochewe
L. Luichart
Garve
Achnasheen
Strath
Up. L. Torridon
Torridon
Milltown
Meig
Strath Conon
2208
Orrin
Glencarron
Scardroy
Moruisg 3026
Glen
3060 Maol Chean-dearg
Achnashellach
Applecross Forest
B. Bhan 2936
Monar Forest
Applecross
L. Monar
3554
Beau
L. Kishorn
Lochcarron
Carron
Strathcarron
Farrar
Struy
Loch Carron
Attadale
Stromemore
N.

ORKNEY ISLANDS
SHETLAND ISLANDS
on same scale
CAITHNESS
ZETLAND
MORAY
NAIRN
BANFF
Kirkwall
Stromness
Thurso
Wick
Lerwick
Inverness
Elgin
Nairn
Forres
Peterhead
Fraserburgh
Pentland Firth
Moray Firth
Dornoch Firth
4 West from Greenwich

NORTHERN IRELAND
Scale 1:1,000,000 (16 miles = 1 inch)
Statute Miles
Kilometres
Railways
Canals
1755 Heights in feet
Projection: Conical with two standard parallels
ATLANTIC
OCEAN
Tory I.
Horn Head
Inishbofin
Bloody Foreland
Dunfanaghy
Falcarragh
Creeslough
Muckish 2197
Gola I.
Inishfree B.
Bunbeg
Gweedore
Errigal 2466
Rosses Bay
The Rosses
Derryveagh Mts.
Aran I.
2240
Burtonport
Dungloe
Crohy Hd.
Gweebarra
Doochary
Trawenagh B.
Gweebarra B.
Gweebarra
DONE
Fintown
Dawros Pt.
Loughros More B.
Cloghan
Glenties
Croagh Gorm 2219
Blue Stack Mts.
1515
Sl Tooey
Ardara
Glen B.
Rossan Pt.
Glencolumbkille
1653
Rathlin O'Birne I.
Slieve League
1972
Carrick
Killybegs
Inver
Donegal
Laghey
Carrigan Hd.
Muckross Hd.
Mc Swyne's B.
Inver B.
Mountcharles
Donegal Harb.
Ballintra
St. John's Pt.
Kildoney Pt.
Donegal Bay
Erne
Ballyshannon
Bundoran
Belleek
Mullaghmore
Inishmurray
Kinlough
Lough Melvin
Cliffoney
Garrison
Roskeeragh Pt.
Truskmore 2113
Glenade
Sligo Bay
Carney
Kiltyclogher
Drumcliff
Manor Hamilton
Dromore B.
Ballysadare Bay
SLIGO
Hazelwood
L. Gill
Dromore West
1446
Lackagh Hs.
Dromahair
Ballysadare
Coolaney
Collooney
Ballintogher
Drumkeeran
SLIGO
Unshin
L. Allen
Ballymote
Bralieve Mts.
Arigna
Achonry
Tobercurry
L. Arrow
Ballinafad
Drumshambo
Curry
Curlew Mts.
L. Key
Leitrim
Carrick
L. Gara
Boyle
Charlestown
Monasteraden
Jamestown
Rinn-a Rodain (Kingsland)
Ballaghaderreen
Clogher
Frenchpark
Bellanagare
Elphin
Lough-glynn
ROSCOMMON
Tulsk
Castlerea
Strokestown
Castleplunket
Ballinlough
Ballintober
CONNACHT
Ballymoe
Suck
Ballyclare
Glennamaddy
Dunamon
Roscommon
Dunmore
Ballymurray
Knockcroghery
Athleague
Mount Talbot
Ballygar
Kiltoom
Newtown Bellew
Ballyforan
Mountbellew Bri.
Castleblakeney
Ahascragh
Kilconnell
Newtown
Ballinasloe
Monivea
Attymon
Claregalway
Clare
GALWAY
Stags of Broadhaven
Benwee Hd.
Broad Haven
Erris Head
Downpatrick Hd.
Bunatrahir B.
Benmore Hd.
Lenadoon Pt.
Portacloy
Belderg
Maumakeogh 1246
Ballycastle
Kilcummin
Killala Bay
Easky
Ross
Rossport
Annagh Hd.
Binghamstown
Mullet Pena.
Belmullet
Carrowmore L.
Oweniny
Killala
Inis crone
Bangor
Belville
North Inishkea South
Gweesalia
Owenmore
Bellacorick
Ballina
Ardnaree
Blacksod Bay
Crossmolina
Slieve Gamph (Ox Mts.)
1338
Moy
Fallmore
Blacksod Pt.
Ridge Pt.
Slieve More
Saddle Hd.
Croaghaun
2369
Nephin Beg 2065
Deel
Lough Conn
Aclare
Nephin 2644
Nephin Beg Ra.
Achill Hd.
2192
2204
Keel
2342
Foxford
Achill I.
Achill
L. Feeagh
L. Cullin
Callow
Swinford
Dooega
Mulrany
Beltra L.
Corraun Pena.
Burrishoole
Achill Sd.
Achillbeg I.
Newport B.
Newport
Bellavary
Kilkelly
Castlebar
Kiltimagh
Clew Bay
Manulla
Ballyglass
Clare I.
Old Hd.
Westport B.
Westport
Ballyhean
MAYO
Balla
Mayo
Westport Quay
Ballyhaunis
Emlagh Pt.
Louisburgh
2510
Croaghpatrick
Caher I.
Killadoon
Knappagh
Partry Mts.
Ballyglass
Claremorris
Inishturk
Murrisk Hs.
Kilknock
Sheeffry Hs. 2504
L. Carra
Ballindine
Inishbofin
Killary Har.
Mweelrea 2688
Erriff
Toormakeady
Hollymount
Rinvyle
Benwee 2237
Lough Mask
Robe
Milltown
Ballynakill Hr.
Salrock
Aasleagh
Leenaun
Inishmaine-finny
Ballinrobe
Clare
Aughrus Pt.
Cleggan
Letterfrack
Maumturk Mts.
Joyce's Country
Cong
Kilconly
Kilbennan
Omey I.
Clifden B.
Clifden
Twelve Pins
Benbaun 2395
2307
Maam
Clonbur
Black
Shrule
Tuam
Connemara
Maam Cross
Recess
Lough Corrib
Headford
Ballyconneely
Toombeola
Ballynahinch
Corrofin
Slyne Hd.
Killabeg
Ballyglunen
Screeb
Oughterard
Ballyconneely B.
Roundstone
Bertraghboy Bay
Glinsk
Rosscahill
Iar Connacht
Moycullen
Carna
Croaghnakeela
Boderg
Rooskee
L. Ree
Lough
Drumsna
Shannon
Kilronan

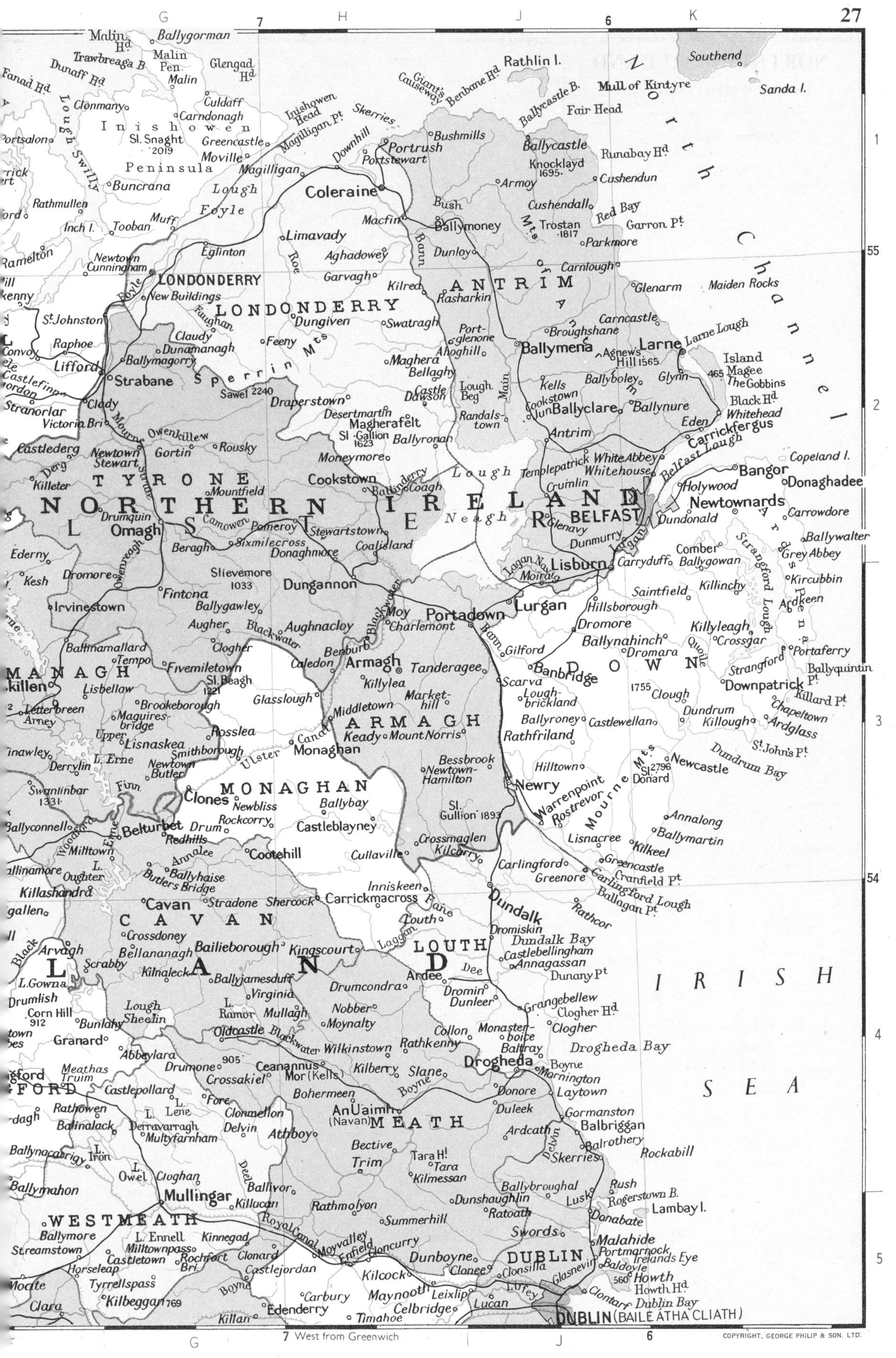
G
7
H
J
6
K
Malin Hd.
Ballygorman
Trawbreaga B.
Malin Pen.
Glengad Hd.
Malin
Dunaff Hd.
Fanad Hd.
Lough Swilly
Clonmany
Culdaff
Carndonagh
Inishowen Peninsula
Sl. Snaght 2019
Greencastle
Moville
Buncrana
Portsalon
Rathmullen
Inch I.
Tooban
Muff
Lough Foyle
Rathmelton
Newtown Cunningham
Inishowen Head
Magilligan Pt.
Skerries
Magilligan
Downhill
Giant's Causeway
Benbane Hd.
Rathlin I.
Ballycastle B.
Mull of Kintyre
Southend
Sanda I.
Fair Head
Portrush
Portstewart
Bushmills
Ballycastle
Knocklayd 1695
Runabay Hd.
Cushendun
Coleraine
Armoy
Cushendall
Red Bay
Garron Pt.
Bush
Macfin
Ballymoney
Trostan 1817
Parkmore
Limavady
Aghadowey
Dunloy
Mts. of Antrim
Carnlough
Eglinton
Garvagh
Glenarm
Maiden Rocks
North Channel
LONDONDERRY
New Buildings
Kilrea
Rasharkin
ANTRIM
Dungiven
Swatragh
Carncastle
St. Johnston
Faughan
Claudy
Feeny
Sperrin Mts.
Port-glenone
Broughshane
Larne
Larne Lough
Raphoe
Dunamanagh
Maghera
Ahoghill
Ballymena
Agnew's Hill 1565
Island Magee
Convoy
Lifford
Ballymagorry
Bellaghy
Ballyboley
Glynn
465
The Gobbins
Castlefinn
Strabane
Sawel 2240
Draperstown
Castle Dawson
Lough Beg
Main
Kells
Cookstown Jun.
Ballyclare
Ballynure
Black Hd.
Whitehead
Stranorlar
Clady
Desertmartin
Magherafelt
Randals-town
Eden
Victoria Bri.
Mourne
Owenkillew
Sl. Gallion 1623
Ballyronan
Antrim
Carrickfergus
Castlederg
Rousky
Newtown Stewart
Gortin
Moneymore
Templepatrick
White Abbey
Whitehouse
Belfast Lough
Copeland I.
Derg
Strule
TYRONE
Mountfield
Cookstown
Ballinderry
Coagh
Lough Neagh
Crumlin
Bangor
Donaghadee
Killeter
Holywood
NORTHERN IRELAND
Newtownards
BELFAST
Carrowdore
Dundonald
Drumquin
Camowen
Pomeroy
Omagh
Stewartstown
Glenavy
Ards Pen.
Ballywalter
Ulster
Dunmurry
Comber
Strangford Lough
Grey Abbey
Ederny
Beragh
Sixmilecross
Donaghmore
Coalisland
Lagan
Owenreagh
Ballygowan
Carryduff
Kircubbin
Kesh
Dromore
Slievemore 1033
Dungannon
Blackwater
Lagan Nav.
Moira
Lisburn
Killinchy
Saintfield
Ardkeen
Fintona
Irvinestown
Ballygawley
Moy
Portadown
Lurgan
Hillsborough
Augher
Aughnacloy
Charlemont
Bann
Dromore
Killyleagh
Crossgar
Quoile
Portaferry
Clogher
Benburb
Ballynahinch
Dromara
Ballinamallard
Tempo
Caledon
Armagh
Tanderagee
Gilford
DOWN
Strangford
Ballyquintin Pt.
Fivemiletown
Sl. Beagh 1221
Banbridge
Downpatrick
Killard Pt.
Killylea
Markethill
Scarva
Lisbellaw
Loughbrickland
1755
Clough
Glasslough
Middletown
ARMAGH
Dundrum
Chapeltown
Letterbreen
Brookeborough
Ballyroney
Castlewellan
Killough
Ardglass
Arney
Maguiresbridge
Keady
Mount Norris
Rathfriland
Upper
Rosslea
Canal
Lisnaskea
Smithborough
Monaghan
Bessbrook
Mourne Mts.
Newcastle
St. John's Pt.
Dundrum Bay
Swanlinbar 1331
Derrylin
L. Erne
Newtown Butler
Finn
Newtown-Hamilton
Hilltown
Sl. Donard 2796
MONAGHAN
Newry
Warrenpoint
Rostrevor
Clones
Newbliss
Ballybay
Sl. Gullion 1893
Annalong
Ballyconnell
Woodford
Erne
Belturbet
Drum
Rockcorry
Castleblayney
Redhills
Lisnacree
Ballymartin
Milltown
Annalee
Cootehill
Crossmaglen
Kilcurry
Cullaville
Kilkeel
Greencastle
Carlingford
Cranfield Pt.
Ballinamore
L. Oughter
Ballyhaise
Butlers Bridge
Greenore
Carlingford Lough
Ballagan Pt.
Killashandra
Cavan
Stradone
Shercock
Carrickmacross
Inniskeen
Fane
Dundalk
Rathcor
CAVAN
Louth
Crossdoney
Dromiskin
Dundalk Bay
Laggan
Arvagh
Bellananagh
Bailieborough
Kingscourt
LOUTH
Castlebellingham
Annagassan
Black
Scrabby
Kilnaleck
Ballyjamesduff
Dee
Ardee
Dunany Pt.
IRISH SEA
L. Gowna
Drumcondra
Dromin
Dunleer
Drumlish
Virginia
L. Ramor
Mullagh
Nobber
Grangebellew
Clogher Hd.
Corn Hill 912
Bunlahy
Lough Sheelin
Moynalty
Collon
Monasterboice
Clogher
Granard
Oldcastle
Blackwater
Wilkinstown
Rathkenny
Baltray
Drogheda Bay
Abbeylara
905
Ceanannus Mor (Kells)
Drumone
Kilberry
Slane
Drogheda
Boyne
Meathas Truim
Crossakiel
Mornington
Castlepollard
L. Lene
Fore
Bohermeen
Boyne
Donore
Laytown
Rathowen
Clonmellon
An Uaimh (Navan)
MEATH
Duleek
Gormanston
Ballinalack
L. Derravarragh
Delvin
Athboy
Ardcath
Balbriggan
Multyfarnham
Bective
Delvin
Balrothery
Ballynacargy
L. Iron
Trim
Tara H.
Tara
Skerries
Rockabill
L. Owel
Cloghan
Deel
Kilmessan
Ballymahon
Ballybroughal
Rush
Ballivor
Mullingar
Killucan
Dunshaughlin
Lusk
Rogerstown B.
Lambay I.
WESTMEATH
Royal Canal
Rathmolyon
Ratoath
Donabate
Ballymore
L. Ennell
Summerhill
Swords
Kinnegad
Malahide
Streamstown
Milltownpass
Moyvalley
Clonard
Enfield
Cloncurry
DUBLIN
Portmarnock
Irelands Eye
Castletown
Rochfort Bri.
Dunboyne
Horseleap
Castlejordan
Clonee
Clonsilla
Baldoyle
Tyrrellspass
Kilcock
Glasnevin
Howth
Moate
560
Howth Hd.
Boyne
Carbury
Maynooth
Leixlip
Liffey
Clontarf
Dublin Bay
Kilbeggan 769
Clara
Edenderry
Celbridge
Lucan
Killan
Timahoe
DUBLIN (BAILE ÁTHA CLIATH)
1
2
3
4
5
55
54
7 West from Greenwich
COPYRIGHT, GEORGE PHILIP & SON, LTD.

A
B
10
C
D
9
E
ATLANTIC
OCEAN
Ballyconneely
Toombeola
Slyne Hd.
Ballyconneely B.
Roundstone
Bertraghboy Bay
Glinsk
Croaghnakeela
Carna
Kilkieran B.
Lettermore I.
Costelloe
Skerd Rks
Mweenish I.
Gorumna I.
Carraroe
Lettermullan
Cashla B.
North Sound
Ballynew
Screeb
Oughterard
Rosscahill
Lough Corrib
Iar Connacht
Moycullen
G A L W A Y
C O N N A U G H T
Killabeg
Ballyglunen
Monivea
Attymon
Clare
Claregalway
Menlough
Athenry
GALWAY
Salthill
Barna
Spiddal
Oranmore
Kiltullagh
Clarinbridge
Kilcolgan Pt.
Tawin I.
Kinvarra B.
Dunkellin
Craughwell
Loughrea
L. Rea
Galway Bay
Black Hd.
Ardrahan
Kilchreest
Brannock Is.
Kilmurvy
Kilronan
Killeany B.
Inishmore
Killeany
Murrough
Bealaclugga
Kinvara
Slieve A
Inishmaan
Ballyvaughan
1134
1073
St. Carran
Kiltartan
Gort
Derrybrien
1207
Aran Islands
South Sound
Inisheer
Doolin Hd.
Lisdoonvarna
Aughrim
L. Cutra
Tubber
Roadford
Kilfenora
1312
L. Graney
Knockannis
Cliffs of Moher
Hags Hd.
Ennistymon
Crusheen
Graney
Mountsh
Liscannor
Liscannor Bay
Lehinch
Corrofin
Scarriff
Inagh
Kilnamona
Tulla
Tuamgraney
Mal Bay
Miltown Malbay
St. Callan 1282
C L A R E
Ennis
Mutton I.
Quilty
Clarecastle
Quin
Kilkishen
St. Bernard
1746
Broadford
Killaloe
872
Doonbeg B.
Newmarket on Fergus
O'Briensbridge
Donegal Pt.
Doon-beg
Creegh
Kilmihill
R. Fergus
Sixmilebridge
Ardnacrusha Power Sta.
Doonbeg
Kilkee B.
Kilkee
Moyasta
Killadysert
Rineanna (Shannon Airport)
Kilrush
Knock
Labasheeda
Pallaskenry
LIMERICK
Carrigaholt
Cross
Scattery I.
River Shannon
Askeaton
Mungret
Boher
Caherconlish
Loop Head
Kilbaha
Foynes
Shanagolden
St. Patrickswell
Dunmore Hd.
Mouth of the Shannon
Ballylongford
Tarbert
Glin
Adare
Ballybunion
Newtown Sandes
Ardagh
Rathkeale
Croom
Maigue
Herbertstown
Lisselton
Galey
L I M E R I C K
Listowel
Athea
1052
Ballingarry
Bruff
Ballyduff
Newcastle
Knockainy
Kerry Hd.
Feale
Kilmeedy
Bruree
Ballyheige
Deel
Feenagh
Seven Hogs
Lixnaw
754
Duagh
Abbeyfeale
Brandon Bay
Ballyheige Bay
Abbeydorney
Glanaruddery Mts.
Kilkinlea
Mullaghareirk Mts.
Rath Luirc (Charleville)
Kilfinnane
Brandon Pt.
Stack's Mts.
1118
Drumcollihera
1341
Rough Pt.
M U N S T E R
Dromina
1696
Ballyhoura
Ballydavid Hd.
Tralee Bay
Fenit
Spa
Tralee
1095
Smerwick Har.
Brandon 3127 Mt.
Stradbally
2713
Castlegregory
Blennerville
Castleisland
Liscarroll
Buttevant
Kildorrery
Awbeg
Sybil Pt.
Ballydavid
Beenoskee
2796
Sl. Mish
Gortatlea
Knockanefune
1441
Newmarket
Doneraile
2713
Currans
Brown Flesk
Ballydesmond
Kanturk
Castletown-roche
Inishtooskert
Dingle
Anascaul
Inch
Castlemaine
Maine
Farranfore
Dunmore Hd.
Ventry
1696
Eagle Mt.
Castlemaine Harb.
Milltown
Cullen
Boherboy
Mallow
Gt. Blasket I.
Dingle Hr.
K E R R Y
Blackwater
Banteer
Lombardstown
Killavullen
Slea Hd.
Killorglin
L. Caragh
Laune
Aghadoe
Rathmore
Inishvickillane
Dingle Bay
Glen-beigh
Dunloe
Killarney
L. Leane
Flesk
Headford
Millstreet
2104
Macgillicuddys Reeks
Gap of Dunloe
2739
Muckross Abbey
The Paps
2284
2273
Boggeragh Mts.
Glenville
Doulus Hd.
Coomacarrea
Caragh
3414
Carrauntoohil
Purple Mt.
2756
Derrynasaggart Mts.
2118
2133
Carriganimmy
Donoughmore
Valentia Hr.
Knights Town
Iveragh Mts.
2541
Mangerton Mt.
C O R K
Cahirciveen
Valentia Har.
Inny
2539
Windy Gap
Ballyvourney
Valentia I.
2245
Kilgarvan
Sullane
Dripsey
Blarney
Bray Hd.
Foilclogh
1639
Kenmare
Mweelin
1603
Coachford
Lee
CORK
Portmagee
Derriana L.
Templenoe
Roughty
Carran
1989
Macroom
Sheen
Ballingeary
Bride
Blackrock
Puffin I.
St. Finian's B.
Ballinskelligs
L. Currane
Sneem
Dromore
Conigar
Lee
Crookstown
Ballincollig
Passage
Parknasilla
Knockboy
2321
1886
Pass of Keimaneigh
Inchigeelagh
Owenboy
Gt. Skellig
Ballinskelligs B.
Waterville
Bolus Hd.
Sheh 1797
Shehy Mts.
Kinneigh
Clara Hills
Kilpatrick
Lit. Skellig
Hog's Hd.
Lauragh
Caha Mts.
Glengarriff
Kealkill
Inishannon
Scariff I.
Kenmare River
Ardgroom
Sugarloaf 1887
Dunmanway
Ballineen
Enniskean
Bandon
Kinsale
Lambs Hd.
Hungry Hill 2251
Adrigole
Whiddy I.
Owen Hill 1762
Bandon
Ballinascarthy
Kilbrittain
Cod's Hd.
Sl. Miskish
Castletown Bere
Bantry
Drimoleague
Ballydonegan B.
Ballydonegan
Ilen
Timoleague
Kinsale Hr.
Dursey I.
Bere I.
Bay
Durrus
Clonakilty
Court-macsherry
Courtmacsherry
Old Hd.
Dursey Hd.
Crow Hd.
Cahermore
Bantry Bay
Skibbereen
Ross-carbery
Barry Pt.
Butlerstown
Ballydehob
Glandore
Clonakilty Bay
Seven Heads
Sheeps Hd.
Schull
Dunmanus Bay
Castle-townshend
Rosscarbery B.
Galley Hd.
Goleen
Roaringwater B.
Glandore Har.
Long I.
Toe Hd.
Mizen Hd.
Baltimore
Crookhaven
Sherkin I.
Baltimore B.
C. Clear
Clear I.
53
52
1
2
3
4

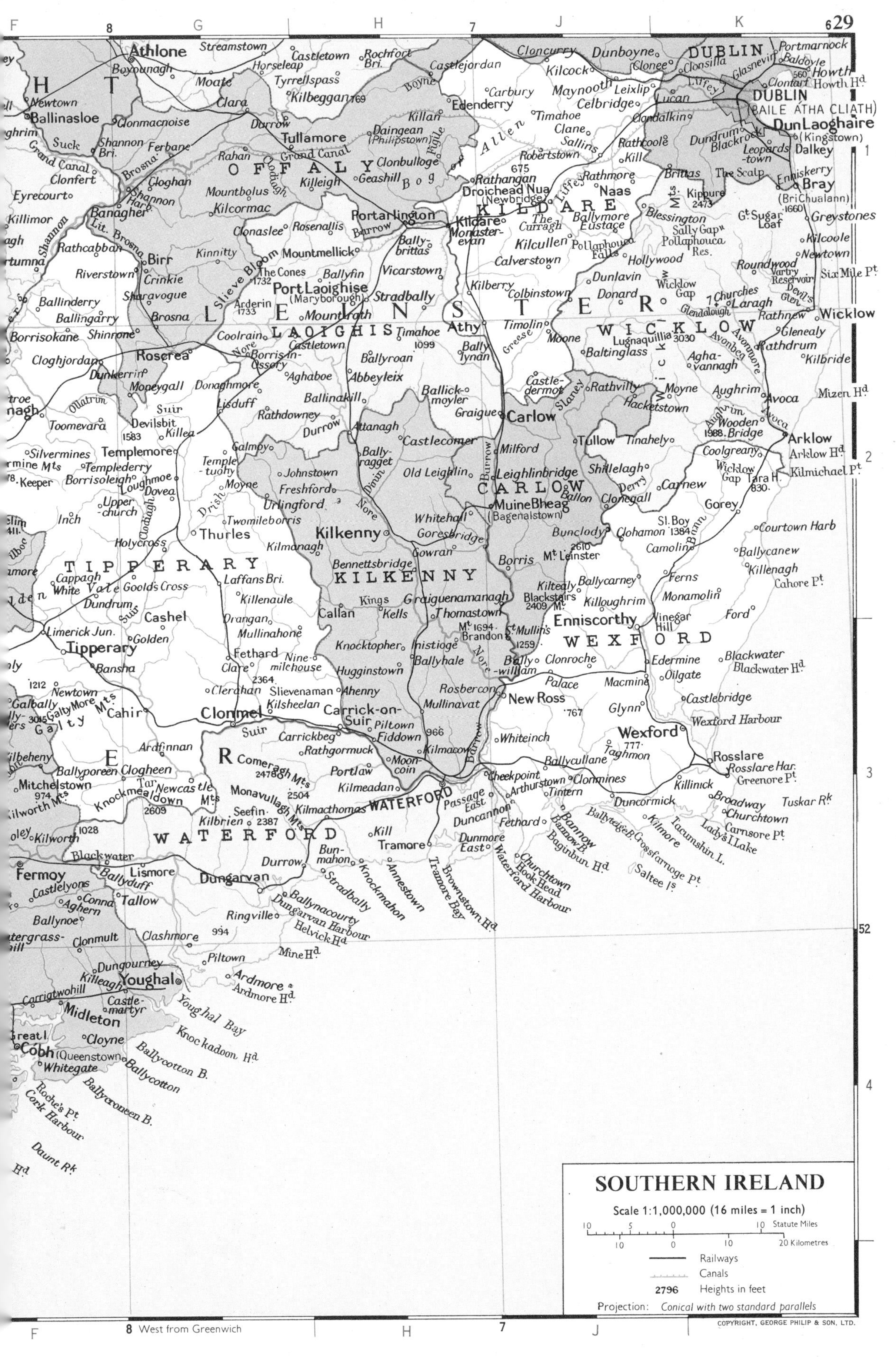
F
8
G
H
7
J
K
Athlone
Streamstown
Castletown
Rochfort Bri.
Horseleap
Castlejordan
Cloncurry
Dunboyne
DUBLIN
Portmarnock
Baldoyle
Howth
Howth Hd.
Clonee
Clonsilla
Glasnevin
Clontarf
DUBLIN
(BAILE ATHA CLIATH)
Dun Laoghaire
(Kingstown)
Dalkey
Boyounagh
Moate
Tyrrellspass
Kilbeggan
769
Boyne
Carbury
Kilcock
Maynooth
Leixlip
Lucan
Liffey
Newtown
Ballinasloe
Clara
Edenderry
Celbridge
Clondalkin
Clonmacnoise
Durrow
Killan
Timahoe
Clane
Rathcoole
Dundrum
Blackrock
Leopards -town
Suck
Shannon Bri.
Ferbane
Tullamore
Grand Canal
Daingean
(Philipstown)
Figile
Bog of Allen
Sallins
Kill
Grand Canal
Rahan
Brosna
OFFALY
Clonbulloge
Robertstown
Clonfert
675
Rathmore
Brittas
The Scalp
Enniskerry
Bray
(BriChualann)
Cloghan
Killeigh
Geashill
Rathangan
Droichead Nua
(Newbridge)
Naas
Kippure
2473
Eyrecourt
Mountbolus
Shannon Harb.
Kilcormac
KILDARE
Blessington
Gt. Sugar Loaf
1660
Greystones
Killimor
Banagher
Portarlington
Kildare
Monasterevan
The Curragh
Ballymore Eustace
Sally Gap
Pollaphouca Res.
Kilcoole
Shannon
Lit. Brosna
Clonaslee
Rosenallis
Barrow
Bally-brittas
Kilcullen
Pollaphouca Falls
Newtown
Rathcabban
Birr
Kinnitty
Mountmellick
Calverstown
Hollywood
Roundwood
Vartry Reservoir
Six Mile Pt.
Riverstown
Crinkie
Slieve Bloom
The Cones
1732
Ballyfin
Vicarstown
Dunlavin
Wicklow Gap
Sharavogue
Port Laoighise
(Maryborough)
Stradbally
Kilberry
Colbinstown
Donard
7 Churches
Laragh
Devil's Glen
Ballinderry
Arderin
1733
Mountrath
Glendalough
Rathnew
Wicklow
Ballingarry
Brosna
LEINSTER
Athy
Timolin
WICKLOW
Glenealy
Borrisokane
Shinrone
Coolrain
LAOIGHIS
Timahoe
1099
Bally Lynan
Moone
Lugnaquillia
3030
Avonbeg
Avonmore
Rathdrum
Castletown
Greese
Baltinglass
Agha-vannagh
Kilbride
Cloghjordan
Roscrea
Nore
Borris-in-Ossory
Ballyroan
Dunkerrin
Aghaboe
Abbeyleix
Castle-dermot
Rathvilly
Moyne
Aughrim
Avoca
Mizen Hd.
Moneygall
Donaghmore
Ballinakill
Ballick-moyler
Slaney
Hacketstown
Ollatrim
Lisduff
Suir
Rathdowney
Graigue
Carlow
Aughrim
Wooden Bridge
1988
Toomevara
Devilsbit
1583
Killea
Durrow
Attanagh
Castlecomer
Tullow
Tinahely
Arklow
Arklow Hd.
Silvermines
Templemore
Galmoy
Bally-ragget
Milford
Coolgreany
Templederry
Temple-tuohy
Johnstown
Old Leighlin
Leighlinbridge
Shillelagh
Wicklow Gap
Tara H.
830
Kilmichael Pt.
Keeper
Borrisoleigh
Loughmoe
Dovea
Moyne
Freshford
Dinin
CARLOW
Derry
Carnew
Upper-church
Drish
Clodagh
Urlingford
Nore
Muine Bheag
(Bagenalstown)
Ballon
Clonegall
Gorey
Inch
Twomileborris
Whitehall
Sl. Boy
1384
Thurles
Kilkenny
Goresbridge
Bunclody
Clohamon
Bann
Courtown Harb.
Holycross
Kilmanagh
Gowran
Mt. Leinster
2610
Camolin
Ballycanew
TIPPERARY
Bennettsbridge
Borris
Ferns
Killenagh
Cappagh White
Vale
Goold's Cross
Laffans Bri.
KILKENNY
Kiltealy
Ballycarney
Cahore Pt.
Killenaule
Kings
Graiguenamanagh
Blackstairs Mt.
2409
Killoughrim
Monamolin
Dundrum
Suir
Cashel
Callan
Kells
Thomastown
Enniscorthy
Vinegar Hill
Ford
Limerick Jun.
Drangan
Mullinahone
Mt. Brandon
1694
St. Mullin's
WEXFORD
Golden
Tipperary
Fethard
Nine-milehouse
Knocktopher
Inistioge
1259
Clonroche
Edermine
Blackwater
Bansha
Clare
Ballyhale
Bally-william
Oilgate
Blackwater Hd.
1212
Newtown
2364
Slievenaman
Ahenny
Hugginstown
Rosbercon
Palace
Macmine
Galbally
Galty More
3015
Galty Mts.
Cahir
Clerihan
Kilsheelan
Clonmel
Carrick-on-Suir
Piltown
Mullinavat
New Ross
767
Glynn
Castlebridge
Wexford Harbour
Suir
Carrickbeg
Fiddown
966
Whiteinch
Wexford
777
Taghmon
Ardfinnan
Rathgormuck
Kilmacow
Barrow
Rosslare
Rosslare Har.
Greenore Pt.
Ballyporeen
Clogheen
Comeragh Mts.
2478
Portlaw
Moon-coin
Ballycullane
Mitchelstown
Tar
Newcastle
Kilmeadan
Cheekpoint
Arthurstown
Clonmines
Killinick
Tuskar Rk.
974
Knockmealdown Mts.
2504
Monavullagh Mts.
WATERFORD
Passage East
Tintern
Duncormick
Broadway
Churchtown
Kilworth Mts.
2609
Seefin
Kilbrien
2387
Kilmacthomas
Duncannon
Fethard
Bannow
Bannow B.
Ballyteige B.
Kilmore
Tacumshin L.
Lady's I. Lake
Carnsore Pt.
1028
Kilworth
WATERFORD
Kill
Dunmore East
Baginbun Hd.
Crossfarnoge Pt.
Blackwater
Tramore
Saltee Is.
Fermoy
Lismore
Ballyduff
Dungarvan
Durrow
Bun-mahon
Knockmahon
Annestown
Tramore Bay
Brownstown Hd.
Waterford Harbour
Churchtown
Hook Head
Castlelyons
Conna
Aghern
Tallow
Stradbally
Ballynacourty
Dungarvan Harbour
Helvick Hd.
Ballynoe
Ringville
994
Clonmult
Clashmore
52
Mine Hd.
Dungourney
Piltown
Killeagh
Youghal
Ardmore
Ardmore Hd.
Carrigtwohill
Castle-martyr
Midleton
Youghal Bay
Great I.
Cloyne
Knockadoon Hd.
Cobh
(Queenstown)
Ballycotton B.
Whitegate
Ballycotton
Roche's Pt.
Cork Harbour
Ballycroneen B.
Daunt Rk.
1
2
3
4
SOUTHERN IRELAND
Scale 1:1,000,000 (16 miles = 1 inch)
10 5 0 10 Statute Miles
10 0 10 20 Kilometres
Railways
Canals
2796 Heights in feet
Projection: Conical with two standard parallels
F
8 West from Greenwich
H
7
J
COPYRIGHT, GEORGE PHILIP & SON, LTD.

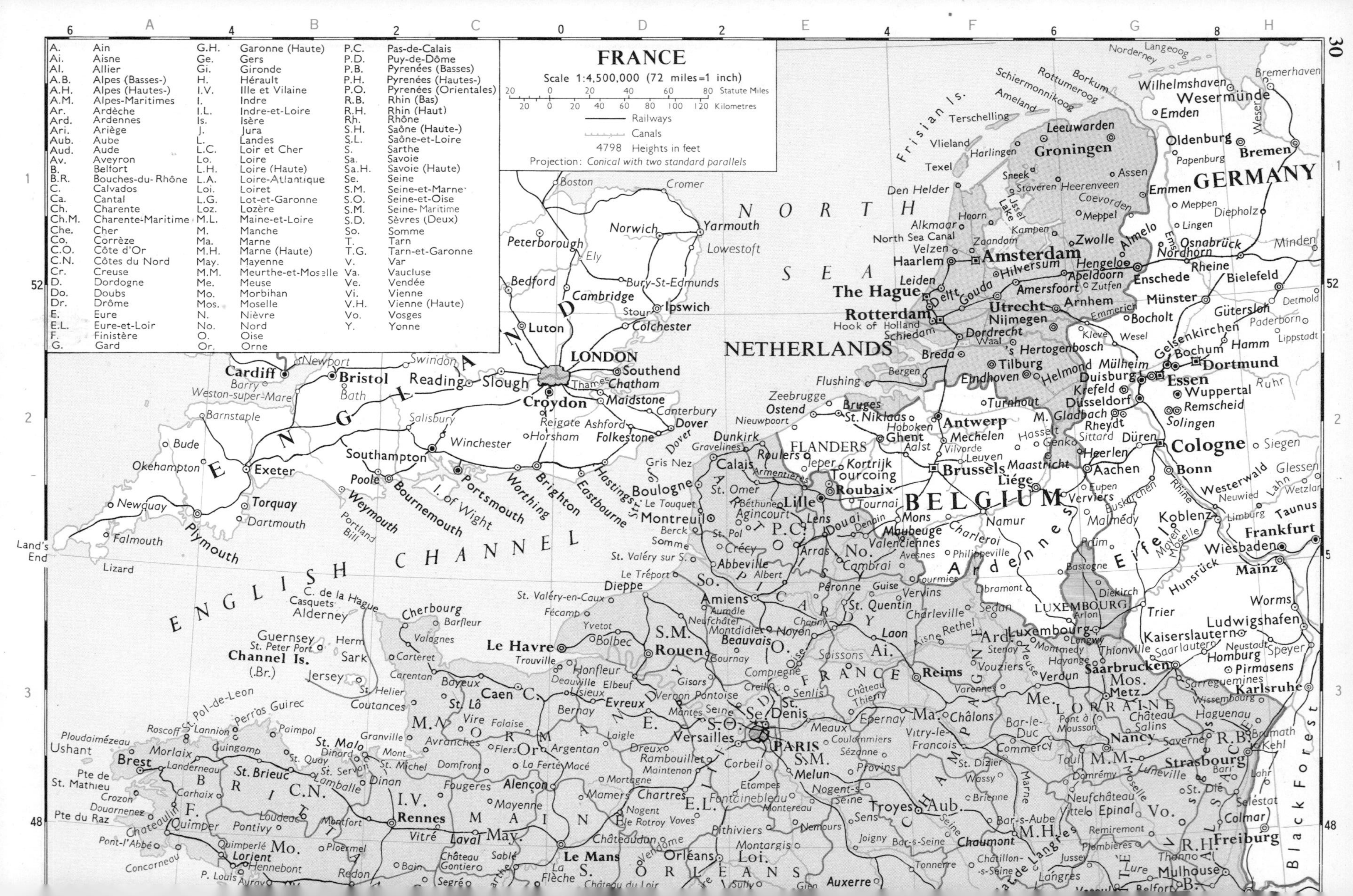
FRANCE
Scale 1:4,500,000 (72 miles=1 inch)
Statute Miles
Kilometres
Railways
Canals
4798 Heights in feet
Projection: Conical with two standard parallels
A. Ain
Ai. Aisne
Al. Allier
A.B. Alpes (Basses-)
A.H. Alpes (Hautes-)
A.M. Alpes-Maritimes
Ar. Ardèche
Ard. Ardennes
Ari. Ariège
Aub. Aube
Aud. Aude
Av. Aveyron
B. Belfort
B.R. Bouches-du-Rhône
C. Calvados
Ca. Cantal
Ch. Charente
Ch.M. Charente-Maritime
Che. Cher
Co. Corrèze
C.O. Côte d'Or
C.N. Côtes du Nord
Cr. Creuse
D. Dordogne
Do. Doubs
Dr. Drôme
E. Eure
E.L. Eure-et-Loir
F. Finistère
G. Gard
G.H. Garonne (Haute)
Ge. Gers
Gi. Gironde
H. Hérault
I.V. Ille et Vilaine
I. Indre
I.L. Indre-et-Loire
Is. Isère
J. Jura
L. Landes
L.C. Loir et Cher
Lo. Loire
L.H. Loire (Haute)
L.A. Loire-Atlantique
Loi. Loiret
L.G. Lot-et-Garonne
Loz. Lozère
M.L. Maine-et-Loire
M. Manche
Ma. Marne
M.H. Marne (Haute)
May. Mayenne
M.M. Meurthe-et-Moselle
Me. Meuse
Mo. Morbihan
Mos. Moselle
N. Nièvre
No. Nord
O. Oise
Or. Orne
P.C. Pas-de-Calais
P.D. Puy-de-Dôme
P.B. Pyrenées (Basses)
P.H. Pyrenées (Hautes-)
P.O. Pyrenées (Orientales)
R.B. Rhin (Bas)
R.H. Rhin (Haut)
Rh. Rhône
S.H. Saône (Haute-)
S.L. Saône-et-Loire
S. Sarthe
Sa. Savoie
Sa.H. Savoie (Haute)
Se. Seine
S.M. Seine-et-Marne
S.O. Seine-et-Oise
S.M. Seine-Maritime
S.D. Sèvres (Deux)
So. Somme
T. Tarn
T.G. Tarn-et-Garonne
V. Var
Va. Vaucluse
Ve. Vendée
Vi. Vienne
V.H. Vienne (Haute)
Vo. Vosges
Y. Yonne

FRANCE
SWITZERLAND
ITALY
SPAIN
BAY OF BISCAY
MEDITERRANEAN SEA
Gulf of Lions
Massif Central
Pyrenees
Monts d'Auvergne
Cevennes
Jura
POITOU
MARCHE
BOURBONNAIS
LYONNAIS
LIMOUSIN
AUVERGNE
ANGOUMOIS
SAINTONGE
AUNIS
GUYENNE
GASCONY
BEARN
DAUPHINE
PROVENCE
ROUSSILLON
TOURAINE
BASQUE PROVINCES
OLD CASTILE
ARAGON
CATALONIA
ANDORRA
Nantes
Bordeaux
Toulouse
Lyons
Marseilles
Bourges
Limoges
Clermont Ferrand
St. Etienne
Grenoble
Geneva
Bern
Lausanne
Fribourg
Turin
Nice
Toulon
Montpellier
Perpignan
Carcassonne
Bilbao
San Sebastian
Santander
Pamplona
Zaragoza
Barcelona
Valladolid
Burgos
Logroño
Vitoria
Lérida
Tarragona
Sierra de la Demanda
Sierra de Guadarrama
Mt. Blanc 15,780
Monte Rosa 15,217
Mt. Pelvoux 13,460
Mte Viso 12,602
Puy de Dome 4806
Mt. Dore 6190
Maladetta 11,168
Mt. Perdu 10,997
Ebro
Duero
Garonne
Dordogne
Rhône
Isère
Durance
Lot
Tarn
CORSICA
On same scale
Bastia
Ajaccio
Corse
Corte
Mte. Cinto 8890
Bonifacio
Str. of Bonifacio
West from Greenwich 0 East from Greenwich

CENTRAL EUROPE
Scale 1:4,500,000 (72 miles = 1 inch)
Statute Miles
Kilometres
Railways
Canals
4460 Heights in feet
Projection: Conical with two standard parallels
DENMARK
NETHERLANDS
BELGIUM
LUX.
FRANCE
GERMANY
SWITZERLAND
ITALY
AUSTRIA
Frisian Islands
Heligoland Bay
Kiel Bay
Fehmarn Belt
Lübeck Bay
SCHLESWIG-HOLSTEIN
LOWER SAXONY
NORTH RHINE-WESTPHALIA
RHINE-LAND PALATINATE
SAAR
BADEN-WÜRTTEMBERG
BAVARIA
LORRAINE
BURGUNDY
FRANCHE COMTÉ
ALSACE
TYROL
TRENTINO ALTO-ADIGE
FRIULI VENEZIA GIULIA
SALZBURG
VORARLBERG
LIECHTENSTEIN
Flensburg
Kiel
Lübeck
Hamburg
Altona
Harburg
Bremerhaven
Bremen
Wilhelmshaven
Emden
Oldenburg
Groningen
Leeuwarden
Amsterdam
Haarlem
The Hague
Leiden
Utrecht
Rotterdam
Dordrecht
Arnhem
Nijmegen
Apeldoorn
Enschede
Osnabrück
Münster
Hanover
Brunswick
Magdeburg
Halle
Leipzig
Dresden
Karl Marx (Chemnitz)
Zwickau
Plauen
Erfurt
Jena
Gera
Weimar
Kassel
Göttingen
Dortmund
Essen
Bochum
Duisburg
Oberhausen
Gelsenkirchen
Wuppertal
Düsseldorf
Cologne (Koln)
Bonn
Aachen
Koblenz
Wiesbaden
Mainz
Frankfurt
Offenbach
Darmstadt
Mannheim
Ludwigshafen
Heidelberg
Karlsruhe
Stuttgart
Würzburg
Bamberg
Fürth
Nürnberg
Regensburg
Ingolstadt
Augsburg
Munich (München)
Ulm
Freiburg
Strasbourg
Mulhouse
Basle
Zürich
Bern
Luzern
Lausanne
Geneva
Metz
Nancy
Reims
Dijon
Besançon
Lyons
Villeurbanne
Antwerp
Brussels
Liege
Maastricht
Luxembourg
Trier
Saarbrücken
Kaiserslautern
Innsbruck
Salzburg
Bolzano
Trento
Como
Udine
Erz Gebirge (Ore Mts.)
Thuringian Forest
Harz Mts.
Black Forest
Swabian Jura
Vosges
Ardennes
Eifel
Hunsrück
Taunus
Westerwald
Rothaar G. 2760
Vogels Berg 2533
Fichtel Geb. 3445
Brocken 3750
Bohemian Forest
Jura Mts.
Plateau de Langres
Rhine
Elbe
Weser
Ems
Danube
Moselle
Main
Neckar
Meuse
Saône
Rhône
Inn
L. Leman
L. Maggiore
L. Como
Bodensee
St. Gotthard P. 6929
Splügen P. 6946
Brenner P. 4511
Gr. Glockner 12,461
Matterhorn 14,701
Mte. Rosa 15,217
Mt. Blanc 15,780
Ortles 12,792
Bernina 13,304
Adamello 11,660
Marmolada 10,965
Carnic Alps
Dolomites

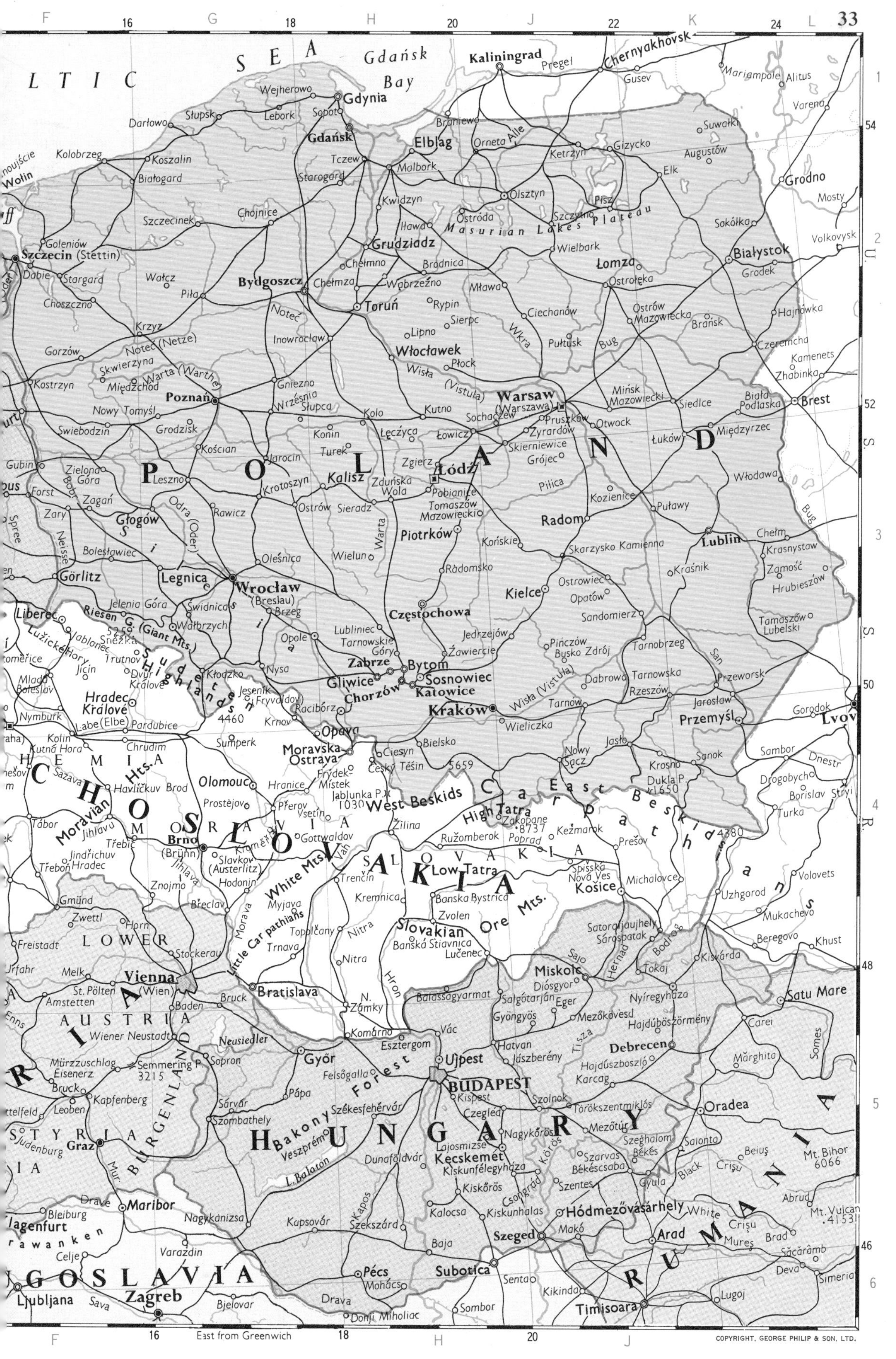
BALTIC SEA
Gdańsk Bay
Kaliningrad
Pregel
Chernyakhovsk
Gusev
Mariampole
Alitus
Varena
Gdynia
Wejherowo
Lebork
Sopot
Słupsk
Darłowo
Gdańsk
Braniewo
Elbląg
Orneta
Alle
Suwałki
Gizycko
Kolobrzeg
Koszalin
Białogard
Tczew
Malbork
Kętrzyn
Augustów
Starogard
Elk
Grodno
Wolin
Olsztyn
Mosty
Kwidzyn
Chojnice
Ostróda
Pisz
Szczecinek
Iława
Masurian Lakes Plateau
Szczytno
Sokółka
Goleniów
Grudziądz
Wielbark
Volkovysk
Szczecin (Stettin)
Chełmno
Brodnica
Łomza
Białystok
Dabie
Stargard
Wałcz
Bydgoszcz
Chełmza
Wąbrzeźno
Mława
Ostrołęka
Grodek
Piła
Choszczno
Noteć
Toruń
Rypin
Ciechanów
Ostrów Mazowiecka
Hajnówka
Sierpc
Brańsk
Krzyż
Lipno
Wkra
Pułtusk
Bug
Noteć (Netze)
Inowrocław
Czeremcha
Gorzów
Włocławek
Kamenets
Skwierzyna
Płock
Zhabinka
Warta (Warthe)
Wisła (Vistula)
Kostrzyn
Międzychód
Gniezno
Warsaw (Warszawa)
Mińsk Mazowiecki
Biała Podlaska
Brest
Poznań
Września
Słupca
Siedlce
Nowy Tomyśl
Kolo
Kutno
Sochaczew
Pruszków
Otwock
Swiebodzin
Grodzisk
Konin
Łęczyca
Łowicz
Żyrardów
Łuków
Międzyrzec
Kościan
Turek
Skierniewice
Grójec
Gubin
Zielona Góra
Jarocin
Zgierz
Łódź
POLAND
Leszno
Krotoszyn
Kalisz
Zduńska Wola
Pabianice
Pilica
Włodawa
Forst
Zagań
Ostrów
Sieradz
Tomaszów Mazowiecki
Kozienice
Puławy
Zary
Odra (Oder)
Rawicz
Radom
Bug
Spree
Głogów
Warta
Piotrków
Końskie
Lublin
Chełm
Neisse
Silesia
Bolesławiec
Wielun
Skarzysko Kamienna
Krasnystaw
Oleśnica
Radomsko
Kraśnik
Zamość
Görlitz
Legnica
Wrocław (Breslau)
Kielce
Ostrowiec
Hrubieszów
Jelenia Góra
Świdnica
Brzeg
Częstochowa
Opatów
Liberec
Riesen G. (Giant Mts.)
Wałbrzych
Sandomierz
Tamaszów Lubelski
Lužické Hory
Jablonec
Sněžka 5259
Opole
Lubliniec
Tarnowskie Góry
Jędrzejów
Tarnobrzeg
Trutnov
Sudeten Highlands
Kłodzko
Zawiercie
Pińczów
Busko Zdrój
San
Jičín
Dvůr Králové
Nysa
Zabrze
Bytom
Mladá Boleslav
Gliwice
Sosnowiec
Dabrowa Tarnowska
Przeworsk
Hradec Králové
Jeseník
Fryvaldov
Chorzów
Katowice
Rzeszów
Nymburk
4460
Racibórz
Kraków
Wisła (Vistula)
Tarnów
Jarosław
Labe (Elbe)
Pardubice
Krnov
Wieliczka
Przemyśl
Gorodok
Lvov
Kolín
Opava
Kutná Hora
Chrudim
Sumperk
Moravska Ostrava
Ciesyn
Bielsko
Nowy Sącz
Jasło
Sanok
Sambor
Dnestr
BOHEMIA
Český Těšín
5659
Krosno
Drogobych
Sázava
Frýdek-Místek
Dukla P. 1650
Havlíčkuv Brod
Olomouc
Hranice
Jablunka P. 1030
West Beskids
CARPATHIANS
East Beskids
Borislav
Stryi
Prostějov
Přerov
High Tatra
Zakopane 8737
Tábor
Moravian Hts.
Vsetín
Turka
CZECHOSLOVAKIA
Žilina
Kežmarok
Jihlava
Ružomberok
Poprad
4380
Brno (Brünn)
Kroměříž
Gottwaldov
Prešov
Třebíč
Jindřichuv Hradec
Slavkov (Austerlitz)
Váh
Spišská Nová Ves
Třeboň
Hodonín
White Mts.
Trenčín
Low Tatra
Košice
Michalovce
Volovets
Znojmo
Jihlava
Kremnica
Banská Bystrica
Uzhgorod
Gmünd
Břeclav
Myjava
Ore Mts.
Zwettl
Morava
Little Carpathians
Zvolen
Mukachevo
Horn
Topolčany
Nitra
Slovakian Ore Mts.
Sátoraljaujhely
Sárospatak
Freistadt
LOWER AUSTRIA
Trnava
Banská Stiavnica
Beregovo
Khust
Stockerau
Lučenec
Sajo
Bodrog
Urfahr
Melk
Nitra
Hernád
Tokaj
Kisvárda
Vienna (Wien)
Bratislava
Hron
Miskolc
Diósgyör
St. Pölten
Amstetten
Baden
Bruck
N. Zámky
Balassagyarmat
Salgótarján
Eger
Nyíregyháza
Satu Mare
Enns
Gyöngyös
Mezőkövesd
Hajdúböszörmény
AUSTRIA
Wiener Neustadt
Komárno
Vác
Tisza
Carei
Neusiedler
Esztergom
Hatvan
Debrecen
Someș
Mürzzuschlag
Semmering P. 3215
Sopron
Győr
Újpest
Jászberény
Hajdúszoboszló
Mărghita
Eisenerz
BURGENLAND
Felsőgalla
Bakony Forest
BUDAPEST
Karcag
Bruck
Kapfenberg
Pápa
Kispest
Szolnok
Törökszentmiklós
Oradea
Leoben
Sárvár
Székesfehérvár
Czegléd
Szombathely
Mezőtúr
STYRIA
HUNGARY
Nagykőrös
Szeghalom
Salonta
Judenburg
Graz
Veszprém
Lajosmizse
Szarvas
Békés
Beiuș
Mt. Bihor 6066
Mur
L. Balaton
Dunaföldvár
Kecskemét
Körös
Békéscsaba
Crișu
Kiskunfélegyháza
Szentes
Gyula
Black
RUMANIA
Drave
Maribor
Kapos
Kiskőrös
Csongrád
Abrud
Bleiburg
Kalocsa
Kiskunhalas
Hódmezővásárhely
White
Mt. Vulcan 4153
Klagenfurt
Nagykanizsa
Kapsovár
Szekszárd
Crișu
Karawanken
Varazdin
Baja
Szeged
Makó
Arad
Mureș
Brad
Celje
Săcărâmb
Pécs
Subotica
Deva
Simeria
YUGOSLAVIA
Mohács
Senta
Kikinda
Ljubljana
Sava
Zagreb
Bjelovar
Drava
Sombor
Timișoara
Lugoj
Donji Miholjac
16
18
20
22
24
F
G
H
J
K
L
1
2
3
4
5
6
54
52
50
48
46
U. S. S. R.
East from Greenwich
COPYRIGHT, GEORGE PHILIP & SON, LTD.

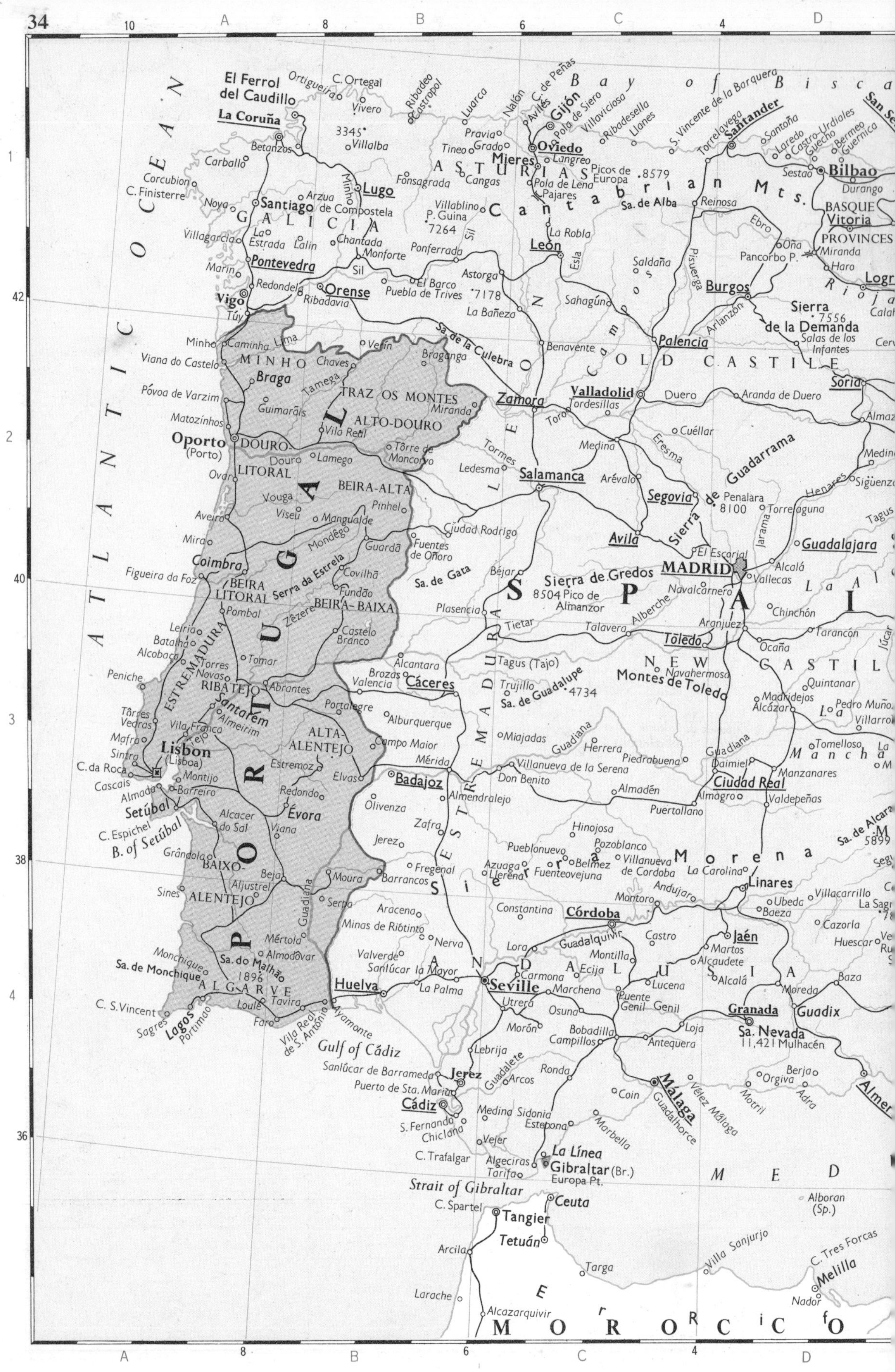

10
A
8
B
6
C
4
D
El Ferrol del Caudillo
Ortigueira
C. Ortegal
Vivero
Ribadeo
Castropol
Luarca
Nalón
C. de Peñas
Avilés
Gijón
Pola de Siero
Villaviciosa
Ribadesella
Llanes
S. Vincente de la Barquera
Torrelavega
Santander
Santoña
Laredo
Castro-Urdiales
Guecho
Bermeo
Guernica
San Se
Bay of Biscay
La Coruña
3345
Villalba
Betanzos
Pravia
Grado
Tineo
Oviedo
Mieres
Langreo
Picos de Europa
8579
Carballo
Corcubion
C. Finisterre
Minho
Lugo
Fonsagrada
Cangas
ASTURIAS
Pola de Lena
Pajares
Sestao
Bilbao
Durango
Noya
Santiago de Compostela
Arzua
GALICIA
Villablino
P. Guina
7264
Cantabrian Mts.
Sa. de Alba
Reinosa
BASQUE PROVINCES
Vitoria
Villagarcia
La Estrada
Lalin
Chantada
Sil
La Robla
Ebro
Oña
Miranda
Haro
Marin
Pontevedra
Monforte
Ponferrada
León
Esla
Saldaña
Pisuerga
Pancorbo P.
Redondela
Orense
Ribadavia
El Barco
Puebla de Trives
Astorga
7178
Sahagún
Burgos
Rioja
Logr
Vigo
Túy
La Bañeza
Arlanzón
Sierra de la Demanda
7556
Calah
Salas de los Infantes
Cerv
Minho
Caminha
Lima
Verín
Sa. de la Culebra
Benavente
Palencia
Viana do Castelo
MINHO
Chaves
Bragança
OLD CASTILE
Soria
Braga
Tamega
TRAZ OS MONTES
Miranda
Zamora
Valladolid
Tordesillas
Duero
Aranda de Duero
Póvoa de Varzim
Guimarães
ALTO-DOURO
Toro
Almaz
Matozinhos
Vila Real
Medina
Cuéllar
Oporto (Porto)
DOURO
Tôrre de Moncorvo
Tormes
Eresma
Sierra de Guadarrama
Medin
Ovar
Douro
Lamego
LITORAL
Ledesma
Salamanca
Arévalo
Sigüenza
Henares
BEIRA-ALTA
Vouga
Pinhel
Segovia
Penalara 8100
Torrelaguna
Aveiro
Viseu
Mangualde
Tagus
Mira
Mondego
Guarda
Ciudad Rodrigo
Fuentes de Oñoro
Avila
Jarama
Guadalajara
Coimbra
Covilhã
El Escorial
Figueira da Foz
BEIRA LITORAL
Serra da Estrela
Fundão
Sa. de Gata
Béjar
Sierra de Gredos
8504 Pico de Almanzor
MADRID
Vallecas
Alcalá
Pombal
BEIRA-BAIXA
Zêzere
Plasencia
Navalcarnero
Alberche
Chinchón
Leiria
Castelo Branco
Tietar
Talavera
Aranjuez
Batalha
ESTREMADURA
Tarancón
Alcobaça
Tomar
Alcantara
Toledo
Ocaña
Júcar
Torres Novas
Tagus (Tajo)
NEW CASTILE
Navahermosa
Peniche
Brozas
Cáceres
Montes de Toledo
Quintanar
RIBATEJO
Abrantes
Valencia
Trujillo
Sa. de Guadalupe
4734
Madridejos
Alcázar
Pedro Muño
Tôrres Vedras
Santarém
Portalegre
Villarro
Almeirim
Alburquerque
ALTA-ALENTEJO
Vila Franca
Tejo
Miajadas
Guadiana
Herrera
Tomelloso
Mafra
Campo Maior
Mancha
Sintra
Lisbon (Lisboa)
Estremoz
Mérida
Villanueva de la Serena
Piedrabuena
Daimiel
Manzanares
C. da Roca
Montijo
Elvas
Badajoz
Don Benito
Cascais
Almada
Barreiro
Redondo
Almadén
Ciudad Real
Setúbal
Alcacer do Sal
Évora
Olivenza
Almendralejo
Puertollano
Almagro
Valdepeñas
C. Espichel
B. of Setúbal
Viana
Zafra
Hinojosa
Sa. de Alcara
5899
Grândola
Jerez
Pueblonuevo
Pozoblanco
BAIXO-ALENTEJO
Beja
Moura
Barrancos
Fregenal
Azuaga
Llerena
Belmez
Villanueva de Cordoba
Sierra Morena
La Carolina
Fuenteovejuna
Sines
Aljustrel
Serpa
Aracena
Andujar
Linares
Villacarrillo
Constantina
Córdoba
Montoro
Ubeda
Baeza
Minas de Riotinto
Cazorla
Nerva
Castro
Jaén
Huescar
Mértola
Guadalquivir
Martos
Monchique
Sa. de Monchique
Sa. do Malhão
Almodôvar
1896
Valverde
Sanlúcar la Mayor
Lora
Montilla
Alcaudete
Carmona
Ecija
Lucena
Alcalá
Baza
ALGARVE
Huelva
La Palma
Seville
Marchena
Moreda
C. S. Vincent
Tavira
Loulé
Utrera
Osuna
Puente Genil
Genil
Granada
Guadix
Sagres
Lagos
Portimão
Faro
Vila Real de S. António
Ayamonte
Morón
Bobadilla
Campillos
Loja
Antequera
Sa. Nevada
11,421 Mulhacén
Gulf of Cádiz
Lebrija
Guadalete
Sanlúcar de Barrameda
Jerez
Arcos
Ronda
Málaga
Vélez Málaga
Berja
Orgiva
Almer
Puerto de Sta. Maria
Coin
Motril
Adra
Cádiz
Medina Sidonia
Guadalhorce
S. Fernando
Chiclana
Estepona
Marbella
Vejer
C. Trafalgar
Algeciras
La Línea
Gibraltar (Br.)
Tarifa
Europa Pt.
MED
Strait of Gibraltar
C. Spartel
Ceuta
Tangier
Alboran (Sp.)
Tetuán
Villa Sanjurjo
C. Tres Forcas
Arcila
Targa
Melilla
Larache
Nador
Alcazarquivir
MOROCCO
PORTUGAL
SPAIN
ATLANTIC OCEAN
LEÓN
ESTREMADURA
ANDALUSIA
1
2
3
4
42
40
38
36

Provincial capitals underlined thus **Murcia**

Note: Bilbao is provincial capital of Viscaya province

San Sebastian	,,	,,	,, Guipuzcoa	,,
Vitoria	,,	,,	,, Alava	,,
Pamplona	,,	,,	,, Navarra	,,

SPAIN AND PORTUGAL

Scale 1:4,500,000 (72 miles = 1 inch)

20 0 40 80 Statute Miles

20 0 40 80 120 Kilometres

Railways

Canals

5899 Heights in feet

Projection: *Conical with two standard parallels*

GERMANY
Freiburg
Tuttlingen
Memmingen
Rosenheim
Salzburg
Bad Ischl
Steyr
Gmunden
Enns
Baden
Bruck
Danube
Zámky
Komárno
Vác
Esztergom
Újpest
BUDAPEST
Vesoul
Belfort
Mulhouse
Rhine
Schaffhausen
Ravensburg
Kempten
Friedrichshafen
Montbéliard
Basle
Winterthur
Konstanz
Constance
St. Gallen
Bregenz
VORARLBERG
Garmisch Partenkirchen
Kufstein
Hallein
Wiener Neustadt
Mürzzuschlag
Eisenerz
Semmering P. 3215
Neusiedler
Sopron
Győr
Felsőgalla
Besancon
Jura Mts
Biel
La Chaux-de-Fonds
Aarau
Zürich
Feldkirch
LIECHTENSTEIN
Innsbruck
Schwaz
SALZBURG
Bruck
Leoben
Kapfenberg
Knittelfeld
BURGENLAND
Sárvár
Szombathely
Pápa
Székesfehérvár
HUNGARY
Neuchâtel
Solothurn
Aare
Luzern
Zug
Schwyz
Glarus
Arlberg P.
Landeck
Ötztal
TYROL
Brenner P. 4511
12 461
Gr Glockner
Badgastein
Judenburg
STYRIA
Graz
Veszprém
Dunaföldvár
L. Balaton
Fribourg
Bern
Thun
Rhine
Chur
Davos
Inn
Lienz
CARINTHIA
Mur
Kiskőrös
Kalocsa
SWITZERLAND
Lausanne
Interlaken
St. Gotthard P. 6929
Ticino
Merano
Bressanone
Carnic Alps
Drave
Villach
Bleiburg
Maribor
Nagykanizsa
Kapsovár
Kapos
Szekszárd
Baja
1230
L. Geneva
Thonon
Geneva
Sion
Rhône
Martigny
Brig
Locarno
Bernina 13,304
Chiavenna
9049
Stelvio P.
Ortles 12,792
TRENTINO
ALTO-ADIGE
Bolzano
Marmolada 10,965
Dolomites
Cortina d'Ampezzo
Piave
FRIULI VENEZIA GIULIA
Triglav 9396
Kobarid (Caporetto)
Klagenfurt
Karawanken
Celje
Varazdin
Pécs
Mohács
Annecy
Domodossola
Matterhorn 14,701
Mte. Rosa 15,217
L. Maggiore
Lugano
Adda
Adamello 11,660
Trento
Belluno
Vittorio Veneto
Tagliamento
Udine
Ljubljana
Sava
SLOVENIA
Zagreb
Bjelovar
Drava
Donji Miholjac
Mt. Blanc 15,780
Gt. St. Bernard P.
Aosta
8113
Dora Baltea
V. D'AOSTA
Verbania
Varese
Como
Cantu
L. Como
Lecco
Bergamo
Oglio
Riva
Rovereto
Adige
Schio
Bassano
Portogruaro
Pordenone
Gorizia
Monfalcone
Isonzo
Cerknica
Kočevje
CROATIA
Osijek
Lit. St. Bernard 7178 P.
Gran Paradiso 13,323
Ivrea
Busto Arsizio
Biella
LOMBARDY
Monza
Treviglio
Brescia
L. Garda
VENETO
Vicenza
Verona
Treviso
Trieste
Karst
YUGOSLAVIA
Kupa
Karlovac
Sisak
Našice
Požega
Novska
Brod
Vinkovci
Moutiers
Mt. Cenis P. 6833
Chivasso
Novara
Milan (Milano)
Crema
Lodi
Vigevano
Ticino
Chiese
Padua (Padova)
Miro
Venice (Venezia)
Gulf of Venice
Capodistria
Istra
Rijeka
Sušak
Kapela
Modane
Vercelli
Casale
Pavia
Adda
Mantua (Mantova)
Legnago
Chioggia
Adige
Mt. Pelvoux 13,460
Briançon
Susa
Turin (Torino)
PIEDMONT
Alessandria
Po
Voghera
Piacenza
Cremona
Po
Rovigo
Adria
Porto Tolle
Rovinj
Krk
Senj
Dinara
BOSNIA
Unac
Bosanska Gradiška
Odžak
Bosna
Brčko
Pinerolo
Mt. Viso 12,602
Saluzzo
Fossano
Tanaro
Asti
Alba
Tortona
Novi Ligure
Trebbia
Mirandola
Parma
Carpi
Bondeno
Copparo
Ferrara
Pula (Pola)
C. Kamenjak
Kvarner
Cres
Kvarnević
Velebit Planina
Bihać
Banja Luka
Sana
Vrbas
Doboj
Tesanj
Tuzla
Embrun
Cúneo
Mondovi
2560
La Bochetta P.
Savona
LIGURIA
Riv. di Ponente
Riv. di Levante
Genoa (Genova)
Rapallo
Chiavari
Sestri Levante
ITALY
Reggio
Modena
EMILIA-ROMAGNA
Bologna
Reno
Portomaggiore
Argenta
Comacchio
Lugo
Ravenna
Imola
Faenza
Lošinj
Pag
Gospić
Kremen 5220
Gračac
Srnetica
HERCEGOVINA
Žepče
Travnik
Zenica
Han Pijesak
10,016
Maritime Alps
Digne
Tenda
Mte. Cimone 7096
Forlì
Cesena
Rubicone
Rimini
ADRIATIC
Dugi Otok
Zadar
6276
Troglav
Dinara Planina
Sarajevo
Grasse
Nice
Menton
San Remo
Imperia
Monaco & Monte Carlo
G. of Genoa
Spezia
Carrara
Massa
Pietrasanta
Viareggio
Pistoia
Porreta P.
Prato
APENNINES
San Marino
Pesaro
Fano
Sibenik
Split
DALMATIA
Jablanica
Konjic
Neretva
Draguignan
Antibes
Cannes
Fréjus
St. Tropez
Arno
Leghorn (Livorno)
Lucca
Pisa
S. Miniato
Pontedera
Florence (Firenze)
Arezzo
Urbino
MARCHES
Senigallia
Ancona
Loreto
Iesi
Brač
Hvar
Mostar
Foča
LIGURIAN SEA
Rossignano Marittimo
Volterra
TUSCANY
Siena
Cortona
Città di Castello
Perugia
Fabriano
Macerata
Civitanova
Fermo
Stolac
Metkovik
Iles d'Hyères
C. Corse
Capraia
L. Trasimeno
Assisi
Foligno
Monti Vettore
San Benedetto
Vis
Korčula
Piombino
Chiusi
Amiata 5689
UMBRIA
Spoleto 8130
Ascoli Piceno
Lastovo
Trebinje
Portoferraio
Bastia
Elba
Ombrone
Grosseto
Orvieto
Tiber
Todi
Teramo
Gran Sasso 9560
Dubrovnik
Calvi
Mte. Cinto 8891
Orbetello
L. Bolsena
Terni
Rieti
Salto
Sabine Mts.
L'Aquila
Chieti
Pescara
Palagruža (Yugoslavia)
Herceg Novi
Kotor
Mte. Argentario
Fiora
Viterbo
Tarquinia
Maremma
ABRUZZI
Avezzano
Mt. Amaro 9170
Ortona
Lanciano
Vasto
Termoli
S. Nicandro
SEA
CORSICA
Aleria
Civitavecchia
Bracciano
Campagna
Tivoli
Sulmona
and MOLISE
Ajaccio
FRANCE
AUSTRIA

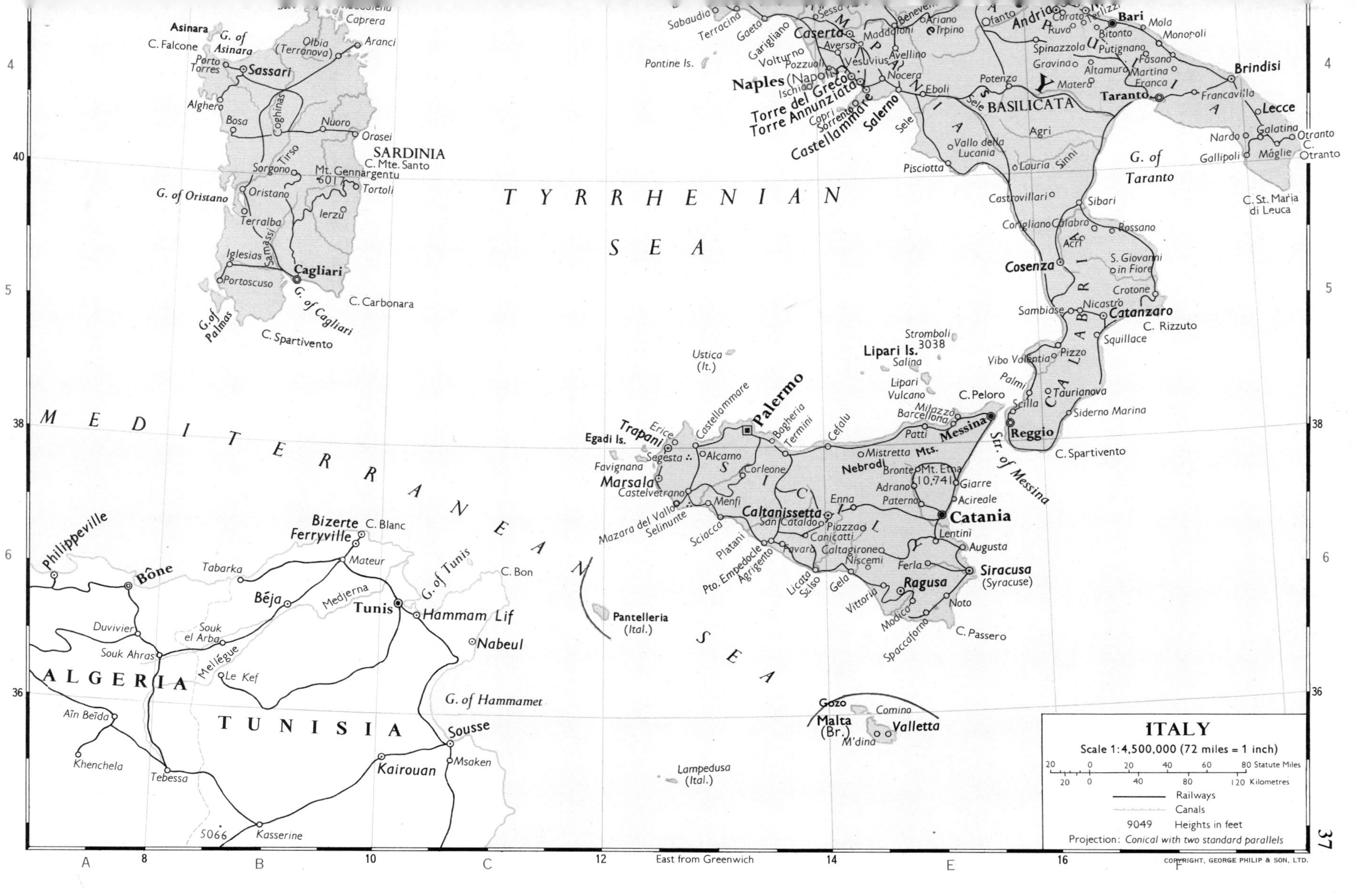
ITALY
Scale 1:4,500,000 (72 miles = 1 inch)
Statute Miles
Kilometres
Railways
Canals
9049 Heights in feet
Projection: Conical with two standard parallels
East from Greenwich
TYRRHENIAN SEA
MEDITERRANEAN SEA
SARDINIA
BASILICATA
ALGERIA
TUNISIA
Asinara
G. of Asinara
C. Falcone
Porto Torres
Sassari
Olbia (Terranova)
Caprera
Aranci
Alghero
Bosa
Coghinas
Nuoro
Orosei
C. Mte. Santo
Mt. Gennargentu 6017
Tortoli
Tirso
Sorgono
Oristano
G. of Oristano
Ierzu
Terralba
Samassi
Iglesias
Cagliari
G. of Cagliari
Portoscuso
C. Carbonara
G. of Palmas
C. Spartivento
Pontine Is.
Sabaudia
Terracina
Gaeta
Garigliano
Volturno
Caserta
Aversa
Pozzuoli
Naples (Napoli)
Ischia
Torre del Greco
Torre Annunziata
Capri
Sorrento
Castellammare
Salerno
Vesuvius
Maddaloni
Avellino
Nocera
Eboli
Sele
Ariano Irpino
Ofanto
Andria
Corato
Ruvo
Bitonto
Bari
Mola
Monopoli
Spinazzola
Putignano
Gravina
Altamura
Fasano
Martina Franca
Matera
Potenza
Taranto
Brindisi
Francavilla
Lecce
Galatina
Otranto
C. Otranto
Nardo
Gallipoli
Máglie
G. of Taranto
C. St. Maria di Leuca
Agri
Vallo della Lucania
Lauria
Sinni
Pisciotta
Castrovillari
Sibari
Corigliano Calabro
Rossano
Acri
Cosenza
S. Giovanni in Fiore
Crotone
Sambiase
Nicastro
Catanzaro
C. Rizzuto
Squillace
Vibo Valentia
Pizzo
Palmi
Taurianova
Scilla
Siderno Marina
Reggio
C. Spartivento
Stromboli 3038
Lipari Is.
Salina
Lipari
Vulcano
C. Peloro
Milazzo
Barcellona
Patti
Messina
Str. of Messina
Ustica (It.)
Castellammare
Palermo
Bagheria
Termini
Cefalu
Mistretta
Nebrodi Mts.
Bronte
Mt. Etna 10,741
Giarre
Acireale
Adrano
Paterno
Catania
Egadi Is.
Erice
Trapani
Segesta
Alcamo
Corleone
Favignana
Marsala
Castelvetrano
Menfi
Enna
Caltanissetta
San Cataldo
Piazza
Canicatti
Mazara del Vallo
Selinunte
Sciacca
Platani
Pto. Empedocle
Agrigento
Favara
Caltagirone
Niscemi
Lentini
Augusta
Ferla
Siracusa (Syracuse)
Licata
Salso
Gela
Vittoria
Ragusa
Modica
Noto
Spaccaforno
C. Passero
Pantelleria (Ital.)
Gozo
Comino
Malta (Br.)
Valletta
M'dina
Lampedusa (Ital.)
Philippeville
Bône
Tabarka
Bizerte
C. Blanc
Ferryville
Mateur
Béja
Medjerna
Tunis
G. of Tunis
Hammam Lif
C. Bon
Nabeul
Duvivier
Souk el Arba
Souk Ahras
Mellégue
Le Kef
G. of Hammamet
Aïn Beïda
Sousse
Msaken
Kairouan
Khenchela
Tebessa
5066
Kasserine

A
C
D
E
F
G
20
22
24
26
28
30
48
46
44
42
1
2
3
CZECHOSLOVAKIA
U.S.S.R.
MOLDAVIA S.S.R.
Bessarabia
HUNGARY
RUMANIA
BULGARIA
YUGOSLAVIA
BOSNIA AND HERCEGOVINA
MONTENEGRO
SERBIA
Carpathian Mts
Transylvania
Transylvanian Alps
Wallachia
Banat
Dobroga
Balkan Mountains
Bakony Forest
BLACK SEA
Danube
Drava
Sava
Tisza
Mureș
Olt
Prut
Dnestr
Siret (Sereth)
Morava
Drina
Iron Gate
Red Tower P.
P. of the Tartars
3054
Pietrosu
7562
6896
Pietrosul
Mt. Bihor
6066
Mt. Vulcan
4153
Godeanu
7313
Peleaga
8238
8297
Mt. Mandra
8346
Mt. Negoiu
Mt. Omul
8222
7116
7211
V. Stalin
9596
8661
8274
Tara
Durmitor
Kopaonik
Chilia Mouth
Sulina Mouth
St. Gheorghe's Mouth
Portiței Mouth
Letea I.
St. Gheorghe I.
Dranov I.
C. Kaliakra
C. Igneada
L. Balaton
L. Shkodër
Trajan's Wall
Trajan's Gate
Shipka P.
BUDAPEST
Újpest
Győr
Szombathely
Miskolc
Debrecen
Szeged
Pécs
Kecskemét
Hódmezővásárhely
Kaposvár
Satu Mare
Oradea
Cluj
Arad
Timișoara
Alba-Iulia
Sibiu
Orașul Stalin
(Brașov)
Iași
Botoșani
Bacau
Galați
Brăila
Ploești
Bucharest
(București)
Craiova
Turnu Severin
Constanța
Izmail
Kishinev
Bendery
Tiraspol
Belgrade
(Beograd)
Novi Sad
Subotica
Osijek
Sarajevo
Niš
Skoplje
Titograd
(Podgorica)
Shkodër
Sofia
Plovdiv
Pleven
Ruse (Ruschuk)
Stalin (Varna)
Burgas

SOUTH-EAST EUROPE
Scale 1:4,500,000 (72 miles = 1 inch)
20 0 20 40 60 80 Statute Miles
20 0 40 80 120 Kilometres
Railways
Canals
9550 Heights in feet
Projection: Conical with two standard parallels
GREECE
TURKEY
Anatolia
MACEDONIA
THRACE
THESSALY
EPIRUS
PELOPONNESE
CRETE
DODECANESE
KIKLÁDHES (Cyclades)
N. Sporades
IONIAN SEA
ÆGEAN SEA
SEA OF CANDIA
MEDITERRANEAN SEA
Str. of Otranto
Sea of Marmara
ITALY
Brindisi
Francavilla
Lecce
Nardo
Galatina
Otranto
C. Otranto
Gallipoli
Máglie
C. St. Maria di Leuca
Tiranë
Shkumbi
Lushnje
Elbasan
Ohridsko L.
Gramsh
Tomorrit 8136
Berat
Seman
Pogradec
Korçë
Ersekë
Sazan
Vlonë
Tepelenë
Vijosë
Përmeto
Gjinokastër
Sarandë
Ohrid
Jablanica
Bitolj (Monastir)
Prespa L.
Florina
Edhessa
Yiannitsa
Veroia
Kastoria
Kozáni
Aliákmon
Smolikas 8652
Pindus Mts
Kateríni
9570 Olympus
Elasson
Piniós
Óssa 6489
Lárisa
Kalabáka
Tríkkala
Kardhítsa
Ioánnina
Igoumenitsa
Kérkira (Corfu)
Kérkira
Árta
Préveza
Levkás
Levkàs (Sta. Maura)
Akhelóös
Agrínion
Kálamos
Itháki
Kefallinía (Cephalonia)
Argostólion
Mesolóngion
Zákinthos
Zákinthos
Vólos
G. of Vólos
Pílion 5075
Farsala
Almirós
Lamía
P. of Thermopylae
Gióna 8235
Amfissa
Návpaktos
Delfoí
Parnassos 8061
Levádhia
Elikon 5735
Thívai
Aíyion
Gulf of Corinth
G. of Pátrai
Pátrai
Erímanthos 7297
Killíni
7795 Corinth
Loutra
Amaliás
Pírgos
Olympia
Mycenae
Mikinai
Árgos
Návplion
Tripolis
Megalópolis
Kiparissía G.
Kiparissía
Filiatrá
Messíni
Kalámai
Spárti
Pílos
Taíyetos Mts.
G. of Messíni
Yíthion
G. of Lakonía
C. Taínaron (Matapan)
Monemvasia
C. Maléa
Kíthira (Cerigo)
Kíthira
Andikíthira
G. of Argolis
Idhra
Mégara
Salamis
G. of Aíyina
Aíyina
Athens (Athínai)
Piraiévs
Marathon
Lávrion
Kéa
Kíthnos
Sérifos
Sífnos
Mílos
Síkinos
Íos
Thíra
Anáfi
Amorgós
Astipálaia
Náxos
Náxos
Páros
Levkai 3313
Rinía
Síros
Ermoúpolis
Tínos
Tínos
Míkonos
Ándros
Ándros
C. Kafirévs
4587
Káristos
Évvoia (Euboea)
Óros 4406
Khalkis
Peli
Aidhipsos
Skíros
Skiathos
Iliodhrómia
Thessaloniki
G. of Thessaloniki
Kalándra
Polýiros
C. Platí
G. of Toronaios
C. Psevdhókavos
Singitikós G.
Kariai
Mt. Athos 6670
Thásos 3947
Samothráki 5249
Imrozo
Límnos
Kástron
Moúdhros
C. Planka
Áyios Evstrátios
Dardanelles (Hellespont)
Troy
Bozca Ada
Lésvos
Mitilíni
Khíos (Chios)
Khíos
Cesme
Sámos
Limin Vatheos
Ikaría
3389
Foúrnoi
Pátmos
Kálimnos
Kos
Kos
Pothea
Tílos
Simi
Khalki
Rhódos
Ródhos (Rhodes)
3986
Karpáthos
3986
Kásos
Sérres
Kilkís
Dojran
Sokhós
Dráma
Kavállao
Xánthi
Komotiní
Alexandroúpolis
Enez
Ergene
Keşan
Malkara
Tekirdağ
Çorlu
İstanbul
Üsküdar
Beykoz
İzmit
Marmara
Imrali
G. of Saros
Gelibolu (Gallipoli)
Eceabat
Çanakkale
Bandirma
Bursa
Ulu Dağ 8343
Simav
Kemalpaşa
Kepsut
Balikesir
Ayvacik
Ida 5797
Edremit
G. of Edremit
C. Burun
Ayvalik
Bergama
Kirkağaç
Akhisar
Çandarli
Karaburun
G. of İzmir
Menemen
Manisa
Gediz
Turgutlu
İzmir (Smyrna)
Ödemiş
Alaşehir
Sarigöl
Uşak
Emet
Aydin
Nazilli
Menderes
Denizli
Çine
Milâs
Muğla
G. of Mandalya
G. of Kerme
Marmaris
Dalaman
G. of Makri
Kastéli
C. Spátha
Khanion B.
Khaniá
Lévka Óri 8045
Soúdhas B.
Réthimnon
Kóra Sfakíon
Mt. Ídhi 8058
Timbákion
C. Líthinon
C. Dia
Iráklion (Candia)
Cnossus
Arkhánai
Dhikti 7048
Ierápetra
Áyios
Merabéllou B.
Sitia
East from Greenwich
COPYRIGHT, GEORGE PHILIP & SON, LTD.

SCANDINAVIA
Scale 1:6,500,000 (104 miles = 1 inch)
50 0 50 100 Statute Miles
50 0 50 100 150 Kilometres
Railways
Canals
8097 Heights in feet
Projection: Conical with two standard parallels
ICELAND
on the same scale
West from 18 Greenwich
Arctic Circle
NORWEGIAN SEA
GULF OF BOTHNIA
Kvarken
FINMARK
TROMS
NORDLAND
N. TRÖNDELAG
SÖR TRÖNDELAG
NORBOTTEN
VÄSTERBOTTEN
JÄMTLAND
LAPPI
OULU
KUOPIO
VAASA
U. S. S. R.
Lofoten
Vesterålen
Vest Fjorden
Lopphavet
Varanger Fjord
Tana Fjord
Lakse Fjord
Porsangen
Rybachi Pen.
Inari L.
Tromsö
Narvik
Kiruna
Gällivare
Boden
Luleå
Haparanda
Tornio (Torneå)
Kemi
Oulu (Uleåborg)
Kajaani
Iisalmi
Kuopio
Jyväskylä
Joensuu
Kokkola
Pietarsaari
Vaasa
Umeå
Skellefteå
Piteå
Lycksele
Östersund
Trondheim
Kristiansund
Molde
Ålesund
Namsos
Mosjöen
Mo i Rana
Bodö
Hammerfest
Vadsö
Vardö
Murmansk
Kandalaksha
Pechenga
Härnösand
Kramfors
Örnsköldsvik
Reykjavik
Akureyri
Husavik
Vatna Jökull
Odadahraun
Siglufjördur
Saudarkrokur
Isafjördur
Seydisfjördur
Akranes
Keflavik
Hafnarfjördur
Faxa Flói
Breidi Fjord

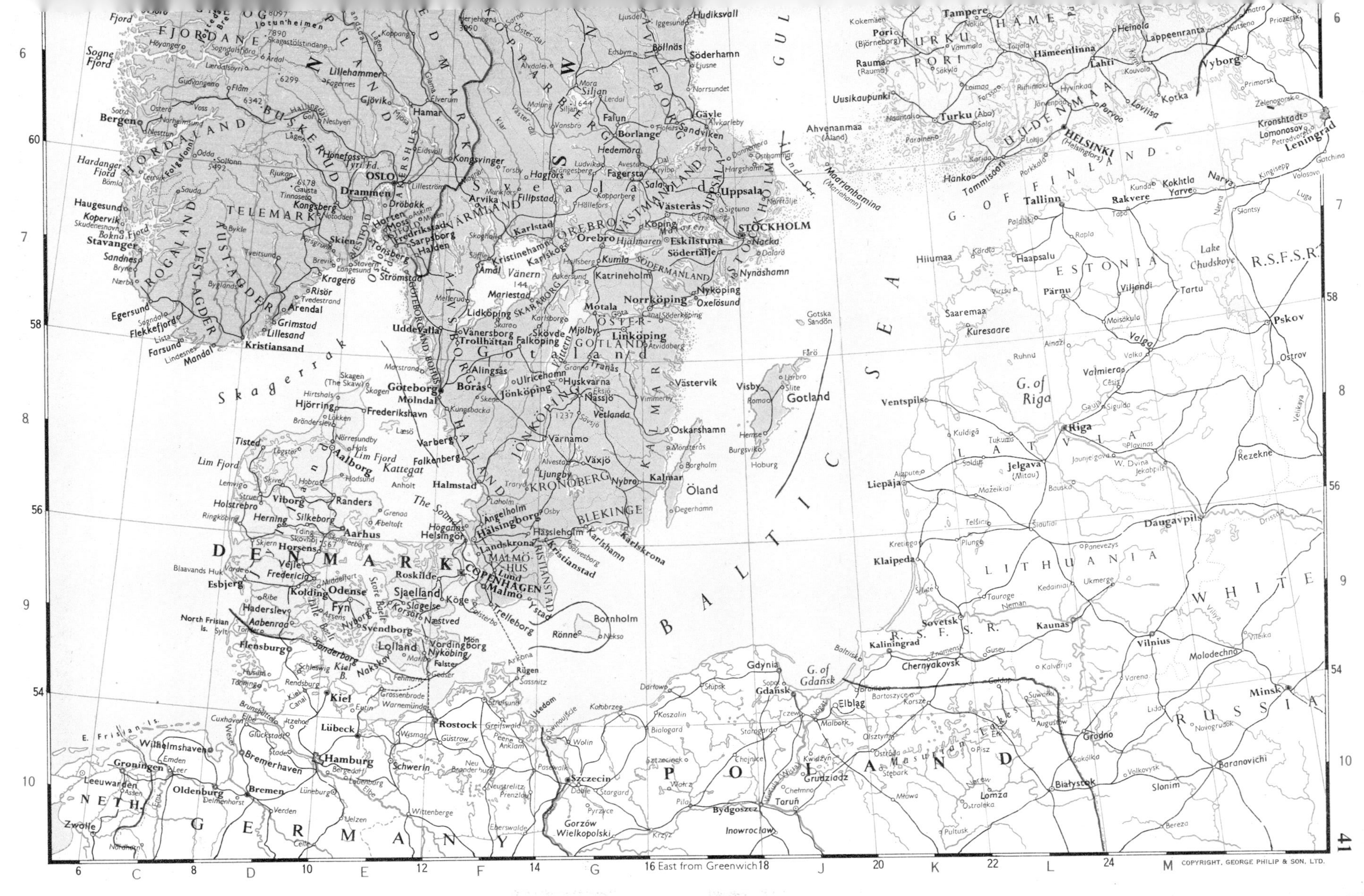
BALTIC SEA
G. OF FINLAND
G. of Riga
G. of Gdańsk
Skagerrak
Kattegat
The Sound
Svealand
Götaland
DENMARK
FINLAND
ESTONIA
LATVIA
LITHUANIA
R.S.F.S.R.
WHITE RUSSIA
POLAND
GERMANY
NETH.
HELSINKI (Helsingfors)
Tallinn
Riga
Leningrad
STOCKHOLM
OSLO
COPENHAGEN
Vilnius
Kaunas
Minsk
Göteborg
Malmö
Gotland
Öland
Bornholm
Saaremaa
Hiiumaa
Lake Chudskoye
Pskov
Narva
Tartu
Pärnu
Daugavpils
Jelgava (Mitau)
Liepāja
Ventspils
Klaipeda
Kaliningrad
Gdańsk
Gdynia
Elbląg
Szczecin
Rostock
Lübeck
Hamburg
Kiel
Bremen
Bremerhaven
Wilhelmshaven
Oldenburg
Groningen
Leeuwarden
Zwolle
Flensburg
Aarhus
Aalborg
Odense
Esbjerg
Bergen
Stavanger
Kristiansand
Uppsala
Västerås
Örebro
Norrköping
Linköping
Jönköping
Karlskrona
Kalmar
Visby
Gävle
Turku (Åbo)
Tampere
Pori (Björneborg)
Vyborg
Białystok
Grodno
Toruń
Bydgoszcz
16 East from Greenwich 18
COPYRIGHT, GEORGE PHILIP & SON, LTD.

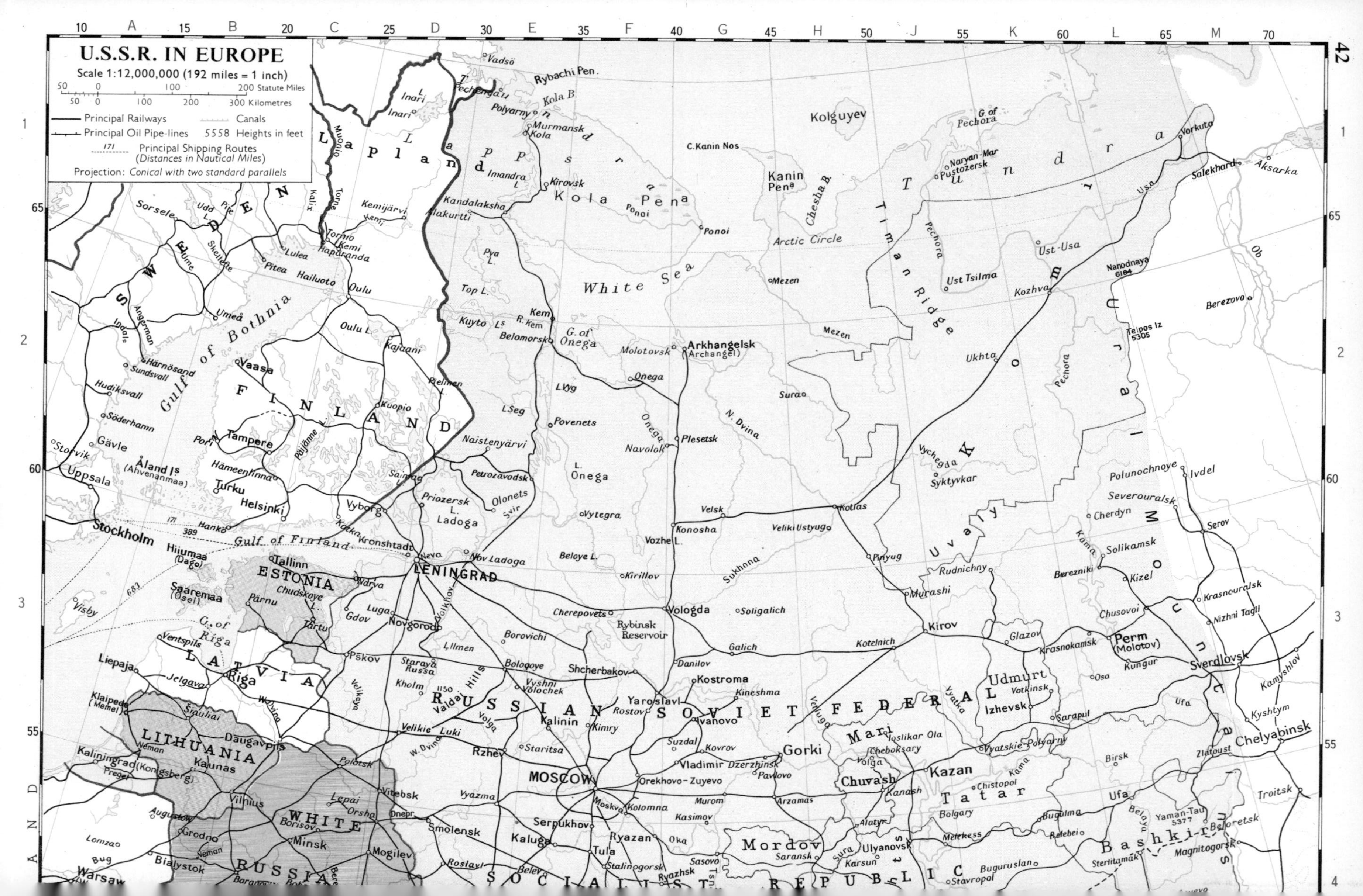
U.S.S.R. IN EUROPE
Scale 1:12,000,000 (192 miles = 1 inch)
50 0 100 200 Statute Miles
50 0 100 200 300 Kilometres
Principal Railways
Principal Oil Pipe-lines
Canals
5558 Heights in feet
171 Principal Shipping Routes (Distances in Nautical Miles)
Projection: Conical with two standard parallels
Vadsö
Rybachi Pen.
Pechenga
Inari L.
Inari
Kola B.
Polyarny
Murmansk
Kola
Lapland
Imandra L.
Kirovsk
Kola Pena
Ponoi
Kandalaksha
Alakurtti
Kemijärvi
Kemi
Tornio
Haparanda
Muonio
Torne
Kalix
Lulea
Pitea
Hailuoto
Oulu
Oulu L.
Sorsele
Udd L.
Pite
Skellefte
Ume
Umeå
Angerman
Indals
Härnösand
Sundsvall
Hudiksvall
Söderhamn
Gävle
Storvik
Uppsala
Stockholm
Åland Is. (Ahvenanmaa)
Gulf of Bothnia
Vaasa
FINLAND
SWEDEN
Kajaani
Kuopio
Pielinen L.
Tampere
Pori
Päijänne
Hämeenlinna
Turku
Helsinki
Hanko
171
389
683
Saimaa
Vyborg
Kotka
Kronshtadt
Gulf of Finland
Hiiumaa (Dagö)
Saaremaa (Ösel)
Visby
Tallinn
ESTONIA
Narva
Chudskoye L.
Pärnu
Tartu
G. of Riga
Ventspils
LATVIA
Riga
Liepaja
Jelgava
Klaipeda (Memel)
Šiauliai
LITHUANIA
Daugavpils
Neman
Kaliningrad (Königsberg)
Pregel
Kaunas
Vilnius
Augustow
Grodno
Bialystok
Lomzao
Bug
Warsaw
Polotsk
Lepai
Orsha
WHITE RUSSIA
Borisov
Minsk
Vitebsk
Dnepr
Mogilev
Smolensk
Roslavl
Pya L.
Top L.
Kuyto Ls
Kem
R. Kem
Belomorsk
G. of Onega
White Sea
LVyg
LSeg
Povenets
Naistenyärvi
Petrozavodsk
Olonets
Svir
Priozersk
L. Ladoga
Neva
LENINGRAD
Nov Ladoga
Volkhov
Luga
Gdov
Novgorod
Pskov
Velikaya
L.Ilmen
Staraya Russa
Kholm
1150
Valdai Hills
Velikie Luki
W. Dvina
Borovichi
Bologoye
Vyshni Volochek
Rzhev
Staritsa
Kalinin
Vyazma
MOSCOW
Moskva
Kolomna
Serpukhov
Kaluga
Belev
Tula
Stalinogorsk
Ryazan
Oka
Ryazhsk
Sasovo
L. Onega
Vytegra
Beloye L.
Kirillov
Cherepovets
Rybinsk Reservoir
Shcherbakov
Kimry
Yaroslavl
Rostov
Ivanovo
Suzdal
Kovrov
Vladimir
Dzerzhinsk
Orekhovo-Zuyevo
Murom
Kasimov
Kostroma
Kineshma
Danilov
Galich
Vologda
Soligalich
Sukhona
Vozhe L.
Konosha
Velsk
Veliki Ustyug
Kotlas
Pinyug
Murashi
Kirov
Kotelnich
Vetluga
Gorki
Pavlovo
Arzamas
Mordov
Saransk
Sura
Alatyr
Ulyanovsk
Karsun
Chuvash
Cheboksary
Volga
Kanash
Kazan
Mari
Yoshkar Ola
Tatar
Chistopol
Bolgary
Melekess
Bugulma
Bugulslan
Stavropol
Bugulma
Molotovsk
Arkhangelsk (Archangel)
Onega
Navolok
Plesetsk
N. Dvina
Sura
Mezen
C.Kanin Nos
Kanin Pena
Chesha B.
Arctic Circle
Kolguyev
Timan Ridge
Tundra
G. of Pechora
Naryan-Mar
Pustozersk
Pechora
Ust Tsilma
Ust-Usa
Ukhta
Kozhva
Usa
Vorkuta
Salekhard
Aksarka
Ob
Berezovo
Narodnaya 6184
Telpos Iz 5305
Ural Mountains
Vychegda
Syktyvkar
Uvaly
Rudnichny
Glazov
Udmurt
Votkinsk
Izhevsk
Vyatka
Sarapul
Vyatskie Polyany
Kama
Krasnokamsk
Perm (Molotov)
Osa
Kungur
Chusovoi
Berezniki
Solikamsk
Kizel
Cherdyn
Severouralsk
Polunochnoye
Ivdel
Serov
Krasnouralsk
Nizhni Tagil
Sverdlovsk
Kamyshlov
Kyshtym
Chelyabinsk
Ufa
Birsk
Zlatoust
Troitsk
Belaya
Yaman-Tau 5377
Beloretsk
Magnitogorsk
Sterlitamak
Bashkir
Rafebei
RUSSIAN SOVIET FEDERAL SOCIALIST REPUBLIC

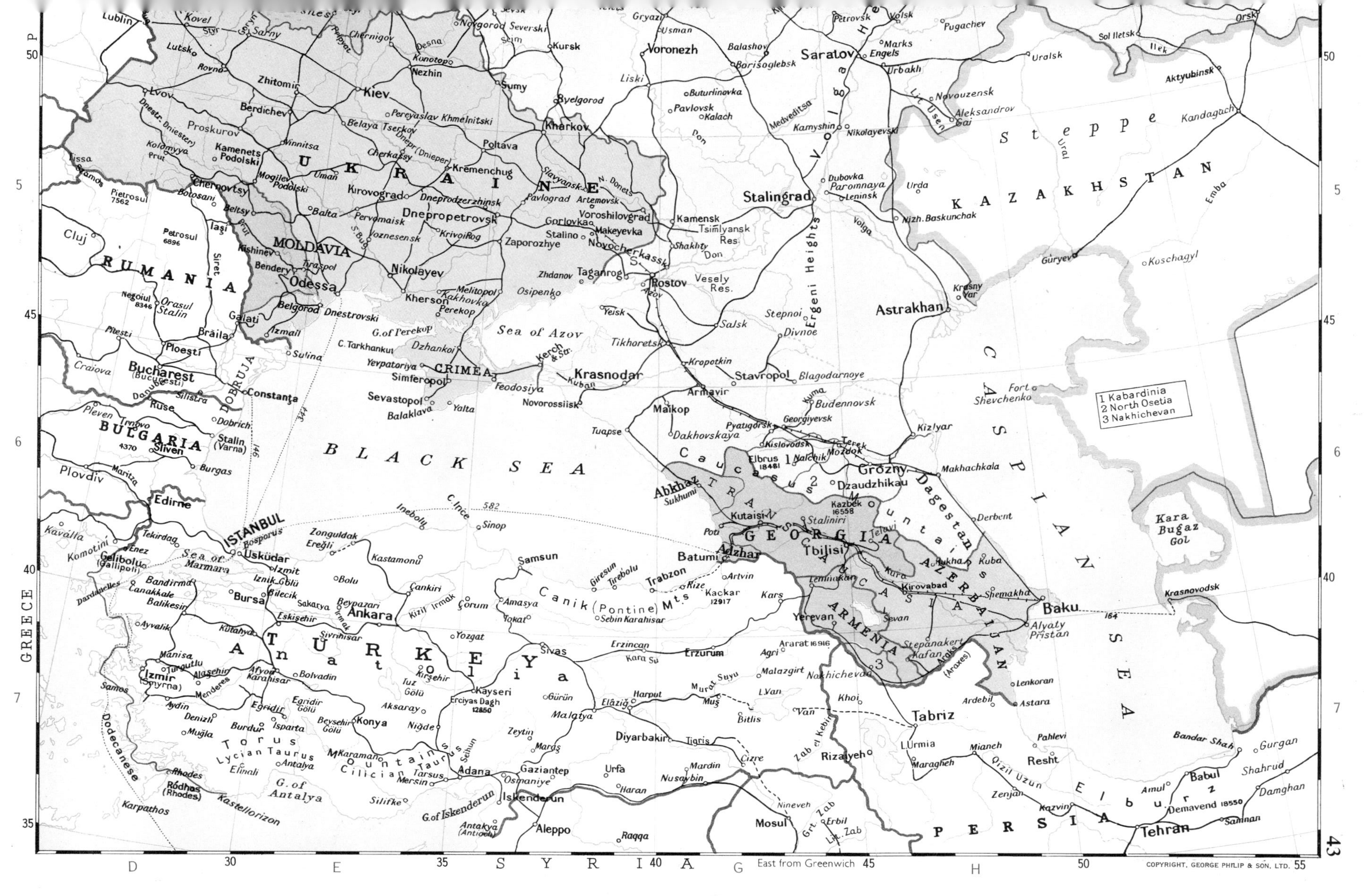

1 Kabardinia
2 North Osetia
3 Nakhichevan
CASPIAN SEA
BLACK SEA
Sea of Azov
KAZAKHSTAN
Steppe
UKRAINE
MOLDAVIA
RUMANIA
BULGARIA
GEORGIA
AZERBAIJAN
ARMENIA
Dagestan
Abkhaz
Adzhar
CRIMEA
TURKEY
Anatolia
SYRIA
PERSIA
Elburz
Caucasus Mountains
Canik (Pontine) Mts.
Taurus Mountains
Cilician Taurus
Lycian Taurus
Kara Bugaz Gol
Stalingrad
Saratov
Astrakhan
Voronezh
Kharkov
Kiev
Rostov
Krasnodar
Stavropol
Grozny
Tbilisi
Baku
Yerevan
Batumi
Odessa
Sevastopol
Simferopol
Dnepropetrovsk
Zaporozhye
Stalino
Bucharest
Constanța
ISTANBUL
Ankara
Izmir (Smyrna)
Trabzon
Erzurum
Tabriz
Tehran
Mosul
Aleppo
Adana
Konya
Kayseri
Samsun
Sinop
Rhodes
Dodecanese
Edirne
Plovdiv
Cluj
Lublin
Lvov
Krasnovodsk
Fort Shevchenko
Guryev
Uralsk
Aktyubinsk
Orsk
Elbrus 18481
Kazbek 16558
Ararat 16916
Demavend 18550
Kackar 12917
Erciyas Dagh 12850
GREECE
East from Greenwich
COPYRIGHT, GEORGE PHILIP & SON, LTD.

R.S.F.S.R.
1. Daghestan A.S.S.R.
2. Kabardinian A.S.S.R.
3. Mari A.S.S.R.
4. Mordvinian A.S.S.R.
5. North Osetian A.S.S.R.
6. Tatar A.S.S.R.
7. Udmurt A.S.S.R.
8. Chuvash A.S.S.R.
AZERBAIJAN
9 Nakhichevan A.S.S.R.
GEORGIA
10. Abkhaz A.S.S.R.
11 Adzhar A.S.S.R.
UNION OF SOVIET SOCIALIST REPUBLICS
Scale 1:25,000,000 (400 miles = 1 inch)
100 0 200 400 Statute Miles
100 0 200 400 600 Kilometres
Railways
Canals
2673 Shipping Routes
(Distances in Nautical Miles)
Projection: Conical Orthomorphic with two standard parallels
80 East from Greenwich

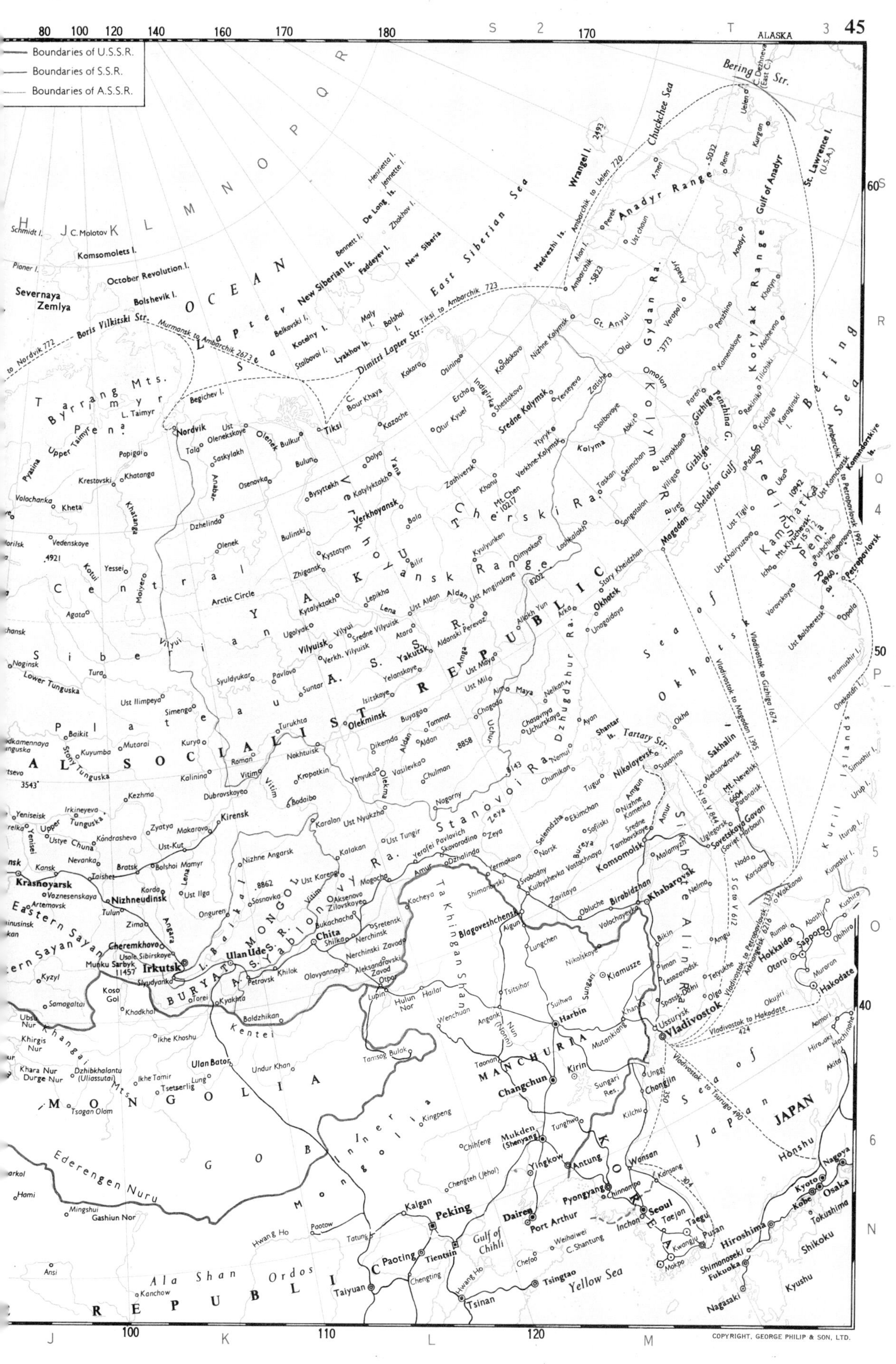
Boundaries of U.S.S.R.
Boundaries of S.S.R.
Boundaries of A.S.S.R.
ALASKA
Bering Str.
C. Dezhnev (East C.)
Chuckchee Sea
Wrangel I.
St. Lawrence I. (U.S.A.)
Gulf of Anadyr
Anadyr Range
Koryak Range
Bering Sea
Komandorskiye Is.
Petropavlovsk
Kamchatka Pen.
Sredinny Ra.
Shelekhov Gulf
Gizhiga G.
Penzhina G.
Magadan
Okhotsk
Sea of Okhotsk
Sakhalin
Kuril Islands
Tartary Str.
Nikolayevsk
Sovetskaya Gavan (Soviet Harbour)
Komsomolsk
Khabarovsk
Sikhote Alin Ra.
Vladivostok
Sea of Japan
JAPAN
Hokkaido
Sapporo
Otaru
Hakodate
Honshu
Nagoya
Kyoto
Osaka
Kobe
Hiroshima
Shikoku
Kyushu
Fukuoka
Shimonoseki
Nagasaki
KOREA
Seoul
Pusan
Pyongyang
Wonsan
Chongjin
Yellow Sea
Gulf of Chihli
Port Arthur
Dairen
Tsingtao
Tsinan
Tientsin
Peking
Kalgan
Paoting
Taiyuan
MANCHURIA
Harbin
Changchun
Mukden (Shenyang)
Kirin
Antung
Yingkow
Ta Khingan Shan
Blagoveshchensk
Chita
Ulan Ude
Irkutsk
L. Baikal
BURYAT MONGOL A.S.S.R.
Yablonovy Ra.
Stanovoi Ra.
Dzhugdzhur Ra.
MONGOLIA
Ulan Bator
GOBI
Inner Mongolia
Ala Shan
Ordos
REPUBLIC
Krasnoyarsk
Nizhneudinsk
Eastern Sayan
Kirensk
Central Siberian Plateau
YAKUTSK A.S.S.R.
Yakutsk
Verkhoyansk
Verkhoyansk Range
Cherski Ra.
Kolyma Ra.
Gydan Ra.
Sredne Kolymsk
Olekminsk
Vilyuisk
Lena
Aldan
Tiksi
Nordvik
Taimyr Pen.
Byrranga Mts.
Severnaya Zemlya
October Revolution I.
Bolshevik I.
Komsomolets I.
Boris Vilkitski Str.
Laptev Sea
New Siberian Is.
Kotelny I.
Dimitri Laptev Str.
East Siberian Sea
De Long Is.
Medvezhi Is.
Arctic Circle
OCEAN
COPYRIGHT, GEORGE PHILIP & SON, LTD.

ARCTIC OCEAN
PACIFIC OCEAN
Iceland
Arctic Circle
British Isles
North Sea
Scandinavia
Baltic Sea
Finland
North Cape
Kola
White Sea
Barents Sea
Novaya Zemlya
Kara Sea
Kara Strait
Taimyr Peninsula
Chelyuskin
Laptev Sea
New Siberian Is.
Wrangel I.
East Cape
Bering Str.
Bering Sea
Aleutian Is.
Kamchatka
Klyuchevsk V.
15,912
Kolyma Ra.
Kolyma
Verkhoyansk Range
Lena
Olenek
Khatanga
Yenisei
Central Siberian Plateau
Lower Tunguska
Upper Tunguska
Angara
Aldan
Sea of Okhotsk
Sakhalin
Kuril Is.
Tuscarora Trough
27,858
La Pérouse Str.
Hokkaido
Stanovoi Ra.
Yablonovy Ra.
Amur
Baikal
Selenga
Sayan Mts.
Altai
Khingan Ra.
Manchurian Plain
Sungari
Sikhote Alin Ra.
Sea of Japan
Honshu
Fujiyama
12,388
Japan
Korea
Korea Str.
Yellow Sea
G. of Chihli
Pei-ho
Plain of North China
Hwang-ho
Bonin Is.
East China Sea
Ryukyu Is.
Tropic of Cancer
Formosa
China
Yangtse-Kiang
Si-kiang
Song-ka (Red)
G. of Tongking
Hainan
Luzon
Philippine Is.
Philippines Deep
35412
Mindanao
Caroline Is.
Pelew Is.
Palawan
Sulu Sea
China Sea
G. of
Further India
Mekong
Menam
Salween
Irrawaddy
Bay of Bengal
Andaman Is.
Plateau of Mongolia
Gobi or Shamo
Koko Nor
Kunlun
Plateau of Tibet
Tsangpo
Everest
Himalaya
Brahmaputra
Ganga
Yamuna
India
Thar
Sutlej
Indus
Sulaiman Ra.
Karakoram Ra.
Pamirs
Stalin Pk.
Hindu Kush
Tarim
Turfan Basin
Tarim Basin
Takla Makan
Lop Nor
Tien Shan
Belukha
15,158
L. Balkhash
Ili
Chu
Kirgiz Steppe
Irtysh
Ob
Tobol
West Siberian Plain
Noradnaya
Ural Mountains
Ural
North European Plain
Central Russian Uplands
Dvina
Volga
Don
Dnieper
Vistula
Elbe
Rhine
Carpathians
Danube
Bosporus
Black Sea
Anatolia
Taurus
Cyprus
Caucasus
Elbrus
18,481
Ararat
16,916
Caspian Sea
Aral Sea
Syr Darya
Amu Darya
Turanian Plain
Hari Rud
Helmand
Elburz Mts.
Demavend
18,380
Salt Desert
Plateau of Iran
Tigris
Euphrates
Mesopotamia
Suez Canal
Sinai
Dead Sea
Syrian Desert
Nile
Arabia
Persian Gulf
G. of Oman
Rub al Khali
Red Sea
G. of Aden
Socotra
C. Guardafui
Somali Peninsula
Arabian Sea
Laccadive Is.
Narbada
Deccan
Western Ghats
Eastern Ghats
Godavari
Kistna
Palk Strait

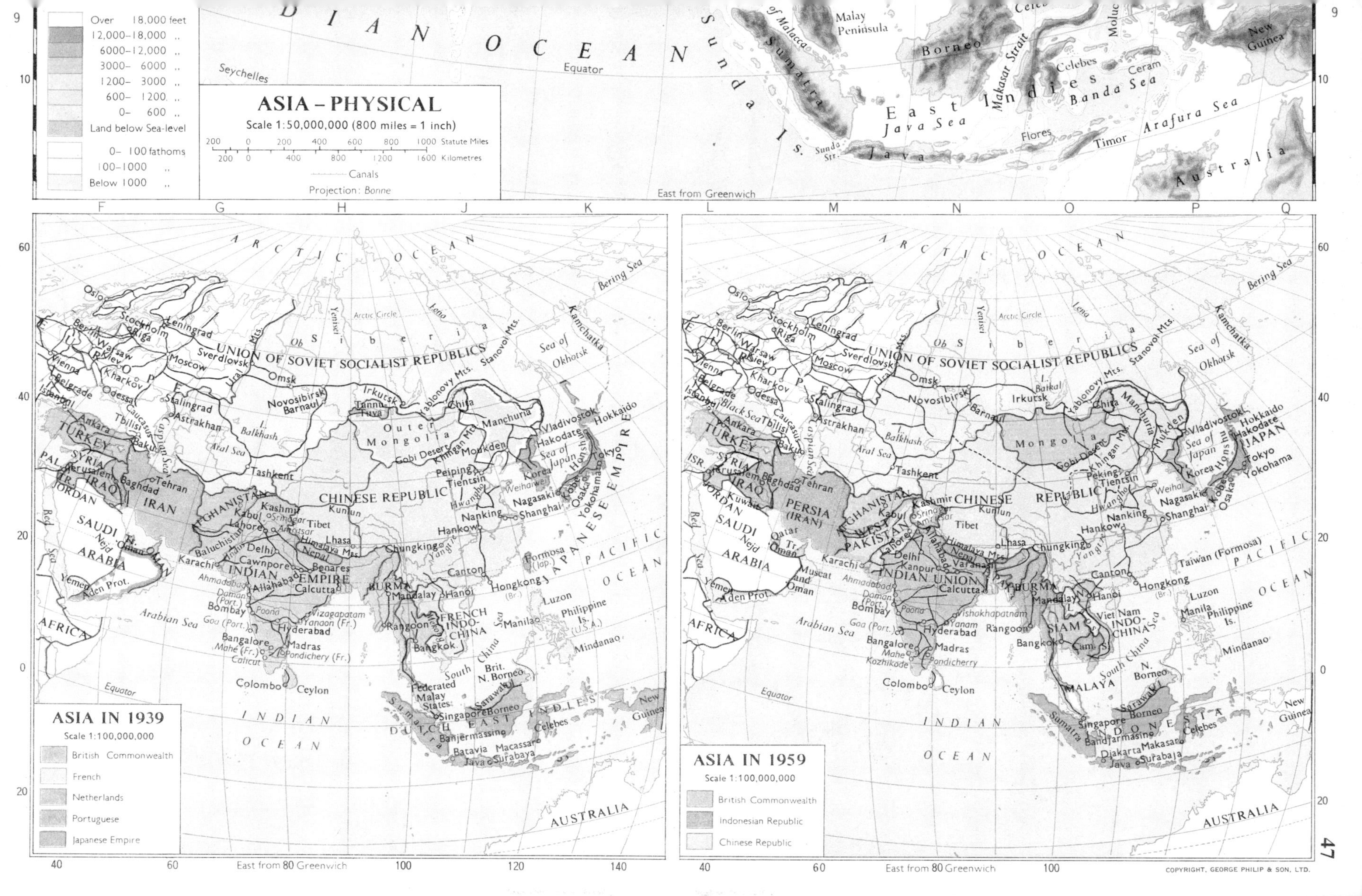

ASIA - PHYSICAL
Scale 1:50,000,000 (800 miles = 1 inch)
Over 18,000 feet
12,000–18,000 ,,
6000–12,000 ,,
3000– 6000 ,,
1200– 3000 ,,
600– 1200 ,,
0– 600 ,,
Land below Sea-level
0– 100 fathoms
100–1000 ,,
Below 1000 ,,
200 0 200 400 600 800 1000 Statute Miles
200 0 400 800 1200 1600 Kilometres
Canals
Projection: Bonne
INDIAN OCEAN
Equator
Seychelles
East from Greenwich
Sunda Is.
Sumatra
Malay Peninsula
Borneo
Makasar Strait
Celebes
East Indies
Java Sea
Java
Banda Sea
Ceram
Flores
Timor
Arafura Sea
New Guinea
Australia
ASIA IN 1939
Scale 1:100,000,000
British Commonwealth
French
Netherlands
Portuguese
Japanese Empire
ARCTIC OCEAN
UNION OF SOVIET SOCIALIST REPUBLICS
CHINESE REPUBLIC
INDIAN EMPIRE
JAPANESE EMPIRE
IRAN
TURKEY
SAUDI ARABIA
FRENCH INDO-CHINA
DUTCH EAST INDIES
PACIFIC OCEAN
INDIAN OCEAN
AUSTRALIA
East from 80 Greenwich
ASIA IN 1959
Scale 1:100,000,000
British Commonwealth
Indonesian Republic
Chinese Republic
PERSIA (IRAN)
WEST PAKISTAN
INDIAN UNION
CHINESE REPUBLIC
JAPAN
INDONESIA
MALAYA
SIAM
BURMA
COPYRIGHT, GEORGE PHILIP & SON, LTD.

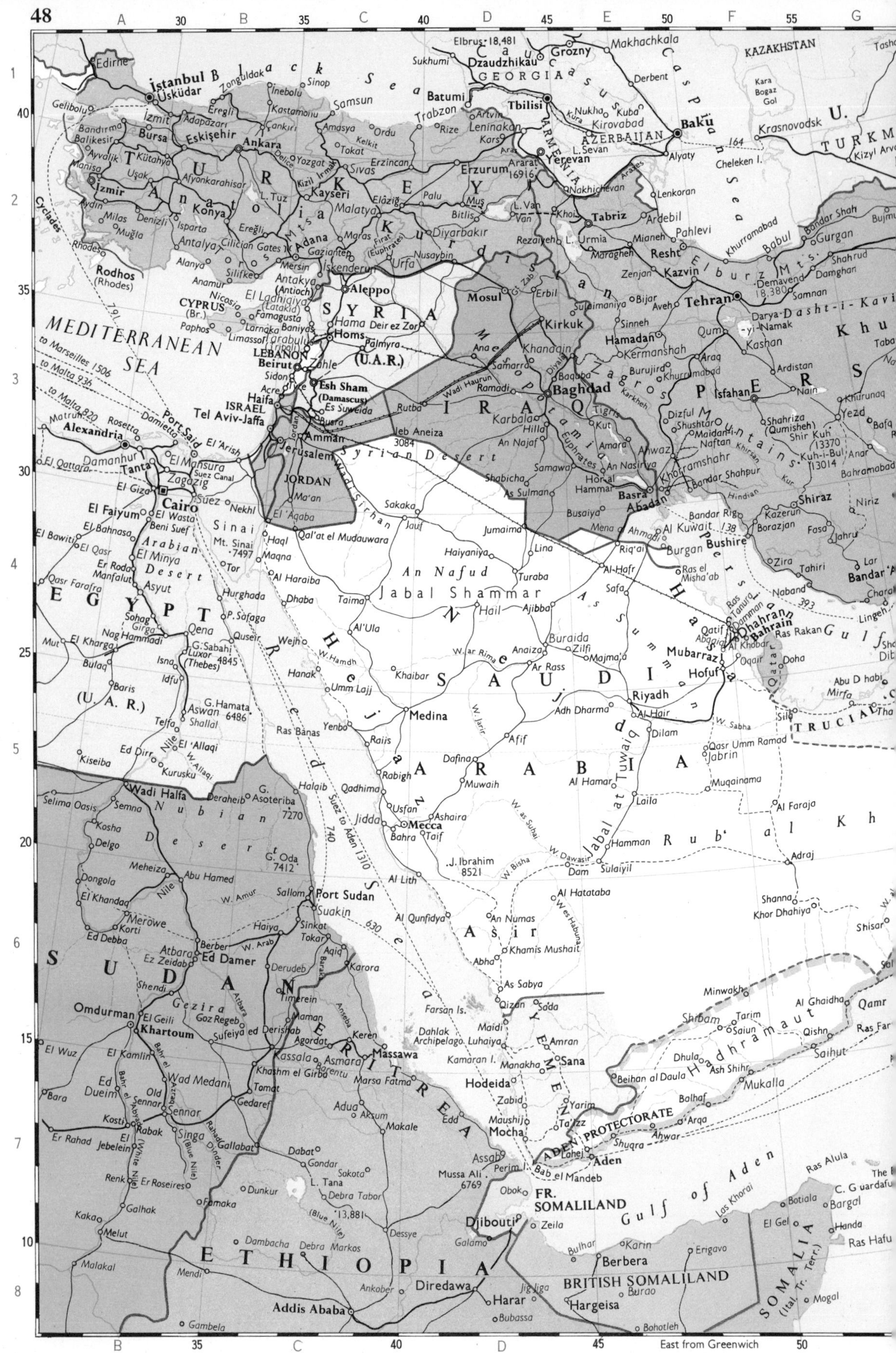
A
30
B
35
C
40
D
45
E
50
F
55
G
1
40
2
35
3
30
4
25
5
20
6
15
7
10
8
Black Sea
Caspian Sea
MEDITERRANEAN SEA
Red Sea
Persian Gulf
Gulf of Aden
Caucasus
KAZAKHSTAN
GEORGIA
AZERBAIJAN
ARMENIA
TURKEY
Anatolia
Taurus Mts
Kurdistan
SYRIA
(U.A.R.)
LEBANON
ISRAEL
JORDAN
IRAQ
Mesopotamia
Syrian Desert
PERSIA
Zagros Mountains
Elburz Mts.
Dasht-i-Kavir
EGYPT
(U. A. R.)
Arabian Desert
Sinai
SAUDI ARABIA
Nejd
Hejaz
Hasa
An Nafud
Jabal Shammar
As Summan
Rub' al Khali
Asir
YEMEN
ADEN PROTECTORATE
Hadhramaut
TRUCIAL
SUDAN
Nubian Desert
Gezira
ERITREA
ETHIOPIA
FR. SOMALILAND
BRITISH SOMALILAND
SOMALIA (Ital. Tr. Terr.)
CYPRUS (Br.)
Rodhos (Rhodes)
Cyclades
Edirne
Istanbul
Üsküdar
Ankara
Izmir
Bursa
Eskişehir
Konya
Kayseri
Adana
Sivas
Erzurum
Trabzon
Samsun
Batumi
Tbilisi
Yerevan
Baku
Grozny
Makhachkala
Elbrus 18,481
Ararat 16916
Tabriz
Tehran
Demavend 18,380
Resht
Kazvin
Hamadan
Kermanshah
Isfahan
Shiraz
Abadan
Khorramshahr
Bushire
Aleppo
Hama
Homs
Beirut
Esh Sham (Damascus)
Haifa
Tel Aviv-Jaffa
Jerusalem
Amman
Mosul
Kirkuk
Baghdad
Basra
Alexandria
Port Said
Cairo
Suez Canal
Suez
Mt. Sinai 7497
Aswan
Luxor (Thebes)
Wadi Halfa
Port Sudan
Khartoum
Omdurman
Medina
Mecca
Jidda
Riyadh
Hofuf
Dhahran
Bahrain
Al Kuwait
Qatar
Doha
Sana
Hodeida
Mocha
Aden
Bab el Mandeb
Perim
Massawa
Asmara
Djibouti
Berbera
Hargeisa
Addis Ababa
Diredawa
Harar
L. Tana
L. Van
L. Urmia
L. Sevan
to Marseilles 1506
to Malta 936
to Malta 820
Suez to Aden 1310
East from Greenwich

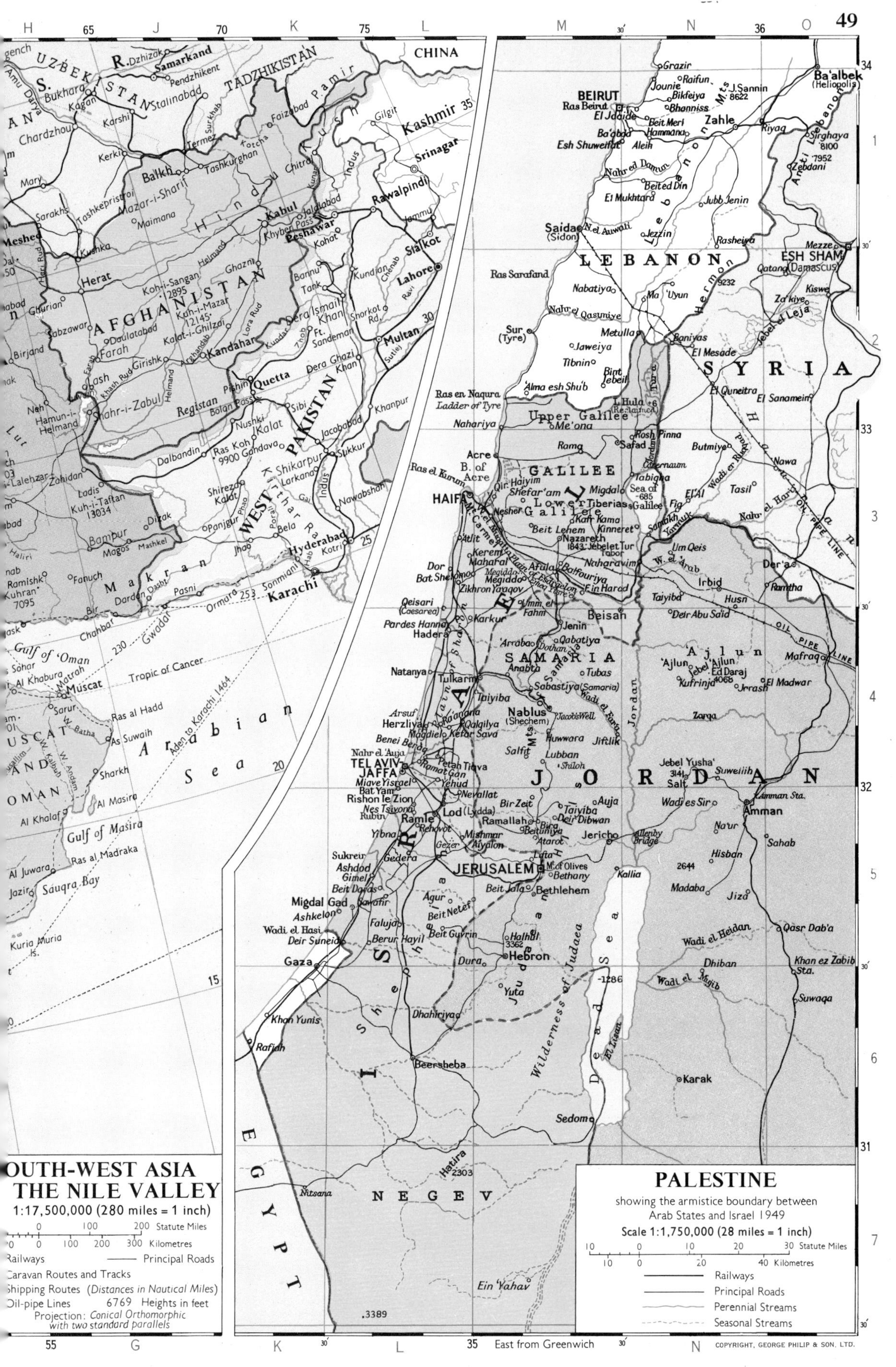

OUTH-WEST ASIA
THE NILE VALLEY
1:17,500,000 (280 miles = 1 inch)
0 100 200 Statute Miles
0 0 100 200 300 Kilometres
Railways
Principal Roads
Caravan Routes and Tracks
Shipping Routes (Distances in Nautical Miles)
Oil-pipe Lines
6769 Heights in feet
Projection: Conical Orthomorphic with two standard parallels
PALESTINE
showing the armistice boundary between Arab States and Israel 1949
Scale 1:1,750,000 (28 miles = 1 inch)
10 0 10 20 30 Statute Miles
10 0 20 40 Kilometres
Railways
Principal Roads
Perennial Streams
Seasonal Streams
East from Greenwich
COPYRIGHT, GEORGE PHILIP & SON, LTD.
CHINA
UZBEKISTAN
TADZHIKISTAN
AFGHANISTAN
WEST PAKISTAN
Kashmir
Samarkand
Bukhara
Stalinabad
Termez
Balkh
Mazar-i-Sharif
Kabul
Peshawar
Rawalpindi
Srinagar
Sialkot
Lahore
Multan
Herat
Kandahar
Quetta
Hyderabad
Karachi
Meshed
Zahidan
Makran
Gwadar
Muscat
Gulf of 'Oman
Tropic of Cancer
Arabian Sea
Gulf of Masira
Hindu Kush
Registan
Aden to Karachi 1464
BEIRUT
LEBANON
SYRIA
ESH SHAM (Damascus)
Ba'albek (Heliopolis)
Zahle
Saida (Sidon)
Sur (Tyre)
Lebanon Mts.
Anti Lebanon
Hermon
Upper Galilee
GALILEE
Lower Galilee
HAIFA
Acre
B. of Acre
Nazareth
Tiberias
Sea of Galilee -685
Jordan
Yarmuk
Irbid
Der'a
Beisan
Jenin
SAMARIA
Nablus (Shechem)
Tulkarm
Natanya
Hadera
TEL AVIV
JAFFA
Ramle
Lod (Lydda)
Ramallah
Jericho
Allenby Bridge
JERUSALEM
Bethlehem
Hebron
Gaza
Khan Yunis
Rafiah
Beersheba
Dead Sea -1286
Wilderness of Judaea
Judaean Hills
Shephelah
ISRAEL
JORDAN
'Ajlun
Amman
Salt
Madaba
Karak
Sedom
NEGEV
EGYPT
OIL PIPE LINE

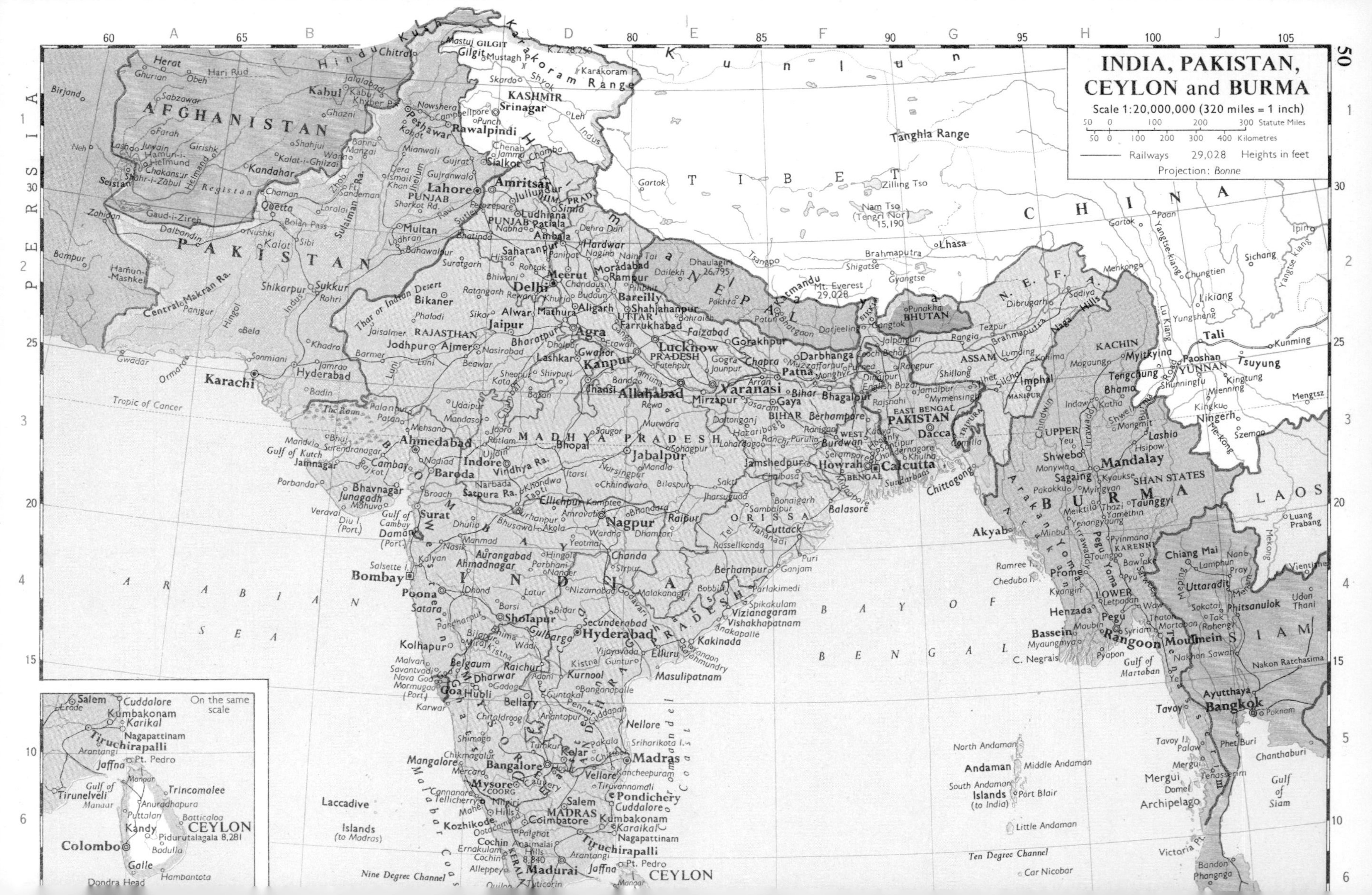
INDIA, PAKISTAN, CEYLON and BURMA
Scale 1:20,000,000 (320 miles = 1 inch)
Statute Miles
Kilometres
Railways
29,028 Heights in feet
Projection: Bonne
AFGHANISTAN
PAKISTAN
PERSIA
TIBET
CHINA
NEPAL
BHUTAN
BURMA
SIAM
LAOS
INDIA
KASHMIR
ARABIAN SEA
BAY OF BENGAL
Tropic of Cancer
Kunlun
Karakoram Range
Hindu Kush
Himalaya
Tanghla Range
Mt. Everest 29,028
Karachi
Bombay
Delhi
Calcutta
Madras
Hyderabad
Lahore
Dacca
Rangoon
Mandalay
Bangkok
Colombo
CEYLON
On the same scale
Laccadive Islands (to Madras)
Andaman Islands (to India)
Nine Degree Channel
Ten Degree Channel
Gulf of Martaban
Gulf of Siam
Mergui Archipelago

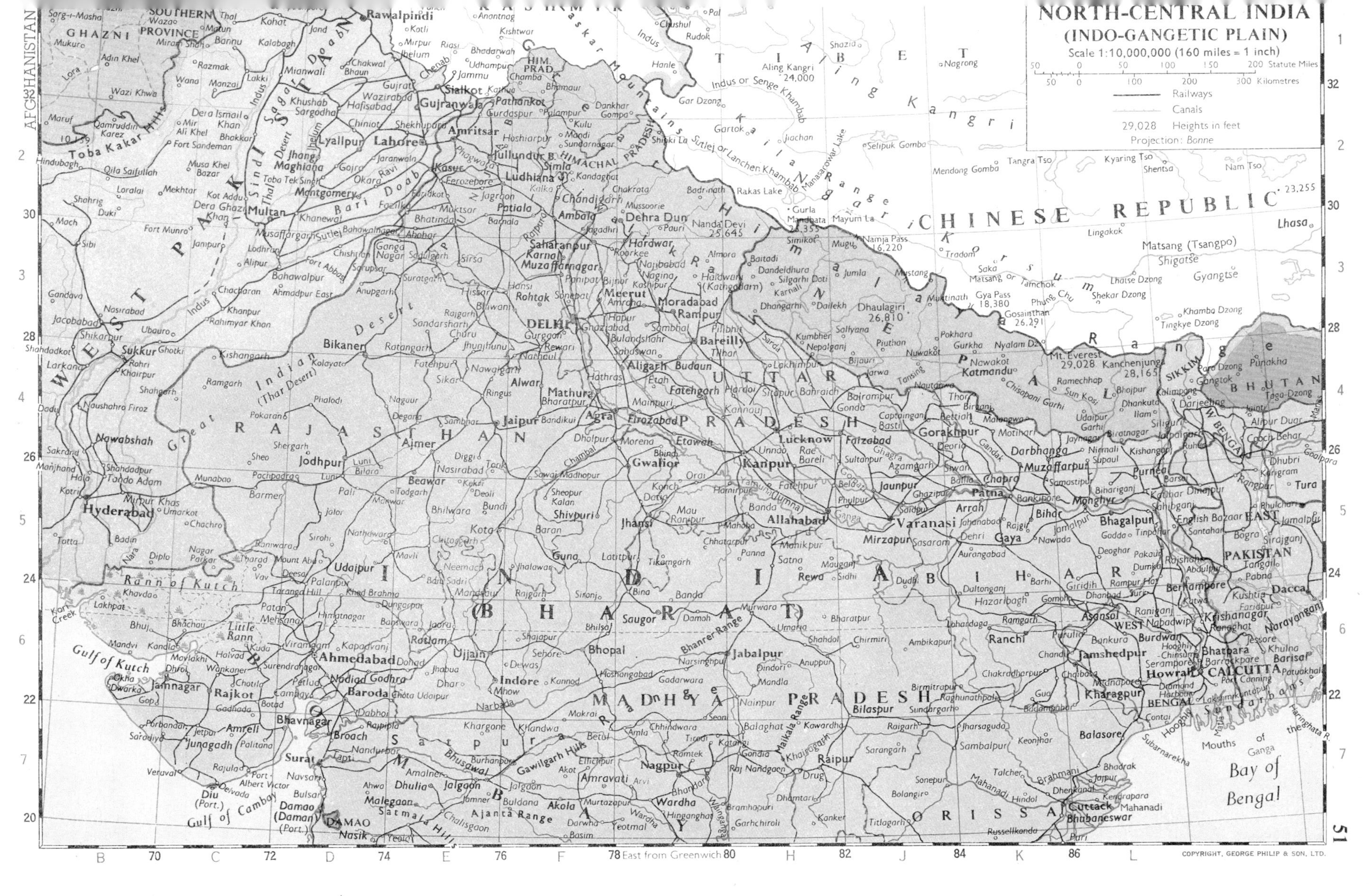
NORTH-CENTRAL INDIA
(INDO-GANGETIC PLAIN)
Scale 1:10,000,000 (160 miles = 1 inch)
50 0 50 100 150 200 Statute Miles
50 0 100 200 300 Kilometres
Railways
Canals
29,028 Heights in feet
Projection: Bonne
CHINESE REPUBLIC
T I B E T
UTTAR PRADESH
MADHYA PRADESH
RAJASTHAN
BIHAR
ORISSA
INDIA (BHARAT)
WEST PAKISTAN
EAST PAKISTAN
NEPAL
BHUTAN
SIKKIM
AFGHANISTAN
Bay of Bengal
Gulf of Kutch
Gulf of Cambay
Indian (Thar) Desert
Himalaya
B 70 C 72 D 74 E 76 F 78 East from Greenwich 80 H 82 J 84 K 86 L
COPYRIGHT, GEORGE PHILIP & SON, LTD.

BURMA
Mandalay
Akyab
Prome
Rangoon
Moulmein
Bassein
C. Negrais
Mergui Archipelago
Andaman Islands
N Andaman
Middle Andaman
S. Andaman
Port Blair
(India)
Lit. Andaman
Ten Degree Channel
Car Nicobar
Nicobar Islands (India)
Great Nicobar
Great Channel
Andaman Sea
Coco Is.
Preparis
SIAM (THAILAND)
Bangkok
Chiang Mai
Ayutthaya
Isthmus of Kra
Gulf of Siam
INDO-CHINA
VIET NAM
LAOS
CAMBODIA
Tonle Sap
Phom Penh
Saigon-Cholon
Hanoi
Haiphong
Gulf of Tonkin
Hue
Tourane
Vientiane
Luang Prabang
Hainan
Nanning (Yungning)
Wuchow (Tsangwu)
Canton
Macao
Kowloon
Paracel Is. (China)
SOUTH CHINA SEA
Spratly I.
Amboyna Cay
Louisa Reef
Luconia Shoals
London Reefs
Fiery Cross Reef
MALAYA
Kuala Lumpur
Georgetown
Penang
Ipoh
Malacca
Johore Bahru
Singapore
Kota Bharu
Kuala Trengganu
Str. of Malacca
SUMATRA
Medan
Kutaradja
Simeulue
Nias
Padang
Palembang
Djambi
Siberut
Mentawai Is.
Barisan Mountains
Bangka
Belitung
Riau Arch.
Lingga Arch.
Anambas Is.
Bunguran Islands
BRUNEI
SARAWAK
Kuching
Pontianak
BORNEO
INDONESIA
Java Sea
Djakarta
Bandung
Semarang
Jogjakarta
Surakarta
Surabaja
JAVA
Sunda Str.
Teluk Betung
Bawean
Christmas I. (British)
INDIAN OCEAN
East from Greenwich

EAST INDIES
AND
FURTHER INDIA
Scale 1:17,000,000 (272 miles = 1 inch)
100 0 100 200 300 Statute Miles
100 0 200 400 Kilometres
Railways
Oil Pipe-line
2736 Shipping Routes (Distances in Nautical Miles)
6430 Heights in feet
Projection: Conical
PACIFIC OCEAN
PHILIPPINES
Formosa (Taiwan)
Tainan
Kaohsiung
Pingtung
Hengchun
Taitung
Huoshao Tao
Hungtou Hsu (Lan Yu)
Y'Ami
Basco
Batan Is.
Balintang Channel
Balintang
Babuyan Is.
Aparri
C. Engaño
Negra Pt.
Laoag
Batac
Bangued
Vigan
Tuguegarao
Palanan
San Fernando
Ilagan
Luzon
Lingayen G.
9612
Solano
Casiguran
C. Bolinao
Baguio
C. San Ildefonso
Lingayen
Dagupan
San Jose
Cabanatuan
Iba
Quezon City
Tarlac
Polillo Is.
San Fernando
Manila
Bataan
San Pablo
Daet
Yog Pt.
Catanduanes
Manila Bay
Cavite
Calauag
Naga
Virac
Manila to Guam 1497
Lucena
Sorsogon
Lubang Is.
Batangas
Boac
Legaspi
Gubat
Calapan
Bulan
Calbayog
Mindoro
Samar
Mindoro Str.
Looc
Masbate
Catbalogan
Busuanga
Masbate
Roxas (Capiz)
Tacloban
Calamian Group
Cuyo Is.
Pandan
Panay
Cebu
Ormoc
Leyte
Iloilo
Baybay
Bacuit
Taytay
San Jose
Bacolod
Cebu
Dinagat
Siargao
Dumaran
Negros
Bohol
Tagbilaran
Tandag
Palawan
Puerto Princesa
Cagayan Is.
Tanjay
Lianga
Dumaguete
Mindanao Sea
Talisayan
Butuan
San Juan
Tubbataha Reefs
Dipolog
Cagayan
Mt. Mantalingajan 6839
Mandih
Iligan
Malaybalay
Mindanao
Liloy
Ozamiz
Davao
Bugsuk
Sulu Sea
Pagadian
Balabac
Bancoran
Cotabato
Apo 9690
Mati
San Miguel Is.
Dulawan
Digos
Davao G.
Banggi
Cagayan Sulu
Zamboanga
C. San Agustin
Labuk B.
Turtle Is.
Pangutaran Group
Lamitan
Basilan
Luan
Kiamba
Glan
Sandakan
Jolo
Tinaca Pt.
Sarangani Is.
Nenusa Is.
Talaud Is.
Karakelong
Beo
Tawitawi
Sulu Arch.
Lahad Datu
Pintasan
Sibutu
Tahuna
Sangihe
Celebes Sea
Sangihe Is.
Siau
Tawau
St. Lucia B.
Bunju
Tarakan
Tandjung Selor
Maratua
Klabat 6545
Maju
Manado
Djailolo
Amurang
Ternate
C. Mangkalihat
Buol
Paleleh
Kuandang
6430
Gorontalo
Kotabuna
Batuputih
Tolitoli 8881
Sangkulirang
Siboa
Tilamuta
Molucca Sea
Muara Antjalung
Tinombo
Togian Is.
(Penju)
Labuha
Batjan
Bontang
Sabang
Gulf of Tomini
Uebonti
Peleng
Mangole
Obi
Samarinda
Donggala
Parigi
Luwuk
Obi Is.
Banggai
Taliabu
Pasangkaju
Palu
Todjo
Sula Is.
Sanana
Balikpapan
Poso
G. of Tolo
Banggai Is.
Lariang
Celebes
Namlea
Balangan
Wamlana
Buru
Masamba
L. Towuti
Salabangka Is.
Palopo
Manui
Leksula
Ambelau
Mamudju
Rantekombola 11,335
Kendari
Wowoni
Kolaka
Kotabaru
Sebuku
Madjene
Parepare
Gulf of Bone
Buapinang
Butung
Watansopeng
Maros
Wangiwangi
Tukangbesi Is.
Makasar
Kadjang
Binongko
Masalima Is.
Makasar Str.
Kabaena
Muna
Pasarwadjo
Takalar
Bonthain
Salajar
Salajar (Benteng)
Postiljon Is.
Kalaotoa
Balabalangan
Tanahdjampea
Flores Sea
Djakarta to Thursday I. 2149
Rindjani 12,224
Mojo
9353
Raba
Reo
Flores
Paloe
Maumere
Larantuka
Adonara
Lomblen
Alor
Pantar
Atapupu
Ombai Str.
Ataúro (Port.)
Dili 9712
Vila Salazar
Vila Nova de Malaca
Nova Sagres
(Port.)
7874
Ende
Geliting
AMBENO (Port.)
Oecussi
Timor
Armindo Monteiro
Ruteng
Sumbawa
Memboro
Waingapu
Sawu Sea
Pariti
Niki Niki
Sumbawa-besar
Lunjuk-besar
Waikabubak
Sumba
Melolo
4019
Seba
Sawu Is.
Baa
Roti
Kupang
Lesser Sunda Islands
Timor Sea
Morotai
Pitu
Galela
Halmahera
Buli
Gotowasi
Patani
Weda
Gebe
Waigeo
Semo
Gani
Asia Is.
Aju Is.
Mapia Is.
Schouten Is.
Equator
Waibeem
Manokwari
Numfoor
Supiori
Biak
Mokmer
Bosnek
Japen
Wakre
Kwoka
Sorong 9842
Vogelkop
Jambe
Mios Num
Wariap
Serui
Samate
Wersar
Mogoi
Windehsi
Geelvink Bay
Klamono
Sege
Misoöl
McCluer G.
Babo
Saga
Kaimana
Kiruru
Ceram Sea
Wahai
Sawai
Bula
Fakfak
Weri
Ibonma
Karufa
Waru
Piru
Ceram
Geser
Gorong I.
Adi
Tehoru
Saparua
Ambon
Bandanaira
Watubela Is.
Manila to Banda Is.
Thursday I.
Ewab Is. (Kai)
Dobo
Wokam
Aru Is.
Kobroor
Tual
Banda Elat
Kai Ketjil
2240
Trangan
Manuk
Penju Is.
Serua
Lucipara Is.
Banda Sea
Nila
Tanimbar Is.
Larat
Teun
West Daja Is.
South Daja Is.
Jamdena
Saumlaki
Gunungapi
Damar
Tepa
Wetar
Roma
Babar
Selaru
Masela
Iliwaki
Kisar
Moa
Sermata
Arafura Sea
Cobourg Pen.
Melville I.
C. Van Diemen
Van Diemen G.
Bathurst I.
Darwin
AUSTRALIA
Pine Creek
Daly
Katherine
Yap Is.
Ngulu Atoll
Caroline Islands (U.S. Trust Terr.)
Palau Is.
Koror
Sonsorol Is.
Pulo Anna
Merir
Tobi
Manila 631
120 G H 130 J K 140
F 120 G H 130
2 3 10 4 5 0 6 7 10 8

MONGOLIA
SINKIANG
TIBET
CHINGHAI (KOKO NOR)
SZECHWAN
YUNNAN
KWEICHOW
KWANGSI
HUNAN
BURMA
SIAM
LAOS
VIET NAM
INDO-CHINA
ASSAM
BHUTAN
E. PAKISTAN
N.E.F.A.
Gobi or Sha
Bay of Bengal
Gulf of Tongking
Ulan-Bator
Urumchi (Tihwa)
Lhasa
Lanchow
Chengtu
Chungking
Kunming
Sian
Hanoi
Haiphong
Rangoon
Mandalay
CALCUTTA
Dacca
Hainan
East from Greenwich

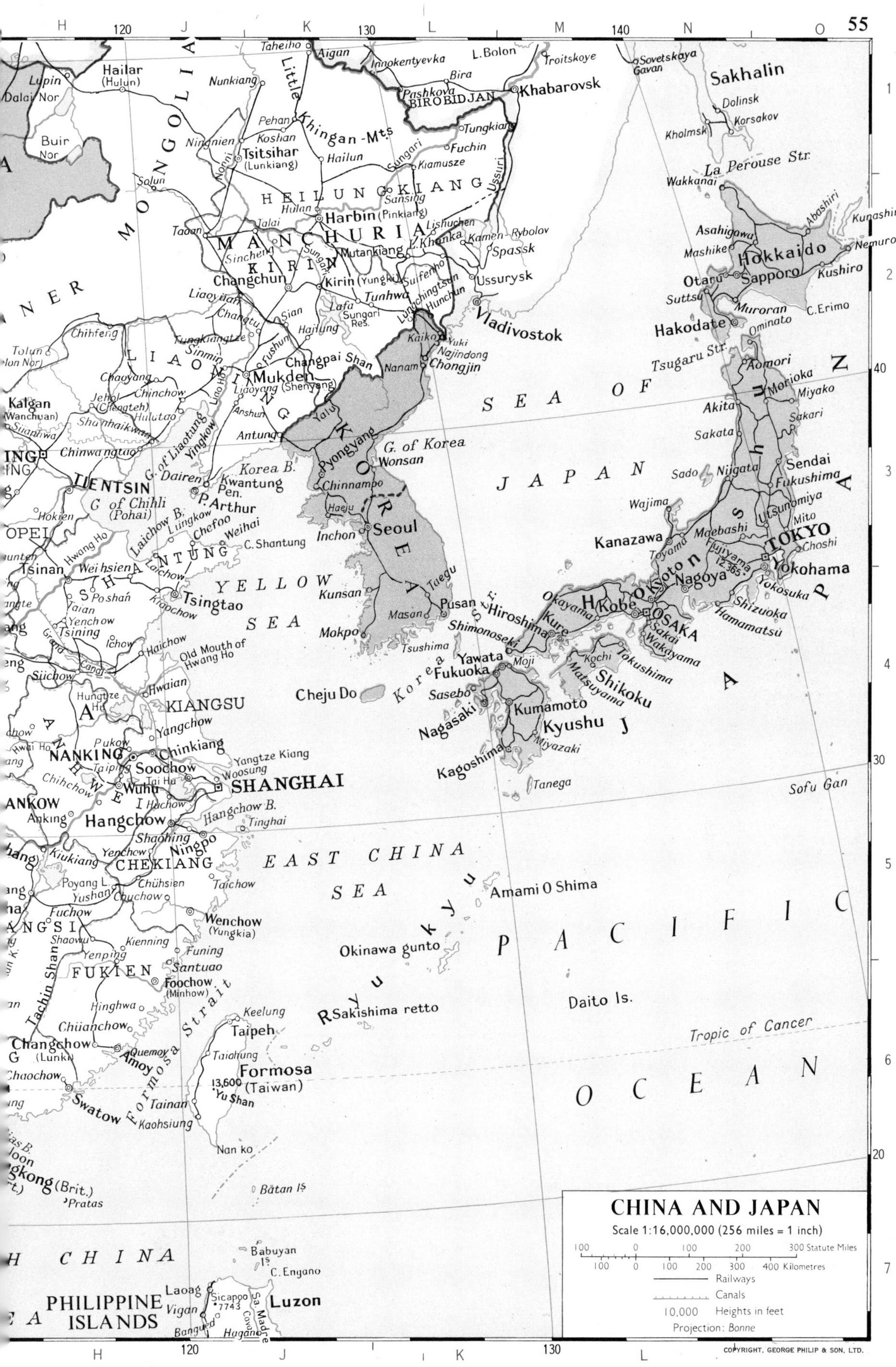
CHINA AND JAPAN
Scale 1:16,000,000 (256 miles = 1 inch)
100 0 100 200 300 Statute Miles
100 0 100 200 300 400 Kilometres
Railways
Canals
10,000 Heights in feet
Projection: Bonne
SEA OF JAPAN
YELLOW SEA
EAST CHINA SEA
PACIFIC OCEAN
Tropic of Cancer
MANCHURIA
KOREA
JAPAN
Hokkaido
Honshu
Shikoku
Kyushu
TOKYO
OSAKA
SHANGHAI
NANKING
TIENTSIN
Formosa (Taiwan)
PHILIPPINE ISLANDS
Luzon
Sakhalin
Vladivostok
Seoul
Mukden (Shenyang)
Harbin (Pinkiang)
Ryukyu
Okinawa gunto
Sakishima retto
Daito Is.
Amami O Shima

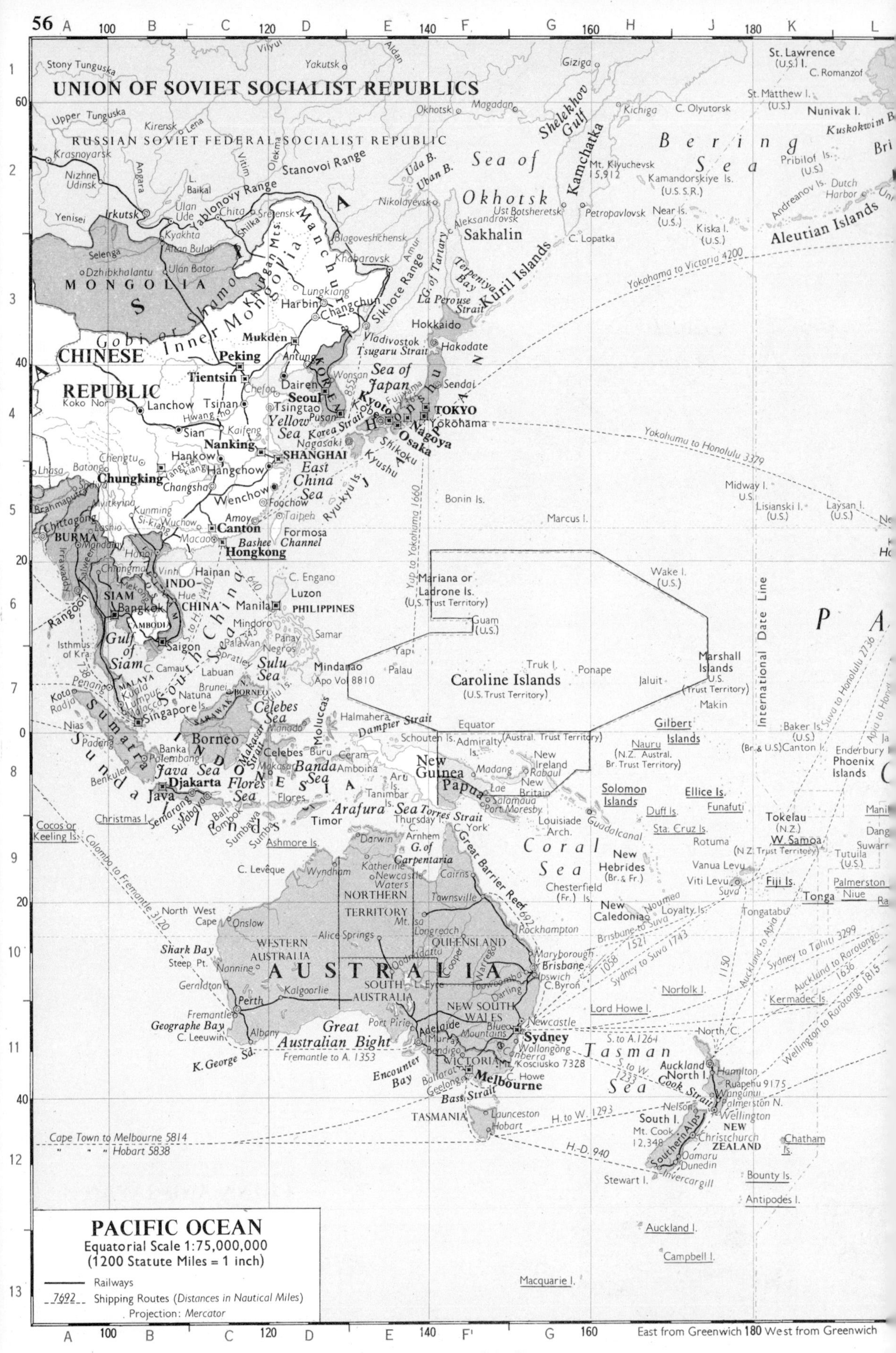
UNION OF SOVIET SOCIALIST REPUBLICS
RUSSIAN SOVIET FEDERAL SOCIALIST REPUBLIC
Stony Tunguska
Upper Tunguska
Vilyui
Yakutsk
Aldan
Gizigа
Okhotsk
Magadan
Kirensk
Lena
Krasnoyarsk
Nizhne Udinsk
Angara
Vitim
Olekma
Stanovoi Range
Uda B.
Uban B.
Sea of Okhotsk
Shelekhov Gulf
Kamchatka
Mt. Klyuchevsk 15,912
Kichiga
C. Olyutorsk
Bering Sea
Kamandorskiye Is. (U.S.S.R.)
Petropavlovsk
Ust Botsheretsk
St. Lawrence (U.S.) I.
C. Romanzof
St. Matthew I. (U.S.)
Nunivak I.
Kuskokwim B.
Pribilof Is. (U.S.)
Dutch Harbor
Andreanov Is.
Aleutian Islands
Near Is. (U.S.)
Kiska I. (U.S.)
C. Lopatka
L. Baikal
Yablonovy Range
Irkutsk
Ulan Ude
Chita
Sretensk
Shilka
Yenisei
Kyakhta
Altan Bulak
Selenga
Ulan Bator
Dzhibkhalantu
MONGOLIA
Nikolayevsk
Aleksandrovsk
Sakhalin
Blagoveshchensk
Amur
Khabarovsk
G. of Tartary
Terpeniya Bay
Kuril Islands
Sikhote Range
La Perouse Strait
Manchuria
Khingan Mts.
Lungkiang
Harbin
Changchun
Inner Mongolia
Gobi or Shamo
Vladivostok
Tsugaru Strait
Hokkaido
Hakodate
Mukden
Antung
CHINESE REPUBLIC
Peking
Tientsin
Koko Nor
Lanchow
Tsinan
Chefoo
Dairen
Wonsan
KOREA
Seoul
Pusan
Sea of Japan
Sendai
Honshu
Fujiyama
Kyoto
Kobe
TOKYO
Yokohama
Nagoya
Osaka
Shikoku
Kyushu
Nagasaki
Korea Strait
Tsingtao
Yellow Sea
Hwang ho
Sian
Kaifeng
Nanking
SHANGHAI
Hankow
Hangchow
Yangtse Kiang
Chengtu
Chungking
Changsha
East China Sea
Wenchow
Foochow
Ryu-kyu Is.
Amoy
Taipeh
Formosa
Bashee Channel
Canton
Macao
Hongkong
Lhasa
Batong
Sadiya
Brahmaputra
Myitkyina
Kunming
Si-kiang
Wuchow
Chittagong
BURMA
Lashio
Mandalay
Irrawaddy
Salween
Hanoi
Vinh
Chiengmai
Mekong
Hainan
INDO-CHINA
Hue
SIAM
Bangkok
CAMBODIA
Rangoon
Saigon
Gulf of Siam
Isthmus of Kra
C. Camau
Penang
MALAYA
Kuala Lumpur
Malacca
Singapore
Kota Radja
Nias
Sumatra
Padang
Banka
Palembang
Benkulen
Sunda Islands
Java Sea
Djakarta
Java
Semarang
Surabaya
Bali
Lombok
Sumbawa
Sumba
Christmas I.
Cocos or Keeling Is.
Ashmore Is.
South China Sea
Spratley
Labuan
Brunei
Natuna
N. BORNEO
SARAWAK
Borneo
INDONESIA
Makasar Strait
Celebes
Makasar
Celebes Sea
Sulu Is.
Sulu Sea
Palawan
Mindoro
Manila
Luzon
PHILIPPINES
C. Engano
Panay
Negros
Samar
Mindanao
Apo Vol 8810
Manado
Moluccas
Halmahera
Dampier Strait
Buru
Ceram
Amboina
Banda Sea
Flores Sea
Flores
Timor
Aru Is.
Tanimbar Is.
Arafura Sea
Torres Strait
Thursday I.
New Guinea
Papua
Schouten Is.
Admiralty Is.
Madang
Lae
Salamaua
Port Moresby
New Ireland
Rabaul
New Britain
Louisiade Arch.
Guadalcanal
Bonin Is.
Marcus I.
Mariana or Ladrone Is. (U.S. Trust Territory)
Guam (U.S.)
Yap
Palau
Truk I.
Ponape
Caroline Islands (U.S. Trust Territory)
Jaluit
Marshall Islands U.S. (Trust Territory)
Makin
Wake I. (U.S.)
Midway I. U.S.
Lisianski I. (U.S.)
Laysan I. (U.S.)
International Date Line
Equator
(Austral. Trust Territory)
Gilbert Islands
Nauru (N.Z. Austral. Br. Trust Territory)
Baker Is. (U.S.)
(Br. & U.S.) Canton I.
Enderbury I.
Phoenix Islands
Solomon Islands
Ellice Is.
Funafuti
Duff Is.
Sta. Cruz Is.
Tokelau (N.Z.)
W. Samoa (N.Z. Trust Territory)
Tutuila (U.S.)
Rotuma
Vanua Levu
Viti Levu
Suva
Fiji Is.
Tonga
Tongatabu
Palmerston
Niue
Coral Sea
New Hebrides (Br. & Fr.)
Chesterfield (Fr.) Is.
New Caledonia
Noumea
Loyalty Is.
Darwin
C. Arnhem
C. York
G. of Carpentaria
Great Barrier Reef
Katherine
Newcastle Waters
Wyndham
C. Levêque
Cairns
Townsville
NORTHERN TERRITORY
Mt. Isa
Longreach
QUEENSLAND
Rockhampton
North West Cape
Onslow
Alice Springs
WESTERN AUSTRALIA
Shark Bay
Steep Pt.
Nannine
AUSTRALIA
Oodnadatta
Cooper
Warrego
Maryborough
Brisbane
Ipswich
Toowoomba
C. Byron
Geraldton
Kalgoorlie
SOUTH AUSTRALIA
Eyre
Darling
Perth
Fremantle
Geographe Bay
C. Leeuwin
Albany
K. George Sd.
Great Australian Bight
Port Pirie
Adelaide
Murray
NEW SOUTH WALES
Blue Mountains
Newcastle
Sydney
Wollongong
Canberra
Mt. Kosciusko 7328
C. Howe
Bendigo
Ballarat
Geelong
VICTORIA
Melbourne
Encounter Bay
Bass Strait
TASMANIA
Launceston
Hobart
Lord Howe I.
Norfolk I.
Kermadec Is.
Tasman Sea
Auckland
North I.
Hamilton
Ruapehu 9175
Wanganui
Palmerston N.
Wellington
Cook Strait
Nelson
South I.
Mt. Cook 12,348
Southern Alps
Christchurch
NEW ZEALAND
Oamaru
Dunedin
Invercargill
Stewart I.
Chatham Is.
Bounty Is.
Antipodes I.
Auckland I.
Campbell I.
Macquarie I.
Yokohama to Victoria 4200
Yokohama to Honolulu 3379
Yap to Yokohama 1660
Suva to Honolulu 2736
Apia to Honolulu
Colombo to Fremantle 3120
Fremantle to A. 1353
S. to A. 1264
S. to W. 1233
H. to W. 1293
H.-D. 940
Brisbane to Suva 1521
Sydney to Suva 1743
Sydney to Tahiti 3299
Auckland to Rarotonga 1636
Wellington to Rarotonga 1815
Auckland to Apia
Cape Town to Melbourne 5814
" " Hobart 5838
East from Greenwich 180 West from Greenwich
PACIFIC OCEAN
Equatorial Scale 1:75,000,000
(1200 Statute Miles = 1 inch)
Railways
7692 Shipping Routes (Distances in Nautical Miles)
Projection: Mercator

CANADA
NORTH AMERICA
UNITED STATES
MEXICO
SOUTH AMERICA
BRAZIL
PERU
BOLIVIA
ARGENTINA
COLOMBIA
VENEZUELA
ECUADOR
PARAGUAY
URUGUAY
GUIANAS
Hudson Bay
Hudson Strait
Gulf of Alaska
Gulf of Mexico
Caribbean Sea
West Indies
Gulf of St. Lawrence
Tropic of Cancer
Equator
Tropic of Capricorn
Hawaiian Islands (U.S.)
Galapagos Is. (Ecuador)
Clipperton I. (Fr.)
Marquesas Is. (Fr.)
Tuamotu Archipelago (Fr.)
Tubuai Is. (Fr.) (Austral Is.)
Easter I. (Chile)
Sala-y-Gomez (Chile)
Juan Fernandez Is. (Chile)
Falkland Is.
Tierra del Fuego
Magellan's Strait
C. Horn
Honolulu to Panama 4711
Honolulu to San Francisco 2098
Honolulu to Vancouver 2419
Tahiti to S. Francisco 3658
Tahiti to Panama 4570
Pitcairn to Panama 3624
Liverpool to Havana 3936
Colon to S'hampton 4563
Kingston to S'hampton 4059
Los Angeles
San Francisco
Seattle
Vancouver
Minneapolis
CHICAGO
Detroit
Montreal
Toronto
NEW YORK
Philadelphia
Baltimore
Washington
Mexico
Havana
Caracas
Bogota
Lima
Santiago
Buenos Aires
Montevideo
COPYRIGHT, GEORGE PHILIP & SON, LTD.

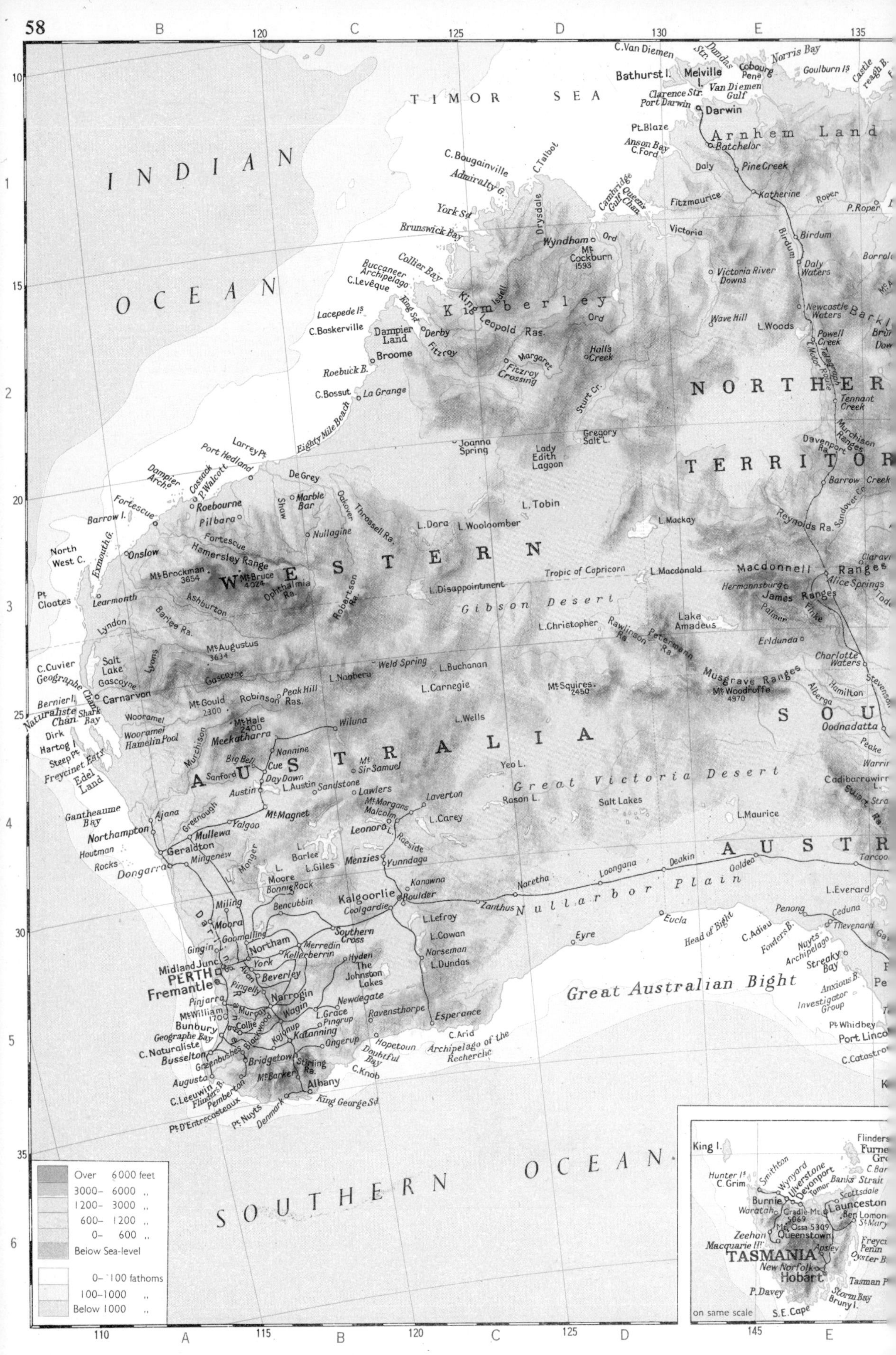
INDIAN OCEAN
TIMOR SEA
SOUTHERN OCEAN
Great Australian Bight
WESTERN AUSTRALIA
NORTHERN TERRITORY
SOUTH AUSTRALIA
Kimberley
Arnhem Land
Gibson Desert
Great Victoria Desert
Nullarbor Plain
Tropic of Capricorn
C. Van Diemen
Dundas Str.
Melville I.
Bathurst I.
Cobourg Pena
Norris Bay
Goulburn Is
Van Diemen Gulf
Clarence Str.
Port Darwin
Darwin
Pt. Blaze
Anson Bay
C. Ford
Batchelor
Daly
Pine Creek
Katherine
Roper
P. Roper
Fitzmaurice
Victoria
Birdum
Daly Waters
Victoria River Downs
Wave Hill
L. Woods
Newcastle Waters
Powell Creek
Telegraph & Motor Route
Tennant Creek
Murchison Ranges
Davenport Ra.
Barrow Creek
Reynolds Ra.
Sandover Cr.
L. Mackay
Macdonnell Ranges
Hermannsburg
Alice Springs
James Ranges
Palmer
Finke
Lake Amadeus
Erldunda
Charlotte Waters
Musgrave Ranges
Mt. Woodroffe 4970
Alberga
Hamilton
Oodnadatta
Peake
Cadibarrawirra
Stuart Ra.
Petermann Ra.
Rawlinson Ra.
L. Christopher
L. Macdonald
Mt. Squires 2450
C. Bougainville
Admiralty G.
C. Talbot
Drysdale
Cambridge Gulf
Queens Chan.
York Sd.
Brunswick Bay
Wyndham
Ord
Mt. Cockburn 1593
Collier Bay
Buccaneer Archipelago
C. Levêque
King Leopold Ras.
Isdell
Lacepede Is.
C. Baskerville
King Sd.
Dampier Land
Derby
Fitzroy
Broome
Margaret
Fitzroy Crossing
Hall's Creek
Sturt Cr.
Roebuck B.
C. Bossut
La Grange
Eighty Mile Beach
Joanna Spring
Lady Edith Lagoon
Gregory Salt L.
L. Tobin
Larrey Pt.
Port Hedland
Dampier Arch.
Cossack
P. Walcott
Roebourne
Pilbara
De Grey
Shaw
Marble Bar
Oakover
Throssell Ra.
Nullagine
L. Dora
L. Wooloomber
Fortescue
Barrow I.
North West C.
Exmouth G.
Onslow
Hamersley Range
Mt. Brockman 3654
Mt. Bruce 4024
Ophthalmia Ra.
Robertson Ra.
L. Disappointment
Pt. Cloates
Learmonth
Ashburton
Lyndon
Barlee Ra.
Mt. Augustus 3634
C. Cuvier
Geographe Chan.
Salt Lake
Lyons
Gascoyne
Weld Spring
L. Buchanan
L. Nabberu
L. Carnegie
Bernier I.
Naturaliste Chan.
Carnarvon
Mt. Gould 2300
Robinson Ra.
Peak Hill
Shark Bay
Dirk Hartog I.
Wooramel
Hamelin Pool
Mt. Hale 2400
Meekatharra
Wiluna
L. Wells
Steep Pt.
Freycinet Est.
Edel Land
Murchison
Nannine
Big Bell
Cue
Mt. Sir Samuel
Yeo L.
Sanford
Day Dawn
Austin
L. Austin
Sandstone
Lawlers
Mt. Morgans
Malcolm
Laverton
Rason L.
Salt Lakes
L. Maurice
Gantheaume Bay
Ajana
Northampton
Greenough
Mullewa
Yalgoo
Mt. Magnet
Leonora
L. Carey
Raeside
Houtman Rocks
Geraldton
Mingenew
Monger
L. Barlee
Menzies
Yunndaga
Dongarra
L. Moore
L. Giles
Bonnie Rock
Kanowna
Kalgoorlie
Boulder
Coolgardie
Naretha
Loongana
Deakin
Ooldea
Tarcoola
Zanthus
Miling
Darling Ra.
Moora
Bencubbin
L. Lefroy
Eucla
L. Everard
Penong
Ceduna
Thevenard
Gingin
Goomalling
Southern Cross
L. Cowan
Eyre
Head of Bight
C. Adieu
Fowlers B.
Nuyts Archipelago
Midland Junc.
PERTH
Fremantle
Northam
Merredin
Kellerberrin
York
Avon
Beverley
Hyden
The Johnston Lakes
Norseman
L. Dundas
Streaky Bay
Anxious B.
Investigator Group
Pingelly
Narrogin
Newdegate
Pinjarra
Murray
Mt. William 1700
Wagin
L. Grace
Pingrup
Ravensthorpe
Esperance
Bunbury
Collie
Geographe Bay
Blackwood
Kojonup
Katanning
Ongerup
C. Arid
Pt. Whidbey
Port Lincoln
C. Naturaliste
Busselton
Greenbushes
Bridgetown
Hopetoun
Archipelago of the Recherche
Doubtful Bay
C. Catastrophe
Stirling Ra.
Augusta
Mt. Barker
C. Knob
C. Leeuwin
Flinders B.
Pemberton
Albany
King George Sd.
Pt. D'Entrecasteaux
Pt. Nuyts
Denmark
Over 6000 feet
3000– 6000 „
1200– 3000 „
600– 1200 „
0– 600 „
Below Sea-level
0– 100 fathoms
100–1000 „
Below 1000 „
King I.
Hunter Is.
C. Grim
Smithton
Wynyard
Ulverstone
Devonport
Tamar
Flinders
Furneaux Group
C. Barren
Banks Strait
Scottsdale
Burnie
Launceston
Waratah
Cradle Mt. 5069
Mt. Ossa 5309
Ben Lomond
St. Marys
Zeehan
Queenstown
Macquarie H.
TASMANIA
Apsley
Freycinet Penin.
Oyster B.
New Norfolk
Hobart
Tasman Pen.
P. Davey
Storm Bay
Bruny I.
S.E. Cape
on same scale
110
115
120
125
130
135
145
10
15
20
25
30
35
A
B
C
D
E
1
2
3
4
5
6

AUSTRALASIA
POLITICAL
Scale 1:92,000,000
TERR. OF NEW GUINEA AND PAPUA
INDONESIA
INDIAN OCEAN
NORTHERN TERRITORY
WESTERN AUSTRALIA
SOUTH AUSTRALIA
QUEENSLAND
N.S.W.
VICT.
TASMANIA
NEW ZEALAND
PACIFIC OCEAN
Tasman Sea
Coral Sea
AUSTRALIA - PHYSICAL
Scale 1:15,000,000 (240 miles = 1 inch)
Statute Miles
Kilometres
Railways
5309 Heights in feet
Projection: Bonne
Gulf of Carpentaria
QUEENSLAND
NEW SOUTH WALES
VICTORIA
PACIFIC OCEAN
Great Dividing Ra.
Great Barrier Reef
Bass Strait
BRISBANE
SYDNEY
MELBOURNE
ADELAIDE
CANBERRA
East from Greenwich

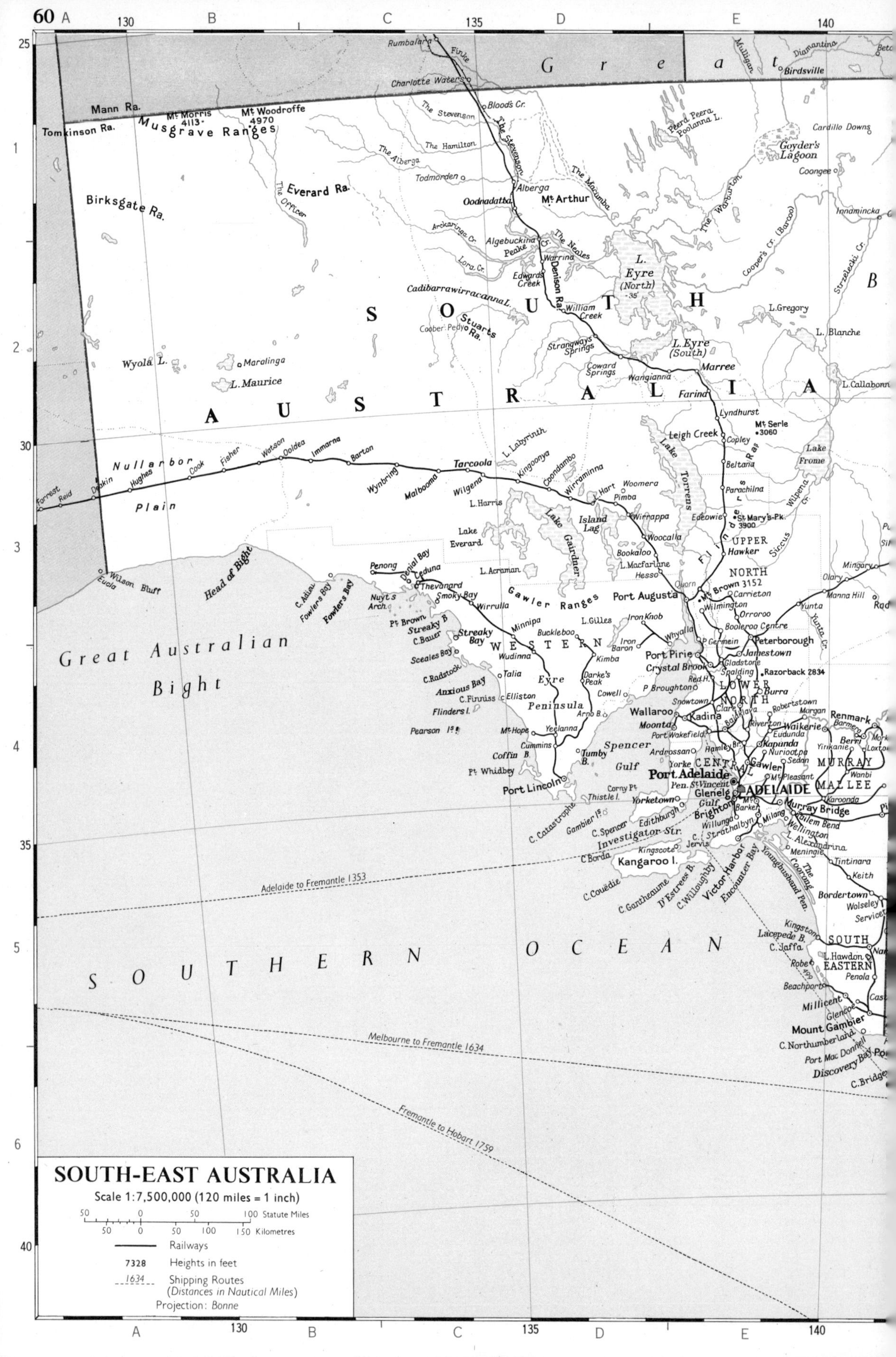
SOUTH-EAST AUSTRALIA
Scale 1:7,500,000 (120 miles = 1 inch)
50 0 50 100 Statute Miles
50 0 50 100 150 Kilometres
Railways
7328 Heights in feet
1634 Shipping Routes
(Distances in Nautical Miles)
Projection: Bonne
SOUTH AUSTRALIA
Great Australian Bight
SOUTHERN OCEAN
Adelaide to Fremantle 1353
Melbourne to Fremantle 1634
Fremantle to Hobart 1759
Mann Ra.
Musgrave Ranges
Tomkinson Ra.
Mt Morris 4113
Mt Woodroffe 4970
Everard Ra.
Birksgate Ra.
Wyola L.
Maralinga
L. Maurice
Nullarbor Plain
Forrest
Reid
Deakin
Hughes
Cook
Fisher
Watson
Ooldea
Immarna
Barton
Wynbring
Malbooma
Tarcoola
Wilgena
Kingoonya
L. Labyrinth
Coondambo
Wirraminna
Pimba
Woomera
Eucla
Wilson Bluff
Head of Bight
Fowlers Bay
Penong
Denial Bay
Ceduna
Thevanard
Smoky Bay
Streaky Bay
Wirrulla
Gawler Ranges
Minnipa
Wudinna
Eyre Peninsula
Port Lincoln
Spencer Gulf
Port Augusta
Whyalla
Port Pirie
Crystal Brook
Wallaroo
Moonta
Kadina
Yorketown
Port Adelaide
ADELAIDE
Glenelg
Brighton
Murray Bridge
Kangaroo I.
Kingscote
Investigator Str.
Victor Harbor
Encounter Bay
Gulf St Vincent
Gawler
Kapunda
Burra
Peterborough
Jamestown
Renmark
Berri
Waikerie
Morgan
Quorn
Hawker
Mt Brown 3152
Flinders Ra.
St Mary's Pk. 3900
Mt Serle 3060
Leigh Creek
Lake Torrens
Lake Frome
Marree
Farina
Lyndhurst
L. Eyre (North)
L. Eyre (South)
L. Gairdner
Oodnadatta
Alberga
Mt Arthur
William Creek
Coober Pedy
Stuarts Ra.
Rumbalara
Finke
Charlotte Waters
Birdsville
Goyder's Lagoon
Innamincka
Mount Gambier
Millicent
Beachport
Robe
Kingston
Naracoorte
Penola
Bordertown
Keith
Tintinara
The Coorong
L. Alexandrina
Tailem Bend
Coffin B.
Tumby B.
Cowell
Blood's Cr.
Strangways Springs
Coward Springs
Hesso
Olary
Yunta
Manna Hill
Razorback 2834
Great
Pearson Is.
Flinders I.
C. Catastrophe
Thistle I.
Gambier Is.
C. Spencer
C. Borda
C. Jervis
Discovery Bay
C. Bridgewater
C. Northumberland
Port Mac Donnell

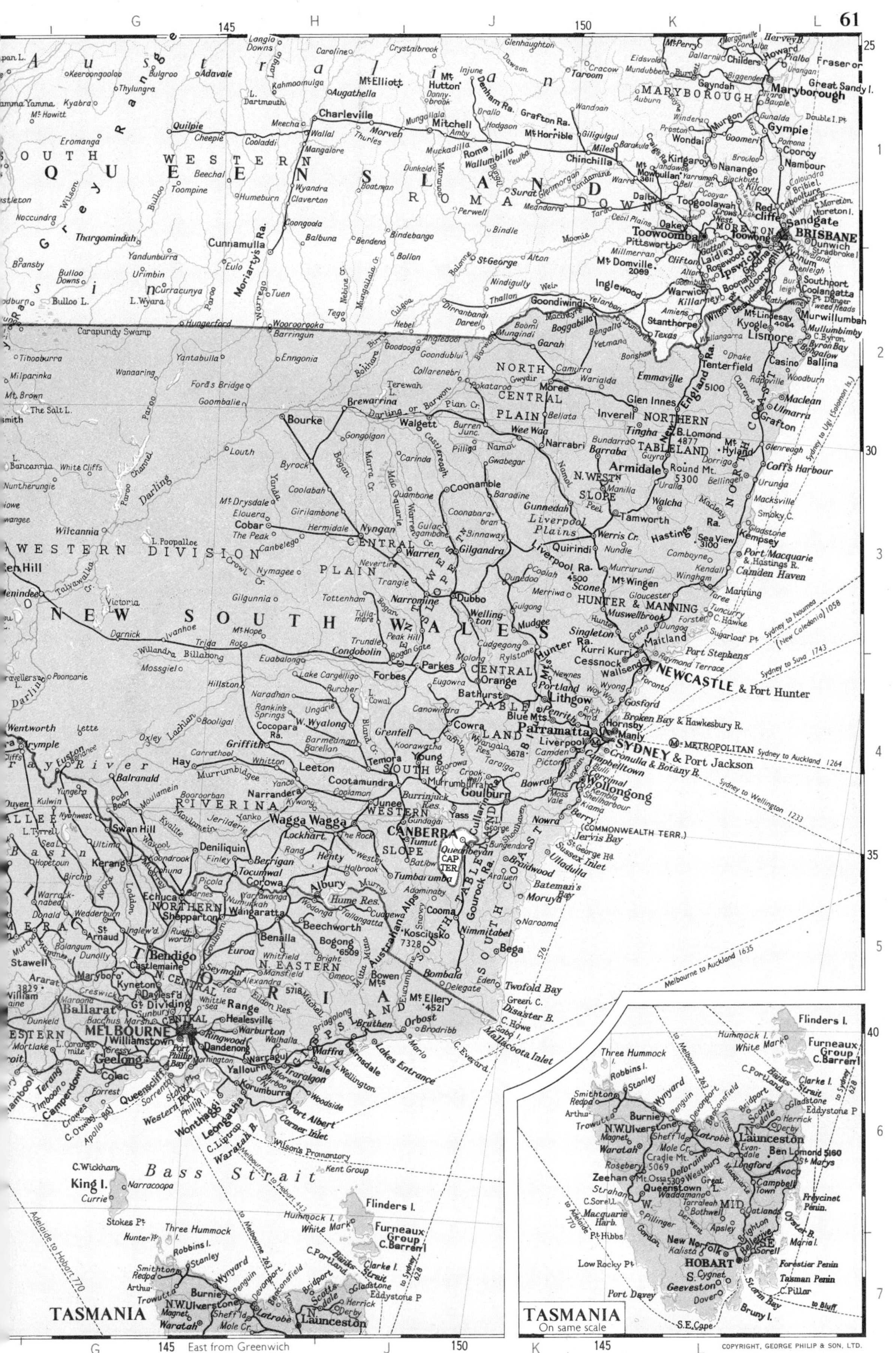
G
H
J
K
L
145
150
25
30
35
40
1
2
3
4
5
6
7
QUEENSLAND
NEW SOUTH WALES
VICTORIA
SOUTH WESTERN
ROMA
DOWNS
MARYBOROUGH
MORETON
NORTH CENTRAL PLAIN
NORTHERN TABLELAND
N. WESTN SLOPE
WESTERN DIVISION
CENTRAL PLAIN
CENTRAL TABLE LAND
HUNTER & MANNING
SOUTH WESTERN SLOPE
RIVERINA
SOUTH COAST
NORTH COAST
SOUTH TABLE LAND
N. EASTERN
N. CENTRAL
NORTHERN
GIPPSLAND
METROPOLITAN
(COMMONWEALTH TERR.)
Grey Range
Great Dividing Range
Liverpool Plains
Liverpool Ra.
New England Ra.
Australian Alps
Blue Mts.
Bass Strait
Charleville
Mitchell
Roma
Miles
Chinchilla
Dalby
Toowoomba
Ipswich
BRISBANE
Sandgate
Southport
Coolangatta
Maryborough
Gympie
Nambour
Warwick
Stanthorpe
Goondiwindi
Cunnamulla
Thargomindah
Quilpie
Adavale
St George
Inglewood
Mt Domville 2099
Lismore
Murwillumbah
Casino
Ballina
Grafton
Tenterfield
Glen Innes
Inverell
Armidale
Tamworth
Moree
Narrabri
Gunnedah
Coffs Harbour
Kempsey
Port Macquarie
Taree
Bourke
Brewarrina
Walgett
Cobar
Nyngan
Dubbo
Wilcannia
Broken Hill
Menindee
Wentworth
Mildura
Mudgee
Orange
Bathurst
Lithgow
Parkes
Forbes
Condobolin
Maitland
Cessnock
NEWCASTLE & Port Hunter
Port Stephens
Gosford
Hornsby
Manly
Parramatta
SYDNEY & Port Jackson
Liverpool
Campbelltown
Wollongong
Cronulla & Botany B.
Broken Bay & Hawkesbury R.
Goulburn
CANBERRA
Queanbeyan
Yass
Young
Cowra
Cootamundra
Temora
Wagga Wagga
Narrandera
Leeton
Griffith
Hay
Deniliquin
Albury
Corowa
Tumut
Tumbarumba
Cooma
Bombala
Bega
Moruya
Nowra
Jervis Bay
Twofold Bay
Eden
Mt Kosciusko 7328
Mt Ellery 4521
Swan Hill
Kerang
Echuca
Shepparton
Wangaratta
Benalla
Beechworth
Bendigo
Castlemaine
Ballarat
Ararat
Stawell
Seymour
Healesville
MELBOURNE
Williamstown
Geelong
Dandenong
Port Phillip Bay
Colac
Warragul
Yallourn
Traralgon
Sale
Bairnsdale
Maffra
Orbost
Lakes Entrance
Wonthaggi
Leongatha
Korumburra
Port Albert
Wilson's Promontory
King I.
Flinders I.
Furneaux Group
C. Barren I.
Three Hummock I.
Robbins I.
Stanley
Wynyard
Burnie
N.W. Ulverstone
Devonport
Latrobe
Launceston
Ben Lomond 5160
Cradle Mt. 5069
Zeehan
Queenstown
Macquarie Harb.
New Norfolk
HOBART
Bellerive
Sorell
Geeveston
Port Davey
S.E. Cape
Bruny I.
Tasman Penin
Freycinet Penin.
Sydney to Auckland 1264
Sydney to Wellington 1233
Sydney to Suva 1743
Sydney to Noumea (New Caledonia) 1058
Melbourne to Auckland 1635
Melbourne to Hobart 443
Adelaide to Hobart 770
TASMANIA
TASMANIA On same scale
East from Greenwich

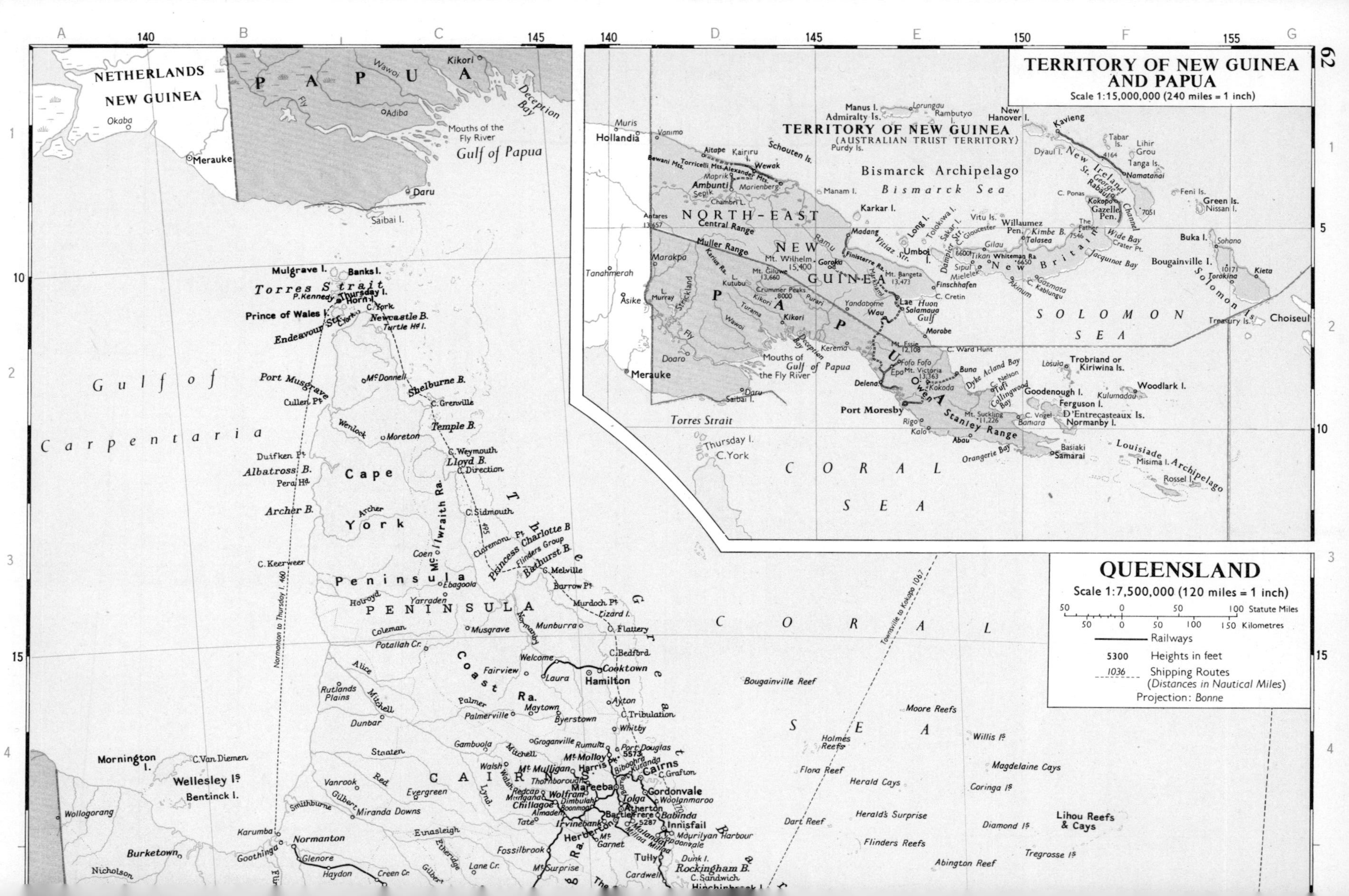
TERRITORY OF NEW GUINEA AND PAPUA
Scale 1:15,000,000 (240 miles = 1 inch)
TERRITORY OF NEW GUINEA
(AUSTRALIAN TRUST TERRITORY)
Bismarck Archipelago
Bismarck Sea
NORTH-EAST NEW GUINEA
PAPUA
SOLOMON SEA
CORAL SEA
Torres Strait
Gulf of Papua
QUEENSLAND
Scale 1:7,500,000 (120 miles = 1 inch)
Statute Miles
Kilometres
Railways
5300 Heights in feet
1036 Shipping Routes
(Distances in Nautical Miles)
Projection: Bonne
NETHERLANDS NEW GUINEA
Gulf of Carpentaria
Cape York Peninsula
CORAL SEA
Great Barrier Reef
Townsville to Kokopo 1067
Normanton to Thursday I. 460
Cooktown
Cairns
Port Moresby
Hollandia
Merauke

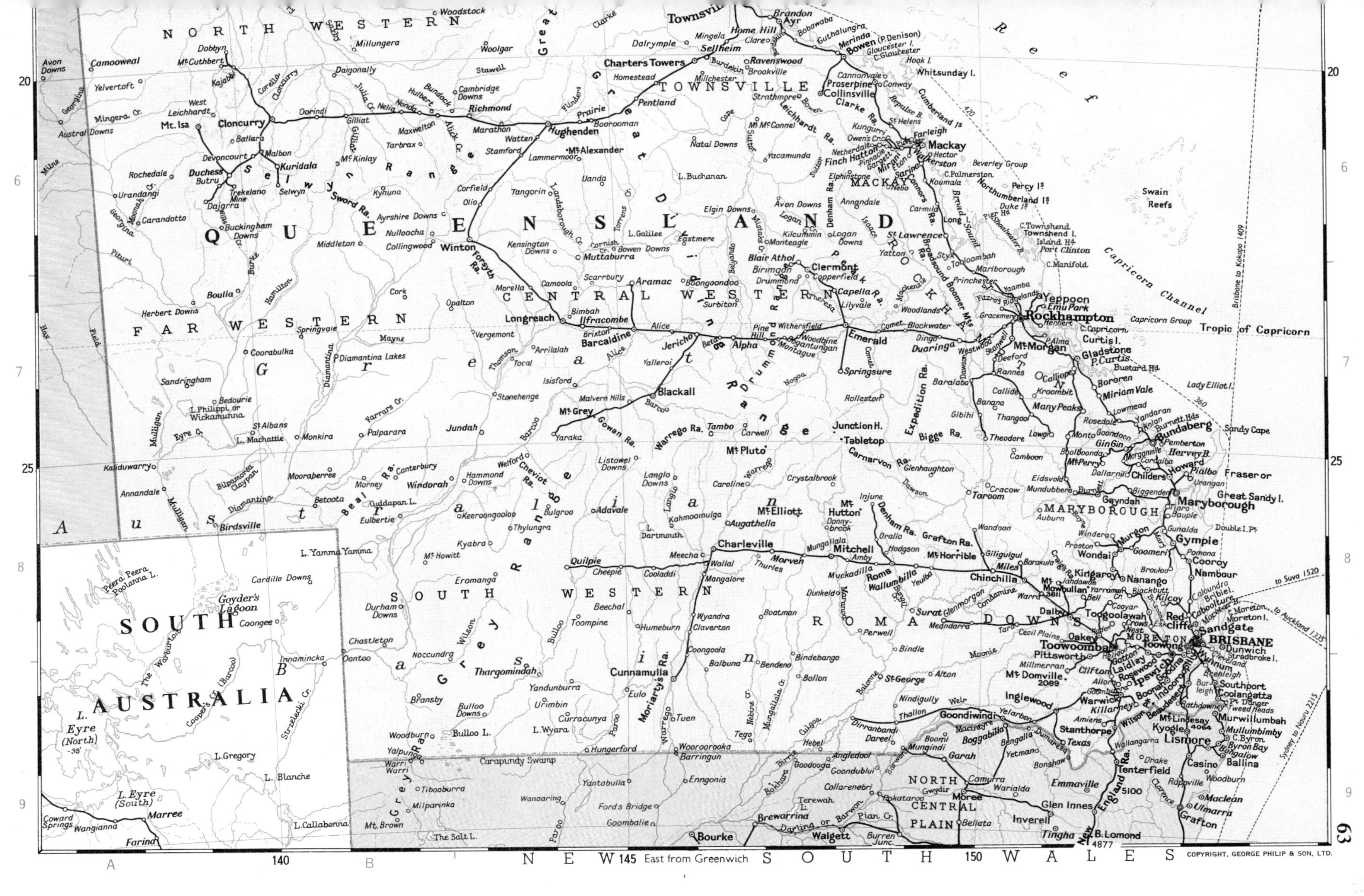

QUEENSLAND
NORTH WESTERN
CENTRAL WESTERN
FAR WESTERN
SOUTH WESTERN
TOWNSVILLE
MACKAY
ROCKHAMPTON
MARYBOROUGH
ROMA DOWNS
MORETON
SOUTH AUSTRALIA
NEW SOUTH WALES
NORTH CENTRAL PLAIN
Great Dividing Range
Great Artesian Basin
Great Barrier Reef
Selwyn Ra.
Grey Range
Capricorn Channel
Tropic of Capricorn
Swain Reefs
Broad Sound
Brisbane
Toowoomba
Ipswich
Gympie
Maryborough
Bundaberg
Gladstone
Rockhampton
Mackay
Bowen
Townsville
Charters Towers
Hughenden
Richmond
Cloncurry
Mt. Isa
Longreach
Barcaldine
Winton
Emerald
Charleville
Roma
Cunnamulla
Quilpie
Boulia
Birdsville
Camooweal
Goondiwindi
Warwick
Stanthorpe
Lismore
Grafton
Bourke
Walgett
Moree
L. Eyre (North)
L. Eyre (South)
Marree
Farina
Goyder's Lagoon
Cooper's Cr.
Diamantina
Brisbane to Kokopo 1409
to Suva 1520
to Auckland 1335
Sydney to Nauru 2215
N E W 145 East from Greenwich S O U T H 150 W A L E S
COPYRIGHT, GEORGE PHILIP & SON, LTD.

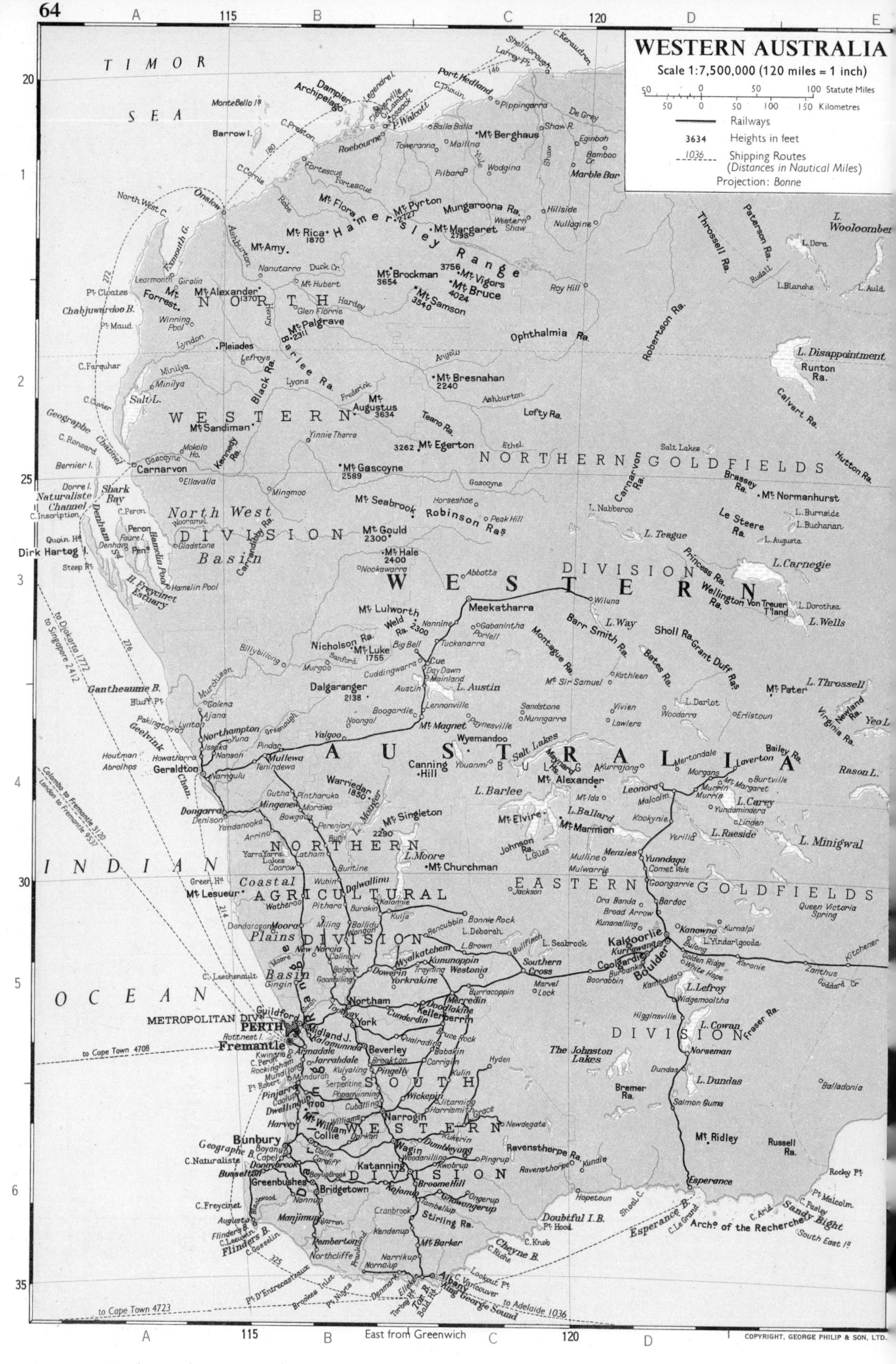
WESTERN AUSTRALIA
Scale 1:7,500,000 (120 miles = 1 inch)
Statute Miles
Kilometres
Railways
3634 Heights in feet
1036 Shipping Routes (Distances in Nautical Miles)
Projection: Bonne
TIMOR SEA
INDIAN OCEAN
NORTH WEST DIVISION
NORTHERN GOLDFIELDS
WESTERN AUSTRALIA
DIVISION
NORTHERN Coastal AGRICULTURAL Plains DIVISION
Basin
EASTERN GOLDFIELDS DIVISION
SOUTH WESTERN DIVISION
METROPOLITAN DIV.
PERTH
Fremantle
Guildford
Midland J.
Kalamunda
Rottnest I.
Armadale
Kwinana
Rockingham
Mandurah
Pinjarra
Harvey
Bunbury
Busselton
Donnybrook
Collie
Bridgetown
Greenbushes
Manjimup
Pemberton
Northcliffe
Augusta
Flinders B.
C. Leeuwin
C. Naturaliste
Geographe B.
C. Freycinet
Albany
King George Sound
Mt. Barker
Stirling Ra.
Katanning
Wagin
Narrogin
Pingelly
Beverley
York
Northam
Toodyay
Merredin
Kellerberrin
Southern Cross
Coolgardie
Kalgoorlie
Boulder
Kanowna
Norseman
Esperance
Esperance B.
Archo. of the Recherche
Ravensthorpe
Hopetoun
Doubtful I.B.
Cheyne B.
Menzies
Leonora
Laverton
Malcolm
Kookynie
Wiluna
Meekatharra
Cue
Mt. Magnet
Yalgoo
Mullewa
Geraldton
Northampton
Dongarra
Houtman Abrolhos
Moora
New Norcia
Gingin
Carnarvon
Shark Bay
Dirk Hartog I.
Onslow
North West C.
Exmouth G.
Roebourne
Port Hedland
Marble Bar
Nullagine
Dampier Archipelago
Barrow I.
Monte Bello Is.
Hamersley Range
Mt. Bruce 4024
Mt. Augustus 3634
Mt. Egerton
L. Disappointment
L. Carnegie
L. Wells
L. Barlee
L. Moore
L. Lefroy
L. Cowan
L. Dundas
L. Minigwal
The Johnston Lakes
Robinson Ras.
to Cape Town 4708
to Cape Town 4723
to Adelaide 1036
Colombo to Fremantle 3120
London to Fremantle 9537
to Djakarta 1772
to Singapore 2412
East from Greenwich
115
120
20
25
30
35

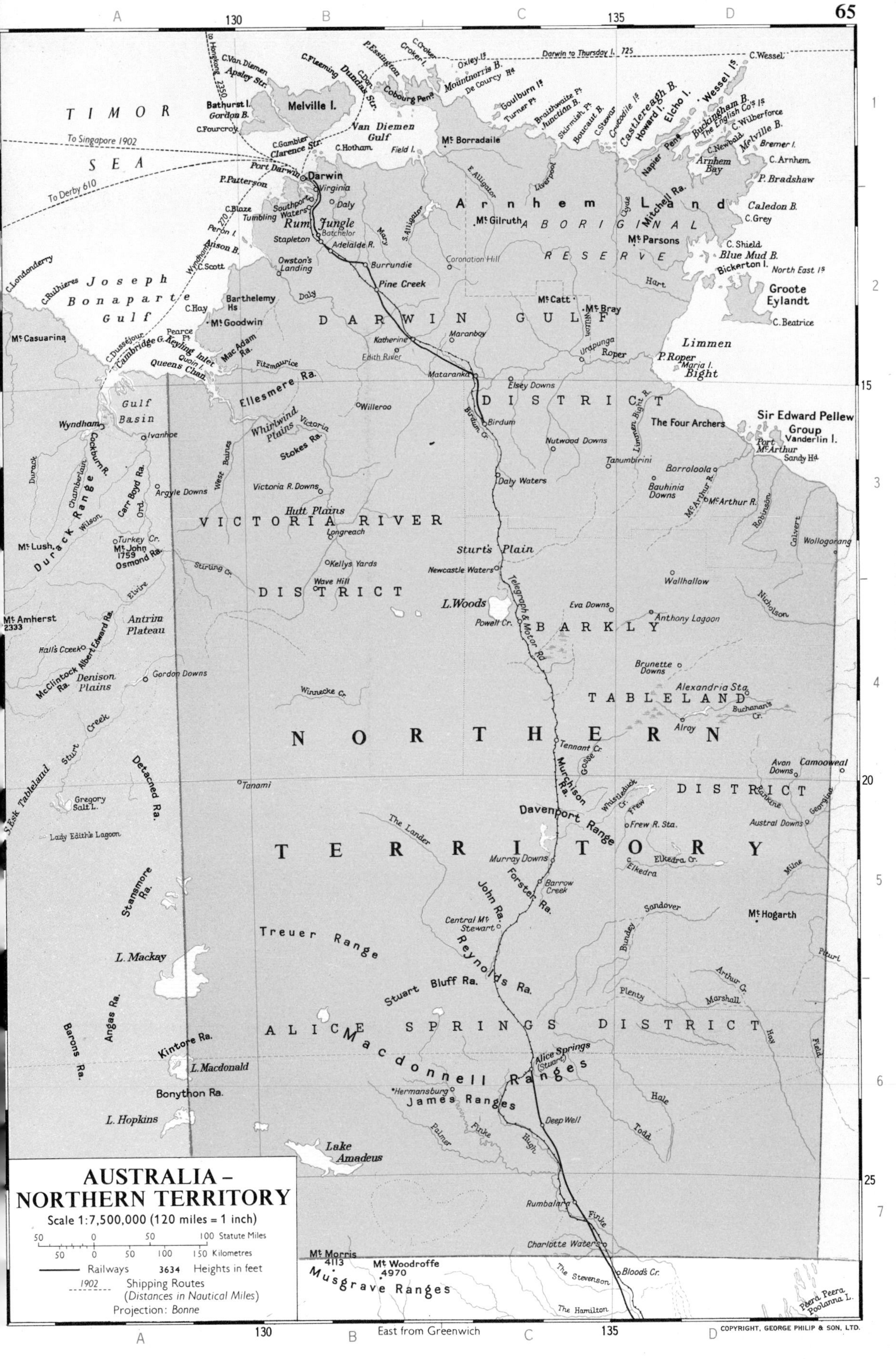
AUSTRALIA – NORTHERN TERRITORY
Scale 1:7,500,000 (120 miles = 1 inch)
Statute Miles
Kilometres
Railways
3634 Heights in feet
1902 Shipping Routes (Distances in Nautical Miles)
Projection: Bonne
East from Greenwich
TIMOR SEA
Darwin
Melville I.
Bathurst I.
Van Diemen Gulf
Arnhem Land
ABORIGINAL RESERVE
DARWIN GULF DISTRICT
VICTORIA RIVER DISTRICT
BARKLY TABLELAND DISTRICT
ALICE SPRINGS DISTRICT
NORTHERN TERRITORY
Joseph Bonaparte Gulf
Groote Eylandt
Limmen Bight
Sir Edward Pellew Group
Katherine
Pine Creek
Rum Jungle
Mataranka
Birdum
Daly Waters
Newcastle Waters
Tennant Cr.
Alice Springs (Stuart)
Macdonnell Ranges
James Ranges
Lake Amadeus
L. Mackay
L. Macdonald
Musgrave Ranges
Mt Woodroffe 4970
Mt Morris 4113
Wyndham
Camooweal
Borroloola
Telegraph & Motor Rd
To Singapore 1902
To Derby 610
Darwin to Thursday I. 725

T A S M A N
S E A
NORTH AUCKLAND
SOUTH AUCKLAND
C. Reinga
North C.
C. Maria van Diemen
Houhora
Rangaunu Bay
Doubtless Bay
Mangonui
Whangaroa Harb.
Ahipara B.
Kaitaia
Reef Pt.
B. of Islands
C. Brett
Opua
Rawene
Kaikohe
Hikurangi
Whangarei
Whangarei Harb.
Bream Hd.
Bream Bay
Hokianga Harb.
Donnelly's Crossing
Dargaville
Waipu
Lit. Barrier I.
Gt. Barrier I.
C. Rodney
C.Colville
Cuvier I.
Hauraki Gulf
Kaipara Harb.
Warkworth
Helensville
Takapuna
Devonport
Coromandel
Whitianga
Mt. Eden
AUCKLAND
Onehunga
Papakura
Thames
Pukekohe
Waiuku
Waikato
Mercer
Paeroa
Waihi
Mayor I.
Tauranga Harb.
Huntly
Te Aroha
Morrinsville
Mt. Maunganui
White I.
C. Runaway
Bay of Plenty
Te Puke
Tauranga
Raglan
Hamilton
Cambridge
Roto Rua
Kawerau
Whakatane
Opotiki
Raukumara Ra.
East C.
Kawhia Harb.
Te Awamutu
Otorohanga
Putaruru
Rotorua
L. Tarawera
Taneatua
Waipiro
Motuhora
Tolaga
GISBORNE
Tocoroa
Kinleith
Mokai
KAINGAROA STATE FOREST
Murupara
Te Kuiti
Mokau
L. Taupo
Ongarue
Taupo
Rangitaiki
Ormond
North Taranaki Bight
TARANAKI
Taumarunui
Kaimanawa Mts.
Waikaremoana
Gisborne
Poverty Bay
Waitara
New Plymouth
Inglewood
Whangamomona
Tarawera
Nuhaka
Waikokopu
Mt. Egmont 8260
C. Egmont
Stratford
Waimarino
Ruapehu 9175
Wairoa
Mahia Peninsula
Opunake
Eltham
Raetihi
Ohakune
Waiouru
Petane
Hawke Bay
Napier
Hawera
South Taranaki Bight
Patea
Waverley
Taihape
Mangaweka
Ruahine Ra.
HAWKE'S BAY
C. Kidnappers
Hastings
Wanganui
Hunterville
Waipawa
Marton
Bulls
Halcomb
Feilding
Waipukurau
Palmerston N.
Dannevirke
Foxton
Shannon
Woodville
Pahiatua
C. Farewell
Golden
C. Turnagain
A
B
C
D
E
F
G
168
170
172
174
176
178
1
2
3
36
38
40

NEW ZEALAND
Scale 1:4,500,000 (72 miles = 1 inch)
Statute Miles
Kilometres
Railways
Principal Roads
5140 Heights in feet
Projection: Conical with two standard parallels
East from Greenwich
P A C I F I C
O C E A N
WELLINGTON
Cook Strait
Petone
Lr. Hutt
Eastbourne
WELLINGTON
Carterton
Greytown
Martinborough
L. Wairarapa
Picton
Havelock
Blenheim
Seddon
Ward
Awatere
Kaikoura Ra.
9465 Taipugenuku
Clarence
Kaikoura
MARLBOROUGH
Nelson
Motueka
Richmond
Wakefield
Wairau
Tadmor
Murchison
Rotoroa
Lyell Ra.
Buller Gorge
Karamea Bight
Seddonville
Granity
Westport
Lyell
Inangahua
Mt. Travers • 7671
Mt. Franklyn • 7671
Spenser Mts.
Reefton
Blackhall
Runanga
Greymouth
Brunner
Kumara
Hokitika
Ross
Ahaura
Mt. Hochstetter 5140
Hanmer
Amuri P.
L. Brunner
Jackson
Otira Gorge
Arthur's Pass
Bealey
L. Coleridge
Waiau
Culverden
Waiai-uha
Hurunui
Waikari
Waipara
Amberley
Oxford
Waimakariri
Rangiora
Pegasus Bay
Kaiapoi
New Brighton
Christchurch
Lyttelton
Riccarton
Lincoln
Banks Peninsula
Akaroa
Little River
L. Ellesmere
Southbridge
Rakaia
Springfield
White Cliffs
Methven
Springburn
L. Tekapo
Rangitata
Plains
Ashburton
Canterbury Bight
Temuka
Timaru
St. Andrews
CANTERBURY
Abut Hd.
Okarito
Hochstetter Dome 9258
Mt. Cook 12,349
Tasman Glacier
Hermitage
Westland Bight
Jackson's B.
Okuru
Haast
WESTLAND
Southern Alps
Fairlie
Pukaki L.
Canterbury
Waitaki
Waimate
Kurow
Mt. Aspiring 9975
Ohau L.
L. Hawea
L. Wanaka
Mt. Earnslaw 9250
Milford Sd.
Mitre Peak 5560
Bligh Sd.
George Sd.
Sutherland Falls
Pembroke
Kinloch
Arrowtown
Dunstan Mts.
Cromwell
Queenstown
Wakatipu
Clyde
Alexandra
Naseby
Tokarahi
Ngapara
Kakanui Mts.
Oamaru
Maheno
Hampden
Dunback
Palmerston
Taieri
Waikouaiti
OTAGO
Secretary I.
Doubtful Sd.
SOUTHLAND
Kingston
L. Te Anau
L. Manapouri
Breaksea Sd.
Resolution I.
Dusky Sd.
Manapouri
Mossburn
Lumsden
Eyre Mts.
Garvie Mts.
Umbrella Mts.
Roxburgh
Clutha
Dunedin
Mosgiel
Port Chalmers
Otago Harbour
C. Saunders
West Harbour
St. Kilda
Green Island
Lawrence
Edievale
Kelso
Tapanui
Nightcaps
L. Poteriteri
Clifden
Tuatapere
Chalky Inlet
Preservation Inlet
Winton
Gore
Clinton
Milton
Balclutha
Kaitangata
Nugget Pt.
Hedgehope
Mataura
Wyndham
Te Waewae B.
Orepuki
Riverton
Invercargill
S. Invercargill
Tokanui
Owaka
Tahakopa
Waikawa Harb.
Bluff
Foveaux Str
Oban
Stewart I.
Port Pegasus
S.W. Cape
COPYRIGHT, GEORGE PHILIP & SON, LTD.

10 West from Greenwich 0 East from Greenwich

EUROPE
ATLANTIC OCEAN
Mediterranean Sea
Sahara
The Sudan
Guinea

C. Clear
London
English Channel
Paris
Seine
Loire
Bay of Biscay
C. Finisterre
Pyrenees
Ebro
Madrid
Tagus
PORTUGAL
Lisbon
C. St. Vincent
Strait of Gibraltar
Madeira
Casablanca
Marrakech
Toubkal 13,661
Great Atlas
Anti Atlas
Canary Islands
C. Juby
Elbe
Berlin
Vistula
Warsaw
Oder
Danube
Rhine
Rhone
Mt. Blanc 15,780
Alps
Vienna
Budapest
Carpathians
Dnestr
Dnepr
Don
Volga
Aral Sea
Caspian Sea
Caucasus
Elbrus 18,481
Black Sea
Istanbul
Danube
Dinaric Alps
Adriatic Sea
Apennines
Corsica
Rome
Sardinia
Tyrrhenian Sea
Balearic Islands
Algiers
Tunis
C. Bon
Sicily
Malta
Maritime Atlas
Plateau of the Shotts
Saharan Atlas
G. of Gabes
Tripoli
G. of Sidra
Athens
Crete
Rhodes
Cyprus
Tuz Golu
L. Van
L. Urmia
Elburz
Tehran
Tigris
Euphrates
Baghdad
Zagros
Syrian Desert
Persian Gulf
Alexandria
Cairo
Suez Canal
Arabian Desert
Nile
Libyan Desert
Red Sea
Tropic of Cancer
Mecca
Wadi Halfa
Nubian Desert
Port Sudan
Kamaran I.
Omdurman
Khartoum
Atbara
Massawa
Perim I.
Bay of Aden
C. Guardafui
Ras Dashan 15,158
L. Tana
White Nile
Blue Nile
Ethiopian Highlands
Addis Ababa
Bahr el Arab
Bahr el Ghazal
Bahr el Jebel
Webi
L. Stefanie
Ubangi
Ahaggar
Tibesti
C. Blanco
Adrar
Senegal
C. Verde
Niger
L. Chad
Shari
Kano
Fouta Djalon
Freetown
Volta
Ibadan
Lagos
Benue
Adamawa Highlands
Accra

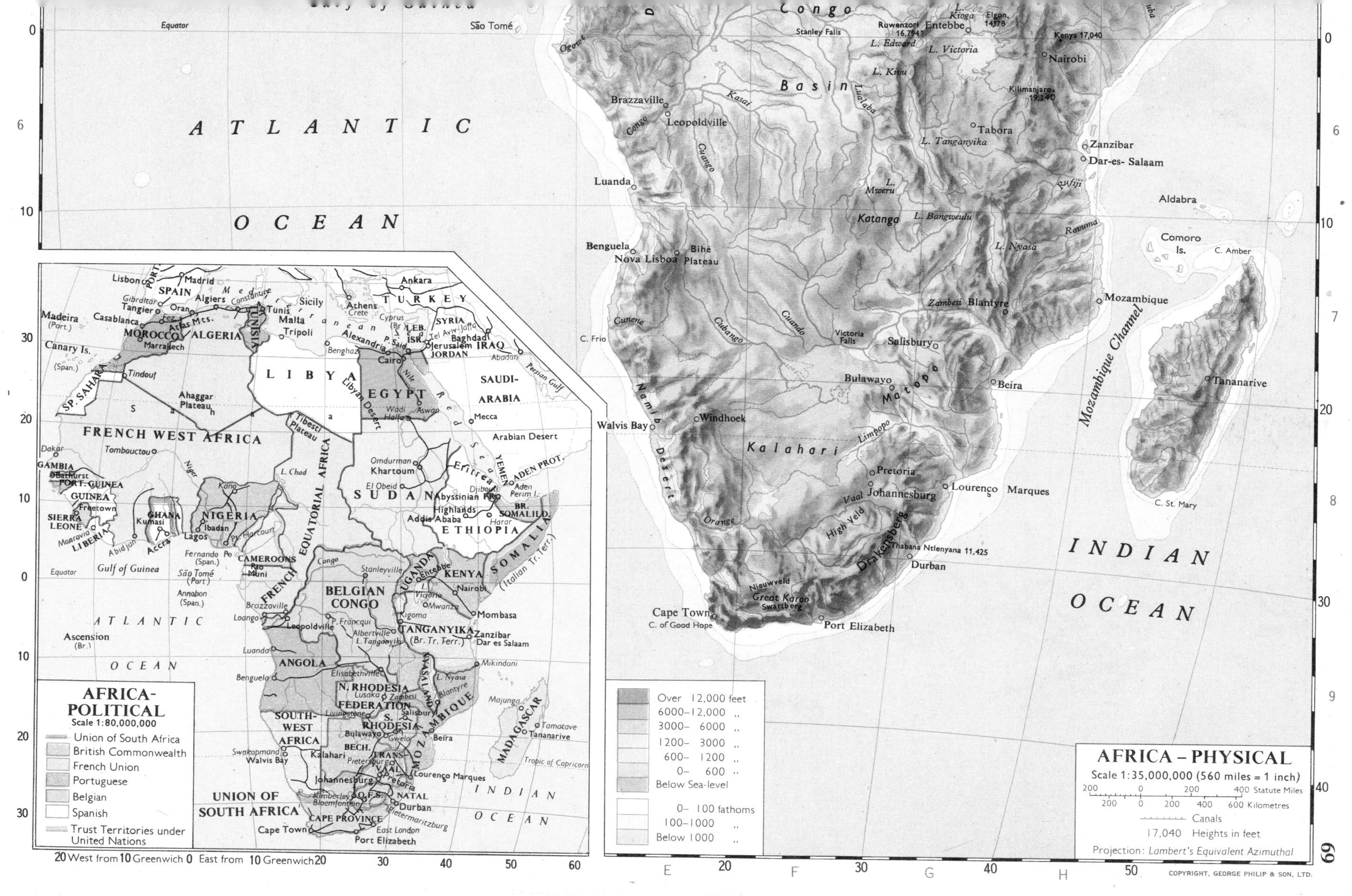
AFRICA – PHYSICAL
Scale 1:35,000,000 (560 miles = 1 inch)
200 0 200 400 Statute Miles
200 0 200 400 600 Kilometres
Canals
17,040 Heights in feet
Projection: Lambert's Equivalent Azimuthal
Over 12,000 feet
6000–12,000 ,,
3000– 6000 ,,
1200– 3000 ,,
600– 1200 ,,
0– 600 ,,
Below Sea-level
0– 100 fathoms
100–1000 ,,
Below 1000 ,,
ATLANTIC
OCEAN
INDIAN
OCEAN
Equator
São Tomé
Congo
Basin
Stanley Falls
Ruwenzori 16,794
Entebbe
L. Kioga
Elgon 14,178
Kenya 17,040
L. Edward
L. Victoria
Nairobi
L. Kivu
Kilimanjaro 19,340
Brazzaville
Leopoldville
Kasai
Lualaba
Tabora
L. Tanganyika
Zanzibar
Dar-es- Salaam
Luanda
Cuango
L. Mweru
Rufiji
Aldabra
Katanga
L. Bangweulu
Ruvuma
Comoro Is.
C. Amber
Benguela
Nova Lisboa
Bihé Plateau
L. Nyasa
Mozambique
Zambesi
Blantyre
Mozambique Channel
Cunene
C. Frio
Cubango
Cuando
Victoria Falls
Salisbury
Tananarive
Bulawayo
Matopo
Beira
Namib
Walvis Bay
Windhoek
Limpopo
Desert
Kalahari
Pretoria
Lourenço Marques
C. St. Mary
Vaal
Johannesburg
Orange
High Veld
Drakensberg
Thabana Ntlenyana 11,425
Durban
Nieuwveld
Great Karoo
Swartberg
Cape Town
C. of Good Hope
Port Elizabeth
E
F
G
H
AFRICA-POLITICAL
Scale 1:80,000,000
Union of South Africa
British Commonwealth
French Union
Portuguese
Belgian
Spanish
Trust Territories under United Nations
Lisbon
PORT.
Madrid
SPAIN
Gibraltar
Tangier
Oran
Algiers
Constantine
Tunis
Sicily
Malta
Tripoli
Athens
Crete
Cyprus
Ankara
TURKEY
SYRIA
LEB.
ISR.
Tel Aviv-Jaffa
Jerusalem
JORDAN
Baghdad
IRAQ
Abadan
Persian Gulf
Madeira (Port.)
Casablanca
MOROCCO
Atlas Mts.
ALGERIA
TUNISIA
Marrakech
Canary Is. (Span.)
Tindouf
SP. SAHARA
Benghazi
Alexandria
P. Said
Cairo
LIBYA
Libyan Desert
EGYPT
Nile
SAUDI-ARABIA
Ahaggar Plateau
Wadi Halfa
Aswan
Mecca
Tibesti Plateau
FRENCH WEST AFRICA
Arabian Desert
Dakar
Tombouctou
GAMBIA
Bathurst
PORT. GUINEA
GUINEA
Freetown
SIERRA LEONE
Monrovia
LIBERIA
Niger
L. Chad
Omdurman
Khartoum
El Obeid
SUDAN
Eritrea
YEMEN
ADEN PROT.
Aden
Perim I.
Djibouti
Abyssinian Highlands
Addis Ababa
ETHIOPIA
Harar
BR. SOMALILD.
Kano
NIGERIA
GHANA
Kumasi
Accra
Abidjan
Ibadan
Lagos
Pt. Harcourt
FRENCH EQUATORIAL AFRICA
Gulf of Guinea
Fernando Po (Span.)
CAMEROONS
Rio Muni
São Tomé (Port.)
Annobon (Span.)
SOMALIA (Italian Tr. Terr.)
UGANDA
Entebbe
KENYA
Stanleyville
Congo
BELGIAN CONGO
Victoria
Mwanza
Nairobi
Mombasa
Brazzaville
Loango
Leopoldville
P. Francqui
Albertville
L. Tanganyika
Kigoma
TANGANYIKA (Br. Tr. Terr.)
Zanzibar
Dar es Salaam
Ascension (Br.)
ATLANTIC
OCEAN
Luanda
ANGOLA
Mikindani
Benguela
Elisabethville
N. RHODESIA
Lusaka
Zambesi
NYASALAND
L. Nyasa
Blantyre
Livingstone
FEDERATION
Salisbury
S. RHODESIA
MOZAMBIQUE
Majunga
MADAGASCAR
Tamatave
Tananarive
SOUTH-WEST AFRICA
Swakopmund
Walvis Bay
Kalahari
Bulawayo
Gwelo
BECH.
Beira
TRANSVAAL
Pietersburg
Tropic of Capricorn
Johannesburg
Pretoria
Lourenço Marques
INDIAN
OCEAN
UNION OF SOUTH AFRICA
Kimberley
Bloemfontein
O.F.S.
NATAL
Durban
Pietermaritzburg
CAPE PROVINCE
East London
Cape Town
Port Elizabeth
20 West from 10 Greenwich 0 East from 10 Greenwich 20

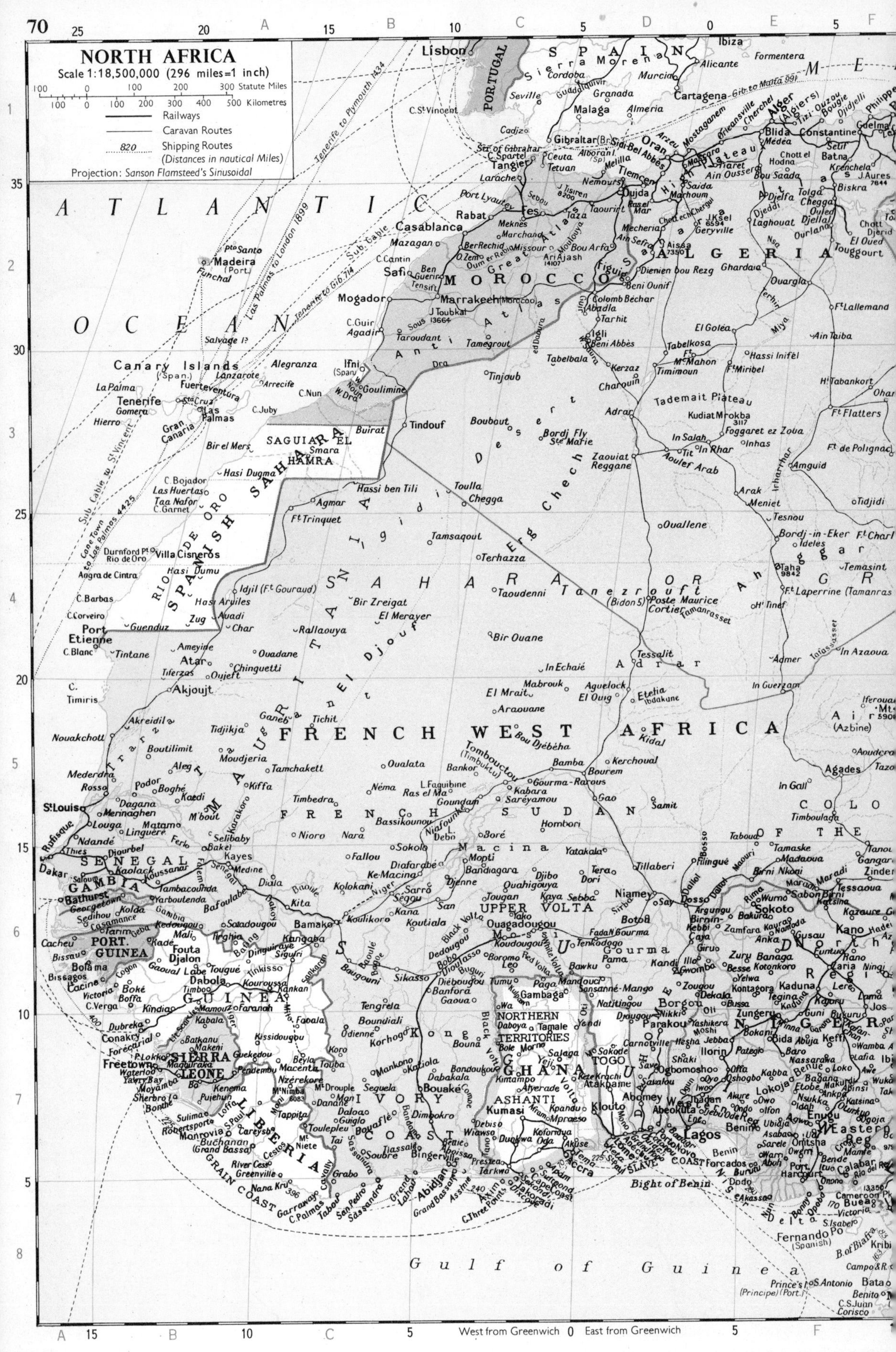
NORTH AFRICA
Scale 1:18,500,000 (296 miles=1 inch)
Statute Miles
Kilometres
Railways
Caravan Routes
Shipping Routes
(Distances in nautical Miles)
Projection: Sanson Flamsteed's Sinusoidal
ATLANTIC OCEAN
SPAIN
PORTUGAL
MOROCCO
ALGERIA
SPANISH SAHARA
RIO DE ORO
SAGUIA EL HAMRA
FRENCH WEST AFRICA
MAURITANIA
FRENCH SUDAN
SENEGAL
GAMBIA
PORT. GUINEA
GUINEA
SIERRA LEONE
LIBERIA
IVORY COAST
UPPER VOLTA
GHANA
TOGO
DAHOMEY
NIGERIA
NORTHERN TERRITORIES
ASHANTI
Gulf of Guinea
Bight of Benin
Canary Islands
Madeira
Lisbon
Casablanca
Dakar
Freetown
Monrovia
Accra
Lagos
Tombouctou (Timbuktu)
Bamako
Niamey
Ouagadougou
Kano
Alger (Algiers)
Oran
Fernando Po (Spanish)
West from Greenwich 0 East from Greenwich

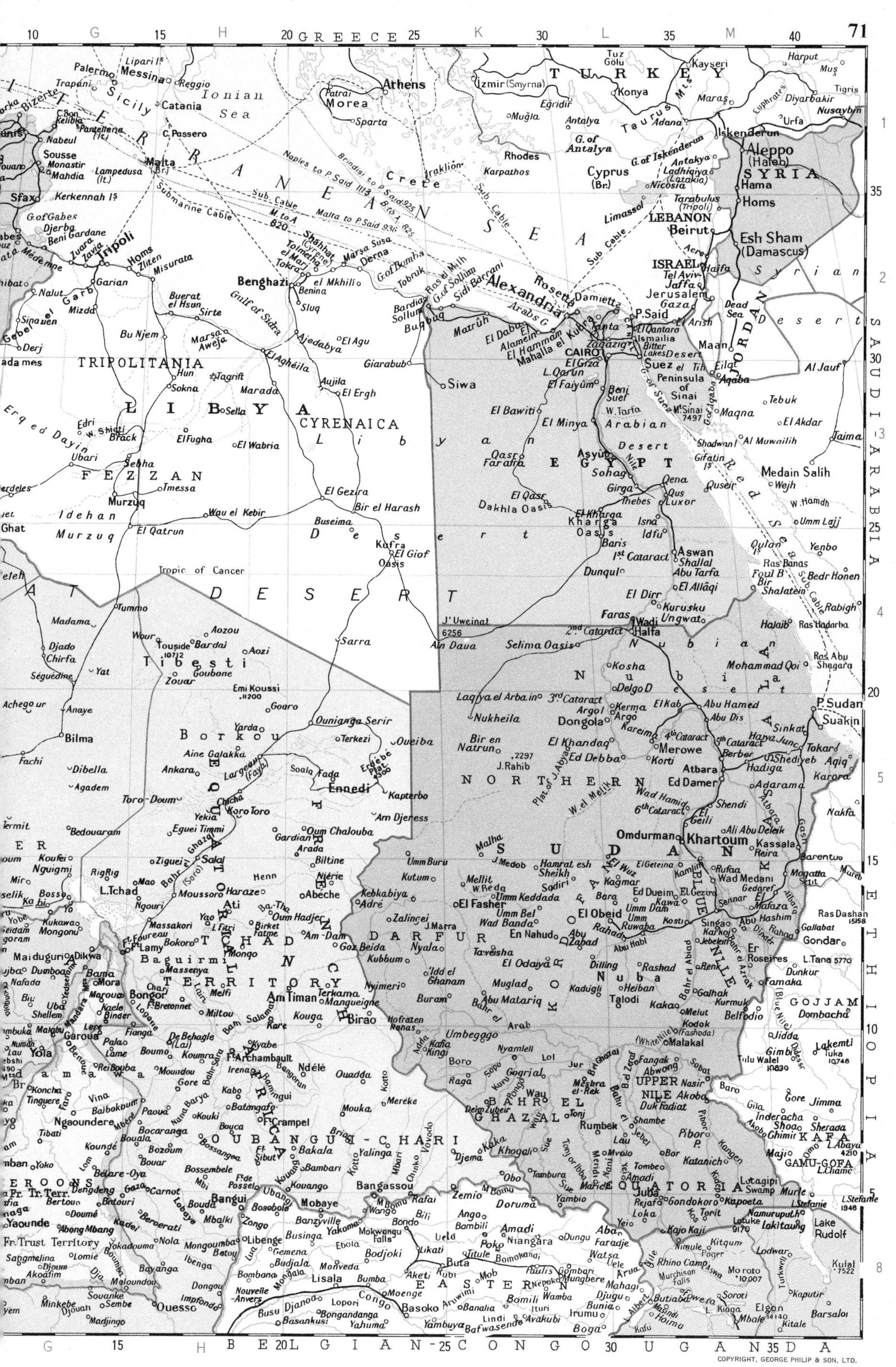

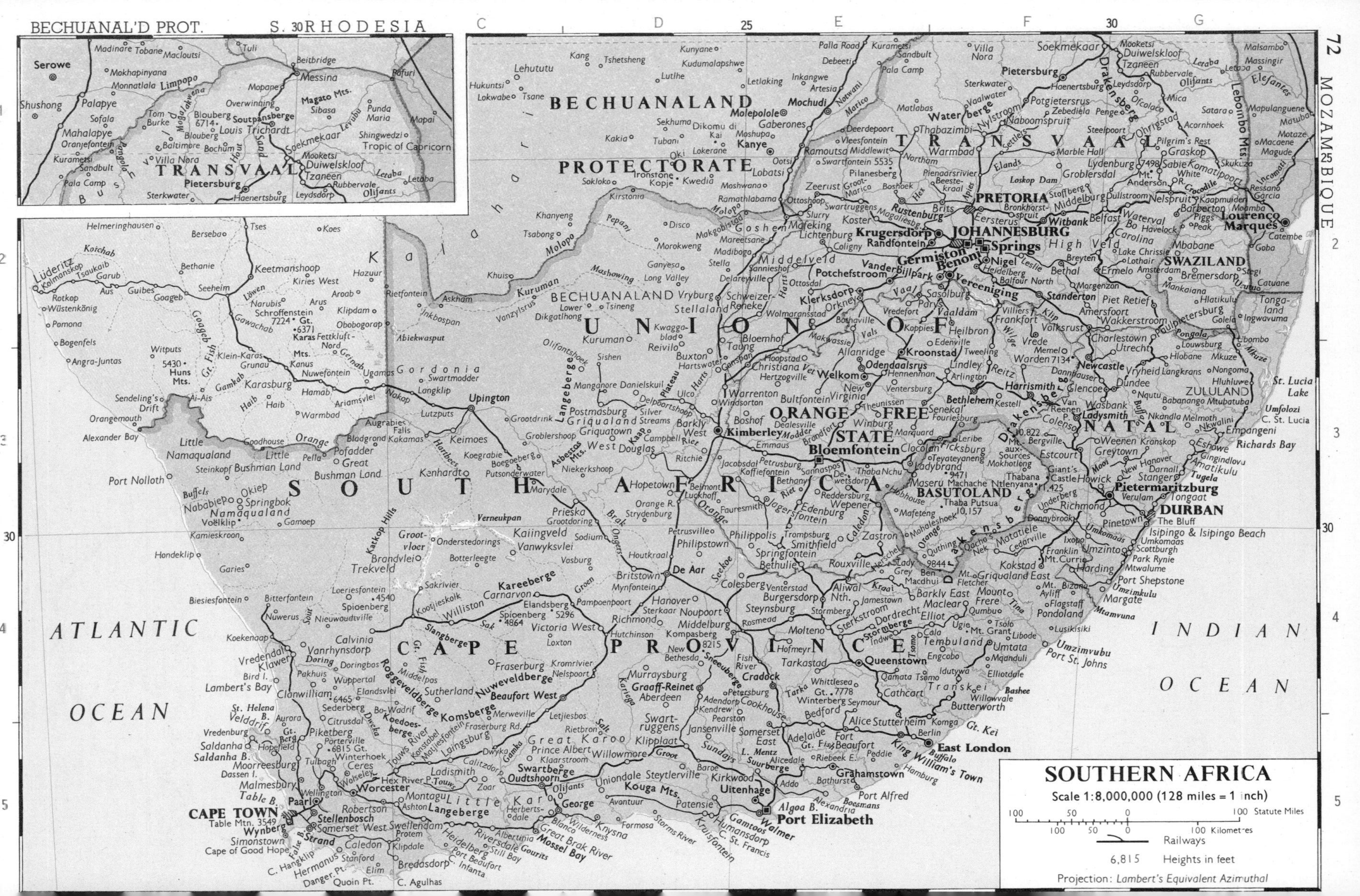
SOUTHERN AFRICA
Scale 1:8,000,000 (128 miles = 1 inch)
Statute Miles
Kilometres
Railways
6,815 Heights in feet
Projection: Lambert's Equivalent Azimuthal
BECHUANAL'D PROT.
S. RHODESIA
MOZAMBIQUE
TRANSVAAL
BECHUANALAND PROTECTORATE
UNION OF SOUTH AFRICA
ORANGE FREE STATE
BASUTOLAND
SWAZILAND
NATAL
ZULULAND
CAPE PROVINCE
ATLANTIC OCEAN
INDIAN OCEAN
Kalahari
Gordonia
Great Karoo
Little Karoo
Namaqualand
Bushman Land
High Veld
Drakensberg
Lebombo Mts.
Transkei
Griqualand West
Griqualand East
Tropic of Capricorn
PRETORIA
JOHANNESBURG
Bloemfontein
Kimberley
DURBAN
Pietermaritzburg
CAPE TOWN
Port Elizabeth
East London
Lourenço Marques
Pietersburg
Mafeking
Upington
De Aar
Beaufort West
Keetmanshoop
Lüderitz
Port Nolloth
Mossel Bay
George
Grahamstown
Queenstown
Maseru
Mbabane
C. Agulhas
Cape of Good Hope

EAST AFRICA
Scale 1:12,000,000 (190 miles=1 inch)
100 0 100 Statute Miles
100 0 100 200 Kilometres
Railways
17,040 Heights in feet
Projection: Lambert's Equivalent Azimuthal
East from Greenwich
COPYRIGHT, GEORGE PHILIP & SON, LTD.
UGANDA
KENYA
SOMALIA
BELGIAN CONGO
RUANDA-URUNDI
(Belgian Trust Territory)
TANGANYIKA
(British Trust Territory)
ZANZIBAR PROTECTORATE
KENYA PROT.
FEDERATION OF RHODESIA AND NYASALAND
NORTHERN RHODESIA
SOUTHERN RHODESIA
NYASALAND
MOZAMBIQUE
INDIAN OCEAN
Lake Victoria
Lake Tanganyika
Lake Nyasa
L. Mweru
L. Bangweulu
L. Rukwa
L. Albert
L. Edward
L. Kivu
L. Kyoga
Stanleyville
Kampala
Nairobi
Mombasa & Kilindini
Tanga
Dar-es-Salaam
Zanzibar & Island
Dodoma
Tabora
Mwanza
Elisabethville
Jadotville
Albertville
Ndola
Broken Hill
Lusaka
Livingstone
Salisbury
Bulawayo
Umtali
Beira
Blantyre
Zomba
Mozambique
Quelimane
Lindi
Mtwara
Kilimanjaro 19,340
Mt. Kenya 17,040
Meru 14,979

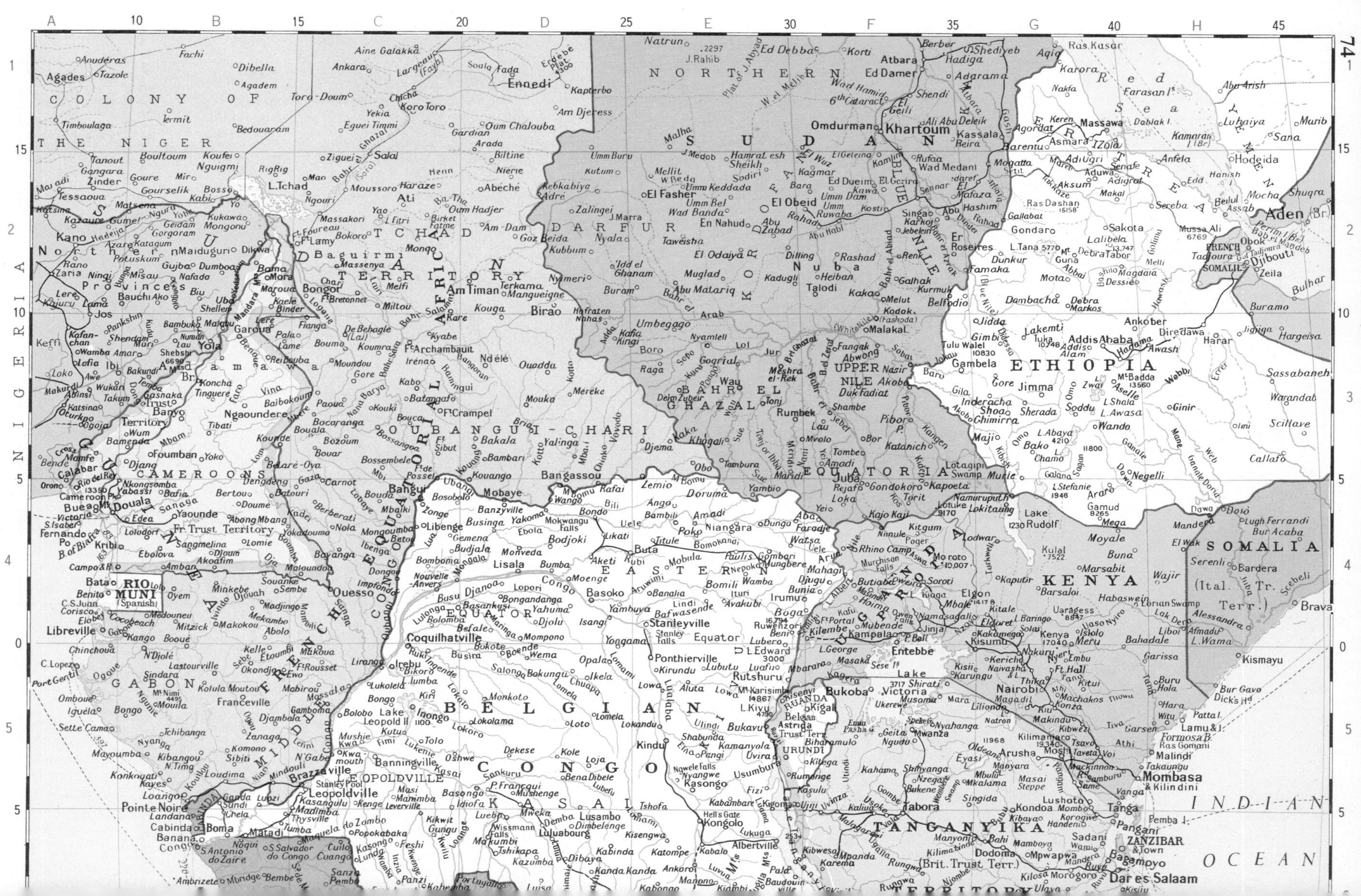
NORTHERN
SUDAN
DARFUR
KORDOFAN
UPPER NILE
BAHR EL GHAZAL
EQUATORIA
BLUE NILE
ETHIOPIA
KENYA
SOMALIA
(Ital. Tr. Terr.)
FRENCH SOMALIL.
UGANDA
TANGANYIKA
(Brit. Trust Terr.)
BELGIAN CONGO
EASTERN
EQUATOR
KASAI
LEOPOLDVILLE
RUANDA URUNDI
OUBANGUI-CHARI
GABON
CAMEROONS
RIO MUNI (Spanish)
NIGERIA
Northern Provinces
COLONY OF THE NIGER
TCHAD
Red Sea
INDIAN OCEAN
Khartoum
Omdurman
Atbara
Kassala
Wad Medani
El Obeid
El Fasher
Malakal
Juba
Wau
Addis Ababa
Asmara
Massawa
Djibouti
Aden
Harar
Gondaro
Jimma
Nairobi
Mombasa
Kampala
Entebbe
Dar es Salaam
ZANZIBAR
Tanga
Tabora
Dodoma
Kisumu
Stanleyville
Coquilhatville
Leopoldville
Brazzaville
Libreville
Pointe Noire
Douala
Yaounde
Bangui
Ft. Lamy
Kano
L.Tchad
Lake Rudolf
L.Albert
L.Edward
L.Kivu
L.Tana

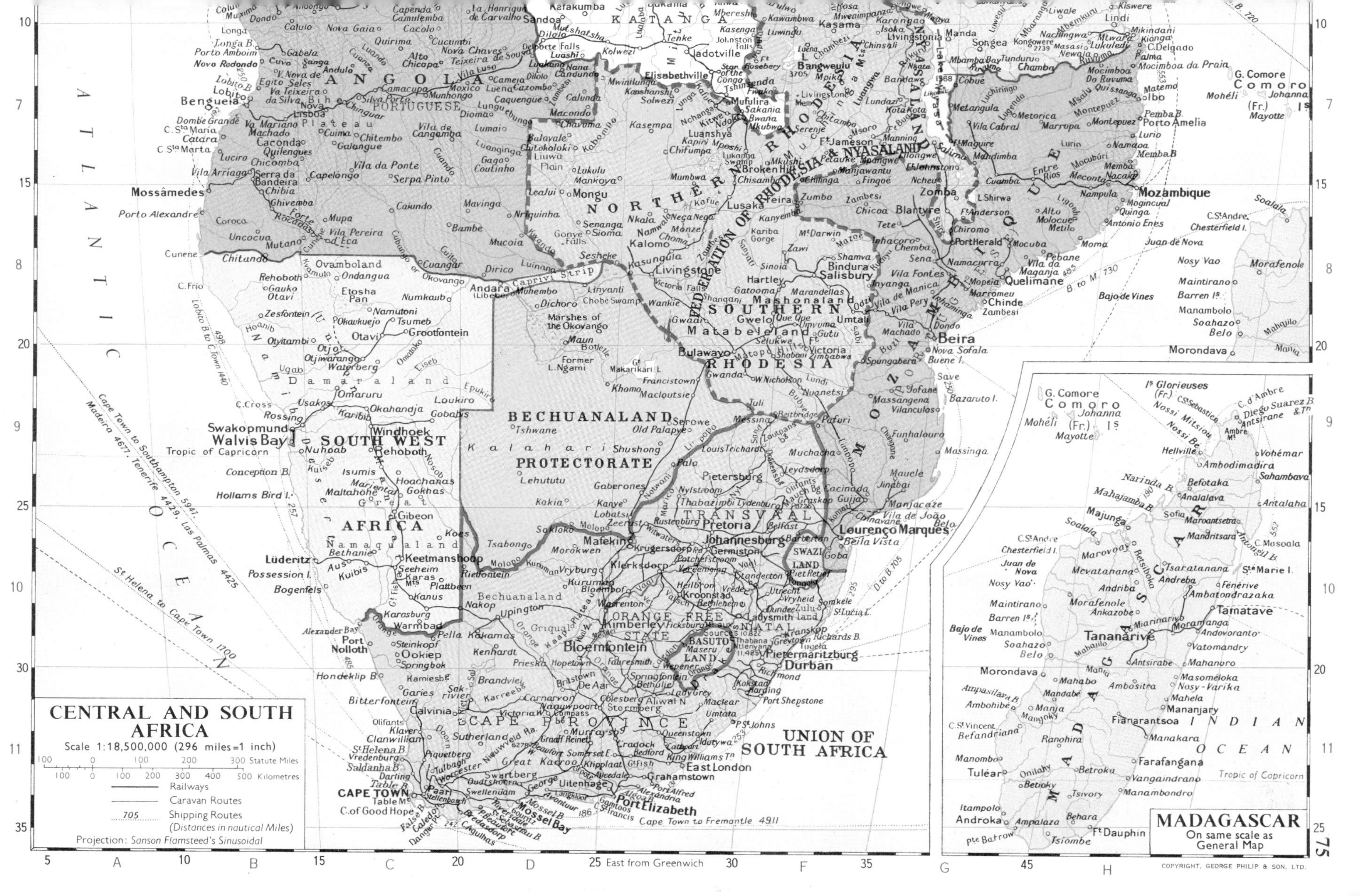
CENTRAL AND SOUTH AFRICA
Scale 1:18,500,000 (296 miles=1 inch)
Statute Miles
Kilometres
Railways
Caravan Routes
Shipping Routes (Distances in nautical Miles)
Projection: Sanson Flamsteed's Sinusoidal
MADAGASCAR
On same scale as General Map
East from Greenwich
ATLANTIC OCEAN
INDIAN OCEAN
ANGOLA
PORTUGUESE
KATANGA
NORTHERN RHODESIA
FEDERATION OF RHODESIA & NYASALAND
NYASALAND
SOUTHERN RHODESIA
Mashonaland
Matabeleland
MOZAMBIQUE
BECHUANALAND PROTECTORATE
Kalahari
SOUTH WEST AFRICA
Ovamboland
Damaraland
Namaqualand
Caprivi Strip
TRANSVAAL
ORANGE FREE STATE
NATAL
BASUTO LAND
SWAZI LAND
CAPE PROVINCE
UNION OF SOUTH AFRICA
Tropic of Capricorn
Cape Town to Southampton 5941
Madeira 4677, Tenerife 4429, Las Palmas 4425
St Helena to Cape Town 1700
Lobito B. to C. Town 1440
Cape Town to Fremantle 4911
Benguela
Lobito
Mossâmedes
Elisabethville
Jadotville
Lusaka
Broken Hill
Livingstone
Salisbury
Bulawayo
Umtali
Zomba
Blantyre
Beira
Quelimane
Mozambique
Lourenço Marques
Pretoria
Johannesburg
Bloemfontein
Kimberley
Mafeking
Pietermaritzburg
Durban
East London
Port Elizabeth
Mossel Bay
CAPE TOWN
C. of Good Hope
Windhoek
Swakopmund
Walvis Bay
Lüderitz
Keetmanshoop
Port Nolloth
Tananarive
Tamatave
Majunga
Fianarantsoa
Tuléar
Morondava
Ft Dauphin
G. Comore
Comoro (Fr.) Is
COPYRIGHT, GEORGE PHILIP & SON, LTD.

ARCTIC OCEAN
Wrangel I.
Bering Strait
St. Lawrence I.
Nunivak I.
C. Barrow
Beaufort Sea
C. Bathurst
Alaska
Yukon
Mt. McKinley 20,320
Mt. St. Elias 18,008
Mt. Logan 19,850
Kodiak I.
Gulf of Alaska
Axel Heiberg Land
Sverdrup Is.
Ellesmere I.
Kane Bay
Parry Is.
Queen Elizabeth Islands
Melville I.
M'Clure Strait
Viscount Melville Sound
Banks I.
Devon I.
Lancaster Sound
Somerset
Prince of Wales I.
Victoria I.
Gulf of Boothia
Greenland
Baffin Bay
Disko I.
Davis Strait
Godthaab
Julianehaab
C. Farewell
Denmark Strait
Reykjavik
Iceland
Baffin Island
Cumberland Sound
Foxe Basin
Foxe Channel
Arctic Circle
Frobisher Bay
Southampton I.
Hudson Strait
C. Chidley
C. Wolstenholme
Chesterfield Inlet
Great Bear L.
Back
Mackenzie
Great Slave L.
Dubawnt
Athabasca L.
Athabasca
Peace
Reindeer L.
Churchill
Nelson
Hudson Bay
Belcher Is.
C. Henrietta Maria
James Bay
Eastmain
Labrador
Hamilton Inlet
C. Charles
Belle Isle Strait
Newfoundland
St. John's
C. Race
Anticosti
Gulf of St. Lawrence
C. Breton I.
Pr. Edward I.
St. Lawrence
Laurentian Plateau
Quebec
Saint John
Nova Scotia
Halifax
Sable I.
C. Sable
Bay of Fundy
White Mts. 6293
Montreal
L. Champlain
Ottawa
C. Cod
Nantucket I.
Long I.
New York
Philadelphia
Washington
L. Huron
Toronto
L. Ontario
Niagara Falls
Hamilton
L. Erie
Detroit
L. Michigan
Chicago
L. Superior
Minneapolis
Mississippi
Lake Winnipeg
Winnipeg
Regina
Queen Charlotte Islands
Queen Charlotte Sound
Coast Range
Stikine
Skeena
Mt. Waddington
Fraser
ROCKY MOUNTAINS
GREAT PLAINS
Robson Pk. 12,972
Yellowhead Pass
Edmonton
N. Saskatchewan
Kicking Horse Pass
Calgary
S. Saskatchewan
Selkirk Mts.
Crowsnest Pass
Missouri
Vancouver I.
Vancouver
Juan de Fuca Strait
C. Flattery
Seattle
Mt. Rainier 14,408
Portland
Columbia
Cascade Range
C. Blanco
C. Mendocino
Coast Range
Mt. Shasta 14,162
Sierra
Snake
Great Salt Lake
N. Platte
Platte
San Francisco
PACIFIC OCEAN

NORTH AMERICA – PHYSICAL
Scale 1:30,000,000 (480 miles = 1 inch)
100 0 100 200 300 400 500 Statute Miles
100 0 200 400 600 800 Kilometres
19,344 Heights in feet
Projection: Bonne
Over 12,000 feet
6000–12,000 ,,
3000– 6000 ,,
1200– 3000 ,,
600– 1200 ,,
0– 600 ,,
Below Sea-level
0– 100 fathoms
100–1000 ,,
Below 1000 ,,
ATLANTIC OCEAN
PACIFIC OCEAN
Gulf of Mexico
Caribbean Sea
West Indies
Greater Antilles
Bahama Islands
Cuba
Havana
Jamaica
Hispaniola
Port au Prince
Puerto Rico
Florida
Florida Strait
C. Sable
Yucatan Strait
C. Catoche
Yucatan
Gulf of Campêche
Gulf of Honduras
C. Gracias á Dios
Sierra Madre
Lower California
Gulf of California
C. San Lucas
C. Corrientes
Guadalupe
Pta. Eugenia
Los Angeles
Colorado
Colorado Plateau
Llano Estacado
Rio Grande del Norte
Monterrey
Guadalajara
Mexico City
Popocatepetl 17,887
Puebla
Citlaltepetl 18,700
Balsas
G. of Tehuantepec
Vol Fuego 12,582
Guatemala
L. Nicaragua
Vol Irazu 11,260
G. of Panama
G. of Darien
Coco I.
Malpelo
C. Corrientes
Houston
Dallas
Red
Arkansas
Ozark Plateau
Mississippi
Memphis
Alabama
New Orleans
Atlanta
Blue Ridge
Sa. Nevada de S. Marta 18,947
G. of Venezuela
L. Maracaibo
Sierra de Merida
Magdalena
Tolima 18,438
Orinoco
Guaviare
Caquetá
Napo
Cotopaxi 19,344
Chimborazo 20,577
Guayaquil
G. of Guayaquil
Marañon
C. San Francisco
Equator
Tropic of Cancer
West from Greenwich
NORTH AMERICA POLITICAL
Scale 1:67,000,000
ARCTIC OCEAN
CANADA
UNITED STATES
MEXICO
CENTRAL AMERICA
WEST INDIES
Hudson Bay
Baffin I.
Banks I.
Victoria I.
Alaska
Alaska Ra.
Fairbanks
Anchorage
Ft. Yukon
Aklavik
Coppermine
Mackenzie
Gt. Bear L.
Gt. Slave L.
Skagway
Queen Charlotte Is.
Kitimat
Pr. George
Cascade Ra.
Edmonton
Calgary
Kamloops
Vancouver
Seattle
Portland
Spokane
Saskatoon
Regina
Winnipeg
L. Winnipeg
Churchill
Schefferville
Laurentian Plateau
Sept-Iles
Newfoundland
St. John's
Cape Breton I.
Halifax
Saint John
St. Lawrence
Quebec
Montreal
Ottawa
Toronto
Sudbury
Pt. Arthur
Ft. William
L. Superior
Hamilton
Buffalo
Detroit
Cleveland
Pittsburgh
Boston
Providence
New York
Philadelphia
Baltimore
Washington
Appalachians
Missouri
Minneapolis
Milwaukee
Chicago
L. Michigan
Sioux City
Omaha
Kansas City
Indianapolis
Columbus
Cincinnati
Louisville
Ohio
St. Louis
Mississippi
Memphis
Atlanta
Birmingham
Charleston
Jacksonville
Florida
Miami
Mobile
New Orleans
Houston
Galveston
Dallas
Fort Worth
Oklahoma City
Denver
Salt Lake City
Great Basin
Pocatello
Sierra Nevada
Sacramento
Oakland
San Francisco
Los Angeles
San Diego
Phoenix
Albuquerque
Santa Fe
San Antonio
Hermosillo
Lower California
G. of California
La Paz
Sierra Madre
Monterrey
Guadalajara
Manzanillo
Mexico
Veracruz
Merida
Gulf of Mexico
Havana
Cuba
Nassau
Bahama Is. (Br.)
Bermuda (Br.)
Hispaniola
Haiti
Dom. Rep.
Pto. Rico
Port au Prince
Jamaica (W.I.)
Kingston
Greater Antilles
Caribbean Sea
BR. HOND.
GUAT.
HONDURAS
SAL.
San Salvador
NICARAGUA
COSTA RICA
San José
Colon
PANAMA
Panama
COL.
VENEZUELA
Maracaibo
PACIFIC OCEAN
ATLANTIC OCEAN
Tropic of Cancer
West from 100 Greenwich

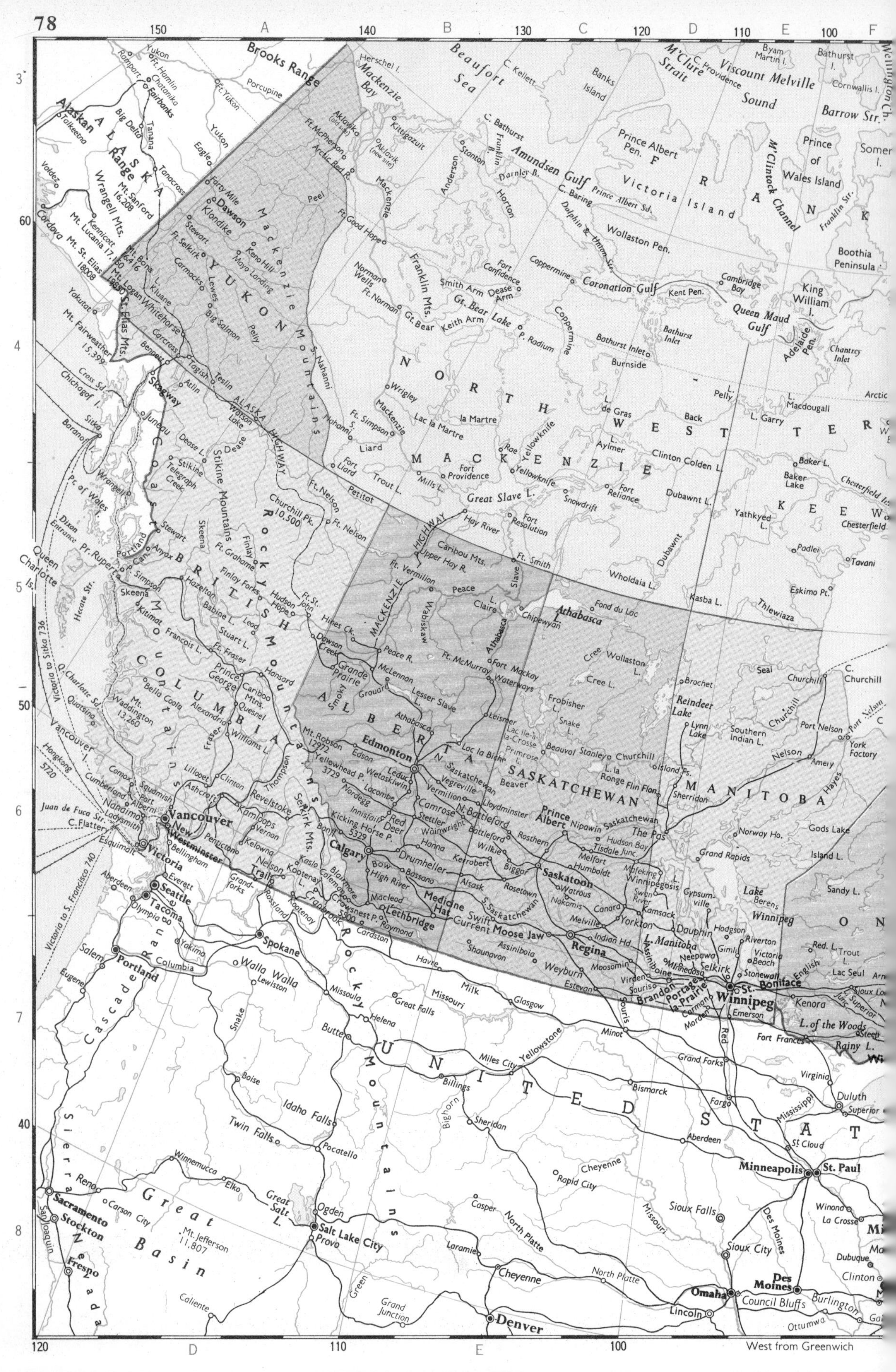

Brooks Range
Beaufort Sea
Mackenzie Bay
Banks Island
M'Clure Strait
Viscount Melville Sound
Prince Albert Pen.
Victoria Island
Amundsen Gulf
Coronation Gulf
Queen Maud Gulf
Gt. Bear Lake
Great Slave L.
Athabasca L.
Reindeer Lake
ALASKA
YUKON
Mackenzie Mountains
NORTH WEST TERRITORIES
MACKENZIE
KEEWATIN
BRITISH COLUMBIA
Coast Mountains
Rocky Mountains
ALBERTA
SASKATCHEWAN
MANITOBA
ALASKA HIGHWAY
MACKENZIE HIGHWAY
Dawson
Whitehorse
Fairbanks
Prince Rupert
Prince George
Vancouver
Victoria
Seattle
Tacoma
Portland
Spokane
Edmonton
Calgary
Lethbridge
Medicine Hat
Moose Jaw
Regina
Saskatoon
Prince Albert
Winnipeg
St. Boniface
L. Winnipeg
L. of the Woods
UNITED STATES
Cascade Range
Sierra Nevada
Great Basin
Salt Lake City
Ogden
Great Salt L.
Denver
Cheyenne
Omaha
Minneapolis
St. Paul
Des Moines
Duluth
Sioux Falls
Sioux City
Bismarck
Sacramento
Stockton
Fresno
Reno
West from Greenwich

CANADA
Scale 1:17,500,000 (280 miles = 1 inch)
100 50 0 100 200 Statute Miles
100 0 100 200 300 Kilometres
Railways
Canals
946 Shipping Routes
(Distances in Nautical Miles)
3206 Heights in feet
Projection: Bonne
GREENLAND
ATLANTIC OCEAN
Baffin Bay
Baffin Island
Davis Strait
Hudson Strait
Hudson Bay
Foxe Basin
Foxe Channel
Ungava Bay
Frobisher Bay
Cumberland Sd.
Cumberland Peninsula
Lancaster Sound
Bylot I.
Pond Inlet
Scott Inlet
C. Aston
Home B.
C. Dyer
Hoare B.
C. Mercy
Resolution I.
C. Chidley
Akpatok I.
Digges Is.
Mansel I.
Coats I.
Southampton I.
Bell Pen.
Melville Peninsula
Fury & Hecla Str.
Prince Charles I.
Nettilling L.
Amadjuak L.
Amadjuak
Foxe Penin.
C. Dorchester
C. Horsburgh
Upernavik
Disko I.
Disko B.
Godhavn
Jacobshavn
Christianshaab
Egedesminde
Søndre Strømfjord
Holsteinsborg
Sukkertoppen
Godthaab
Fiskenaesset
Frederikshaab
Ivigtut
Julianehaab
Sydpröven
C. Farewell
Angmagssalik
King Christian IX's Land
Mt. Forel 11,100
King Frederick VI Coast
Ûmánaq Fd.
Churchill to Liverpool 2956
P. Nelson to Liverpool 2966
QUEBEC
LABRADOR
NEWFOUNDLAND
NEW BRUNSWICK
NOVA SCOTIA
PR. EDWARD I.
ONTARIO
Gulf of St. Lawrence
James Bay
Lake Superior
Lake Huron
L. Michigan
L. Ontario
Lake Erie
Georgian Bay
L. Champlain
MONTREAL
Quebec
Ottawa
Toronto
Hull
Three Rivers
Sherbrooke
St. Hyacinthe
Sorel
Joliette
Shawinigan Fs.
La Tuque
Levis
Thetford Mines
Chicoutimi
Jonquière
Roberval
Dolbeau
L. St. John
Saguenay
Tadoussac
Rivière du Loup
Rimouski
Matane
Gaspé
Gaspé Pen.
Campbellton
Dalhousie
Bathurst
Chatham
Newcastle
Moncton
Fredericton
Saint John
Woodstock
Edmundston
Perth
Amherst
Springhill
Truro
New Glasgow
Pictou
Halifax
Dartmouth
Windsor
Kentville
Digby
Yarmouth
Bridgewater
Liverpool
Shelburne
C. Sable
Sydney
Glace Bay
Cape Breton I.
Port Hawkesbury
Mulgrave
C. Canso
C. North
Charlottetown
Summerside
Tignish
Magdalen Is.
Cabot Str.
Anticosti I.
C. Gaspé
St. John's
Corner Brook
Grand Falls
Gander
Lewisporte
Twillingate
Bonavista
Carbonear
Harbour Grace
Bell I.
Placentia
Trepassey
C. Race
P. aux Basques
C. Ray
Millertown
Millertown Jc.
Miquelon I. (Fr.)
St. Pierre I. (Fr.)
Belle Isle
C. Bauld
Str. of Belle Isle
Notre Dame B.
Trinity B.
Battle Harb.
Cartwright
Rigolet
Goose
Hamilton
L. Melville
North West R.
Michikamau L.
Grand Falls
Hopedale
Nain
Zoar
Nutak
Hebron
C. Harrison
Indian Harb.
Domino Harb.
Schefferville
Burnt Creek
Dyke L.
Petitsikapau
Lobstick L.
Ashuanipi L.
Lac Joseph
Moisie
Sept Iles
Mingan
Natashquan
Romaine
St. Augustin
Ft. Chimo
Koksoak
George R.
Whale
Kaniapiskau
Leaf
Larch
L. Minto
Lower Seal L.
Upper Seal L.
Lac Bienville
Clearwater L.
Gt. Whale
Kanaaupscow
Ft. George
Nitchequon L.
Eastmain
Rupert House
Rupert
L. Evans
Mistassini
Albanel L.
Peribonca
Bersimis
Manicouagan
Baie Comeau
Betsiamites
Chibougamau
Nottaway
Harricanaw
Gouin Reservoir
Cabonga Reservoir
Mattagami
Abitibi
Cochrane
Timmins
Kirkland Lake
Rouyn
Taschereau
Senneterre
Doucet
Weymont
St. Maurice
Englehart
Haileybury
Cobalt
L. Timiskaming
Sudbury
North Bay
Coppercliff
Sault Ste. Marie
Michipicoten Hr.
Franz
Heron Bay
Oba
Hearst
Kenogami
Nakina
Longlac
Moosonee
Moose
Missinaibi
Albany
Ft. Albany
Kapiskau
Attawapiskat
Winisk
Sutton L.
Akimiski I.
Twin Is.
Charlton I.
C. Henrietta Maria
C. Jones
Belcher Is.
Baker's Dozen
King George Is.
The Sleepers
Portland Promontory
Port Harrison
Ottawa Is.
Payne L.
Payne
Kingwa
Kovik
Wakeham Bay
Pembroke
Arnprior
Chalk River
Parry Sound
Peterboro'
Belleville
Kingston
Cobourg
Oshawa
Orillia
Owen Sound
Guelph
Kitchener
Stratford
London
Brantford
Hamilton
Niagara Falls
Sarnia
Chatham
Windsor
DETROIT
Toledo
Cleveland
Erie
Buffalo
Jamestown
Rochester
Syracuse
Utica
Albany
Binghamton
Elmira
Scranton
Allentown
Trenton
Philadelphia
Wilmington
Harrisburg
Pittsburg
Youngstown
Akron
Canton
NEW YORK
New Haven
Hartford
Springfield
Worcester
Boston
Providence
C. Cod
Lowell
Manchester
Portland
Lewiston
Augusta
Bangor
Burlington
Granby
Lachine
Cornwall
Saginaw
Muskegon
Grand Rapids
Kalamazoo
Racine
South Bend
Ft. Wayne
Mackinaw
B. of Fundy
Northumberland Str.
Quebec to Glasgow 2558
Liverpool 2625
Montreal to Southampton 2907
St. John's to Liverpool 1926
Quebec to Liverpool 2872
Halifax to St. John's 540
Halifax to St. Johns 540
New York to Liverpool 3043, Southampton 3117
New York to Gibraltar 3206, Genoa 4054, Naples 4176
Boston to Halifax 369
New York to Halifax 599
Halifax to Bermuda 760
Sub. Cable
G 80 H 70 J 60 K 50 L 40 M 30 2
3 60 4 5 50 6 7 40 8
G 80 H 70 J

BRITISH COLUMBIA
ALBERTA
SASKATCHEWAN
CANADA
PACIFIC OCEAN
WASHINGTON
OREGON
IDAHO
MONTANA
WYOMING
NORTH DAKOTA
SOUTH DAKOTA
NEBRASKA
CALIFORNIA
NEVADA
UTAH
COLORADO
ARIZONA
NEW MEXICO
TEXAS
KANSAS
MEXICO
SONORA
CHIHUAHUA
COAHUILA
LOWER CALIFORNIA
Gulf of California
Great Basin
Rocky Mountains
Sierra Nevada
Sierra Madre
Coast Range
Lesser Slave Lake
Lac Île à la Crosse
Primrose Lake
Snake Lake
Churchill
Flin Flon
Sherridon
Lac la Ronge
Moose Lake
Cedar L.
Reindeer L.
Edmonton
Athabasca
Beaver
Queen Charlotte Sound
Moresby I.
Ocean Falls
Prince George
Fraser
Cariboo Mts.
Quesnal Lake
Jasper
Leduc
Vegreville
N. Saskatchewan
Lloydminster
North Battleford
Prince Albert
The Pas
Mt. Waddington 13,260
Clinton
Ashcroft
Red Deer
Penhold
Drumheller
Saskatoon
Rosthern
Melfort
Hudson Bay
Mafeking
Swan Lake
Swan River
Lake Winnipegosis
Duck Mt.
Campbell River
Kamloops
Lytton
Vernon
Upper Arrow Lake
Columbia
Mt. Assiniboine 11,500
Banff
Calgary
Gleichen
Quill Lakes
Assiniboine
Vancouver Is.
Union
Jervis Inlet
Str. of Georgia
Vancouver
New Westminster
Barkley Sd.
Juan de Fuca Str.
Esquimalt
Victoria
C. Flattery
Hope
Mt. Baker 10,750
Bellingham
Grand Forks
Lower Arrow Lake
Kootenay Lake
Nelson
Trail
Rossland
Steele
Fernie
Crow's Nest Pass 4,460
Macleod
Belly
Lethbridge
Raymond
Bow
South Saskatchewan
Medicine Hat
Swift Current
Maple Creek
Moose Jaw
Regina
Last Mountain Lake
Indian Head
Qu'appelle
L. Manitoba
Minnedosa
Neepawa
Moosomin
Moose Mt.
Virden
Brandon
Boissevain
Olympic Mts.
Puget Sd.
Everett
Seattle
Tacoma
Olympia
Greys Harb.
Aberdeen
Cape Disappointment
Lake Chelan
Wenatchee
Spokane
Sandpoint
Lake Pend Oreille
Kalispell
Glacier Nat. Park
Lewis Range
Milk
Wood Mt.
Marias
Teton
Havre
Missouri
Great Falls
Fort Peck Reservoir
Big Muddy
Plateau du Coteau du Missouri
Williston
Minot
Souris
Devils Lake
Mt. Rainier 14,408
Mt. Adams 12,470
Ellensburg
Columbia Plateau
Yakima
Pasco
Kennewick
Kellogg
Moscow
Lewiston
Clearwater
Bitter Root Mts.
Clark Fork
Missoula
Helena
Big Belt Mts.
Lewistown
Musselshell
Glendive
Miles City
Yellowstone
Mandan
Bismarck
Jamestown
Dickinson
Cannon Ball
Astoria
St. Helens
Portland
McMinnville
C. Foulweather
Mt. Hood 11,253
The Dalles
Pendleton
Walla Walla
Blue Mountains
La Grande
Grangeville
Salmon
Anaconda
Butte
Bozeman
Livingston
Billings
Big Horn
Tongue
Powder
Little Missouri
Grand
Mobridge
Moreau
Owl
Salem
Albany
Corvallis
John Day
Deschutes
Eugene
Springfield
North Bend
C. Blanco
Bend
Baker
Roseburg
Mt. Thielsen 9,178
Umpqua Mts.
Rogue
Grants Pass
Harney L.
Summer L.
Malheur L.
Owyhee
Payette
Caldwell
Nampa
Boise
Hyndman Pk. 12,078
Hailey
Salmon Riv. Mts.
Yellowstone National Park
Absaroka Range
Big Horn Mts.
Sheridan
Buffalo
Belle Fourche
Black Hills
Rapid City
Bad Lands
Cheyenne
Pierre
White
Mitchell
St. Anthony
Rexburg
Teton Mt. 13,766
Idaho Falls
Blackfoot
Pocatello
Gannett Pk. 13,785
Wind River Mts.
Klamath L.
Klamath Falls
Goose L.
Humboldt Bay
Eureka
C. Mendocino
Mt. Shasta 14,162
Pit
Rupert
Burley
Malad City
Preston
Bear L.
Logan
Brigham
Casper
South Pass
Pathfinder Res.
Rawlins
Laramie Mts.
Chadron
Niobrara
Redding
Mt. Lassen 10,465
Mt. Linn 8,600
Honey L.
Winnemucca
Humboldt
Elko
Great Salt Lake
Ogden
Rock Springs
Green
Laramie
Evans Pass
North Platte
Scotts Bluff
Alliance
Arena Pt.
Ukiah
Chico
Pyramid L.
Reno
Marysville
Carson Sink
Sparks
Carson City
Tahoe
Pyramid Pk. 10,020
Salt Lake City
Tooele
Great Salt Lake Desert
Utah L.
Spanish Fork
Provo
Springville
Uinta Mts.
Yampa
Fort Collins
Greeley
Cheyenne
Sidney
Sterling
South Platte
Grand Island
Santa Rosa
Sacramento
Vallejo
Richmond
Golden Gate
San Francisco
Berkeley
Oakland
San Mateo
Santa Cruz
San Jose
Monterey
Salinas
Stockton
Yosemite National Park
Merced
Mt. Lyell 13,090
White Mt. 14,242
Walker Lake
Candelaria
Hot Creek Ra.
Tonopah
Goldfield
Wheeler Pk. 13,055
Nephi
Sevier
Sevier L.
Manti
Richfield
Price
Grand Junction
Park Range
Mt. Elbert 14,431
Leadville
Longmont
Boulder
Denver
Fort Morgan
McCook
Republican
Goodland
Beloit
Fresno
San Joaquin
Hanford
Visalia
Sequoia Nat. Park
Tulare
Mt. Whitney 14,495
Owens Lake
Death Valley -276
Las Vegas
Virgin
Lake Mead
Cedar City
Zion Nat. Park
St. George
Colorado
Abajo Pk. 11,446
Montrose
Gunnison
Sawatch Mts.
Pikes Pk. 14,110
Colorado Springs
Canon City
Pueblo
Salida
Arkansas
La Junta
Smoky Hill
Hays
Garden City
Dodge City
Gt. Bend
McPherson
Hutchinson
Pratt
Sa. Santa Lucia
San Luis Obispo
Bakersfield
Tehachapi Pass
C. Concepcion
Santa Barbara
Grand Canyon Nat. Park
Colorado Plateau
Painted Desert
Roof Butte 9,575
San Juan
San Juan Mts.
Durango
Alamosa
Sangre de Cristo Mts.
Blanca Pk. 14,363
Walsenburg
Trinidad
Raton
Cimarron
Liberal
San Miguel I.
Santa Cruz I.
Hollywood
Santa Monica
Glendale
Pasadena
Mohave Desert
San Bernardino
San Bernardino Mts.
Colorado Desert
LOS ANGELES
Long Beach
Santa Barbara Is.
S. Nicolas
S. Clemente
Sta. Catalina
Riverside
Redlands
Santa Ana
Salton Sea
San Diego
El Centro
San Francisco Pk. 12,655
Flagstaff
Verde
Mogollon Mesa
Winslow
Havasu Lake
Prescott
Phoenix
Salt
Mesa
Globe
Gila
Baldy Pk. 11,590
Gallup
Mt. Taylor 11,389
Los Alamos
Santa Fe
Chama
Las Vegas
Albuquerque
San Jose
Rio Grande
Socorro
Elephant Butte Res.
Black Mts.
Silver City
Lordsburg
Deming
Las Cruces
S. Andres Mts.
Santa Blanca Pk. 11,898
Alamogordo
Sacramento Mts.
Pecos
Roswell
Hobbs
Carlsbad
Tucumcari
Clovis
Llano Estacado
Amarillo
Dalhart
Pampa
Red or Canadian
Woodward
North Canadian
Alva
Enid
Clinton
Chickasha
Lawton
Altus
Vernon
Mangum
Quanah
Plainview
Lubbock
Wichita Falls
Brazos
Breckenridge
Fort Worth
Abilene
Sweet Water
Midland
Odessa
San Angelo
Edwards Plateau
Austin
New Braunfels
San Antonio
Del Rio
Uvalde
Eagle Pass
Crystal City
Laredo
Nuevo Laredo
Tucson
Douglas
Ciudad Juarez
El Paso
Marfa
Alpine
Rio Grande del Norte
Ensenada
St. Quintin
Magdalena
Cananea
Angel de la Guarda I.
Tiburon I.
Sebastian Vizcaino Bay
Hermosillo
Ures
Guaymas
S. Rosalia
Yaqui
Ciudad Obregon
Alamos
Carmen I.
Los Mochis
Topolobampo
Fuerte
Sinaloa
Mocorito
Batopilas
Hidalgo del Parral
Guerrero
Moctezuma
Chihuahua
Llano de los Christianos
Conchos
S. Pedro
Bolson de Mapimi
Jimenez
Sierra Mojada
Monclova
Gomez Palacio
Torreon
San Pedro
Monterrey
Piedras Negras
San Carlos
Sabinas
Nuevo Rosito
Lampazos
Salado
Harlingen
McAllen
Matamoros
ALEUTIAN IS.
Scale 1:45,000,000
(720 miles = 1 inch)
Unimak I.
Dutch Harbor
Unalaska I.
Umnak I.
Fox Is.
Attu I.
Aleutian Islands
Near Is.
Kiska I.
Rat Is.
Amchitka I.
Andreanof Is.
Atka I.
PACIFIC OCEAN
ALASKA
Scale 1:45,000,000
(720 miles = 1 inch)
Barrow
Brooks Range
Baird Mts.
Kotzebue
Chandalar
Fort Yukon
Yukon
Seward Pen.
Nome
Tanana
Rampart
Circle
Fairbanks
Dawson
Bering Strait
St. Lawrence I.
Anvik
Ophir
Mt. McKinley 20,300
Alaska Range
Talkeetna
Nunivak I.
Matanuska
Valdez
Cordova
Anchorage
Whittier
Kuskokwim Bay
Bristol Bay
Homer
Yakutat
Whitehorse
Skagway
Juneau
Sitka
Petersburg
Wrangell
Ketchikan
Prince Rupert
GULF OF ALASKA
Chichagof I.
Alexander Archipelago
Baranof I.
Prince of Wales I.
Afognak I.
Kodiak I.
Alaska Peninsula
Unimak I.
Trinity Is.
Chirikof I.
Sanak I.
Shumagin Is.
Graham I.

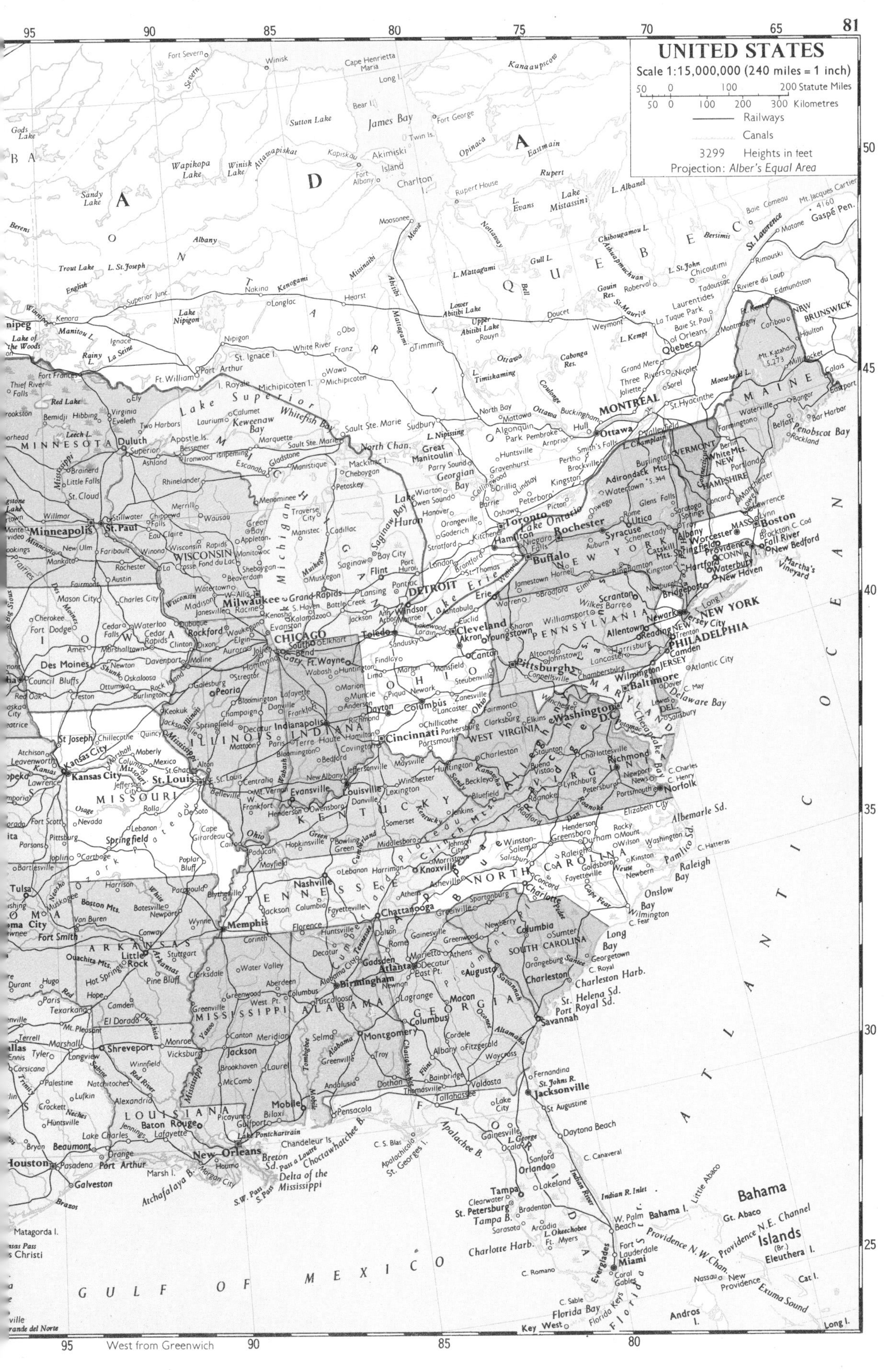
UNITED STATES
Scale 1:15,000,000 (240 miles = 1 inch)
50 0 100 200 Statute Miles
50 0 100 200 300 Kilometres
Railways
Canals
3299 Heights in feet
Projection: Alber's Equal Area
95 90 85 80 75 70 65
50 45 40 35 30 25
West from Greenwich
CANADA
ONTARIO
QUEBEC
NEW BRUNSWICK
James Bay
Lake Superior
Lake Michigan
Lake Huron
Lake Erie
Lake Ontario
Georgian Bay
Saginaw Bay
Green Bay
L. Nipissing
L. Mistassini
L. Champlain
Moosehead L.
Lake of the Woods
Lake Nipigon
MINNESOTA
WISCONSIN
MICHIGAN
IOWA
ILLINOIS
INDIANA
OHIO
MISSOURI
KENTUCKY
TENNESSEE
WEST VIRGINIA
VIRGINIA
NORTH CAROLINA
SOUTH CAROLINA
GEORGIA
ALABAMA
MISSISSIPPI
LOUISIANA
ARKANSAS
FLORIDA
PENNSYLVANIA
NEW YORK
NEW JERSEY
MARYLAND
DEL.
CONN.
R.I.
MASS.
VERMONT
NEW HAMPSHIRE
MAINE
Duluth
Minneapolis
St. Paul
Milwaukee
CHICAGO
DETROIT
Toledo
Cleveland
Buffalo
Rochester
Toronto
Hamilton
Ottawa
MONTREAL
Quebec
Boston
Providence
Hartford
NEW YORK
Newark
PHILADELPHIA
Baltimore
Washington D.C.
Pittsburgh
Cincinnati
Columbus
Indianapolis
Louisville
St. Louis
Kansas City
Memphis
Nashville
Knoxville
Chattanooga
Atlanta
Birmingham
Montgomery
Mobile
New Orleans
Baton Rouge
Jackson
Shreveport
Little Rock
Houston
Galveston
Jacksonville
Tampa
St. Petersburg
Orlando
Miami
Charleston
Savannah
Columbia
Charlotte
Richmond
Norfolk
Ozark Plateau
Boston Mts.
Ouachita Mts.
Cumberland Plateau
Blue Ridge
Piedmont
Adirondack Mts. 5,344
White Mts.
Mt. Katahdin 5,273
Mt. Jacques Cartier 4160
Gaspé Pen.
Cape Cod
Long I.
Martha's Vineyard
Delaware Bay
Chesapeake Bay
Albemarle Sd.
Pamlico Sd.
C. Hatteras
C. Fear
Long Bay
Onslow Bay
Raleigh Bay
Charleston Harb.
St. Helena Sd.
Port Royal Sd.
C. Canaveral
L. Okeechobee
Everglades
Florida Bay
Florida Keys
Key West
C. Sable
C. Romano
Charlotte Harb.
Tampa B.
Apalachee B.
C. S. Blas
Choctawhatchee B.
Delta of the Mississippi
S.W. Pass
S. Pass
Pass a Loutre
Chandeleur Is.
Breton Sd.
Atchafalaya B.
Lake Pontchartrain
Marsh I.
Matagorda I.
GULF OF MEXICO
ATLANTIC OCEAN
Bahama Islands (Br.)
Gt. Abaco
Little Abaco
Bahama I.
Andros I.
Eleuthera I.
Cat I.
Long I.
Exuma Sound
Nassau
New Providence
Providence N.W. Chan.
Providence N.E. Channel
Straits of Florida

MEXICO AND
CENTRAL AMERICA
Scale 1:17,500,000 (280 miles = 1 inch)
100 50 0 100 200 300 Statute Miles
100 0 100 200 300 400 Kilometres
Railways
Canals
18,204 Heights in feet
Projection: Bonne
PANAMA
CANAL
1:1,000,000 (16m. – 1in.)
Canal Zone
UNITED STATES
MEXICO
PACIFIC OCEAN
GULF OF MEXICO
Gulf of Campêche
Caribbean Sea
Gulf of California
Lower California
Sierra Madre
Yucatan
Yucatan Strait
Florida Str.
Tropic of Cancer
G. of Tehuantepec
Isthmus of Tehuantepec
Gulf of Honduras
GUATEMALA
BR. HONDURAS
HONDURAS
SALVADOR
NICARAGUA
COSTA RICA
PANAMA
CUBA
JAMAICA
San Diego
Tijuana
Mexicali
Yuma
Tucson
Nogales
Ciudad Juarez
El Paso
Chihuahua
Hermosillo
Guaymas
La Paz
Mazatlan
Durango
Torreon
Monterrey
Saltillo
Laredo
Nuevo Laredo
Matamoros
Brownsville
Tampico
San Luis Potosi
Aguascalientes
Guadalajara
Leon
Queretaro
MEXICO
Toluca
Puebla
Veracruz
Jalapa
Orizaba
Oaxaca
Acapulco
Morelia
Colima
Manzanillo
Tepic
Zacatecas
Coatzacoalcos
Villahermosa
Campeche
Merida
Progreso
Valladolid
Cozumel I.
Belize
Guatemala
San Salvador
Tegucigalpa
Managua
Leon
Granada
San José
Puntarenas
Limón
Colón
Panama
Fort Worth
Dallas
Houston
San Antonio
Austin
Corpus Christi
Galveston
Shreveport
Jackson
New Orleans
Baton Rouge
Mobile
Pensacola
Tallahassee
Jacksonville
Tampa
St. Petersburg
Orlando
Miami
Havana
Matanzas
Cienfuegos
Camagüey
Key West
Nassau
Andros I.
Grand Bahama I.
I. of Pines
Grand Cayman (Br.)
Revilla Gigedo Is. (Mexico)
Popocatepetl 17,887
Citlaltepetl 18,700
Colima Vol. 12,664
Vol. Fuego 12,582
Vol. Irazú 11,260
Gatun
Gatun Lake
Gamboa
Madden L.
Madden Dam
Balboa
La Boca
Ancon
Cristobal
Silver City
Margarita
Pedro Miguel
Miraflores Locks
Culebra
Las Delicias
La Chorrera
Bay of Panama

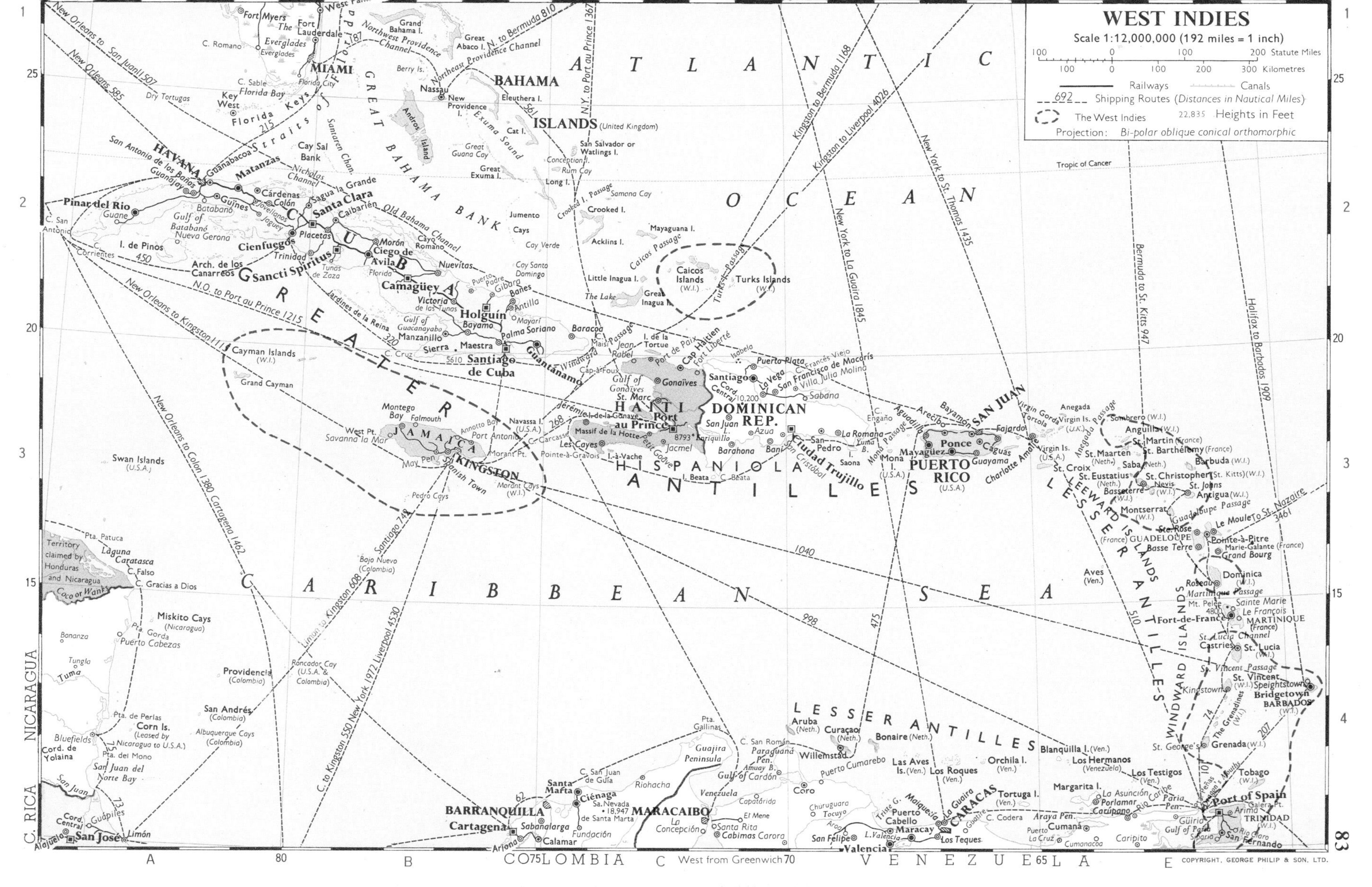
WEST INDIES
Scale 1:12,000,000 (192 miles = 1 inch)
100 0 100 200 Statute Miles
100 0 100 200 300 Kilometres
Railways
Canals
692 Shipping Routes (Distances in Nautical Miles)
The West Indies
22,835 Heights in Feet
Projection: Bi-polar oblique conical orthomorphic
ATLANTIC OCEAN
CARIBBEAN SEA
GREATER ANTILLES
LESSER ANTILLES
LEEWARD ISLANDS
WINDWARD ISLANDS
Tropic of Cancer
BAHAMA ISLANDS (United Kingdom)
GREAT BAHAMA BANK
CUBA
HAVANA
Matanzas
Pinar del Rio
Santa Clara
Cienfuegos
Sancti Spiritus
Ciego de Avila
Camagüey
Holguín
Santiago de Cuba
Guantánamo
I. de Pinos
MIAMI
Fort Myers
Fort Lauderdale
Key West
Florida Keys
Straits of Florida
Nassau
Andros Island
Cayman Islands (W.I.)
Grand Cayman
JAMAICA
KINGSTON
Montego Bay
Spanish Town
HAITI
Port au Prince
Cap Haïtien
Gonaïves
DOMINICAN REP.
Ciudad Trujillo
Santiago
HISPANIOLA
Windward Passage
Turks Islands (W.I.)
Caicos Islands (W.I.)
Mona Passage
PUERTO RICO (U.S.A.)
SAN JUAN
Ponce
Mayagüez
Anegada Passage
Virgin Is. (U.S.A.)
Anguilla (W.I.)
St. Martin (France)
St. Christopher (St. Kitts) (W.I.)
Antigua (W.I.)
Montserrat (W.I.)
GUADELOUPE (France)
Dominica (W.I.)
MARTINIQUE (France)
St. Lucia (W.I.)
St. Vincent (W.I.)
BARBADOS (W.I.)
Bridgetown
Grenada (W.I.)
Tobago (W.I.)
TRINIDAD (W.I.)
Port of Spain
Aruba (Neth.)
Curaçao (Neth.)
Bonaire (Neth.)
VENEZUELA
CARACAS
La Guaira
Valencia
Maracay
MARACAIBO
COLOMBIA
BARRANQUILLA
Cartagena
Santa Marta
Ciénaga
NICARAGUA
C. RICA
San José
Limón
Bluefields
Miskito Cays (Nicaragua)
C. Gracias a Dios
Swan Islands (U.S.A.)
Providencia (Colombia)
San Andrés (Colombia)
Corn Is. (Leased by Nicaragua to U.S.A.)
Territory claimed by Honduras and Nicaragua
New Orleans to San Juan 1507
New Orleans 585
New Orleans to Kingston 1115
N.O. to Port au Prince 1215
New Orleans to Colon 1380 Cartagena 1462
N.Y. to Port au Prince 1367
N. to Bermuda 810
Kingston to Bermuda 1168
Kingston to Liverpool 4026
New York to La Guaira 1845
New York to St. Thomas 1435
Bermuda to St. Kitts 947
Halifax to Barbados 1909
To St. Nazaire 3461
C. to Kingston 550 New York 1972 Liverpool 4530
Limon to Kingston 608
Santiago 748
West from Greenwich
COPYRIGHT, GEORGE PHILIP & SON, LTD.

SOUTH AMERICA – PHYSICAL

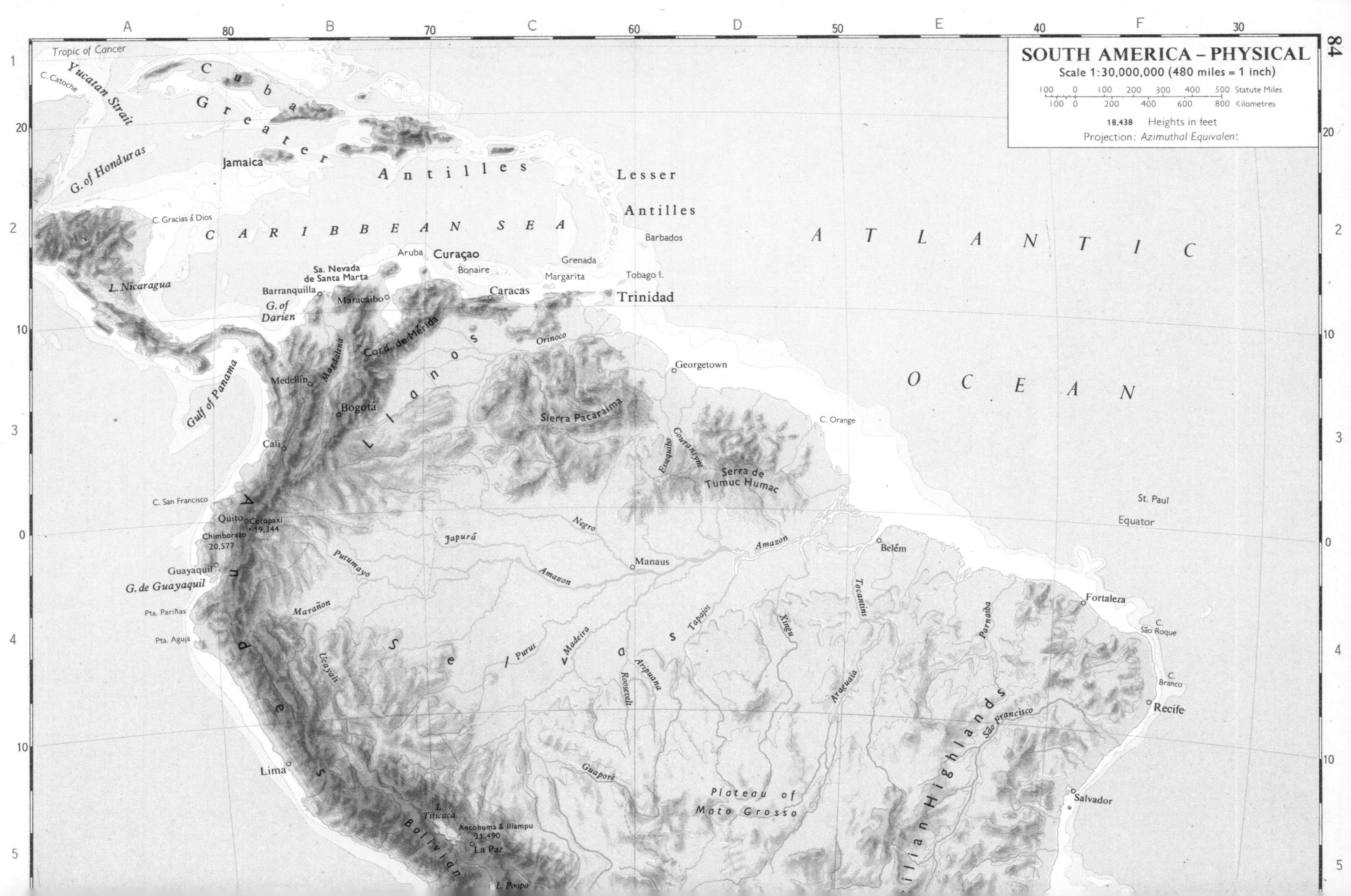

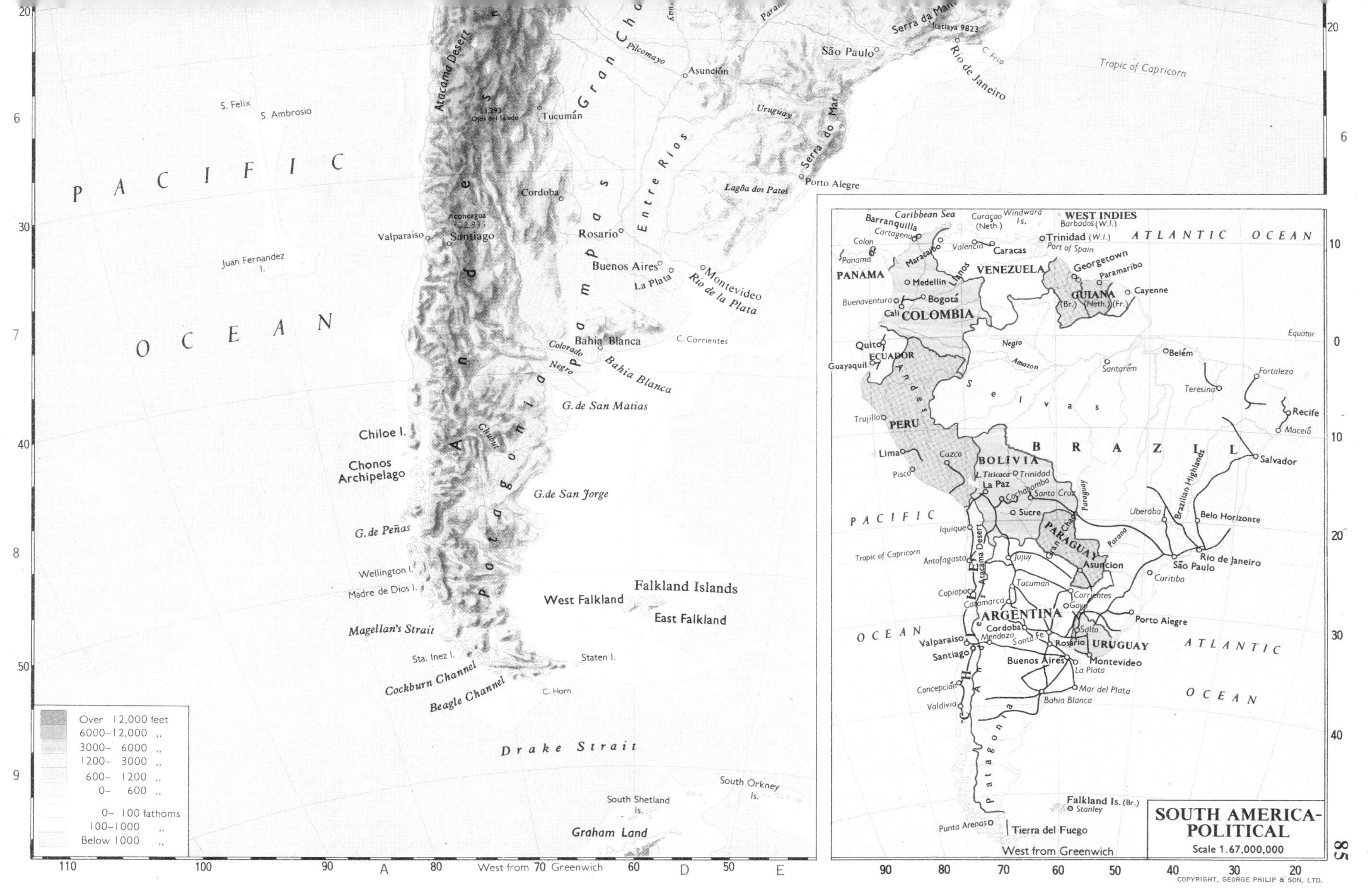
PACIFIC OCEAN
S. Felix
S. Ambrosio
Juan Fernandez I.
Atacama Desert
23,293 Ojos del Salado
Tucumán
Gran Chaco
Pilcomayo
Asunción
São Paulo
Serra da Mantiqueira
Itatiaya 9823
Rio de Janeiro
C. Frio
Tropic of Capricorn
Uruguay
Serra do Mar
Entre Rios
Porto Alegre
Lagôa dos Patos
Cordoba
Aconcagua 22,835
Valparaiso
Santiago
Rosario
Pampas
Buenos Aires
La Plata
Montevideo
Rio de la Plata
Andes
Bahia Blanca
C. Corrientes
Colorado
Negro
G. de San Matias
Patagonia
Chubut
Chiloe I.
Chonos Archipelago
G. de San Jorge
G. de Peñas
Wellington I.
Madre de Dios I.
West Falkland
Falkland Islands
East Falkland
Magellan's Strait
Sta. Inez I.
Staten I.
Cockburn Channel
Beagle Channel
C. Horn
Drake Strait
South Orkney Is.
South Shetland Is.
Graham Land
Over 12,000 feet
6000–12,000 ,,
3000– 6000 ,,
1200– 3000 ,,
600– 1200 ,,
0– 600 ,,
0– 100 fathoms
100–1000 ,,
Below 1000 ,,
West from 70 Greenwich
SOUTH AMERICA-POLITICAL
Scale 1.67,000,000
Caribbean Sea
Barranquilla
Cartagena
Colon
Panama
PANAMA
Curaçao (Neth.)
Windward Is.
WEST INDIES
Barbados (W.I.)
Trinidad (W.I.)
Port of Spain
ATLANTIC OCEAN
Maracaibo
Valencia
Caracas
VENEZUELA
Llanos
Georgetown
Paramaribo
Cayenne
GUIANA
(Br.) (Neth.) (Fr.)
Medellin
Bogotá
Buenaventura
Cali
COLOMBIA
Equator
Quito
ECUADOR
Guayaquil
Negro
Amazon
Santarém
Belém
Fortaleza
Teresina
Recife
Maceió
Andes
Selvas
Trujillo
PERU
Lima
Pisco
Cuzco
BOLIVIA
L. Titicaca
Trinidad
La Paz
Cochabamba
Santa Cruz
Sucre
Paraguay
BRAZIL
Brazilian Highlands
Salvador
Uberaba
Belo Horizonte
PACIFIC
Iquique
Tropic of Capricorn
Antofagasta
Atacama Desert
Jujuy
Gran Chaco
PARAGUAY
Parana
Asuncion
Rio de Janeiro
São Paulo
Curitiba
Copiapo
Catamarca
Tucuman
Corrientes
Goya
ARGENTINA
Porto Alegre
Cordoba
Mendoza
Santa Fe
Salto
Valparaiso
Santiago
Rosario
URUGUAY
Buenos Aires
Montevideo
La Plata
OCEAN
ATLANTIC OCEAN
Concepcion
Mar del Plata
Valdivia
Bahia Blanca
Chile
Patagonia
Falkland Is. (Br.)
Stanley
Punta Arenas
Tierra del Fuego
West from Greenwich

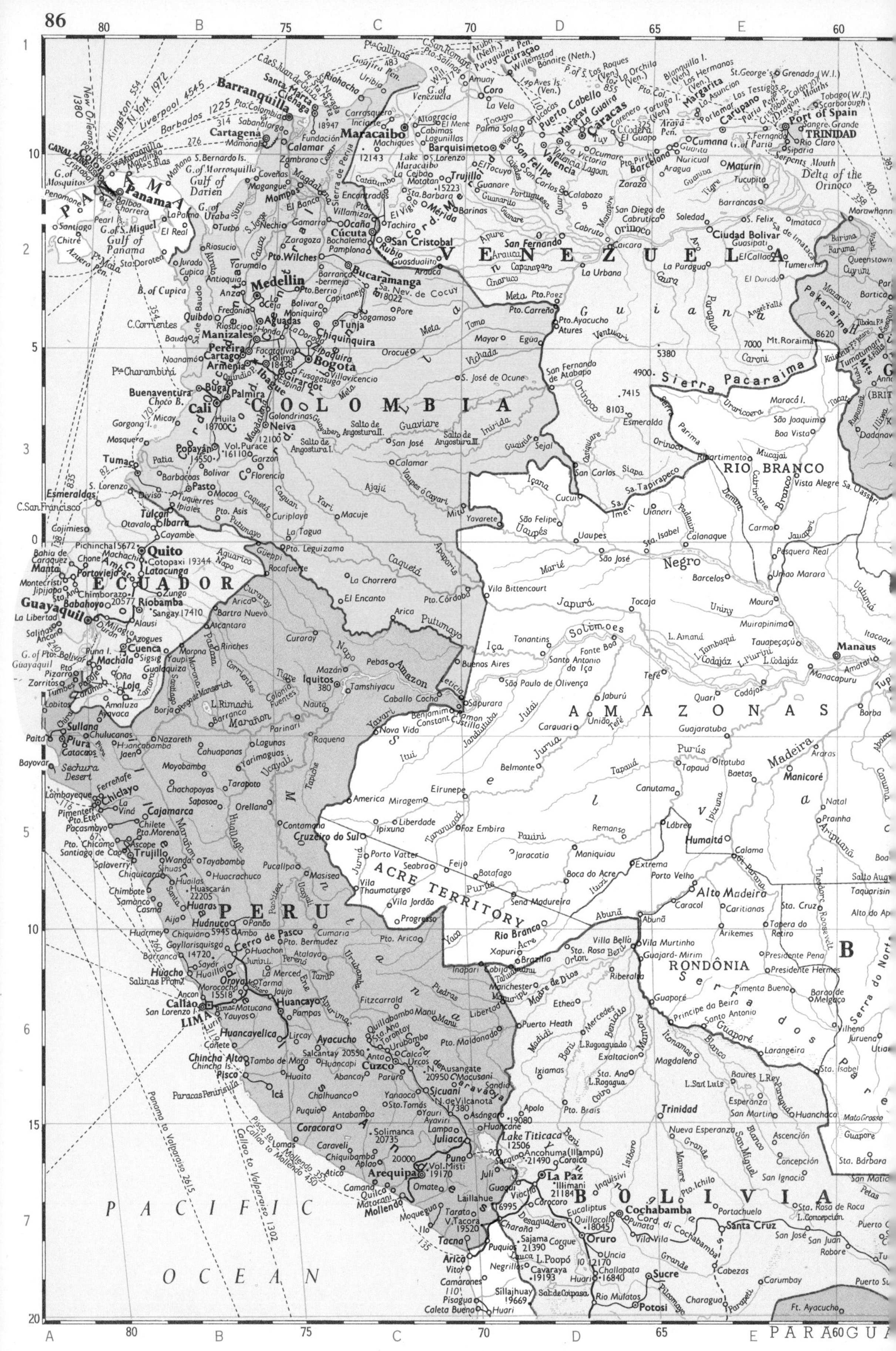
80
B
75
C
70
D
65
E
60
PANAMA
Panama
Colon
CANAL ZONE
G. of Mosquitos
Gulf of Panama
G. of S. Miguel
Pearl Is.
Azuero Pen.
Gulf of Darien
G. of Uraba
Barranquilla
Cartagena
Santa Marta
Ciénaga
Riohacha
Pta. Gallinas
Guajira Pen.
Aruba (Neth.)
Curaçao
Bonaire (Neth.)
Willemstad
Paraguana Pen.
G. of Venezuela
Maracaibo
Lake Maracaibo
Coro
Barquisimeto
Puerto Cabello
Maracay
La Guaira
Caracas
Valencia
Barcelona
Cumana
Margarita
Carupano
Port of Spain
TRINIDAD
Tobago (W.I.)
Grenada (W.I.)
Scarborough
Dragon Mouths
Serpents Mouth
G. of Paria
Delta of the Orinoco
Maturin
Ciudad Bolivar
Tucupita
Calabozo
San Fernando
Orinoco
VENEZUELA
Guiana
Sierra Pacaraima
Mt. Roraima
Pakaraima Mts
Cúcuta
San Cristobal
Mérida
Trujillo
Barinas
Bucaramanga
Medellin
Manizales
Pereira
Armenia
Ibague
Bogota
Tunja
Girardot
Neiva
Cali
Buenaventura
Palmira
Buga
Popayán
Pasto
Tumaco
COLOMBIA
Cord. Oriental
Cord. Central
Magdalena
Cauca
Meta
Guaviare
Vichada
Inirida
Caquetá
Putumayo
Vaupes
Apaporis
Leticia
Esmeraldas
Tulcan
Ibarra
Quito
Cotopaxi 19344
Latacunga
Chimborazo 20577
Riobamba
Sangay 17410
ECUADOR
Manta
Portoviejo
Guayaquil
G. of Guayaquil
Puna I.
Cuenca
Machala
Loja
Tumbes
Sullana
Piura
Paita
Sechura Desert
Chiclayo
Cajamarca
Trujillo
Chimbote
Huaraz
Huascarán 22205
Huánuco
Cerro de Pasco
Huacho
Callao
LIMA
Huancayo
Huancavelica
Ayacucho
Cuzco
Chincha Alta
Pisco
Icá
Arequipa
Mollendo
Puno
Juliaca
Lake Titicaca
Tacna
Arica
Iquitos
Amazon
Marañon
Ucayali
Huallaga
Napo
PERU
PACIFIC OCEAN
Panama to Valparaiso 2615
Callao to Valparaiso 1302
Callao to Mollendo 450
AMAZONAS
Solimoes
Japurá
Negro
Manaus
Purús
Juruá
Madeira
Humaitá
Porto Velho
Manicoré
ACRE TERRITORY
Rio Branco
Cruzeiro do Sul
RIO BRANCO
Boa Vista
RONDÔNIA
Guaporé
Alto Madeira
BOLIVIA
La Paz
Illimani 21184
Ancohuma (Illampú) 21490
Oruro
Cochabamba
Cord. di Cochabamba
Santa Cruz
Sucre
Potosi
Trinidad
Beni
Mamore
Madre de Dios
L. Poopó
Sajama 21390
PARAGUA
A
B
C
D
E
1
2
3
4
5
6
7
8
9
10
20

SOUTH AMERICA
NORTH
Scale 1:16,000,000 (256 miles = 1 inch)
100 0 100 200 300 Statute Miles
100 0 100 200 300 400 Kilometres
Railways
Canals
1075 Shipping Routes
Distances in Nautical Miles
550 Heights in feet
Projection: Sanson-Flamsteed Sinusoidal
55 G 50 H 45 J 40 K 35
N O R T H
A T L A N T I C
O C E A N
Barbados to Belem 1089
Recife to New York 3678
Belem to Liverpool 4043
New York to Belem
Equator
Paramaribo
Nieuw Amsterdam
Nieuw Nickerie
Coronie
Groningen
Paranam
Moengo
Albina
St. Laurent
St. Jean
Mana
Iracoubo
Sinnamary
Kourou
I. du Diable (Devil's I.)
Macouria
Cayenne
Kwakoegron
Dam
Montsinery
Caux
Approuague
C. Orange
C. Cassiporé
SURINAME
(NETH.)
(FRENCH)
St. Georges
St. Paul
Souvenir
Petit François
Cormontibo
Popakai
Ajoewa
3050
Pierre
Peio
1476
Cunani
Montenegro (Amapá)
Maracá I.
C. Raso
Serra de Tumuc Humac
Sa. do Agumiuare
AMAPÁ
Mapari
Araguari
Pta Grossa
Mouths of the Amazon
Caviana I.
Mexiana I.
2855
Macapá
Paru
Curuá
Jari
Mazagao
Afuá
Chaves
Soure
C. Magoarinho
Curuçá
Salinopolis
Vigia
Bragança 357
Marajo Island
R. Pará
Prata
Belém (Pará)
Gurupá I.
Almeirim
Belem 860
Monte Alegre
to Prainha
Gurupá
Melgaço
Muaná
Obidos
Manaus
Amazon
Juruti
Santarém
Parintins
Belterra
Aveiro
Fordlandia
Itaituba
Tapajóz
Porto de Moz
Vitória
Altamira
Xingú
Abaetuba
Acará
Cametá
Baião
Curralinho
Vizeu
Pta Turi
Cururupu
Turiaçu
Guimarães
Alcântara
São Marcos B.
São Luis (Maranhão)
Montes Aureos
Turissú
Viana
Rosário
Itapecurú
Coroatá
Codó
Caxias
Teresina
Barreirinhas
Tutoia
Luis Correia (Amarração)
384
Camocim
Pta Tabagé
Parnaiba
Piracuruca
Miguel Alves
Barras
Granja
Sobral
Umari
Fortaleza (Ceará)
Maranguape
Baturite
Ipueiras
Quixadá
Oticica
Crateus
Senador Pompeu
Aracati
Areia Branca
Macau
408
Caiçara
C. São Roque
Natal
Mossoró
RIO GRANDE DO NORTE
Caraúbas
Limoeiro
União
CEARÁ
Iguatú
Carius
Oros
Crato
Caicó
Jardim do Serido
Nova Cruz
Canguaretama
Mamanguape
Cabedelo
Sousa
Pombal
Alagôa Grande
Cajazeiras
PARAIBA
Campina Grande
Umbuzeiro
João Pessôa (Paraíba)
Nazare-da-Mata
Recife (Pernambuco)
Sa. do Araripe
Ouricuri
Paulistana
Mofrense
PERNAMBUCO
Sertânia
Rio Branco
Pesqueira
Cabrobó
Garanhuns
Petrolandia
Palmeira
Palmares
Barreiros
Maragoji
Atalaia
Maceió
Piranhas
ALAGÔAS
Paulo Afonso Falls
Petrolina
Joazeiro
Casa Nova
Remanso
São Francisco
Vaza Barris
Propriá
SERGIPE
Penedo
Coruripe
Capela
Aracaju
São Christovao
Estância
Barracão
Alagoinhas
389
Bonfim
Campo Formoso
Queimadas
Itapicuru
Jacobina
Serrinha
Mundo Novo
Jacuipe
Feira
Bom Jardim
Cachoeira
São Felix
Sto. Amaro
Itaberaba
Salvador (Baia)
Todos B.
Itaeté
Paraguassú
Amargosa
Sincorá
Valença
Nazaré
Jequié
Marau
Col. Itapira
Ilhéus
Serra do Periperi
Itabuna
Canavieiras
Belmonte
Porto Seguro
Comoxatiba
Prado
Caravelas
Abrolhos Arch
Itaúnas
Conceição da Barra
São Mateus
Mucuri
Aimores
Nova Venécia
Doce
Ibiraçu
Rio de Janeiro to Recife 1075
472
To Southampton from Rio de Janeiro 5034
Montevideo 6009
MARANHÃO
Barra do Corda
Itapecurú
Picos
Sa. do Valentin
Amarante
Valença
Oeiras
Floriano
Nova Iorque
Sa. do Itapecurú
Loreto
Uruçui
PIAUI
Tranqueira
Correntes
Gurguéia
São João do Piaui
Sta. Filomena
Sa. do Penitente
Parnaiba
Sa. das Covodas
Balsas
Caracol
Sa. do Piaui
Sta. Teresa
Parnaguá
Sa. Grande
Sa. Negra
Grajaú
Mearim
Serra da Desordem
Gurupi
Ferreira
Capim
Patos
Alcobaça
Breu Branco
Agua Limpa
Areião
Tocantins
Marabá
São João
Sa. da Cachoeira Gde.
Tocantinopolis
Carolina
Riachão
Sa. do Estrondo
Araguaia
Sobrado
Sa. dos Carajas
Itacaiunas
Triumpho
Fresco
Sa. dos Gradaús
Gameleira
Conceição
Araguacema
Salles
Serra
Pacajá
Jacundá
Anapú
Grande Pacajá
Iriri
Bacabel
Jamanchim
Crepori
Curuá
Manoel
Sa. do Cachimbo
Pedro Afonso
Sono
Pto. Franco
Mangabeiras
Sa. das Mangabeiras
Sa. dos Javaés
Chavantes
Balsas
Porto Nacional
Natividade
Manoel Alves
Taguatinga
Peixe
Parana
Campos Belos
São Domingos
Sa. Dourada
Sa. da Sta. Luzia dos Tocantins
Sta. Tereza
Palma
Serra de Goiás
BRAZIL
GOIAS
Bananal I.
Braço Maior
Braço Menor
Aldea Cumaré
Sta. Isabel do Morro
Carajo
Serra do Roncador
Culuene
São Domingos
Mortes
Araguaia
Redempção
Pouso Alegre
Serra Formosa
Steinen
Pôrto Artur
Batovi
Paranatinga
Pôrto Caneco
Independencia
Sta. Isabel
MATO GROSSO
Corrego Fundo
Diamantina
Plateau of Mato Grosso
Brotas
Mortes
Cuiabá
Pres. Mintinho
Gen. Carneiro
Registro do Araguaia
Balisa
Macedina
Aruana
Pirenopolis
Goias
Anápolis
Goiania
Bela Vista
Vianopolis
Luzinia
Brazilia
Corumbá
Formosa
Planaltina
Sa. do Rio Preto
Sa. do Rio Claro
Alto Araguaia
Jataí
Rio Verde
Verde
Claro
Morrinhos
Paranaiba
Catalão
Ouvidor
Araguari
Roncador
Paracatú
Patos de Minas
Pirapora
Bocaiuva
Montes Claros
São Francisco
Januária
Monte Azul (Tremedal)
Rio Pardo
Grão Mogul
Salinas
Jequitinhonha
Fortaleza
Arassuai
Minas Novas
Sa. do Chifre
Teófilo-Otoni
Igreja Nova
Diamantina
Itambe 6705
Carinhanha
Sta. Maria da Victoria
Bom Jesus da Lapa
Caetité
Ituaçu
Contendas
Bom Jesus dos Meiras
Condeúba
Gavião
Conquista
Pardo
Itabuna
Paratinga
Serra do Tombador
Jardinopolis
Barreiras
Formosa
Barra
Grande
Altos do Parana
Cique-Cique
BAIA
Sta. Barbara
Pilar
São José do Tocantins
Forte
MINAS GERAIS
Uberlandia
Patrocinio
Tiros
Paraopeba
Sete Lagôas
Sabará
Itabira
Caete
Sta. Barbara
Belo Horizonte
Ibiá
Indaia
Araxá
Uberaba
Prata
Frutal
Igarapava
Grande
Aimorés
Caratinga
Figueira
Bahúsinho
Coxim
Aparé
Pto. da Ilha
Santana do Paranaiba
Sucuriu
Verde
Pequiri
Taquari
São Lourenço
Esperança
Antonio
Sta. Barbara
West from Greenwich
55 50 H 45 J 40 K
COPYRIGHT, GEORGE PHILIP & SON, LTD.
1 10 2 5 3 0 4 5 10 6 15 7

BOLIVIA
PARAGUAY
MATO GROSSO
BRAZIL
GOIAS
MINAS GERAIS
BAHIA
RONDÔNIA
ESPIRITO SANTO
RIO DE JANEIRO
SÃO PAULO
PARANÁ
SANTA CATARINA
RIO GRANDE DO SUL
URUGUAY
PERU
La Paz
Cochabamba
Sucre
Potosí
Oruro
Santa Cruz
Asunción
Concepción
Corumbá
Cuiabá
Goiania
Belo Horizonte
Niterói
Santos
Curitiba
Florianópolis
Pôrto Alegre
Pelotas
Rio Grande
Corrientes
Resistencia
Santa Fé
Paraná
Rosario
Córdoba
Tucumán
Salta
Jujuy
Santiago del Estero
Catamarca
La Rioja
San Juan
Antofagasta
Iquique
Arica
Tacna
Arequipa
Mollendo
Cuzco
Lake Titicaca
Tropic of Capricorn
Montevideo to Rio de Janeiro
Montevideo to Recife 2047
Callao 1302
Panama 2615
San Francisco 5138
Honolulu 5916
Yokohama 9939

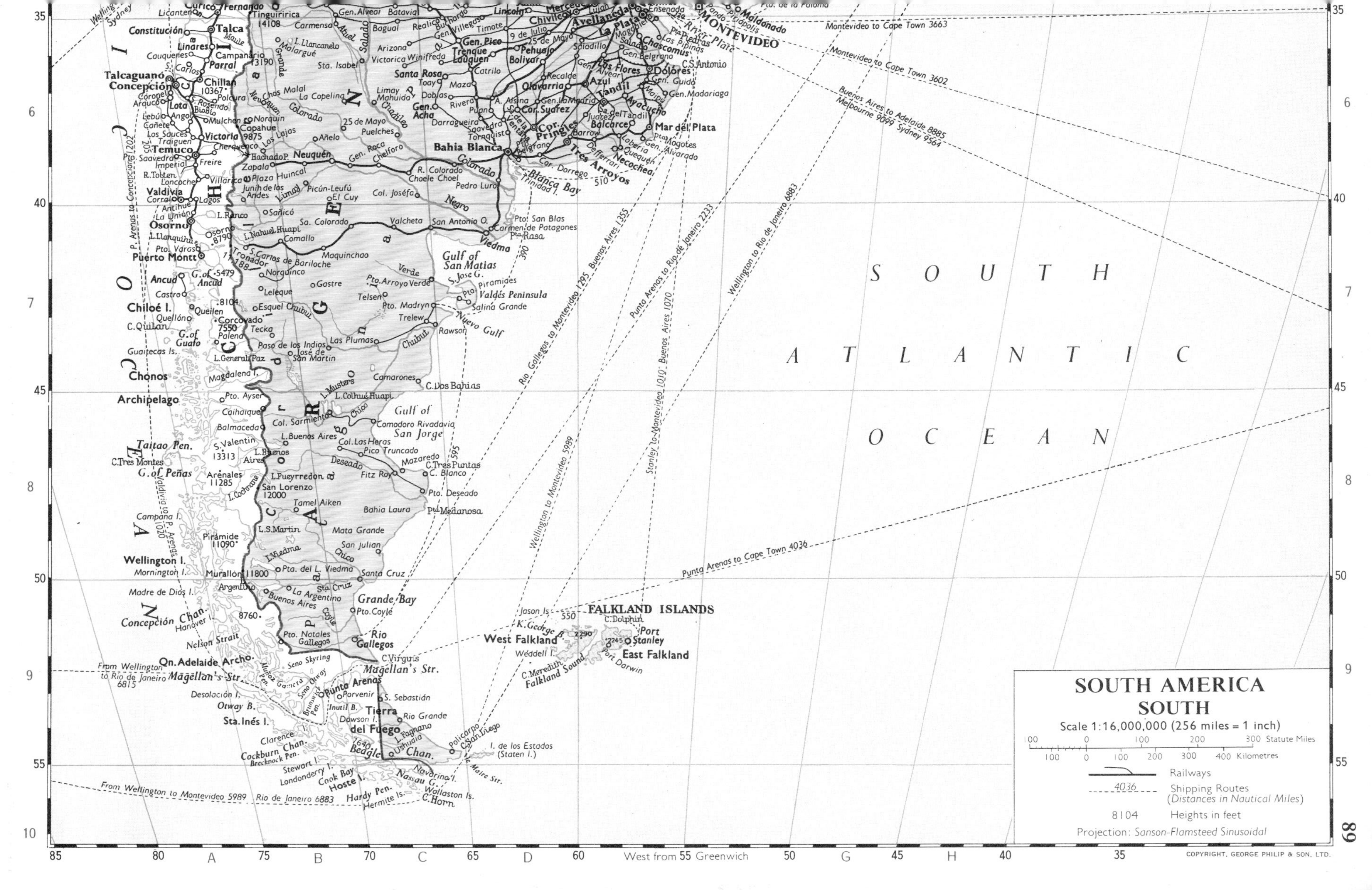

SOUTH AMERICA
SOUTH
Scale 1:16,000,000 (256 miles = 1 inch)
Statute Miles
Kilometres
Railways
4036 Shipping Routes (Distances in Nautical Miles)
8104 Heights in feet
Projection: Sanson-Flamsteed Sinusoidal
SOUTH ATLANTIC OCEAN
FALKLAND ISLANDS
West Falkland
East Falkland
Port Stanley
Falkland Sound
MONTEVIDEO
Maldonado
River Plate
Mar del Plata
Bahia Blanca
Blanca Bay
Gulf of San Matias
Valdés Peninsula
Nuevo Gulf
Gulf of San Jorge
Comodoro Rivadavia
Grande Bay
Rio Gallegos
Magellan's Str.
Tierra del Fuego
Punta Arenas
Beagle Chan.
C. Horn
Talca
Concepción
Temuco
Valdivia
Osorno
Puerto Montt
Chiloé I.
Chonos Archipelago
Taitao Pen.
G. of Peñas
Wellington I.
Neuquén
Viedma
Montevideo to Cape Town 3663
Montevideo to Cape Town 3602
Buenos Aires to Adelaide 8885
Melbourne 9099 Sydney 9564
Wellington to Rio de Janeiro 6883
Punta Arenas to Rio de Janeiro 2233
Rio Gallegos to Montevideo 1295 Buenos Aires 1355
Stanley to Montevideo 1010 Buenos Aires 1070
Wellington to Montevideo 5989
Punta Arenas to Cape Town 4036
From Wellington to Montevideo 5989 Rio de Janeiro 6883
From Wellington to Rio de Janeiro 6815
West from 55 Greenwich

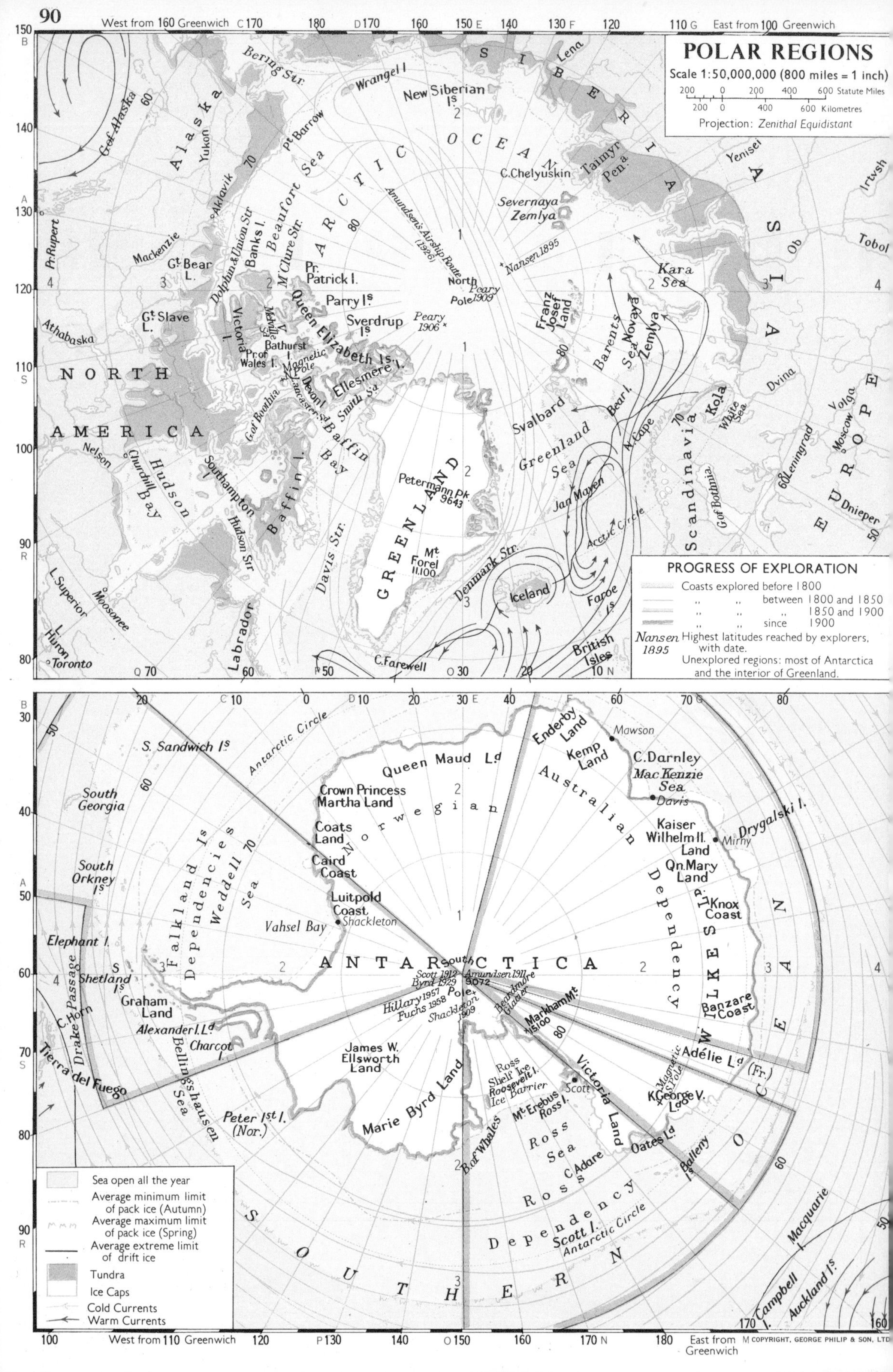
POLAR REGIONS
Scale 1:50,000,000 (800 miles = 1 inch)
Statute Miles
Kilometres
Projection: Zenithal Equidistant
West from 160 Greenwich
East from 100 Greenwich
PROGRESS OF EXPLORATION
Coasts explored before 1800
,, ,, between 1800 and 1850
,, ,, ,, 1850 and 1900
,, ,, since 1900
Nansen 1895 Highest latitudes reached by explorers, with date.
Unexplored regions: most of Antarctica and the interior of Greenland.
ARCTIC OCEAN
SIBERIA
NORTH AMERICA
EUROPE
Alaska
Yukon
G. of Alaska
Bering Str.
Wrangel I.
New Siberian Is.
Pt. Barrow
Beaufort Sea
Aklavik
Mackenzie
Gt. Bear L.
Gt. Slave L.
Athabaska
Pr. Rupert
Dolphin & Union Str.
Banks I.
M'Clure Str.
Pr. Patrick I.
Parry Is.
Sverdrup Is.
Queen Elizabeth Is.
Victoria I.
Melville Sd.
Bathurst I.
Pr. of Wales I.
Magnetic N. Pole
Devon I.
Lancaster Sd.
Ellesmere I.
Smith Sd.
G. of Boothia
Baffin Bay
Baffin I.
Southampton I.
Hudson Bay
Churchill
Nelson
Hudson Str.
Labrador
Davis Str.
L. Superior
L. Huron
Toronto
Moosonee
Amundsen's Airship Route (1926)
Peary 1906
Peary 1909
North Pole
Nansen 1895
C. Chelyuskin
Severnaya Zemlya
Taimyr Pen.
Lena
Yenisei
Irtysh
Ob
Tobol
Kara Sea
Franz Josef Land
Barents Sea
Novaya Zemlya
Svalbard
Bear I.
N. Cape
Greenland Sea
Jan Mayen
Arctic Circle
GREENLAND
Petermann Pk. 9643
Mt. Forel 11,100
Denmark Str.
Iceland
Faroe Is.
British Isles
C. Farewell
Scandinavia
Kola
White Sea
G. of Bothnia
Dvina
Volga
Moscow
Leningrad
Dnieper
ANTARCTICA
South Pole
Scott 1912
Amundsen 1911
Byrd 1929
Hillary 1957
Fuchs 1958
Shackleton 1909
9072
Queen Maud Ld.
Crown Princess Martha Land
Coats Land
Caird Coast
Luitpold Coast
Vahsel Bay
Shackleton
Norwegian
Enderby Land
Kemp Land
Mawson
C. Darnley
MacKenzie Sea
Davis
Australian Dependency
Kaiser Wilhelm II. Land
Mirny
Drygalski I.
Qn. Mary Land
Knox Coast
WILKES LD.
Banzare Coast
Adélie Ld. (Fr.)
Magnetic S. Pole
K. George V. Ld.
Oates Ld.
Balleny Is.
Victoria Land
Scott
Markham Mt. 15100
Beardmore Glacier
Ross Shelf Ice
Roosevelt I.
Ice Barrier
Mt. Erebus
Ross I.
Ross Sea
C. Adare
B. of Whales
Ross Dependency
Scott I.
Antarctic Circle
Marie Byrd Land
James W. Ellsworth Land
Peter Ist. I. (Nor.)
Bellingshausen Sea
Charcot I.
Alexander I. Ld.
Graham Land
S. Shetland Is.
Elephant I.
South Orkney Is.
South Georgia
S. Sandwich Is.
Falkland Is. Dependencies
Weddell Sea
Drake Passage
C. Horn
Tierra del Fuego
SOUTHERN OCEAN
Macquarie I.
Campbell I.
Auckland Is.
Sea open all the year
Average minimum limit of pack ice (Autumn)
Average maximum limit of pack ice (Spring)
Average extreme limit of drift ice
Tundra
Ice Caps
Cold Currents
Warm Currents
West from 110 Greenwich
East from Greenwich
COPYRIGHT, GEORGE PHILIP & SON, LTD.

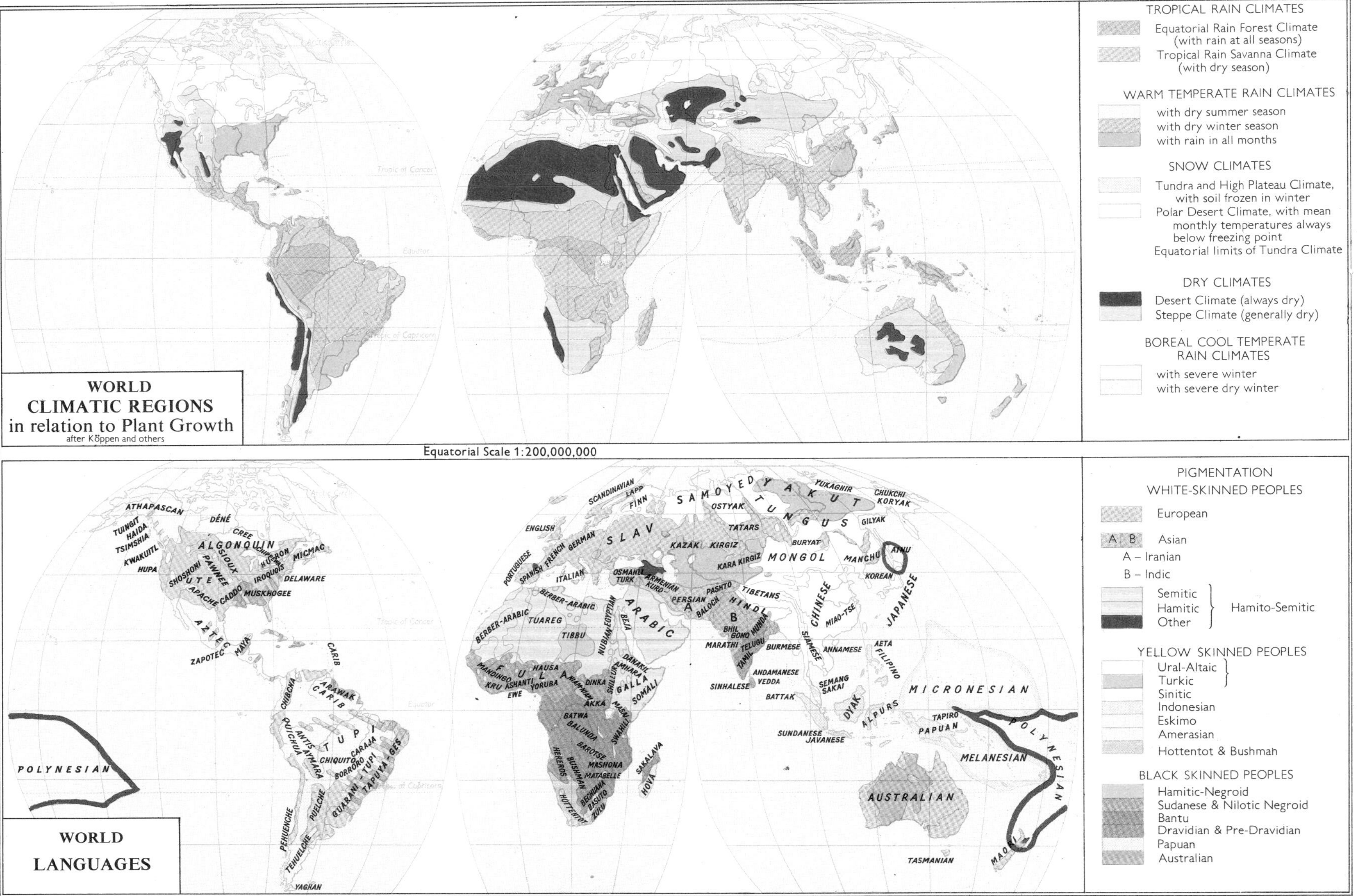
WORLD
CLIMATIC REGIONS
in relation to Plant Growth
after Köppen and others
TROPICAL RAIN CLIMATES
Equatorial Rain Forest Climate (with rain at all seasons)
Tropical Rain Savanna Climate (with dry season)
WARM TEMPERATE RAIN CLIMATES
with dry summer season
with dry winter season
with rain in all months
SNOW CLIMATES
Tundra and High Plateau Climate, with soil frozen in winter
Polar Desert Climate, with mean monthly temperatures always below freezing point
Equatorial limits of Tundra Climate
DRY CLIMATES
Desert Climate (always dry)
Steppe Climate (generally dry)
BOREAL COOL TEMPERATE RAIN CLIMATES
with severe winter
with severe dry winter
Tropic of Cancer
Equator
Tropic of Capricorn
Equatorial Scale 1:200,000,000
WORLD
LANGUAGES
PIGMENTATION
WHITE-SKINNED PEOPLES
European
A B Asian
A – Iranian
B – Indic
Semitic
Hamitic
Other
Hamito-Semitic
YELLOW SKINNED PEOPLES
Ural-Altaic
Turkic
Sinitic
Indonesian
Eskimo
Amerasian
Hottentot & Bushman
BLACK SKINNED PEOPLES
Hamitic-Negroid
Sudanese & Nilotic Negroid
Bantu
Dravidian & Pre-Dravidian
Papuan
Australian
ATHAPASCAN
DÉNÉ
TUINGIT
HAIDA
TSIMSHIA
KWAKUITL
HUPA
CREE
ALGONQUIN
SIOUX
CHIPPEWAS
HURON
MICMAC
SHOSHONI
PAWNEE
UTE
IROQUOIS
DELAWARE
APACHE
CADDO
MUSKHOGEE
AZTEC
MAYA
ZAPOTEC
CARIB
CHIBCHA
ARAWAK
CARIB
QUICHUA
ANTIS
AYMARA
TUPI
CHIQUITO
CARAJA
BORRORO
TUPI
GUARANI
TAPUYA-GES
PUELCHE
PEHUENCHE
TEHUELCHE
YAGHAN
POLYNESIAN
SCANDINAVIAN
LAPP
FINN
ENGLISH
PORTUGUESE
SPANISH
FRENCH
GERMAN
SLAV
ITALIAN
OSMANLI
TURK
ARMENIAN
KURD
BERBER-ARABIC
TUAREG
TIBBU
NUBIAN-EGYPTIAN
BEJA
ARABIC
PERSIAN
BALOCH
PASHTO
HINDI
BHIL
GONO
MUNDA
MARATHI
TELUGU
TAMIL
SINHALESE
VEDDA
ANDAMANESE
MANDINGO
KRU
ASHANTI
EWE
HAUSA
FULA
YORUBA
NIAMNIAM
DINKA
SHILLUK
AMHARA
DANAKIL
GALLA
SOMALI
AKKA
MASAI
SWAHILI
BATWA
BALUNDA
BAROTSE
MASHONA
MATABELLE
HEREROS
BUSHMAN
BECHUANA
BASUTO
ZULU
HOTTENTOT
SAKALAVA
HOVA
SAMOYED
OSTYAK
YAKUT
YUKAGHIR
CHUKCHI
KORYAK
TUNGUS
GILYAK
TATARS
KAZAK
KIRGIZ
KARA KIRGIZ
BURYAT
MONGOL
MANCHU
AINU
KOREAN
TIBETANS
CHINESE
MIAO-TSE
JAPANESE
BURMESE
SIAMESE
ANNAMESE
AETA
FILIPINO
SEMANG
SAKAI
BATTAK
DYAK
ALFURS
SUNDANESE
JAVANESE
MICRONESIAN
TAPIRO
PAPUAN
MELANESIAN
POLYNESIAN
AUSTRALIAN
TASMANIAN
MAORI

WORLD
DENSITY OF POPULATION

Equatorial Scale 1:100,000,000

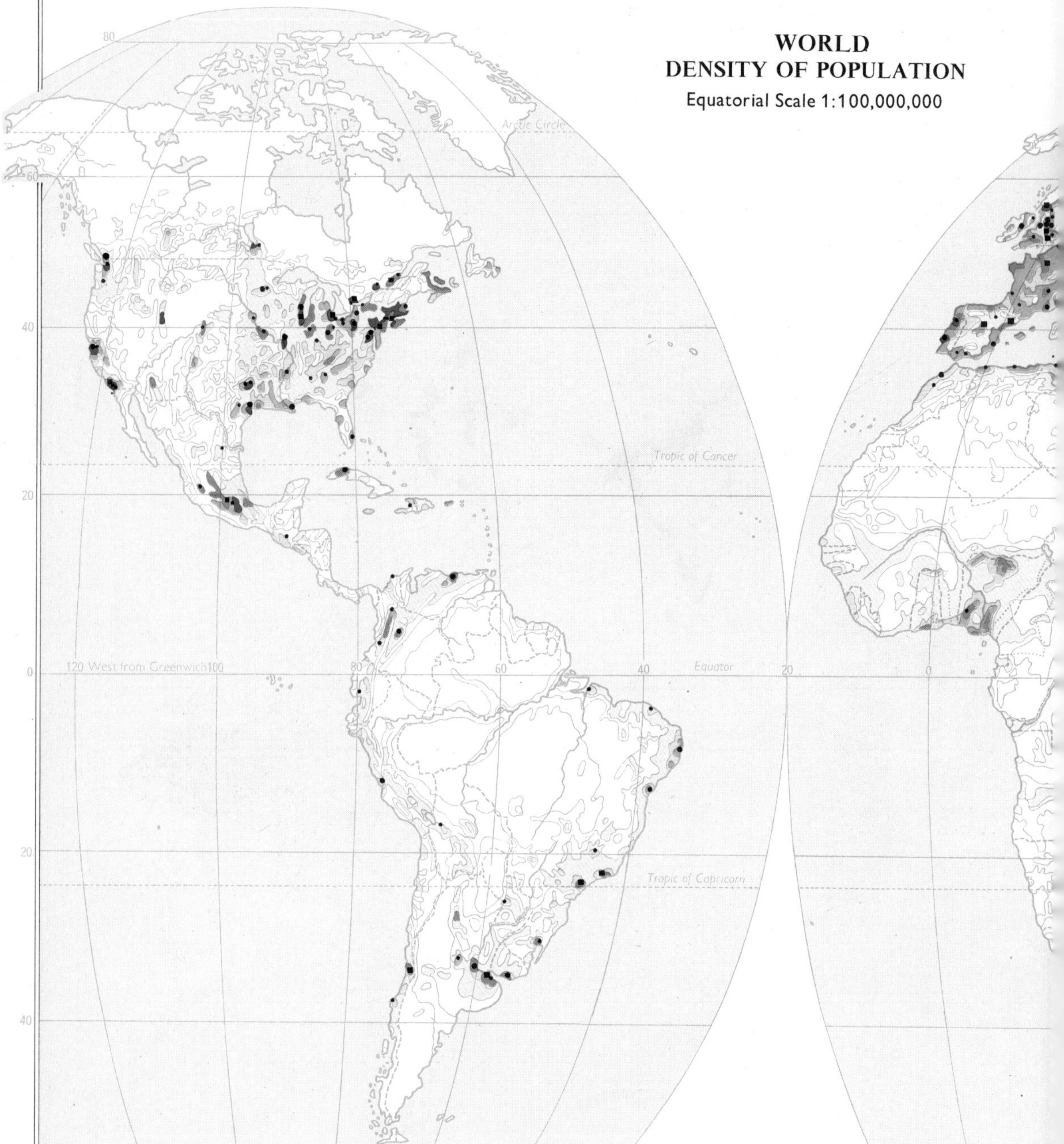

Arctic Circle

Tropic of Cancer

120 West from Greenwich 100

80

60

40

Equator

20

0

Tropic of Capricorn

Antarctic Circle

Inhabitants
per square mile
Under 1
1— 8
9— 16
17— 64
65—128
129—256
257—512
Over 512
Towns with over 1,000,000 inh.
,, 500,000—1,000,000 ,,
,, 100,000— 500,000 ,,
140 East from Greenwich 160

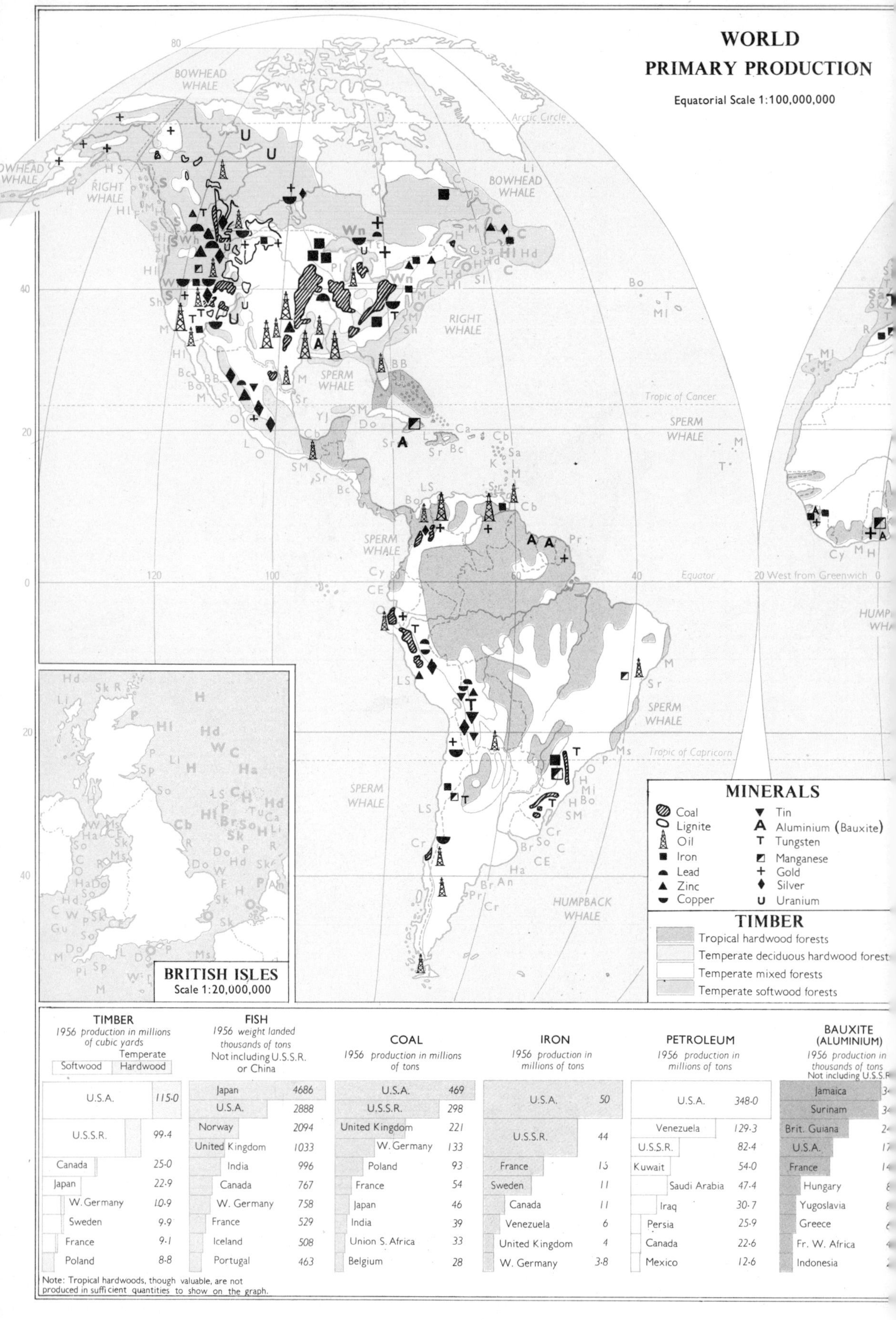

WORLD
PRIMARY PRODUCTION
Equatorial Scale 1:100,000,000
BOWHEAD WHALE
RIGHT WHALE
SPERM WHALE
HUMPBACK WHALE
Arctic Circle
Tropic of Cancer
Equator
Tropic of Capricorn
20 West from Greenwich
MINERALS
Coal
Lignite
Oil
Iron
Lead
Zinc
Copper
Tin
Aluminium (Bauxite)
Tungsten
Manganese
Gold
Silver
Uranium
TIMBER
Tropical hardwood forests
Temperate deciduous hardwood forests
Temperate mixed forests
Temperate softwood forests
BRITISH ISLES
Scale 1:20,000,000
TIMBER
1956 production in millions of cubic yards
Softwood
Temperate Hardwood
U.S.A. 115·0
U.S.S.R. 99·4
Canada 25·0
Japan 22·9
W. Germany 10·9
Sweden 9·9
France 9·1
Poland 8·8
Note: Tropical hardwoods, though valuable, are not produced in sufficient quantities to show on the graph.
FISH
1956 weight landed thousands of tons
Not including U.S.S.R. or China
Japan 4686
U.S.A. 2888
Norway 2094
United Kingdom 1033
India 996
Canada 767
W. Germany 758
France 529
Iceland 508
Portugal 463
COAL
1956 production in millions of tons
U.S.A. 469
U.S.S.R. 298
United Kingdom 221
W. Germany 133
Poland 93
France 54
Japan 46
India 39
Union S. Africa 33
Belgium 28
IRON
1956 production in millions of tons
U.S.A. 50
U.S.S.R. 44
France 13
Sweden 11
Canada 11
Venezuela 6
United Kingdom 4
W. Germany 3·8
PETROLEUM
1956 production in millions of tons
U.S.A. 348·0
Venezuela 129·3
U.S.S.R. 82·4
Kuwait 54·0
Saudi Arabia 47·4
Iraq 30·7
Persia 25·9
Canada 22·6
Mexico 12·6
BAUXITE (ALUMINIUM)
1956 production in thousands of tons
Jamaica
Surinam
Brit. Guiana
U.S.A.
France
Hungary
Yugoslavia
Greece
Fr. W. Africa
Indonesia

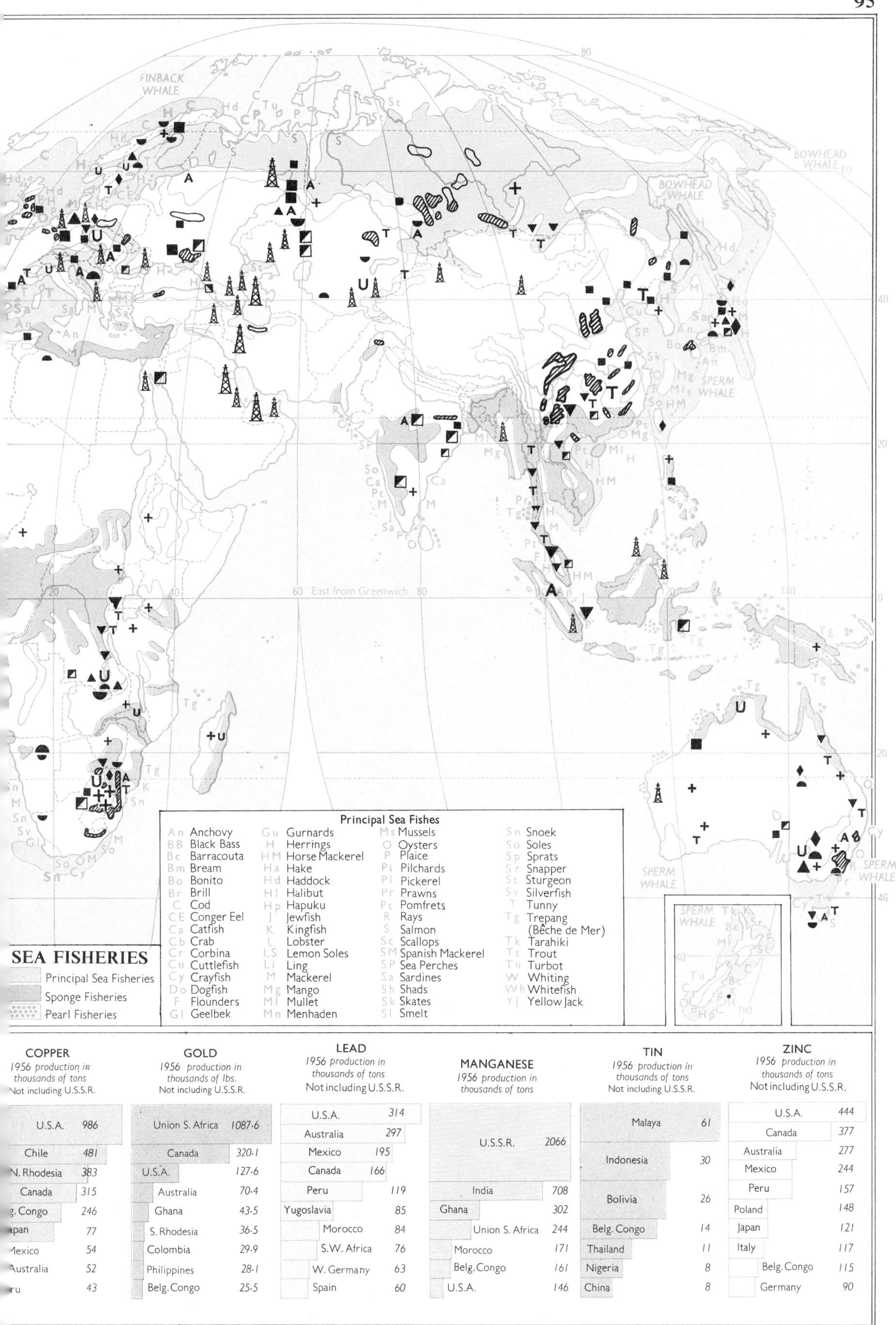

SEA FISHERIES
Principal Sea Fisheries
Sponge Fisheries
Pearl Fisheries
Principal Sea Fishes
An Anchovy
BB Black Bass
Bc Barracouta
Bm Bream
Bo Bonito
Br Brill
C Cod
CE Conger Eel
Ca Catfish
Cb Crab
Cr Corbina
Cu Cuttlefish
Cy Crayfish
Do Dogfish
F Flounders
Gl Geelbek
Gu Gurnards
H Herrings
HM Horse Mackerel
Ha Hake
Hd Haddock
Hl Halibut
Hp Hapuku
J Jewfish
K Kingfish
L Lobster
LS Lemon Soles
Li Ling
M Mackerel
Mg Mango
Ml Mullet
Mn Menhaden
Ms Mussels
O Oysters
P Plaice
Pi Pilchards
Pl Pickerel
Pr Prawns
Pt Pomfrets
R Rays
S Salmon
Sc Scallops
SM Spanish Mackerel
SP Sea Perches
Sa Sardines
Sh Shads
Sk Skates
Sl Smelt
Sn Snoek
So Soles
Sp Sprats
Sr Snapper
St Sturgeon
Sv Silverfish
T Tunny
Tg Trepang (Bêche de Mer)
Tk Tarahiki
Tt Trout
Tu Turbot
W Whiting
Wh Whitefish
YJ Yellow Jack
FINBACK WHALE
BOWHEAD WHALE
SPERM WHALE
60 East from Greenwich 80
COPPER
1956 production in thousands of tons
Not including U.S.S.R.
U.S.A. 986
Chile 481
N. Rhodesia 383
Canada 315
Belg. Congo 246
Japan 77
Mexico 54
Australia 52
Peru 43
GOLD
1956 production in thousands of lbs.
Not including U.S.S.R.
Union S. Africa 1087·6
Canada 320·1
U.S.A. 127·6
Australia 70·4
Ghana 43·5
S. Rhodesia 36·5
Colombia 29·9
Philippines 28·1
Belg. Congo 25·5
LEAD
1956 production in thousands of tons
Not including U.S.S.R.
U.S.A. 314
Australia 297
Mexico 195
Canada 166
Peru 119
Yugoslavia 85
Morocco 84
S.W. Africa 76
W. Germany 63
Spain 60
MANGANESE
1956 production in thousands of tons
U.S.S.R. 2066
India 708
Ghana 302
Union S. Africa 244
Morocco 171
Belg. Congo 161
U.S.A. 146
TIN
1956 production in thousands of tons
Not including U.S.S.R.
Malaya 61
Indonesia 30
Bolivia 26
Belg. Congo 14
Thailand 11
Nigeria 8
China 8
ZINC
1956 production in thousands of tons
Not including U.S.S.R.
U.S.A. 444
Canada 377
Australia 277
Mexico 244
Peru 157
Poland 148
Japan 121
Italy 117
Belg. Congo 115
Germany 90

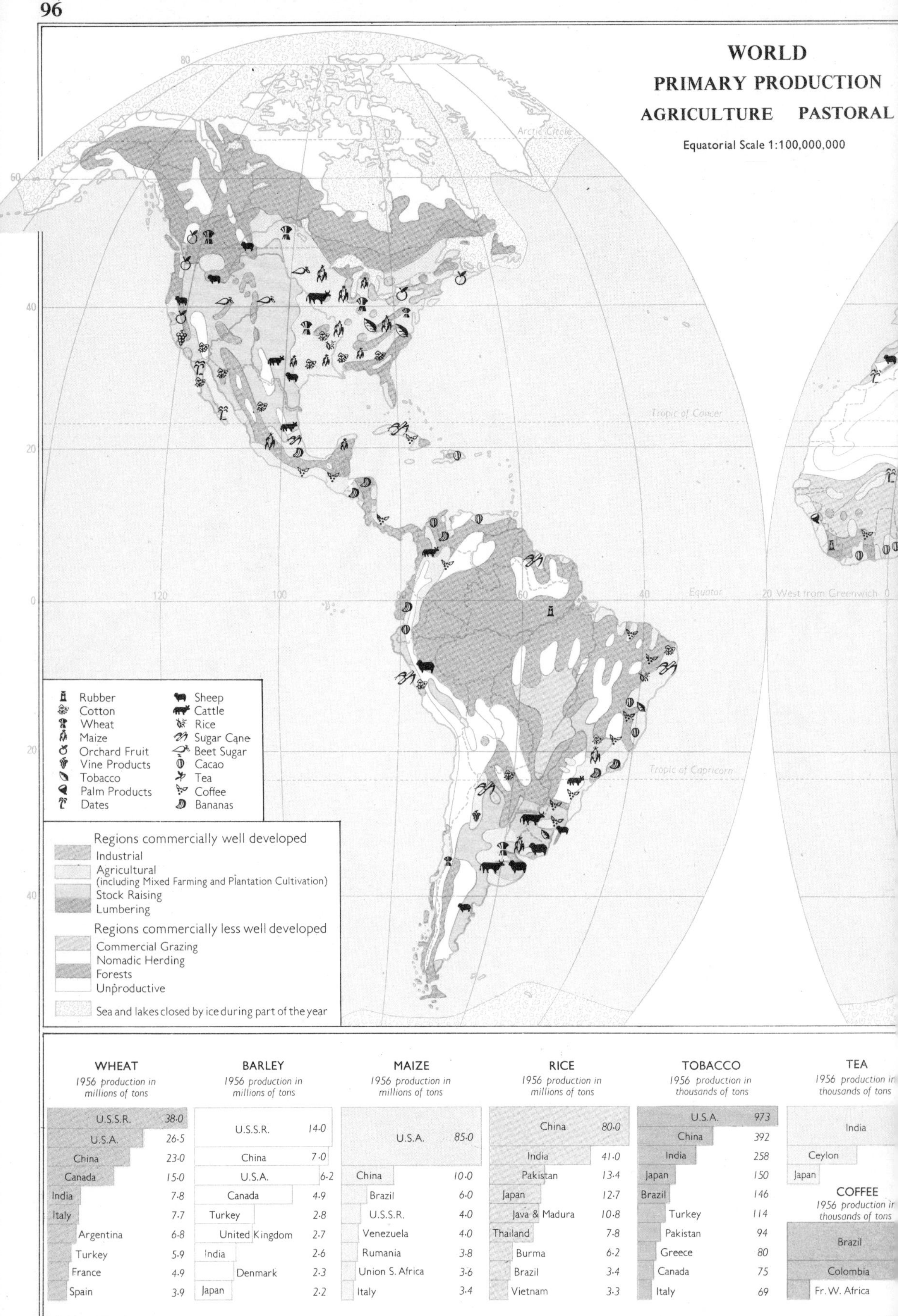
WORLD
PRIMARY PRODUCTION
AGRICULTURE PASTORAL
Equatorial Scale 1:100,000,000
Arctic Circle
Tropic of Cancer
Equator
Tropic of Capricorn
20 West from Greenwich 0
80
60
40
20
0
20
40
120
100
80
60
40
Rubber
Cotton
Wheat
Maize
Orchard Fruit
Vine Products
Tobacco
Palm Products
Dates
Sheep
Cattle
Rice
Sugar Cane
Beet Sugar
Cacao
Tea
Coffee
Bananas
Regions commercially well developed
Industrial
Agricultural
(including Mixed Farming and Plantation Cultivation)
Stock Raising
Lumbering
Regions commercially less well developed
Commercial Grazing
Nomadic Herding
Forests
Unproductive
Sea and lakes closed by ice during part of the year
WHEAT
1956 production in millions of tons
U.S.S.R. 38·0
U.S.A. 26·5
China 23·0
Canada 15·0
India 7·8
Italy 7·7
Argentina 6·8
Turkey 5·9
France 4·9
Spain 3·9
BARLEY
1956 production in millions of tons
U.S.S.R. 14·0
China 7·0
U.S.A. 6·2
Canada 4·9
Turkey 2·8
United Kingdom 2·7
India 2·6
Denmark 2·3
Japan 2·2
MAIZE
1956 production in millions of tons
U.S.A. 85·0
China 10·0
Brazil 6·0
U.S.S.R. 4·0
Venezuela 4·0
Rumania 3·8
Union S. Africa 3·6
Italy 3·4
RICE
1956 production in millions of tons
China 80·0
India 41·0
Pakistan 13·4
Japan 12·7
Java & Madura 10·8
Thailand 7·8
Burma 6·2
Brazil 3·4
Vietnam 3·3
TOBACCO
1956 production in thousands of tons
U.S.A. 973
China 392
India 258
Japan 150
Brazil 146
Turkey 114
Pakistan 94
Greece 80
Canada 75
Italy 69
TEA
1956 production in thousands of tons
India
Ceylon
Japan
COFFEE
1956 production in thousands of tons
Brazil
Colombia
Fr. W. Africa

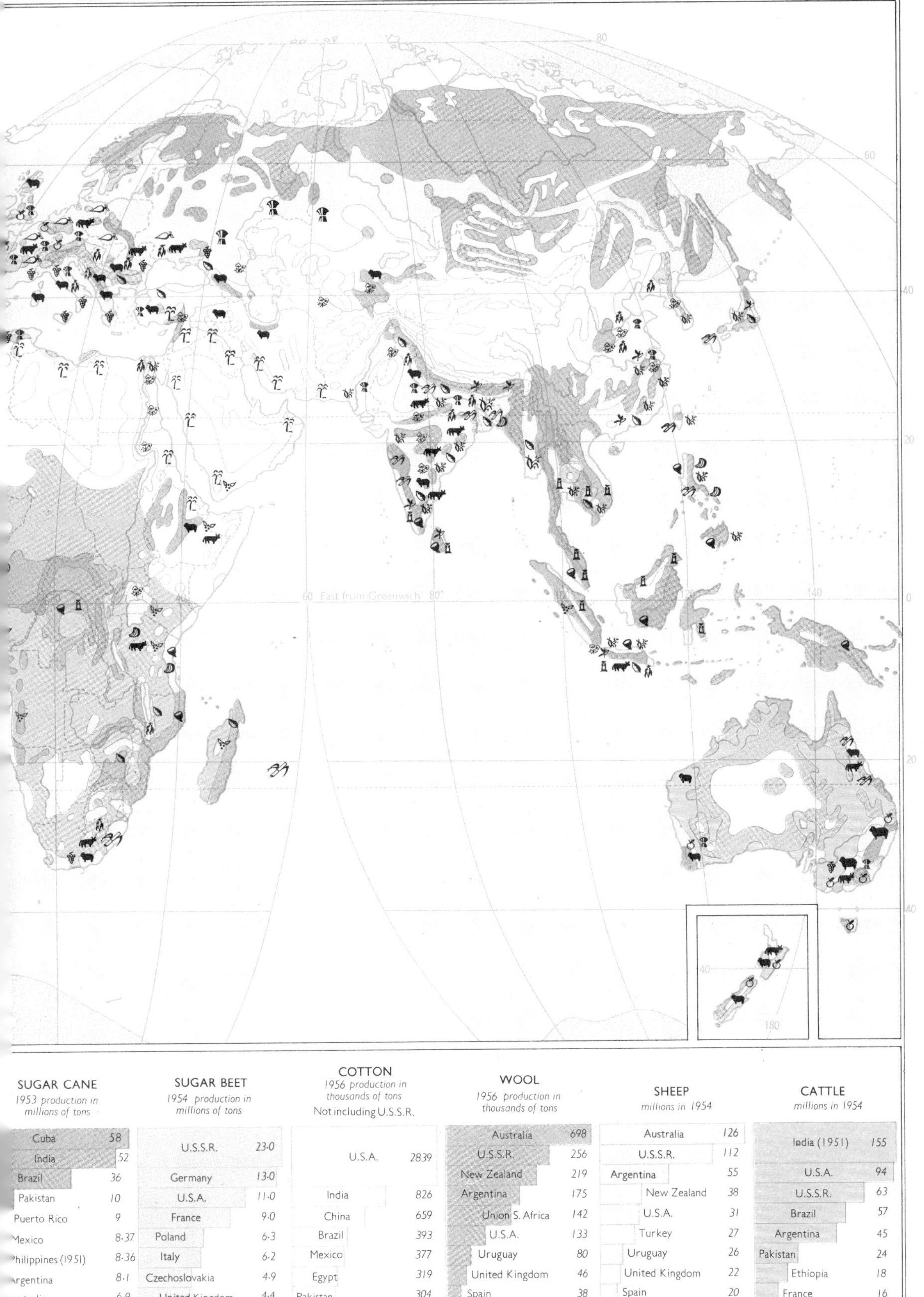

SUGAR CANE
1953 production in millions of tons

Country	Production
Cuba	58
India	52
Brazil	36
Pakistan	10
Puerto Rico	9
lexico	8·37
hilippines (1951)	8·36
rgentina	8·1
ustralia	6·9
.S.A.	6·3

SUGAR BEET
1954 production in millions of tons

Country	Production
U.S.S.R.	23·0
Germany	13·0
U.S.A.	11·0
France	9·0
Poland	6·3
Italy	6·2
Czechoslovakia	4·9
United Kingdom	4·4
Netherlands	2·9

COTTON
1956 production in thousands of tons
Not including U.S.S.R.

Country	Production
U.S.A.	2839
India	826
China	659
Brazil	393
Mexico	377
Egypt	319
Pakistan	304
Turkey	162

WOOL
1956 production in thousands of tons

Country	Production
Australia	698
U.S.S.R.	256
New Zealand	219
Argentina	175
Union S. Africa	142
U.S.A.	133
Uruguay	80
United Kingdom	46
Spain	38
Turkey	38

SHEEP
millions in 1954

Australia	126
U.S.S.R.	112
Argentina	55
New Zealand	38
U.S.A.	31
Turkey	27
Uruguay	26
United Kingdom	22
Spain	20
Persia	17

CATTLE
millions in 1954

India (1951)	155
U.S.A.	94
U.S.S.R.	63
Brazil	57
Argentina	45
Pakistan	24
Ethiopia	18
France	16
Australia	15

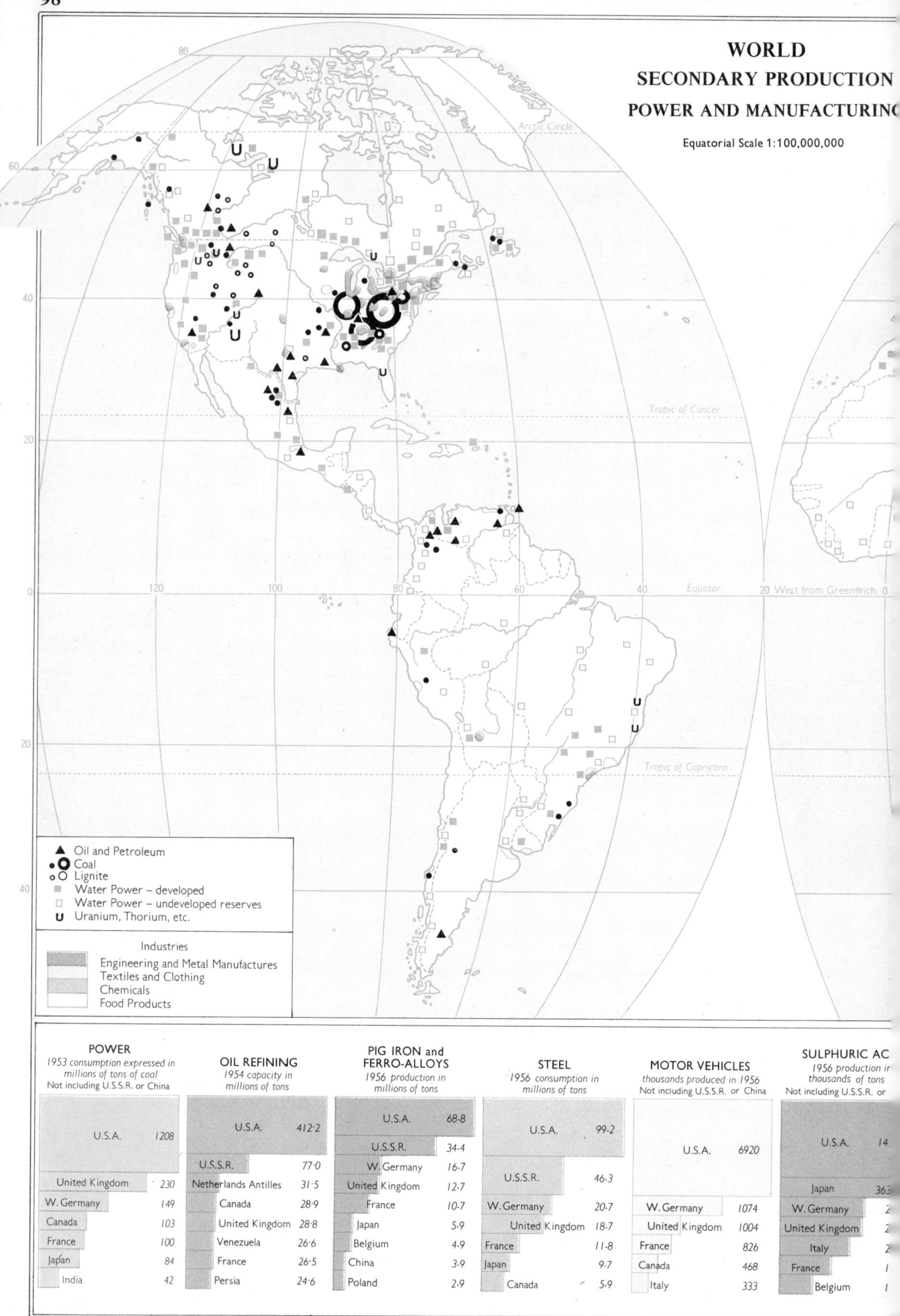

WORLD
SECONDARY PRODUCTION
POWER AND MANUFACTURIN
Equatorial Scale 1:100,000,000
Arctic Circle
Tropic of Cancer
Equator
Tropic of Capricorn
20 West from Greenwich 0
80
60
40
20
0
120
100
80
60
40
20
40
Oil and Petroleum
Coal
Lignite
Water Power – developed
Water Power – undeveloped reserves
Uranium, Thorium, etc.
Industries
Engineering and Metal Manufactures
Textiles and Clothing
Chemicals
Food Products
POWER
1953 consumption expressed in millions of tons of coal
Not including U.S.S.R. or China
U.S.A. 1208
United Kingdom 230
W. Germany 149
Canada 103
France 100
Japan 84
India 42
OIL REFINING
1954 capacity in millions of tons
U.S.A. 412·2
U.S.S.R. 77·0
Netherlands Antilles 31·5
Canada 28·9
United Kingdom 28·8
Venezuela 26·6
France 26·5
Persia 24·6
PIG IRON and FERRO-ALLOYS
1956 production in millions of tons
U.S.A. 68·8
U.S.S.R. 34·4
W. Germany 16·7
United Kingdom 12·7
France 10·7
Japan 5·9
Belgium 4·9
China 3·9
Poland 2·9
STEEL
1956 consumption in millions of tons
U.S.A. 99·2
U.S.S.R. 46·3
W. Germany 20·7
United Kingdom 18·7
France 11·8
Japan 9·7
Canada 5·9
MOTOR VEHICLES
thousands produced in 1956
Not including U.S.S.R. or China
U.S.A. 6920
W. Germany 1074
United Kingdom 1004
France 826
Canada 468
Italy 333
SULPHURIC AC
1956 production ir thousands of tons
Not including U.S.S.R. or
U.S.A. 14
Japan 363
W. Germany
United Kingdom
Italy
France
Belgium

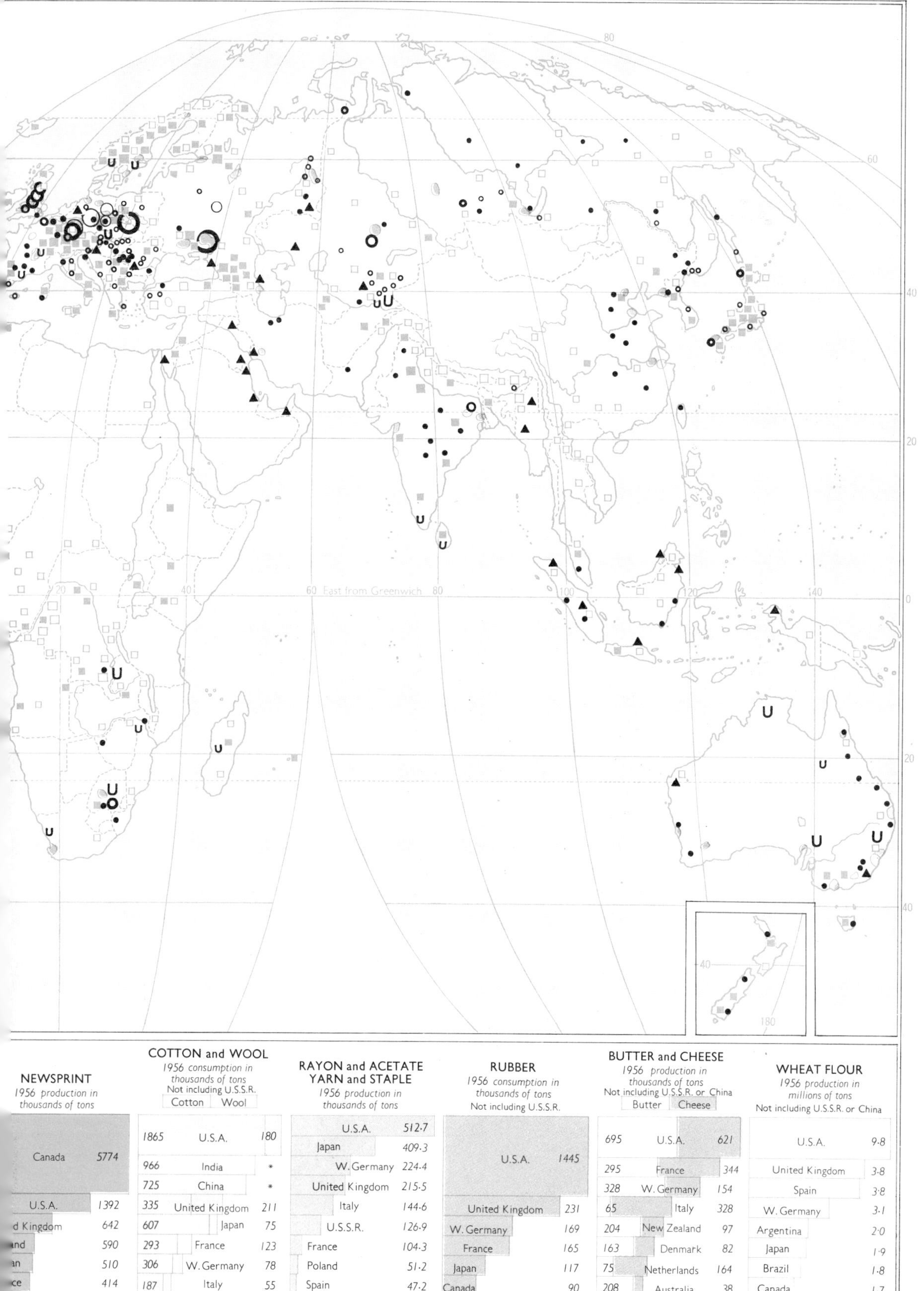

NEWSPRINT
1956 production in thousands of tons

Country	Production
Canada	5774
U.S.A.	1392
d Kingdom	642
and	590
an	510
ce	414
en	408

COTTON and WOOL
1956 consumption in thousands of tons
Not including U.S.S.R.

Cotton	Country	Wool
1865	U.S.A.	180
966	India	*
725	China	*
335	United Kingdom	211
607	Japan	75
293	France	123
306	W. Germany	78
187	Italy	55
219	Brazil	*

**No data for wool consumption*

RAYON and ACETATE YARN and STAPLE
1956 production in thousands of tons

Country	Production
U.S.A.	512·7
Japan	409·3
W. Germany	224·4
United Kingdom	215·5
Italy	144·6
U.S.S.R.	126·9
France	104·3
Poland	51·2
Spain	47·2
Austria	43·3

RUBBER
1956 consumption in thousands of tons
Not including U.S.S.R.

U.S.A.	1445
United Kingdom	231
W. Germany	169
France	165
Japan	117
Canada	90
Italy	72

BUTTER and CHEESE
1956 production in thousands of tons
Not including U.S.S.R. or China

Butter	Country	Cheese
695	U.S.A.	621
295	France	344
328	W. Germany	154
65	Italy	328
204	New Zealand	97
163	Denmark	82
75	Netherlands	164
208	Australia	38
144	Canada	41

WHEAT FLOUR
1956 production in millions of tons
Not including U.S.S.R. or China

Country	Production
U.S.A.	9·8
United Kingdom	3·8
Spain	3·8
W. Germany	3·1
Argentina	2·0
Japan	1·9
Brazil	1·8
Canada	1·7
Yugoslavia	1·3

EUROPE
LAND USE, AGRICULTURE AND MINERALS

Scale 1:27,500,000
(440 miles = 1 inch)

100 0 100 200 300 400 Statute Miles
100 0 200 400 600 Kilometres

Projection: *Bonne*

- Industrial and Mining
- Forest
- Tundra, Alpine and Desert
- Unimproved Pasture and Steppe
- Improved Pasture
- Arable
- Arboriculture

- Coal
- Lignite
- Oil
- Iron
- Copper
- Zinc
- Lead
- Manganese
- Antimony
- Silver
- Gold
- Uranium
- Potassium Salt
- Tin
- Aluminium (Bauxite)
- Nickel
- Natural Gas

- Wheat
- Maize
- Sugar Beet
- Vine
- Potatoes
- Olives
- Tobacco
- Sheep
- Cattle
- Lumbering

Arctic Circle

ASIA
LAND USE, AGRICULTURE AND MINERALS

Scale 1:60,000,000 (960 miles = 1 inch)

200 0 200 400 600 800 1000 Statute Miles
200 0 400 800 1200 1600 Kilometres

Projection: *Bonne*

- Industrial and Mining
- Forest
- Tundra, Alpine and Desert
- Steppe and Poor Pasture
- Mainly Pastoral
- Arable and Pastoral
- Arable and Plantation

Minerals	Agriculture
Oil	Wheat
Coal	Rice
Iron	Maize
Copper	Barley
Lead	Oats
Zinc	Rye
Manganese	Tobacco
Antimony	Cotton
T Tungsten	Sugar
Tin	Coffee
+ Gold	Tea
Silver	Jute
Asbestos	Vine
Mica	Citrus Fruit
Chrome	Groundnuts
Aluminium (Bauxite)	Rubber
U Uranium and Thorium	Silk
	Cattle
	Sheep
	Lumbering

Note: There is a large number of cattle in India; their economic importance is however reduced by sociological and religious restrictions.

Industrial and Mining
Forest and Bush
Desert or Alpine Wastes
Steppe and Semi-desert
Open Grazing and Ranging
Pastoral with Stock-raising
Agriculture, Stock-raising and Plantations

AFRICA
LAND USE, AGRICULTURE AND MINERALS

Scale 1:50,000,000 (800 miles = 1 inch)

200 0 200 400 600 800 1000 Statute Miles

200 0 400 800 1000 1200 Kilometres

Projection: *Lambert's Equivalent Azimuthal*

Oil
Coal
Iron
Manganese
Copper
Gold
Tin
Silver
Asbestos
Zinc
Lead
Diamonds
Uranium
Chrome
Cobalt
Vanadium
Phosphates
Salt
Bauxite (Aluminium)

Wheat
Maize
Rice
Tea
Cotton
Coffee
Cacao
Tobacco
Ginger
Groundnuts
Palm Products
Vine
Esparto
Dates
Rubber
Cattle
Sheep
Sisal
Olives
Bananas
Sugar

Tropic of Cancer
Equator
Tropic of Capricorn

30 West from 20 Greenwich 10 0 10 East from 20 Greenwich 30 40 50

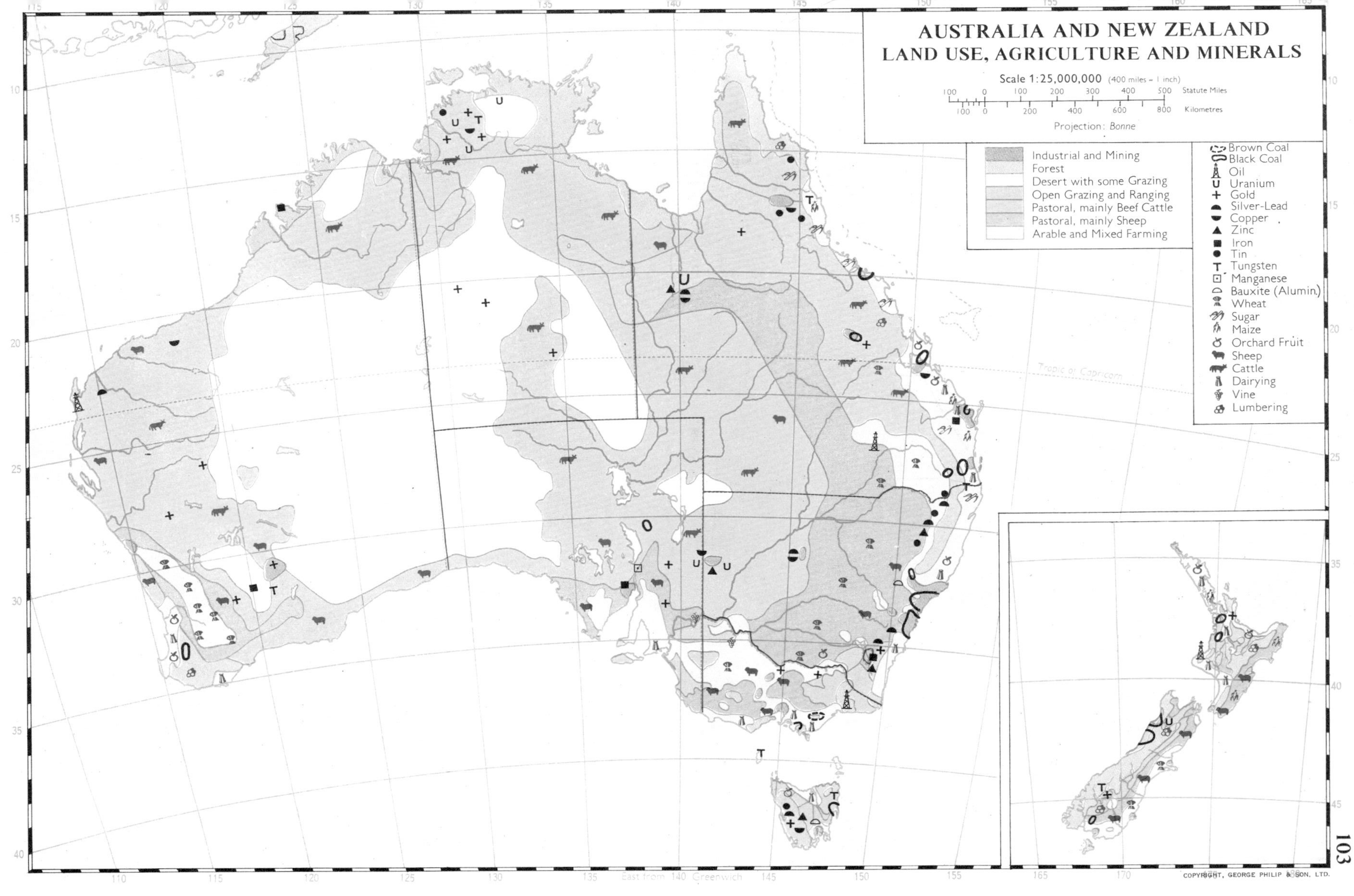
AUSTRALIA AND NEW ZEALAND
LAND USE, AGRICULTURE AND MINERALS
Scale 1:25,000,000 (400 miles = 1 inch)
Statute Miles
Kilometres
Projection: Bonne
Industrial and Mining
Forest
Desert with some Grazing
Open Grazing and Ranging
Pastoral, mainly Beef Cattle
Pastoral, mainly Sheep
Arable and Mixed Farming
Brown Coal
Black Coal
Oil
Uranium
Gold
Silver-Lead
Copper
Zinc
Iron
Tin
Tungsten
Manganese
Bauxite (Alumin.)
Wheat
Sugar
Maize
Orchard Fruit
Sheep
Cattle
Dairying
Vine
Lumbering
Tropic of Capricorn
East from 140 Greenwich

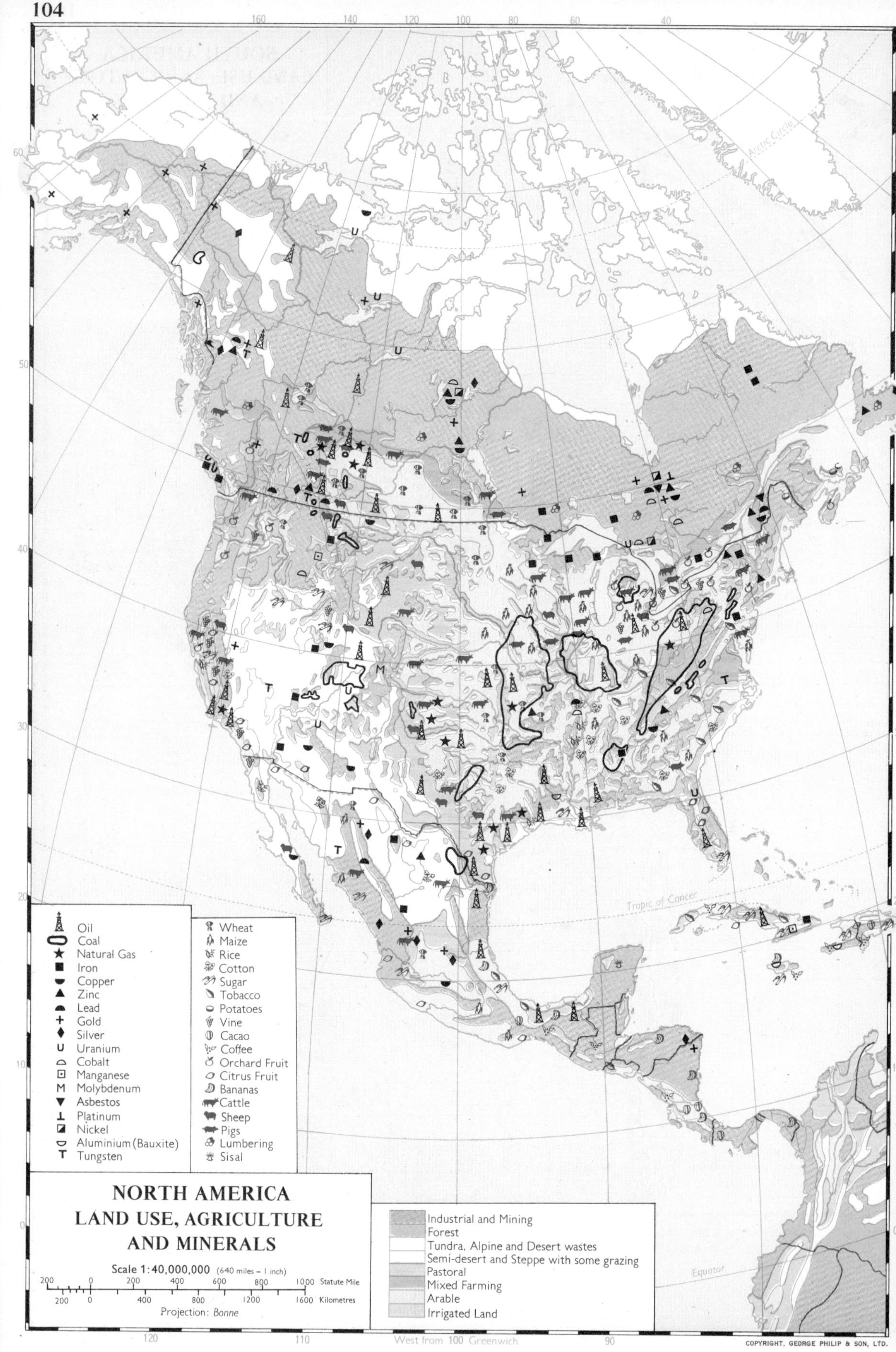

NORTH AMERICA
LAND USE, AGRICULTURE AND MINERALS

Scale 1:40,000,000 (640 miles = 1 inch)

200 0 200 400 600 800 1000 Statute Miles

200 0 400 800 1200 1600 Kilometres

Projection: *Bonne*

SOUTH AMERICA
LAND USE, AGRICULTURE
AND MINERALS
Scale 1:35,000,000
(560 miles = 1 inch)
Statute Miles
Kilometres
Projection: Bonne
Tropic of Capricorn
West from 60 Greenwich
Coal
Oil
Iron
Copper
Silver-Lead
Tin
Manganese
Vanadium
Gold
Platinum
Aluminium (Bauxite)
Diamonds
Salt
Nitrates
Uranium & Thorium
Tungsten
Wheat
Maize
Cotton
Rice
Sugar
Coffee
Cacao
Vine
Tobacco
Citrus Fruit
Bananas
Dairying
Cattle
Sheep
Rubber
Industrial and Mining
Forest with some native agriculture, hunting and collecting
Tropical Forest with some native agriculture
Desert or Alpine wastes
Semi-desert with grazing
Pastoral with agriculture
Agriculture, stock-raising and plantations

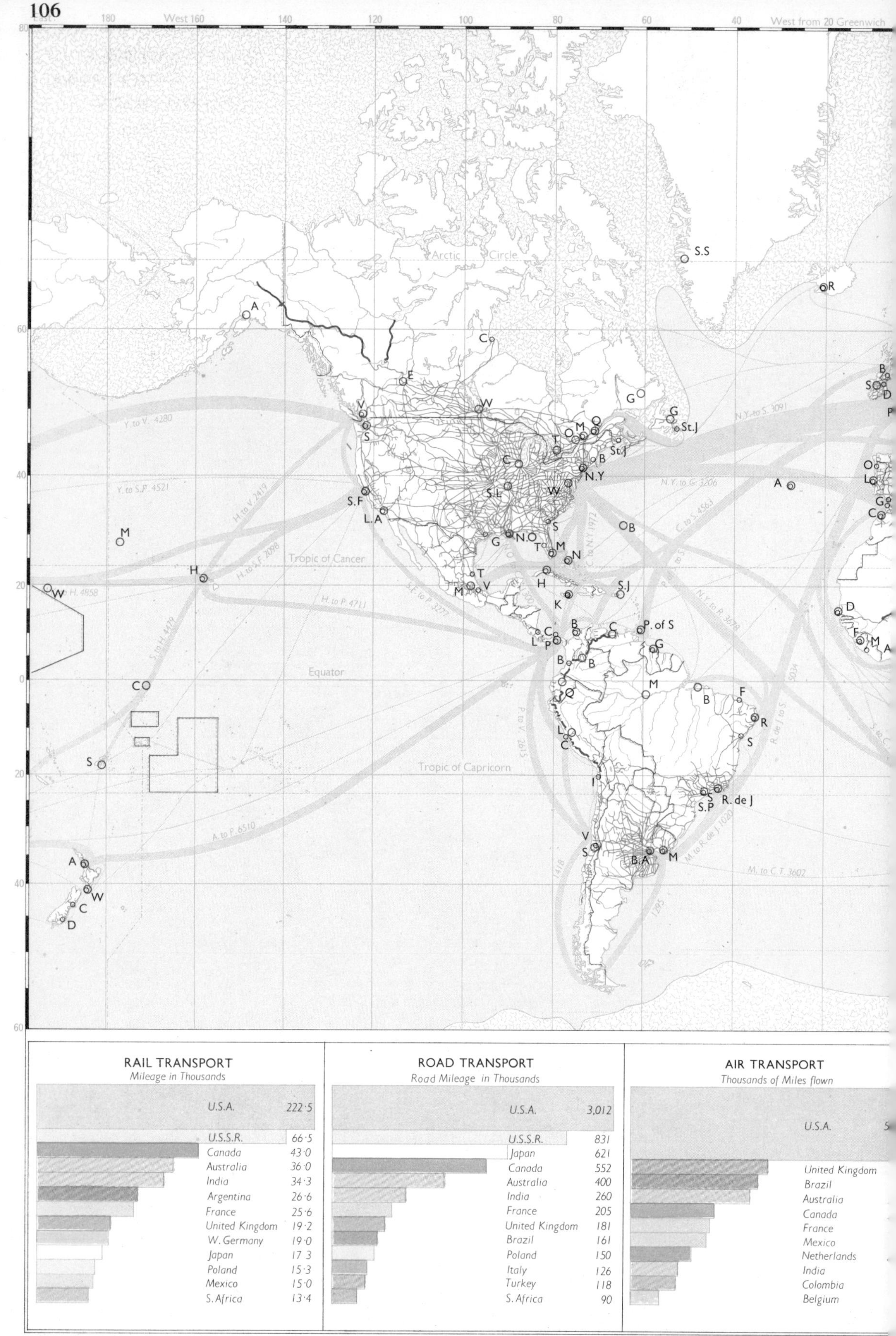

East 180 West 160 140 120 100 80 60 40 West from 20 Greenwich
Arctic Circle
Tropic of Cancer
Equator
Tropic of Capricorn
Y. to V. 4280
Y. to S.F. 4521
H. to V. 2419
H. to S.F. 2098
H. to P. 4711
S.F. to P. 3277
S. to H. 4479
A. to P. 6510
P. to V. 2615
N.Y. to S. 3091
N.Y. to G. 3206
C. to S. 4563
N.Y. to R. 3678
M. to R. de J. 1020
M. to C.T. 3602
S.S
R
A
C
E
V
S
W
T
M
O
Q
G
St.J
B
N.Y
S.F
L.A
S.L
N.O
H
K
S.J
P. of S
L
P
F
R. de J
S.P
I
B.A
D
RAIL TRANSPORT
Mileage in Thousands
U.S.A. 222·5
U.S.S.R. 66·5
Canada 43·0
Australia 36·0
India 34·3
Argentina 26·6
France 25·6
United Kingdom 19·2
W. Germany 19·0
Japan 17 3
Poland 15·3
Mexico 15·0
S. Africa 13·4
ROAD TRANSPORT
Road Mileage in Thousands
U.S.A. 3,012
U.S.S.R. 831
Japan 621
Canada 552
Australia 400
India 260
France 205
United Kingdom 181
Brazil 161
Poland 150
Italy 126
Turkey 118
S. Africa 90
AIR TRANSPORT
Thousands of Miles flown
U.S.A.
United Kingdom
Brazil
Australia
Canada
France
Mexico
Netherlands
India
Colombia
Belgium

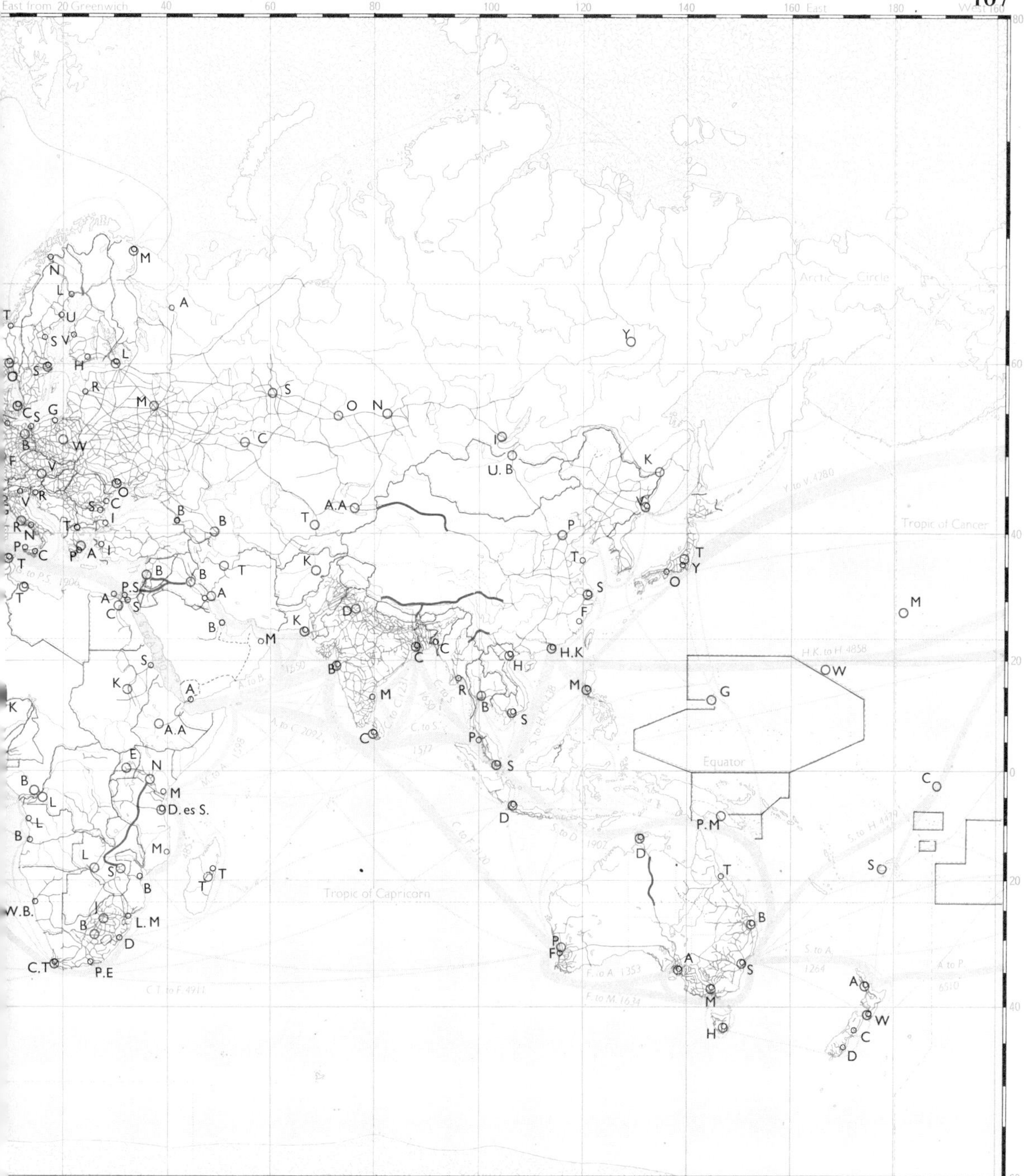

INLAND WATERWAYS

Navigable Miles (in Thousands)

Country	Miles
U.S.S.R.	68·3
U.S.A.	25·4
Brazil	23·6
India	20·0
Bolivia	12·0
China	10·5
Germany	8·1
Belgian Congo	7·2
Fr. Eq. Africa	5·9
Colombia	5·0
Poland	3·5
Pakistan	2·8
Kenya	2·7
United Kingdom	2·4

MERCHANT SHIPPING

Gross Registered Tonnage (in Millions)

Country	Tonnage
U.S.A.	26·4
United Kingdom	19·4
Norway	7·2
Panama	3·9
France	3·9
Italy	3·9
Netherlands	3·7
Japan	3·7
Sweden	2·8
W. Germany	2·6
Canada	1·5
Denmark	1·7
Liberia	4·0

WORLD TRANSPORT

Equatorial Scale 1:140,000,000

Projection: Mercator

- *Railways*
- *Railways under construction*
- *Airports* ○ *Seaports*
- *Roads (see note)*
- *Steamship Routes (width according to importance)*
- *Seas or lakes blocked by ice during part of year*

Notes: See pages 4-5 for Air Routes. Roads are shown only where the railway network is sparse.

See pages 4-5 for Air Routes.

WORLD TRADE

Scale 1:175,000,000

Exports | Imports

Total value of trade in 1953 (or last year for which statistics are available) expressed in millions of U.S. dollars.

25,280
10,000
5000
1000
500
100
10

West from Greenwich
East from Greenwich
Arctic Circle
Tropic of Cancer
Equator
Tropic of Capricorn
Antarctic Circle

U.S.S.R.
Post-war information not available

China
Post-war information not available

Canada
Greenland
Iceland
Faeroe Islands
Norway
Sweden
Finland
Estonia (1938)
Latvia (1938)
Lithuania (1938)
U.S.S.R. (1938)
United States
Bermuda
Bahamas
Mexico
Ecuador
Peru
Bolivia (1953)
Paraguay (1951)
C. Verde Is. (1953)
Surinam
Brazil
Uruguay
Chile
Argentina
Falkland Is. (1953)
Greece
Turkey
Syria
Afghanistan (1948)
Morocco
Gibraltar
Tangier (1952)
Malta & Gozo
Lebanon
Israel
Tunisia
Algeria
Cyprus
Iraq
Persia (1953)
Libya
French Cameroons
Egypt
Jordan (1953)
French West Africa
French Equatorial Africa
Aden (1953)
Pakistan
Gambia
Sierra Leone
Fr. Togoland
Nigeria
Sudan
Ethiopia & Eritrea
Brit. Somaliland
Fr. Somaliland
Liberia (1953)
São Tomé
Belgian Congo
Somalia
Kenya-Uganda
Zanzibar
Gold Coast
Angola
Tanganyika
Nyasaland (1953)
N. Rhodesia (1953)
Mozambique (1953)
South West Africa
S. Rhodesia (1953)
Union of South Africa
Madagascar
Mauritius
Reunion
India
Portuguese India (1952)
Burma
Ceylon
Malaya
Indonesia
China (1938)
Korea (1938)
Hong Kong
Formosa
Thailand (1938)
Indo-China (1953)
Brunei
North Borneo
Sarawak
Japan
Ryukyu Is. (1953)
Guam
Philippines
N.E. New Guinea (1953)
New Guinea (1953)
Papua
Western Samoa
Fiji Is.
New Caledonia
Australia
New Zealand

Central America

Scale 1:40,000,000

Tropic of Cancer
Cuba (1953)
Brit. Honduras
Honduras
Guatemala
Salvador
Nicaragua
Costa Rica
Panama
Jamaica
Haiti
Dominican Republic
Virgin Islands (1953)
Leeward Islands
Guadeloupe
Martinique
Barbados (1953)
Windward Islands
Netherlands Antilles
Trinidad & Tobago
British Guiana
French Guiana
Colombia
Venezuela

Note: Imports c.i.f. and Exports f.o.b. are taken from United Nations' Yearbook of International Trade Statistics 1954, and are expressed in millions of U.S. dollars.

Central Europe

Scale 1:27,500,000

Denmark
Eire
United Kingdom
Netherlands
Belgium with Luxembourg
West Germany
Poland (1948)
Czechoslovakia (1948)
Austria
Hungary (1948)
France
Switzerland
Italy
Bulgaria (1938)
Rumania (1938)
Yugoslavia
Albania (1938)
Portugal
Spain

FACTS AND FIGURES

A SUMMARY OF USEFUL INFORMATION

THE EARTH, CONTINENTS AND OCEANS

Dimensions of the Earth

Polar diameter of the Earth	7,900·0 miles
Equatorial diameter of the Earth	7,926·7 „
Polar circumference of the Earth	24,861·0 „
Equatorial circumference of the Earth	24,902·5 „
Volume of the Earth	259,913,575,000 cubic „
Area of the Earth	196,957,772 square „

Comparative Areas of the Continents and Oceans

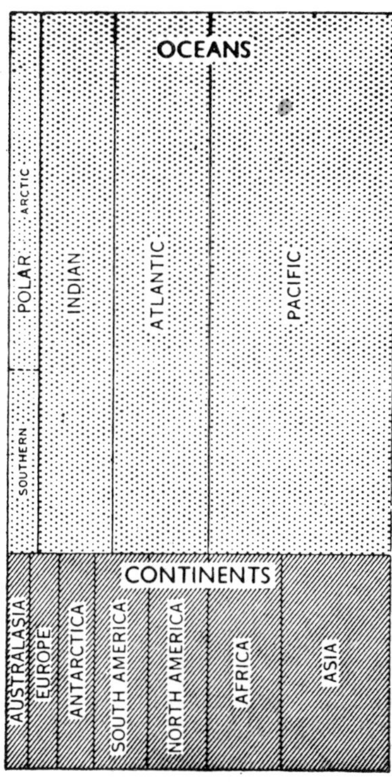

Length of degrees of Latitude and Longitude

Latitude	Length of a degree on a meridian Miles	Length of a degree on a parallel Miles
0°	68·70	69·17
10°	68·73	68·13
20°	68·79	65·03
30°	68·88	59·96
40°	68·99	53·06
50°	69·11	44·55
60°	69·23	34·67
70°	69·32	23·73
80°	69·39	12·05
90°	69·41	0·00

The mean length of a degree of latitude measured on a meridian is 364,566 feet, or nearly 69·15 statute miles (60 geographical miles). Owing to the earth being flattened at the poles, the length of a degree measured on a meridian gradually increases towards the poles in the above proportion.

Populations of the World, Continents and regions, 1955, in millions[1]

WORLD [2]	2,691
AFRICA	223
Northern Africa	78
Tropical and Southern Africa	145
AMERICA	366
Northern America	183
Middle America	58
South America	125
ASIA [3]	1,481
South West Asia [3]	73
South Central Asia	499
South East Asia	185
East Asia	724
EUROPE [4]	409
North and Western Europe	137
Central Europe	134
Southern Europe	138
OCEANIA	14·6
U.S.S.R. [5]	200

[1] Estimates include adjustments for overestimation and underenumeration.
[2] Includes allowance for population of the U.S.S.R.
[3] Including Turkey but excluding the U.S.S.R. shown.
[4] Excluding the U.S.S.R. shown separately below and the European part of Turkey included in Asia.
[5] Official estimate, 1956.

Length of the longest and shortest day in different Latitudes

Latitude	Longest Day hrs. mins.		Shortest Day hrs. mins.	
0°	12	9	11	58
15°	12	59	11	11
30°	14	2	10	8
45°	15	36	8	40
***51½°**	**16**	**34**	**7**	**44**
60°	18	45	5	42
66½° (Arctic Circle)	24	0	0	0

North of the Arctic Circle the number of 24-hour days in a year are:

70°	65 days
80°	134 days
90°	186 days

* Latitude of London

THE POPULATIONS OF THE PRINCIPAL CITIES OF THE WORLD

Towns with over one million inhabitants are in heavy type, and where obtainable the metropolitan populations are given, e.g. Greater New York and Greater Montreal, etc. Figures are based on the latest census where available and reliable estimates, and are given in thousands.

EUROPE

ENGLAND & WALES (1951)
- **London**, Greater . . 8,250
- „ County . . 3,348
- **Birmingham** . 1,103
- Liverpool . 768
- Manchester . 682
- Leeds . 510
- Sheffield . . 498
- Bristol . . 439
- Nottingham . 312
- Hull . . 300
- Bradford . 287
- Leicester . 281
- Coventry . . 277
- Newcastle . 275
- Stoke . . 271
- Croydon . 249

SCOTLAND (1951)
- **Glasgow** . . 1,089
- Edinburgh . 467

N. IRELAND
- Belfast . . 444

IRELAND
- Dublin . . 539

AUSTRIA
- **Vienna** . . 1,616

BELGIUM
- Brussels . . 985
- Antwerp . . 256

BULGARIA
- Sofia . . . 726

CZECHO-SLOVAKIA
- Prague (Praha) 978
- Brno . . . 306

DENMARK
- Copenhagen . 753

FINLAND
- Helsinki . . 425

FRANCE
- **Paris** . . . 2,850
- Marseilles . 661
- Lyons . . 471
- Toulouse . . 269
- Bordeaux . 258

GERMANY
- **Berlin** . . 3,363
- **Hamburg** . . 1,751
- Munich . . 962
- Cologne . . 713
- Essen . . 699
- Düsseldorf . 654
- Frankfurt . 623
- Leipzig . 613
- Dortmund . 607
- Stuttgart . 601
- Hanover . . 536
- Bremen . . 507
- Dresden . . 496
- Duisburg . 476
- Nuremberg . 424
- Wuppertal . 406
- Gelsenkirchen 374
- Bochum . . 345
- Karl Marxstadt 290
- Halle . . 289
- Mannheim . 287
- Magdeburg . 261
- Kiel . . 256

GREECE
- **Athens and Piraeus** . 1,368

HUNGARY
- **Budapest** . 1,757

ITALY
- **Rome** . . 1,702
- **Milan** . . 1,277
- **Naples** . . 1,025
- Turin . . 722
- Genoa . . 687
- Palermo . 503
- Florence . . 391
- Bologna . . 351
- Venice . . 322
- Catania . . 302
- Bari . . . 274
- Trieste . . 270

NETHERLANDS
- Amsterdam . 871
- Rotterdam . 722
- The Hague . 606

NORWAY
- Oslo . . . 451

POLAND
- **Warsaw** . . 1,069
- Lodz . . . 683
- Krakow . 461
- Wroclaw . 389
- Poznan . . 379

PORTUGAL
- Lisbon . . 790
- Oporto . . 284

RUMANIA
- **Bucharest** . 1,236

SPAIN
- **Madrid** . . 1,843
- **Barcelona** . 1,403
- Valencia . . 511
- Seville . . 405
- Malaga . . 277
- Zaragoza . 274

SWEDEN
- Stockholm . 794
- Göteborg . 387

SWITZERLAND
- Zürich . . 390

U.S.S.R.
- **Moscow** . . 4,847
- **Leningrad** . 3,182
- Kiev . . . 991
- Baku . . . 901
- Kharkov . . 877
- Gorky . . 876
- Tashkent . . 778
- Kuibyshev . 760
- Novosibirsk . 731
- Sverdlovsk . 707
- Tbilisi . . 635
- Stalino . . 625
- Chelyabinsk . 612
- Odessa . . 607
- Dnepropetrovsk 576
- Kazan . . 565
- Riga . . . 565
- Rostov-on-Don . 552
- Perm . . . 538
- Stalingrad . 525
- Saratov . . 518
- Omsk . . . 505
- Ufa . . . 471
- Minsk . . 412
- Voronezh . 400
- Lvov . . . 387
- Yerevan . . 385
- Zaporozhe . 381
- Yaroslavl . 374
- Karaganda . 350
- Stalinsk . . 347

YUGOSLAVIA
- Belgrade . . 522
- Zagreb . . 350

ASIA

BURMA
- Rangoon . . 737

CAMBODIA
- Pnompenh . 500

CEYLON
- Colombo . 425

CHINA*
- **Shanghai** . 6,204
- **Peking** . . 5,420
- **Tientsin** . . 2,693
- **Mukden** . . 2,290
- **Wuhan** . . 1,800
- **Chungking** . 1,620
- **Sian** . . . 1,500
- **Canton** . . 1,496
- **Dairen** . . 1,054
- **Nanking** . . 1,020
- Tsingtao . . 850
- Harbin . . 760
- Taiyuan . . 500
- Anshan . . 400

HONGKONG
- Victoria . . 700
- Kowloon . 301

INDIA
- **Bombay** . . 2,839
- **Calcutta** . . 2,549
- **Madras** . . 1,416
- **Delhi** . . . 1,191
- **Hyderabad** . 1,086
- Ahmedabad . 788
- Bangalore . 779
- Kanpur (Cawnpore) 705
- Lucknow . 497
- Poona . . 481
- Nagpur . . 449
- Howrah . . 433
- Agra . . . 376
- Madurai . . 362
- Varanasi . 356
- Allahabad . 332
- Amritsar . . 326
- Indore . . 311
- Jaipur . . 291
- Patna . . 283
- Sholapur . 266
- Jabalpur . . 257

INDONESIA
- **Djakarta** . 3,000
- Surabaja . . 341

IRAQ
- **Baghdad** . 1,085

ISRAEL
- Tel Aviv-Jaffa 371

JAPAN
- **Tokyo** . . 8,638
- **Osaka** . . 2,542
- **Nagoya** . . 1,336
- **Kyoto** . . 1,204
- **Yokohama** . 1,143
- Kobe . . . 979
- Fukuoka . 544
- Kawasaki . 445
- Sapporo . . 426
- Sendai . . 375
- Hiroshima . 357
- Amagasaki . 335
- Kumamoto . 332
- Kanazawa . 303
- Yokosuka . 295

KOREA
- **Seoul** . . 1,574
- **Pusan** . . 1,045
- Taegu . . 487
- Inchon . . 318
- Pyongyang . 286

LEBANON
- Beirut . . 400

PAKISTAN
- **Karachi** . . 1,009
- Lahore . . 849
- Dacca . . 411
- Chittagong . 294

PERSIA
- **Tehran** . . 1,513
- Tabriz . . 290

PHILIPPINES
- **Manila** . . 1,200

SIAM
- **Bangkok** . 1,208

SINGAPORE
- **Singapore** . 1,466

SYRIA
- *Aleppo . . 398
- Damascus . 395
- Homs . . 294

TURKEY
- **Istanbul** . . 1,215
- Ankara . . 453

VIETNAM
- **Saigon-Cholon** 1,800
- Hanoi . . 298

AUSTRALASIA

AUSTRALIA
- **Sydney** . . 1,975
- **Melbourne** . 1,677
- Brisbane . . 543
- Adelaide . 529
- Perth . . 376

NEW ZEALAND
- Auckland . 401

AFRICA

ALGERIA
- Algiers . . 361
- Oran . . . 299

EGYPT
- **Cairo** . . 2,091
- Alexandria . 919

ETHIOPIA
- Addis Ababa 400

MOROCCO
- Casablanca . 700

NIGERIA
- Ibadan . . 459
- Lagos . . 272

TUNISIA
- Tunis . . 410

UNION OF SOUTH AFRICA
- Johannesburg 884
- Cape Town . 578
- Durban . . 480
- Pretoria . . 285

NORTH AMERICA

CANADA
- **Montreal** . 1,109
- Toronto . . 667
- Vancouver . 365
- Winnipeg . 255
- Hamilton . 239
- Ottawa . . 222
- Quebec . . 170

UNITED STATES
- **New York** . 7,795
- **Chicago** . . 3,620
- **Los Angeles** . 2,243
- **Philadelphia** . 2,072
- **Detroit** . . 1,850
- Baltimore . 950
- Cleveland . 941
- St. Louis . 857
- Washington . 802
- Boston . . 801
- San Francisco 775
- Pittsburgh . 677
- Milwaukee . 656
- Houston . . 596
- Buffalo . . 580
- New Orleans 570
- Cincinnati 562
- Minneapolis 522
- Seattle . . 516
- Atlanta . . 503
- San Diego . 494
- Kansas City (Mo.) . . 457
- Columbus . 450
- Newark . . 438
- Dallas . . 434
- San Antonio . 430
- Indianapolis . 427
- Denver . . 416
- Memphis . 396
- Oakland . . 384
- Portland (Oreg.) . 374
- Louisville . 369
- Toledo . . 335
- Rochester . 332
- Birmingham . 326
- St. Paul . . 311
- Akron . . 299
- Jersey City . 299
- Ft. Worth . 278
- Omaha . . 251
- Long Beach . 251

MEXICO
- **Mexico City** . 2,235
- Guadalajara . 378
- Monterrey . 333
- Puebla . . 211

CENTRAL AMERICA

CUBA
- Havana . . . 787

GUATEMALA
- Guatemala . 294

HAITI
- Port au Prince 200

SOUTH AMERICA

ARGENTINA
- **Buenos Aires** . 3,703
- Rosario . . 761
- Córdoba . 352
- La Plata . . 325

BOLIVIA
- La Paz . . 321

BRAZIL
- **Rio de Janeiro** 2,303
- **Sao Paulo** . 2,017
- Recife . . 512
- Salvador . 389
- Pôrto Alegre . 375
- Belo Horizonte 338

CHILE
- **Santiago** . . 1,350

COLOMBIA
- Bogotá . . 648
- Medellin . 358
- Cali . . . 284
- Barranquilla . 280

ECUADOR
- Guayaquil . 296

PERU
- **Lima** . . . 1,135

URUGUAY
- Montevideo . 838

VENEZUELA
- **Caracas** . . 1,102

* Incomplete Data

WORLD ORGANIZATIONS, ALLIANCES, TREATIES, ETC.

1. THE UNITED NATIONS ORGANIZATION

During the Second World War it became obvious to the nations opposing Nazi Germany and her allies that, when peace came, some new international organization would be needed to take the place of the League of Nations. A beginning was made with the declaration of 1st January 1942, by which the United Kingdom, U.S.A., U.S.S.R. and China bound themselves to the purposes and principles of the Atlantic Charter. The foundations of the new organization were laid by the 'Moscow Pact' (1st November 1943) and its detailed design was shaped at meetings at Dumbarton Oaks, near Washington, D.C., in which the same four powers took part. The plan was discussed at the San Francisco Conference (25th April to 26th June 1945) and on the last day of the conference the Charter of the United Nations was signed by the representatives of fifty nations

For Peace and Progress

The Preamble of the Charter contains a general statement of policy and runs thus:

'We, the peoples of the United Nations, determined to save succeeding generations from the scourge of war, which twice in our lifetime has brought untold sorrow to mankind, and to reaffirm faith in fundamental human rights, in the dignity and worth of the human person, in the equal rights of men and women and of nations large and small; and to establish conditions under which justice and respect for the obligations arising from treaties and other sources of international law can be maintained; and to promote social progress and better standards of life in larger freedom; and for these ends to practise tolerance and live together in peace with one another as good neighbours; and to unite our strength to maintain international peace and security; to ensure by the acceptance of principles and the institution of methods, that armed force shall not be used, save in the common interest; and to employ international machinery for the promotion of the economic and social advancement of all peoples, Have resolved to combine our efforts to accomplish these aims.'

The United Nations formally came into existence on 24th October 1945. Its permanent headquarters are at Manhattan, New York. There are six principal organs:

1. The General Assembly

This consists of all members. Each may be represented at meetings by five representatives, but has only one vote. Each has the right to be represented on the Main Committees (Political and Security; Economic and Financial; Social, Humanitarian and Cultural; Trusteeship; Administrative and Budgetary; Legal). The General Assembly normally meets once a year (on the third Tuesday in September), but special sessions may also be held.

2. The Security Council

This consists of five *permanent* members (U.K.. U.S.A., U.S.S.R., France, China) and six non-permanent members (elected for a two-year term). As its name suggests, the Security Council has as its prime purpose the maintenance of peace and security.

On procedural matters an affirmative vote by seven members of the Council is sufficient, but on all other questions the concurring votes of the permanent members are essential. In other words, the power of veto can be exercised by any permanent member. But no permanent member may vote on any measure put forward for a peaceful settlement of any dispute in which he is a party.

3. Economic and Social Council

Standards of living, human rights, economic, social and cultural matters, education—these and kindred matters are the concern of the Economic and Social Council, which has established various important commissions and agencies. These include: United Nations Children's Fund (UNICEF); United Nations Educational, Scientific and Cultural Organization (UNESCO); Food and Agriculture Organization (FAO); International Civil Aviation Organization (ICAO); International Labour Organization (ILO); International Trade Organization (ITO); World Health Organization (WHO); Universal Postal Union (UPO); International Telecommunications Union (ITU); International Bank for Reconstruction and Development; International Monetary Fund; World Meteorological Organization (WMO); Inter-Governmental Maritime Consultative Organization (IMCO).

Certain of these organizations, e.g., the ILO, were operating before the United Nations Organization was established.

4. The Trusteeship Council

This body deals with territories administered by Trustees, approved by the Council. The territories held under this system are: Tanganyika. British Cameroons, (Britain); Nauru (administered by Australia on behalf of Australia, Britain and New Zealand), New Guinea (Australia); Western Samoa (New Zealand); French Cameroons, (France); Ruanda Urundi (Belgium); Somalia (Italy); Pacific Islands—the Marshalls, Marianas and Carolines (U.S.A.).

5. The International Court of Justice

This Court is the chief judicial organ of the United Nations. It has fifteen judges, elected by the Security Council and General Assembly. Its meetings are held at The Hague (Netherlands).

6. The Secretariat

This is composed of the Secretary-General and an international staff appointed by him under regulations made by the General Assembly.

MEMBERS OF THE UNITED NATIONS

Original Members, 1945

1. Argentina
2. Australia
3. Belgium
4. Bolivia
5. Brazil
6. Byelorussian S.S.R.
7. Canada
8. Chile
9. China
10. Colombia
11. Costa Rica
12. Cuba
13. Czechoslovakia
14. Denmark
15. Dominican Rep.
16. Ecuador
17. Egypt*
18. El Salvador
19. Ethiopia
20. France
21. Greece
22. Guatemala
23. Haiti
24. Honduras
25. India
26. Iran
27. Iraq
28. Lebanon
29. Liberia
30. Luxemburg
31. Mexico
32. Netherlands
33. New Zealand
34. Nicaragua
35. Norway
36. Panama
37. Paraguay
38. Peru
39. Philippine Rep.
40. Poland
41. Saudi Arabia
42. Syria*
43. Turkey
44. Ukrainian S.S.R.
45. Union of South Africa
46. U.S.S.R.
47. United Kingdom
48. United States
49. Uruguay
50. Venezuela
51. Yugoslavia

**On March 7th, 1958, the credentials were accepted of the delegation of the United Arab Republic, which became a single member of the United Nations in place of Egypt and Syria.*

Members subsequently admitted

Member	*Instrument of Adherence presented*	Member	*Instrument of Adherence presented*
52. Afghanistan	10th November 1946	68. Rumania	14th December 1955
53. Iceland	" "	69. Bulgaria	" "
54. Sweden	" "	70. Finland	" "
55. Siam	16th December 1946	71. Ceylon	" "
56. Pakistan	30th September 1947	72. Nepal	" "
57. Yemen	" "	73. Cambodia	" "
58. Burma	19th April 1949	74. Laos	" "
59. Israel	11th May 1949	75. Spain	" "
60. Indonesia	28th September 1950	76. Libya	" "
61. Albania	14th December 1955	77. Tunisia	12th November 1956
62. Jordan	" "	78. Morocco	" "
63. Ireland	" "	79. Sudan	" "
64. Portugal	" "	80. Japan	18th December 1956
65. Hungary	" "	81. Ghana	8th March 1957
66. Italy	" "	82. Malaya	17th September 1958
67. Austria	" "	83. Guinea*	12th December 1958

**But there are now only 82 member-nations, Egypt and Syria having been replaced by the United Arab Republic (see footnote on previous page).*

2. ALLIANCES, TREATIES, ETC.

Afro-Asian Peoples Solidarity Conference

This is a non-governmental but very influential grouping of more than 40 nations of the Asian and African continents, including the Soviet Union as an Asian power, to strengthen Afro-Asian solidarity movements and concert their efforts in the international field. The Conference was established at a meeting in Cairo on January 1st, 1958, and its permanent Secretariat is in Cairo. At the United Nations, 28 delegations of the Afro-Asian bloc meet from time to time to concert policy on matters affecting them.

ANZUS Pact

This Pacific security pact was signed in San Francisco on 1st September 1951 by the representatives of Australia, New Zealand and the United States (hence the name ANZUS). Each country concerned recognizes than 'an armed attack in the Pacific area on any of the parties would be dangerous to its own peace and security' and agrees to 'act to meet the common danger in accordance with its constitutional processes.' From the Australian and New Zealand viewpoint, the pact is a guarantee of American help in the event of any aggression. From the American viewpoint, the pact is one of several treaties by which the United States has built up a security system in the Pacific Area.

Arab League

The Arab League, to preserve the independence and sovereignty of its members and to further their common interests, was brought into being on March 22nd, 1945, by the signature of the Alexandria Convention by Egypt, Iraq, Saudi Arabia, Lebanon, Jordan, Syria, and the Yemen. Libya joined the League in March, 1953, and the Sudan was admitted to membership in January 1956, after achieving independent statehood. Membership dropped by one in February, 1958, when the complete union of Egypt and Syria created the new state called the United Arab Republic. At the end of September, 1958, the North African Arab states of Tunisia and Morocco were admitted to the League as full members, bringing membership up to ten, and overtures were being made to some of the oil-rich sheikdoms of the Persian Gulf, particularly Kuwait.

Baghdad Pact

A treaty of mutual co-operation in security and defence was signed by the representatives of Turkey and Iraq in February 1955 at Baghdad. Shortly after, the United Kingdom concluded a defence agreement with Iraq and acceded to the Baghdad Pact. In September 1955 Pakistan joined the treaty countries and was followed in October by Persia. The United States, which gave its support to the treaty, maintained military and political liaison with the treaty organization from the outset and joined the Military Committee in June, 1957. Baghdad is the seat of the permanent council. It would appear that, following the revolution which made her a republic (July, 1958), Iraq has been content to let her membership of the Pact lapse.

Brussels Treaty

See *Western European Union.*

Colombo Plan

The 'Colombo Plan for Co-operative Economic Development in South and South-East Asia' was first published on 28th November 1950 and was initially a British Commonwealth scheme to help the development and economic progress of the Asian lands of the British Commonwealth. It was not long, however, before the scheme was widened to bring in other Asian countries. The first members of the Consultative Committee were Australia, Canada, Ceylon, India, New Zealand, Pakistan, the United Kingdom, Malaya and British Borneo. Countries which later joined were: Vietnam, Cambodia, Laos (1950); Burma, Nepal (1952); Indonesia (1953); Japan, the Philippine Republic, Thailand (1954). The United States is also associated with the venture and there is close liaison with certain of the specialized agencies of the United Nations.

The provision of grants and loans, especially by the western member countries; the training of scientists, engineers and other technicians, doctors and teachers, mutual consultation and help; the launching of new agricultural, industrial and other projects—all these are aspects of the Colombo Plan.

Council of Europe

See *Western European Union.*

EEC (European Economic Community)

This organisation was brought into being by a treaty signed in Rome on 25th March, 1957, whereby France, Italy, Belgium, West Germany, Luxemburg and Holland formed themselves into an economic group pledged to achieve a customs-free "common-market" in progressive stages over 12 to 17 years. At this same Rome meeting these six "Little Europe" nations also signed a treaty setting up *Euratom* (European Atomic Energy Community) for cooperation in all matters appertaining to the development and use of atomic energy. This and the previously established European Coal and Steel Community have machinery linking them closely with EEC. About the same time Britain put forward a plan for a wider European Free Trade Area within OEEC (see below) which brought counter-proposals from France and Italy which led to long negotiations. The machinery of EEC consists of a Council of Ministers (Cabinet), the European Commission consisting of nine independent members as the executive organ to superintend and organise the working of the Treaty, the Court of Justice of seven judges to settle disputes or disagreements between members (also to serve Euratom and the Coal and Steel Community), an Assembly of 142 members from the six States, and the Economic and Social Committee which is a special consultative body of experts. Euratom and the Coal and Steel Community have similar structures.

GATT (General Agreement on Tariffs and Trade)

This is a multilateral contract which entered into force on 1st January, 1948, with 23 nations as contracting parties and now is subscribed to by 37 countries responsible for well over three-quarters of the world's trade. It lays down a common code of conduct in international trade, provides machinery for reducing and stabilising tariffs, and the opportunity for regular consultation on trade problems at meetings held in Geneva. The key provision is a guarantee of most-favoured-nation treatment in trade between contracting nations.

ICA (International Cooperation Administration)

This American organisation, a semi-autonomous unit within the Department of State at Washington, D.C., administers the foreign aid programmes whereby the United States furnishes economic aid of a wide variety to her friends and allies and also to "uncommitted" nations to help them resist economic influence from the Communist bloc of States. This includes both defence and civil aid, technical assistance and the provision of machinery and raw materials. ICA has taken the place of what was previously called FOA (Foreign Operations Administration) which itself had succeeded earlier organisations stemming from the Marshall Plan for European Recovery.

NATO (North Atlantic Treaty Organization)

On 4th April 1949 the North Atlantic Treaty was signed in Washington by the representatives of Belgium, Canada, Denmark, France, Iceland, Italy, Luxemburg, the Netherlands, Norway, Portugal, the United Kingdom and the United States. The treaty, which amounted to an extension of the Brussels Treaty of 1948 (see *Western European Union* below), pledges the member countries to mutual assistance should any of them be attacked in Europe or North America. Greece and Turkey were admitted to the NATO Organization in 1952; Western Germany in 1955. The headquarters of NATO are in Paris.

OAS (Organization of American States)

Since 1890 conferences of the American republics have been held to promote understanding and co-operation between these countries. In 1948, at the Ninth International Conference of American States at Bogota, Colombia, the Charter of the Organization of American States was adopted. The twenty-one member countries of OAS are: Argentina, Bolivia, Brazil, Chile, Colombia, Costa Rica, Cuba, the Dominican Republic, Ecuador, El Salvador, Guatemala, Haiti, Honduras, Mexico, Nicaragua, Panama, Paraguay, Peru, the United States, Uruguay and Venezuela. The headquarters of OAS are in Washington, D.C.; its principal permanent body is the Pan-American Union.

OCAS (Organization of Central American States)

Although this organization was formed in 1951, its first formal conference was not held until August 1955, when representatives of the member countries (Costa Rica, Guatemala, El Salvador, Honduras, Nicaragua) met at Antigua, Guatemala. Panama was represented only by observers, not wishing to join the organization. The purpose of OCAS is to promote economic, social and cultural co-operation between member countries.

OEEC (Organization for European Economic Co-operation)

OEEC was set up in 1948 to administer the European Recovery Programme proposed by Mr. Marshall, the U.S. Secretary of State, and accepted by sixteen nations (Austria, Belgium, Denmark, France, Greece, Iceland, the Irish Republic, Italy, Luxemburg, the Netherlands. Norway, Portugal, Sweden, Switzerland, Turkey and the United Kingdom) and the western zones of Germany. The 'Marshall Plan' itself was completed by 1952, and in more recent years OEEC has been chiefly concerned with monetary matters and with removing trade restrictions between the member countries. Its technical experts have advised on problems in agriculture, industry, transport, power and other matters. A special agency was set up in 1953 to help the co-ordination of productivity in the member countries. A Nuclear Energy Committee was created in February 1956.

SEATO (South-East Asia Treaty Organization)

This treaty for the collective defence of south-East Asia was signed in Manila on 8th September 1954 by the representatives of Australia, France, New Zealand, Pakistan, the Philippines, Thailand (Siam), the United Kingdom and the United States. The Pacific Charter, issued by the member countries, declared their wish 'to establish a firm basis for common action to maintain peace and security in South-East Asia and the South-West Pacific.' The headquarters of SEATO are at Bangkok.

Warsaw Treaty Organization

In May 1955, at Warsaw, a twenty-year 'treaty of friendship, co-operation and mutual assistance' was signed by the representatives of Albania, Bulgaria, Czechoslovakia, the German Democratic Republic (Eastern Germany), Hungary, Poland, Rumania and the Soviet Union. China also pledged her support to the treaty. The treaty provided for the establishment of a unified military command.

WEU (Western European Union)

Closer cooperation between the countries of Western Europe has been brought about by a number of agreements, the first major one of which was the Brussels Treaty signed on 17th March, 1948, by the Foreign Ministers of Belgium, France, Luxemburg, the Netherlands and the United Kingdom. This treaty provided for collective defence—later to be broadened into the North Atlantic Treaty—and for economic, cultural and social cooperation. The next major step was the London Nine-Power Conference (26th September to 3rd October, 1954), at which Belgium, Canada, France, Western Germany, Italy, the Netherlands, Luxemburg, the United States and the United Kingdom were represented. At this conference it was decided to end the occupation of Western Germany; to invite both Western Germany and Italy to join the Brussels Treaty system; and to invite Western Germany to enter NATO. Western Union was officially inaugurated on 7th May, 1955, two days after Western Germany received full sovereign rights.

Western Union found its political expression in the **Council of Europe**, comprising a Committee of Ministers and a Consultative Assembly established on 5th May, 1949, by Belgium, Denmark, France, the Irish Republic, Italy, Luxemburg, the Netherlands, Sweden and the United Kingdom. Other countries which joined subsequently were Turkey, Greece, Iceland, Western Germany, Austria. The first Assembly took place at Strasbourg in 1949, and that city is the seat of the Council and of the annual meetings of the Assembly. London is the headquarters of WEU.

World Council of Churches

The Council dates from 23rd August 1948, when more than 350 delegates (representing some 147 churches in 44 countries) met at Amsterdam. But its history has roots in much earlier endeavours, such as the World Conference on Christian Missions (Edinburgh, 1910); the International Missionary Council (1921) and its conferences; the conferences of the Faith and Order Movement, and of the Life and Work Movement.

The Council has its headquarters at Geneva and maintains regional offices in London and New York.

THE OCEANS AND SEAS

Name	Area (in sq. miles)	Av. Depth (in feet)	Gt. Depth (in feet)	Name	Area (in sq. miles)	Av. Depth (in feet)	Gt. Depth (in feet)
Pacific Ocean ...	64,000,000	14,000	35,640	Okhotsk Sea ...	590,000	2,750	11,060
Atlantic Ocean ...	31,830,000	12,900	30,246	East China Sea ...	480,000	615	8,920
Indian Ocean ...	28,350,000	13,000	24,440	Yellow Sea ...	480,000	160	348
Southern Ocean ...	5,731,350	4,920	18,850	Japan Sea	405,000	4,835	13,000
Arctic Ocean ...	5,440,000	4,200	17,850	North Sea	222,000	180	2,165
Med. Sea	965,000	4,500	14,449	Red Sea	170,000	1,490	9,301
South China Sea ...	895,000	5,400	16,456	Black Sea	164,000	4,300	7,360
Bering Sea	878,000	4,716	13,422	Caspian Sea ...	163,800	597	2,518
Caribbean Sea ...	750,000	8,400	22,788	Baltic Sea	163,000	180	1,519
Gulf of Mexico ...	700,000	4,700	12,426				

THE CONTINENTS

Name	Area (in sq. miles)	Principal Lakes (area in sq. m.)	Principal Rivers (length in miles)	Greatest Height (in feet)
EUROPE	c. 3,700,000	Ladoga 7,100	Volga 2,290	18,491
		Onega 3,800	Danube 1,750	(Elbruz)
		Vänern 2,141	Dnieper 1,420	
		Chudskoye c. 1,400	Kama 1,262	
		Vättern 733	Don 1,222	
ASIA	16,900,000	Aral 24,635	Yangtze 3,430	29,028
		Baikal 12,150	Hwang Ho 2,900	(Mt. Everest)
		Balkhash 6,680	Amur 2,700	
		Issyk Kul c. 2,395	Lena 2,648	
		Koko-Nor (salt) 2,300	Mekong 2,600	
		Van (salt) 2,100	Ob 2,494	
		Urmia (salt) 1,900	Yenise -Selenga 3,261	
			Irtysh 2,300	
			Indus 2,000	
			Brahmaputra 1,800	
			Euphrates 1,650	
			Syr Darya 1,600	
			Ganga (Ganges) 1,555	
			Angara 1,550	
			Ural 1,500	
			Salween 1,500	
			Irrawaddy 1,400	
			Amu Darya 1,350	
AFRICA	c. 11,500,000	Victoria 26,828	Nile 4,164	19,340
		Tanganyika 12,700	Congo 2,900	(Kilimanjaro)
		Nyasa 10,900	Niger 2,600	
		Chad c. 8,000	Zambesi 1,600	
		Rudolf 3,500	Orange 1,300	
		Bangweulu 2,000		
		Leopold II 1,700		
		Albert c. 1,640		
NORTH AMERICA	c. 8,443,000	Superior 31,820	Mississippi-Missouri 4,240	20,300
		Huron 23,010	Mackenzie-Slave-Peace-Finlay 2,541	(Mt. McKinley)
		Michigan 22,400	Missouri 2,466	
		Great Bear c. 12,000	Mississippi 2,330	
		Great Slave 11,170	Yukon 1,979	
		Erie 9,940	Rio Grande 1,800	
		Winnipeg 8,555	Arkansas 1,450	
		Ontario 7,450	Colorado 1,450	
		Nicaragua 3,000	St. Lawrence (proper) 744	
		Athabaska 3,000		
		Reindeer 2,400		
		Winnipegosis 2,085		
		Manitoba 1,800		
		Great Salt 1,800		
SOUTH AMERICA	c. 6,850,000	Titicaca 3,700-3,200	Amazon 4,000	22,835
		Poopo 970	Purus 2,100	(Aconcagua,
		Buenos Aires 865	Parana 2,050	or possibly
		Chiquita 580	São Francisco 1,800	Ojos del Salado
			Tocantins 1,640	now thought to be
			Orinoco 1,600	23,293)
			Araguaia 1,600	
			Pilcomayo 1,550	
			Paraguay 1,300	
			Negro 1,300	
AUSTRALIA	2,948,000	There are no true lakes of any size in Australia. Large salt lakes are:		7,328
		Eyre 3,700	Darling-Murray c. 2,300	(Kosciusko)
		Torrens 2,400		
		Gairdner 1,500	Murray c. 1,600	
ANTARCTICA	5,000,000 —6,000,000			15,100 (Mt. Markham)

LARGEST ISLANDS OF THE WORLD

Name & Possession, Ocean	Area (in sq. miles)
Greenland (Danish), Arctic	837,000
New Guinea (Brit.-Neth.), Pacific	340,000
Borneo (Brit.-Indonesian), Pacific	290,000
Madagascar (French), Indian	228,500
Baffin Land (Canadian), Arctic	200,000
Sumatra (Indonesian), Pacific-Indian	164,000
Great Britain, Atlantic	88,745
Honshu (Japanese), Pacific	87,500
Victoria (Canadian), Arctic	80,000
Ellesmere (Canadian), Arctic	77,000
Celebes (Indonesian), Pacific-Indian	73,000
South Island (New Zealand), Pacific	58,092
Java (Indonesian), Pacific-Indian	48,842
North Island (New Zealand), Pacific	44,281
Cuba (W. Indies), Atlantic	44,000
Newfoundland (Canadian), Atlantic	42,750
Luzon (Philippine), Pacific	41,000
Iceland, N. Atlantic	40,000
Mindanao (Philippine), Pacific	36,900
Ireland (Whole island), Atlantic	31,840
Hokkaido (Japanese), Pacific	30,000
Novaya Zemlya (U.S.S.R.), Arctic	30,000
Hispaniola (W. Indies), Atlantic	29,500
Sakhalin (U.S.S.R.), Pacific	29,100
Tasmania (Australian), Pacific	26,215
Banks (Canadian), Arctic	26,000
Ceylon, Indian	25,400
Devon (Canadian), Arctic	22,000
Tierra del Fuego (Argentinean-Chilean), Atlantic-Pacific	18,500
Southampton (Canadian), Hudson Bay—Atlantic	17,800
Melville (Canadian), Arctic	16,500
Kyushu (Japanese), Pacific	16,250
West Spitzbergen (Norway), Arctic	15,250
New Britain (British), Pacific	14,600
Prince of Wales (Canadian), Arctic	14,000
Formosa, Pacific	13,850
Hainan (Chinese), Pacific	13,000
Timor (Indonesian-Port.), Pacific-Indian	13,000
Vancouver (Canadian), Pacific	12,450

HIGHEST MOUNTAINS OF THE WORLD
(Heights in feet)

EUROPE

Elbruz (Caucasus)	18,481
Dykh-Tau (Caucasus)	17,054
Shkara (Caucasus)	17,037
Koshtan-Tau (Caucasus)	16,880
Mont Blanc (Alps)	15,780
Monte Rosa (Alps)	15,217
Weisshorn (Alps)	14,803
Matterhorn (Alps)	14,678
Finsteraarhorn (Alps)	14,026
Jungfrau (Alps)	13,668
Mulhacen (Sierra Nevada)	11,420
Pico de Aneto (Pyrenees)	11,168
Perdido (Perdu) (Pyrenees)	10,997
Etna (Sicily)	10,741

ASIA

Mt. Everest (Himalaya)	29,028
K2 (Karakoram) (Himalaya)	28,250
Kanchenjunga (Himalaya)	28,146
Lhotse (Himalaya)	27,890
Makalu (Himalaya)	27,790
Cho-Oyu (Himalaya)	26,867
Dhaulagiri (Himalaya)	26,810
Nanga Parbat (Himalaya)	26,660
Annapurna (Himalaya)	26,503
Gasherbrum (Himalaya)	26,470
Gosainthan (Himalaya)	26,291
Nanda Devi (Himalaya)	25,643
Rakaposhi (Himalaya)	25,550
Kamet (Himalaya)	25,447
Namcha Barwa (Himalaya)	25,445
Ulugh Muztagh (Kunlun)	25,340
Tirich Mir (Hindu Kush)	25,230
Stalin Pk. (Pamirs)	24,590
Pobeda Pk. (Tun Shan)	24,406
Demavend (Iran)	18,550
Ararat (Turkey)	16,945
Kinabalu (Borneo)	13,455

AFRICA

Kilimanjaro (East Africa)	19,340
Mt. Kenya (East Africa)	17,040
Mt. Stanley (Ruwenzori)	16,794
Ras Dashan (Simen Mts.)	15,158
Meru (East Africa)	14,979
Elgon (East Africa)	14,178
Toubkal (Atlas Mts.)	13,661
Cameroon Peak (W. Africa)	13,350
Pico de Teide (Canary Islands)	12,162
Thabana Ntlenyana (Drakensberg)	11,425
Emi Kusi (Tibesti Mts.)	11,204
Piton des Neiges (Réunion)	10,069

NORTH AMERICA

McKinley (Alaska Range)	20,300
Logan (St. Elias Mts.)	19,850
Citlaltepetl (Orizaba) (Mexico)	18,700
Saint Elias (St. Elias Mts.)	18,008
Popocatepetl (Mexico)	17,883
Foraker (Alaska)	17,395
Ixtaccihuatl (Mexico)	17,342
Lucania (St. Elias Mts.)	17,150
King (Canada)	17,130
Steele (Canada)	16,439
Bona (Alaska)	16,421
Sandford (Wrangell Mts.)	16,206
Blackburn (Wrangell Mts.)	16,140
Mt. Whitney (Sierra Nevada)	14,495
Elbert (Rocky Mts.)	14,431
Rainier (Cascade Ra.)	14,408
Blanca Pk. (Rocky Mts.)	14,363
Grays Pk. (Rocky Mts.)	14,341
Taumulco (Guatemala)	13,816
Waddington (Coast Ra., Canada)	13,260
Robson (Rocky Mts., Canada)	12,972
Günnbjörn, Greenland	12,139

SOUTH AMERICA

Aconcagua (Andes, Argentina)	22,835
Ojos del Salados (now reputed to be 23,293)	22,575
Huascaran (Andes, Peru)	22,205
Llullaillaco (Andes, Argentina-Chile)	22,146
Tupungato (Andes, Argentina-Chile)	21,490
Ancohuma (Andes, Bolivia)	21,490
Illampu (Andes, Bolivia)	21,275
Illimani (Andes, Bolivia)	21,185
Chimborazo (Andes, Ecuador)	20,577
Cotopaxi (Andes, Ecuador)	19,334

AUSTRALASIA

Carstenz (Nassau Ra., New Guinea)	16,404
Wilhelmina (Orange Ra., New Guinea)	15,585
Luitpold (New Guinea)	14,435
Mt. Victoria (Owen Stanley Ra., Papua)	13,240
Albert Edward (Owen Stanley Ra., Papua)	13,000
Mt. Cook (Southern Alps, New Zealand)	12,349
Kosciusko (Australian Alps)	7,328

ANTARCTICA

Markham (Queen Alexandra Ra.)	15,100
Kirkpatrick (Queen) Alexandra Ra.)	14,603
Andrew Jackson (Eternity Ra.)	13,750
Lister (Royal Society Ra.)	13,350
Erebus (Ross I.)	13,202
Fridtjof Nansen (Gilbert Grosvenor Ra.)	13,156

OCEANIA

Mauna Kea (Hawaii)	13,784
Mauna Hoa (Hawaii)	13,680
Balbi (Solomon Is.)	10,170
Haleakala (Hawaii)	10,032

PRINCIPAL SHIP CANALS OF THE WORLD

	Miles
White Sea (U.S.S.R.)	140
Göta (Sweden)	115
Suez (Egypt)	101
Volga-Moscow (U.S.S.R.)	80
Albert (Belgium)	80
Kiel (Germany)	61
Volga-Don (U.S.S.R)	60
Panama (U.S.A.)	50½
Houston (U.S.A.)	50
Amsterdam-Rhine	45
Elbe & Trave (Germany)	41
Beaumont-Port Arthur (U.S.A.)	40
Manchester (England)	35½
Chicago Sanitary and Ship (U.S.A.)	28
Ghent-Terneuzen (Belgium and Netherlands)	21
Roupel (Belgium)	20
Chesapeake & Delaware (U.S.A.)	14
Lake Washington (U.S.A.)	8½
Cape Cod (U.S.A.)	8
Bruges (Belgium)	6⅓
New Orleans Industrial (U.S.A.)	6
Corinth (Greece)	4
Sault Ste. Marie (U.S.A. & Canada)	3
Keeweenaw (U.S.A.)	2

Note: Canalized rivers are not included.

NOTABLE VOLCANOES OF THE WORLD

The volcanoes listed here are active, except those indicated by (Q), which are volcanoes of notable activity in the past but are now quiescent. The degree of activity varies, some erupt at frequent intervals, others smoulder or steam or rumble; all however, have erupted in recent years.

Name	*Country*	*Height in feet*	*Name*	*Country*	*Height in feet*
Cotopaxi	Ecuador	19,344	Asama	Japan	8,340
Kibo, Kilimanjaro (Q)	Tanganyika	19,340	Sumbing	Sumatra	8,225
Misti (Q)	Peru	19,031	Tandikat	Sumatra	7,999
Popocatepetl	Mexico	17,887	Mayon	Philippine Is.	7,943
Sangay	Ecuador	17,749	Ngauruhoe	New Zealand	7,515
Tungurahua	Ecuador	16,512	Galunggung	Java	7,113
Cotacachi	Ecuador	16,197	Amburombu	Indonesia	7,051
Klyuchevskaya	U.S.S.R.	15,912	Sorik Marapi	Sumatra	7,037
Purace	Colombia	15,604	Petarangan	Java	7,005
Wrangell	Alaska	14,006	Katmai (Q)	Alaska	7,000
Mauna Loa	Hawaii	13,680	Tongariro	New Zealand	6,458
Cameroons Mt.	Nigeria	13,350	Sangeang	Indonesia	6,395
Tacana	Guatemala	13,333	Kaba	Sumatra	6,355
Erebus	Antarctica	13,200	Awu	Indonesia	6,102
Acatenango	Guatemala	12,992	Trident	Alaska	6,090
Colima	Mexico	12,631	Soputan	Celebes	5,994
Fuego	Guatemala	12,582	Siau	Indonesia	5,853
Kerintji	Sumatra	12,484	Kelud	Java	5,679
Fujiyama	Japan	12,389	Ternate	Halmahera	5,627
Santa Maria	Guatemala	12,362	Hibok Hibok	Philippine Is.	5,619
Rindjani	Indonesia	12,225	Lewotobi Perampuan	Indonesia	5,591
Semeru	Java	12,060	Lamongan	Java	5,482
Nyiragongo	Belgian Congo	11,384	Boleng	Indonesia	5,443
Slamat	Java	11,247	Gamkunoro	Halmahera	5,364
Spurr	Alaska	11,070	Aso	Japan	5,225
Etna	Sicily	10,755	Lewotobi Lakilaki	Indonesia	5,217
Torbert	Alaska	10,600	Sarychev	Kurile Islands	4,872
Agung	Bali	10,308	Pelée (Q)	Martinique	4,799
Llaima	Chile	10,249	Hekla (Q)	Iceland	4,747
Tjareme	Java	10,098	Long Island	Bismarck Arch.	4,278
Nyamlagira	Belgian Congo	10,023	Akutan	Aleutians	4,244
Iliamna	Aleutian Is.	10,016	Kilauea	Hawaii	4,090
Gede	Java	9,705	Soufrière (Q)	St. Vincent Is.	4,048
Merapi	Java	9,551	Augustine	Alaska	3,927
Villarrica	Chile	9,318	Vesuvius (Q)	Italy	3,891
Fogo	Cape Verde Is.	9,281	Werung	Indonesia	3,678
Ruapehu	New Zealand	9,175	Alecedo	Galapagos Is.	3,599
Paricutin (Q)	Mexico	9,100	Lamington	New Guinea	3,500
Big Ben	Heard Island	9,000	Stromboli	Italy	3,038
Pavlof	Alaska	8,900	Paloe	Indonesia	2,871
Telong	Sumatra	8,530	Krakatoa	Indonesia	2,667
Cleveland	Aleutians	8,500	Vulcano (Q)	Italy	1,637

GEYSERS

Most notable are:—

Iceland: Great Geyser (Geysir), Strokkr (Churn).
New Zealand: Waikite, Pohutu, Waimauku.
United States:
Yellowstone National Park:—
(*a*) Worris Geyser Basin:—
Valentine, Steamboat, Fearless, Veteran, Vixen, Corporal, Whirligig, and Pinwheel.
(*b*) Lower Geyser Basin:—
Clepsydra, Great Fountain.
(*c*) Midway Geyser Basin:—
Grand Prismatic Spring, Excelsior.
(*d*) Upper Geyser Basin:—
Artemisia, Riverside, Rocket, Grotto, Giant, Daisy, Old Faithful, Giantess.
Lion Group: Lion, Cub, Lioness, Castle.

HIGHEST WATERFALLS (Height in feet)

Angel Falls, Venezuela	3,212	(highest fall 2,648)
Tugela, Natal	3,110	„ „ 1,350)
Upper Yosemite, Yosemite, U.S.A.	2,565	„ „ 1,430)
Kunenaan, Venezuela	2,000	
Sutherland, New Zealand	1,900	(highest fall 815)
Wollomombie, New South Wales	1,700	(„ „ 1,100)
Ribbon Fall, Yosemite, U.S.A.	1,612	
King George VI (Uitshi), British Guiana	1,600	
Gavarnie, France	1,385	
Takakkaw, Canada	1,200	
Staubbach, Switzerland	980	
Gersoppa, Mysore, India	960	(highest fall 829)
Trummelbach, Switzerland	950	

PRINCIPAL DESERTS OF THE WORLD

AFRICA
Sahara, Northern Africa
Libyan (part of Sahara), N.E. Africa
Nubian, Northern Africa
Kalahari, S.W. Africa
Namib, S.W. Africa
ASIA
Great Arabian:—
Rub' al Khali, S.E. Arabia
Syrian (El Hamad), N. Arabia
Nefud (Red Desert), N. & C. Arabia
Ad Dahna, E. Arabia
Gobi, Mongolia
Dasht-i-Lub, E. Iran
Dasht-i-Kavir, C. Iran
Taklamakan, Sinkiang
Kara Kum, Turkestan
Kyzyl Kum, Turkestan
Thar, N.W. India
N. AMERICA
Mohave, S. California
Colorado, S. California
Vizcaino, N.W. Mexico
Grande, N.W. Mexico
Painted, N.E. Arizona
Great Salt Lake, N.W. Utah
S. AMERICA
Atacama, N. Chile
Sechura, W. Peru
AUSTRALIA
Great Australian:—
Great Sandy (Warburton's), N.W. Aust.
Great Victoria, S.W. Aust.
Gibson's, W. Australia
Arunta, C. Australia

PRINCIPAL DAMS (* under construction)

Name	Location	Height in feet	Date
EUROPE			
Grande Dixence	Dixence R., Switzerland	921	*
Mauvoism	Drance de Bagnes R., Switzerland	776	*
Tignes	Isère R., France	590	1953
Zeuzier	Lienne R., Switzerland	524	*
Santa Giustina	Noce R., Italy	500	1951
Canelles	N. Ribgorzana, Spain	500	*
Dnieper	Dnieper R., U.S.S.R.	121	1949
Kuibyshev	Volga R., U.S.S.R.	131	1956
ASIA			
Bhakra	Sutlej R., India	680	*
Kurobe No. 4	Kurobe R., Japan	590	*
Berkhme	Greater Zah R., India	550	*
Okutadami	Tadami R., Japan	508	*
Bratsk	Angara R., U.S.S.R.	426	1958
Sanmen Gorge	Yellow R., China	360	*
Mettur	Cauvery R., India	214	1934
Maithon	Damoda R., India	162	1957
AFRICA			
Aswan	Nile R., Eg.	176	1933
Owen Falls	Uganda	100	1953

Name	Location	Height in feet	Date
NORTH AMERICA			
Hoover	Colorado R., U.S.A.	726	1936
Shasta	Sacramento R., U.S.A.	602	1945
Hungry Horse	Flathead R., U.S.A.	564	1952
Grand Coulee	Columbia R., U.S.A.	550	1942
Fontana	Little Tennessee R., U.S.A.	480	1944
Anderson Ranch	Boise R., U.S.A.	456	1955
San Gabriel	San Gabriel R., U.S.A.	381	1938
Salt Springs	Mokelumne R., U.S.A.	328	1931
Friant	San Joaquin R., U.S.A.	319	1944
Elephant Butte	Rio Grande, U.S.A.	301	1916
Lazaro Cárdenas (El Palmito)	Nazas R., Mexico	295	1948
CENTRAL AMERICA			
Gatun	Chagres R., Panama	115	1912
AUSTRALIA			
Adaminaby	Eucumbene R.	380	1958
Burrinjuck	MurrumbidgeeR. N.S.W.	247	1922
Eildon	Goulbourn R. Central Victoria	135	1956
Hume	Murray R.	110	1936

EXTREMES OF CLIMATE

The **maximum shade temperature of the air** on record in the world is 136° F. at Azizia (Uzzizia) in Tripoli on September 13, 1922; The **extreme lowest recorded temperature** in the world is −94 F. (126° below freezing point) at Verkhoyansk, Siberia. There are reports however of lower temperatures in E. Siberia, and when records have been analysed it may be found that lower temperatures have been recorded in Antarctica during the I.G.Y. 1957-8.

In the **upper air temperatures** as low as −133° F. have been recorded—e.g. over Agra (India) at a height of 16½ kilometres (54,000 ft.).

The **wettest place** in the world is generally allowed to be Cherrapunji in Assam, where different stations have given averages of 424 and 499 inches per year, of which 90 per cent. fell in the six months April to September. However, at Mawsyhram, a village in N.E. India, 670·35 inches were recorded in 1957.

The greatest recorded rainfall in 24 hours is believed to be 46 inches on July 14-15, 1911, at Baguio, Luzon, Philippines.

United Kingdom: The **maximum shade temperature** recorded in the air at 4 feet above the ground is 100° F. at Greenwich Observatory (Aug. 9, 1911).

The **lowest shade temperatures** are −17° F. at Braemar (Feb. 11, 1895) and −16° F. at Kelso (Dec. 3, 1879).

The **greatest rainfall** recorded in a day was at Martinstown, near Dorchester, 11.00 inches in the 24 hours commencing 9 a.m. (July 18, 1955). **Annual** totals exceeding 240 inches were recorded at The Stye, Borrowdale, in 1872, 1923, 1928 and 1954; at Ben Nevis Observatory in 1898 and at Llyn Llydaw, Snowdon, in 1909. The **smallest annual total** is 9.29 inches at Margate in 1921.

The maximum **wind-velocity** on record occurred on the top of Costa Hill, Orkney, on Jan. 31, 1953, in a gust of 125 miles per hour.

FAMOUS WINDS

FÖHN.

Warm wind blowing from the south down into the narrow northern Alpine valleys, resulting in large and sudden rises of temperature. Wind is sometimes of gale force and usually lasts one or two days. Similar winds occur in other mountainous areas, e.g. the Rockies and the Andes.

CHINOOK.

A westerly wind blowing over the Rockies and descending on the east side as a dry wind, warm in winter, cool in summer. The wind causes a rapid rise in temperature thus stimulating snow-melt.

SCIROCCO.

A hot dry wind blowing all the year, but particularly in spring, from the Sahara across the southern coasts of the eastern Mediterranean. The air is drawn north over the deserts of North Africa and Arabia by the depressions which pass from west to east along the Mediterranean, and it is thus very dry and dusty.

Local names for winds similar to the Scirocco are Leveche in south-east Spain, Chili in Tunisia, Ghibli in Libya and Khamsin in Egypt.

MARIN

Scirocco type of wind blowing on to the Gulf of Lions. Very strong wind bringing stormy weather.

HARMATTAN

Blows as a moderate or strong warm and dry wind from the north in the east of the Sahara, and from the north-east in the west of the Sahara. It is often calm on the surface at night. The wind is often extremely dry in the summer. In January it sweeps over the Guinea lands sometimes reaching the coast.

BERG WINDS

These occur in south-west Africa, and are easterly winds, most frequent in winter, blowing from the plateau down to the coast and giving clear skies, very low humidities and high temperatures.

KARABURAN

Violent east-north easterly wind blowing over the desert areas of Central Asia. It carries clouds of dust along with it, earning its name of "black storm". It blows in daytime in early spring.

GREGALE

Strong wind blowing from Greece towards Malta, bringing variable weather. A similar wind known as Levante blows on the Spanish coast and off Algeria.

MISTRAL

Strong dry cold wind blowing from the north onto the shores of the Gulf of Lions. It is felt over all north-west Mediterranean coasts but especially in the Rhône delta. It brings dry, clear, cold weather and blows especially in winter and spring.

BORA

Strong cold north and north easterly wind similar to the Mistral, but blowing down on to the Dalmatian and Istrian coasts bringing clear, dry weather.

NORTHERS

Cold dry winds blowing from the north to the Gulf region of U.S.A. in winter.

PAMPERO

Cold south-westerly winds blowing on to the Pampas area of South America, bringing a short spell of stormy weather, then clear cold conditions. Another similar wind is the Southerly Burster of New South Wales. These winds are most frequent in spring and summer.

TYPHOONS, ETC.

The strongest winds occur in the tropical and subtropical typhoons, cyclones and hurricanes. Typhoons originate in the west Pacific and South China Sea, hurricanes in the West Indies and cylones in the Bay of Bengal.

ALTERNATIVE SPELLINGS OF PLACE NAMES

Aachen: Aix la Chapelle
Aalst: Alost
Abéché: Abeshi
Abeshr, *see* Abéche
Abidjan: Abijan
Abo, see Turku
Adrianople, see Edirne
Agram, see Zagreb
Agrigento: Girgenti
Ahvenanmaa: Åland Is.
Aix la Chapelle, *see* Aachen
Akkerman, *see* Belgorod-Dnestrovski
Åland Is., *see* Ahvenanmaa
Alba Iulia: Karlsburg
Aleppo: Haleb
Alexandretta, *see* Iskenderon
Alexandria: El Iskandariya
Alexandropol, *see* Leninakan
Allenstein, *see* Olsztyn
Alma-Ata: Verny
Alost, *see* Aalst
Altdamm, *see* Dabie Lubuskie
Alto Madeira: Santo Antonio
Amarração, *see* Luis Correia
Amravati: Amraoti
An Geata Mór: Binghamstown
An Uaimh: Navan
Angora, *see* Ankara
Ankara: Angora
Anking: Hwaining
Antakya: Antioch
Antioch, *see* Antakya
Antivari, *see* Bar
Anvers: Antwerp, Antwerpen
Apollonia, *see* Marsa Susa
Arkhangelsk: Archangel
Arlon: Aarlen
Artemovsk: Bakhmut
Aruãna: Leopoldina
Ashdod Gimel: Isdud
Athinai: Athens
Auschwitz, *see* Oswiecim
Aussig, *see* Usti

Baan, *see* Paan
Bagenalstown, *see* Muine Bheag
Bahia, *see* Salvador
Baia, *see* Salvador
Baile Átha Cliath: Dublin
Baile Deasmhumhna: Ballydesmond, Kingwilliamstown
Bakhmut, *see* Artemovsk
Ballydesmond, *see* Baile Deasmhumhna
Baltiisk: Pillau
Banaras, *see* Varanasi
Bandirma: Panderma
Bar: Stari Bar, Antivari
Barce, *see* El Marj
Basel, *see* Basle
Basle: Basel
Batang, *see* Paan
Batavia, *see* Djakarta
Bayan Tumen, *see* Choibalsan
Beit Nabala *see* Nevallat
Belém: Para
Belgard, *see* Bialogard

Belgorod-Dnestrovski: Akkerman, Cetatea Albâ
Benares, *see* Varanasi
Benguela Velha, *see* Porto Amboim
Beograd: Belgrade
Berdiansk, *see* Osipenko
Bern: Berne
Beuthen, *see* Bytom
Bezwada, *see* Vijayavada
Bharat: India
Bialogard: Belgard
Binghamstown, *see* An Geata Mór
Bitolj: Monastir
Björneborg, *see* Pori
Blue Mountains: Toowoomba
Bobo Dioulasso: Bobo Diulasso
Bogor: Buitenzorg
Bolzano: Bozen
Borgå, *see* Porvoo
Brahestad, *see* Raahe
Braniewo: Braunsberg
Brasov, *see* Orasul Stalin
Bratislava: Pressburg
Braunsberg, *see* Braniewo
Breslau, *see* Wroclaw
Bressanone: Brixen
Brest: Brest Litovsk
Brixen, *see* Bressanone
Brno: Brunn
Bromberg, *see* Bydgoszcz
Brugge: Bruges
Brunn, *see* Brno
Brusa, *see* Bursa
Brussels, *see* Bruxelles
Bruxelles: Brussel, Brussels
Buchanan: Grand Bassa
Bucuresti: Bucharest
Budweis, *see* Ceske Budejovice
Bukavu: Costermansville
Buitenzorg, *see* Bogor
Bunclody: Newtownbarry
Bursa: Brusa
Bydgoszcz: Bromberg
Bytom: Beuthen

Caesarea, *see* Qeisari
Cairo: El Qahira
Calicut, *see* Kozhikode
Candia, *see* Iraklion
Canton: Panyu, Punyu, Kwangchow
Caporetto, *see* Kobarid
Caribrod, *see* Dimitrovgrad
Carlsbad, *see* Karlovy Vary
Cattaro, *see* Kotor
Cawnpore, *see* Kanpur
Ceanannus Mor: Kells
Ceará, *see* Fortaleza
Cerigo, *see* Kíthera
Cernauti, *see* Chernovtsy
Ceske Budejovice: Budweis
Cetatea Alba, *see* Belgorod-Dnestrovski
Chad, *see* Tchad
Changan, *see* Sian
Changchow, *see* Lungki
Charleville, *see* Rath Luirc
Cheb: Eger
Cheju-do: Quelpart
Chemnitz, *see* Karl Marx Stadt
Chemulpho, *see* Inchon
Cheribon, *see* Tjirebon
Chernovtsy: Cernauti, Czernowitz
Chernyakovsk: Insterberg

Chihli: Pohai
Chimoia, *see* Vila Pery
Chios, *see* Khios
Chisinau, *see* Kishinev
Chkalov, *see* Orenburg
Choibalsan: Bayan Tumen
Chongjin: Seishin
Cieszyn: Teschen
Cluj: Klausenburg
Coatzacoalcos: Pto. Mexico
Cóbh: Queenstown
Cocanada, *see* Kakinada
Cologne: Koln
Constance, *see* Konstanz
Constanta: Küstenje
Constantinople, *see* Istanbul
Copenhagen: Köbenhavn
Corfu, *see* Kerkira
Corunna, *see* La Coruña
Costermansville, *see* Bukavu
Courtrai, *see* Kortrijk
Crete, *see* Kriti
Cyclades, *see* Kikladhes
Cyrene, *see* Shahhat
Czernowitz, *see* Chernovtsy

Dabie Lubuskie. Altdamm, Dabie
Daingean: Philipstown
Damascus, *see* Esh Sham
Damietta: Dumyat
Danzig, *see* Gdansk
Daugavpils: Dvinsk
Delfoi: Delphi
Deutsch Krone, *see* Walcz
Dimitrovgrad (Bulg.): Kamenets
Dimitrovgrad (Y-Slav.): Caribrod
Dimitrovo: Pernik
Diushambe, *see* Stalinabad
Djakarta: Batavia
Djatinegara: Meeste Cornelis
Djibouti: Jibut
Djokjakarta: Jogjakarta
Dnepropetrovsk: Yekaterinoslav
Dobrich, *see* Tolbukhin
Doornik, *see* Tournai
Dor: Tantura
Dorpat, *see* Tartu
Droichead Nua: Newbridge
Dublin, *see* Baile Átha Cliath
Dubrovnik: Ragusa
Dulcigno, *see* Ulcinj
Dumyat, *see* Damietta
Dunkerque: Dunquerque, Dunkirk
Dun Laoghaire: Kingstown
Dupnitsa, *see* Marek
Durres: Durazzo
Dvinsk, *see* Daugavpils
Dzargalantu: Kobdo, Dzirgalantu
Dzaudzhikau: Ordzhonikodze
Dzibkhatantu: Uliassutai

Edgeworthstown, *see* Meathas Truim
Edirne: Adrianople
Eger, *see* Cheb
Eilat: Um Rashrash

El Arish, *see* Larache
El 'Auja, *see* Nitsana
El Chaco: Presidente Peron
El Iskandariya, *see* Alexandria
El Ladhiqiya: Latakia
El Lajjun, *see* Megiddo
El Majdal, *see* Migdal Gad
El Marj: Barce
El Qahira, *see* Cairo
El Qubab, *see* Mishmar Aiyalon
El Suweis, *see* Suez
Elblag: Elbing
Eldorado, *see* Port Radium
Eluru: Elluru, Ellore
Enzeli, *see* Pahlevi
Erevan, *see* Yerevan
Escaut, *see* Schelde
Esh Sham: Damascus
Esseg, *see* Osijek
Eva Peron, *see* La Plata
Evvoia: Euboe

Faizabad: Fyzabad
Ferdinand, *see* Mikhailovgrad
Firenze, *see* Florence
Fiume, *see* Rijeka
Flanders: Vlaanderen
Florence: Firenze
Flushing, *see* Vlissingen
Foochow: Minhow
Formosa: Taiwan
Fortaleza: Ceará
Fort Shevchenko: Fort Alexandrovski
Frauenburg, *see* Frombork
Fredrikshald, *see* Halden
Fribourg: Freiburg
Frombork: Frauenburg
Frunze: Pishpek
Fünfkirchen, *see* Pécs
Fusan, *see* Pusan
Fyzabad, *see* Faizabad

Gallipoli, *see* Gelibolu
Gamlakarleby, *see* Kokkola
Gand, *see* Gent
Gävle: Gefle
Gdansk: Danzig
Gelibolu: Gallipoli
Geneva (Lake), *see* Leman
Genève: Geneva (Town)
Genoa: Genova
Gensan, *see* Wonsan
Gent: Gand, Ghent
Ghent, *see* Gent.
Girgenti, *see* Agrigento
Glatz, *see* Klodzko
Gliwice: Gleiwitz
Glubczyce: Leobschütz
Goleniòw: Gollnow
Gorki: Nijni-Novgorod
Göteborg: Gothenburg
Gottwaldov: Zlin
Grosswardein, *see* Oradea
Grünberg, *see* Zielona Gora
Guaporé, *see* Rondônia

Haeju: Haiju
Hailar: Hulun
Halden: Fredrikshald
Haleb, *see* Aleppo
Hämeenlinna: Tavastehus
Hannover: Hanover
Harbin: Pinkiang
Heijo, *see* Pyong-yang

ALTERNATIVE SPELLINGS OF PLACE NAMES

Helsinki: Helsingfors
Hermannstadt, *see* Sibiu
Hirschberg, *see* Jelenia Góra
Homs (Libya): Leptis Magna
Hot Springs *see* Truth or Consequences
Hulun, *see* Hailar
Hwaining, *see* Anking

Iasi: Jassy
Ibiza: Iviza
Ieper: Ypres
Inchon: Chemulpho
India, *see* Bharat
Insterberg, *see* Chernyakovsk
Iraklion: Candia
Iran: Persia
Irian: Netherlands New Guinea
Ishdud, *see* Ashdod Gimel
Iskenderon: Alexandretta
Istanbul: Constantinople
Iviza, *see* Ibiza
Izmir: Smyrna

Jabalpur: Jubbulpore
Jaffa, *see* Tel Aviv-Jaffa
Jamnagar: Navanagar
Jassy, *see* Iasi
Jelenia Góra: Hirschberg
Jelgava: Mitau
Jibuti, *see* Djibouti
João Pessoa: Paraiba
Jogjakarta: Djokjakarta
Jubbulpore, *see* Jabalpur

Kakinada: Cocanada
Kalgan: Wanchüan
Kalinin: Tver
Kaliningrad: Königsberg
Kamenets, see Dimitrovgrad
Kanchow: Kanhsien
Kanhsien, *see* Kanchow
Kanpur: Cawnpore
Kaolan, *see* Lanchow
Kara-Kliss, *see* Kirovakin
Karl Marx Stadt: Chemnitz
Karlovac: Karlstad
Karlsburg, *see* Alba Iulia
Karlstad, *see* Karlovac
Karlovy Vary: Carlsbad
Kaschau, *see* Kosice
Kaskinen: Kaskö
Katowice: Stalinogrod
Kaunas: Kovno
Keelung: Kiirun
Keijo, *see* Seoul
Kells, *see* Ceanannus Mor
Kerkira: Corfu
Khibinogorsk, *see* Kirovsk
Khios: Chios
Kikladhes: Cyclades
Kiirun, *see* Keelung
Kingstown, *see* Dun Laoghaire
Kingswilliamstown, *see* Baile Deasmhumhna
Kirin: Yungki
Kirov: Viatka, Vyatka
Kirovakin: Kara-Kliss
Kirovgrad: Kirovo Yelisavetgrad, Zinovyevsk
Kirovsk: Khibinogorsk
Kishinev: Chisinau
Kithira: Cerigo
Klaipeda: Memel
Klausenburg, *see* Cluj
Klodzko: Glatz
Knob Lake, *see* Schefferville
Kobarid: Caporetto
Kobdo, *see* Dzargalantu
København, *see* Copenhagen
Kodzhent, *see* Leninabad
Kokkola: Gamlakarleby
Kolarovgrad: Shumen
Kolchugino, *see* Leninsk Kuznetski
Koln, *see* Cologne
Kolobrzeg: Kolberg
Köningsberg, *see* Kaliningrad
Konstanz: Constance
Kortrijk: Courtrai
Kosice: Kaschau
Kosseir, *see* Quseir
Koszalin: Köslin
Kotor: Cattaro
Kovno, *see* Kaunsas
Kozhikode: Calicut
Kozlov, *see* Michurinsk
Krasnodar: Yekaterinodar
Kristiinankaupunki: Kristinestad
Kriti: Krete, Crete
Kropotkin: Romanovsk
Kuibyshev: Samara
Kunming: Yunnan
Küstenje, *see* Constanta

La Coruña: Corunna
La Plata: Eva Peron
Laibach, *see* Ljubljana
Lanchow: Kaolan
Lappeenranta: Vilmanstrand
Larache: El Arish
Latakia, *see* El Ladhiqiya
Lauenburg, *see* Lebork
Lebork: Lauenburg
Leghorn: Livorno
Legnica: Liegnitz
Lemburg, *see* Lvov
Leman, Lake: Geneva, Lake
Leninabad: Kodzhent
Leninakan: Alexandropol
Leningrad: Petrograd
Leninsk Kuznetski: Lenino, Kolchugino
Leobschütz, *see* Glubczyce
Leopoldina, *see* Aruaña
Leptis Magna, *see* Homs
Leuven: Louvain
Libau, *see* Liepaja
Liberec: Reichenberg
Liegnitz, *see* Legnica
Liepaja: Libau
Lisbon: Lisboa
Livorno, *see* Leghorn
Ljubljana: Laibach
Loanda, *see* Luanda
Lod: Lydda
Louvain, *see* Leuven
Luanda: Loanda
Lucerne: Luzern
Lugansk, *see* Voroshilovgrad
Luis Correia: Amarração
Lungki: Changchow, Lunki
Lungkiang, *see* Tsitsihar
Luxembourg: Luxemburg
Lvov, Lwow, Lemburg
Lwow, *see* Lvov
Lydda, *see* Lod
Lyons: Lyon

Maas, *see* Meuse
Macequece, *see* Vila de Manica
Madurai: Madura
Magallanes, *see* Punta Arenas
Majorca, *see* Mallorca
Malbork: Marienburg, Malborg
Malines, *see* Mechelen
Mallorca: Majorca
Mantova: Mantua
Maranhão:, see São Luiz
Marburg, *see* Maribor
Marek: Dupnitsa
Maria Theresiopel, *see* Subotica
Mariánske Lázně: Marienbad
Maribor: Marburg
Marienburg, *see* Malbork
Mariupol, *see* Zhdanov
Marrakech: Morocco
Marsa Susa: Apollonia
Marseille: Marseilles
Maryborough, *see* Port Laoighise
Mathura: Muttra
Meathas Truim: Edgeworthstown
Mechelen: Malines
Meester Cornelis, *see* Djatinegara
Megiddo: El Lajjun
Memel, *see* Klaipeda
Menorca: Minorca
Me'ona: Tarshiha
Meuse: Maas
Michurinsk: Kozlov
Migdal Gad: El Majdal
Mikhailovgrad: Ferdinand
Mikkeli: Sankt Michel
Milano: Milan
Minhow, *see* Foochow
Minorca, *see* Menorca
Mishmar Aiyalon: El Qubab
Mitau, *see* Jelgava
Molotov, *see* Perm
Monastir, *see* Bitolj
Monte Azul: Tremedal
Morocco, *see* Marrakech
Moskva: Moscow
Mountcharles, *see* Tantallon
Muine Bheag: Bagenalstown
Mukden: Shenyang
Munich: München
Muttra, *see* Mathura

Najin: Rashin
Namen, *see* Namur
Namur: Namen
Nanning: Yungning
Naples: Napoli
Navan, *see* An Uaimh
Navanagar, *see* Jamnagar
Neisse, *see* Nysa
Neemuch: Nimach
Neusatz, *see* Novi Sad
Neustettin, *see* Szczecinek
Nevallat: Beit Nabala
Newbridge (Ire.), *see* Droichead Nua
Newmarket (Flint), *see* Trelawnyd
Newtownbarry, *see* Bunclody
Nictheroy, *see* Niteroi
Nieuwpoort: Nieuport
Nijni Novgorod, *see* Gorki
Nikolaistad, *see* Vaasa
Nimach, *see* Neemuch
Nisa, *see* Nysa
Nisibin *see* Nusaybin
Niteroi: Nictheroy
Nitsana: El'Auja
Novi Sad: Neusatz
Novosibirsk: Novo Nikolaevsk
Nürnberg: Nuremburg
Nusaybin: Nisibin
Nykarleby *see* Uusikaarlepyy
Nysa: Nisa, Neisse
Nystad, *see* Uusikaupunk
Nyslott, *see* Savonlinna

Ödenburg, *see* Sopron
Olomouc: Olmutz
Olsztyn: Allenstein
Opava: Troppau
Opole: Oppeln
Oporto: , *see* Pôrto
Oradea: Grosswardein
Orasul Stalin: Brasov
Ordzhonikidze, *see* Vladikavkaz
Ordzhonikodze, *see* Dzaudzhikau
Orenburg: Chkalov
Osijek: Esseg
Osipenko: Berdiansk
Ostende: Oostende, Ostend
Oswiecim: Auschwitz
Ouagadougou, Wagadugu
Ouargla: Wargla
Oulu: Uleåborg

Paan: Baan, Batang
Pahlevi: Enzeli
Panderma, *see* Bandirma
Panyu, *see* Canton
Paoshan: Yungchang
Paoting: Tsingyuan
Para, *see* Belém
Paraiba, *see* Joao Pessoa
Patrai: Patras
Pécs: Fünfkirchen
Peking: Peiping
Perm: Molotov
Pernambuco, *see* Recife
Pernik, *see* Dimitrovo
Persia, *see* Iran
Petrograd, *see* Leningrad
Philippopolis, *see* Plovdiv
Philipstown, *see* Daingean
Pillau, *see* Baltiisk
Pilsen, *see* Plzen
Pingyang, *see* Pyong-yang
Pinkiang, *see* Harbin
Piraevs: Piraeus, Peiraieus, Pireefs
Pishpek, *see* Frunze
Pleven: Plevna
Plovdiv: Philippopolis
Plzen: Pilsen
Podgorica, *see* Titograd
Pohai, *see* Chihli
Pola, *see* Pula

ALTERNATIVE SPELLINGS OF PLACE NAMES

Pondicherry: Pondichery
Pori: Björneborg
Port Laoighise: Maryborough
Port Radium: Eldorado
Pôrto: Oporto
Porto Amboim: Benguela Velha
Porvoo: Borgå
Poznan: Posen
Praha: Prague
Presidente Peron, *see* El Chaco
Pressburg, *see* Bratislava
Puerto Mexico, *see* Coatzacoalcos
Pula: Pola
Punta Arenas: Magallanes
Pusan: Fusan
Pyong-yang: Pingyang Heijo

Qeisari: Caesarea
Queenstown, *see* Cóbh
Quelpart, *see* Cheju-do
Quseir: Kosseir

Raahe: Brahestad
Raciborz: Ratibor
Ragusa, *see* Dubrovnik
Raheng, *see* Tak
Rankovicevo: Kraljevo
Rashid, *see* Rosetta
Rashin, *see* Najin
Rath Luirc: Charleville
Ratibor, *see* Raciborz
Ratisbon, *see* Regensburg
Recife: Pernambuco
Regensburg: Ratisbon
Reichenberg, *see* Liberec
Reval, *see* Tallinn
Rhodes, *see* Rodhós
Rijeka: Fiume
Rodhós: Rhodes
Roeselare: Roulers
Roma: Rome
Romanovsk, *see* Kropotkin
Rondônia: Guaporé
Rosetta: Rashid
Roulers, *see* Roeselare
Rovinj: Rovigno
Ruse: Ruschuk
Rybinsk, *see* Shcherbakov

Saida: Sidon
Saint Gall: Sankt Gallen
Saint Nicolas, *see* Sint Niklaas
Salonika, *see* Thessaloniki
Salvador: Baia, Bahia
Samara, *see* Kuibyshev
Sankt Gallen, *see* Saint Gall
Sankt Michel: Mikkeli
Santo Antonio, *see* Alto Madeira
São Luis: Maranhão
Saragossa, *see* Zaragoza
Savonlinna: Nyslott
Schässburg, *see* Sighisoara
Schefferville: Knob Lake
Schelde: Escaut, Scheldt
Schweinitz, *see* Swidnica
Scutari (Albania), *see* Shkodër
Scutari (Turkey), *see* Usküdar
Sedom: Sodom
Seishin, *see* Chongjin
Semlin, *see* Zemun
Seoul: Keijo
Sept Îles: Seven Islands
Sevilla: Seville
S'Gravenhage: The Hague
Shahhat: Cyrene
Shcherbakov: Rybinsk
Shenyang, *see* Mukden
Shetland: Zetland
Shkodër: Scutari
Shivpuri: Sipri
Shumen, *see* Kolarovgrad
Sibiu: Hermannstadt
Siam, *see* Thailand
Sian: Changan
Sidon, *see* Saida
Sighisoara: Schässburg
Simbirsk, *see* Ulyanovsk
Singora, *see* Songkhla
Sint Niklaas: Saint Nicolas
Sipri, *see* Shivpuri
Siracusa: Syracuse
Skoplje: Usküb
Skutari, *see* Shkodër
Sliten, *see* Zliten
Slupsk: Stolp
Smyrna, *see* Izmir
Sodom, *see* Sedom
Sofiya: Sofia
Sombor: Zombor
Songjin: Siongchin
Songkhla: Singora
Soochow: Wu
Sopron: Ödenburg
Sousse: Susa
Sovetsk: Tilsit
Spitsbergen, *see* Svalbard
Split: Spalato
Stalin: Varna
Stalinabad: Duishambe
Stalino: Yuzovka
Stalingrad: Tsaritzin
Stalinogrod, *see* Katowice
Stari Bar, *see* Bar
Stavropol: Voroshilovsk
Stettin, *see* Szczecin
Stolp, *see* Slupsk
Stolpmünde, *see* Ustka
Stuhlweissenburg, *see* Székesfehérvár
Subotica: Maria Theresiopel
Suez: El Suweis
Sur: Tyre
Suriname: Netherlands Guiana
Susa, *see* Sousse
Svalbard: Spitsbergen
Sverdlovsk: Yakaterinburg
Swidnica: Schweinitz
Syracuse, *see* Siracusa
Szczecin: Stettin
Szczecinek: Neustettin
Székesfehérvár: Stuhlweissenburg

Taegu: Taiku
Taihoku, *see* Taipeh
Taiku: Taegu
Taipeh: Taihoku
Taiwan, *see* Formosa
Taiyüan: Yangku
Tak: Raheng, Rahaeng
Tali: Tungchow
Tallinn: Reval
Tammerfors, *see* Tampere
Tampere: Tammerfors
Tantallon: Mountcharles
Tantura, *see* Dor
Tarabulus: Tripoli
Tarshiha, *see* Me'ona
Tartu: Dorpat
Tavastehus, *see* Hameenlinna
Tbilisi: Tiflis
Tchad: Chad
Tel Aviv-Jaffa: Jaffa, Tel Aviv
Tende: Tenda
Teschen, *see* Cieszyn
Thailand: Siam
Thebes, *see* Thivai
The Hague: *see* S'Gravenhage
Thessaloniki: Salonika
Thivai: Thebes
Tiflis, *see* Tbilisi
Tihwa, *see* Urumchi
Tilsit, *see* Sovetsk
Timbuktu, *see* Tombouctou
Tiruchirapalli: Trichinopoly
Titograd: Podgorica
Tjirebon: Cheribon
Tolbukhin: Dobrich
Tombouctou: Timbuktu
Toowoomba, *see* Blue Mountains
Tornio: Tornea
Tournai: Doornik
Trabzon: Trebizond
Trelawnyd: Newmarket
Tremedal, *see* Monte Azul
Trèves: Trier
Trichinopoly, *see* Tiruchirapalli
Tripoli, *see* Tarabulus
Troppau, *see* Opava
Truth or Consequences: Hot Springs
Tsingyuan, *see* Paoting
Tsitsihar: Lungkiang
Tsangwu, *see* Wuchow
Tsaritzin, *see* Stalingrad
Tungchow, *see* Tali
Turin: Torino
Turku: Abo
Tver, *see* Kalinin
Tyre, *see* Sur

Ulan Ude: Verkhneudinsk
Ulcinj: Dulcigno
Uleåborg, *see* Oulu
Uliassutai, *see* Dzhibkhalantu
Ulyanovsk: Simbirsk
Um Rashrash, *see* Eilat
Urumchi: Tihwa
Usküb, *see* Skoplje
Usküdar: Scutari
Ussurysk: Voroshilov
Usti: Aussig
Ustka: Stolpmünde
Uusikaarlepyy: Nykarleby
Uusikaupunki: Nystad

Vaasa: Nikolaistad
Varanasi: Banaras, Benares
Varna, *see* Stalin
Verkhneudinsk, *see* Ulan Ude
Venice: Venezia
Ventimiglia: Vintimille
Ventspils: Windau, Vindava
Verny, *see* Alma-Ata
Viborg: Viipuri
Vienna: Wien
Vijayavada: Bezwada
Vila de Manica: Macequece
Vila Pery: Chimoia
Vilmanstrand, *see* Lappeenranta
Vilnius: Vilna, Vilno Wilno
Vilvoorde: Vilvorde
Vindava, *see* Ventspils
Vintimille, *see* Ventimiglia
Visagapatam, *see* Vishakhapatnam
Vishakhapatnam: Vizagapatam, Visakakhapatnam
Vlaanderen, *see* Flanders
Vladikavkaz, *see* Ordzhonikidze
Vlissingen: Flushing
Voroshilov, *see* Ussurysk
Voroshilovgrad: Lugansk
Voroshilovsk, *see* Stavropol
Vyatka, *see* Kirov

Wagadugu, *see* Ouagadougou
Walbrzych: Waldenburg
Walcz: Deutch Krone
Waldenburg, *see* Walbraych
Wanchüan, *see* Kalgan
Wargla, *see* Ouargla
Warszawa: Warsaw
Weihai: Weihaiwei
Wenchow: Yungkia
Wien, *see* Vienna
Wilno, *see* Vilnius
Windau, *see* Ventspils
Wonsan: Gensan
Wroclaw: Breslau
Wuchow: Tsangwu
Wuhsien, *see* Soochow

Yanam: Yanaon
Yangku, *see* Taiyüan
Yekaterinburg, *see* Sverdlovsk
Yekaterinodar, *see* Krasnodar
Yekaterinoslav, *see* Dnepropetrovsk
Yelisavetgrad, *see* Kirovgrad
Yerevan: Erevan
Ypres, *see* Ieper
Yungchang, *see* Paoshan
Yungki, *see* Kirin
Yungkia, *see* Wenchow
Yungning, *see* Nanning
Yunnan, *see* Kunming
Yuzovka, *see* Stalino

Zadar: Zara
Zagreb: Agram
Zaragoza: Saragossa
Zemun: Semlin
Zetland: Shetland
Zhdanov: Mariupol
Zielona Gora: Grünberg
Zinovyevsk, *see* Kirovgrad
Zlin, *see* Gottwaldov
Zliten: Sliten
Zombor, *see* Sombor

INDEX

ABBREVIATIONS

AA – *Autonomous Area*
AR – *Autonomous Region*
Admin. Div. – *Administrative Division*
Afghan. – *Afghanistan*
Afr. – *Africa*
Ala. – *Alabama*
Alas. – *Alaska*
Alb. – *Albania*
Alg. – *Algeria*
Alta. – *Alberta*
Amaz. – *Amazonas*
Amer. – *America*
And. P. – *Andhra Pradesh*
Ang. – *Angola*
Antarc. – *Antarctica*
Arab. – *Arabia*
Arch. – *Archipelago*
Arg. – *Argentina*
Ariz. – *Arizona*
Ark. – *Arkansas*
A.S.S.R. – *Autonomous Soviet Socialist Republic*
Aust. – *Austria*
Austral. – *Australia*
B. – *Bay, Bight (Baie, Baia)*
Baden-Württ. – *Baden-Württemburg*
Baluch. – *Baluchistan*
Basut. – *Basutoland*
Bav. – *Bavaria*
B.C. – *British Columbia*
Bech. – *Bechuanaland*
Beds. – *Bedfordshire*
Belg. – *Belgium, Belgian*
Belg. Cong. – *Belgian Congo*
Berks. – *Berkshire*
Bg. – *Berg.*
Bk. – *Bank*
Bol. – *Bolivia*
Bom. – *Bombay*
Brand. – *Brandenburg*
Braz. – *Brazil*
Br., Brit. – *British*
Br. Gui. – *British Guiana*
Bri. – *Bridge*
Br. Somal. – *British Somaliland*
Bucks. – *Buckinghamshire*
Bulg. – *Bulgaria*
C. – *Cape (Cabo)*
Calif. – *California*
Cambod. – *Cambodia*
Cambs. – *Cambridgeshire*
Can. – *Canada, Canal*
Can. Is. – *Canary Islands*
Cards. – *Cardiganshire*
Cas. – *Castle*
Cat. – *Cataract*
Cel. – *Celebes*
Cent. – *Central*
Cey. – *Ceylon*
Chan. – *Channel*
Ches. – *Cheshire*
Chih. – *Chihuahua*
Co. – *County*
Col. – *Colombia, Colony*
Colo. – *Colorado*
Conn. – *Connecticut*
Cont. – *Continent*
C. Prov. – *Cape Province*
Cr. – *Creek*
C. Rica – *Costa Rica*
Cumb. – *Cumberland*
Cz. – *Czechoslovakia*
D.C. – *District of Columbia*
Del. – *Delaware*
Den. – *Denmark*
Dépt. – *Département, Department*
Des. – *Desert*
Dist. – *District*
Div. – *Division*
Dj. – *Djebel*
Dom. Rep. – *Dominican Republic*
E. – *East*
Ec. – *Ecuador*
Eg. – *Egypt*
Eng. – *England*
E. Pak. – *East Pakistan*
Eq., Equat. – *Equatorial*
Erit. – *Eritrea*
Est. – *Estuary*
Eur. – *Europe*
Falk. Is. – *Falkland Islands*
Fd. – *Fiord, Fjord*
Fed. – *Federal, Federation*
Fin. – *Finland*
Fla. – *Florida*
For. – *Forest*
Fr. – *France, French*
Fr. Eq. Afr. – *French Equatorial Africa*
Fr. Guin. – *French Guinea*
Fr. Somal. – *French Somaliland*
Fr. W. Afr. – *French West Africa*
Fs. – *Falls*
Ft. – *Fort*
G. – *Gulf, Gebel*
Ga. – *Georgia*
Gam. – *Gambia*
Ger. – *Germany*
Gl. – *Glacier*
Glos. – *Gloucestershire*
Gr. – *Greece*
Green. – *Greenland*
Grp. – *Group*
Gt. – *Great*
Guat. – *Guatemala*
Gui. – *Guiana*
Guin. – *Guinea*
Hants. – *Hampshire*
Harb. – *Harbor, Harbour*
Hd. – *Head*
Here. – *Herefordshire*
Herts. – *Hertfordshire*
Him. P. – *Himachal Pradesh*
Hond. – *Honduras*
Hs. – *Hills*
Hts. – *Heights*
Hung. – *Hungary*
Hunts. – *Huntingdonshire*
I.(s) – *Island(s) (Isle, Île)*
Ice. – *Iceland*
Ill. – *Illinois*
Ind. – *Indiana*
Indon. – *Indonesia*
Ind. U. – *Indian Union*
Inf. – *Inférieure*
I. of M. – *Isle of Man*
I. of W. – *Isle of Wight*
Ire. – *Ireland*
Isr. – *Israel*
Isth. – *Isthmus*
It. – *Italy*
J. – *Jebel, Jabel*
Jam. – *Jamaica*
Jap. – *Japan*
Jc., Junc. – *Junction*
Kan. – *Kansas*
Ken. Col. – *Kenya Colony*
King. – *Kingdom*
Ky. – *Kentucky*
L. – *Lake, Lough, Loch, Lago, Lac*
La. – *Louisiana*
Lab. – *Labrador*
Lag. – *Lagoon, Laguna, Lagoa*
Lancs. – *Lancashire*
Ld. – *Land*
Leics. – *Leicestershire*
Lib. – *Liberia*
Lim. – *Limerick*
Lincs. – *Lincolnshire*
Lit. – *Little*
Lr. – *Lower*
Lr. Sax. – *Lower Saxony*
Lux. – *Luxembourg*
Mad. P. – *Madhya Pradesh*
Madag. – *Madagascar*
Man. – *Manitoba*
Manch. – *Manchuria*
Mass. – *Massachusetts*
Maur. – *Mauritius*
Md. – *Maryland*
Me. – *Maine*
Meck. – *Mecklenburg*
Medit. – *Mediterranean*
Mex. – *Mexico*
Mich. (U.S.A.) – *Michigan*
Mich. (Mex.) – *Michoacan*
Mid. – *Middle*
Min. Ger. – *Minas Gerais*
Minn. – *Minnesota*
Miss. – *Mississippi*
Mo. – *Missouri*
Mon. – *Monmouthshire*
Mong. – *Mongolia*
Mont. – *Montana*
Mor. – *Morocco*
Mozam. – *Mozambique*
Mt. – *Mountain, Mount*
Mte. – *Monte*
Mti. – *Monti*
Mts. – *Mountains, Monts.*
N. – *North, Northern*
Nat. – *Natal*
Nat. Mon. – *National Monument*
Nat. Pk. – *National Park*
N.B. – *New Brunswick*
N.C. – *North Carolina*
N.D. – *North Dakota*
Neb. – *Nebraska*
Neth. – *Netherlands*
Neth. Gui. – *Netherlands Guiana*
Nev. – *Nevada*
Newf. – *Newfoundland*
N. Guin. – *New Guinea*
N.H. – *New Hampshire*
Nic. – *Nicaragua*
Nig. – *Nigeria*
N. Ire. – *Northern Ireland*
N.J. – *New Jersey*
N. Mex. – *New Mexico*
Nor. – *Norway*
Northants. – *Northamptonshire*
Northumb. – *Northumberland*
Notts. – *Nottinghamshire*
N. Rhod. – *Northern Rhodesia*
N. Rh.-W.phal. – *North Rhine-Westphalia*
N.S. – *Nova Scotia*
N.S.W. – *New South Wales*
N. Terr. – *Northern Territory, Australia*
N.W. Terr. – *North-West Territories, Canada*
N.Y. – *New York*
Nyasa. – *Nyasaland*
N.Z. – *New Zealand*
O. – *Oasis*
Oc. – *Ocean*
O.F.S. – *Orange Free State*
Okla. – *Oklahoma*
Ont. – *Ontario*
Ore. – *Oregon*
P. – *Paso, Pass, Passo*
Pa. – *Pennsylvania*
Pac. – *Pacific*
Pak. – *Pakistan*
Pan. – *Panama*
Par. – *Paraguay*
Pass. – *Passage*
P.E.I. – *Prince Edward Island*
Pen. – *Peninsula*
Phil. – *Philippines*
Pk. – *Peak, Park*
Pl. – *Plain, Planina*
Plat. – *Plateau*
Pol. – *Poland*
Port. – *Portugal, Portuguese*
Préf. – *Préfecture*
P. Rico. – *Puerto Rico*
Prom. – *Promontory*
Prot. – *Protectorate*
Prov. – *Province, Provincial*
Pt. – *Point, Port*
Pta. – *Punta (Point)*
Pte. – *Pointe (Point)*
Pto. – *Porto, Puerto (Port)*
Que. – *Quebec*
Queens. – *Queensland*
R. – *River, Rio, Riviers*
Ra. – *Range*
Raj. – *Rajasthan*
Rd. – *Road*
Reg. – *Region*
Rep. – *Republic*
Res. – *Reserve, Reservoir*
Rf. – *Reef*
Rhld.-Pal. – *Rhineland-Palatinate*
R.I. – *Rhode Island*
Rks. – *Rocks*
Rosc. – *Roscommon*
R.S.F.S.R. – *Russian Soviet Federal Socialist Republic*
Rum. – *Rumania*
S. – *Sea, South*
Sa. – *Sierra, Serra*
Sal. – *Salvador*
Salop. – *Shropshire*
Sar. – *Sarawak*
Sask. – *Saskatchewan*
Sax. – *Saxony*
Sax.-Anh. – *Saxony-Anhalt*
S. Austral. – *South Australia*
S.C. – *South Carolina*
Scot. – *Scotland*
S.D. – *South Dakota*
Sd. – *Sound*
Sen. – *Senegal*
S.-Holst. – *Schleswig-Holstein*
Si.-Arab. – *Saudi Arabia*
S. Leone – *Sierra Leone*
Som. – *Somerset*
Somal. – *Somaliland, Somalia*
Sp., Span. – *Spain, Spanish*
S. Rhod. – *Southern Rhodesia*
S.S.R. – *Soviet Socialist Republic*
St. – *State*
St. – *Saint, also see note below*
Sta. – *Santa*
Ste. – *Sainte*
Sto. – *Santo*
Staffs. – *Staffordshire*
Stn. – *Station*
Str. – *Strait*
Sud. – *Sudan*
S.W. Africa – *South-West Africa*
Swazi. – *Swaziland*
Swed. – *Sweden*
Switz. – *Switzerland*
Tang. Terr. – *Tanganyika Territory*
Tas. – *Tasmania*
Tenn. – *Tennessee*
Terr. – *Territory*
Tex. – *Texas*
Tipp. – *Tipperary*
Tn. – *Town*
Trans. – *Transvaal*
Tur. – *Turkey*
U. – *Union*
U.A.R. – *United Arab Republic*
Ukr. – *Ukraine*
U. of S. Africa – *Union of South Africa*
Ut. P. – *Uttar Pradesh*
Up. – *Upper*
Urug. – *Uruguay*
U.S.A. – *United States of America*
U.S.S.R. – *Union of Soviet Socialist Republics*
V. – *Vale*
Va. – *Virginia*
Val. – *Valley*
Ven. – *Venezuela*
Vic. – *Victoria*
Vol. – *Volcano*
Vt. – *Vermont*
W. – *West, Wadi, Wady*
War. – *Warwickshire*
Wash. – *Washington*
W. Austral. – *Western Australia*
W. Ind. – *West Indies*
Wick. – *Wicklow*
Wilts. – *Wiltshire*
Wind. Is. – *Windward Islands*
Wis. – *Wisconsin*
Worcs. – *Worcestershire*
W. Pak. – *West Pakistan*
W. Va. – *West Virginia*
Wyo. – *Wyoming*
Yorks. – *Yorkshire*
Y.-slav. – *Yugoslavia*
Zan. – *Zanzibar*
Zulu. – *Zululand*

For physical features such as Bays, Capes, Headlands, Mountains, Points, Rivers, etc., see under Proper name.

Names beginning with M', Mc, M'c are indexed under Mac.

The following names meaning Saint are indexed under St. (Saint):— Saint, Sanct, Sankt, Sant', Sent, Sint, Svaty, Sveti, Svety, Szent.

Printed in Great Britain